PUBLISHER'S

May 2004

Welcome to the 2004 edition of Olympic Track & Field History! This amazing resource guide is the work of Mel Watman, the co-editor of Athletics International. Shooting Star Media, Inc. has worked with Mel since 1996 on this project.

This publication is to give you a perspective on all of the modern Olympic Games – from 1896 through 2000. Mel has provided not only features on all Olympic Track & Field events, but also results of each games!

The Olympic Games are one of the few events that bring our world, all 280 plus countries, together. Track and field athletics is one of the most popular sports worldwide.

Who will be the new heroes of Athens 2004? We hope that Olympic Track & Field History is a resource that adds to your enjoyment of our sport and the Olympic Games.

Regards,

Larry Eder

Larry Eder

ATF presents the Olympic Track & Field History by Mel Watman; published in the U.S.A. Copyrights are with Mel Watman for all content. American Track & Field logo is registered trademark of Shooting Star Media, Inc, Ft. Atkinson, WI. No part of this publication may be stored in any way or with any media without written permission of the Publisher. **Publisher:** Larry Eder, **Designer:** Kristen Cerer, **Photographer:** Mark Shearman. Published 2004. All Rights Reserved.

ISBN 0 9528011 6 7

Los Angeles 1984. Carl Lewis (USA), photo by Mark Shearman.

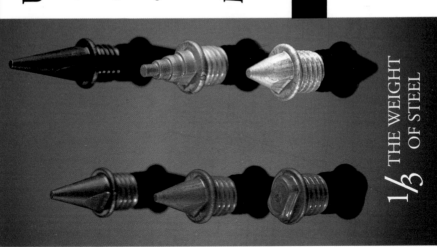

Sydney 2000. Stacy Dragila (USA), photo by Mark Shearman

**PROPER HYDRATION
ISN'T ROCKET SCIENCE.
IT'S CHEMISTRY.**

Athletes perform at their best when they replace the essential elements they sweat out.
Water doesn't have them. Gatorade® does. Nothing rehydrates, replenishes, and refuels athletes better.

is it in you?

CAROLINA KLUFT
HEPTATHLON WORLD CHAMPION

1033

PARIS 2003 ST-DEMS

Sydney 2000. Heike Drechsler (Germany), photo by Mark Shearman

GREG THREW AWAY GIRLFRIENDS' PHONE NUMBERS, TICKET STUBS EVEN HIS COLLEGE DIPLOMA. **HE ONLY KEPT WHAT WAS IMPORTANT**

Reebok

OUTPERFORM

THE REEBOK PREMIER SERIES. ADVANCED TECHNOLOGY FOR ADVANCED HUMANITY. DMX FOAM AND DMX SHEAR PROVIDE CUSHIONING AND BALANCE FROM HEEL TO FOREFOOT. COMBINATION CARBON AND BLOWN RUBBER OUTSOLE FOR MAXIMUM TRACTION AND DURABILITY/PLAY DRY MOISTURE MANAGEMENT LINING/OPEN WEAVE MESH UPPER FOR BREATHABILITY + SUPPORT.

Sydney 2000. Jonathan Edwards (Gt Britain), photo by Mark Shearman

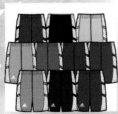

Sydney 2000. Maurice Greene (USA), photo by Mark Shearman

HIND

TEAM SPORTS®

G-FORCE LYCRA TOP

15067   Women's   **S-XL**

Shell: 83% Nylon, 17% Spandex n Liner: 83%
Nylon, 17% Spandex • Longer length for tuck-
in rule requirements • Flatseam construction •
Comfortable bra liner • Streamlined fit for the
serious athlete

Colors: Scarlet/White (SC), Navy/White (NY),
Maroon/White (MR), Black/White (BK), Purple/
White (PU), Cobalt/White (CB), Forest/White
(FR)

NEW COLORS: Maize/White (MZ), Kelly/White
(KY), Navy/Columbia (NY/CO), Navy/Maize
(NY/MZ), Maroon/Maize (MR/MZ), Scarlet/
Black (SC/BK), Orange/Black (OR/BK)

ll for your nearest dealer
800-376-7787

lew for Track 2004!

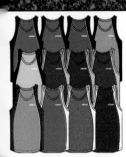

RAVE SINGLET

15059   Men's   **S-XXXL**
15069   Women's   **S-XXXL**

Multi-colored, dual-paneled singlet • Contemporary, athletic cut n 100% Coolmax polyester
closed-hole mesh • Comfortable matching neck
and armhole piping

Colors: Cobalt/Black, Scarlet/Black,
Forest/Black, Orange/Black, Maize/Black,
Maroon/Maize, Navy/Maize, Purple/Maize,
Columbia/Navy, Cobalt/White, Scarlet/White,
Navy/White

RAVE SHORT

10071   Unisex   **XS-XXXL**

Solid color training/racing short • Contemporary, athletic cut with 6" inseam • "Sure Fit"
elastic waistband with drawstring • HTS textur-
ized nylon shell •HTS 100% Drylete liner

Colors: Scarlet (SC), Black (BK), Cobalt (CB),
Maroon (MR), Navy (NY), Forest (FR), Maize
(MZ), Purple (PU), Orange (OR), Columbia
(CO)

M-F Athletics • Kessler's • Dick Pond Sports
• On Track • Anaconda Sports
ailable at these dealers and many others!

Sydney 2000. Marion Jones (USA), photo by Mark Shearman

Sydney 2000. Marion Jones (USA) wins the 100m, photo by Mark Shearman

Sydney 2000. Jan Zelezny (Czech Republic), photo by Mark Shearman

Sydney 2000. Haile Gebrselassie (Ethiopia, 1658) wins the 10,000m from Paul Tergat (Kenya, 2393), photo by Mark Shearman

INTRODUCTION

The Modern Olympics come full circle this year, for they will be staged in Athens, the site of the inaugural Games in 1896. Even more symbolically, two of the track and field events – the men's and women's shot – will take place at Olympia itself, where the ancient Games were held for over a thousand years from 776 BC.

In this comprehensive history of Olympic track and field athletics, which contains much new material since the edition of four years ago, I have attempted to present the highlights and flavour of each of the Games since 1896 together with the statistics and trivia so dear to the hearts and minds of track and field fans. Of course, it's the Olympic champions who attract most attention, but it has been my intention also to honour those athletes who may not have won gold medals but still played an important part in the rich pageant that is Olympic history. Indeed, this work is dedicated to all who have fulfilled the ambition of every youngster who comes into our sport: to represent his or her country in an Olympic Games.

Once again it is my hope that readers will derive as much enlightenment and pleasure from this book as I did in researching and writing the material.

Mel Watman, London, May 2004

THE ANCIENT GAMES

LOST IN the swirling mists of Greek antiquity is the exact date of the first Olympic Games. They were definitely held at Olympia in the year 776 BC, and it is recorded that a local man from the district of Elis by the name of Koroibos or Coroibis won the sprint race, but the origins may go back considerably further in time.

Certainly, sporting events were a common feature of life in ancient Greece. Homer, who may have lived in about 900 BC, referred in The Iliad to Games – organised by Achilles – at the funeral of Patroclus, while there are various legends suggesting that Heracles (Hercules), son of Zeus, was responsible for inaugurating the Olympic Games in honour of his father.

Whatever and whenever their origin, the Olympic Games developed into the foremost sports festival in all of Greece. They were staged every four years at Olympia, a shrine to Zeus from around 1000 BC, and the Games contained a large element of religious ceremony including the sacrificing of 100 oxen on the great altar of Zeus.

To begin with, the only Olympic event contested was the stade, a sprint race of 192.27 metres – the length of the stadium, a Latin word deriving from stade. Competitors used a form of starting blocks ... grooved stone slabs set into the ground. The runners, and there could be as many as 20 in a single race, would start from a standing position, with torso bent forward. Woe betide anyone who deliberately false started; rules were strictly enforced and offenders could be flogged by the judges!

A two stades (384m) race, known as diaulos, was instituted in 724 BC. It was an out and back sprint, the runners having to swing round posts at the end of the straight and head back for the start. Negotiating the turn adeptly, as in swimming today, was crucial. The generic Greek word for an athletic contest was agon, from which comes our word agony – appropriate, no doubt, as the runners became engulfed in lactic acid on the second stade.

Long distance runners were catered for from 720 BC when a 24 stades (approx 4600m) race known as dolichos entered the programme, and in 708 BC – by which time, it is believed, the custom of competing naked had been established – the classic all round test, the pentathlon, was inaugurated. That consisted of throwing the discus, standing long jump (involving hand-held weights of up to 4.6 kilograms), throwing the javelin and the stade sprint. Only if the issue had not yet been settled (only victories counted) was the fifth discipline – wrestling –contested.

The javelin, used to lethal effect in hunting and battle, was modified for competitive purposes by the inclusion of a blunt tip. The wooden spear would usually be about six feet (1.83 metres) in length (the modern javelin can be up to 8ft 10in or 2.70 metres long) and it was thrown quite differently. The athlete's middle and index finger would be inserted into a leather thong looped near the javelin's centre of gravity and when he hurled the javelin the thong would uncoil, adding spin as well as thrust to the spear's flight.

It has been calculated that the stadium at Olympia could hold up to 40,000 spectators, but for several centuries women were not allowed to watch. Any woman discovered in the crowd would be hurled to her death from a high rock. However, at a non-Olympic festival staged at Olympia there was a sprint race for unmarried girls. A similar event was held at the other three Games on the pan-Hellenic "circuit".

The only prize awarded at the Olympic Games, at least in the earlier days, was a wreath of wild olive leaves ... although winners were often heaped with riches when they got back home for the honour (and, presumably, the gods' benevolence) they had brought their city.

Later, professionalism and corruption crept in, and as the Greek civilisation declined so too did the Olympic Games. Eventually they were abolished in AD 393 by decree of the Christian emperor Theodosius I, who ordered an end to all pagan ceremonies.

Nevertheless, it is an astonishing achievement, and indicative of the Olympic Games' extraordinary popular appeal, that despite all the wars and political and social upheavals during that time the Games were held without a break every four years for over a thousand years.

THE OLYMPIC REVIVAL

THE ONCE sacred buildings at Olympia were demolished in the fifth century AD, and such natural disasters as floods and earthquakes ultimately left the site buried under some 20 feet of soil. For over a thousand years the Olympic Games were forgotten.

The renewal of interest began not in Greece but early in the 17th century in England, where Robert Dover, a lawyer born in 1582, anticipated Baron de Coubertin by nearly three centuries in being fired by the desire to revive the ancient Olympic ideal. The Cotswold Games, a rural sports meeting, had been held in Gloucestershire since Saxon times, but by bestowing upon the event the grandiose title "Mr Robert Dover's Olimpick Games upon the Cotswold Hills" this rustic festival – which included races for men and women, jumping and throwing as well as such pursuits as dancing and shin kicking – won itself a place in sports history.

Another English contribution was the founding in 1850 by Dr William Penny Brookes, a local surgeon, of the Much Wenlock Olympian Society in Shropshire. That same year the society organised the first Much Wenlock Olympic Games, events including races, high jump and long jump, with the winners being presented with laurel leaves as in ancient Greece.

Two years later, a German archaelogist Ernst Curtius – who had worked at Olympia – advocated the restaging of the Olympic Games in a lecture delivered in Berlin, while in 1859 Major Evangelis Zappas put on a pan-Hellenic sports festival, probably the first since the Olympics' demise, and some 20,000 spectators turned up.

However, the man who is universally regarded as the founder of the modern Olympic Games was an enlightened French aristocrat, Pierre de Fredi, baron de Coubertin (1863-1937). It was he who translated the dream into reality.

Coubertin, an educationalist who passionately believed that mental development could not be divorced from physical development and subscribed to the mens sana in corpore sano (sound mind in a sound body) concept, was only 26 when he was commissioned by the French Government in 1889 to study physical culture in other countries. He was particularly impressed by the English public school sporting tradition. At age 12 he had read Tom Brown's Schooldays, a great influence on him for the rest of his life, and Rugby School was one of his ports of call when he visited England. He also met the aged Dr Brookes, of the Much Wenlock Olympian Society. A devoted Hellenist, Coubertin visited the excavations at Olympia, further enhancing his Olympic vision.

It was in Paris in November 1892 that he first publicly advocated a revival of the Olympic Games. The suggestion was met with cheers. The next step was the organisation, again in Paris, of an international conference. That was held in June 1894, with twelve countries represented, and Coubertin's motion that "sports competitions should be held every fourth year on the lines of the Greek Olympic Games, and every nation should be invited to participate" was approved unanimously.

Coubertin had envisaged reviving the Games in 1900 as part of the International Exposition in Paris, but the Greek delegates at the conference produced an emotional argument in favour of Athens and it was further agreed that the inaugural modern Olympic Games should be staged in 1896. The International Olympic Committee, with Coubertin as secretary general and a Greek, Demetrius Vikelas, as president, came into existence in November 1894 and had less than 18 months to get the show on the road.

Their task was fraught with problems, mainly in relation to the Greek government, which was close to bankruptcy at the time and wanted nothing to do with such a costly exercise. However, public interest ran high and Crown Prince Constantine chaired an Hellenic Olympic Committee.

The Greek people came up with the money required, with businessman Georgios Averoff donating what was then a huge amount to pay for the reconstruction of the Panathenean Stadium. The work was completed in time and all was ready for the opening of the Games on Easter Monday of 1896. The Olympic flame had at last been rekindled after fifteen centuries.

GREEKS HAIL A NEW HERO

THE OPENING ceremony on April 6 was a momentous event. The Games had captured the imagination of the Greek public and over 60,000 people packed the splendid marble stadium, in a state of great excitement and pride as King George I declared the Games open. Thousands more climbed hills which overlooked the open stadium ... "spectators who were too poor to pay the small price of admission to the stadium, but who were determined to see the revival of the ancient Greek festival", according to a contemporary newspaper account.

The Times of April 7 1896 reported: "The coincidence of the 75th anniversary of the declaration of Greek independence, and the celebration of the national festival, with the revival of the ancient Olympic Games is an event calculated to stimulate in the highest degree the patriotic enthusiasm of the Greek nation, recalling as it does, not only the heroic deeds of past generations, but also the noble institutions of a remote and illustrious age.

"If the concourse of strangers [foreign visitors] is not quite so great as was expected, the deficiency is fully made up by the immense crowd of Greeks who have arrived from every part of the world. Great enthusiasm prevails among the people, and it is fully warranted by the success with which all the preparations for the festival have been carried out."

Although nine countries were represented, barely half of the 75 athletics competitors were non-Greek and few of those were officially entered by their countries' national sports bodies. The highly successful American track and field team was drawn only from Princeton University and the Boston Athletic Association, while none of the four Britons who competed was of top national standard. They entered as individuals, for although Charles Herbert, honorary secretary of the AAA, was a member of the International Olympic Committee and helped draw up the programme of twelve athletics events, the AAA decided against sending a British team on the grounds of expense.

Among the leading British athletes of the day were Charles Bradley and Alf Downer (both 9.8 for 100 yards), Edgar Bredin (48.5 440 yards), Fred Bacon (4:17.0 mile) and Godfrey Shaw (15.8 120 yards hurdles), while Irish stars included James Ryan (1.94 high jump) and Denis Horgan (14.16 shot). The greatest Americans, none of whom travelled to Athens either, were Bernie Wefers (9.8 100 yards), Charles Kilpatrick (1:53.4 880 yards), Tom Conneff (4:15.6 mile), Stephen Chase (15.4 120 yards hurdles) and Mike Sweeney (1.97 high jump). Those British, Irish and American performances give an indication of performances achieved by 1896, and one should not be misled by the mediocre marks recorded in Athens.

Despite all the distinguished absentees, English-speaking athletes dominated the track and field events, with nine victories for the Americans and two for a London-based Australian accountant, Edwin Flack, who – like several other competitors from overseas – had heard about the Olympic Games and thought it would be fun to take a holiday trip there. The 333.33m track, with its hairpin bends, was difficult to negotiate but even so Flack's winning times of 2:11.0 for 800m and 4:33.2 for 1500m were nothing to write home about.

There were three other double winners. Tom Burke, the reigning American 440 yards champion, took the 100m in 12.0 after having previously won the 400m in 54.2 – having to reduce speed drastically on the loose cinders before each of the tight bends. Later in the year, at the USA Championships, he showed his true worth by running 48.8 for 440 yards. Ellery Clark, who would later become a successful author, high jumped 1.81 and long jumped 6.35 for a pair of silver medals ... those, not gold medals, were awarded the winners in Athens.

The other double winner, and the most versatile athlete of the Games, was Bob Garrett. In addition to winning the shot (11.22) and discus (29.15) he also placed second in the high jump and long jump. The 20 year-old from Princeton amazed the Greeks by beating their experts in the discus, having never previously seen the 2kg platter to be used in the Games. His only practice had been with a much heavier and unwieldy copy of an ancient Greek implement. Sixth in the discus was 23 year-old Greek scholar George Stuart Robertson, an Oxford blue at hammer throwing who was in Athens primarily to compose and recite the valedictory Greek ode.

Of the other British competitors, Launceston Elliott was fourth in his 100m heat (but he did win the single-handed weightlifting title), Charles Gmelin was third in the 400m to become Britain's first Olympic athletics medallist, and Grantley Goulding was second to Tom Curtis (USA) in the 110m hurdles. The other American winners were Bill Hoyt in the pole vault and James Connolly in what was then known as the hop step and jump, although in fact he took two hops and a jump to register 13.71 and become the first Olympic champion to be crowned for some 15 centuries.

The final event, the marathon, brought glory at last to the Greeks. But it was thanks to the French historian Michel Breal, aided and abetted by Baron de Coubertin, that the race was part of the Olympic programme. Inspired by the (probably apocryphal) story of the military courier Pheidippides, or Philippides, who ran 40 kilometres from Marathon to Athens to bring news of a famous Greek victory over the Persians in 490 BC and promptly collapsed and died after uttering the words "Rejoice; we conquer", the two Frenchmen urged the organising committee to stage a commemorative race over the route. The Greeks agreed.

When first the Frenchman Albin Lermusiaux, and then Edwin Flack led the field of 18 runners, 14 of whom were Greeks, the onlookers groaned. But both front runners collapsed from exhaustion, and excitement ran high as the news spread that a Greek shepherd by the name of Spiridon Louis was out in front. The starter, Colonel Papadiamantopoulos, entered the stadium on horseback and rushed over to the royal box. By the time Louis reached the entrance to the stadium ("all dust and perspiration", as an American observed), Prince George and Crown Prince Constantine were on hand to escort him to the finish.

Louis, who was 23 and had finished only fifth in a trial race over the course in 3:18:27, covered the 40k route in 2:58:50 ... and became a national hero.

"The scene in the stadium when it was discovered that a Greek was leading baffles description," reported The Times. "The winner, a young peasant named Louis from a village two hours distant from Athens, was running in good form as he entered the stadium and approached the winning post close by the royal box, amid a rain of flowers and bouquets. His success was quite unexpected. The result of the marathon race was quickly telegraphed to all the chief towns of Greece, and demonstrations in honour of the victor are reported from many parts of the country."

The euphoria in Greece over the Olympic revival was not reflected everywhere. A sniffy leading article in London's Sunday Times stated: "The Olympic Games, which have been held at Athens during the past week, have aroused an interest which is, perhaps, a good deal in excess of their importance. They are the first of an international tournament which is intended to be held annually [sic]. Athens was selected as the scene of the first because, we presume, it was in Greece that the ancient Olympic Games were played. But the modern Greeks are evidently degenerates as athletes. Except in the 26 miles foot race, from Marathon to Athens, Grecian competitors have carried off very few of the prizes. England does not appear to have figured very prominently, but the probability is that the English competitors in the Games are by no means the best athletes we could put in the arena. The prizes were not attractive enough to draw our champions."

Even more sour was the writer of this piece

STAR OF THE GAMES

SPIRIDON LOUIS
(born 12 Jan 1873; died 26 Mar 1940)

How appropriate that the marathon, run over the legendary route from Marathon to Athens, should be won by a Greek ... transforming the previously unheralded Spiridon Louis into a national icon.

in The Spectator, dated April 11 1896. "It is impossible to get honestly interested in the revival of the Olympic Games. They are not contested in the old place, but in Athens, or in the old way, but among the representatives of outsiders whom the Hellenes would have contemptuously styled barbarians, or in the old spirit, for the last thing the spectators are thinking of is the comparative beauty of the combatants or the effect of their training upon the beauty of the race. The people of Athens are interested ... but, to the rest of the world, the 'revival' is little more than an ordinary international contest of athletics.

"One wonders what Pericles would have said if he could have known that, when the Olympic Games were revived 2,300 years after his death, nearly all the honours would be carried away by barbarians from a continent of the existence of which he had never dreamed ... or that they would have so mastered the secrets of nature that they could send accounts of a victory or defeat at Athens instantaneously under the ocean to their own abodes."

Critics and sceptics notwithstanding, the modern Olympic Games were away and running. There would be crises to come, but one of man's nobler exercises had been enthusiastically relaunched.

Please note that there are discrepancies among historians concerning some of the 1896 Olympic results. Those below are believed to be accurate, but it's not possible to be dogmatic about it. In these and results of some later Games, certain place times are estimates.

1896 - ATHENS

100m: 1, Tom Burke USA 12.0; 2, Fritz Hofmann GER 12.2; 3, Alajos Szokolyi HUN 12.6.

400m: 1, Tom Burke USA 54.2; 2, Herbert Jamison USA 56.2; 3, Charles Gmelin GBR 56.6; 4, Fritz Hofmann GER 56.6 (although some sources give 3rd to Hofmann and 4th to Gmelin).

800m: 1, Edwin Flack AUS 2:11.0; 2, Nándor Dani HUN 2:11.8; 3, Dimitrios Golemis GRE 2:28.0.

1500m: 1, Edwin Flack AUS 4:33.2; 2, Arthur Blake USA 4:34.2; 3, Albin Lermusiaux FRA 4:36.0.

Marathon: (40k) 1, Spiridon Louis GRE 2:58:50; 2, Charilaos Vasilakos GRE 3:06:03; 3, Gyula Kellner HUN 3:06:35.

110mH: 1, Tom Curtis USA 17.6; 2, Grantley Goulding GBR 17.7 (only 2 ran in final).

HJ: 1, Ellery Clark USA 1.81; eq2, James Connolly USA & Bob Garrett USA 1.65.

PV: 1, Bill Hoyt USA 3.30; 2, Albert Tyler USA 3.20; eq3, Evangelos Damaskos GRE & Ioannis Theodoropoulos GRE 2.60.

LJ: 1, Ellery Clark USA 6.35; 2, Bob Garrett USA 6.18; 3, James Connolly USA 6.11.

TJ: 1, James Connolly USA 13.71; 2, Alexandre Tuffere FRA 12.70; 3, Ioannis Persakis GRE 12.56.

SP: 1, Bob Garrett USA 11.22; 2, Miltiades Gouskos GRE 11.20; 3, Georgios Papasideris GRE 10.36.

DT: 1, Bob Garrett USA 29.15 (world best); 2, Panagiotis Paraskevopoulos GRE 28.95; 3, Sotirios Versis GRE 28.78.

WORLD BESTS AT THE START OF 1900

The following are listed as the best marks as at January 1 1900 in the IAAF's "Progression of World Best Performances & Official World Records" compiled by Richard Hymans.
100m: 10.8 Cecil Lee GBR 1892, Etienne de Ré BEL 1893, L Atcherley GBR 1895, Harry Beaton GBR 1895, Harald Andersson SWE 1896 & Isaac Westergren SWE 1898/1899; 200m/220y: 21.4y James Maybury USA 1897; 400m/440y: 48.5y Henry Lenox Tindall GBR 1889 & Edgar Bredin GBR 1895; professional: 48.3y Richard Buttery GBR 1873; 800m/880y: 1:53.4y Charles Kilpatrick USA 1895; 1500m: 4:10.4 Albin Lermusiaux FRA 1896; Mile: 4:15.6 Thomas Conneff USA 1895; pro: 4:12.8 Walter George GBR 1886; 3 Miles: 14:24.0 Sidney Thomas GBR 1893; pro: 14:19.5 Peter Cannon GBR 1888; 6 Miles: 30:17.8 Thomas 1892; pro: 29:50.0 Jack White GBR 1863; 120yH: 15.2y Alvin Kraenzlein USA 1898; 400mH/440yH: 56.4y Jerome Buck USA 1896; HJ: 1.97 Michael Sweeney USA 1895; PV: 3.62 Raymond Clapp USA 1898; LJ: 7.43 Kraenzlein 1899; TJ: 14.94 James Connolly USA 1896; pro: 14.96 Tom Aitken GBR 1873; SP: 14.75 George Gray CAN 1898; DT: 36.19 Charles Henneman USA 1897; HT: 51.10 John Flanagan IRL 1899; JT: 49.32 Eric Lemming SWE 1899.

THE 1896 Games in Athens were well organised and a great popular success although most of the world's best athletes were absent and performance levels were low. By way of contrast, the 1900 edition in Paris did attract many of the world's elite and several fine performances were registered, but the organisation was adjudged to be appalling and little interest was taken by the Parisian public in what was merely a sideshow at the great Paris International Exhibition.

A writer in the British magazine The Field, dated July 28 1900, did not pull any punches. "The whole series of sports produced nothing but muddles, bad arrangements, bad management, bad prizes and any amount of ill-feeling amongst the nationalities engaged."

One source of friction was the 500m grass track at the Racing Club of France's grounds in the Bois de Boulogne. As late as mid-May circulars were still being issued by the organisers stating that all races would be run on a cinder track – but it never materialised. Instead there was uneven turf, which was not helped by excessive watering. Field event facilities were not any better, and another disappointment was the smallness of the crowds. The first day of athletics drew only a thousand spectators, at least half of whom were Americans. The exuberance of the transatlantic visitors, who had plenty to celebrate, did not endear them to the few local fans who turned up.

"The introduction of the American college cheers was a complete revelation to the Frenchmen and other foreigners," related an American newspaper dispatch. "At the first yell they apparently imagined some invasion of wild Indians had occurred, but after hearing the various cries about a hundred times during the day they appreciated the fact that it was simply an outburst of American enthusiasm or encouragement of the college men. The Frenchmen, however, could not be reconciled to this form of cheering, and they were heard to frequently exclaim: 'what a band of savages!'"

Franco-American relations were not improved by a dispute over the timetable of events. Again, there was no official USA team; it was a collection of individuals representing various universities and clubs, and the universities involved were against any competition on a Sunday. Apparently, the university authorities were given an assurance that their athletes would not be required to compete on a Sunday, only to find that the timetable had been fixed, several finals were scheduled for Sunday and no changes could be made. As a result, several leading American athletes had to withdraw.

That angered a Daily Express correspondent who saw it all as a dastardly plot by the French following an impressive showing by the Americans in the AAA Championships shortly before the Games. "The crack athletes of the United States made a great success in London. The Parisian argument seems to be that, if they can beat the best Great Britain can produce, France has no sort of chance. Hence the choice of a Sunday for the international sports. There is one phrase which describes this to all of us. It is 'unEnglish'. Unfortunately, both the literal and the sentimental meanings of it are unknown to our neighbours across the Channel."

The most famous victim was Meyer Prinstein, of the University of Syracuse, a predominantly Methodist seat of learning. On the Saturday, Prinstein – the world long jump record holder with 7.50 – led the qualifying competition with a leap of 7.17, well ahead of his predecessor as world record holder, Alvin Kraenzlein (6.93). In those days performances made in a qualifying round of a field event counted towards the final placings, and having – so he thought – made an agreement with Kraenzlein that both would miss the final next day Prinstein reckoned the gold medal was safely his. To his consternation, howev-

STAR OF THE GAMES

ALVIN KRAENZLEIN
(born 12 Dec 1876; died 6 Jan 1928)

The only athlete to win four individual titles in one Games, the versatile American scored in the 60m, 110m hurdles, 200m hurdles and long jump, setting world bests in the short sprint and high hurdles.

er, Kraenzlein did show up for the final, and with a jump of 7.18 snatched victory by a centimetre. A furious Prinstein punched his rival on the nose. The irony of it all was that Polish-born Prinstein, forbidden by his college to compete on a Sunday, was himself Jewish!

That controversy notwithstanding, the 23 year-old Kraenzlein was the star of the Games as he won four individual titles, the most by any athlete at a single Olympics, although two of them came in events which were only briefly on the Olympic programme: the 60m, in which he set a world best of 7.0, and the 200m low hurdles in which he clocked 25.4 which was far inferior to the 23.6 he recorded for 220 yards hurdles on a straight track in 1898. Kraenzlein's other victory came in the 110m hurdles, where his time of 15.4 was a world best.

Even more medals (actually, prizes were awarded instead of medals in Paris) were won by fellow-American Walter Tewksbury, who not only triumphed in the 200m and 400m hurdles but was also second in the 60m and 100m and third in the 200m hurdles. To the chagrin of the home supporters, his 400m hurdles win came at the expense of the French champion, Henri Tauzin, and although the time of 57.6 now looks exceedingly slow one should make allowances for the fact that the first nine hurdles were actually 30-foot long telegraph poles strung across the track at the requisite height and the final barrier was a 16-foot water jump! No wonder the Canadian who finished third, George Orton, had earlier won the 2500m steeplechase – a race which reportedly included "stone fences, a water jump, hurdles and other obstacles."

In fact, there were two steeplechase races and the other, over 4000m, resulted in a British clean sweep as John Rimmer, a 22 year-old Liverpool policeman, won from Charles Bennett and Sidney Robinson. The small British team of five (one an Irishman, Patrick Leahy) performed remarkably well, winning a total of nine medals, four of them gold.

The star was Bennett, who outshone his second place in the steeplechase with wins in the 1500m and 5000m team race, setting 'world records' in both. In fact, there were no official world records prior to the IAAF's creation in 1912 but Bennett's 1500m victory (Britain's first

ever Olympic gold medal) in 4:06.2 was the fastest time yet registered although considerably inferior to the world best mile time of 4:15.6 by Tom Conneff (USA), never mind Walter George's professional mark of 4:12.8 (actually 4:12 3/4) back in 1886. The pace varied wildly as the first 500m lap was covered in 81.2, the second in 94.8 and the third in 70.2!

Bennett (29), an engine driver based at Bournemouth who ran for Finchley Harriers, went on to finish first in the 5000m in 15:29.8 (some sources give 15:20.0), again a world best but not to be compared with Sidney Thomas' amateur 3 miles best of 14:24.0 in 1893. This was not an individual event (it did not enter the Olympic programme as such until 1912) but a team race. Five runners per team were required, and only France and Britain lined up. In truth, Britain could field only four runners, but they were permitted to complete the team with the Australian Stanley Rowley, who had finished third in all three sprints. He had no intention of running the full distance and after seven laps of jogging and walking was allowed to retire without penalising the team.

The remaining British victory occurred in the 800m where Alfred Tysoe, a farm worker from Lancashire, put together 400's of 65.0 and 56.2 to win in 2:01.2. That didn't represent the speed at which he could run, for he had won the AAA 880 yards in 1:57.8, the fastest in the world that year. Tragically, the Salford Harrier went down with pleurisy the following year and died 15 months after his Olympic success at the age of 27.

As Ireland did not compete in the Olympics as a separate entity until 1924, Patrick Leahy participated as a member of the Great Britain & Ireland team, finishing second in the high jump, third in the long jump and fourth in the triple jump, won by Prinstein. Both the high jump and pole vault were won by Irving Baxter, whose medal tally rose to five with three second places to the phenomenal Ray Ewry in the standing jumps events - held all on one day!. Ewry, who as a boy was confined to a wheelchair after contracting polio, had no peer in his particular field and would go on to win a record total of ten Olympic titles if one includes the 1906 Interim Games. Another athlete who was embarking upon a great Olympic career was hammer thrower John Flanagan, a New York policeman who emigrated to the USA in 1896 from County Limerick in Ireland. He won the first of three titles.

As in Athens, so in Paris it was the marathon which produced the only home winner – although research by French statistician Alain Bouillé suggests that Michel Theato was actually born a citizen of Luxembourg. On a boiling hot day only three men broke four hours for the twisting, poorly marked 40.26k (25 miles) course, and there are lingering suspicions that Theato might not have run the full distance. The American, Arthur Newton maintained he took the lead at halfway and was never passed, but he was officially placed fifth in 4:04:12.

It was symptomatic of a Games which would have won a gold medal for confusion. "We have made a hash of our work," admitted Baron de Coubertin, who had succeeded as International Olympic Committee president in 1896 and would remain so until 1925. "It's a miracle that the Olympic movement survived that celebration."

1900 - PARIS

60m: 1, Alvin Kraenzlein USA 7.0 (world best); 2, Walter Tewksbury USA 7.0; 3, Stanley Rowley AUS 7.1; 4, Edmund Minahan USA 7.2.

100m: 1, Frank Jarvis USA 11.0 (10.8 heat; equals world best); 2, Walter Tewksbury USA 11.1 (10.8 semi-final; equals world best); 3, Stanley Rowley AUS 11.2; Arthur Duffey USA dnf.

200m: 1, Walter Tewksbury USA 22.2; 2, Norman Pritchard GBR 22.6; 3, Stanley Rowley AUS 22.7; 4, William Holland USA 22.7.

400m: 1, Maxie Long USA 49.4; 2, William Holland USA 49.9; 3, Ernst Schultz DEN 51.5.

800m: 1, Alfred Tysoe GBR 2:01.2; 2, John Cregan USA 2:01.6; 3, David Hall USA 2:02.5; 4, Henri Deloge FRA.

1500m: 1, Charles Bennett GBR 4:06.2 (world best); 2, Henri Deloge FRA 4:06.6; 3, John Bray USA 4:09.2; 4, David Hall USA 4:09.5.

5000m (team race): 1, Great Britain & Ireland 26pts (1, Charles Bennett 15:29.8 – world best; 2, John Rimmer 15:35.5; 6, Sidney Robinson; 7, Alfred Tysoe; 10, Stanley Rowley AUS); 2, France 29 (3, Henri Deloge 15:42.0; 4, Gaston Ragueneau; 5, Jacques Chastanie; 8, Andre Castanet; 9, Michel Champoudry).

Marathon: (40.26k) 1, Michel Théato FRA/LUX 2:59:45; 2, Emile Champion FRA 3:04:17; 3, Ernst Fast SWE 3:37:14; 4, Eugene Besse FRA 4:00:43.

2500mSC: 1, George Orton CAN 7:34.4; 2, Sidney Robinson GBR 7:35.8; 3, Jacques Chastanie FRA 7:42.0; 4, Arthur Newton USA.

4000mSC: 1, John Rimmer GBR 12:58.4; 2, Charles Bennett GBR 12:58.6; 3, Sidney Robinson GBR 12:58.8; 4, Jacques Chastanie FRA 13:00.4; 5, George Orton CAN.

110mH: 1, Alvin Kraenzlein USA 15.4 (world best); 2, John McLean USA 15.5; 3, Fred Moloney USA 15.6; 4, Jean Lécuyer FRA.

200mH: 1, Alvin Kraenzlein USA 25.4; 2, Norman Pritchard GBR 25.9; 3, Walter Tewksbury USA 26.0; 4, Eugene Choisel FRA 26.5.

400mH: 1, Walter Tewksbury USA 57.6; 2, Henri Tauzin FRA 58.1; 3, George Orton CAN 58.9; William Lewis USA dns

HJ: 1, Irving Baxter USA 1.90; 2, Patrick Leahy GBR/IRL 1.78; 3, Lajos Gönczy HUN 1.75; eq4, Carl-Albert Andersen NOR, Eric Lemming SWE & Waldemar Steffen GER 1.70.

PV: 1, Irving Baxter USA 3.30; 2, Meredith Colkett USA 3.25; 3, Carl-Albert Andersen NOR 3.20; eq4, Eric Lemming SWE, Jakab Kauser HUN (age 13!) & Emile Gontier FRA 3.10.

LJ: 1, Alvin Kraenzlein USA 7.18; 2, Meyer Prinstein USA 7.17; 3, Patrick Leahy GBR/IRL 6.95; 4, William Remington USA 6.82.

TJ: 1, Meyer Prinstein USA 14.47; 2, James Connolly USA 13.97; 3, Lewis Sheldon USA 13.64; 4, Patrick Leahy GBR/IRL 13.36.

SP: 1, Richard Sheldon USA 14.10; 2, Josiah McCracken USA 12.85; 3, Robert Garrett USA 12.35; 4, Rezso Crettier HUN 12.05.

DT: 1, Rudolf Bauer HUN 36.04; 2, Frantisek Janda-Suk BOH 35.25; 3, Richard Sheldon USA 34.60; 4, Panagiotis Paraskevopoulos GRE 34.04.

HT: 1, John Flanagan USA 51.01; 2, Truxton Hare USA 46.25; 3, Josiah McCracken USA 44.50; 4, Eric Lemming SWE.

Standing HJ: 1, Ray Ewry USA 1.65 (world best); 2, Irving Baxter USA 1.52; 3, Lewis Sheldon USA 1.50.

Standing LJ: 1, Ray Ewry USA 3.30; 2, Irving Baxter USA 3.13; 3, Emile Torcheboeuf FRA 3.03.

Standing TJ: 1, Ray Ewry USA 10.58; 2, Irving Baxter USA 9.95; 3, Robert Garrett USA 9.50.

AN ALL-AMERICAN AFFAIR

THE INTERNATIONAL Olympic Committee, meeting in Paris in May 1901, came out in favour of Chicago as the venue for the 1904 Games ... but St Louis, due to stage a World's Fair that year, threatened to upstage the "windy city" by arranging a big sports meeting of its own. The IOC weakly allowed the dispute between the two American cities to be decided by President "Teddy" Roosevelt, who plumped for St Louis. The IOC rubber-stamped the decision, despite being only too aware, after Paris, of the problems of allowing the Olympic Games to be a mere sideshow at a world exposition instead of being a great international festival in its own right.

It was a mistake which could have sounded the death knell for the Olympic movement. There was little public interest in, or even awareness of, the Olympic Games in St Louis; and, as in Paris, even many of the participating athletes did not realise the historic significance of the competition. In fact, as there were so few foreign competitors (only ten countries were represented in athletics, compared with 16 in Paris) the 1904 Olympics were little more than a glorified American inter-club contest. Indeed, official club scores were kept with the New York Athletic Club just beating the Chicago Athletic Association in a bitterly contested battle.

Over a four and a half month period so many sports events were staged in St Louis in connection with the exposition to celebrate the centenary of the purchase of Louisiana from France that it was not always obvious which were, or were not, deemed Olympic contests. The track and field programme was staged between August 29 and September 3 ... so it's a moot point whether the triathlon and 'decathlon', held at the beginning of July, really had much to do with the Olympics as such. Performance levels at the meeting were high, thanks to the strength of the American athletes, but the event was of little international significance and even Baron de Coubertin did not bother to attend.

Only two events eluded the athletes from the USA: the 56 pound weight throw, won by Montreal policeman Etienne Desmarteau

(who died of typhoid the very next year, aged 32), and the aforementioned 'decathlon'. This was actually styled as the US All-Around Championship, and although it was a ten-event test it didn't bear much resemblance to the decathlon as we now know it. The events were, in this sequence: 100 yards, shot, high jump, 880 yards walk, hammer, pole vault, 120 yards hurdles, 56 pound weight throw, long jump and mile ... oh, and all on one day! The winner was a remarkable 35 year-old Irishman, Tom Kiely, five times AAA hammer champion between 1897 and 1902 and a 15.47 triple jumper (two hops and a jump actually) back in 1892.

Two other Irish-born athletes won titles, but as American citizens. John Flanagan, who hailed from County Limerick, retained his hammer laurels, this time throwing from a 7ft (2.13) circle as against 9ft (2.74) in 1900, while County Mayo's Martin Sheridan, a member of New York's finest, won the discus. It was a close call for Sheridan, as both he and Ralph Rose threw the same distance of 39.28. For the first and only time in Olympic history, a throw-off was ordered, and Sheridan came out on top. Rose had previously won the shot (from a 7ft circle rather than the 7ft square at the two previous Olympics) with a world's best equalling 14.81. Only 19, he was 1.98 (6'6") tall and weighed 106kg at the time of the Games although he would later balloon to 130kg (over 20 stones). Tragically, both Rose and Sheridan died young ... 28 and 36 respectively.

On the grounds of expense, no British team was sent to St Louis, and so the Games were deprived of Alf Shrubb, who that year established himself as the greatest distance runner the world had yet seen with a season which included the international cross country championship and such world bests as 9:09.6 for 2 miles, 14:17.2 for 3 miles, 29:59.4 for 6 miles, 31:02.4 for 10,000m and 50:40.6 for 10 miles, that last mark surviving until 1928. The 5000m and 10,000m did not enter the Olympic programme until 1912 but Shrubb would have been well capable of winning the 1500m, which went to James Lightbody in a world best (but a very weak one compared to the mile) of 4:05.4.

There was, however, one British-born

winner in St Louis: marathon champion Tom Hicks, a 29 year-old professional clown who first saw the light of day in Birmingham.

The clown of the race, though, was his American team-mate Fred Lorz, who actually crossed the finishing line in first place but was disqualified when it transpired that he had covered much of the course in a car! Apparently, after an attack of cramp at 9 miles he was offered a lift back to the stadium but when the car broke down at the 20 miles mark Lorz got out and started running again. He claimed it was all a joke but the authorities took a dim view of it and he was disqualified 'for life', although the ban was lifted so quickly that the following spring he won the Boston Marathon in 2:38:24.

Hicks, like Spiridon Louis before him, never raced again after his Olympic triumph. The intense heat, the hilly nature of the 40k course, the dust thrown up by passing cars, and the fact that no water was provided en route other than one well at about halfway made it a particularly gruelling test for the runners, as can be judged from the times. Hicks, who had clocked 2:39:35 when finishing second at Boston four months earlier, was timed at 3:28:53 and was in a dreadful state at the finish. About seven miles from the end, with a big lead, he was close to collapse but his helpers insisted he kept going. There being no rules prohibiting drugs in those days, he was given a mixture of strychnine and raw egg white. That kept him shuffling along, and further doses plus the odd nip of brandy enabled him to reach the finish six minutes ahead of Albert Corey, a Frenchman who worked as a professional strike-breaker in Chicago. The race was notable also for the appearance of the first black African runners in Olympic history. Two Kaffir tribesmen from South Africa, who happened to be at the World's Fair as part of a Boer War exhibit, took part and finished ninth and twelfth.

The Games also produced the first black medallists in the Americans George Poage, who was third in the 200m hurdles and 400m hurdles, and Joseph Stadler, second in the standing high jump and third in the standing triple jump. Both those titles were retained by

Ray Ewry, as was the standing long jump in which Ewry propelled himself to a world best of 3.47.

The winner of the 400m hurdles, Harry Hillman, was credited with 53.0, a sensational time considering the world best then stood at 57.2. The explanation was that the race was run over 2'6" (76cm) hurdles instead of 3'0" (91.4cm), although Hillman might well have run around 55 sec over the full size barriers. He had earlier won the flat 400m in 49.2 in a straight final of 13 runners! Hillman, who also won the 200m hurdles, and Scottish-born Lawson Robertson (third in the standing high jump and sixth in the 100m) would, several years later in 1909, team up to set a remarkable world best of 11.0 for the 100 yards three-legged race.

The predominant sprinter in St Louis was Archie Hahn, "the Milwaukee whirlwind", who captured the 60m in a world best equalling 7.0, the 200m in 21.6 (on a straight course, the track measuring three laps to a mile or 536.6 metres), and the 100m against a strong wind in 11.0. As the 60m was discontinued, the 1.65 (5'5") tall Hahn became the only triple sprint winner in Olympic history. Incidentally, in the 200m a domestic false start rule was applied, and all three of Hahn's rivals in the final received a two-yard penalty for beating the gun. As there wasn't too much space behind the start line that was commuted to one yard – but Hahn won by three yards anyway.

Another triple winner was James Lightbody, whose world best 1500m came after victories in the steeplechase (2590m) and 800m, while Meyer Prinstein became the only man to win both the long jump and triple jump. That he achieved on the same day, thus retaining his triple jump laurels and finally gaining the long jump title which had eluded him so narrowly and controversially four years earlier. Another whose patience was rewarded was pole vaulter Charles Dvorak, one of the men who had been withdrawn from the 1900 Games because his event was contested on a Sunday. The first vaulter to use a bamboo pole, in preference to ash or hickory, he cleared 3.50 for victory and unsuccessfully attempted a world best of 3.71.

1904 - ST LOUIS

60m: 1, Archie Hahn USA 7.0 (equals world best); 2, William Hogenson USA 7.1 (7.0 heat, eq world best); 3, Fay Moulton USA 7.1; 4, Clyde Blair USA 7.1 (7.0 heat, equals world best).

100m: 1, Archie Hahn USA 11.0; 2, Nate Cartmell USA 11.2; 3, William Hogenson USA 11.3; 4, Fay Moulton USA 11.4.

200m: (straight track) 1, Archie Hahn USA 21.6; 2, Nate Cartmell USA 21.9; 3, William Hogenson USA 22.1; 4, Fay Moulton USA.

400m: 1, Harry Hillman USA 49.2; 2, Frank Waller USA 49.8; 3, Herman Groman USA 50.0; 4, Joseph Fleming USA 50.6; 5, Meyer Prinstein USA 50.7.

800m: 1, James Lightbody USA 1:56.0; 2, Howard Valentine USA 1:56.3; 3, Emil Breitkreutz USA 1:56.4; 4, George Underwood USA 1:57.2.

1500m: 1, James Lightbody USA 4:05.4 (world best); 2, William Verner USA 4:06.8; 3, Lacey Hearn USA; 4, David Munson USA.

Marathon: (40k) 1, Tom Hicks USA 3:28:53; 2, Albert Corey FRA 3:34:52; 3, Arthur Newton USA 3:47:33; 4, Felix Carvajal CUB.

2590mSC: 1, James Lightbody USA 7:39.6; 2, John Daly GBR/IRL 7:40.6; 3, Arthur Newton USA; 4, William Verner USA.

110mH: 1, Frederick Schule USA 16.0; 2, Thaddeus Shideler USA 16.2; 3, Lesley Ashburner USA 16.4; 4, Frank Castleman USA.

200mH: (straight track) 1, Harry Hillman USA 24.6; 2, Frank Castleman USA 24.9; 3, George Poage USA 25.2; 4, George Varnell USA.

STAR OF THE GAMES

RAY EWRY

(born 14 Oct 1873; died 29 Sep 1937)

The standing jumps are now an historical curiosity, but in his day the American, Ray Ewry, was one of the world's outstanding athletes. He won all ten of the Olympic events he contested between 1900 and 1908, an all-time record, three of them in St Louis

400mH: (2'6"/76cm hurdles) 1, Harry Hillman USA 53.0; 2, Frank Waller USA 53.2; 3, George Poage USA 58.4; 4, George Varnell USA.

HJ: 1, Sam Jones USA 1.80; 2, Garrett Serviss USA 1.77; 3, Paul Weinstein GER 1.77; 4, Lajos Gönczy HUN 1.75.

PV: 1, Charles Dvorak USA 3.50; 2, Leroy Samse USA 3.43; 3, Louis Wilkins USA 3.35; 4, Ward McLanahan USA 3.35; 5, Claude Allen USA 3.35.

LJ: 1, Meyer Prinstein USA 7.34; 2, Daniel Frank USA 6.89; 3, Robert Stangland USA 6.88; 4, Fred Englehardt USA 6.63.

TJ: 1, Meyer Prinstein USA 14.35; 2, Fred Englehardt USA 13.90; 3, Robert Stangland USA 13.36; 4, John Fuhler USA 12.91.

SP: 1, Ralph Rose USA 14.81 (eq world best); 2, Wesley Coe USA 14.40; 3, Leon Feuerbach USA 13.37; 4, Martin Sheridan USA 12.39.

DT: 1, Martin Sheridan USA 39.28; 2, Ralph Rose USA 39.28; 3, Nikolaos Georgantas GRE 37.68; 4, John Flanagan USA 36.14.

HT: 1, John Flanagan USA 51.23; 2, John DeWitt USA 50.26; 3, Ralph Rose USA 45.73; 4, Charles Chadwick USA 42.78.

Triathlon: 1, Max Emmerich USA 35.7pts (LJ-6.58, SP-9.81, 100yards-10.6); 2, John Grieb USA 34.0; 3, William Merz USA 32.95.

'Decathlon': 1, Tom Kiely GBR/IRL 6036 (100yards-11.2, SP-10.82, HJ-1.52, 880yards walk-3:59.0, HT-36.76, PV-2.74, 120yards H-17.8, 56lb weight-8.91, LJ-5.94, mile-5:51.0); 2, Adam Gunn USA 5907; 3, Truxtun Hare USA 5813.

4 Miles (team race): 1, New York AC 27pts (1, Arthur Newton 21:17.8; 5, George Underwood; 6, Paul Pilgrim; 7, Howard Valentine; 8, David Munson); 2, Chicago AA 28 (2, James Lightbody; 3, William Verner; 4, Lacey Hearn; 9, Albert Corey FRA; 10, Sidney Hatch).

56lb Weight: 1, Etienne Desmarteau CAN 10.46; 2, John Flanagan USA 10.16; 3, James Mitchel USA 10.13.

Standing HJ: 1, Ray Ewry USA 1.60; 2, Joseph Stadler USA 1.45; 3, Lawson Robertson USA 1.45.

Standing LJ: 1, Ray Ewry USA 3.47 (world best); 2, Charles King USA 3.27; 3, John Biller USA 3.25.

Standing TJ: 1, Ray Ewry USA 10.54; 2, Charles King USA 10.16; 3, Joseph Stadler USA 9.60.

WAS IT or was it not an Olympic celebration? The status of the Interim or Intercalated or Athenian Games of 1906 is still a subject for argument. In one sense they cannot count as a normal Olympics as they took place halfway through an Olympiad, and one of the historic foundations of the Olympic Games was that they were held every fourth year. But, although they are considered unofficial by the International Olympic Committee, the 1906 Games were certainly promoted by the Greeks as Olympic Games and Olympic medals were awarded.

As in 1896, but unlike the 1900 and 1904 editions, the Games were an immense success with the public, with huge crowds flocking to the Panathenean Stadium each day. As Capt F A M Webster wrote a few years later: "The Games of 1906, although not partaking of the nature of a regular Olympiad, yet had great importance in the development of the scheme in that they formed by far the most important gathering of athletes which had ever up to that time been brought together."

The Greeks had, from the outset, wanted to stage the Games permanently in Athens but Baron de Coubertin's view that the Games should be hosted throughout the world prevailed. As a compromise, therefore, the Greeks proposed to hold their own Olympic-style series of international events halfway between each official celebration but it wasn't until 1906 that the notion became a reality ... and it turned out to be the last such meeting, for after the 1908 Games in London the future of the Olympic movement was assured anyway.

These 1906 Games were taken seriously by the two main athletics powers, for the USA held trials for the first time and the formation of the British Olympic Association in May 1905 and the funds raised by that body enabled Britain to be properly represented.

Southampton-born Lieutenant Henry Hawtrey (24) of the Royal Engineers won the only long distance track race on the programme, a 5 miles event, in 26:11.8. He would go on to be decorated in the First World War, reach the rank of Brigadier and become an aide-de-camp to King George V.

The other "British" winners were in fact men from the Emerald Isle who still had no alternative but to be entered as from Great Britain & Ireland. Con Leahy, one of seven brothers all of whom became distinguished athletes, went one place better than Patrick Leahy in 1900 by winning a long drawn out high jump with a modest leap of 1.77, while Peter O'Connor – decisively beaten by Meyer Prinstein in the long jump, 7.20 to 7.02, after fouling several of his efforts – made amends by winning the triple jump (14.07) ahead of Con Leahy. He celebrated by shinning up the flagpole, removing the Union Jack and replacing it with the Irish flag ... an early example of the Games being used for political purposes. Despite being a heavy pipe smoker, O'Connor was an athlete ahead of his time, for his world long jump record of 7.61 set in Dublin in 1901 stood as a world record for 20 years and as an Irish record for almost 90! Of that jump, a quarter inch short of 25 feet, Harold Abrahams (whose elder brother Sidney placed fifth in the 1906 long jump) would write: "I always marvel at the integrity of the judges who measured O'Connor's jump. I think I should have been tempted to make it 25 feet."

The London-born Scot, Wyndham Halswelle, came away with two medals. In the 400m he was second to Paul Pilgrim, who was allowed to accompany the USA team to Athens at his own expense after failing to be

STAR OF THE GAMES

PAUL PILGRIM
(born 26 Oct 1883; died 7 Jan 1958)

Not until Alberto Juantorena 70 years later would anyone emulate Paul Pilgrim's feat of winning both the 400m and 800m. The American beat Wyndham Halswelle (the 400m winner in 1908) and James Lightbody (the 800m champion in 1904) respectively officially selected. The next day, Pilgrim took the 800m with Halswelle third. Not until Alberto Juantorena in 1976 would that particular Olympic double be achieved again. Another Scot, Irish-born John McGough, finished second in the 1500m.

Among other new events was the javelin, which despite its ancient Greek origins was dominated in those days by the Swedes. In what was labelled "freestyle javelin throwing", enabling competitors to throw the spear in any manner of their choice, the Stockholm policeman Eric Lemming used a conventional technique to reach 53.90, surpassing his own world best. Fifth of the 22 entrants for that event, and winner of an ancient Greek style discus contest (no spinning allowed), was 36 year-old Verner Järvinen, an important figure in Olympic history. Not only did he win Finland's first ever gold medal but one of his sons, Matti, would win the Olympic javelin title in 1932; another, Akilles, would twice take the decathlon silver medal (1928 and 1932).

Hopes of another Greek victory in the marathon came to nothing, the highest placed local runner finishing fifth. The winner was Canada's Billy Sherring, a railwayman from Hamilton, Ontario, who only scraped together his fare to Athens thanks to a bet on a horse which came in at 6-1. Sherring covered the 41.86k (26 miles) course in 2:51:24, his bodyweight dropping from 112 to 98lb during the race! The non-finishers included a 20 year-old Italian who had a 42k time of 2:42 to his credit. He dropped out at 24k with stomach trouble. Two years later his name would be on everybody's lips ... Dorando Pietri.

1906 - ATHENS (Interim Games)

100m: 1, Archie Hahn USA 11.2; 2, Fay Moulton USA 11.3; 3, Nigel Barker AUS 11.3.
400m: 1, Paul Pilgrim USA 53.2; 2, Wyndham Halswelle GBR 53.8; 3, Nigel Barker AUS 54.1.
800m: 1, Paul Pilgrim USA 2:01.5; 2, James Lightbody USA 2:01.6; 3, Wyndham Halswelle GBR 2:03.0.
1500m: 1, James Lightbody USA 4:12.0; 2, John McGough GBR/IRL 4:12.6; 3, Kristian Hellström SWE 4:13.4.

5 Miles: 1, Henry Hawtrey GBR 26:11.8; 2, John Svanberg SWE 26:19.4; 3, Edward Dahl SWE 26:26.2.
Marathon: (41.86k) 1, Billy Sherring CAN 2:51:24; 2, John Svanberg SWE 2:58:21; 3, William Frank USA 3:00:47.
110mH: 1, Robert Leavitt USA 16.2; 2, Alfred Healey AUS 16.2; 3, Vincent Duncker GER 16.3.
HJ: 1, Con Leahy GBR/IRL 1.77; 2, Lajos Gönczy HUN 1.75; eq3, Themistoklis Diakidis GRE & Herbert Kerrigan USA 1.72.
PV: 1, Fernand Gonder FRA 3.50; 2, Bruno Söderström SWE 3.40; 3, Edward Glover USA 3.35.
LJ: 1, Meyer Prinstein USA 7.20; 2, Peter O'Connor GBR/IRL 7.02; 3, Hugo Friend USA 6.96.
TJ: 1, Peter O'Connor GBR/IRL 14.07; 2, Con Leahy GBR/IRL 13.98; 3, Thomas Cronan USA 13.70.
SP: 1, Martin Sheridan USA 12.32; 2, Mihaly David HUN 11.83; 3, Eric Lemming SWE 11.26.
DT: 1, Martin Sheridan USA 41.46; 2, Nicolaos Georgantas GRE 38.06; 3, Verner Järvinen FIN 36.82.
JT: (freestyle) 1, Eric Lemming SWE 53.90 (world best); 2, Knut Lindberg SWE 45.17; 3, Bruno Söderström SWE 44.92.
DT: (Greek style) 1, Verner Järvinen FIN 35.17; 2, Nicolaos Georgantas GRE 32.80; 3, Istvan Mudin HUN 31.91.
Throwing The Stone (6.4kg): 1, Nicolaos Georgantas GRE 19.92; 2, Martin Sheridan USA 19.03; 3, Michel Dorizas GRE 18.58.
Pentathlon: (Standing LJ, DT, JT, 192m, Greco-Roman Wrestling) 1, Hjalmar Mellander SWE 24pts; 2, Istvan Mudin HUN 25; 3, Eric Lemming SWE 29.
1500m Walk: 1, George Bonhag USA 7:12.6; 2, Donald Linden CAN 7:19.8; 3, Konstantin Spetsiotis GRE 7:22.0.
3000m Walk: 1, György Sztantics HUN 15:13.2; 2, Hermann Müller GER 15:20.0; 3, Georgios Saridakis GRE 15:33.0.
Standing HJ: 1, Ray Ewry USA 1.56; eq2, Leon Dupont BEL, Lawson Robertson USA & Martin Sheridan USA 1.40.
Standing LJ: 1, Ray Ewry USA 3.30; 2, Martin Sheridan USA 3.09; 3, Lawson Robertson USA 3.05.

DORANDO PIETRI, still perhaps the most famous marathon runner in history, is the name most closely associated with the London Olympics of 1908. Few people recall that the actual marathon winner on that occasion was the American Johnny Hayes, but the legend of Dorando (see page 18) lives on. The other happening synonymous with these Games was the bizarre 'walkover', the only one in Olympic athletics history, by Britain's Wyndham Halswelle in the 400m (see page 16).

The Games were originally awarded to Rome, but in 1906 the Italian authorities gave notice that, due to the country's parlous financial state, it would not be possible to proceed. The IOC invited Britain to take over and despite the short notice the White City Stadium, claimed to be the most advanced in the world at that time, was constructed at Shepherds Bush in West London. The Games would be held in conjunction with the Franco-British Exhibition, but unlike Paris and St Louis they stood on their own feet.

A crowd of nearly 50,000 saw King Edward VII declare open the Games, but straight away there were problems. The American and Swedish flags were unaccountably missing from those fluttering over the stadium, and the athletes from Finland (then part of the Russian empire) refused to march behind the hated Czarist flag.

There was no Irish flag on display either, but athletes born in the Emerald Isle or of Irish parentage won no fewer than seven gold medals. Representing the USA, Martin Sheridan retained his discus title and also succeeded in the Greek-style version of the event, John Flanagan won his third hammer title, and Johnny Hayes, born in New York but whose parents emigrated from Co Tipperary, became marathon champion. Bobbie Kerr, born in Co Fermanagh but who moved with his family to Canada at the age of seven, carried the Maple Leaf to victory in the 200m; Tim Ahearne from Co Limerick, competing for the Great Britain & Ireland team, set a world hop step and jump record of 14.92; and Edmond Barrett from Co Derry – fifth in the shot – won a gold medal as a member of the City of London Police team which took the tug-of-war title on behalf of the British Isles. In addition, Kerr finished third in the 100m won by 19 year-old South African Reggie Walker, Con Leahy was equal second in the high jump, Sheridan was third in the standing long jump (Ray Ewry won that and the standing high jump yet again), Dennis Horgan from Co Cork was second in the shot, while in the hammer there was an Irish clean sweep for behind the USA's Flanagan and Matt McGrath (born in Co Tipperary) came Con Walsh of Co Cork and Canada.

It was a pretty good meeting for athletes from the British mainland too. In addition to the controversial 400m victory by Wyndham Halswelle (Edinburgh H), who set an Olympic and British record of 48.4 in his semi, there were gold medals for Manchester's Emil Voigt in the 5 miles, Arthur Russell of Walsall in the 3200m steeplechase and Brighton policeman George Larner in the 3500m and 10 miles walking events, his time in the latter of 1:15:57.4 being a world amateur best. In addition, Joe Deakin (14:39.6), Archie Robertson and Bill Coales finished one-two-three in the 3 miles team race. Deakin, a member of Herne Hill Harriers, was a veteran of the Boer War, went on to be gassed in the First World War and yet continued to race until he was ninety! When he died in 1972, aged 93, he was Britain's oldest Olympic gold medallist.

The Americans came up with several of

STAR OF THE GAMES

MEL SHEPPARD
(born 5 Sep 1883; died 4 Jan 1942)

First he triumphed in the 1500m, and then he ran away with the 800m in a world best of 1:52.8 following a near suicidal first lap of 53.0. He later collected a third gold medal by anchoring the USA to victory in the medley relay.

the most sparkling performances and in Mel Sheppard they had the man of the Games. Sheppard, who had been rejected by the New York police on the grounds of a weak heart, first outsprinted Britain's Harold Wilson, the first man to break four minutes for the distance (3:59.8 in the Olympic trials), in the 1500m and a week later he survived a sensational 53.0 first 400m to finish well ahead in the 800m in a world's best of 1:52.8. He also anchored the USA team to victory in the 1600m medley relay, with John Taylor – who ran the 400m stint – becoming the first black athlete to strike Olympic gold. Tragically, Taylor died of typhoid just four months after the Games at the age of 24.

The American duo of Forrest Smithson and Charles Bacon set neatly rounded world hurdles bests of 15.0 and 55.0 respectively, while another world mark fell in the javelin where Eric Lemming threw 54.82. He had reached 57.33 in Stockholm the previous month but that was never ratified as a Swedish record.

For the only time in athletics history an individual Olympic title was shared: it happened in the pole vault and involved two Americans. Edward Cook, aged only 19, cleared 3.71 in the qualifying competition, while that height was matched by Alfred Gilbert in the final. As qualifying performances in field events were carried forward to the finals at that time, both men received gold medals. Gilbert later made his name and fortune in another sphere, as the inventor of that popular toy, the Erector set.

In view of all the excellent competition it was a pity that the crowds were usually so small that they were lost in the vast stadium. The high price of tickets was one reason, but that great Olympic authority Capt F A M Webster – writing in 1914 – pinpointed another factor which contributed to the disappointing attendance. "Here in England we have an absolute plethora of sporting fixtures all the year round, and to the man in the street the Olympic Games do not represent anything very much out of the ordinary, and are certainly not as important as an inter-varsity match, the Boat Race, or the English FA Cup final at the Crystal Palace." The Olympics still had a way to go.

Halswelle That Ends Well

THE WORLD of athletics first began to take note of a London-born Scot by the name of Wyndham Halswelle in 1905. This dashing young lieutenant in the Highland Light Infantry, a veteran of the Boer War, succeeded in winning the AAA 440 yards title. Next year, at the Interim Olympics in Athens he finished second in the 400m and third in the 800m, and went on to win four Scottish titles (100-880 yards) in a single afternoon and retain the AAA championship in a personal best of 48.8.

Halswelle's form as the 1908 Games approached was brilliant. In the space of a fortnight he recorded a British best 300 yards time of 31.2, set a British 440y record of 48.4 that was to survive for 26 years, and romped away with the AAA title in 49.4 at the newly opened White City. It was to this stadium, then claimed to be "the largest, most costly and best appointed the world has yet known", that he returned later in July for the Olympic Games.

Halswelle, the favourite, began well by winning his 400m heat in 49.4 and fared even better in the semi-finals with victory in the Olympic record time of 48.4. The next fastest qualifier, at 49.0, was William Robbins, one of three Americans to join Halswelle in the four-man final the following day on the three-laps-to-the-mile track. The draw resulted in John Carpenter taking the inside position, then Halswelle, Robbins and John Taylor. The race was not run in lanes (or 'strings' as known in those days) and consequently something of a free-for-all developed. Halswelle was baulked by Robbins within the first 50m but that was nothing compared to what was to happen later.

Here, in Halswelle's own words, is what occurred.

"I did not attempt to pass the Americans until the last corner, reserving my efforts for the finishing straight. Here I attempted to pass Carpenter on the outside, since he was not far enough from the kerb to do so on the inside, and I was too close up to have crossed behind him. Carpenter's elbow undoubtedly touched my chest, for as I moved outwards to pass him he did likewise, keeping his right arm in front of me. In this manner he bored me across quite two-thirds of the track, and entirely stopped my running. As

I was well up to his shoulder and endeavouring to pass him, it is absurd to say I could have come up on the inside. I was too close after half-way round the bend to have done this; indeed to have done so would have necessitated chopping my stride, and thereby losing anything from two to four yards. When about 30 or 40 yards from the tape I saw the officials holding up their hands, so I slowed up, not attempting to finish all out."

The judges (all appointed by the Amateur Athletic Association) declared 'no race' and an official inquiry into the alleged obstruction was held that evening. Dr A R Badger, a vice-president of the AAA stationed as an umpire on the bend just before the beginning of the finishing straight, said in evidence: "The position of Robbins at that point was that he was leading and about a yard in front of Carpenter. Robbins and Carpenter were in such a position as to compel Halswelle to run very wide all round the bend, and as they swung into the straight Halswelle made a big effort and was gaining hard; but running up the straight the further they went the wider Carpenter went out from the verge, keeping his right shoulder sufficiently in front of Halswelle to prevent his passing. When they had run 30 yards up the straight Carpenter was about 18 inches off the outside of the track. I at once ran up the track, waving my hands to the judges to break the worsted."

The outcome was that Carpenter, whose 'winning' time has been quoted as anything from 47.8 to 48.6, was disqualified and a re-run ('in strings') ordered for two days later. Halswelle was the only taker, for Taylor and Robbins – in a gesture of sympathy for Carpenter – boycotted the re-run. Thus the spectators were offered the bizarre spectacle of their man running the distance solo in 50 seconds dead for his gold medal.

For a contemporary American point of view on the controversy, let's hear from journalist John Kieran who wrote: "Here were three runners from the United States competing against a single Englishman. It was hinted in some of the less conservative London newspapers that the Briton could expect nothing but the worse of it, and the spectators were requested to bear in mind that, in an emergency, the old instructions issued by Lord Nelson at Trafalgar were still in force; England expected every man to do his duty. The team leaders of the United States group looked upon all this as nothing less than inciting to riot. Mike Murphy, veteran coach and trainer to the United States team, warned his three finalists of this feeling and urged them to keep clear of trouble, which they promised to do.

"It was a stirring contest and as the runners came into the stretch Carpenter was in the lead with Robbins second and Halswelle third. Suddenly somebody along the track set up a yell of 'foul', and in a moment a dozen officials leaped out on the track. An unidentified official ran up and broke the worsted string across the finish line and thus there was no tape for the first runner to breast when he arrived at the end of his journey. Taylor, in the trailing position, found his way obstructed by floundering officials and he did not finish the race, but Carpenter, Robbins and Halswelle finished in that order.

"The United States group didn't know what all the disorder was about, but the information was soon furnished. British officials bobbed up with eye-witnesses to prove that Halswelle had been impeded and crowded towards the outside of the track by Carpenter, and perhaps by Robbins also. They were not sure of the team work but they were willing to swear that Carpenter was guilty of high crimes and misdemeanours. The British officials declared it 'no race' and ordered it re-run on the last day of the week. The United States officials told them they might as well make it the Day of the Greek Kalends, because their runners would not be in it, and didn't have any interest in the date. In loud language they said the United States was being rooked, bilked, cheated, swindled and robbed to put it mildly. If there had been a boat leaving Shepherd's Bush that night for New York the United States athletes and officials probably would have torn down what they could of the Stadium and then rushed up the gang-plank for home. But overnight, all hands and heads cooled out enough to stick by the decision to remain and finish out the meet."

Halswelle ran his final race the following week and was killed in 1915 by a sniper's bullet while serving in France during the First World War. He was 32.

LONDON 1908

The First London Marathon

THE MARATHON truly captured the public's imagination, to such a degree that some 90,000 people packed into the stadium to see one of the most dramatic finishes in athletics history.

The odd distance (26 miles 385 yards or 42,195m) that has come to be accepted as the standard length of a marathon was a legacy of this race, and it came about by accident rather than design. The race was intended to be precisely 26 miles but in fact the course from the grounds of Windsor Castle to the finish opposite the royal box in the White City Stadium extended for that extra 385 yards.

In unusually hot and humid conditions, the front runners cut out too fast a pace. Britain's Jack Price held a 41 sec lead at 13 miles (1:15:13), but he dropped out a mile or so later, leaving the English-born South African Charles Hefferon two minutes clear of his nearest challenger at 15 miles. By 20 miles Hefferon - operating at 2:40 pace - was almost four minutes ahead of Dorando Pietri, who succeeded in halving the deficit by 24 miles. One mile later Pietri moved into the lead, with Johnny Hayes passing Hefferon for second place.

Here is how a correspondent for The Times graphically described the scene in the stadium:

"And at last he comes. A tired man, dazed, bewildered, hardly conscious, in red shorts and white vest, his hair white with dust, staggers on to the track. It is Dorando, the Italian. He looks about him, hardly knowing where he is. Just the knowledge that somehow, by some desperate resolve of determination, he must get round that 200 yards to the tape of the finish keeps him on his feet. Fifty yards, and he cannot even do that. He falls on the track, gets up, staggers on a few yards and falls again, and yet again; and then he reaches the last turn. The goal is in sight, though his closed eyes cannot see it. He is surrounded by officials almost, if not quite, supporting him, urging and cheering him on. If they were not there he would fall. He cannot run straight. And yet 50 yards from the end he suddenly bursts into a pathetic, almost a horrible, parody of a spurt, drops again ten yards from the tape, rises, staggers forward over those last terrible few yards, and has reached the goal.

"But not with much to spare. Hayes, of the United States, follows him into the Stadium, a long way behind him in time, but comparatively a fresh and strong man, who can actually run, and is fast catching him up. Not quite, however, though he has run a magnificent race.

"The Americans protested against Dorando's win on the ground that he received assistance, and the protest was finally sustained by the council. So that, after all, the unfortunate man had his agonised struggles to no purpose. Altogether the finish of the race was far from satisfactory. The rule about attendants not being allowed on the course was flagrantly broken. The position of those in authority was undoubtedly difficult. It seemed inhuman to leave Dorando to struggle on unaided, and inhuman to urge him to continue. It did not seem right that thousands of people should witness a man suffering as he did. It seemed hard that he should lose the victory after having reached the Stadium so long before any one else. And yet, after all, the race was not to the Stadium entrance, but to the finish in front of the royal box, and it is extremely doubtful whether, by his own unaided exertions, Dorando could ever have got so far."

Happily, Dorando Pietri (Dorando was used erroneously as his surname whereas in fact that was his first name) made such a swift recovery from his ordeal that he was back at the stadium the following day to receive a special gold cup, the idea of Sir Arthur Conan Doyle, from the hands of Queen Alexandra. Pietri (whose time was 2:54:47) and Hayes (2:55:19) both quickly turned professional and in New York in November 1908 Pietri won in 2:44:21 to his rival's 2:45:06 ...in a full marathon run over more than 260 laps of the Madison Square Garden indoor track!

1908 - LONDON

100m: 1, Reggie Walker SAF 10.8; 2, James Rector USA 10.9; 3, Bobbie Kerr CAN 10.9; 4, Nate Cartmell USA 11.0.

200m: 1, Bobbie Kerr CAN 22.6; 2, Robert Cloughen USA 22.6; 3, Nate Cartmell USA 22.7; 4, George Hawkins GBR 22.9.

400m: 1, Wyndham Halswelle GBR 50.0 (walkover; 48.4 semi-final). Other original finalists: John Carpenter USA, William Robbins USA & John Taylor USA.

800m: 1, Mel Sheppard USA 1:52.8 (world best); 2, Emilio Lunghi ITA 1:54.2; 3, Hanns Braun GER 1:55.2; 4, Odön Bodor HUN 1:55.4; 5, Theodore Just GBR 1:56.4; 6, John Halstead USA.

1500m: 1, Mel Sheppard USA 4:03.4; 2, Harold Wilson GBR 4:03.6; 3, Norman Hallows GBR 4:04.0; 4, John Tait CAN 4:06.8; 5, Ivo Fairbairn-Crawford GBR 4:07.6; 6, Joe Deakin GBR 4:07.9.

5 Miles: 1, Emil Voigt GBR 25:11.2; 2, Edward Owen GBR 25:24.0; 3, John Svanberg SWE 25:37.2; 4, Charles Hefferon SAF 25:44.0; 5, Archie Robertson GBR 26:13.0; 6, Frederick Meadows CAN.

Marathon: (42.2k) 1, Johnny Hayes USA 2:55:19; 2, Charles Hefferon SAF 2:56:06; 3, Joseph Forshaw USA 2:57:11; 4, Alton Welton USA 2:59:45; 5, William Wood CAN 3:01:44; 6, Frederick Simpson CAN 3:04:29 ... Dorando Pietri ITA disqualified (2:54:47).

3200mSC: 1, Arthur Russell GBR 10:47.8; 2, Archie Robertson GBR 10:48.4; 3, John Eisele USA 11:00.8; 4, Guy Holdaway GBR; 5, Harold Sewell GBR; 6, William Galbraith CAN.

110mH: 1, Forrest Smithson USA 15.0 (world best); 2, John Garrells USA 15.7; 3, Arthur Shaw USA 15.8; 4, William Rand USA 16.0.

400mH: 1, Charles Bacon USA 55.0 (world best); 2, Harry Hillman USA 55.3; 3, Leonard (Jimmy) Tremeer GBR 57.0; Leslie Burton GBR dnf.

1600m Medley Relay: (200m, 200m, 400m, 800m) 1, USA (Bill Hamilton, Nate Cartmell, John Taylor, Mel Sheppard) 3:29.4; 2, Germany (Arthur Hoffman, Hans Eicke, Otto Trieloff, Hanns Braun) 3:32.4; 3, Hungary (Pal Simon, Frigyes Mezey-Wiesner, József Nagy, Odön Bodor) 3:32.5.

HJ: 1, Harry Porter USA 1.90; eq2, Georges André FRA, Con Leahy GBR/IRL & Istvan Somodi HUN 1.88; eq5, Herbert Gidney USA & Thomas Moffitt USA 1.85.

PV: eq1, Edward Cook USA & Alfred Gilbert USA 3.71; eq3, Ed Archibald CAN, Charles Jacobs USA & Bruno Söderström SWE 3.58; eq6, Georgios Banikas GRE & Sam Bellah USA 3.50.

LJ: 1, Frank Irons USA 7.48; 2, Dan Kelly USA 7.09; 3, Calvin Bricker CAN 7.08; 4, Edward Cook USA 6.97; 5, John Brennan USA 6.86; 6, Frank Mount-Pleasant USA 6.82.

TJ: 1, Tim Ahearne GBR/IRL 14.92 (world best); 2, Garfield MacDonald CAN 14.76; 3, Edvard Larsen NOR 14.39; 4, Calvin Bricker CAN 14.10; 5, Platt Adams USA 14.07; 6, Frank Mount-Pleasant USA 13.97.

SP: 1, Ralph Rose USA 14.21; 2, Dennis Horgan GBR/IRL 13.62; 3, John Garrells USA 13.18; 4, Wesley Coe USA 13.07; 5, Edmond Barrett GBR/IRL 12.89; 6, Marquis Horr USA 12.82.

DT: 1, Martin Sheridan USA 40.89; 2, Merritt Giffin USA 40.70; 3, Marquis Horr USA 39.44; 4, Verner Järvinen FIN 39.42; 5, Arthur Dearborn USA 38.52; 6, James Talbott USA 38.40.

HT: 1, John Flanagan USA 51.92; 2, Matt McGrath USA 51.18; 3, Con Walsh CAN 48.50; 4, Tom Nicolson GBR 48.09; 5, Lee Talbott USA 47.86; 6, Marquis Horr USA 46.94.

JT: 1, Eric Lemming SWE 54.82 (world best); 2, Arne Halse NOR 50.57; 3, Otto Nilsson SWE 47.10; 4, Aarne Salovaara FIN 45.89; 5, Armas Pesonen FIN 45.18; 6, Juho Halme FIN 44.96.

3 Miles Team Race: 1, Great Britain & Ireland 6pts (1, Joe Deakin 14:39.6; 2, Archie Robertson 14:41.0; 3, Bill Coales 14:41.6); 2, USA 19 (4, John Eisele 14:41.8; 6, George Bonhag; 9, Herbert Trube); 3, France 32 (8, Louis de Fleurac; 11, Joseph Dreher; 13, Paul Lizandier).

3500m Walk: 1, George Larner GBR 14:55.0; 2, Ernest Webb GBR 15:07.4; 3, Harry Kerr NZL 15:43.4.

10 Miles Walk: 1, George Larner GBR 1:15:57.4 (world best); 2, Ernest Webb GBR 1:17:31.0; 3, Edward Spencer GBR 1:21:20.2.

Standing HJ: 1, Ray Ewry USA 1.57; eq2, John Biller USA & Constantin Tsiklitiras GRE 1.55.

Standing LJ: 1, Ray Ewry USA 3.33; 2, Constantin Tsiklitiras GRE 3.23; 3, Martin Sheridan USA 3.22.

DT: (Greek style) 1, Martin Sheridan USA 38.00; 2, Marquis Horr USA 37.32; 3, Verner Järvinen FIN 36.48.

JT: (Freestyle) 1, Eric Lemming SWE 54.44; 2, Michel Dorizas GRE 51.36; 3, Arne Halse NOR 49.73.

A SWEDISH RHAPSODY

TWO MEN, one a Finn obliged to wear the Russian emblem on his vest and the other an American Indian who would later be stripped of his honours, shared the limelight at the highly successful Stockholm Olympics.

"Hannes" (actually Johan Pietari) Kolehmainen won the inaugural 5000m and 10,000m titles, the former after an epic duel with Frenchman Jean Bouin in a startling world record time. He also set a world 3000m record and won the cross country.

The Finnish athletics historian Matti Hannus has written that because he had been able to prepare full-time for four months, thanks to brother Viljami's financial aid from America, Hannes Kolehmainen was in fantastic shape for the Games. Here, in Hannus' words, is what he achieved in Stockholm:

July 7: Won his 10,000m heat in 33:49.0.

July 8: Starting the 10,000m final like a maniac, he passed 400m in 64 sec, 1500m in 4:13.0 (faster than Lasse Viren 64 years later in Montreal), 3000m in 8:52.0 and halfway in 15:11.4. Leading in the oppressive heat by half a lap, he was able to slow down and yet won - almost jogging - in 31:20.8 way ahead of the American Hopi Indian, Louis Tewanima, and Finnish countryman Albin Stenroos, who was destined to win the Olympic marathon in Paris 12 years later. This was Finland's first athletics gold medal in an official Olympic Games.

July 9: Won 5000m heat in 15:38.9.

July 10: The 5000m final: a race to savour and wonder at, especially as during the three preceding days Hannes had raced a total of 25k, as opposed to Jean Bouin's 5k (winning his heat in a world class 15:05.0). After a slowish start,

the barrel-chested Frenchman began to press on, passing 3000m in 8:44, at which point all his rivals - save for a rather tired looking Hannes - had been dropped. For lap after lap the two gladiators strode on at a speed which had not been dreamt of before. The finishing moments of this epic duel have never been surpassed. Hannes, with the Russian emblem on his vest (Finland was then under Russian rule), gave all he had and inched past his great rival, breasting the tape in an astonishing 14:36.6 - nearly 25 sec under Arthur Robinson's 1908 world record! At just 22 he was the youngest 5000m world record breaker until Haile Gebrselassie in 1994, and also the youngest Olympic 10,000m champion until Brahim Boutayeb in 1988.

July 12: Won 3000m team race heat in a world record 8:36.9, but Finland did not qualify for the three-team final.

July 15: Easily won the cross country gold medal, also taking silver in the team competition. Thus, six races in a little more than a week, three of them finals and each one of them golden!

Whereas Jean Bouin never returned from the battlefields of World War I (he lost his life in September 1914 aged 25), Kolehmainen would again make his mark on the Olympics eight years later, this time representing an independent Finland, when he won the over-distance (42.75k) marathon title in 2:32:36, the fastest by an amateur up to that time although brother Viljami was timed at a barrier-breaking 2:29:40 as a professional in the USA in 1912. Even that was not the end of Hannes' Olympic involvement.

At the opening ceremony of the 1952 Games in Helsinki, by then aged 62, Kolehmainen received the torch from 55 year-old Paavo Nurmi - the man for whom Hannes had been a boyhood idol - and carried it up the stairs to the top of Helsinki Olympic Tower. It was a richly deserved honour, for it was Kolehmainen, who died on January 11 1966, who was the first of the Flying Finns.

Jim Thorpe (see page 22) established himself as the greatest all-round athlete the world would see for a long time to come by winning both the decathlon and pentathlon, while another American double winner was Ralph Craig, who was to return to the USA Olympic team THIRTY SIX YEARS later! The man who took the 100m (after reportedly committing three of the seven false starts in the final without being penalised) and 200m in

---

STAR OF THE GAMES

HANNES KOLEHMAINEN
(born 9 Dec 1889; died 11 Jan 1966)

The first of the "Flying Finns" dominated the 10,000m, smashed the world record to snatch a thrilling 5000m victory, set another world record in the 3000m team race heats, and took the cross-country title.

Stockholm was a travelling reserve for the yachting team in 1948, at the age of 59, and was given the honour of carrying the flag at the opening ceremony.

James "Ted" Meredith, who was only 20 and hadn't yet started college, also came away with two golds. Closely following defending champion Mel Sheppard through a storming 52.4 first 400m (on a 383m track), he came past for a narrow 800m victory in the world record time of 1:51.9, collecting a second world record by carrying on to the 880 yards mark in 1:52.5 and a third when he contributed to the USA team's inaugural Olympic 4x400m relay win in 3:16.6.

Other American winners included Albert Gutterson who improved in the long jump from 7.33 to 7.60, just a centimetre away from the world record, and the Irish-born pair of Pat McDonald (from Co Clare) and Matt McGrath (from Co Tipperary) in the shot and hammer respectively. In the standing high jump, Platt and Benjamin Adams became the first brothers to score an Olympic one-two, the first brothers to have won an Olympic medal apiece being Dick (1st shot) and Lewis (3rd standing high jump and triple jump) Sheldon in 1900. Another curiosity: George Bonhag became the only man ever to win gold medals as a walker and runner. The 1906 1500m walk champion this time was a member of the winning 3000m team.

Two other events for which the Americans were favourites went instead to the British. The USA 4x100m relay squad clocked a world record 42.2 in the semis but were disqualified, enabling the second placed British team (43.0) to advance to the final, where Welshman David Jacobs, Scotsman Henry Macintosh, Londoner Vic D'Arcy and Yorkshireman Willie Applegarth sped round in 42.4 for victory.

Like two other medallists in these Games, 5000m runners Jean Bouin and George Hutson, Macintosh was killed in action during the First World War which was to begin two years later.

Destined to live until 1991, when he was 99, was Abel Kiviat, the world record holder for 1500m with 3:55.8 which he had set a month before the Games when still only 19. He was expected to win but was confounded by Arnold Jackson, who went up to Oxford in October 1910 and only took up running in 1911. His approach was casual, even by Oxbridge standards. His training consisted less of running than of massages, walking and golf, while he was certainly not averse to smoking and drinking. He won the mile against Cambridge in 1912 in his best time of 4:21.4, which won him selection for the Olympic 1500m along with eight other Britons. In those days countries were not restricted to a maximum of three per event.

At the bell in Stockholm, Kiviat was in the lead with Jackson, a novice in this class of competition, in seventh place after having run well wide all the way. Gradually Jackson worked his way into the bunch of four in pursuit of Kiviat rounding the final bend and, in a thrilling finish, burst past for victory in 3:56.8, an Olympic and British record.

His later life was as remarkable as his Olympic breakthrough. During the First World War he gained the DSO and three bars (one of only seven officers to achieve that distinction), was wounded three times and became, at 27, the youngest brigadier-general in the British Army. He ultimately changed his name to Arnold Strode-Jackson and was a member of the British delegation to the Paris Peace Conference before settling in America. He became a naturalised US citizen in 1945 but died in his beloved Oxford in 1972.

English-born, but representing Canada, was the winner of the new Olympic walk event at 10,000m, George Goulding. A man of few words, it would seem, he telegraphed his wife: "Won - George".

South Africa scored a one-two in the 40.2k (25 miles) marathon, run again in gruelling conditions with the afternoon sun beating down on the runners. The winner Ken McArthur, a Transvaal policeman who was born in Co Antrim and had emigrated from Ireland seven years earlier, told reporters "I went out to win or die." Unfortunately, the latter applied to a 21 year-old Portuguese runner, Francisco Lazaro, who collapsed from a combination of sunstroke and heart trouble and died in hospital the next day.

That tragedy cast a cloud over the Games, but nevertheless they were a triumph for the Swedish organisers. As Lord Noel-Baker (who placed sixth in the 1500m as Philip Baker) has written: "The Games were what Coubertin had planned and believed that they would be - a great international festival of sporting friendship and goodwill." The world looked forward to the next Olympics, due for Berlin in 1916 ... but the dark shadow of war was to intervene.

HERO & VICTIM

JIM THORPE was hailed as the world's greatest athlete at the 1912 Olympics, but spent the rest of his life coming to terms with being the champion who didn't officially exist.

Of all the athletes whose achievements brought glory to the Olympic Games none was treated so shabbily by the Olympic hierarchy as Jim Thorpe, who was the world's first outstanding all-round athlete, a man so far ahead of his time that in 1950 - 38 years after his greatest triumphs in athletics - he was voted the top sportsman of the first half of the century by an Associated Press poll of sports writers. At about that time a Hollywood feature film (Jim Thorpe - All-American, known as Man of Bronze in Britain) loosely based on his life, and starring Burt Lancaster in the title role, brought his astonishing story to the attention of new generations.

Born in Oklahoma on May 28 1888 with the tribal name of Wa-tho-huck ("Bright Path"), he was predominantly a mixture of American Indian and Irish with a little French blood thrown in. His grandfather had been an Irish blacksmith, while his grandmother was descended from the great Sac and Fox chief Black Hawk.

Thorpe developed into virtually a one-man team in track and field as well as excelling in football and baseball and it was his prowess in the latter sport which led to his downfall, for in 1909/10 he was paid a trifling amount in a small-time professional league in North Carolina, something that leaked out after he became a famous athlete and resulted in the loss of his amateur status and the forfeit of his Olympic medals.

The pentathlon came first in Stockholm and he dominated the competition, winning four of the five events and finishing third of the 26 entrants in the other for a near perfect score. In sixth place was American team-mate Avery Brundage, a man who would become a millionaire and President of the International Olympic Committee, a stickler for amateurism who all his life was implacably opposed to any reprieve for Thorpe.

The decathlon was spread over three days because of the large entry of 29. Thorpe took the lead in the shot, the last of the three events on day one, and built up a huge advantage during the four events contested on day two. At the finish he had accumulated 8412 points on the scoring tables of the day, which were based on each of the Olympic records prior to 1912 being worth 1000 points. He won by a whopping 688 points from Sweden's Hugo Wieslander, and added over a thousand points to the previous world best! On the tables in use today, Thorpe's score works out at 6564 ... which would have won him the silver medal at the 1948 Olympics.

Presenting Thorpe with his medals and trophies, King Gustav V of Sweden shook his hand and told him: "Sir, you are the greatest athlete in the world", to which accolade Thorpe famously replied: "Thanks, King."

The following year he was declared a professional by the USA's governing body, the AAU, and the IOC demanded the return of Thorpe's medals and awards. His name was struck from the Olympic records, although to their credit Ferdinand Bie and Wieslander - who were promoted to pentathlon and decathlon champions - always acknowledged, as did everyone else bar pompous, hypocritical officialdom, that Thorpe was the true Olympic gold medallist.

Thorpe went on to play professional football and baseball until 1928 but, despite later appearing in some Hollywood films, he fell upon hard times and became an alcoholic. At the time of his death from a heart attack in 1953 at the age of 64 Thorpe was still in Olympic limbo - a supreme champion stripped of his medals and honours.

After much campaigning, Thorpe's amateur status was eventually restored by the AAU in 1973 but it wasn't until 1982, by which time the more enlightened Lord Killanin was President, that the IOC finally acknowledged that Thorpe did indeed win those two gold medals all those years ago.

1912 - STOCKHOLM

100m: 1, Ralph Craig USA 10.8; 2, Alvah Meyer USA 10.9; 3, Donald Lippincott USA 10.9; 4, George Patching SAF 10.9; 5, Frank Belote USA

11.0; Howard Drew USA dns.

200m: 1, Ralph Craig USA 21.7; 2, Donald Lippincott USA 21.8; 3, Willie Applegarth GBR 22.0; 4, Richard Rau GER 22.2; 5, Charles Reidpath USA 22.3; 6, Donnell Young USA 22.3.

400m: 1, Charles Reidpath USA 48.2; 2, Hanns Braun GER 48.3; 3, Edward Lindberg USA 48.4; 4, Ted Meredith USA 49.2; 5, Carroll Haff USA 49.5.

800m: 1, Ted Meredith USA 1:51.9 (world rec); 2, Mel Sheppard USA 1:52.0; 3, Ira Davenport USA 1:52.0; 4, Melville Brock CAN 1:52.7; 5, David Caldwell USA 1:52.8; 6, Hanns Braun GER 1:53.1.

1500m: 1, Arnold Jackson GBR 3:56.8; 2, Abel Kiviat USA 3:56.9; 3, Norman Taber USA 3:56.9; 4, John Paul Jones USA 3:57.2; 5, Ernst Wide SWE 3:57.6; 6, Philip Baker GBR 4:01.0.

5000m: 1, Hannes Kolehmainen FIN 14:36.6 (world rec); 2, Jean Bouin FRA 14:36.7; 3, George Hutson GBR 15:07.6; 4, George Bonhag USA 15:09.8; 5, Tell Berna USA 15:10.0; 6, Mauritz Carlsson SWE 15:18.6.

10,000m: 1, Hannes Kolehmainen FIN 31:20.8; 2, Louis Tewanima USA 32:06.6; 3, Albin Stenroos FIN 32:21.8; 4, Joseph Keeper CAN 32:36.2; 5, Alfonso Orlando ITA 33:31.2.

Marathon: (40.2k) 1, Ken McArthur SAF 2:36:55; 2, Christian Gitsham SAF 2:37:52; 3, Gaston Strobino USA 2:38:43; 4, Andrew Sockalexis USA 2:42:08; 5, James Duffy CAN 2:42:19; 6, Sigfrid Jacobsson SWE 2:43:25.

Steeplechase: not held.

110mH: 1, Fred Kelly USA 15.1; 2, James Wendell USA 15.2; 3, Martin Hawkins USA 15.3; 4, John Case USA 15.3; 5, Kenneth Powell GBR 15.5; John Nicholson USA dnf.

400mH: not held.

4x100m Relay: 1, Great Britain (David Jacobs, Henry Macintosh, Vic D'Arcy, Willie Applegarth) 42.4; 2, Sweden (Ivan Möller, Charles Luther, Ture Persson, Knut Lindberg) 42.6; Germany (Otto Röhr, Max Herrmann, Erwin Kern, Richard Rau) disq (42.3 semi-final, world record).

4x400m Relay: 1, USA (Mel Sheppard, Ed Lindberg, Ted Meredith, Charles Reidpath) 3:16.6 (world rec); 2, France (Charles Lelong, Robert Schurrer, Pierre Failliot, Charles Poulenard) 3:20.7; 3, Great Britain (George Nicol, Ernest Henley, James Soutter, Cyril Seedhouse) 3:23.2.

HJ: 1, Alma Richards USA 1.93; 2, Hans Liesche GER 1.91; 3, George Horine USA 1.89; eq4, Egon Erickson USA & Jim Thorpe USA 1.87; eq6, Harry Grumpelt USA & John Johnstone USA 1.85.

PV: 1, Harry Babcock USA 3.95; eq2, Frank Nelson USA & Marcus Wright USA 3.85; eq4, William Hapenny CAN, Frank Murphy USA & Bertil Uggla SWE 3.80.

LJ: 1, Albert Gutterson USA 7.60; 2, Calvin Bricker CAN 7.21; 3, Georg Aberg SWE 7.18; 4, Harry Worthington USA 7.03; 5, Eugene Mercer USA 6.97; 6, Fred Allen USA 6.94.

TJ: 1, Gustaf Lindblom SWE 14.76; 2, Georg Aberg SWE 14.51; 3, Erik Almlöf SWE 14.17; 4, Erling Vinne NOR 14.14; 5, Platt Adams USA 14.09; 6, Edvard Larsen NOR 14.06.

SP: 1, Pat McDonald USA 15.34; 2, Ralph Rose USA 15.25; 3, Lawrence Whitney USA 13.93; 4, Elmer Niklander FIN 13.65; 5, George Philbrook USA 13.13; 6, Imre Mudin HUN 12.81.

DT: 1, Armas Taipale FIN 45.21; 2, Richard Byrd USA 42.32; 3, James Duncan USA 42.28; 4, Elmer Niklander FIN 42.09; 5, Hans Tronner AUT 41.24; 6, Arlie Mucks USA 40.93.

HT: 1, Matt McGrath USA 54.74; 2, Duncan Gillis CAN 48.39; 3, Clarence Childs USA 48.17; 4, Robert Olsson SWE 46.50; 5, Carl Johan Lind SWE 45.61; 6, Denis Carey GBR/IRL 43.78.

JT: 1, Eric Lemming SWE 60.64; 2, Julius Saaristo FIN 58.66; 3, Mor Koczan HUN 55.50; 4, Juho Halme FIN 54.65; 5, Väinö Sikaniemi FIN 52.43; 6, Richard Abrink SWE 52.20.

Dec: 1, Jim Thorpe USA 8412 (world rec; 6564 as rescored on present tables) (100m-11.2, LJ-6.79, SP-12.89, HJ-1.87, 400m-52.2, DT-36.98, 110mH-15.6, PV-3.25, JT-45.70, 1500m-4:40.1); 2, Hugo Wieslander SWE 7724 (5965); 3, Charles Lomberg SWE 7414 (5721); 4, Gösta Holmer SWE 7348 (5748); 5, James Donahue USA 7083 (5701); 6, Eugene Mercer USA 7075 (5825).

Cross Country: I, Hannes Kolehmainen FIN 45:12; 2, Hjalmar Andersson SWE 45:45; 3, John Eke SWE 46:38. Teams: I, Sweden 10pts (2, Andersson; 3, Eke; 5, Josef Ternström); 2, Finland 11 (1, Kolehmainen; 4, Jalmari Eskola; 6, Albin Stenroos); 3, Great Britain 49 (15, Fred Hibbins; 16, Ernest Glover; 18, Tom Humphreys).

3000m Team Race: I, USA 9pts (1, Tell Berna 8:44.6; 3, Norman Taber 8:45.2; 5, George Bonhag 8:46.6); 2, Sweden 13 (2, Thorild Olsson 8:44.6; 4, Ernst Wide 8:46.2; 7, Bror Fock 8:47.1); 3, Great Britain 23 (6, William Cottrill 8:46.8; 8, George Hutson 8:47.2; 9, Cyril Porter 8:48.0); Hannes Kolehmainen 8:36.9 (world rec) in heat, but Finland eliminated.

10,000m Walk: I, George Goulding CAN 46:28.4; 2, Ernest Webb GBR 46:50.4; 3, Fernando Altimani ITA 47:36.6.

Standing HJ: I, Platt Adams USA 1.63; 2, Benjamin Adams USA 1.60; 3, Constantin Tsiklitiras GRE 1.55.

Standing LJ: I, Constantin Tsiklitiras GRE 3.37; 2, Platt Adams USA 3.36; 3, Benjamin Adams USA 3.28.

SP: (aggregate of both hands) I, Ralph Rose USA 27.70 (15.23 & 12.47); 2, Pat McDonald USA 27.53; 3, Elmer Niklander FIN 27.14.

DT: (aggregate of both hands) I, Armas Taipale FIN 82.86 (44.68 & 38.18); 2, Elmer Niklander FIN 77.96; 3, Emil Magnusson SWE 77.37.

JT: (aggregate of both hands) I, Julius Saaristo FIN 109.42 (61.00 & 48.42); 2, Väino Siikaniemi FIN 101.13; 3, Urho Peltonen FIN 100.24.

Pen: I, Jim Thorpe USA 7pts (LJ-7.07, JT-46.71, 200m-22.9, DT-35.75, 1500m-4:44.8); 2, Ferdinand Bie NOR 21; 3, James Donahue USA 29.

BRITAIN'S OLYMPIC CHAMPIONS

ABRAHAMS Harold: 1924 100m
AHEARNE Tim (IRL): 1908 Triple Jump
AINSWORTH-DAVIS John: 1920 4x400m
APPLEGARTH Willie: 1912 4x100m
BENNETT Charles: 1900 1500m & 5000m team
BRASHER Chris: 1956 3000mSC
BROWN Godfrey: 1936 4x400m

BURGHLEY Lord: 1928 400mH
BUTLER Guy: 1920 4x400m
CHRISTIE Linford: 1992 100m
COALES Bill: 1908 3 Miles team
COE Seb: 1980 & 1984 1500m
D'ARCY Vic: 1912 4x100m
DAVIES Lynn: 1964 Long Jump
DEAKIN Joe: 1908 3 Miles team
EDWARDS Jonathan: 2000 Triple Jump
GREEN Tommy: 1932 50k Walk
GRIFFITHS Cecil: 1920 4x400m
HALSWELLE Wyndham: 1908 400m
HAMPSON Tom: 1932 800m
HAWTREY Henry: 1906 5 Miles
HEMERY David: 1968 400mH
HILL Albert: 1920 800m & 1500m
HODGE Percy: 1920 3000mSC
JACKSON Arnold: 1912 1500m
JACOBS David: 1912 4x100m
KIELY Tom (IRL): 1904 'Decathlon'
LARNER George: 1908 3500m & 10M Walk
LEAHY Con (IRL): 1906 High Jump
LIDDELL Eric: 1924 400m
LINDSAY Robert: 1920 4x400m
LOWE Douglas: 1924 & 1928 800m
MACINTOSH Henry: 1912 4x100m
MATTHEWS Ken: 1964 20k Walk
O'CONNOR Peter (IRL): 1906 Triple Jump
OVETT Steve: 1980 800m
RAMPLING Godfrey: 1936 4x400m
RIMMER John: 1900 5000m team & 4000mSC
ROBERTS Bill: 1936 4x400m
ROBERTSON Archie: 1908 3 Miles team
ROBINSON Sidney: 1900 5000m team
RUSSELL Arthur: 1908 3200mSC
THOMPSON Daley: 1980 & 1984 Dec
THOMPSON Don: 1960 50k Walk
TYSOE Alfred: 1900 800m & 5000m team
VOIGT Emil: 1908 5 Miles
WELLS Allan: 1980 100m
WHITLOCK Harold: 1936 50k Walk
WOLFF Freddie: 1936 4x400m

Women

GUNNELL Sally: 1992 400mH
LEWIS Denise: 2000 Heptathlon
PACKER Ann: 1964 800m
PETERS Mary: 1972 Pentathlon
RAND Mary: 1964 Long Jump
SANDERSON Tessa: 1984 Javelin

THE WAR to end all wars – a forlorn hope as it turned out – came to its conclusion in November 1918 and within weeks the International Olympic Committee had awarded the next Games to Antwerp in war-ravaged Belgium. The hosts had a tough task, particularly as they had barely a year and a half to make all the preparations, and in the circumstances they did an admirable job. A total of 25 nations, two less than in 1912, participated, including New Zealand in its own right (previously there had been combined Australasian teams), but not surprisingly the defeated Central Powers – Germany, Austria, Bulgaria, Hungary and Turkey – were not invited.

The British team fared well, with victories in the 800m, 1500m, steeplechase and 4x400m relay, plus other medals in the 100m, 200m, 400m, 1500m, 10,000m, 10,000m walk and the cross country and 3000m team races, yet there were some influential figures who felt Britain should no longer support the Olympic Games!

One of them was Sir Theodore Cook, a member of the British Olympic Council, who wrote to The Times complaining that the Olympic movement had "become entirely alien to English thought and character" and suggesting that Britain should withdraw.

His letter prompted an indignant reply from athletics team captain Philip Baker, co-signed by over 40 members of his team. "We can only suppose that Sir Theodore Cook shares the views of the numerous but ill-informed critics of the Games who for so many years have spread the belief that the Olympic Games are not carried out in a sporting spirit, that they lead to 'bad blood' among the nations who take part in them, and that they lead also inevitably to professionalism. But we wish as emphatically as we can to deny that they are in any way correct. On the contrary, these contests have without exception been run in a spirit of fairness and good sportsmanship which we believe to be equal to the highest standards of British tradition."

Philip Baker, who won a silver medal in the Antwerp 1500m, remained a great Olympic enthusiast for the rest of his long and distinguished life. As Philip Noel-Baker, MP, he served as Minister of Fuel and Power in Clement Attlee's Labour Government and in 1959 he was awarded the Nobel Peace Prize for his campaigning for an international arms control treaty.

The man who beat Baker for the 1500m crown was Albert Hill (see page 27), whose feat of winning both the 800m and 1500m would not be repeated on the Olympic stage until Peter Snell in 1964.

Britain's other individual champion was Guernsey-born Percy Hodge, winner of the 3000m steeplechase, run on a grass course set inside the cinder track. Hodge, a member of Surrey Athletic Club, won by about 100m in a British best of 10:00.4 and was annoyed he didn't run faster. He failed to hear the bell and, unaware he was approaching the finish, the 29 year-old did not produce his normal sprint.

That vivid chronicler of our sport, F A M Webster, referred to Hodge in one of his books as a "pale, long-limbed, red-headed fellow" and described his style as "most peculiar". As he wrote: "The USA coaches agreed that never had they seen an athlete with so many glaring faults travel and take his obstacles at such an astounding speed. He was like a man who is running to save himself from falling flat on his face. His shoulders were bowed, his body bent in at the waist and, in the early stages of the race, he took each hurdle in the old-fashioned, bent-legged manner. But so soon as he felt the least sign of fatigue overtaking him he altered his action. His leading leg then went straight up and was thrown outwards across the hurdle, over which he passed with a sort of falling-forward action. This looked ludicrous but was, in reality, far faster and less exhausting than the style he had employed earlier in the race. His speed increased as he

STAR OF THE GAMES

ALBERT HILL
(born 24 Mar 1889; died 8 Jan 1969)

Aged 31 and after serving with the Royal Flying Corps in France during the First World War, London-born Albert Hill captured both the 800m and 1500m titles, the last man to do so until Peter Snell 44 years later.

approached each water-jump, which he did with set determination. He went over the hedge in such a way that he always landed with one foot in the water and the other on the slope leading to dry land. This meant that he always got back into his running stride at once, and so was away quicker than any of his rivals."

Who is the only junior to have won an Olympic gold medal for Britain? The answer is Cecil Griffiths, Hodge's Surrey AC clubmate, who at the age of 19 (he was born on Jan 20 1901) gave his team the lead on the first leg of the 4x400m relay. The London-born Scot, Robert Lindsay of Blackheath Harriers, kept Britain ahead on the second stage as did Welsh-born John Ainsworth-Davis of the newly created Achilles Club on the third. Another Achilles man, Guy Butler, anchored the squad to a 15m victory in 3:22.2 ... slightly slower than the British women's team when they placed fourth in the 1991 World Championships! Butler was to win two more medals in the next Games, and his total of four Olympic medals – equalled by Seb Coe in 1980/84 – has never been surpassed by a British athlete.

His arch-rival was Bevil Rudd, a chain smoking Rhodes Scholar at Oxford who had deadheated with Cambridge undergraduate Butler at 440 yards in the 1920 varsity match. Rudd could have been selected for the British team as he was born in Devon and had earlier run for England but he opted instead for South Africa, where he went to school and lived before going up to Oxford in 1913. Rudd, who won the Military Cross in the First World War, came out on top in Antwerp. After finishing third in the 800m he triumphed in the 400m despite being far from well, his winning time of 49.6 also reflecting the sorry state of the rain-sodden track.

The USA team ended up with "only" nine victories and were shocked to find the Finns achieving the same number thanks mainly to their outstanding distance runners and field event specialists.

However, world records were set by Frank Loomis with 54.0 in the 400m hurdles, Frank Foss who vaulted 4.09, and the sprint relay team with 42.2. Pat McDonald became the oldest ever athletics gold medallist when, at 42, he took the last 56 pound weight title to be contested, while another of the Irish-American 'whales', Pat Ryan (he was born in Co Limerick and emigrat-

ed to New York in 1910), won the hammer. His throw of 57.77 in 1913 would last as a world record for 25 years.

The most charismatic of the Americans was sprinter Charley Paddock, only just turned 20 but already a great showman who delighted the fans with his spectacular leap for the tape. About twelve feet from the line he would spring forward, arms flung wide. It probably didn't get him to the tape any faster, but it did appear to daunt any close opponent at that stage.

Paddock, who in 1921 was destined to be timed at an astonishing 10.2 for 110 yards (100.58m), won the 100m gold in 10.8 but the race was surrounded by controversy. Just before the pistol was fired the assistant starter told Paddock to move his fingers behind the line, and some of his opponents – believing the instruction was for them to get up – relaxed. American team-mate Loren Murchison was totally left when the gun went off, and the British hope, Harry Edward, also lost valuable ground at the start and did well to fight his way into third place. Second went to Morris Kirksey, who joined Paddock in the winning relay team and is one of only four men to have won gold medals in two sports ... for he was also in the victorious American rugby team!

Paddock was surprisingly beaten in the 200m by Allen Woodring, who only made the US team as a reserve, while Edward picked up another bronze medal despite a heavily bandaged hamstring. Edward, who was in Germany when the First World War broke out and spent the duration in an internment camp, was the first great black sprinter to represent Britain (he was born in what was then British Guiana, now Guyana) and in 1922 he was to score an astonishing AAA Championships triple – 100, 220 and 440 yards – all within an hour.

The Games produced one other world best on the track: Earl Thomson of Canada took the 110 metres hurdles in 14.8 although that didn't come close to his world mark of 14.4 for the slightly shorter 120 yards (109.73m).

But perhaps the finest performance came from the 1912 5000m/10,000m champion Hannes Kolehmainen in the marathon. This time representing Finland as an independent, sovereign country he covered the over-distance 42.75

kilometres course in 2:32:36, a world's best by an amateur ... although not a Kolehmainen family record as brother Viljami had in 1912 covered 42.2 kilometres in a professional record of 2:29:40. Estonia, which made its Olympic comeback as a separate entity at Barcelona in 1992, claimed the silver medal through Jüri Lossman, who finished only 13 seconds behind in what was until 1996 the closest of all Olympic marathon races.

The Games also heralded the birth of an even more celebrated Finnish Olympian in Paavo Nurmi. The tiny Frenchman Joseph Guillemot outkicked him in the 5000m, but Nurmi turned the tables in the 10,000m (a race in which Scotsman James Wilson finished third), and followed up with two further gold medals in the cross country (team and individual). The Games were a resounding success for the Finnish team, and of particular significance was the result of the javelin ... Finns occupied the first four places with world record holder Jonni Myyrä, only eighth in 1912 with 51.32, this time winning with 65.78.

Philip Noel-Baker was to write of the Antwerp Games:"They were an important factor in the world's psychological recovery from the war. They showed that not even a world war, lasting more than the period of a whole Olympiad, could break or weaken the Olympic Movement."

Symbolising that spirit was the Olympic flag designed by Baron de Coubertin and flown for the first time at these Games. The five interlinked coloured rings of blue, yellow, black, green and red (at least one of those colours appears in every national flag) are meant, according to the founder of the Modern Games, to "represent the five parts of the world won over to Olympism and ready to accept its bountiful rivalries". Also making its bow in Antwerp was the IOC motto of Citius, Altius, Fortius – faster, higher, stronger.

ALBERT HILL'S TWIN PEAKS

BRITAIN'S ATHLETE of the Games was undoubtedly Albert Hill, who completed the 800m/1500m double – the last to do so until Peter Snell in 1964.

Born in Tooting (South London) on March 24 1889, Hill first made a name for himself as a cross country and long distance track runner – he won the AAA 4 miles title in 1910 – but was to be the first link in a chain of brilliant half milers that graced British athletics between the two world wars.

After serving in France for three years as a wireless operator with the Royal Flying Corps he was 30 years of age by the time he was able to resume his athletics career, but he quickly made his mark by winning the AAA 880 yards and mile double in 1919, equalling Joe Binks' 1902 British mile record of 4:16.8 later in the year. Hill, a railway ticket collector and a member of London's Polytechnic Harriers, wanted to go for the Olympic double but after finishing second to Bevil Rudd in the 1920 AAA 880 yards and not contesting the mile he was at first definitely selected only for the 800m.

As he recalled many years later: "I well remember the strong argument I had with Sir Harry Barclay, the secretary of the AAA, when the teams were being selected, for the committee were opposed to my attempting the 800 and 1500m. But I was adamant on tackling the double and in the end Sir Harry bowed to my arguments. Most of the critics, too, were against my decision – the more so because I had been defeated by Bevil Rudd, the Oxford runner and South Africa's representative in the half mile championship that year. Many considered Rudd as the greatest middle distance runner of that era. But when he beat me at Stamford Bridge my leg was still troubling me. Shortly afterwards, with the aid of a bandage above the ankle, it improved 100 per cent and I was determined to show the critics that I was not the has-been they thought I was."

Show them he did. First came the 800m on August 17, and this is what Hill wrote about it:"I considered Rudd my most dangerous opponent. He was a hot favourite to take the 800m, but I had other ideas. Knowing that Earl Eby, the American, always ran a fast first quarter I was determined to move to the front just after the bend, and take the field along at a fast pace. I realised that, whatever the earlier pace, Rudd always made his great effort at the 300 yard mark and he did so this time. Soon, he had a big lead and, entering the home straight with 120 yards to go, was still leading by three to four yards. Everyone expected an easy victory, but I was watching him closely, and noticed his arms beginning to come up high, and his body getting stiff. The stiffer his action became the more I forced myself to relax, arms down, body slightly forward. And turning on full speed, I caught up with him 20 yards out, going on to beat Eby by a yard with Rudd third.

"Of all the contests in my long years on the track, that one stands out as the victory based most satisfyingly on judgment and tactics. It was, moreover, a case of 'all's well that ends well', for about a month before the British team were to leave for Antwerp I severely strained the shin muscles in my left leg. In spite of medical attention, the injury persisted and two weeks before our departure it was doubtful whether I would be able to make the trip."

As a bonus, Hill's time of 1:53.4 was a British record. Eby was timed at 1:53.6 and Rudd, who turned his ankle when leading in the finishing straight, recorded 1:54.0. Fourth was Hill's 19 year-old team-mate Edgar Mountain, while in seventh place was the Dutchman Adriaan Paulen, who would serve as President of the IAAF from 1976 to 1981.

Two days later Hill lined up for the 1500m final, run in pouring rain on a very heavy cinder track. "My chief opponent," Hill wrote, "was Joie Ray of America, a great little runner, who always made his third lap very fast. Aware of this, I was determined to be with him at the bell, then take him along at a fast pace. But unfortunately Ray was not at his best. In the third lap he lost the kick, and I had the easiest of victories." His time was 4:01.8, with Philip Baker, who sacrificed his own chances by sheltering Hill during the race, runner-up in 4:02.4.

The Times described Hill's double in these terms: "It was the greatest individual achievement of the Games. He showed himself to be not only one of the greatest of runners, but also a runner of unbeaten courage and a great track tactician to boot."

At 31 Hill remains the oldest man ever to have won an Olympic 800 or 1500m title. His labours weren't over yet, for on August 22 he took part in the final of the 3000m team race, in which he won a silver medal.

The post-script to Hill's career came in 1921. He and his coach, Sam Mussabini, planned for him to lower the world mile record (then 4:12.6) to 4:08 by running four laps of 62 sec-

onds each at the AAA Championships, but the pressures of competition and the large size of the field caused an even pace schedule to be thrown to the winds. Leading all the way, with young Henry Stallard at his shoulder, Hill unreeled the first three laps in 59.6, 64.4 and 67.2. Stallard made a sustained challenge over the last furlong but Hill resisted to win in 4:13.8, a full three seconds inside the British record. Hill later turned to coaching, his most successful pupil being Sydney Wooderson who in 1937 was to succeed in bringing the world mile record to Britain. Hill settled in Canada, where he died in 1969 at the age of 79.

1920 - ANTWERP

100m: 1, Charley Paddock USA 10.8; 2, Morris Kirksey USA 10.8; 3, Harry Edward GBR 10.9; 4, Jackson Scholz USA 10.9; 5, Emile Ali Khan FRA 11.1; 6, Loren Murchison USA 11.2.

200m: 1, Allen Woodring USA 22.0; 2, Charley Paddock USA 22.1; 3, Harry Edward GBR 22.2; 4, Loren Murchison USA 22.2; 5, George Davidson NZL 22.3; 6, Jack Oosterlaak SAF 22.4.

400m: 1, Bevil Rudd SAF 49.6; 2, Guy Butler GBR 49.9; 3, Nils Engdahl SWE 50.0; 4, Frank Shea USA 50.1; 5, John Ainsworth-Davis GBR 50.3; 6, Harry Davel SAF 50.4.

800m: 1, Albert Hill GBR 1:53.4; 2, Earl Eby USA 1:53.6; 3, Bevil Rudd SAF 1:54.0; 4, Edgar Mountain GBR 1:54.6; 5, Donald Scott USA 1:56.0; 6, Albert Sprott USA 1:56.4.

1500m: 1, Albert Hill GBR 4:01.8; 2, Philip Baker GBR 4:02.4; 3, Lawrence Shields USA 4:03.1; 4, Vaclav Vohralik TCH 4:04.6; 5, Sven Lundgren SWE 4:06.3; 6, André Audinet FRA 4:06.4.

5000m: 1, Joseph Guillemot FRA 14:55.6; 2, Paavo Nurmi FIN 15:00.0; 3, Erik Backman SWE 15:13.0; 4, Teodor Koskenniemi FIN 15:17.0; 5, Charles Blewitt GBR 15:19.0; 6, William Seagrove GBR 15:21.0.

10,000m: 1, Paavo Nurmi FIN 31:45.8; 2, Joseph Guillemot FRA 31:47.2; 3, James Wilson GBR 31:50.8; 4, Augusto Maccario ITA 32:02.0; 5, James Hatton GBR 32:14.0; 6, Jean Manhes FRA 32:26.0.

Marathon: (42.75k) 1, Hannes Kolehmainen FIN 2:32:36 (world best); 2, Jüri Lossman EST 2:32:49; 3, Valerio Arri ITA 2:36:33; 4, Auguste Broos BEL 2:39:26; 5, Juho Tuomikoski FIN 2:40:11; 6, Sofus Rose DEN 2:41:18.

3000mSC: 1, Percy Hodge GBR 10:00.4; 2, Patrick Flynn USA 10:21.1; 3, Ernesto Ambrosini ITA 10:23.6; 4, Gustaf Mattsson SWE 10:23.7; 5, Michael Devaney USA 10:26.0; 6, Albert Hulsebosch USA 10:32.0.

110mH: 1, Earl Thomson CAN 14.8 (world rec); 2, Harold Barron USA 15.1; 3, Frederick Murray USA 15.1; 4, Harry Wilson NZL 15.2; 5, Walker Smith USA 15.2; 6, Carl-Axel Christiernsson SWE 15.3.

400mH: 1, Frank Loomis USA 54.0 (world rec); 2, John Norton USA 54.6; 3, August Desch USA 54.7; 4, Georges André FRA 54.8; 5, Carl-Axel Christiernsson SWE 55.6; 6, Charles Daggs USA 56.4.

4x100m Relay: 1, USA (Charley Paddock, Jackson Scholz, Loren Murchison, Morris Kirksey) 42.2 (world rec); 2, France (René Lorain, René Tirard, René Mourlon, Emile Ali Khan) 42.6; 3, Sweden (Agne Holmström, William Petersson, Sven Malm, Nils Sandström) 42.9; 4, Great Britain 43.1; 5, Denmark 43.5; 6, Luxembourg 43.9.

4x400m Relay: 1, Great Britain (Cecil Griffiths, Robert Lindsay, John Ainsworth-Davis, Guy Butler) 3:22.2; 2, South Africa (Harry Davel, Clarence Oldfield, Jack Oosterlaak, Bevil Rudd) 3:24.2; 3, France (Georges André, Gaston Fery, Maurice Delvart, Jean Devaux) 3:24.8; 4, USA 3:25.2; 5, Sweden; 6, Belgium.

HJ: 1, Richmond Landon USA 1.94; 2, Harold Muller USA 1.90; 3, Bo Ekelund SWE 1.90; 4, Walter Whalen USA 1.85; 5, John Murphy USA 1.85; 6, Howard Baker GBR 1.85.

PV: 1, Frank Foss USA 4.09 (world rec); 2, Henry Petersen DEN 3.70; 3, Edwin Myers USA 3.60; 4, Edward Knourek USA 3.60; 5, Ernfrid Rydberg SWE 3.60; 6, Lauritz Jörgensen DEN 3.60.

LJ: 1, William Petersson (later Björnemann) SWE 7.15; 2, Carl Johnson USA 7.09; 3, Erik Abrahamsson SWE 7.08; 4, Dink Templeton USA 6.95; 5, Erling Aastad NOR 6.88; 6, Rolf Franksson SWE 6.73.

TJ: 1, Vilho Tuulos FIN 14.50; 2, Folke Jansson SWE 14.48; 3, Erik Almlöf SWE 14.27; 4, Ivar Sahlin SWE 14.17; 5, Sherman Landers USA 14.17; 6, Dan Ahearn USA 14.08.

SP: 1, Ville Pörhölä FIN 14.81; 2, Elmer Niklander FIN 14.15; 3, Harry Liversedge USA 14.15; 4, Pat McDonald USA 14.08; 5, Einar Nilsson SWE 13.87; 6, Harald Tammer EST 13.60.

DT: 1, Elmer Niklander FIN 44.68; 2, Armas Taipale FIN 44.19; 3, Augustus Pope USA 42.13; 4, Oscar Zallhagen SWE 41.07; 5, William Bartlett USA 40.87; 6, Allan Eriksson SWE 39.41.

HT: 1, Pat Ryan USA 52.87; 2, Carl Lind SWE 48.43; 3, Basil Bennett USA 48.25; 4, Malcolm Svensson SWE 47.29; 5, Matt McGrath USA 46.67; 6, Tom Nicolson GBR 45.70.

JT: 1, Jonni Myyrä FIN 65.78; 2, Urho Peltonen FIN 63.60; 3, Paavo Johansson (later Jaale) FIN 63.09; 4, Julius Saaristo FIN 62.39; 5, Alexander Klumberg EST 62.39; 6, Gunnar Lindström SWE 60.52.

Dec: 1, Helge Lövland NOR 6803 (5803 on present tables) (12.0, 6.28, 11.19, 1.65, 54.8, 16.2, 37.34, 3.20, 48.01, 4:48.4); 2, Brutus Hamilton USA 6771 (5739); 3, Bertil Ohlson SWE 6580 (5639); 4, Gösta Holmer SWE 6532 (5551); 5, Evert Nilsson SWE 6433 (5371); 6, Valdemar Wickholm FIN 6405 (5630).

8k Cross Country: 1, Paavo Nurmi FIN 27:15; 2, Erik Backman SWE 27:18; 3, Heikki Liimatainen FIN 27:38; 4, James Wilson GBR 27:46; 5, Frank Hegarty GBR 27:57; 6, Teodor Koskenniemi FIN 27:58. Teams: 1, Finland 10pts (Nurmi, Liimatainen, Koskenniemi); 2, Great Britain 21 (Wilson, Hegarty; 12, Arthur Nichols); 3, Sweden 23 (Backman; 10, Gustaf Mattsson; 11, Hilding Ekman).

3000m Team Race: 1, USA 10pts (1, Horace Brown 8:45.4; 3, Arlie Schardt 8:46.4; 6, Ivan Dresser); 2, Great Britain 20 (5, Charles Blewitt; 7, Albert Hill; 9, William Seagrove); 3, Sweden 24 (2, Erik Backman 8:45.6; 13, Sven Lundgren; 15, Edvin Wide). Note: non-scoring runners were ignored in calculating team scores.

3000m Walk: 1, Ugo Frigerio ITA 13:14.2; 2, George Parker AUS 13:20.6; 3, Richard Remer USA 13:23.6; 4, Cecil McMaster SAF 13:22.2; 5, Thomas Maroney USA 13:25.08; 6, Charles Dowson GBR 13:28.0.

10,000m Walk: 1, Ugo Frigerio ITA 48:06.2; 2, Joseph Pearman USA 49:40.8; 3, Charles Gunn GBR 49:43.2; 4, Cecil McMaster SAF 50:00.4; 5, William Hehir GBR 50:11.8; 6, Thomas Maroney USA 50:24.4.

56lb Weight: 1, Pat McDonald USA 11.26; 2, Pat Ryan USA 10.96; 3, Carl Lind SWE 10.25.

Pen: 1, Eero Lehtonen FIN 14pts (LJ-6.63, JT-54.67, 200m-23.0, DT-34.64, 1500m-4:40.2); 2, Everett Bradley USA 24; 3, Hugo Lahtinen FIN 26.

FINNISH RUNNERS DOMINATE

SO PRE-EMINENT was Finland in middle and long distance running in Paris that between 1500m and the marathon, including the steeplechase, the men of Suomi won all eight of the gold medals available!

The first went to New York-based Ville Ritola, number 14 among 20 brothers and sisters, who in the 10,000m survived a 15:00.2 first half to set a world record of 30:23.2. Ritola followed that with an equally convincing 3000m steeplechase win in 9:33.6, just a fifth of a second outside the unofficial world's best. He would proceed to win two more gold medals (as a member of the cross country and 3000m teams) and two silvers for a record six medals in a single Games ... and yet ultimately he was overshadowed by his compatriot Paavo Nurmi (see page 33) who ended up with five gold medals, the most ever to have been won at one Olympics.

Nurmi beat Ritola in the 5000m – less than an hour after winning the 1500m – and a particularly gruelling cross country race, as well as finishing in front of him in the team race over 3000m. The other Finnish running star was 35 year-old Albin Stenroos, the 1912 10,000m bronze medallist, who in only his second marathon race in 15 years achieved victory by a margin of almost six minutes, the widest in Olympic history not counting the interim Games of 1906.

With Jonni Myrrä retaining the javelin title

STAR OF THE GAMES

PAAVO NURMI
(born 13 Jun 1897; died 2 Oct 1973)

Hicham El Guerrouj thrilled fans last year by going so close to a 1500m/5000m double in the World Championships, but – also in Paris – the most famous of all Finnish athletes took both Olympic titles within the space of an hour ... and went on to win the cross country and 3000m team race!

and Eero Lehtonen winning the pentathlon, Finland gained ten titles – as against 12 by the USA, three by Britain and two by the rest of the world combined: Nick Winter of Australia, who triple jumped a world record 15.52, and Italy's 10,000m walk winner Ugo Frigerio. A record 40 nations took part in the athletics, but – as in 1920 – Germany was not invited.

Chariots of Fire heroes Harold Abrahams in the 100m and Eric Liddell in the 400m (see page 31) both scored unexpected victories, while Douglas Lowe won the 800m on his 22nd birthday when he wasn't even considered to be Britain's best at the distance.

Lowe, born in Manchester on August 7 1902 and a member of the Achilles club (Oxford and Cambridge University past and present) which dominated British athletics at that time, travelled to Paris as second string to Henry Stallard, who had beaten him for the AAA half mile title in 1:54.6.

Right from the start of the final Stallard (despite a painful foot injury) set a swift pace, which suited Lowe perfectly although Stallard was quick to point out after the race that his intention was to win and not simply draw out his team-mate. At 400m Lowe was in sixth place but with 200m to go he and Paul Martin of Switzerland were closing. Stallard was caught at 700m, leaving Lowe and Martin to fight for the gold medal and it was the Englishman, yet to win even his own national title, who proved the stronger. His time of 1:52.4 took a second off Albert Hill's British record. The gallant Stallard gave his all and was just edged out of the bronze medal by Schuyler Enck (USA), but finished third in the 1500m two days later, one place ahead of Lowe, a novice at the distance.

These Games saw a remarkable display by Britain's sprinters and middle distance runners, with gold in the 100m (Abrahams), bronze in the 200m (Liddell), gold and bronze (Liddell and Guy Butler) in the 400m, gold in the 800m (Lowe), bronze in the 1500m (Stallard), silver in the 4x100m and bronze in the 4x400m – and both of those might have been gold had Liddell been available for the relays. There were medals also in the 3000m team race and for Gordon Goodwin in the walk and for Malcolm Nokes in the hammer.

This last was especially notable, for he was the first non-Irish British representative to win a field event medal ... and there wouldn't be another UK throws medallist until Dave Ottley and Tessa Sanderson sixty years later.

Two Americans were double champions: Harold Osborn and Clarence "Bud" Houser. The latter was the last man to date to win both the shot and discus, while Osborn achieved the unique feat of winning both the decathlon and an individual event. Osborn, who used the Western Roll style, was the world high jump record holder at 2.03, although 1.98 sufficed for victory in Paris.

Curiously, a world long jump record was registered by a man who failed to make his national team for that event! While William DeHart Hubbard leapt 7.44 for victory in the long jump to become the first black athlete to win an individual Olympic gold medal, Bob LeGendre (an American born of French parents) touched down at 7.76 in the opening event of the pentathlon, in which he finished third overall. Another bizarre chain of events occurred in the 400m hurdles, in which the man who actually crossed the line third – Finland's Erik Wilen – was credited with a new Olympic record of 53.8. Morgan Taylor won the gold medal but his time of 52.6 was disallowed as a world and Olympic record because he knocked over a hurdle, while Charles Brookins, a close second in 52.8, was disqualified for running out of his lane.

Taylor was to father a noted athlete in Morgan Taylor Jr, who was second ranked long jumper in the world in 1952 with 7.77, and Commodore Cochran, who ran the first leg for the USA's world record breaking 4x400m team, was to be followed as an Olympic gold medallist 24 years later by his brother, Roy Cochran, winner of the 400m hurdles and 4x400m in London in 1948. Commodore (that was his name, not rank) was born in 1902, Roy in 1919.

Other American winners included Lee Barnes, who captured the pole vault title one week before his 18th birthday. The world record holder, Charles Hoff of Norway, was unable to compete in his speciality because of injury ... and so he contested the 800m instead and reached the final!

CHARIOTS OF FIRE

THANKS TO an Oscar-winning film released in 1981, certain events at the 1924 Olympics are familiar to millions of people who were born decades later, and the names of Harold Abrahams and Eric Liddell became famous again. Chariots of Fire focused on the contrasting background and motivation of the two athletes ... but, for dramatic effect, the screenplay often deviated from the known facts. For instance, much was made in the film of Liddell discovering only on the journey to Paris that the 100m heats would be held on a Sunday, but actually he was aware of the timetable several months earlier.

Harold Abrahams, born in Bedford on December 15 1899, was encouraged to become an athlete by his elder brothers, one of whom, Sidney, competed in the Olympics of 1908 and 1912. Coached by Sam Mussabini, he trained diligently during the winter of 1923/24 ... it was almost unheard of in those days for a sprinter to train as often as three times a week, as Abrahams did!

"My training sessions consisted largely of perfecting the start and practising arm action over and over again," wrote Abrahams. "No starting blocks in those days, and we took meticulous care with the placing and digging of starting holes and the accurate control of the first few strides. We paid infinite attention to my length of stride. I shall always believe that the vital factor in my running in Paris was that by conscientious training I had managed to shorten my stride an inch or two and get an extra stride into my 100 metres."

His improvement was evident in June 1924 when he set an English long jump record of 7.38 and ran a wind-assisted 9.6 for 100 yards. Nevertheless, Abrahams travelled to the Games in Paris with no great hopes. "Truthfully, I did not think I had any chance of a gold medal, nor did anyone else. The Americans appeared to me to be in a different class from myself." There was Charley Paddock, the reigning 100m champion and world record holder at 10.4, Jackson Scholz, Loren Murchison and Chester Bowman. All were much faster on paper than the tall, powerfully built Briton whose fastest legal 100 yards time was 9.9, equivalent to 10.8 for 100m.

However, it became apparent in the second round heats that Abrahams had timed his peak to perfection as he streaked to victory in an Olympic and British record equalling 10.6. In the semi-finals next day he won again in 10.6 despite being left at the start. He knew then he could win the gold medal and during the three and three-quarter hours interval before the final "I felt like a condemned man feels just before going to the scaffold".

By halfway Abrahams was fractionally ahead of the American pair of Scholz and Bowman. "Scudding like some vast bird with outstretched wings, a spectacle positively appalling in its grandeur," as one observer described him, the 24 year-old London Athletic Club and Achilles star soared through the tape well clear of Scholz in another 10.6 to become the first European to win the blue riband of sprinting. Arthur Porritt, who would become surgeon to the British royal family and Governor-General of his native New Zealand, unexpectedly took the bronze medal ahead of Bowman, with Paddock only fifth.

Abrahams went on to finish last in the 200m final, won by Scholz in 21.6, but picked up a silver medal in the relay along with Walter Rangeley, Lancelot Royle and William Nichol, the British team finishing in 41.2, only two metres behind the Americans' world record equalling 41.0, after having themselves established a short-lived record of 42.0 in a heat.

That, effectively, was the end of Abrahams' active career. He seriously damaged a leg while long jumping in May 1925 and never competed again, but went on to make an enormous contribution to the sport in other ways: as an administrator, writer, statistician and radio commentator. He died in 1978, aged 78.

Alas, Eric Liddell was to die all too young, at the hands of the Japanese in 1945 when he was 43.

The son of a Scottish missionary, Liddell was born at Tientsin, China, on January 16 1902 and brought to Britain aged five. As a student at Edinburgh University he won his first Scottish sprint titles in 1921 but made more impact as a rugby three-quarter, gaining his first Scottish 'cap' the following year, until in 1923 he captured the AAA sprint double in 9.7 and 21.6. That British 100 yards record was only a tenth outside the world mark.

As the Olympic 100m heats would be run on a Sunday, that event was ruled out by Liddell, a devout Christian. He prepared instead for 400m, but it was not until he won the AAA 440 yards title (49.6) in June 1924 that he broke 50 sec for the first time. His chances of winning in Paris against a cluster of men credited with times around 48 sec seemed fairly remote ... but, like Abrahams, Liddell was to reach unexpected heights in Paris.

His third place in the 200m final behind Scholz and Paddock could have been seen as a pointer, but 400m heats in 50.2 and a personal best of 49.0 attracted little attention. However, he caused a minor stir by taking the second semi-final in 48.2, only 0.4 slower than the Olympic record set by Horatio Fitch (USA) in the first semi. For the final a few hours later Liddell was drawn in the outside lane – a particular disadvantage for a relative novice at the event.

From the gun Liddell sprinted away like a man possessed and flashed past the halfway mark in an unheard of 22.2, some four metres clear of his nearest opponent, team-mate Guy Butler. Liddell's head was thrown back, his arms all over the place, his knee drive exaggerated ... the experts shook their heads knowingly; they were watching a classic example of a sprinter misjudging his effort. Any other man would have blown up but the inspired 22 year-old Scot somehow summoned up hidden reserves of stamina. At the tape he had six metres to spare over Fitch, with Butler third.

His time of 47.6 was only 0.2 outside the best on record. Absurdly, it was ratified as a world record because, reasoned the IAAF, Ted Meredith's 47.4 was made over 440 yards and not 400 metres, ignoring the fact that 440y is actually 2.34m longer! As a European and UK best, Liddell's mark stood for a dozen years and it represented a gain of some 1.7 sec over his pre-Olympic fastest although it should be noted that the Stade Colombes track measured 500m.

Liddell bowed out of international athletics the following week with a 440 yards relay leg timed at 47.6 and in 1925 became a missionary in China. He spent the rest of his life there, becoming an ordained minister of the Congregational Church. He died of a brain haemorrhage during internment in a Japanese prison camp.

THE IMMORTAL PAAVO NURMI

AS THE years roll by, the names of some of the great champion athletes of their day become increasingly obscure or forgotten. Not so in the case of Paavo Nurmi. Eighty years after his astonishing Olympic exploits in Paris he remains one of the best known and most revered figures in athletics history. A readers' poll conducted by Athletics International at the end of 1999 named Nurmi as the second greatest male athlete of the century.

What he achieved at the 1924 Games is still difficult to comprehend. On July 10 (the very same day that his hero Hannes Kolehmainen won the 1912 Olympic 5000m title in world record time) Nurmi killed off his rivals in the 1500m, flashing past 800m in 1:58.5 and easing up in the closing stages when victory was assured to reach the finish in 3:53.6, just a second outside his own world record. That would have been a good day's work in itself, but the reason why the 27 year-old Finn conserved his energy was that 42 minutes later he was due back on the track to contest the 5000m final against his compatriot Ville Ritola, who had already won the 10,000m in a world record 30:23.2 and the steeplechase in 9:33.6.

Nurmi's rivals cannily made the pace very fast, the first kilometre of 2:46.4 being 13:52 pace whereas his world record stood at 14:28.2, but nothing could throw Nurmi. He stayed in touch, took the lead at about halfway and kept Ritola at bay as the two came home half a minute ahead of the next finisher. Nurmi's time of 14:31.2 was second only to his world record. Needless to add, this particular Olympic double has remained unique, as also Nurmi's feat in Helsinki three weeks earlier when – again within about an hour but without serious competition – he set the world records of 3:52.6 and 14:28.2.

There was more to come from Nurmi in Paris. On July 12, on one of the hottest days ever known in the French capital, he encountered Ritola again, but this time it was no contest. While only 15 of the 38 runners reached the finish line of the 10.65k cross country race, and most of those were reduced to little more than a jog, Nurmi appeared totally oblivious to the terrifying conditions and came home some 400m ahead of Ritola, with the bronze medallist another minute behind. As that was a team as well as individual

race Nurmi collected another two gold medals for his efforts, and his fifth gold came the following day when he led Finland to victory in the 3000m team race. No individual award this time, but again he dominated Ritola with his time of 8:32.0 close to his own official world record of 8:28.6.

Nurmi, born in Turku on June 13 1897, was to amass the greatest number of Olympic medals by an athlete: nine golds and three silvers between 1920 and 1928. He would surely have gained another in the 1932 Olympic marathon had he not been disqualified from amateur competition shortly before the Los Angeles Games.

His collection of world records was equally impressive: between 1921 and 1931 he set new figures at distances ranging from 1500m to 20,000m including such times as 4:10.4 for the mile, 8:20.4 for 3000m, 8:59.6 for 2 miles and 30:06.2 for 10,000m. His consistency was legendary. He was never beaten in a race longer than 5000m, while between 1921 and 1925 his only defeats came in a 5000m he failed to finish due to illness and one race at the rather short distance for him of 800m.

Nurmi "became the most famous Finnish person in history", declared Matti Hannus in his book Flying Finns. "Even before the era of TV, Paavo Nurmi became a full-blooded entertainer, a star beside other stars: Greta Garbo, Charlie Chaplin, Douglas Fairbanks, Rudolph Valentino." A hurdling contemporary of Nurmi's, Martti Jukola, wrote: "He became a running giant who was surrounded by the mythical aura of a fairy-tale. During a whole decade, more was written and spoken about him everywhere than about any other athlete – perhaps more than about any human spirit. Millions of people wanted to see him."

But Nurmi never played to the gallery; he went about his business of winning races for his own satisfaction. As Jukola put it: "He became austere and withdrawn. Without smiling, cold and unapproachable, he went on destroying past feats, then, having done his job, went away like an executioner – without feelings, without noticing anyone. There was something inhumanly barren and cruel in him, but he conquered the world with his bright weapons: his will, his super-natural power."

Perhaps his dour personality grew from the hardship he encountered as a youngster. His father died when Paavo was 12 and he had to

PAAVO NURMI CONTINUED

work as an errand boy and assume family responsibilities at that young age. Running was his release, and he was inspired by the news of Kolehmainen's Olympic triumphs in Stockholm, when Nurmi was a highly impressionable 15.

Nurmi set new standards of training, sometimes working out as often as three times a day and becoming the first distance runner to include regular speedwork in his sessions. Here is his schedule for May 1924. In the early morning he would walk 10-12k, with the occasional sprint thrown in, followed by some gym work and a bath. Already warmed up nicely he would, after about an hour, start his track training which might include a set of 4-5 x 80-120m sprints, a time trial at 400-1000m and an even paced run of 3000-4000m with a fast last lap. In the evening he would run between 4000 and 7000m cross country, speeding up considerably over the final kilometre or two.

Although debarred from the 1932 Games, Nurmi re-entered the Olympic arena 20 years later when, to the delight of the crowd packing the stadium in Helsinki (outside of which there is a statue to Finland's greatest athlete), it was he who was given the honour of carrying the Olympic torch on its lap of honour. It was in Helsinki in 1973 that Nurmi died, aged 76, but his deeds continue to live on in the minds of all who appreciate athletics.

1924 - PARIS

100m: 1, Harold Abrahams GBR 10.6; 2, Jackson Scholz USA 10.8; 3, Arthur Porritt NZL 10.9; 4, Chester Bowman USA 10.9; 5, Charley Paddock USA 10.9; 6, Loren Murchison USA 11.0.

200m: 1, Jackson Scholz USA 21.6; 2, Charley Paddock USA 21.7; 3, Eric Liddell GBR 21.9; 4, George Hill USA 22.0; 5, Bayes Norton USA 22.0; 6, Harold Abrahams GBR 22.3.

400m: 1, Eric Liddell GBR 47.6; 2, Horatio Fitch USA 48.4; 3, Guy Butler GBR 48.6; 4, David Johnson CAN 48.8; 5, John Coard Taylor USA 56.0 (fell); Josef Imbach SUI dnf.

800m: 1, Douglas Lowe GBR 1:52.4; 2, Paul Martin SUI 1:52.5; 3, Schuyler Enck USA 1:52.9; 4, Henry Stallard GBR 1:53.0; 5, William Richardson USA 1:53.7; 6, Ray Dodge USA 1:54.2.

1500m: 1, Paavo Nurmi FIN 3:53.6; 2, Willy Schärer SUI 3:55.0; 3, Henry Stallard GBR 3:55.6; 4, Douglas Lowe GBR 3:57.0; 5, Raymond Buker USA 3:58.6; 6, Lloyd Hahn USA 3:59.0.

5000m: 1, Paavo Nurmi FIN 14:31.2; 2, Ville Ritola FIN 14:31.4; 3, Edvin Wide SWE 15:01.8; 4, John Romig USA 15:12.3; 5, Eino Seppälä FIN 15:18.3; 6, Charles Clibbon GBR 15:20.4.

10,000m: 1, Ville Ritola FIN 30:23.2 (world rec); 2, Edvin Wide SWE 30:55.2; 3, Eero Berg FIN 31:43.0; 4, Väinö Sipilä FIN 31:50.2; 5, Ernie Harper GBR 31:58.0; 6, Halland Britton GBR 32:06.0.

Marathon: (42.2k) 1, Albin Stenroos FIN 2:41:23; 2, Romeo Bertini ITA 2:47:20; 3, Clarence DeMar USA 2:48:14; 4, Lauri Halonen FIN 2:49:48; 5, Sam Ferris GBR 2:52:26; 6, Manuel Plaza CHI 2:52:54.

3000mSC: 1, Ville Ritola FIN 9:33.6; 2, Elias Katz FIN 9:44.0; 3, Paul Bontemps FRA 9:45.2; 4, Marvin Rick USA 9:56.4; 5, Karl Ebb FIN 9:57.5; 6, Evelyn Montague GBR 9:58.0.

110mH: 1, Dan Kinsey USA 15.0; 2, Sid Atkinson SAF 15.0; 3, Sten Pettersson SWE 15.4; 4, Carl-Axel Christiernsson SWE 15.5; 5, Karl Anderson USA (fell); George Guthrie USA disq.

400mH: 1, Morgan Taylor USA 52.6 (unratified world rec); 2, Erik Wilen FIN 53.8; 3, Ivan Riley USA 54.1; 4, Georges André FRA 55.6; Charles Brookins USA & Fred Blackett GBR disq.

4x100m Relay: 1, USA (Frank Hussey, Louis Clarke, Loren Murchison, Al Leconey) 41.0 (eq world rec set in semi-final); 2, Great Britain (Harold Abrahams, Walter Rangeley, Lancelot Royle, William Nichol) 41.2; 3, Netherlands (Jacob Boot, Henricus Broos, Jan de Vries, Marinus van den Berge) 41.8; 4, Hungary 42.0; 5, France 42.2; Switzerland disq.

4x400m Relay: 1, USA (Commodore Cochran, Bill Stevenson, Oliver MacDonald, Alan Helffrich)

FINLAND'S OLYMPIC DISTANCE RUNNING WINNERS

Hannes Kolehmainen: 1912: 5000m, 10,000m & Cross Country; 1920 Marathon; Paavo Nurmi: 1920 10,000m & Cross Country; 1924 1500m, 5000m & Cross Country (1st 3000m Team Race); 1928 10,000m; Ville Ritola: 1924 10,000m & 3000mSC; 1928 5000m; Albin Stenroos: 1924 Marathon; Harri Larva: 1928 1500m; Toivo Loukola: 1928 3000mSC; Lauri Lehtinen: 1932 5000m; Volmari Iso-Hollo: 1932 & 1936 3000mSC; Gunnar Höckert: 1936 5000m; Ilmari Salminen: 1936 10,000m; Pekka Vasala: 1972 1500m; Lasse Viren: 1972 & 1976 5000m & 10,000m

3:16.0 (world rec); 2, Sweden (Artur Svensson, Erik Bylehn, Gustaf Wejnarth, Nils Engdahl) 3:17.0; 3, Great Britain (Edward Toms, George Renwick, Richard Ripley, Guy Butler) 3:17.4; 4, Canada 3:22.8; 5, France 3:23.4; 6, Italy 3:28.0.

HJ: 1, Harold Osborn USA 1.98; 2, Leroy Brown USA 1.95; 3, Pierre Lewden FRA 1.92; 4, Thomas Poor USA 1.88; 5, Jenö Gaspar HUN 1.88; 6, Helge Jansson SWE 1.85.

PV: 1, Lee Barnes USA 3.95; 2, Glenn Graham USA 3.95; 3, James Brooker USA 3.90; 4, Henry Petersen DEN 3.90; 5, Victor Pickard CAN 3.80; 6, Ralph Spearow USA 3.70.

LJ: 1, William De Hart Hubbard USA 7.44; 2, Ed Gourdin USA 7.27; 3, Sverre Hansen NOR 7.26; 4, Vilho Tuulos FIN 7.07; 5, Louis Wilhelme FRA 6.99; 6, Christopher Mackintosh GBR 6.92.

TJ: 1, Nick Winter AUS 15.52 (world rec); 2, Luis Brunetto ARG 15.42; 3, Vilho Tuulos FIN 15.37; 4, Väinö Rainio FIN 15.01; 5, Folke Jansson SWE 14.97; 6, Mikio Oda JPN 14.35.

SP: 1, Bud Houser USA 14.99; 2, Glenn Hartranft USA 14.98; 3, Ralph Hills USA 14.64; 4, Hannes Torpo FIN 14.45; 5, Norman Anderson USA 14.29; 6, Elmer Niklander FIN 14.26.

DT: 1, Bud Houser USA 46.15; 2, Vilho Niittymaa FIN 44.95; 3, Thomas Lieb USA 44.83; 4, Augustus Pope USA 44.42; 5, Ketil Askildt NOR 43.40; 6, Glenn Hartranft USA 42.49.

HT: 1, Fred Tootell USA 53.29; 2, Matt McGrath USA 50.84; 3, Malcolm Nokes GBR 48.87; 4, Erik Eriksson FIN 48.74; 5, Ossian Skjöld SWE 45.28; 6, James McEachern USA 45.22.

JT: 1, Jonni Myrrä FIN 62.96; 2, Gunnar Lindström SWE 60.92; 3, Eugene Oberst USA 58.35; 4, Yrjö Ekqvist FIN 57.56; 5, William Neufeld USA 56.96; 6, Erik Blomqvist SWE 56.85.

Dec: 1, Harold Osborn USA 7711 (world rec; 6476 on present tables) (11.2, 6.92, 11.43, 1.97, 53.2, 16.0, 34.51, 3.50, 46.69, 4:50.0); 2, Emerson Norton USA 7351 (6117); 3, Aleksandr Klumberg-Kolmpere EST 7329 (6056); 4, Anton Huusari FIN 7005 (5952); 5, Edward Sutherland SAF 6794 (5928); 6, Ernst Gerspach SUI 6744 (5765).

10.65k Cross Country: 1, Paavo Nurmi FIN 32:55; 2, Ville Ritola FIN 34:20; 3, Earle Johnson USA 35:21; 4, Ernie Harper GBR 35:36; 5, Henri Lauvaux FRA 36:45; 6, Arthur Studenroth USA 36:46. Teams: 1, Finland 11pts (Nurmi, Ritola, Heikki Liimatainen); 2, USA 14 (Johnson, Studenroth, August Fager); 3, France 20 (Lauvaux, Gaston Heuet, Maurice Norland).

3000m Team Race: 1, Finland 8pts (1, Paavo Nurmi 8:32.0; 2, Ville Ritola 8:40.6; 5, Elias Katz 8:45.4); 2, Great Britain 14 (3, Bernard Macdonald 8:44.0; 4, "Johnny" Johnston 8:45.2; 7, George Webber); 3, USA 25 (6, Edward Kirby 8:53.0; 8, William Cox; 11, Willard Tibbetts).

10,000m Walk: 1, Ugo Frigerio ITA 47:49.0; 2, Gordon Goodwin GBR 48:37.9; 3, Cecil McMaster SAF 49:08.0; 4, Donato Pavesi ITA 49:17.0; 5, Arthur Tell Schwab SUI 49:50.2; 6, Frederick Clark GBR 49:59.2.

Pen: 1, Eero Lehtonen FIN 14pts (LJ-6.68, JT-50.93, 200m-23.0, DT-40.44, 1500m-4:47.0); 2, Elemer Somfay HUN 16; 3, Bob LeGendre USA 18 (7.76 LJ, world rec).

WORLD RECORDS OF THE DAY

The IAAF, founded in 1912, issued its inaugural list of world records in 1914. Here are the records for "Olympic" events as at January 1 1925. Note the preponderance of Americans, and the fact that several of the performances are roughly comparable to today's world records for women. However, two current women's world records, for the marathon (2:15:25) and pole vault (4.86, admittedly with far more advanced equipment), would have been undreamt of for men of that era.

100: 10.4 Charley Paddock USA 1921
200: 21.2 Willie Applegarth GBR 1914
400: 47.4 Ted Meredith USA 1916
800: 1:51.9 Ted Meredith USA 1912
1500: 3:52.6 Paavo Nurmi FIN 1924
5000: 14:28.2 Paavo Nurmi FIN 1924
10,000: 30:06.2 Paavo Nurmi FIN 1924
Mar: 2:32:36 Hannes Kolehmainen FIN 1920
3000SC: 9:33.4 Paul Bontemps FRA 1924
110H: 14.8 Earl Thomson CAN 1920
400H: 52.6 Morgan Taylor USA 1924
4x100: 41.0 USA 1924
4x400: 3:16.0 USA 1924
HJ: 2.03 Harold Osborn USA 1924
PV: 4.21 Charles Hoff NOR 1923
LJ: 7.76 Robert LeGendre USA 1924
TJ: 15.52 Dan Ahearn USA 1911 & Nick Winter AUS 1924
SP: 15.54 Ralph Rose USA 1909
DT: 47.61 Thomas Lieb USA 1924
HT: 57.77 Pat Ryan USA 1913
JT: 66.62 Gunnar Lindström SWE 1924
Dec: 7711 Harold Osborn USA 1924 (=6476 on present tables; 6564 by Jim Thorpe USA 1912)

THE EMPIRE STRIKES BACK

THE AMERICANS, used to being the dominant force in the shorter track events at the Olympics, received a nasty shock in Amsterdam. Their highly touted sprinters failed to win any medals as Percy Williams of Canada scored a double triumph, while other representatives of the British Empire in Sid Atkinson of South Africa and Lord Burghley of Britain took care of the two hurdling events. Sixteen year-old Betty Robinson did win the inaugural women's 100m (see page 38) but the only American male to triumph in an individual track event was Ray Barbuti, who took the 400m in 47.8.

The New York Times correspondent placed the blame on the team coaches and management. "Many explanations and suggestions were offered," he wrote, "but the ones heard most frequently were that the team, puffed up with conceit, hasn't trained seriously since its arrival at Amsterdam and that it might be well for the American committee hereafter to return to rough-house methods when an athlete who broke rules was immediately dismissed from the team, and as another critic said 'when coaches were coaches instead of newspaper correspondents'. Head coach Lawson Robertson from his seat in the press stand, which he has occupied throughout every event in the Olympics, admitted he could not understand what, indeed, is the matter with his boys. This is more understandable when it is explained that the press stand is a long distance from the quarters of the athletes. Patrick Walsh, manager of the track and field team, could not understand either – also from his seat in the press stand. General Douglas MacArthur, President of the American Olympic Committee, likewise shook his head sadly – from his seat in the press stand. The American team has been a great disappointment and despite the fact that it enjoys better training and living facilities and has more coaches, trainers and managers than the team of any other nation, it will perhaps be listed as the poorest team that ever represented the United States in the Olympics."

Too much ice cream was the reason for the Yanks' demise, according to a writer from the London Evening Standard who commented that some members of the US team had put on too much weight from over-indulgence.

Not that the Americans left Amsterdam exactly empty handed. They still won eight men's events, while the next most successful team, Finland, took five. Britain won two titles through Douglas Lowe and Lord Burghley, with Jack London and Walter Rangeley picking up silver medals and the sprint relay team finishing third.

Douglas Lowe, newly qualified as a barrister, made Olympic history by becoming the first runner (if one excludes 1906) to successfully defend a title. An unexpected winner of the 800m in Paris, Lowe had scaled new heights in 1926 ... although he met his match in Dr Otto Peltzer of Germany. Excitement ran high for their 880 yards clash at the AAA Championships. Peltzer had run 800m in 1:52.8, the world's fastest in 1925, while Lowe had tuned up for the race with a world 600 yards record of 1:10.4. It was a thriller, with both men beating Ted Meredith's world record of 1:52.2. Lowe led at halfway in 54.6, repelled Peltzer's persistent challenges along the back straight but found himself unable to counter the German's final sprint. Peltzer won in 1:51.6, with Lowe's time untaken but estimated at 1:52.0.

As in Paris, Lowe ran no faster than necessary in the Olympic preliminaries and it was to his advantage that whereas he was able to stroll through his semi-final in a relaxed 1:56.0 (eliminating an ill Peltzer) three of his most dangerous rivals – Lloyd Hahn (USA), Phil Edwards (Canada) and Séra Martin (France) – were caught up in a hectic battle which necessitated their running

STAR OF THE GAMES

PERCY WILLIAMS
(born 19 May 1908; died 29 Nov 1982)

At 15 Percy Williams suffered from rheumatic fever and was told to avoid undue excitement and exertion. Five years later the diminutive Canadian was crowned double sprint champion – to the dismay of the Americans, who won no medals at all either in the 100m or 200m.

1:53 or faster to qualify. Lowe was ideally placed throughout the final. Hahn, who had set a short lived world record of 1:51.4 in the US Olympic Trials, led at 400m in 55.2 with Lowe (55.6) second and the situation remained unchanged until the final bend, at which point Lowe accelerated clean away to win by a full second in the Olympic and British record time of 1:51.8.

Lowe later contributed a 47.6 400m relay leg and ended his career on a high note by improving his British 800m record to 1:51.2 when defeating Peltzer in Berlin a few weeks later. He continued to make a valuable contribution to athletics as an administrator, serving as honorary secretary of the AAA from 1931 (when he was still only 29) to 1938. He enjoyed a distinguished legal career; he took silk in 1964 and became a Recorder of the Crown Court. He died in 1981 at the age of 78.

Britain's other Olympic champion of 1928, Lord Burghley, also lived until 1981, when he was 76. Like Lowe (and Harold Abrahams) he was a product of Cambridge University but unlike them had made no impression at the 1924 Games. Only 19, he fell in his heat of the 110m hurdles. He would eventually set British 120 yards hurdles records of 14.8 in 1927 and 14.5 in 1930, only a tenth of a second outside the world record, but from small beginnings (61.2 for his first 440 yards hurdles in 1924) it was as a 400m hurdler that he became renowned.

In 1927 Lord Burghley (David George Brownlow Cecil) not only lowered his British 440 yards hurdles mark to 54.2 in the AAA Championships at Stamford Bridge but, thanks to time zoning, became joint world record holder for a few hours. The same afternoon, in Nebraska, John Gibson took the American title in a startling 52.6. Gibson failed to reach the final in Amsterdam, the favourite being defending champion Morgan Taylor, who had set a world 400m hurdles record of 52.0 at the US Olympic Trials, whereas Lord Burghley's latest British 440 yards hurdles record of 54.0 was the equivalent of 53.7 for the metric event. But the "peerless peer", serving as a lieutenant in the Grenadier Guards at the time, scored a magnificent upset victory. He led the American pair of Taylor and Frank Cuhel into the finishing straight, deliberately chopped his stride in order to make sure of clearing the last hurdle cleanly

and withstood all assaults to snap the tape a metre clear of the US duo in a British record of 53.4. It was the first time the USA had failed to win this Olympic title.

Not a single medal was won by an American in the sprints, the only time (apart from the boycotted 1980 Games) that has ever happened. Frank Wykoff, only 18, was the USA's big hope for the 100m but he was overweight and placed only fourth, as did defending champion Jackson Scholz in the 200m.

Both titles went to a frail-looking 20 year-old Canadian, Percy Williams. At 15 he had suffered from rheumatic fever, which left him with a damaged heart and he was told to avoid undue excitement and exertion. However, he was spotted in 1926 by coach Bob Granger who straight away decided that within two years he could transform the scrawny teenager into an Olympic champion. He was proved right: in Amsterdam he equalled the Olympic record of 10.6 in a heat, and a time of 10.8 sufficed to win the gold medal a metre ahead of statuesque British Guiana-born Jack London, representing Britain. At 57kg (126lb) the 1.70m (5'7") tall Canadian became the lightest ever man to win an Olympic sprint crown. Williams beat another Briton, fast finishing Walter Rangeley, to take the 200m in 21.8. In his diary for that day, Williams noted: "Well, it's done. Won the 200m. Not so bad. Telegrams galore. The girls' team sent flowers to me. Hot dog!"

With the men's programme being trimmed to 22 events there were not as many medal chances in long distance running as previously and Paavo Nurmi and Ville Ritola had to settle for one victory apiece. The 10,000m came first, and Nurmi overtook Ritola in the finishing straight to win in 30:18.8 for his ninth and last Olympic gold medal. Ritola turned the tables in the 5000m in 14:38.0 for the fifth gold of his career. Third in both races (he was also third in the 1924 5000m and 1920 3000m team race, second in the 1924 10,000m) was Edvin Wide, a Swedish citizen since 1918 but – wouldn't you know it – actually a Finn by birth.

Nurmi and Ritola clashed again the day after the 5000m in the steeplechase final, but although Nurmi – whose barrier technique was pretty rudimentary – finished inside the previous unofficial world best he was a well beaten second and Ritola dropped out injured at the bell. The race was still a clean sweep for Finland, victory going to Toivo Loukola in 9:21.8. Five years earlier this Helsinki policeman had been discharged from military service because of suspected tuberculosis. In the 1500m, Finland had to settle for only two of the medals as Frenchman Jules Ladoumegue, the man destined to become the first to break 3:50 for 1500m and 4:10 for the mile before being declared a professional, finished second to 21 year-old Harri Larva, who was born (as Harry Lagerström) of Swedish parents. Just a 3:59.6 performer in 1927 he improved to 3:52.0, only a second outside the world record, and won the title in 3:53.2.

Finnish runners in those days exerted the sort of hold over distance running that the Africans have now, but a highly significant result was achieved in the marathon which was won in 2:32:57 by Boughera El Ouafi, an Algerian who represented France – the first non-South African to strike Olympic gold for that continent. Asia also reached the top rung for the first time as the 1.67m (5'6") tall Mikio Oda of Japan took the triple jump title. Another landmark was Pat O'Callaghan's victory in the hammer. There was nothing new about an Irish-born athlete winning that event (only in 1924 had it been won by anybody else!) but the doctor from County Cork became the first athlete to be crowned Olympic champion while officially representing Ireland. He had only taken up the event the previous year.

Among the medals for the first, and last, time was Haiti in the person of its Olympic soccer team captain, Silvio Cator. He long jumped 7.58 to place second to Ed Hamm (USA) ... and in Paris less than six weeks later he added 3cm to Hamm's world record with a leap of 7.93 to become the first 26-foot jumper.

On the subject of world records, the Amsterdam Games threw up five officially ratified marks in the men's events.

LADIES FIRST!

ALTHOUGH THERE was Olympic competition for women in golf and tennis as early as 1900 and swimming was introduced in 1912, it was not until 1928 that the Olympic Games admitted female track and field athletes ... and even then the number of events on the programme was a derisory five: 100m, 800m, 4x100m relay,

high jump and discus. The Women's AAA, founded in 1922, was so disgusted by this token offer that it refused to send a British team to Amsterdam.

Britain had previously been in the forefront of international women's athletics. In 1921, at the first international women's meeting, staged in Monte Carlo, British athletes won six of the ten events. Co-founders of an international women's governing body, Federation Sportive Feminine Internationale, later that year were Britain, France, USA, Czechoslovakia, Italy and Spain. The body staged a "Women's Olympic Games" in Paris in 1922, organised as a gesture of defiance after FSFI's demand for women's events at the 1924 Olympics was rejected by the IOC. Following objections by the IOC and IAAF to the use of the word Olympic, the meeting was renamed World Games.

The WAAA staged its first full-scale championships in 1923 and the following year the novelty of a women's international meeting drew 25,000 spectators to Stamford Bridge. Yet there was still much male opposition to overcome. The 1924 Olympic 100m champion Harold Abrahams wrote at about that time: "I do not consider that women are built for really violent exercise of the kind that is the essence of competition. One has only to see them practising to realise how awkward they are on the running track." Never in his wildest dreams could he have foreseen that one day women would run faster and long jump farther than himself, or that a female would cover 10,000m more quickly than Paavo Nurmi and Ville Ritola did when winning their Olympic titles!

Even an enthusiast like Capt F A M Webster, who wrote Athletics Of Today For Women in 1930, could not conceal his patronising attitude. He was a victim of his times and social background. "It is hard to see how it can be contended that the throwing of a light javelin can impose a greater strain upon a woman than the use of the overhead tennis service, since both actions call for the employment of exactly the same set of muscles. Again, how can it be said that a short cross country race of two and three-quarter miles is likely to prove any more harmful than a day out with the beagles? Or what argument can be advanced to prove that a sane system of athletics will not the better fit a young woman for the daily household tasks, which frequently involve the moving and lifting of heavy pieces of furniture? On the score of endurance, women have at least as much 'staying power' as men, as is proved at the end of a hard day's hunting, or a long night's dancing, when the man usually finishes rather more 'shop soiled' than his sister."

Not surprisingly, the women athletes attracted a good deal of press attention, but much of what was reported was of a disparaging nature. So much was written about the collapse of several competitors at the end of the 800m final that the event was deleted from the Olympic programme until 1960. In 1932 and 1936 the longest event was 100m, and from 1948 to 1956 inclusive it was all of 200m. The 400m would not be introduced until 1964, the 1500m was added in 1972, the 3000m and marathon in 1984.

One contemporary account of the 800m stated: "If it served any purpose at all, it showed that the modern young woman is apt to attempt too much in the name of sport. As a spectacle, however, it was one for which I had no liking. To run roughly half a mile at breakneck speed is surely too much for any girl. Of the girls who came within reasonable distance of winning, four were so exhausted that they fell all of a heap on the grass, utterly weary and overwrought. Some of them collapsed as much from disappointment and failure as from fatigue."

In fact it was a remarkable race in which the first three finished inside the previous world best, and the winning time of 2:16.8 by Lina Radke (who became Germany's first ever Olympic champion) was not officially surpassed until 1944. Second in 2:17.6 was the great Japanese all-rounder Kinue Hitomi (she was actually born a Korean), who took part in this event as the long jump, at which she held the world record of 5.98, was not on the programme. During an all too brief career she also set world marks for 100m, 200m, 220 yards, 400m and triple jump. She died of tuberculosis in 1931, aged just 23.

World records fell in three other events. US-born Ethel Catherwood (18) of Canada, voted by newspapermen as the prettiest competitor in the Games (she later married 1924 Olympic high jump and decathlon champion Harold Osborn), high jumped 1.59, Halina Konopacka of Poland threw the discus 39.62 (she was the first female champion to be crowned), and Canada won the sprint relay in 48.4 — which helped make up for the disappointment of the 100m final.

Myrtle Cook, who had set a world record of 12.0 in the Canadian Championships, was disqualified for two false starts and her teammate Fanny Rosenfeld disputed the result, feeling she had won. However, the appeal was rejected and the title went in 12.2 to Betty Robinson, a 16 year-old American schoolgirl who was competing in only the fourth meeting of her life, having made her racing debut just four months earlier. Robinson was badly injured in a plane crash in 1931, unable to walk properly or bend her knee for a couple of years, but made a remarkable comeback to qualify for the 1936 Olympic team. Although she couldn't use a crouch start, she placed fifth in the 100m trial and won her place on the relay squad which took the gold medal in Berlin.

1928 - AMSTERDAM
100m: 1, Percy Williams CAN 10.8; 2, Jack London GBR 10.9; 3, Georg Lammers GER 10.9; 4, Frank Wykoff USA 11.0; 5, Wilfred Legg SAF 11.0; 6, Bob McAllister USA 11.0.
200m: 1, Percy Williams CAN 21.8; 2, Walter Rangeley GBR 21.9; 3, Helmut Körnig GER 21.9; 4, Jackson Scholz USA 21.9; 5, John Fitzpatrick CAN 22.1; 6, Jakob Schüller GER 22.2.
400m: 1, Ray Barbuti USA 47.8; 2, James Ball CAN 48.0; 3, Joachim Büchner GER 48.2; 4, John Rinkel GBR 48.4; 5, Werner Storz GER 48.8; 6, Herman Phillips USA 49.0.
800m: 1, Douglas Lowe GBR 1:51.8; 2, Erik Byléhn SWE 1:52.8; 3, Hermann Engelhard GER 1:53.2; 4, Phil Edwards CAN 1:54.0; 5, Lloyd Hahn USA 1:54.2 ; 6, Séra Martin FRA 1:54.6.
1500m: 1, Harri Larva FIN 3:53.2; 2, Jules Ladoumegue FRA 3:53.8; 3, Eino Purje FIN 3:56.4; 4, Hans-Georg Wichmann GER 3:56.8; 5, Cyril Ellis GBR 3:57.6; 6, Paul Martin SUI 3:58.4.
5000m: 1, Ville Ritola FIN 14:38.0; 2, Paavo Nurmi FIN 14:40.0; 3, Edvin Wide SWE 14:41.2; 4, Leo Lermond USA 14:50.0; 5, Ragnar Magnusson SWE 14:59.6; 6, Armas Kinnunen FIN 15:02.0.
10,000m: 1, Paavo Nurmi FIN 30:18.8; 2, Ville Ritola FIN 30:19.4; 3, Edvin Wide SWE 31:00.8;

THE EMPIRE STRIKES BACK CONTINUED

4, Jean-Gunnar Lindgren SWE 31:26.0; 5, Arthur Muggridge GBR 31:31.8; 6, Ragnar Magnusson SWE 31:37.2.

Marathon: 1, Boughera El Ouafi FRA 2:32:57; 2, Manuel Plaza CHI 2:33:23; 3, Martti Marttelin FIN 2:35:02; 4, Kanematsu Yamada JPN 2:35:29; 5, Joie Ray USA 2:36:04; 6, Seiichiro Tsuda JPN 2:36:20.

3000mSC: 1, Toivo Loukola FIN 9:21.8 (world best); 2, Paavo Nurmi FIN 9:31.2; 3, Ove Andersen FIN 9:35.6; 4, Nils Eklöf SWE 9:38.0; 5, Henri Dartigues FRA 9:40.0; 6, Lucien Duquesne FRA 9:40.5.

110mH: 1, Sid Atkinson SAF 14.8; 2, Steve Anderson USA 14.8 (14.8 semi, equals world rec); 3, John Collier USA 14.9; 4, Leighton Dye USA 15.0 (14.8 semi, equals world rec); 5, George Weightman-Smith SAF 15.0 (14.6 semifinal, world rec); 6, Fred Gaby GBR 15.2.

400mH: 1, Lord Burghley GBR 53.4; 2, Frank Cuhel USA 53.6; 3, Morgan Taylor USA 53.6; 4, Sten Pettersson SWE 53.8; 5, Tom Livingstone-Learmonth GBR 54.2; 6, Luigi Facelli ITA 55.8.

4x100m Relay: 1, USA (Frank Wykoff, Jimmy Quinn, Charley Borah, Henry Russell) 41.0 (eq world rec); 2, Germany (Georg Lammers, Richard Corts, Hubert Houben, Helmut Körnig) 41.2; 3, Great Britain (Cyril Gill, Edward Smouha, Walter Rangeley, Jack London) 41.8; 4, France 42.0; 5, Switzerland 42.4; Canada disq.

4x400m Relay: 1, USA (George Baird 48.2, Fred Alderman 47.8, Bud Spencer 49.4, Ray Barbuti 48.8) 3:14.2 (world rec); 2, Germany (Otto Neumann, Richard Krebs, Werner Storz, Hermann Engelhard) 3:14.8; 3, Canada (Alex Wilson, Phil Edwards, Stanley Glover, James Ball 47.6) 3:15.4; 4, Sweden 3:15.8; 5, Great Britain 3:16.4; 6, France 3:19.4.

HJ: 1, Bob King USA 1.94; 2, Ben Hedges USA 1.91; 3, Claude Ménard FRA 1.91; 4, Simeon Toribio PHI 1.91; 5, Harold Osborn USA 1.91; 6, Kazuo Kimura JPN 1.88.

PV: 1, Sabin Carr USA 4.20; 2, Bill Droegemuller USA 4.10; 3, Charles McGinnis USA 3.95; 4, Victor Pickard CAN 3.95; 5, Lee Barnes USA 3.95; 6, Yonataro Nakazawa JPN 3.90.

LJ: 1, Ed Hamm USA 7.73; 2, Silvio Cator HAI 7.58; 3, Al Bates USA 7.40; 4, Willi Meier GER 7.39; 5, Erich Köchermann GER 7.35; 6, Hannes de Boer NED 7.32.

TJ: 1, Mikio Oda JPN 15.21; 2, Levi Casey USA 15.17; 3, Vilho Tuulos FIN 15.11; 4, Chuhei Nambu JPN 15.01; 5, Toimi Tulikoura FIN 14.70; 6, Erkki Järvinen FIN 14.65.

SP: 1, John Kuck USA 15.87 (world rec); 2, Herman Brix USA 15.75; 3, Emil Hirschfeld GER 15.72; 4, Eric Krenz USA 14.99; 5, Armas Wahlstedt FIN 14.69; 6, Wilhelm Uebler GER 14.69.

DT: 1, Bud Houser USA 47.32; 2, Antero Kivi FIN 47.23; 3, James Corson USA 47.10; 4, Harald Stenerud NOR 45.80; 5, John Anderson USA 44.87; 6, Eino Kenttä FIN 44.17.

HT: 1, Pat O'Callaghan IRL 51.39; 2, Ossian Skjöld SWE 51.29; 3, Edmund Black USA 49.03; 4, Armando Poggioli ITA 48.37; 5, Donald Gwinn USA 47.15; 6, Frank Connor USA 46.75.

JT: 1, Erik Lundqvist SWE 66.60; 2, Béla Szepes HUN 65.26; 3, Olav Sunde NOR 63.97; 4, Paavo Liettu FIN 63.86; 5, Bruno Schlokat GER 63.40; 6, Eino Penttilä FIN 63.20.

Dec: 1, Paavo Yrjölä FIN 8053 (world rec; 6587 on present tables)(11.8, 6.72, 14.11, 1.87, 53.2, 16.6, 42.09, 3.30, 55.70, 4:44.0); 2, Akilles Järvinen FIN 7932 (6645); 3, Ken Doherty USA 7707 (6428); 4, James Stewart USA 7624 (6310); 5, Thomas Churchill USA 7417 (6165); 6, Helge Jansson SWE 7286 (6111).

Women's Events

100m: 1, Betty Robinson USA 12.2; 2, Fanny Rosenfeld CAN 12.3; 3, Ethel Smith CAN 12.3; 4, Erna Steinberg GER 12.4; Myrtle Cook CAN & Leni Schmidt GER disq.

800m: 1, Lina Radke GER 2:16.8 (world rec); 2, Kinue Hitomi JPN 2:17.6; 3, Inga Gentzel SWE 2:18.8; 4, Jenny Thompson CAN 2:21.6; 5, Fanny Rosenfeld CAN 2:22.4; 6, Florence McDonald USA 2:22.6.

4x100m Relay: 1, Canada (Fanny Rosenfeld, Ethel Smith, Florence Bell, Myrtle Cook) 48.4 (world rec); 2, USA (Mary Washburn, Jessie Cross, Loretta McNeil, Betty Robinson) 48.6; 3, Germany (Rosa Kellner, Leni Schmidt, Anni Holdmann, Leni Junker) 49.0; 4, France 49.6; 5, Netherlands 49.8; 6, Italy 53.6.

HJ: 1, Ethel Catherwood CAN 1.59 (world rec); 2, Carolina Gisolf NED 1.56; 3, Mildred Wiley USA 1.56; 4, Jean Shiley USA 1.51; 5, Helma Notte GER 1.48; 6, Marjorie Clark SAF 1.48.

DT: 1, Halina Konopacka POL 39.62 (world rec); 2, Lillian Copeland USA 37.08; 3, Ruth Svedberg SWE 35.92; 4, Milly Reuter GER 35.86; 5, Grete Heublein GER 35.56; 6, Liesl Perkaus AUT 33.54.

THE DEPRESSION was forgotten for a while as the Games of the Tenth Olympiad were celebrated in the vast Los Angeles Coliseum with spectacular results for the American athletes. Eleven of the 23 men's events were won by Uncle Sam's representatives and the success rate on the women's side (see page 44) was even more impressive: five American wins out of six ... and the one that got away was won by an athlete who had lived most of her life in the USA.

Eddie Tolan, at 1.64m (under 5'5"), became the shortest of all Olympic male sprint champions, and the first black man to win either the 100 or 200m. Although in 1930 Tolan ran an unratified 10.2 for 100m, the favourite was Ralph Metcalfe, double winner over Tolan in the US Trials. He had also been timed in 10.2, although that was never accepted as a world record either, and run 220 yards (straight track) in a best on record 20.5.

Their 100m duel could not have been closer. Metcalfe drew level with Tolan at 80m and it was impossible with the naked eye to determine who had won. The judges took a long time to decide, referring to the Kirby Two-Eyed Camera photo finish equipment which also provided electrical times to a hundredth of a second. Tolan was given the verdict but Metcalfe shared the winning time of 10.38. The hand time of 10.3 for both men equalled the ratified world record. Many years later, Metcalfe – who became a US Congressman – said he had never been convinced he was defeated and the result should have been a tie.

Metcalfe had a second chance in the 200m but wound up third, some three metres behind Tolan's winning 21.2 (21.12 electrical). However, his chances were diminished by an official's error, for he was told to dig his holes about a metre behind the true starting line in his lane. When the mistake was acknowledged after the race Metcalfe was offered a re-run but, as he didn't want to jeopardise the American sweep of the medals, he declined. Metcalfe didn't even get a gold medal in the sprint relay, for the top three American sprinters were not considered for the squad, which still won by a huge margin in a world record 40.0 (40.10).

Bill Carr had one of the most astonishing, but all too brief, careers in athletics history. His best 440 yards time was merely 48.4 before scoring a sensational win over Ben Eastman at Berkeley on July 2, 47.0 to 47.2. Eastman had, in March, removed a full second from the world record with a phenomenal 46.4 (one turn) and followed up in June with a world mark of 1:50.9 for 880 yards. Carr and Eastman clashed again in the US Olympic 400m trial at Palo Alto on July 16, and again the strong finish of the diminutive Carr prevailed, 46.9 to 47.1.

The Olympic final on August 5 was held only two hours after the semis, won by Carr (Olympic record of 47.2) and Eastman (47.6). Eastman in lane two held a slight lead over Carr (lane four) through 100m (10.8 to 10.9), 200m (21.9 to 22.1) and 300m (33.7 to 33.8), but again Carr passed his opponent in the closing stages to win in a world record 46.2 (46.28) to Eastman's 46.4 (46.50).

Carr, coached by 1904 Olympic medallist Lawson Robertson, later anchored the USA team – minus Eastman – to a world record 3:08.2 (3:08.14) in the relay, but that was the end of his career for in March 1933 he was severely injured in a road accident and never ran again. He only ever ran nine 400m/440y races in his life. More tragic, though, was the case of 110m hurdles winner George Saling, who was also involved in a car crash the following year. He was killed, aged 23.

Coach Dink Templeton (who placed fourth in the 1920 Olympic long jump) may have made a mistake in insisting his man, Eastman, go for the 400m instead of the 800m ... but then that race was a complete triumph

STAR OF THE GAMES

"BABE" DIDRIKSON
(born 26 Jun 1911; died 27 Sep 1956)

What a pity the pentathlon did not become an Olympic event until 1964. Restricted to three events in Los Angeles, Mildred Ella "Babe" Didrikson put up an astonishing all-round display. She won the 80m hurdles in a world record 11.7 and the javelin with 43.69, and after clearing a world record 1.65 had to settle for the silver medal in the high jump following a jump-off.

for the tall, bespectacled English schoolmaster Tom Hampson, whose time was a barrier-breaking 1:49.8 (1:49.70 electrical). It was the fourth consecutive British victory in this event.

Born at Clapham in South London on October 28 1907, Hampson – who failed to gain a full "Blue" at Oxford – first made his mark in 1930 when he won the 880 yards in 1:52.4 in the inaugural British Empire Games. A feature of his appearances in 1932 was his remarkable pace judgment. "I was convinced," he wrote, "having studied some of Professor Hill's researches and knowing the working of the 'oxygen-debt' theory, that the Finnish runners were correct when they maintained that the most economical method of running was to keep as near as possible to an even pace throughout. I found that only very rarely did my lap times show a discrepancy of more than two-fifths of a second, which showed that I had mastered the difficult subject of pace."

The small British team of 17 men and five women took nearly a fortnight for the journey to California, starting with a five-day voyage from Southampton to Quebec on the Empress of Britain. "By taking a little exercise of some sort – skipping, trotting or walking on deck, a little PT in the gym, interspersed with visits to the ship's pool which did not altogether please the 'old-timers' – I kept my fitness," recalled Hampson. "Three days' break in Toronto enabled us all to regain our land legs, but the worst part of the journey was to come – the five days' train trip across America in the cramped confines of a tourist coach. Even here, however, we were able to stretch our legs with an occasional trot on the station platforms, and five days clear after our arrival in Los Angeles was sufficient to put on the finishing touches."

Hampson ran a perfectly planned and executed race in the Games, a classic example of the merits of even pace, but on the day his supporters must have been swallowing hard at seeing their man some 20 metres behind the leader, Canada's Phil Edwards, at the half distance reached in 52.3 after an opening 200m of 24.4! Hampson was fifth in the field of nine in 54.8, dead on schedule for the 1:50 timing that he estimated would be sufficient for victory.

Shortly after the start of the second lap Hampson began to pick off the men ahead and soon only Edwards was in front. Hampson passed the flagging leader along the back straight

but the real race was only just beginning, for another Canadian, Alex Wilson, had been running at his heels all this time and went ahead as the pair reached the final bend. The men were locked in mortal combat all the way to the tape, first one and then the other edging in front, but it was Hampson who prevailed. His magnificent time (54.8 + 54.9) was almost a second inside Séra Martin's listed world record. Eastman, who had earlier run an unofficial world best of 1:50.0, said of Hampson: "He is the greatest middle distance man the world has ever seen".

Hampson later collected a silver medal in the 4x400m with a 47.6 leg and maintained a keen interest in athletics for the rest of his life (he died in 1965). He was among the first senior honorary AAA coaches to be appointed and was an official at the 1948 Olympics .

Britain's other winner was Tommy Green in the first Olympic 50k road walk. The 38 year-old railwayman, a member of Belgrave Harriers, was slowed by the very hot weather to a time of 4:50:10, but he still won by seven minutes. It was remarkable that he ever became an athlete, never mind an Olympic champion, for as Ian Buchanan relates in his book British Olympians Green (born Fareham, Hampshire, on March 30 1894) was unable to walk until he was five because of rickets, at 16 he was invalided out of the Army with injuries sustained when a horse fell on him, and while serving in France during the First World War he was wounded three times and badly gassed. Despite all that, he lived to one day short of his 81st birthday.

The red letter day in Irish athletics history was August 1 1932 when, within an hour, both Bob Tisdall and Pat O'Callaghan struck Olympic gold. Indeed, Ireland sent only one other competitor to LA, Eamonn Fitzgerald, and he placed fourth in the triple jump!

Born of Irish parents in Ceylon, Tisdall began hurdling at the English public school, Shrewsbury, when he was 14 and by the time he went up to Cambridge in 1928 he was already a fine all-rounder. His 400m hurdling career began with a 55.0 win on the tight Athens track in 1930. His next attempt, in Dublin on June 3 1932, produced a 440 yards time of 56.2, outside the Irish selection standard of 55.0, but 15 days later on the same track he won the Irish final trial, again at 440 yards, in 54.2. That was the full extent of his experience when he set out for Los Angeles.

He arrived in such a poor physical state that for eight days he spent 15 hours out of every 24 in bed in an attempt to recuperate. Only three days before his heat did he begin to jog. The unorthodox preparation paid off, for he was almost bursting with pent-up energy and after cruising to victory in his heat in 54.8 he won his semi in 52.8, equalling the Olympic record just set by Glenn Hardin (USA).

Next day in the final, taking fifteen strides between each hurdle, he led all the way. As no one was close as he approached the final barrier he decided to aim for safety by leaping higher than necessary. But fatigue and smarting eyes caused him to misjudge the clearance and he knocked down the hurdle with the calf of his leading leg. He managed to preserve his balance sufficiently to scramble to victory by a metre or so but the mishap cost him a world record of 51.7 (51.67 electrical) since a rule in force until 1938 decreed that all hurdles must be left standing to qualify for a record. Consequently, Hardin in second place was credited with a world record of 51.9! The 1924 champion Morgan Taylor narrowly beat the 1928 gold medallist Lord Burghley for third, although the latter – by then an MP – did set a UK record which was to last for 22 years.

Meanwhile, Dr O'Callaghan was encountering problems in defence of his hammer title. After five rounds, the leader with 52.27 was Ville Pörhölä, the Finn who had won the Olympic shot title 12 years earlier ... but with his final attempt O'Callaghan reached 53.92 and for the seventh time in eight Olympic contests the hammer had been won by a son of Ireland. O'Callaghan, who was also an international high jumper (best of 1.88), would produce his longest throw of 59.56 in 1937 but that was not accepted as a world record as the Irish federation was not at that time affiliated to the IAAF. For similar reasons he was unable to defend his title in Berlin. He died in 1991, aged 86.

American football star Jim Bausch amassed a world record decathlon score of 8462 to win by 170 points from Finland's Akilles Järvinen, whose younger brother Matti took the javelin title and whose father Verner won the Greek-style discus at the 1906 Games. Akilles was unlucky in that, as in 1928, he came away with silver although his points when rescored on the current (1985) tables were higher than the winner's.

Another world record fell to Chuhei Nambu of Japan in the triple jump. He was better known as a long jumper, having set a world record of 7.98 in 1931, but – bothered by a leg injury – placed only third in that event. Two days later, in the fifth round of the triple jump, he leapt 15.72 for a world record in that event too.

The last-minute banning of Paavo Nurmi for transgressing the amateur rules probably cost him the marathon title. After running 25 miles (40.2k) in 2:22:03 in June, he looked all set to add a final glorious chapter to his Olympic saga. Instead, Juan Carlos Zabala (20) of Argentina became South America's first Olympic winner, in 2:31:36, but it was close as Britain's Sam Ferris ended full of running (in comparison to Zabala's collapse) only 19 sec behind. It was the nearest so far that a British runner had got to winning the Olympic marathon. Ferris, who was born in Northern Ireland, was over four minutes behind Zabala at halfway and still only sixth after 20 miles.

Janusz Kusocinski of Poland outkicked Volmari Iso-Hollo in the 10,000m, but the Finn won the steeplechase in which, due to an error by the lap scorer, the athletes ran one lap (460m) too many! Iso-Hollo was some 40m ahead of Joe McCluskey (USA) and Britain's Tom Evenson at the true finish, and eventually won by nearly twice that margin while Evenson overtook the American on the extra lap to snatch the silver.

There had earlier been controversy in the 5000m when Lauri Lehtinen of Finland, challenged by Ralph Hill in the final 50m, twice veered across the track to prevent the American passing him. As Lehtinen crossed the line narrowly ahead (both men were timed in 14:30.0) the crowd booed, prompting public address announcer Bill Henry to remonstrate: "Please remember, folks, that these people are our guests".

The Games were notable for their sportsmanship, leading to this comment from famed American sportswriter Grantland Rice: "These Olympic Games have done more than any others to bring the nations of the world closer in a better understanding." Sir Harold Bowden, chairman of the British Olympic Association, mused: "It will be increasingly difficult for misguided politicians to lead any nation into war after this." However, symbolising the changing political order was Luigi Beccali, the Italian who outkicked Britain's Jerry Cornes in the 1500m and gave the Fascist salute at the medal ceremony. It was but a foretaste of the next Games in Berlin ...

TRACK & FIELD TEAM

THE MOST successful athlete of the Los Angeles Games was a young Texan woman who would soon leave behind the world of track and field and find even greater fame as a golfer. Mildred "Babe" Didrikson was a huge hit with the vast crowds which flocked to the Coliseum, although much less popular with her opponents on account of her overbearing personality. As Jean Shiley, who shared a world high jump record with her, put it in Tales of Gold, an oral history of the Olympics as told by American gold medallists: "The Babe was very brash, and she bragged a lot. It wasn't Muhammad Ali who started this 'I'm number one' stuff. Babe started it. She was just so different from all the rest of the girls that it grated on their nerves".

The bestselling American author, Paul Gallico, a sportswriter at the time, pulled no punches in his descriptions of Babe in Farewell to Sport ... "a hard-bitten, hawk-nosed, thin-mouthed little hoyden from Texas ... the muscle moll to end all muscle molls ... she had a boy's body, slim, straight, curveless ... she hated women and loved to beat them". Gallico's theory was that she became the greatest all-round athlete "simply because she would not or could not compete with women at their own and best game – man-snatching. It was an escape, a compensation". Whatever her motivation, Babe Didrikson became the only athlete in Olympic history to win medals on the track, in a jumping event and a throwing event.

There has always been some confusion both over the spelling of her name and her age. She was actually born Mildred Ella Didriksen, of Norwegian parents, in Port Arthur, Texas, but preferred to be known as Didrikson. "I didn't want no one to think I was a Swede," she is said to have drawled. When was she born? She wrote 1913 when filling out her Olympic team information form, making her 19 at the time of the Games, while in her autobiography she stated 1914, but in his book Track's Greatest Women Jon Hendershott claims a baptismal certificate and the headstone above her grave indicate 1911 was the year of her birth and it is now acknowledged that her actual date of birth was 26 June 1911.

She shone first at baseball (she was nick-named after "Babe" Ruth) and basketball, but in June 1930 she took part in athletics for the first time and her natural talent quickly became apparent. Within a month she had won the American javelin title with an unofficial world record of 40.68 and in 1931 she ran an 11.0 100 yards. She was literally a one-woman team, for at the 1932 American Championships, which incorporated the Olympic Trials, she competed in eight events in one afternoon and as the only representative of the Employers Casualty Insurance Company of Dallas Athletic Association scored sufficient points to win the team title single-handed ahead of the 22-strong Illinois Women's AC!

Restricted by some arcane rule to three events, she won her first Olympic gold medal in the javelin, which she threw 43.69. "It slee-uped right out of mah hand", she drawled, assuring reporters that otherwise she would have thrown it 155 feet (47.24), which would have been well beyond the world record. Next came the 80m hurdles over 2'6" barriers, in which she tied the world record of 11.8 in her heat and lowered it to 11.7 in the final in a very close decision over team-mate Evelyne Hall.

"This is no place for anaemic dudes; I'm out to win the high jump, too", she announced in her usual bashful way, but despite sharing in a world record she had to settle for the silver medal. Both she and Jean Shiley, who had placed fourth in Amsterdam at 16, first equalled the world record of 1.62 and then broke it with 1.65, Shiley clearing at the first attempt with her scissors style and Didrikson, using the Western roll, at the second. Both failed at 1.67. Under present rules Shiley would therefore have won, but a jump-off was demanded in those days and both women cleared 1.67 at the first try. However, at that point Didrikson's style was suddenly declared to be diving and therefore illegal – as it was against the rules for the jumper's head to go over the bar before the rest of her body – and the title was awarded to Shiley.

Later that year she was branded a professional because her photo was used in a car ad, even though she had never given her permission and had received no payment. The AAU reinstated her but she had decided to turn professional anyway. She took up golf and as "Babe" Zaharias (she married pro wrestler George Zaharias in 1938) she became the most successful woman player of all time. Voted the greatest female sportswoman of the first half of the 20th century, she died of cancer in 1956.

American women also won the discus and sprint relay in Los Angeles, the only other event on the programme going to an athlete who very nearly represented the USA also but who decided at the last moment to opt for her native Poland. That was Stanislawa Walasiewicz, who had been brought over to the States as a child and was known there as Stella Walsh. A prolific record setter, between 1929 (when she was 18) and 1945 she was credited with 37 world marks, 14 of them officially ratified, at distances ranging from 60m to 1000m plus long jump. In Los Angeles, she equalled the world 100m record of 11.9 in heat, semi-final and final but was pressed hard for the title by Hilda Strike of Canada, who was also timed in 11.9.

It is difficult in retrospect to know how to evaluate Walasiewicz's achievements for in 1980, after being shot dead in Cleveland, Ohio, an autopsy revealed she had male sex organs. Should Hilda Strike be regarded as the rightful Olympic 100m champion of 1932? The Canadian always believed that the title should have been hers.

Britain did send a women's team this time, and the sprint relay squad of Eileen Hiscock, Gwendoline Porter, Violet Webb (mother of Janet Simpson, who would herself win an Olympic relay bronze medal in 1964) and Nellie Halstead finished third to the USA and Canada in a time well inside the previous world record.

1932 - LOS ANGELES
(significant electrical 1/100th of a second times are also given where known)
100m: 1, Eddie Tolan USA 10.3 (eq world rec/10.38); 2, Ralph Metcalfe USA 10.3/10.38; 3, Arthur Jonath GER 10.4/10.50; 4, George Simpson USA 10.5/10.53; 5, Daniel Joubert SAF 10.6/10.60; 6, Takayoshi Yoshioka JPN 10.7/10.79.
200m: 1, Eddie Tolan USA 21.2/21.12; 2,

George Simpson USA 21.4; 3, Ralph Metcalfe USA 21.5; 4, Arthur Jonath GER 21.5; 5, Carlos Lutti ARG 21.6; 6, William Walters SAF 21.9.
400m: 1, Bill Carr USA 46.2 (world rec/46.28); 2, Ben Eastman USA 46.4/46.50; 3, Alex Wilson CAN 47.4; 4, William Walters SAF 48.2; 5, James Gordon USA 48.2; 6, George Golding AUS 48.8.
800m: 1, Tom Hampson GBR 1:49.8 (world rec/1:49.70); 2, Alex Wilson CAN 1:49.9; 3, Phil Edwards CAN 1:51.5; 4, Edwin Genung USA 1:51.7; 5, Edwin Turner USA 1:52.5; 6, Charles Hornbostel USA 1:52.7.
1500m: 1, Luigi Beccali ITA 3:51.2; 2, Jerry Cornes GBR 3:52.6; 3, Phil Edwards CAN 3:52.8; 4, Glenn Cunningham USA 3:53.4; 5, Eric Ny SWE 3:54.6; 6, Norwood Hallowell USA 3:55.0.
5000m: 1, Lauri Lehtinen FIN 14:30.0; 2, Ralph Hill USA 14:30.0; 3, Lauri Virtanen FIN 14:44.0; 4, John Savidan NZL 14:49.6; 5, Jean-Gunnar Lindgren SWE 14:54.7; 6, Max Syring GER 14:59.0.
10,000m: 1, Janusz Kusocinski POL 30:11.4; 2, Volmari Iso-Hollo FIN 30:12.6; 3, Lauri Virtanen FIN 30:35.0; 4, John Savidan NZL 31:09.0; 5, Max Syring GER 31:35.0; 6, Jean-Gunnar Lindgren SWE 31:37.0.
Marathon: 1, Juan Carlos Zabala ARG 2:31:36; 2, Sam Ferris GBR 2:31:55; 3, Armas Toivonen FIN 2:32:12; 4, Dunkie Wright GBR 2:32:41; 5, Seiichiro Tsuda JPN 2:35:42; 6, Kim Eun-bae KOR/JPN 2:37:28.
3000mSC: (actually 3460m) 1, Volmari Iso-Hollo FIN 10:33.4; 2, Tom Evenson GBR 10:46.0; 3, Joe McCluskey USA 10:46.2; 4, Martti Matilainen FIN 10:52.4; 5, George Bailey GBR 10:53.2; 6, Glen Dawson USA 10:58.0.
110mH: 1, George Saling USA 14.6/14.57 (14.4 eq world rec/14.55 semi-final); 2, Percy Beard USA 14.7/14.69; 3, Don Finlay GBR 14.8/14.74; 4, Jack Keller USA 14.8/14.81; 5, Lord Burghley GBR 14.8/14.83; Willi Welscher GER disq.
400mH: 1, Bob Tisdall IRL 51.7 (unratified world rec/51.67; 2, Glenn Hardin USA 51.9 (world rec/51.85); 3, Morgan Taylor USA 52.0/51.96; 4, Lord Burghley GBR 52.02/52.01; 5, Luigi Facelli ITA 53.0; 6, Johan Areskoug SWE 54.6.
4x100m Relay: 1, USA (Bob Kiesel, Emmett

Toppino, Hec Dyer, Frank Wykoff) 40.0 (world rec/40.10); 2, Germany (Helmut Körnig, Friedrich Hendrix, Erich Borchmeyer, Arthur Jonath) 40.9; 3, Italy (Giuseppe Castelli, Ruggero Maregatti, Gabriele Salviati, Edgardo Toetti) 41.2; 4, Canada 41.3; 5, Japan 41.3; 6, Great Britain 41.4.

4x400m: 1, USA (Ivan Fuqua 47.1, Ed Ablowich 47.6, Karl Warner 47.3, Bill Carr 46.2) 3:08.2 (world rec/3:08.14); 2, Great Britain (Crew Stoneley 48.8, Tom Hampson 47.6, Lord Burghley 46.7, Godfrey Rampling 48.1) 3:11.2; 3, Canada (Raymond Lewis 49.5, James Ball 49.9, Phil Edwards 48.1, Alex Wilson 47.3) 3:12.8; 4, Germany 3:14.4; 5, Japan 3:14.6; 6, Italy 3:17.8.

HJ: 1, Duncan McNaughton CAN 1.97; 2, Bob Van Osdel USA 1.97; 3, Simeon Toribio PHI 1.97; 4, Cornelius Johnson USA 1.97; 5, Ilmari Reinikka FIN 1.94; 6, Kazuo Kimura JPN 1.94.

PV: 1, Bill Miller USA 4.31; 2, Shuhei Nishida JPN 4.30; 3, George Jefferson USA 4.20; 4, Bill Graber USA 4.15; 5, Shizuo Mochizuki JPN 4.00; 6, Lucio de Castro BRA 3.90.

LJ: 1, Ed Gordon USA 7.64; 2, Charles Redd USA 7.60; 3, Chuhei Nambu JPN 7.45; 4, Erik Svensson SWE 7.41; 5, Richard Barber USA 7.39; 6, Naoto Tajima JPN 7.15.

TJ: 1, Chuhei Nambu JPN 15.72 (world rec); 2, Erik Svensson SWE 15.32; 3, Kenkichi Oshima JPN 15.12; 4, Eamonn Fitzgerald IRL 15.01; 5, Willem Peters NED 14.93; 6, Sol Furth USA 14.88.

SP: 1, Leo Sexton USA 16.00; 2, Harlow Rothert USA 15.67; 3, Frantisek Douda TCH 15.61; 4, Emil Hirschfeld GER 15.56; 5, Nelson Gray USA 15.46; 6, Hans-Heinrich Sievert GER 15.07.

DT: 1, John Anderson USA 49.49; 2, Henri Laborde USA 48.47; 3, Paul Winter FRA 47.85; 4, Jules Noel FRA 47.74; 5, István Donogán HUN 47.08; 6, Endre Madárasz HUN 46.52.

HT: 1, Pat O'Callaghan IRL 53.92; 2, Ville Pörhölä FIN 52.27; 3, Peter Zaremba USA 50.33; 4, Ossian Skjöld SWE 49.25; 5, Grant McDougall USA 49.12; 6, Federico Kleger ARG 48.33.

JT: 1, Matti Järvinen FIN 72.71; 2, Matti Sippala FIN 69.80; 3, Eino Penttilä FIN 68.70; 4,

Gottfried Weimann GER 68.18; 5, Lee Bartlett USA 64.46; 6, Kenneth Churchill USA 63.24.

Dec: 1, Jim Bausch USA 8462 (world rec; 6735 on present tables)(11.7, 6.95, 15.32, 1.70, 54.2, 16.2, 44.58, 4.00, 61.91, 5:17.0); 2, Akilles Järvinen FIN 8292 (6879); 3, Wolrad Eberle GER 8031 (6661); 4, Wilson Charles USA 7985 (6716); 5, Hans-Heinrich Sievert GER 7941 (6515); 6, Paavo Yrjölä FIN 7688 (6385).

50k Walk: 1, Tommy Green GBR 4:50:10; 2, Janis Dalins LAT 4:57:20; 3, Ugo Frigerio ITA 4:59:06; 4, Karl Hähnel GER 5:06:06; 5, Ettore Rivolta ITA 5:07:39; 6, Paul Sievert GER 5:16:41.

Women's Events

100m: 1, Stanislawa Walasiewicz POL 11.9 (eq world rec; 11.9 heat & semi-final); 2, Hilda Strike CAN 11.9; 3, Wilhelmina Von Bremen USA 12.0; 4, Marie Dollinger GER 12.2; 5, Eileen Hiscock GBR 12.3; 6, Elizabeth Wilde USA 12.3.

80mH: 1, Mildred "Babe" Didrikson USA 11.7 (world rec; 11.8 ht, eq world rec); 2, Evelyne Hall USA 11.7 (world rec); 3, Marjorie Clark SAF 11.8; 4, Simone Schaller USA 11.9; 5, Violet Webb GBR 11.9; 6, Alda Wilson CAN 12.0.

4x100m Relay: 1, USA (Mary Carew, Evelyn Furtsch, Annette Rogers, Wilhelmina Von Bremen) 46.9 (world rec/46.86); 2, Canada (Mildred Frizzel, Lilian Palmer, Mary Fizzell, Hilda Strike) 47.0; 3, Great Britain (Eileen Hiscock, Gwendoline Porter, Violet Webb, Nellie Halstead) 47.6; 4, Netherlands 47.7; 5, Japan 48.9; 6, Germany 50.0.

HJ: 1, Jean Shiley USA 1.65 (world rec; 1.67 in jump-off); 2, Mildred "Babe" Didrikson USA 1.65 (world rec); 3, Eva Dawes CAN 1.60; 4, Carolina Gisolf NED 1.58; 5, Marjorie Clark SAF 1.58; 6, Annette Rogers USA 1.58.

DT: 1, Lillian Copeland USA 40.58; 2, Ruth Osburn USA 40.12; 3, Jadwiga Wajsowna POL 38.74; 4, Tilly Fleischer GER 36.12; 5, Grete Heublein GER 34.66; 6, Stanislawa Walasiewicz POL 33.60.

JT: 1, Mildred "Babe" Didrikson USA 43.69; 2, Ellen Braumüller GER 43.50; 3, Tilly Fleischer GER 43.15; 4, Masako Shinpo JPN 39.08; 5, Nan Gindele USA 37.95; 6, Gloria Russell USA 37.74.

THE OLYMPICS should have been staged in Berlin in 1916 but plans were scrapped when war broke out and Germany was not even allowed back into the Games until 1928. Yet, only three years later, the International Olympic Committee awarded Berlin the Games of 1936, the German capital being chosen in preference to Barcelona.

When the International Olympic Committee voted for Berlin, in May 1931, the aged von Hindenburg was presiding over the shaky but internationally acceptable Weimar Republic but the political situation in Germany was to change menacingly as preparations were made for staging the Olympics, and opposition – particularly from the USA – grew as Hitler rose to power. After Hitler was appointed Chancellor of Germany in January 1933 anti-Semitic attacks became increasingly common, and in August 1934, on the death of von Hindenburg, Hitler became head of state – and, in effect, absolute dictator – as Fuehrer and Reich Chancellor. Nothing now stood in his way.

Liberal opinion throughout the world was appalled by these developments and in June 1933 Count Henri de Baillet-Latour, the Belgian who had succeeded Baron de Coubertin as IOC President in 1925, requested Germany's IOC's representatives to guarantee observance of the Olympic Charter (which would require Jewish competitors in Germany to be considered for selection); otherwise the Games would be taken away from Berlin. The Germans gave that guarantee, but soon afterwards Germany's two IOC members, Dr Theodore Lewald (who was half-Jewish by birth) and Dr Karl Ritter von Halt were replaced as Presidents of the Organising Committees for Berlin and Garmisch-Partenkirchen (Winter Olympics) respectively by Hitler's newly appointed State Director of Sport. Baillet-Latour was incensed, demanded to see Hitler and told him in no uncertain terms that "if our two colleagues should cease to be Presidents of the Organising Committees, the IOC would be obliged to withdraw the Games". Hitler conceded.

Discrimination against Jews continued to grow, though, and in November 1933 delegates at the American AAU convention voted for a boycott of the Games unless Germany permitted Jews to qualify for the Olympic team. In June 1934 the German Olympic Committee announced that 21 Jewish sportsmen had been nominated for training camps, and American Olympic Committee President, Avery Brundage, returned from a trip to Germany confirming that all was well. Consequently, the American Olympic Committee agreed to participate in the Games. However, discrimination did continue and at least one Jewish medal contender, high jumper Gretl Bergmann, failed to be selected ... the Germans preferring to pick "Dora" Ratjen, who turned out to be Hermann Ratjen, a man!

In September 1935 Hitler brought in new decrees, depriving Jews of their German citizenship and civil rights, prompting one of the USA's three IOC representatives, Ernest Lee Jahncke, to step up his opposition to US participation. That infuriated the increasingly influential Brundage, a man of right-wing sympathies, who accused Jahncke of betraying the USA's athletes. Jahncke declined to back off and on the eve of the Games he was expelled from the IOC and replaced by Brundage, who had earlier become President of the AAU (Amateur Athletic Union, the US governing body for amateur sports, including athletics) after Jeremiah Mahoney – who had been in favour of a boycott – had resigned.

Aware of the immense propaganda value

STAR OF THE GAMES

JESSE OWENS
(born 12 Sep 1913; died 31 Mar 1980)

The passage of time has not dimmed the stunning effect that Jesse Owens had on the Berlin Olympics. Despite the odious political atmosphere, the modest and graceful Afro-American, the grandson of slaves, won the hearts of the spectators by winning gold medals in the 100m, 200m, long jump and 4x100m relay of staging the Games, Hitler spared no expense and the Games attracted greater worldwide attention than any previously. A record 49 countries were represented (42 in athletics) and the opening reached new ceremonial heights as, for the first time, an Olympic torch, lit at Olympia, was transported by a relay of runners across Europe to be carried into the vast stadium.

With his four gold medals, Jesse Owens (see page 50) was the star of the Games, while another American sprinter, Helen Stephens, dominated the women's events with her pair of gold medals.

A 6ft (1.83) tall farmgirl from Missouri, Stephens had astonished her high school coach in 1933 when he timed her at 5.8 for 50 yards, which equalled the world best, during a routine physical education fitness test. Two years later, still only 17, she beat Olympic 100m champion Stella Walsh for the US 100m title (indeed she never lost a race during her brief career) and that season, 1935, was timed at an astonishing 10.4 for 100 yards when the official world record stood at 11.0. In Berlin she ran a wind assisted 11.4 in a 100m heat and took the final by some two metres from Walsh (Walasiewicz) in a windy 11.5. She later anchored the USA relay team to victory in 46.9, although she would have had her work cut out trying to catch the Germans (who set a world record of 46.4 in a heat) if their final runner hadn't dropped the baton when close to ten metres ahead.

Although the USA easily came out on top again with a total of 14 victories, and the state-aided German team was next best with five wins, the British team acquitted itself well enough with gold medals for 50k walker Harold Whitlock and the 4x400m relay squad, plus silvers for Godfrey Brown in the 400m, Ernie Harper in the marathon, Don Finlay in the 110m hurdles, Dorothy Odam in the high jump and the women's 4x100m relay team which included Godfrey Brown's sister Audrey.

It was clear from the result of the individual 400m that Britain would stand a great chance in the relay for, in a desperately close finish, Brown (46.68) in the outside lane just failed to catch world record holder Archie Williams, whose time was 46.66. Brown, who

had broken Eric Liddell's British record with 47.3 in his semi-final, held the lead at the first bend but, endeavouring to relax, eased off a shade too much along the back straight. The outcome was that Williams built up a lead of 2-3 metres. Brown edged ever closer to the American, but when the tape intervened Williams was still seven inches ahead. The official hand times of 46.5 and 46.7 gave no indication of just how close it was. Brown's time stood as the British best until 1958. In another tight finish, Jimmy LuValle held on from Britain's Bill Roberts, 46.84 to 46.87.

Neither Williams nor LuValle was included in the USA's relay squad, yet even so the best 400m times of the Americans added up to 3:07.2 as against the Britons' 3:09.6. On paper, then, the Americans should have won by close to 20 metres. Britain's weak link was Hong Kong-born Freddie Wolff on the first leg, for his best ever was only a modest 48.6, but his 49.2 opener laid the foundations for the British win for he finished only three or four metres down on his American rival, who had run 46.5 that year. The situation was tailor-made for Godfrey Rampling, who had come close to making the individual 400m final with a personal best of 47.5. The father of the acclaimed film actress Charlotte Rampling clocked 46.7 to sweep Britain into a three metre lead; Roberts (46.4) added another couple of metres and the Indian-born Brown (46.7) snapped the tape 15m clear in 3:09.0, the second fastest time on record.

Britain's newly established Olympic 50k walk tradition was brilliantly upheld by Harold Whitlock. Only ninth after 20k he moved into third place by the halfway mark, second position at 30k and took the lead just before 35k. A severe case of sickness at 38k caused Whitlock's lead to shrink but he recovered to finish well clear in 4:30:42. A motor racing car mechanic, Whitlock enjoyed a long career as a competitor, finishing 11th in the 1952 Olympics at the age of 48, and he coached Don Thompson to Olympic gold in 1960.

Another gritty Briton was marathoner Ernie Harper (34), fourth in the 1924 Olympic cross country won by Paavo Nurmi, who surpassed all expectations by matching Japan's Kitei Son (who was actually a Korean, Sohn

Kee-chung) stride for stride for mile after mile. Even though the pair ignored the fast start by defending champion Juan Carlos Zabala their own pace was a cracking one.

At halfway Zabala was timed in 1:11:29, Son and Harper in 1:12:19. Zabala was overhauled at 28k (he retired at 32k) and although the blistered Harper ran his heart out to clock 2:31:24 he could not hold Son, whose time was 2:29:20 as compared with his world best of 2:26:42 in 1935. Son, who like his fellow Korean who finished third was forced by the occupying power to adopt a Japanese name, never ran another marathon but made an emotional return to the Olympic arena when in 1988, at the age of 76, he carried the torch at the opening ceremony in Seoul. Incidentally, 30th in the Berlin marathon was Canada's Percy Wyer (3:00:11) who at 52 remains the oldest ever Olympic athletics competitor.

Britain's other two silver medallists would astonish the world with their athletic longevity. Don Finlay, third in 1932, snatched second place in the 110m hurdles in 14.4, a British record, two metres down on Forrest Towns (USA), who three weeks later in Oslo was to smash the world record of 14.1 (which he tied in his Berlin semi-final) with 13.7. Finlay was to compete in the 1948 Olympics and set a British 120 yards hurdles record of 14.4 in 1949, aged 40!

Dorothy Odam, only 16 in Berlin, went on to compete as Dorothy Tyler in the Olympics of 1948, 1952 and 1956. She was unlucky to come away with the silver rather than gold medal for she cleared 1.60 at the first attempt, while the Hungarian Ibolya Csak managed it at the second try and Elfriede Kaun of Germany at the third. All three failed at 1.62, so under the rules now in effect Odam would have been the winner. But in 1936 a jump-off was decreed, and Csak – who this time succeeded at 1.62 – won. In a tie for sixth place was an 18 year-old from Holland by the name of Fanny Koen, of whom much more would be heard at the next Olympics 12 years hence.

Although Dr Jack Lovelock represented his native New Zealand, his 1500m triumph was specially acclaimed by British fans as from the time he arrived at Oxford in 1931 as a 21 year-old Rhodes scholar and a mere 4:26 miler,

he studied and worked in England. Seventh in the 1932 Olympics, he became world mile record holder the following year with 4:07.6 and although he was outsprinted by the new British sensation Sydney Wooderson in the 1936 AAA mile championship Lovelock travelled to Berlin happy in the knowledge that he was in the finest condition of his life. Among the world's top stars, only Wooderson – who was eliminated in his heat the victim of an ankle injury – was missing from the 1500m final.

The slowish tempo of the race (2:05.0 at 800m) suited Lovelock perfectly; he knew his prolonged sprint was a match for anyone and the slower the pace the earlier he would be able to launch that finishing drive ... with the consequent bonus of surprise. Glenn Cunningham, the American who had succeeded Lovelock as world mile record holder with 4:06.8, sized up the situation and powered into the lead, covering the half lap from 800 to 1000m in 30 sec flat. He was still in front at the bell (2:51.0) but Lovelock was at his shoulder. With fully 300m to go the New Zealander struck; in a flash he was several metres ahead and streaking for the tape, and even though Cunningham produced a phenomenal turn of speed he was unable to make any noticeable impression upon the dainty black-clad figure ahead of him. Little wonder, for Lovelock covered that final 300m in 40.9, the last lap in 55.7. His time of 3:47.8 smashed the world record by a second, with Cunningham also inside the previous figures and defending champion Luigi Beccali third. Sadly, Lovelock fell to his death under a subway train in Brooklyn in 1949, aged 39.

Among other world record breakers were Japan's Naoto Tajima, who triple jumped a barrier-breaking 16 metres, Volmari Iso-Hollo, who helped maintain Finnish supremacy in the longer track events by retaining his steeplechase title (covering the requisite 3000m this time!) in 9:03.8, and Glenn Morris, an American whose entire decathlon career consisted of victories in the 1936 Kansas Relays in May (US record of 7576), Olympic Trials in May (world record of 7884) and Olympic Games in August (world record of 7900, worth 7254 on the present scoring tables). Hollywood was impressed and he went on to play Tarzan on the silver screen.

AHEAD OF HIS TIME

MORE THAN sixty years after his heyday the reputation of Jesse Owens remains undimmed. Mention the 1936 Olympics and the first name that comes to mind is Owens, winner of four gold medals (100m, 200m, long jump, 4x100m relay), and as anyone who has seen Leni Riefenstahl's classic film of those Games can testify he was the supreme stylist. While others pounded the track he seemed to float over the surface; while his rivals contorted their features he was relaxation and serenity personified. His contemporaries appeared rooted to their time but the Owens of 1936 would not look out of place in this year's Olympics.

James Cleveland Owens, born to poor sharecroppers in Oakville, Alabama, on September 12 1913, in a Deep South rife with racial prejudice and segregation, is a key figure in sports history. He was to become one of the most famous and acclaimed personalities in the world and, although he couldn't break down all the barriers, his achievements, good looks and gentle demeanour did make it easier for the complete acceptance of later generations of black American sports stars.

Contrary to popular myth, Owens was not snubbed by Hitler ... but he was by his own President. The question of whether Hitler would congratulate Owens was never put to the test because after greeting German and Finnish medallists from the opening events he was asked to desist by the IOC. More significantly, Owens was never congratulated by President Roosevelt. As Owens told Jon Hendershott of Track & Field News: "I came back to my native country and I couldn't ride in the front of the bus. I had to go to the back door, I couldn't live where I wanted. I wasn't invited up to shake hands with Hitler – but I wasn't invited to the White House to shake hands with the President either".

Owens was inspired at the age of 15 by a meeting with Charley Paddock in 1928. Already physically mature (he was married and a father before his 19th birthday) he was so fast in high school that his coach, Charles Riley, thought his stopwatch wasn't functioning properly. He ran a wind assisted 10.3 100m in 1932 and the following year set American high school records of 9.4 for 100 yards (equal to the world record but never submitted for ratification), 20.7 for the straight 220 yards and 7.60 for the long jump.

At Ohio State University he came under the coaching influence of Larry Snyder, and it was at the 'Big Ten' Championships at Ann Arbor, Michigan, that he made athletics history on May 25 1935. In the space of 45 minutes he set six world records! First came the 100 yards at 3.15 pm when he equalled the record of 9.4, followed ten minutes later by his only long jump of the day ... a phenomenal 8.13 (the first ever 8m effort) which would survive as world record for 25 years. At 3.45 he covered the straight 220 yards in 20.3, which was also superior to the record for the slightly shorter 200m, and at 4 pm he clocked a record 22.6 for 200m and 220 yards hurdles.

The following year he travelled to Berlin with another world record under his belt, having run 100m in 10.2, and that event provided his first gold medal on August 3. Two metres clear at halfway, he held off the closing rush of Ralph Metcalfe in 10.3 and the 110,000 spectators gave Owens a standing ovation. He proceeded to win the long jump on August 4 with a wind-assisted 8.06, the 200m on August 5 by a four-metre margin in 20.7 (world best around a turn) and helped the USA win the 4x100m relay on August 9 in a world record 39.8.

The most dramatic event was the long jump, for it nearly ended in disaster. Preparing for the morning's qualifying round (in front of 90,000 fans!), Owens – still clad in his sweats –took what he thought was a practice run, only to find an official waving a red flag and counting it as a no-jump. With his second jump he fouled. Crisis. He only needed 7.15 to qualify, but one more mistake and he would be out.

Aware of his rival's predicament, Germany's Luz Long suggested Owens should go for a safety jump way behind the board. Owens did just that ... and qualified. The final that afternoon was a classic. After three rounds, Owens led only narrowly from Long, 7.87 to 7.84, and with his fifth jump the German electrified the crowd by matching Owens' 7.87 ... and he was ahead on second best jumps, 7.84 to 7.75. Owens responded like the great champion he was; his fifth round reply was 7.94 and while Long fouled his final attempt Owens ended with 8.06, the second longest ever jump although wind assisted. Long and Owens became fast friends that day, a heartening indication of how the Olympic spirit can cut across national and racial barriers, and continued to correspond. Long died on the Eastern front in 1943.

Prejudice did surface, however, in the sprint

relay. Owens was not originally named to the squad, as it was usual American policy to select a number of athletes who did not run in the individual 100m. Three days before the relay heats, head coach Lawson Robertson said the team would be Marty Glickman, Sam Stoller, Frank Wykoff and either Foy Draper or Ralph Metcalfe, and only on the day of the heats was it revealed that Glickman and Stoller, who just happened to be the only Jewish members of the US athletics team, had been excluded.

The excuse trotted out was that the opposition was better than expected and therefore the strongest team would be needed to ensure victory. Owens wanted Glickman and Stoller in the team ("I've already won my three gold medals; let them run, they deserve it"), but was ordered by assistant head coach Dean Cromwell to do as he was told.

In his study of Olympic 100m champions, The Fastest Men On Earth, Neil Duncanson quotes Glickman as saying: "Mere coincidence, was it, that we were both Jewish or out and out anti-semitism? As it turned out later, Avery Brundage, head of the AOC, and Cromwell turned out to be America Firsters, which was the group that was sympathetic to the Nazi cause. Brundage was one of the founders so there was no question about his sympathies".

As it turned out, the USA won with a dozen metres to spare, and so Owens won his fourth gold medal, Metcalfe his first ... and Frank Wykoff made history by being a member of the winning foursome for a third time running.

Although he was only 22, that was virtually the end of Owens' athletics career. The day after the relay he competed in Cologne, winning the long jump but beaten by Metcalfe over 100m; he then ran in a relay race in London and returned to the USA instead of taking part in a European tour negotiated by the AAU. Despite being an amateur and therefore a free agent, Owens was summarily suspended for life by the US governing body, the President of which was Brundage. As a professional, Owens was reduced to such gimmicks as sprinting against race horses. He kept in great shape, though, and in 1948 claimed to have run 9.7 for 100y and long jumped 7.90, while even in 1955, aged 41, he was supposed to have clocked 9.8. A cigarette smoker since his teens, he died of lung cancer in 1980, at the age of 66.

1936 - BERLIN

100m: (+2.7m wind) 1, Jesse Owens USA 10.3w; 2, Ralph Metcalfe USA 10.4; 3, Martinus Osendarp NED 10.5; 4, Frank Wykoff USA 10.6; 5, Erich Borchmeyer GER 10.7; 6, Lennart Strandberg SWE 10.9.

200m: (2.0) 1, Jesse Owens USA 20.7 (world best); 2, Mack Robinson USA 21.1; 3, Martinus Osendarp NED 21.3; 4, Paul Hänni SUI 21.6; 5, Lee Orr CAN 21.6; 6, Wijnand van Beveren NED 21.9.

400m: 1, Archie Williams USA 46.5/46.66; 2, Godfrey Brown GBR 46.7/46.68; 3, Jimmy LuValle USA 46.8/46.84; 4, Bill Roberts GBR 46.8/46.87; 5, William Fritz CAN 47.8; 6, John Loaring CAN 48.2.

800m: 1, John Woodruff USA 1:52.9; 2, Mario Lanzi ITA 1:53.3; 3, Phil Edwards CAN 1:53.6; 4, Kazimierz Kucharski POL 1:53.8; 5, Charles Hornbostel USA 1:54.6; 6, Harry Williamson USA 1:55.8.

1500m: 1, Jack Lovelock NZL 3:47.8 (world rec); 2, Glenn Cunningham USA 3:48.4; 3, Luigi Beccali ITA 3:49.2; 4, Archie San Romani USA 3:50.0; 5, Phil Edwards CAN 3:50.4; 6, Jerry Cornes GBR 3:51.4.

5000m: 1, Gunnar Höckert FIN 14:22.2; 2, Lauri Lehtinen FIN 14:25.8; 3, Henry Jonsson (later Kälarne) SWE 14:29.0; 4, Kohei Murakoso JPN 14:30.0; 5, Jozef Noji POL 14:33.4; 6, Ilmari Salminen FIN 14:39.8.

10,000m: 1, Ilmari Salminen FIN 30:15.4; 2, Arvo Askola FIN 30:15.6; 3, Volmari Iso-Hollo FIN 30:20.2; 4, Kohei Murakoso JPN 30:25.0; 5, Alec Burns GBR 30:58.2; 6, Juan Carlos Zabala ARG 31:22.0.

Marathon: 1, Sohn Kee-chung (Kitei Son) KOR/JPN 2:29:20; 2, Ernie Harper GBR 2:31:24; 3, Nam Seung-yong (Shoryu Nan) KOR/JPN 2:31:42; 4, Erkki Tamila FIN 2:32:45; 5, Vaino Muinonen FIN 2:33:46; 6, Johannes Coleman SAF 2:36:17.

3000mSC: 1, Volmari Iso-Hollo FIN 9:03.8 (world best); 2, Kaarlo Tuominen FIN 9:06.8; 3, Alfred Dompert GER 9:07.2; 4, Martti Matilainen FIN 9:09.0; 5, Harold Manning USA 9:11.2; 6, Lars Larsson SWE 9:16.6.

110mH: 1, Forrest Towns USA 14.2 (14.1 semifinal, eq world rec); 2, Don Finlay GBR 14.4; 3, Fred Pollard USA 14.4; 4, Hakan Lidman SWE 14.4; 5, John Thornton GBR 14.7; 6, Larry O'Connor CAN 14.8.

400mH: 1, Glenn Hardin USA 52.4; 2, John Loaring CAN 52.7; 3, Miguel White PHI 52.8; 4,

Joseph Patterson USA 53.0; 5, Sylvio de Magalhäes Padilha BRA 54.0 ; 6, Christos Mantikas GRE 54.2.

4x100m Relay: I, USA (Jesse Owens, Ralph Metcalfe, Foy Draper, Frank Wykoff) 39.8 (world rec); 2, Italy (Orazio Mariani, Gianni Caldana, Elio Ragni, Tullio Gonnelli) 41.1; 3, Germany (Wilhelm Leichum, Erich Borchmeyer, Erwin Gillmeister, Gerd Hornberger) 41.2; 4, Argentina 42.2; 5, Canada 42.7; Netherlands disq.

4x400m Relay: I, Great Britain (Freddie Wolff 49.2, Godfrey Rampling 46.7, Bill Roberts 46.4, Godfrey Brown 46.7) 3:09.0; 2, USA (Harold Cagle 48.7, Robert Young 47.6, Edward O'Brien 46.7, Alfred Fitch 48.0) 3:11.0; 3, Germany (Helmut Hamann 49.3, Friedrich von Stülpnagel 48.3, Harry Voigt 46.6, Rudolf Harbig 47.6) 3:11.8; 4, Canada 3:11.8; 5, Sweden 3:13.0; 6, Hungary 3:14.8.

HJ: I, Cornelius Johnson USA 2.03; 2, Dave Albritton USA 2.00; 3, Delos Thurber USA 2.00; 4, Kalevi Kotkas FIN 2.00; 5, Kimio Yada JPN 1.97; eq6, Yoshiro Asakuma JPN, Lauri Kalima FIN, Hiroshi Tanaka JPN & Gustav Weinkötz GER 1.94.

PV: I, Earle Meadows USA 4.35; 2, Shuhei Nishida JPN 4.25; 3, Sueo Oe JPN 4.25; 4, Bill Sefton USA 4.25; 5, Bill Graber USA 4.15; eq6, Kiyoshi Adachi JPN, Sylvanus Apps CAN, Peter Bacsalmasi HUN, Josef Haunzwickel AUT, Danilo Innocenti ITA, Jan Korejs TCH, Bo Ljungberg SWE, Alfred Proksch AUT, Wilhelm Sznajder POL, Dick Webster GBR & Viktor Zsuffka HUN 4.00.

LJ: (wind assisted) I, Jesse Owens USA 8.06; 2, Luz Long GER 7.87; 3, Naoto Tajima JPN 7.74; eq4, Wilhelm Leichum GER & Arturo Maffei ITA 7.73; 6, Bob Clark USA 7.67.

TJ: I, Naoto Tajima JPN 16.00 (world rec); 2, Masao Harada JPN 15.66; 3, John Metcalfe AUS 15.50; 4, Heinz Wöllner GER 15.27; 5, Rolland Romero USA 15.08; 6, Kenkichi Oshima JPN 15.07.

SP: I, Hans Woellke GER 16.20; 2, Sulo Bärlund FIN 16.12; 3, Gerhard Stöck GER 15.66; 4, Samuel Francis USA 15.45; 5, Jack Torrance USA 15.38; 6, Dimitri Zaitz USA 15.32.

DT: I, Ken Carpenter USA 50.48; 2, Gordon Dunn USA 49.36; 3, Giorgio Oberweger ITA 49.23; 4, Reidar Sörlie NOR 48.77; 5, Willy Schröder GER 47.93; 6, Nicolaos Syllas GRE 47.75.

HT: I, Karl Hein GER 56.49; 2, Erwin Blask GER 55.04; 3, Fred Warngard SWE 54.83; 4, Gustaf Koutonen FIN 51.90; 5, William Rowe USA

51.66; 6, Donald Favor USA 51.01.

JT: I, Gerhard Stöck GER 71.84; 2, Yrjö Nikkanen FIN 70.77; 3, Kalervo Toivonen FIN 70.72; 4, Lennart Attervall SWE 69.20; 5, Matti Järvinen FIN 69.18; 6, Alton Terry USA 67.15.

Dec: I, Glenn Morris USA 7900 (world rec; 7254 on present tables)(11.1, 6.97, 14.10, 1.85, 49.4, 14.9, 43.02, 3.50, 54.52, 4:33.2); 2, Bob Clark USA 7601 (7063); 3, Jack Parker USA 7275 (6760); 4, Erwin Huber GER 7087 (6658); 5, Reindert Brasser NED 7046 (6570); 6, Armin Guhl SUI 7033 (6618).

50k Walk: I, Harold Whitlock GBR 4:30:42; 2, Arthur Schwab SUI 4:32:10; 3, Adalberts Bubenko LAT 4:32:43; 4, Jaroslav Stork TCH 4:34:01; 5, Edgar Bruun NOR 4:34:54; 6, Fritz Bleiweiss GER 4:36:49.

Women's Events

100m: (3.5) I, Helen Stephens USA 11.5w; 2, Stanislawa Walasiewicz POL 11.7; 3, Käthe Krauss GER 11.9; 4, Marie Dollinger GER 12.0; 5, Annette Rogers USA 12.2; 6, Emmy Albus GER 12.3.

80mH: I, Trebisonda Valla ITA 11.7/11.75; 2, Anni Steuer GER 11.7/11.81; 3, Elizabeth Taylor CAN 11.7/11.82; 4, Claudia Testoni ITA 11.7/11.82; 5, Catharina ter Braake NED 11.8/11.94; 6, Doris Eckert GER 12.0/12.19.

4x100m Relay: I, USA (Harriet Bland, Annette Rogers, Betty Robinson, Helen Stephens) 46.9; 2, Great Britain (Eileen Hiscock, Violet Olney, Audrey Brown, Barbara Burke) 47.6; 3, Canada (Dorothy Brookshaw, Mildred Dolson, Hilda Cameron, Aileen Meagher) 47.8; 4, Italy 48.7; 5, Netherlands 48.8; Germany (Emmy Albus, Käthe Krauss, Marie Dollinger, Ilse Dörffeldt) disq (46.4 heat, world rec).

HJ: I, Ibolya Csak HUN 1.60 (1.62 in jump-off); 2, Dorothy Odam GBR 1.60; 3, Elfriede Kaun GER 1.60; 4, Dora Ratjen* GER 1.58; 5, Marguerite Nicolas FRA 1.58; eq6, Doris Carter AUS, Fanny Koen NED & Annette Rogers USA 1.55. * later classified as a man.

DT: I, Gisela Mauermayer GER 47.63; 2, Jadwiga Wajsowna POL 46.22; 3, Paula Mollenhauer GER 39.80; 4, Toyoko Nakamura JPN 38.24; 5, Hide Mineshima JPN 37.35; 6, Birgit Lundström SWE 35.92.

JT: I, Tilly Fleischer GER 45.18; 2, Luise Krüger GER 43.29; 3, Maria Kwasniewska POL 41.80; 4, Herma Bauma AUT 41.66; 5, Sadako Yamamoto JPN 41.45; 6, Lydia Eberhardt GER 41.37.

BY COMPARISON with the immense suffering and destruction caused by the Second World War, the loss of two Olympic celebrations was a relatively trivial consequence of the conflict. But, in the context of athletics history, it was unfortunate that so many gifted athletes were denied their chance of Olympic glory.

The 1940 Games were awarded to Tokyo, but – following Japanese aggression in China in 1938 – the International Olympic Committee invited Helsinki to take over. Looking further ahead, in June 1939 the IOC chose London as the venue for 1944 but it all became academic when war was declared on September 3 1939.

It's only conjecture, of course, but the stars of the 1940 Games might well have been Rudolf Harbig of Germany, who in 1939 had set world records of 46.0 for 400m and 1:46.6 for 800m (the latter standing until 1955); Britain's Sydney Wooderson, the 1938 European 1500m champion who had lowered the world mile record to 4:06.4 the previous year; Taisto Mäki of Finland, a world record breaker at 5000m (14:08.8) and 10,000m (29:52.6) in 1939; and Cornelius Warmerdam of the USA, the first 15-foot vaulter who reached 4.60 in 1940. Britain's Dorothy Odam might have won the gold which so narrowly eluded her in 1936 and (as Dorothy Tyler) in 1948, for in 1939 she raised the world high jump record to 1.66.

Harbig was killed at the Eastern front in March 1944, and Mäki had been replaced as Finland's distance running star by Viljo Heino (world 10,000m record of 29:35.4 in 1944), but Wooderson, Warmerdam (4.77 in 1942) and Odam/Tyler would still have been major forces had the Games of 1944 taken place. So too would have been the Swedish middle distance marvels, Gunder Hägg (world records of 3:43.0 for 1500m in 1944 and 13:58.2 for 5000m in 1942) and Arne Andersson (world mile record of 4:01.6 in 1944). Happily, Fanny Blankers-Koen (see page 57), who set an astonishing array of world records during the war years, including 10.8 100 yards in 1944, 11.5 100m (unratified) in 1943, 11.3 80m hurdles in 1942, 1.71 high jump in 1943 and 6.25 long jump in 1943, was able to make her mark on Olympic history in 1948.

It was in 1946 that the IOC awarded the Games to London. With only two years to prepare, the organising committee – chaired by 1928 Olympic 400m hurdles champion Lord Burghley – faced a formidable task, particularly in view of the austerity of immediate post-war Britain, but although there weren't too many frills (the male competitors were housed in military camps, the women in colleges) the Games were a great success. Big crowds, often in excess of 80,000, flocked to Wembley Stadium each day. Although, unsurprisingly, Germany and Japan were not invited, and the Soviet Union would not make its Olympic debut until 1952, a record 59 nations (52 in athletics) participated in these Games of the 14th Olympiad. They were actually the eleventh Games to be held, but the four-year Olympiads are numbered regardless of whether war stopped play.

Wing-Commander Donald Finlay, an RAF war hero and twice an Olympic 110m hurdles medallist, took the Olympic Oath on behalf of all his fellow competitors and the Games were declared open by King George VI.

For the first time this century no Olympic titles were won by representatives from Great Britain or Ireland, although the home fans were able to cheer no fewer than six second places.

Fanny Blankers-Koen was the heroine of these Games with her four gold medals, but her successes came mainly at Britain's expense for in

STAR OF THE GAMES

FANNY BLANKERS-KOEN
(born 26 Apr 1918; died 25 Jan 2004)

Stung by a suggestion that at 30 she was too old to win an Olympic title, the "Flying Dutchwoman" proceeded to win four ... at 100m, 200m, 80m hurdles and 4x100m! Had she been able to compete also in the high jump and long jump, where she was world record holder, it could have been six golds.

her three individual triumphs she was chased home by Dorothy Manley (100m), Audrey Williamson (200m) and Maureen Gardner (80m hurdles). Blankers-Koen outclassed the opposition in the sprints but in the hurdles she had to pull out all the stops to get the better of the 19 year-old ballet teacher from Oxford.

The other British runner-up in the women's events was high jumper Dorothy Tyler, now a 28 year-old mother of two, who duplicated her placing of 12 years earlier. She raised her British record to 1.68 with a second-time clearance, but the USA's Alice Coachman went over at the first attempt to take the title and become the first black woman to become an Olympic champion. Third place at 1.61 went to the French concert pianist Micheline Ostermeyer, who had already won the shot and discus titles! However, her winning distances of 13.75 and 41.92 didn't reflect prevailing world standards. The Soviet Union, who did not send a team as it was not yet affiliated to the IOC and IAAF, could have fielded Tatyana Sevryukova, who put the shot 14.59 in Moscow the very same day Ostermeyer was winning the title, and Nina Dumbadze, who threw the discus 53.25 a few days later.

Although the women's programme was extended to include the 200m, long jump and shot, there was still no attempt to cater for endurance runners. Ludicrously, the 200m would remain the longest event at Olympic level until the 800m was reintroduced in 1960. The 400m was added in 1964, 1500m in 1972, 3000m and marathon in 1984, 10,000m in 1988.

The men's programme in 1948 was identical to the present Olympic schedule, with one exception. Instead of a 20k road walk (introduced in 1956) there was a 10,000m track walk, back for the first time since 1924. Werner Hardmo, the Swede who set numerous world records during the war years including a scarcely credible 42:39.6 for 10,000m but whose style was suspect, was disqualified in the final, but Sweden won anyway thanks to the scrupulously fair John Mikaelsson, who actually went faster in his heat (45:03.0) than in the final. Another Swede, John Ljunggren, took the 50k with Britain's Terence ("Tebbs") Lloyd Johnson finishing third to become, at 48, the oldest medallist

in Olympic athletics history.

At the other end of the age scale was Bob Mathias (see page 56), a high school student from California who won the gruelling decathlon at the age of 17 years and eight months to rank to this day as the youngest male ever to win an Olympic title.

History was in the making also when Imre Németh of Hungary, weighing only 84kg and fresh from a world record throw of 59.02 a fortnight earlier, won the hammer title with 56.07. Twenty-eight years later his son, Miklós, would claim the javelin crown with a world record throw of 94.58.

Roy Cochran, who won the 400m hurdles in 51.1 and helped the USA to victory in the 4x400m relay, also contributed to a family gold medal double, for his brother Commodore Cochran was a member of the winning 4x400m team 24 years earlier. Another notable father-son combination were the Swiss walkers Arthur Schwab (second in 1936 50k) and Fritz Schwab, third in the 10,000m at Wembley.

Britain's two silver medals in the men's events occurred in dramatic circumstances. The story of the 4x100m relay is told on page 57, while the other came in the marathon, which started in Wembley Stadium and took the runners through Kingsbury, Canons Park, Stanmore, Boreham Wood, Elstree, Radlett and back.

British hopes rested with the venerable 41 year-old Jack Holden, four times international cross country champion before the war, but he fell victim to blisters. In order to safeguard against sore feet he had pickled his feet in potassium permanganate but when blisters developed under the leather-like outer skin he had no alternative but to drop out. Not that it was the end of a long and honourable career: in 1950 he went on to win the British Empire Games and European marathon titles!

Holden was not the only poignant figure in the Olympic marathon, for Etienne Gailly, a Belgian paratrooper, experienced the mortification of reaching Wembley Stadium first but in such an exhausted state that two men overtook him during the lap of the track. Argentina's Delfo Cabrera, like Gailly making his marathon debut, won in 2:34:52 while Welshman Tom Richards

(38), finishing very fast in the manner of Sam Ferris in 1932, came the closest yet to a British victory in this event by taking second place only 16 seconds behind.

Destined to succeed Cabrera as champion four years hence was Emil Zátopek, who became a great favourite with the crowd as he ran away with the 10,000m and only narrowly failed to win the 5000m, but who could have foreseen that the British runner who finished a bitterly disappointed eighth in the 10,000m, a lap behind Zátopek, would go on to revolutionise marathon running? Jim Peters was his name.

Zátopek opened his account with a remarkably easy victory in the 10,000m. The favourite was the latest in the long line of Flying Finns, world record holder Viljo Heino, but he ran off the track exhausted in the seventh kilometre attempting to stay with the Czechoslovak first lieutenant. Those two had drawn far ahead of anyone else and thus Zátopek won by a margin of close to 300m in 29:59.6. In the 5000m final three days later, contested on a rain-sodden track, Gaston Reiff of Belgium managed to open up a 40m advantage over Captain Zátopek (he had been promoted in the meantime) by the bell and it looked all over. But Zátopek burst into a frenzied sprint and in a desperately exciting finish failed by only a stride to catch Reiff, whose time was 14:17.6.

Zátopek certainly captivated the fans but the most popular winner of all was Arthur Wint in the 400m. He may have been representing Jamaica, but the 28 year-old medical student with the nine-foot stride had made his home in Britain after serving with the RAF and was a member of London's Polytechnic Harriers.

The son of a Jamaican Presbyterian minister and a Scottish mother, Wint had already excelled himself by finishing second to the elegant American, Mal Whitfield, in the 800m in a personal best of 1:49.5. Three days later, running his fifth race of the Games, Wint chopped 0.7 from his fastest 400m with a 46.3 victory in his 400m semi-final. That was needlessly extravagant, for the final was to be run just 105 minutes later and his main rival, US-based team-mate Herb McKenley, cruised through his semi in 47.3.

McKenley, who had placed a close fourth in the 200m won by the USA's Mel Patton, was considered a certainty. He had, in recent weeks, established world records for both 440 yards (46.0) and 400m (45.9). But McKenley made a fatal error of pace judgment. Attempting to run the legs off Wint, and shooting for a time of 45.6, he went much too fast in the early stages, particularly in view of the heavy state of the cinder track. At 200m he was some seven metres up on Wint (22.2) in 21.4, only 0.3 slower than Patton's winning time, but began to tie up when the finishing straight was reached. Hardly daring to believe his luck, Wint caught his flailing rival 20m from the finish to become Jamaica's first ever Olympic gold medallist in his fastest ever time of 46.2.

With George Rhoden also close to making the 400m final, Jamaica fancied their chances of beating the Americans in the relay but disaster struck when Wint, on the third stage, pulled up with cramp and left the track in tears. Four years later it would be a different story.

That 4x400m relay was the final track event of a Games which rekindled the Olympic flame. Sigfrid Edström, the Swedish President of the IOC, summed up London's achievement in a message printed in the British Olympic Association's Official Report.

"The staging of the Olympic Games in London this year was recognised as the most crucial occasion in the history of sport. How could such a project in the Grand Manner be accomplished in the threadbare and impoverished world of 1948? It was a challenge to the British genius for improvisation, for Britain had to hold the Games in a city afflicted with an unparalleled housing shortage – yet homes had to be found for tens of thousands of foreign visitors, not to mention some 6000 athletes. The great test was taken; and the organisation rose gloriously to the supreme challenge. The visitors were housed and fed; the athletes were made at home in camps where every care was taken of their waking and sleeping hours. Wembley Stadium itself, where day after day huge crowds assembled, surpassed in magnificence and convenience any previous homes of the Games. The first Olympic Games for 12 years have come and gone – an unqualified success."

THE BOY WONDER

WHO WOULD have predicted, when he was an anaemic young boy, that Bob Mathias would grow up to become the world's greatest all-round athlete and the only world-ranked decathlete to go through an entire career unde-feated. Indeed, such was his precociousness, once he had overcome his early health problems, that the Californian won his first Olympic title at the breathtakingly young age of 17.

It was in May 1948 that his coach, Virgil Jackson, told him: "I've just heard about some event called the decathlon that will be included in a meet in Los Angeles about a week after you graduate. It'll give you something to do after you get out of school."

Jackson was convinced that with sufficient work Mathias - at that time primarily a discus thrower - could make the Olympic decathlon team in 1952, but those calculations had to be revised after he scored 7094 (6609 on the present tables) when winning that decathlon on June 10/11. He went on to win the Olympic trial on June 26/27 with 7224 (6713) and the Olympic crown on August 5/6 with 7139 (6628).

Kids of 17, even if they do stand 1.83 (6'0") tall and weigh over 84kg (185lb), are not sup-posed to be world beaters in the gruelling ten event test, but Mathias had no real weaknesses and coped brilliantly in difficult conditions with the accumulating fatigue and pressure. Third at the end of his first day of Olympic competition, he took the lead after the seventh event, the dis-cus, and gutted it out to the finish of the 1500m for a clearcut victory. "Never again", he gasped. Asked how he would celebrate, he quipped: "I'll start shaving, I guess".

Looking back to the London Games some 40 years later, he said: "I was just too young to be intimidated. I really didn't understand what the Olympics were all about. Don't forget, there had been no Games for 12 years, and there was no television then."

The adult Mathias went on to even greater deeds: three world records, the last of which was when retaining his Olympic title in 1952. Later he starred in the Hollywood version of his life story and served four terms as a Republican US Congressman.

The Man Who Won The "Wrong" Event

ONE OF the classic Olympic fairy-tales involved Harrison Dillard, who went to the same school in Cleveland, Ohio, as Jesse Owens and who as a 13 year-old, after cheering his hero in a post-Olympic victory parade, ran back home and excitedly told his mother: "I just saw Jesse Owens, and I'm going to be just like him". The chances against Dillard growing up to become a multiple Olympic gold medallist also must have been millions to one ... and yet it came to pass.

Dillard had shown promise with a 14.8 120 yards hurdles in 1943 and in May 1945, hav-ing served in Italy with an all-black infantry divi-sion, he was recruited for the Fifth Army team for what was dubbed the "GI Olympics" in Frankfurt. The sergeant who selected him was one Roscoe Lee Browne, who in 1951 would become the world's fastest 800m runner of the year with 1:49.3 and develop into one of America's most distinguished actors. Dillard won four gold medals at that meeting, impressing the legendary General George "Old Blood and Guts" Patton, who back in 1912 had finished fifth in the Olympic modern pentathlon contest in Stockholm.

Nicknamed "Bones" from an early age because he was so skinny, Dillard ran a 10.3 100m in 1947 but it was as a sprint hurdler that he made his name. Between May 1947 and June 1948 he chalked up 82 consecutive victories, including a world 120 yards hurdles record of 13.6 in April 1948.

It looked a foregone conclusion that he would take the Olympic crown ... until, at the US Trials, he slammed into several hurdles and failed to finish. First three past the post made the team, and so Dillard had lost his chance of Olympic glory. Or had he? The day before he had scraped into the 100m team by finishing third to Barney Ewell (who tied the world record of 10.2) and Mel Patton (10.3) in 10.4, inches ahead of Ed Conwell.

Although he clocked the fastest first round time of 10.4 at Wembley, repeated that time in the second round (with Patton also running 10.4) and won the first semi in 10.5 (Patton took the other in 10.4), Dillard was not expected to beat his two team-mates in the final, which – unlike many later events which were held in rain-sodden conditions – was staged in gorgeous weather. Patton was away to a ruinous start, as was an out-of-sorts McDonald Bailey of Britain, and it was Dillard who led all the way. Ewell, a 30 year-old who had been American junior 100m champion back in 1936, closed fast at the end and broke into a joyous dance, convinced he had won, but when the official result came through he was the first to congratulate the 25 year-old Dillard – the man who had become Olympic champion in the 'wrong' event.

A proud spectator in London was Dillard's coach, Eddie Finnigan, who after embracing his star pupil dashed out of the stadium and made for his hotel. There he left a note for a journalist friend: "This was the day we waited for so long. To think it came not in the hurdles but in the event we all thought Dillard couldn't win. Fate is strange and wonderful. I'm going out to find a church somewhere. My heart is bursting."

Dillard's time was a fast 10.3 but barely a metre behind in fourth place (10.4) was Lt Alistair McCorquodale of the Coldstream Guards, a 22 year-old Scot coached by four-time Olympic medallist Guy Butler. More interested in cricket than athletics, McCorquodale had only two seasons as a serious athlete and despite improving by the equivalent of four metres from a best of 9.9 for 100 yards in 1947 he slipped away from the sport after the Games.

But first he had the thrill of standing atop the medal dais and hearing "God Save The King" played in honour of himself, 1946 European 100m champion Jack Archer and rugby internationals Ken Jones and Jack Gregory.

It wasn't quite for real, though. The American quartet of Ewell, long jumper Lorenzo Wright (deputising for an ill Conwell), Dillard and Patton had waltzed away with the 4x100m relay as expected, winning by seven metres from the British squad in 40.6, but then came a sensational announcement: the USA had been disqualified because of an illegal first change-over and Britain were therefore the winners. The USA team management lodged a protest but it was not until three days later, after the jury of appeal had studied films of the race, that the disqualification was withdrawn and the medals reallocated.

The Flying Dutchwoman

AS THE 1936 Olympics will forever be associated primarily with the exploits of Jesse Owens, so the Games of 1948 will be remembered chiefly for the sprinting and hurdling triumphs of the 30 year-old Dutch housewife, Fanny Blankers-Koen. She became the first and only woman to win four gold medals in a single Games and had she competed in the high jump and long jump, for which she was also entered and at which she was world record holder, it's feasible she could have gone home with six golds!

Born Francina Koen in Amsterdam on April 26 1918, she actually started off as a swimmer and 800m runner, but in 1936 she competed in the Berlin Olympics in the high jump (she tied for sixth place) and relay. Coached by former international triple jumper Jan Blankers (they married in 1940), she picked up a couple of bronze medals in the sprints at the 1938 European Championships and during the years when Holland was occupied by the Germans she set world records in a variety of events. In 1942 she ran 80m hurdles in 11.3; in 1943 (having produced a son) she high jumped 1.71 and long jumped 6.25 as well as clocking 11.5 for 100m in a race against men; in 1944 she was timed at 10.8 for 100 yards. A second child, a daughter, was born in 1945 and the following year Fanny won her first international title, the European 80m hurdles championship.

She displayed great form as the Olympics approached, setting a new official world 100m record of 11.5 and record figures of 11.0 for the hurdles in June 1948, but what really motivated her as she prepared for Wembley was a printed remark of British team manager Jack Crump that she was too old to win at the Olympics. "It was just the thing to rouse me, to make me go out there and prove to them that, even if I was 30 years old and the mother of two children, I could still be a champion."

First came the 100m, where on a slow track and into the wind she won by almost three metres from Britain's Dorothy Manley and Australia's Shirley Strickland in 11.9. She had made her point, but there was no relaxing now. The next test was the hurdles, a race which she nominates as the most memorable - but nervewracking – of her career.

THE FLYING

"Never shall I forget the day of the heats. I went to the warm-up track behind Wembley Stadium that morning as the Olympic 100m gold medallist, but nobody could ever have felt less like a champion. My knees trembled. Never had I been so nervous before a race. I went through my warming-up as usual, but my mind was not on it. All the time I was waiting for a glimpse of my rival, Maureen Gardner, whom I had never seen before. She arrived by car, and made a considerable impression on me when I saw that she had brought her own hurdles. An athlete who carries her own hurdles around must really be in the top class, I thought.

"There were no other hurdles available on the training track and because I felt in need of a little practice over the flights before the first heat, I summoned up my courage and asked if I could use hers. We shook hands and I noticed immediately that I was not the only one who was nervous. Both of us were on tenterhooks. Just how good Maureen was I was soon to see. In her semi-final, she scraped a hurdle and lost her balance, but she still managed to achieve third position and a place in the final. My husband was cautious. 'Fanny,' he said, 'no long jumping for you tomorrow. You must concentrate on the hurdles, because this English girl knows her business'".

She certainly did, and the 19 year-old, in only her second season at the event, was ready

DID YOU KNOW?

Dave Bolen, fourth in the 400m, became US Ambassador to Botswana, Lesotho, Swaziland and the GDR ... Bill Nankeville, sixth in the 1500m, is the father of comedian and impressionist Bobby Davro ... Ottavio Missoni, sixth in the 400m hurdles, would find wider fame as head of the Italian fashion house of Missoni ... Guinn Smith, a US Air Force war hero, became the last man to win an Olympic vault gold medal using a bamboo pole ... Decathlon bronze medallist Floyd Simmons became a Hollywood actor and appeared in South Pacific ... Happier times ahead: Josy Barthel, destined to win the 1500m in 1952, placed 10th of 12 in the London final, while Bob McMillen (who would place 2nd to Barthel) fell three times in his steeplechase heat.

to run the race of her life. The final was a thriller, and for a while it looked as though she would become the first British woman to win an Olympic athletics title. Blankers-Koen got away to a dreadful start but managed to draw level with Gardner approaching the fifth hurdle. Then disaster loomed up again for the Dutch star: "I was going so fast that I went too close to the hurdle, hit it, and lost my balance. What happened after that is just a blurred memory. It was a grim struggle, in which my hurdling style went to pieces. I staggered like a drunkard."

It was close, but by a matter of inches Blankers-Koen had won as both athletes were timed at 11.2, a British record for Gardner. "Maureen and I shook hands. It had been a wonderful race and I was proud to have beaten such a brilliant athlete. We left the ground and went to our waiting coaches. My husband was feeling as delighted as I was. 'Well done, Fanny', he said, 'you aren't too old, after all' – and he left his congratulations at that! But there was Geoff Dyson, giving Maureen a long, long kiss. Ah well ... as somebody standing near said afterwards, 'that's the difference between an engaged couple and a staid old married pair!'" Maureen, who married Britain's first national athletics coach six weeks later, finished second again to Fanny in the 1950 European Championships. Tragically, she died of cancer at 45.

Next on Fanny's Wembley agenda was the 200m, an Olympic event for the first time. By now she was tired and homesick, and wanted to withdraw. Husband Jan coaxed her into continuing and, on a muddy track which held her time down to 24.4, she won by an enormous six metre margin over Audrey Williamson, who won an Olympic silver medal in her first and only appearance for Britain. Audrey Patterson (USA) was placed third but in 1975 statistician Bob Sparks gained access to a photo finish print and discovered that it was Shirley Strickland, bronze medallist in the 100m and 200m, who was actually third, although the official result has never been amended.

Strickland may have been excused for believing a gold medal was coming her way after Australia emerged from the final change-over of the 4x100m relay in the lead with Holland only fourth. But Blankers-Koen was not to be denied, and she stormed through for her fourth victory and an indelible place in Olympic history.

1948 - LONDON

100m: (1.6) 1, Harrison Dillard USA 10.3; 2, Barney Ewell USA 10.4; 3, Lloyd LaBeach PAN 10.4; 4, Alistair McCorquodale GBR 10.4; 5, Mel Patton USA 10.5; 6, McDonald Bailey GBR 10.6.
200m: 1, Mel Patton USA 21.1; 2, Barney Ewell USA 21.1; 3, Lloyd LaBeach PAN 21.2; 4, Herb McKenley JAM 21.2; 5, Cliff Bourland USA 21.3; 6, Les Laing JAM 21.6.
400m: 1, Arthur Wint JAM 46.2; 2, Herb McKenley JAM 46.4; 3, Mal Whitfield USA 46.9; 4, Dave Bolen USA 47.2; 5, Morris Curotta AUS 47.9; 6, George Guida USA 50.2.
800m: 1, Mal Whitfield USA 1:49.2; 2, Arthur Wint JAM 1:49.5; 3, Marcel Hansenne FRA 1:49.8; 4, Herb Barten USA 1:50.1; 5, Ingvar Bengtsson SWE 1:50.5; 6, Bob Chambers USA 1:52.1.
1500m: 1, Henry Eriksson SWE 3:49.8; 2, Lennart Strand SWE 3:50.4; 3, Willie Slijkhuis NED 3:50.4; 4, Vaclav Cevona TCH 3:51.2; 5, Gösta Bergkvist SWE 3:52.2; 6, Bill Nankeville GBR 3:52.6.
5000m: 1, Gaston Reiff BEL 14:17.6; 2, Emil Zátopek TCH 14:17.8; 3, Willie Slijkhuis NED 14:26.8; 4, Erik Ahlden SWE 14:28.6; 5, Bertil Albertsson SWE 14:39.0; 6, Curt Stone USA 14:39.4.
10,000m: 1, Emil Zátopek TCH 29:59.6; 2, Alain Mimoun FRA 30:47.4; 3, Bertil Albertsson SWE 30:53.6; 4, Martin Stokken NOR 30:58.6; 5, Severt Dennolf SWE 31:05.0; 6, Abdallah ben Said FRA 31:07.8.
Marathon: 1, Delfo Cabrera ARG 2:34:52; 2, Tom Richards GBR 2:35:08; 3, Etienne Gailly BEL 2:35:34; 4, Johannes Coleman SAF 2:36:06; 5, Eusebio Guinez ARG 2:36:36; 6, Sid Luyt SAF 2:38:11.
3000mSC: 1, Tore Sjöstrand SWE 9:04.6; 2, Erik Elmsäter SWE 9:08.2; 3, Göte Hagström SWE 9:11.8; 4, Alex Guyodo FRA 9:13.6; 5, Pentti Siltaloppi FIN 9:19.6; 6, Petar Segedin YUG 9:20.4.
110mH: 1, Bill Porter USA 13.9; 2, Clyde Scott USA 14.1; 3, Craig Dixon USA 14.1; 4, Alberto Triulzi ARG 14.6; 5, Peter Gardner AUS 14.7; 6, Hakan Lidman SWE 14.9.
400mH: 1, Roy Cochran USA 51.1; 2, Duncan White CEY 51.8; 3, Rune Larsson SWE 52.2; 4, Dick Ault USA 52.4; 5, Yves Cros FRA 53.3; 6, Ottavio Missoni ITA 54.2.
4x100m Relay: 1, USA (Barney Ewell, Lorenzo Wright, Harrison Dillard, Mel Patton) 40.6; 2,

Great Britain (Jack Archer, Jack Gregory, Alistair McCorquodale, Ken Jones) 41.3; 3, Italy (Enrico Perucconi, Antonio Siddi, Carlo Monti, Michele Tito) 41.5; 4, Hungary 41.6; 5, Canada 41.9; 6, Netherlands 41.9.
4x400m Relay: 1, USA (Art Harnden 48.0, Cliff Bourland 47.3, Roy Cochran 47.8, Mal Whitfield 47.3) 3:10.4; 2, France (Jean Kerebel, Francois Schewetta, Robert Chef d'Hotel, Jacques Lunis) 3:14.8; 3, Sweden (Kurt Lundquist, Lars Wolfbrandt, Folke Alnevik, Rune Larsson) 3:16.0; 4, Finland 3:24.8; Jamaica & Italy dnf.
HJ: 1, John Winter AUS 1.98; 2, Björn Paulsen NOR 1.95; 3, George Stanich USA 1.95; 4, Dwight Eddleman USA 1.95; 5, Georges Damitio FRA 1.95; 6, Arthur Jackes CAN 1.90.
PV: 1, Guinn Smith USA 4.30; 2, Erkki Kataja FIN 4.20; 3, Bob Richards USA 4.20; 4, Erling Kaas NOR 4.10; 5, Ragnar Lundberg SWE 4.10; 6, Richmond "Boo" Morcom USA 3.95.
LJ: 1, Willie Steele USA 7.82; 2, Theo Bruce AUS 7.55; 3, Herb Douglas USA 7.54; 4, Lorenzo Wright USA 7.45; 5, Prince Adedoyin GBR 7.27; 6, Georges Damitio FRA 7.07.
TJ: 1, Arne Ahman SWE 15.40; 2, George Avery AUS 15.36; 3, Ruhi Sarialp TUR 15.02; 4, Preben Larsen DEN 14.83; 5, Geraldo de Oliveira BRA 14.82; 6, Valdemar Rautio FIN 14.70.
SP: 1, Wilbur Thompson USA 17.12; 2, Jim Delaney USA 16.68; 3, Jim Fuchs USA 16.42; 4, Mieczyslaw Lomowski POL 15.43; 5, Gösta Arvidsson SWE 15.37; 6, Yrjö Lehtilä FIN 15.05.
DT: 1, Adolfo Consolini ITA 52.78; 2, Giuseppe Tosi ITA 51.78; 3, Fortune Gordien USA 50.77; 4, Ivar Ramstad NOR 49.21; 5, Ferenc Klics HUN 48.21; 6, Veikko Nyqvist FIN 47.33.
HT: 1, Imre Németh HUN 56.07; 2, Ivan Gubijan YUG 54.27; 3, Bob Bennett USA 53.73; 4, Sam Felton USA 53.66; 5, Lauri Tamminen FIN 53.08; 6, Bo Ericson SWE 52.98.
JT: 1, Tapio Rautavaara FIN 69.77; 2, Steve Seymour USA 67.56; 3, Joszef Várszegi HUN 67.03; 4, Pauli Vesterinen FIN 65.89; 5, Odd Maehlum NOR 65.32; 6, Martin Biles USA 65.17.
Dec: 1, Bob Mathias USA 7139 (6628 on present tables) (11.2, 6.61, 13.04, 1.86, 51.7, 15.7, 44.00, 3.50, 50.32, 5:11.0); 2, Ignace Heinrich FRA 6974 (6559); 3, Floyd Simmons USA 6950 (6531); 4, Enrique Kistenmacher ARG 6929 (6542); 5, Erik Peter Andersson SWE 6877 (6486); 6, Peter Mullins AUS 6739 (6334).

10,000m Walk: 1, John Mikaelsson SWE 45:13.2; 2, Ingemar Johansson SWE 45:43.8; 3, Fritz Schwab SUI 46:00.2; 4, Jim Morris GBR 46:04.0; 5, Harry Churcher GBR 46:28.0; 6, Emile Maggi FRA 47:02.8.

50k Walk: 1, John Ljunggren SWE 4:41:52; 2, Gaston Godel SUI 4:48:17; 3, Tebbs Lloyd Johnson GBR 4:48:31; 4, Edgar Bruun NOR 4:53:18; 5, Harry Martineau GBR 4:53:58; 6, Rune Bjurström SWE 4:56:43.

Women's Events

100m: 1, Fanny Blankers-Koen NED 11.9; 2, Dorothy Manley GBR 12.2; 3, Shirley Strickland AUS 12.2; 4, Viola Myers CAN 12.3; 5, Patricia Jones CAN 12.4; 6, Cynthia Thompson JAM 12.6.

200m: (0.0) 1, Fanny Blankers-Koen NED 24.4; 2, Audrey Williamson GBR 25.1; 3 (4?), Audrey Patterson USA 25.2; 4 (3?), Shirley Strickland AUS 25.2; 5, Margaret Walker GBR 25.6; 6, Daphne Robb SAF 25.7.

80mH: (1.9) 1, Fanny Blankers-Koen NED 11.2; 2, Maureen Gardner GBR 11.2; 3, Shirley Strickland AUS 11.4; 4, Yvette Monginou FRA 11.8; 5, Maria Oberbreyer AUT 11.8; 6, Libuse Lomska TCH 11.9.

4x100m Relay: 1, Netherlands (Xenia Stad-de-Jong, Jeanette Witziers-Timmer, Gerda van der Kade-Koudijs, Fanny Blankers-Koen) 47.5; 2, Australia (Shirley Strickland, Joyce King, June Maston, Elizabeth McKinnon) 47.6; 3, Canada (Diane Foster, Nancy MacKay, Patricia Jones, Viola Myers) 47.8; 4, Great Britain 48.0; 5, Denmark 48.2; 6, Austria 49.2.

HJ: 1, Alice Coachman USA 1.68; 2, Dorothy Tyler (née Odam) GBR 1.68; 3, Micheline Ostermeyer FRA 1.61; eq4, Vinton Beckett JAM & Doreen Dredge CAN 1.58; 6, Bertha Crowther GBR 1.58.

LJ: 1, Olga Gyarmati HUN 5.69; 2, Noëmi Simonetto de Portela ARG 5.60; 3, Ann-Britt Leyman SWE 5.57; 4, Gerda van der Kade-Koudijs NED 5.57; 5, Neeltje Karelse NED 5.54; 6, Kathleen Russell JAM 5.49.

SP: 1, Micheline Ostermeyer FRA 13.75; 2, Amelia Piccinini ITA 13.09; 3, Ine Schäffer AUT 13.08; 4, Paulette Veste FRA 12.98; 5, Jaroslava Komárková TCH 12.92; 6, Anni Bruk AUT 12.50.

DT: 1, Micheline Ostermeyer FRA 41.92; 2, Edera Gentile ITA 41.17; 3, Jacqueline Mazeas FRA 40.47; 4, Jadwiga Wajsowna-Marcinkiewicz POL 39.30; 5, Lotte Haidegger AUT 38.81; 6, Anna Panhorst Niesink NED 38.74.

JT: 1, Herma Bauma AUT 45.57; 2, Kaisa Parviainen FIN 43.79; 3, Lily Carlstedt DEN 42.08; 4, Dorothy Dodson USA 41.96; 5, Johanna Tenunissen Waalboer NED 40.92; 6, Johanna Koning NED 40.33.

WORLD RECORDS OF 50 YEARS AGO (as at January 1 1950)

100: 10.2 Jesse Owens USA 1936, Hal Davis USA 1941, Lloyd LaBeach PAN 1948 & Barney Ewell USA 1948
200: 20.7 Jesse Owens USA 1936, Mel Patton USA 1948 & Barney Ewell USA 1948
400: 45.9 Herb McKenley JAM 1948
800: 1:46.6 Rudolf Harbig GER 1939
1500: 3:43.0 Gunder Hägg SWE 1944 & Lennart Strand SWE 1947
5000: 13:58.2 Gunder Hägg SWE 1942
10,000: 29:21.2 Emil Zátopek TCH 1949
Marathon: 2:25:39 Yun Bok Suh KOR 1947
3000SC: 8:59.6 Eric Elmsäter SWE 1944
110H: 13.7 Forrest Towns USA 1936 & Fred Wolcott USA 1941
400H: 50.6 Glenn Hardin USA 1934
4x100: 39.8 USA 1936
4x400: 3:08.2 USA 1932
HJ: 2.11 Les Steers USA 1941
PV: 4.77 Cornelius Warmerdam USA 1942
LJ: 8.13 Jesse Owens USA 1935
TJ: 16.00 Naoto Tajima JPN 1936
SP: 17.79 Jim Fuchs USA 1949
DT: 56.97 Fortune Gordien USA 1949
HT: 59.57 Imre Németh HUN 1949
JT: 78.70 Yrjö Nikkanen FIN 1938
Dec: 7900 (7254 on present tables) Glenn Morris USA 1936

Women

100: 11.5 Fanny Blankers-Koen NED 1948
200: 23.6 Stanislawa Walasiewicz POL 1935
400: 56.8 Nellie Halstead GBR 1932
800: 2:13.8 Anna Larsson SWE 1945
1500: 4:37.8 Olga Ovsyannikova URS 1946
80H: 11.0 Fanny Blankers-Koen NED 1948
4x100: 46.4 Germany 1936
HJ: 1.71 Fanny Blankers-Koen NED 1943
LJ: 6.25 Fanny Blankers-Koen NED 1943
SP: 14.86 Klavdiya Tochenova URS 1949
DT: 53.25 Nina Dumbadze URS 1948
JT: 53.41 Natalya Smirnitskaya URS 1949
Pen: 4608 Aleksandra Chudina URS 1949

THE FINNISH capital of Helsinki, originally awarded the Games of 1940 and with a population of less than half a million the smallest city to host a summer Olympics, was a superb choice to stage the world's greatest athletics festival. The Finns are second to none in their knowledge and appreciation of the sport, and – particularly in distance running and javelin throwing – had already made a tremendous impact on Olympic history.

Alas, no Finn was to win a gold medal this time, but there was an emotional reminder of the nation's past glories at the opening ceremony. A huge roar erupted as the Olympic torch was carried into the stadium by Suomi's greatest athlete, 55 year-old Paavo Nurmi, who in turn handed it to the man who was his own inspiration, and the man who in 1912 sparked off Finland's fabulous distance running tradition, 62 year-old Hannes Kolehmainen.

It was the start of a glorious Games. Germany and Japan were participants again, and for the first time the Soviet Union fielded a team (winning 17 medals, although only two of them were gold). The USA were even more dominating than usual, amassing 15 victories (including no fewer than 14 of the 24 men's events) – the next highest total being four by the Zátopek family! By winning the 5000m, 10,000m and marathon – a feat which captivated Finnish connoisseurs of distance running – Emil Zátopek (see page 65) joined Paavo Nurmi and Jesse Owens in the pantheon of Olympic legends, and wife Dana played her part by taking the javelin title on the same day he won the 5000m.

On the face of it, Britain's team had a disappointing Games. A number of British athletes were considered to be gold medal prospects, but at the final count had to settle for one silver (high jumper Sheila Lerwill) and four bronze (McDonald Bailey in the 100m, steeplechaser John Disley, long jumper Shirley Cawley and the women's sprint relay team). However, a flurry of fourths and the fact that Britons placed in the first six in as many as 18 different events prompted Harold Abrahams to state in the British Olympic Association's Official Report: "Taken all round, I say that the 1952 British athletics team was the best ever sent to an Olympics and that they performed better than

any previous team." The British press and public disagreed.

Lerwill, the first female straddle jumper and holder of the world record with 1.72, came closest to striking gold. She was assured of at worst the silver medal by clearing 1.65 at the final attempt, the only other to succeed being South Africa's Esther Brand (who cleared at the second try), but her hopes of victory were not helped by a high temperature and a calf bleeding from a spike scratch. With the bar at 1.67 Lerwill failed for a third time while Brand, a scissors jumper who had briefly held the world record with 1.66 in 1941, got over to become the first South African Olympic champion for 20 years ... and the last until 1996. The bronze went to the 1.88 (6'2") tall Soviet, Aleksandra Chudina, who would surely have won the pentathlon had it been on the programme. She was also second in the long jump to Yvette Williams of New Zealand and in the javelin to Dana Zátopková.

World records were established in five of the nine women's events. Galina Zybina of the USSR reached 15.28 with her final put to become the first woman shot putter over 50 feet; while Shirley Strickland of Australia equalled Fanny Blankers-Koen's 80m hurdles figures of 11.0 in a heat before becoming sole owner of

STAR OF THE GAMES

EMIL ZÁTOPEK
(born 19 Sep 1922; died 21 Nov 2000)

No one appreciates distance running more than the Finns, with their great traditions, so how fitting that the most astonishing display of endurance in athletics history should occur in their capital city. The Czech ran away with the 10,000m, kicked to victory in the 5000m and – in his debut at the event – won the marathon by over two minutes!

the record with 10.9 (11.01 on electrical timing) in the final, in which the ailing Dutch heroine of the previous Games smashed into the first two hurdles and failed to finish. That distraction ruined the medal chances of Britain's Jean Desforges (who would later marry the celebrated coach and TV commentator Ron Pickering), in the adjoining lane. She finished fifth in 11.6 after having been timed in a wind-assisted 10.9 in a semi-final won by Strickland in 10.8.

Desforges, who would become European long jump champion two years later, did however gain a medal in the 4x100m relay when, together with Sylvia Cheeseman (who was to marry steeplechase medallist John Disley), June Foulds and Heather Armitage, the British team placed third in 46.2, which was inside the pre-Games world record. That stood at 46.4 by the ill-fated Germans in a heat of the 1936 Olympics. Well, history repeated itself. In Berlin, the highly touted Germans dropped the baton in the final, enabling the Americans to win ... in Helsinki, the Americans won again, this time profiting from a mistake by the cast-iron favourites, Australia.

Marjorie Jackson, a 20 year-old typist from Lithgow, New South Wales, had already established herself as the female star of the Games and a worthy successor to Fanny Blankers-Koen by winning both sprint titles by impressive margins. She had taken the 100m by a good three metres in 11.5 (11.67 electrical timing), equalling the world record held by Blankers-Koen and tied by Jackson herself in a semi-final in which Fanny (on doctor's orders) was a non-starter, and she had a similar margin of victory in the 200m. After equalling Stanislawa Walasiewicz's 1935 world record of 23.6 in her heat and lowering it to 23.4 (23.59 electrical) in her semi, it was a little disappointing that she was reduced to 23.7 in the final after setting off too quickly and losing ground in the closing stages to the Dutch beauty queen Bertha Brouwer.

The Aussie squad of Strickland, Verna Johnston, Winsome Cripps and Jackson set a world record of 46.1 in their heat and were well on their way to victory in the final when, at the last change-over, the outgoing Jackson hit Cripps' knee and dropped the baton. She quickly retrieved it but even she could not make up all the deficit and crossed the line fifth in 46.6. The American team, which included Barbara Jones who at 15 years and 123 days became the youngest ever Olympic gold medallist, snatched the opportunity to win in 45.9 – a world record time shared by the Germans, although the electrical times were 46.14 and 46.18.

New Zealander Yvette Williams missed yet another of Blankers-Koen's world records, her 6.25 long jump mark in 1943, by a single centimetre but first she had to overcome a crisis. After fouling her first two jumps in the 24-woman final, she had to wait an eternity before her third and potentially last attempt. She prudently opted for safety, a 5.90 leap entitling her to three more jumps. At that point Aleksandra Chudina (6.14) led from Shirley Cawley, whose 5.92 broke a 22 year-old British record. Williams was able to relax for her fourth jump and sailed out to 6.24.

There was no such happy outcome in the men's long jump for George Brown, the American who easily topped the 1952 world rankings with a leap of precisely eight metres and who was reported to have jumped 8.34 from take off to landing in Japan the previous year. He fouled three times in a row in the final and gallingly watched his team-mate Jerome Biffle take the title with a mediocre 7.57, the shortest winning mark since 1924.

The triple jump threw up one of five world records in the men's events. Adhemar Ferreira da Silva, the Brazilian bouncing ball, deservedly took a lap of honour after four times exceeding his previous record of 16.01. He jumped 16.12 in the second round, 16.09 in the fourth, 16.22 in the fifth and 16.05 in the sixth, with Leonid Shcherbakov (USSR) setting a European record of 15.98 in second place. Another towering field event achievement came from the 20 year-old Hungarian, József Csermák, who became the first 60 metre hammer thrower in history with a third round effort of 60.34. He thus succeeded as record holder and Olympic champion his own coach, Imre Németh, who in Helsinki finished third.

One 1948 champion who not only successfully defended his title but also smashed the world record was Bob Mathias, now all of 21. Second to his 18 year-old American colleague Milt Campbell after the first two events, Mathias swept ahead in the shot and at the end of the first day (4367 points) was 352 points clear of Campbell. A thigh injury he had sustained in the long jump held him back in the 110m hurdles but a good pole vault (he was using an early fibre glass implement) put him ahead of world record pace and at the finish his score was 7887, which translates to 7592 on the tables used today. His winning margin over Campbell was an extraordinary 912 points.

The remaining men's world records broken in Helsinki were those for the 4x400m relay (Jamaica 3:03.9, see page 66) and – although not yet accorded official status as a world record event – the steeplechase. Josy Barthel's 1500m victory may have been a big surprise, but even fewer people would have mentioned Horace Ashenfelter III as an Olympic medal contender in the steeplechase. This 27 year-old FBI agent, who used to train at night over park benches as a substitute for hurdles, had hardly set the world's tracks alight prior to the Games and did not appear to be in the class of such opponents as Vladimir Kazantsev (USSR) who had set a world best of 8:48.6, Germany's Helmut Gude or Britain's John Disley.

Ashenfelter created a sensation in the heats. Kazantsev won the first in 8:58.0 to smash Volmari Iso-Hollo's 1936 Olympic record, and Disley took the second in a British record of 8:59.4 ... and then along came the American to knock over 15 sec from his national record with a startling 8:51.0. It was no flash in the pan, either, for in the final Ashenfelter – racing the distance for only the sixth time – sprinted away from Kazantsev for a time of 8:45.4. "FBI Man Runs Down Russian" was one typical American newspaper headline. Disley, who made a mistake in tracking an out-of-form Gude, charged through for the bronze medal in another UK record of 8:51.8.

Meanwhile, one man who had waited four long years for his date with destiny was Harrison Dillard who, as related on page 56, won the "wrong" event in 1948. This time the world's finest 110m hurdler made no mistake. At the Olympic Trials he remained ice cool while his rivals melted under the strain of six false starts and in Helsinki, now aged 29, he took the Olympic crown after a tremendous battle with team-mate Jack Davis as both were timed in 13.7 although the electrical times show Dillard won by 9/100ths. "Good things come to those who wait", he told reporters with a smile. Gold medal number four (equalling his old hero Jesse Owens' tally) came in the sprint relay in which he teamed up with Dean Smith, Lindy Remigino and Andy Stanfield.

Remigino had surprisingly succeeded Dillard as Olympic 100m champion. Of the three top Americans, Jim Golliday was injured before the Trials, Art Bragg was hurt at the Games and Andy Stanfield opted for the 200m. The previously unconsidered Remigino (he was only fifth in the US Collegiate Championships and failed to make the American Championships final) snatched second place behind Bragg in the Trials, and went on to gain the narrowest of verdicts in the closest ever Olympic final as half a metre separated first from fourth. As Remigino leaned into the tape, he felt the Jamaican 400m specialist Herb McKenley had won and went over to congratulate him, but the photo finish showed the New Yorker to have won by a hundredth of a second. "Gosh, Herb, it looks as though I won the darn thing," he muttered apologetically. Britain's Trinidad-born McDonald Bailey (who had tied the world record of 10.2 the previous year) was tantalisingly near in third place ahead of Dean Smith. All four were credited with 10.4, although the electrical timing was markedly slower with 10.79 for the winner.

Bailey (31) may have lost the gold medal by maintaining his textbook sprinting style through the line. Although drawn in one of the worst two lanes, which had been saturated by rainwater dripping from the overlapping grandstand roof, Bailey was on terms with Remigino and McKenley ten metres from the finish. But whereas his two rivals lunged for the tape Bailey maintained his upright form. "It was one of those times," commented Bailey ruefully, "when if I'd stuck out my chest I might have won".

Bailey resolved to win the 200m instead, recalling how Mel Patton had made up for his 100m disappointment at Wembley, but he tied up in the straight to finish fourth behind three Americans led in by the favourite, Andy Stanfield, in 20.7.

The Americans could hardly put a foot wrong, with other victories for Mal Whitfield in the 800m (clocking the same time, 1:49.2, as when he won in London and being followed home by the same opponent in Arthur Wint), Charles Moore in the 400m hurdles (with a near world record 50.8), former polio sufferer Walt "Buddy" Davis in the high jump, the "vaulting vicar" Bob Richards in the pole vault, the innovative Parry O'Brien in the shot, long armed Sim Iness in the discus and Cy Young, who celebrated his 24th birthday by becoming the first and only American to win the javelin. Davis, at 2.04m (a shade over 6ft 8in), remains the tallest of all Olympic athletics champions.

Unless you were a Jamaican 400m runner or your name was Zátopek, that did not leave much for the rest, and even in the 1500m there was nearly an American victory, but Sweden and Italy enjoyed moments of glory in the walks. John Mikaelsson retained his 10,000m track title but there were so many arguments over disqualifications (including British hopes Roland Hardy and Lol Allen in the heats) and non-disqualifications (the judges turning a blind eye to blatant lifting by the silver and bronze medallists in the closing stages of the final) that the event was permanently dropped from the Olympic programme. The 50k road walk, won by Giuseppe Dordoni, saw 1936 champion Harold Whitlock (aged 48) finish 11th ... with his 41 year-old brother Rex within a minute of a medal in fourth place.

Another, much more publicised British athlete to finish fourth, was Roger Bannister – still nearly two years away from his pioneering sub-four minute mile but already being built up as a possible Olympic 1500m champion. A bronze medallist over 800m at the 1950 European Championships, he topped the world mile rankings in 1951 with 4:07.8 and he became the greatest crowd-puller in British athletics. A mystique surrounded the lanky, long striding medical student. Almost god-like in action, he seemed to epitomise the ancient Greek concept of athletic perfection. A somewhat remote figure, he only rarely competed and thus every race was something of a special occasion.

He provoked criticism in 1952 by his method of preparation for the only race that mattered to him: the Olympic 1500m final. He decided well in advance not to run any serious mile or 1500m races prior to the Games, presumably taking it for granted that his 1951 form and obvious potential would automatically win him selection . What was not revealed to the public until after the Games was his astonishing time trial at Motspur Park ten days before the Olympic final when he covered three-quarters of a mile in a phenomenal 2:52.9 – nearly four seconds inside the world best. Like Jack Lovelock 16 years earlier his unwavering single-mindedness had brought him to a timely peak ... but fate intervened to deny him Olympic glory. At the eleventh hour the Olympic organisers decided to insert a semi-final round and Bannister's hopes were dashed. All his training had been directed towards running a well separated heat and final; now he was obliged to race on three consecutive days. He left for Helsinki a beaten man, psychologically. No longer did he believe in his own invincibility and, being a thoroughbred type of runner heavily dependent upon nervous energy, he could not hope to succeed unless his mind was attuned to victory. In the circumstances his fourth place in the British record time of 3:46.0 was no mean achievement, but that did not prevent several British newspapermen labelling him a flop. In one sense it was a blessing in disguise. Had Bannister won that race he would probably have retired but in order to compensate for his own personal disappointment he decided to extend his running career for another two years ... and, by running the first sub-four minute mile in 1954, achieved undying fame.

Few people now associate the Helsinki 1500m final with Bannister's unfulfilled ambition; it has gone down in history as the race won by a rank outsider, Luxembourg's Josy Barthel. Werner Lueg, who had equalled the world record of 3:43.0 the previous month, led into the final straight but Barthel sensed the German was running out of steam and overtook him 40m from the line. Finishing faster than anybody, but coming from too far back after being boxed in at a crucial stage (he "looked like a fire engine driver in a traffic jam", wrote Norris McWhirter), was the equally unconsidered American Bob McMillen, and his spectacular finish carried him to within a metre of Barthel, who smashed his previous best of 3:48.5 with an Olympic record of 3:45.2 – a time shared by McMillen, who improved by an even bigger margin. It was the stuff of dreams and legends.

The Bouncing Czech

ONLY ONE man had ever won Olympic gold medals in the 5000m, 10,000m and marathon. That was Hannes Kolehmainen, and it took him eight years to complete the treble: he won the track events in 1912 and the marathon in 1920. At the Helsinki Games, Emil Zátopek captured all three titles in the space of one week.

Zátopek, dubbed "The Bouncing Czech" (although that was a more suitable soubriquet for the late Robert Maxwell), was as dominating in his era as was Paavo Nurmi in his, largely on account of training harder than anyone before him. But there was an important difference between the two men. Nurmi may have been admired and respected but he was not particularly liked, for he was an introvert who kept himself to himself. On the other hand, the ever cheery Zátopek was loved by the public and affectionately regarded by his opponents with whom he would chat (even during races) in a variety of languages. At a time when the Cold War was at its chilliest, this Czechoslovak Army officer broke through all the barriers with his sparkling personality and prodigious deeds.

Born at Koprivnice, in northern Moravia, on September 19 1922 (the very same day but six hours before a baby girl by the name of Dana Ingrová came into the world at a place called Tryskat), Zátopek faced his first big international test in the 1946 European Championships, finishing fifth in the 5000m won by Britain's Sydney Wooderson. Two years later he won the Olympic 10,000m (only two months after making his debut at the event) and was a close second in the 5000m. He won 38 consecutive 10,000m races between May 1948 and July 1954 (between October 1948 and June 1952 he was unbeaten at 5000m as well) and among many world records were such barrier breakers as 28:54.2 for 10,000m and 59:51.8 for 20,000m. His margin of supremacy in 10,000m championship races was extraordinary: he had 47.8 sec to spare at the 1948 Olympics and 69.0 sec at the 1950 Europeans, with the Algerian-born Frenchman Alain Mimoun second each time. In Helsinki, with Mimoun collecting another silver medal, the gap was 15.8 sec, with Zátopek running the second half of the race in 14:33.6 for a time of 29:17.0. British hopes were pinned on the youthful Gordon Pirie, a man who had been inspired by and trained in the ruthless manner of Zátopek, but he paid the penalty of trying to match strides with him and dropped back to seventh. The British hero was Frank Sando, fifth in a British record of 29:51.8 despite losing a shoe on the third of the 25 laps.

The 10,000m was on July 20; two days later Zátopek eased through a 5000m heat in 14:26.0 with the final run on July 24. That was a classic race and proved that Zátopek, renowned as a front runner, also had the deadliest of sustained kicks when needed. Four men were left in contention at the bell: Herbert Schade of Germany, Britain's Chris Chataway, Mimoun and Zátopek. With 300m to go, Chataway burst into

DID YOU KNOW?

Two British team members later became Conservative Members of Parliament: Chris Chataway (5th in 5000m) and Terry [now Lord] Higgins (5th in 4x400m) ... Discus thrower Lia Manoliu of Romania made the first of a record six Olympic appearances ... Dr Arthur Wint, a member of the victorious 4x400m team, became Jamaican High Commissioner in London from 1974 to 1978 ... The gold and silver medallists in the pole vault, Bob Richards and Don Laz (who used steel poles), produced sons who would go higher than themselves – thanks to the advent of the fibre glass pole: Bob Richards Jr cleared 5.33 in 1973 and Brandon Richards 5.60 in 1990, while Doug Laz made 5.30 in 1976 ... Charles Moore Sr, the father of the 400m hurdles gold medallist, was a reserve in the 110m hurdles at the 1924 Olympics ... Yelisaveta Bagryantseva, second to team-mate Nina Romashkova (the USSR's first ever Olympic champion) in the discus, is the mother of Irina Nazarova, a 4x400m relay gold medallist at the 1980 Games ... Martin Stokken, who placed 10th in the 10,000m (he was 4th in 1948), won a silver medal in the Winter Olympics in Oslo in February 1952 as a member of the Norwegian 4x10k cross country skiing team ... Sweden's Arne Ljungqvist, now senior vice-president of the IAAF, placed 15th in the high jump, having been Europe's joint number one in 1951.

the lead but on the crown of the last bend, just after the other three had swept past, the exhausted Briton tripped over the track kerb and went sprawling. Zátopek, thanks to a 57.9 last lap, galloped to victory over Mimoun and Schade in 14:06.6 to complete the first Olympic 5000/10,000m double for 40 years.

As if that was not enough excitement, the Zátopek family gained a second gold medal that day. The former Dana Ingrová, who had become Emil's wife in October 1948, threw 50.47 to become Olympic javelin champion. What are the odds against two people born on the same day marrying each other, never mind both winning Olympic titles on the same day!

In World Sports the previous summer, Harold Abrahams had written: "What that phenomenal runner, Zátopek, will essay is anyone's guess, for he is quite capable of having another crack at both the 5000 and 10,000m and then throwing in the marathon on the last Sunday just for the fun of the thing". That's just what he did. Three days after that pulsating 5000m final, Zátopek lined up for his first marathon. The favourites were two Britons, both of whom had been outclassed by Zátopek in the 1948 Olympic 10,000m but had since emerged as the two fastest marathoners in history: Jim Peters, who had won the Polytechnic Marathon from Windsor to Chiswick six weeks earlier in a mind-blowing 2:20:43 (the previous world best was 2:25:39!), and Stan Cox, runner-up in 2:21:42. After three consecutive silver medals in the event, there seemed a distinct possibility of Britain winning the event for the first time ... but it wasn't to be. Cox blacked out shortly after halfway and Peters, the early leader, dropped out with leg cramp when in third place at around 20 miles.

Despite his inexperience Zátopek judged it absolutely right. He prudently allowed Peters to shoot off, but by 20k he and Sweden's Gustav Jansson were 10 sec ahead. At 30k Zátopek was timed at 1:38:42, Jansson 1:39:08, Peters 1:39:53. Warned by Dana not to overtax himself, he ran well within himself and yet still had practically half a mile to spare at the finish over Reinaldo Gorno of Argentina. "That was probably my easiest victory", he said. His time of 2:23:04 was the third fastest on record, the quickest on an out and back course.

Jamaican Triumph

FOUR YEARS earlier Arthur Wint left the track in tears after an attack of cramp on the third leg put paid to Jamaica's chance of winning the Olympic 4x400 metres relay. Wint had won the individual 400 metres title ahead of team-mate Herb McKenley, and with two other good runners in George Rhoden and Les Laing it had looked like a now or never opportunity for the Jamaicans to topple the mighty Americans.

Miraculously, all four Jamaicans made it to Helsinki ... and this time their prospects seemed even brighter, for in the individual final Rhoden (who had in 1950 succeeded McKenley as world record holder with 45.8) won in 45.9, with McKenley second in the same time and Wint – who won his semi in 46.3 – tying up to finish fifth. Laing was in good form, too, for he placed fifth in the 200m. Not that the Americans would be a pushover: they would field a formidable team in Ollie Matson (the 400m bronze medallist), Gene Cole (a 400m semi-finalist), 400m hurdles winner Charles Moore and 800m champion Mal Whitfield. It proved to be a race that for sustained excitement ranks with any before or since.

Wint, on the lead-off leg, covered his lap in 46.8 marginally behind Matson (46.7), who had finished two places ahead of him in the individual final. The crucial stage for Jamaica would be the second, with Laing, whose fastest out of blocks was 47.5, up against Cole, who had run 46.7. Laing dug in and ran 47.0, but still he was no match for an inspired Cole, who built up a seemingly impregnable lead of 13-14 metres with a leg timed at 45.5.

It was then that Herb McKenley, running in his sixth Olympic final but without a gold medal yet to his name, displayed the full extent of his prodigious talent.

At the age of 30 McKenley knew this was his last shot at Olympic glory, and it was astonishing that he was in Helsinki at all. Only two months earlier he went down with mumps, was confined to bed for three weeks and lost 20 pounds in weight. A month before the Games he finished last in his heat at the American Championships in a pathetic 49.2. He was found to be anaemic and McKenley contacted coach

Joe Yancey to inform officials in Jamaica that he was withdrawing from the team. Fortunately, the said officials instructed McKenley to make his way to Helsinki anyway, and – just in time – he regained form.

But the McKenley who stormed round that third leg was not just a man in form; it was a man inspired. Moore wasn't exactly dawdling as he covered his lap in 46.3, but McKenley not only slowly but inexorably cut back that huge deficit but managed to hand over just ahead. His time was a monumental 44.6, still impressive today when the world record stands at 43.18 ... so imagine the impact that had at a time when the world record was 45.8! McKenley's run was a peep into the future.

The tension throughout the last lap was almost unbearable, as, with Whitfield breathing down his neck, Rhoden resolutely stayed ahead. They finished as they started, both timed at 45.5, and Jamaica had won a famous victory. The USA's world record of 3:08.2, which had stood for 20 years, was smashed to smithereens as Jamaica finished in 3:03.9 (for a sub-46 average) and the USA in 3:04.0.

1952 - HELSINKI

100m: 1, Lindy Remigino USA 10.4/10.79; 2, Herb McKenley JAM 10.80; 3, McDonald Bailey GBR 10.83; 4, Dean Smith USA 10.84; 5, Vladimir Sukharev URS 10.88; 6, John Treloar AUS 10.91.

200m: (1.0) 1, Andy Stanfield USA 20.7/20.81; 2, Thane Baker USA 20.97; 3 Jim Gathers USA 21.08; 4, McDonald Bailey GBR 21.14; 5, Les Laing JAM 21.45; 6, Gerardo Bonnhoff ARG 21.59.

400m: 1, George Rhoden JAM 45.9/46.09; 2, Herb McKenley JAM 46.20; 3, Ollie Matson USA 46.94; 4, Karl-Friedrich Haas GER 47.22 (46.56sf); 5, Arthur Wint JAM 47.24 (46.38sf); 6, Mal Whitfield USA 47.30 (46.64sf).

800m: 1, Mal Whitfield USA 1:49.2/1:49.34; 2, Arthur Wint JAM 1:49.63; 3, Heinz Ulzheimer GER 1:49.78; 4, Gunnar Nielsen DEN 1:49.84; 5, Albert Webster GBR 1:50.47; 6, Gunter Steines GER 1:50.81.

1500m: 1, Josy Barthel LUX 3:45.2/3:45.28; 2, Bob McMillen USA 3:45.39; 3, Werner Lueg GER 3:45.67; 4, Roger Bannister GBR 3:46.30; 5, Patrick El Mabrouk FRA 3:46.35; 6, Rolf Lamers

GER 3:47.18.

5000m: 1, Emil Zátopek TCH 14:06.6/14:06.72; 2, Alain Mimoun FRA 14:07.58; 3, Herbert Schade GER 14:08.80, 4, Gordon Pirie GBR 14:18.31; 5, Chris Chataway GBR 14:18.38; 6, Les Perry AUS 14:23.16.

10,000m: 1, Emil Zátopek TCH 29:17.0; 2, Alain Mimoun FRA 29:32.8; 3, Aleksandr Anufriyev URS 29:48.2; 4, Hannu Posti FIN 29:51.4; 5, Frank Sando GBR 29:51.8; 6, Valter Nyström SWE 29:52.8.

Marathon: 1, Emil Zátopek TCH 2:23:04; 2, Reinaldo Gorno ARG 2:25:35; 3, Gustav Jansson SWE 2:26.07; 4, Choi Yoon-chil KOR 2:26:36; 5, Veikko Karvonen FIN 2:26:42; 6, Delfo Cabrera ARG 2:26:43.

3000mSC: 1, Horace Ashenfelter USA 8:45.4/8:45.68 (world best); 2, Vladimir Kazantsev URS 8:51.52; 3, John Disley GBR 8:51.94; 4, Olavi Rinteenpää FIN 8:55.60; 5, Curt Soderberg SWE 8:55.87; 6, Gunther Hesselmann GER 8:55.98.

110mH: 1, Harrison Dillard USA 13.7/13.91; 2, Jack Davis USA 14.00; 3, Art Barnard USA 14.40; 4, Yevgeny Bulanchik URS 14.73; 5, Ken Doubleday AUS 14.82; 6, Ray Weinberg AUS 15.15.

400mH: 1, Charles Moore USA 50.8/51.06 (50.98ht); 2, Yuriy Lituyev URS 51.51; 3, John Holland NZL 52.26; 4, Anatoliy Yulin URS 52.81; 5, Harry Whittle GBR 53.36; 6, Armando Filiput ITA 54.49.

4x100m Relay: 1, USA (Dean Smith, Harrison Dillard, Lindy Remigino, Andy Stanfield) 40.1/40.26; 2, USSR (Boris Tokaryev, Levan Kalyayev, Levan Sanadze, Vladimir Sukharev) 40.58; 3, Hungary (Laszlo Zarándi, Geza Varasdi, Gyorgy Csányi, Bela Goldoványi) 40.83; 4, Great Britain 40.85; 5, France 41.10; 6, Czechoslovakia 41.41.

4x400m Relay: 1, Jamaica (Arthur Wint 46.8, Les Laing 47.0, Herb McKenley 44.6, George Rhoden 45.5) 3:03.9/3:04.04 (world rec); 2, USA (Ollie Matson 46.7, Gene Cole 45.5, Charles Moore 46.3, Mal Whitfield 45.5) 3:04.21; 3, Germany (Hans Geister 47.3, Gunther Steines 46.9, Heinz Ulzheimer 46.5, Karl-Friedrich Haas 45.9) 3:06.78; 4, Canada 3:09.37; 5, Great Britain 3:10.23; 6, France 3:10.33.

HJ: 1, Walt Davis USA 2.04; 2, Ken Wiesner USA 2.01; 3, José Telles da Conceicao BRA 1.98; 4, Gosta Svensson SWE 1.98; 5, Ron Pavitt GBR 1.95, 6 Ion Söter ROM 1.95.

PV: 1, Bob Richards USA 4.55; 2, Don Laz USA 4.50; 3, Ragnar Lundberg SWE 4.40; 4, Pyotr Denisenko URS 4.40; 5, Valto Olenius FIN 4.30; 6, Bunkichi Sawada JPN 4.20.

LJ: 1, Jerome Biffle USA 7.57; 2, Meredith Gourdine USA 7.53; 3, Odon Földessy HUN 7.30; 4, Ary Facanha de Sa BRA 7.23; 5, Jorma Valtonen FIN 7.16; 6, Leonid Grigoryev URS 7.14 ... George Brown USA (7.32 qual) no mark.

TJ: 1, Adhemar Ferreira da Silva BRA 16.22 (world rec); 2, Leonid Shcherbakov URS 15.98; 3, Arnoldo Devonish VEN 15.52; 4, Walter Ashbaugh USA 15.39; 5, Rune Nilsen NOR 15.13; 6, Yoshio Iimuro JPN 14.99.

SP: 1, Parry O'Brien USA 17.41; 2, Darrow Hooper USA 17.39; 3, Jim Fuchs USA 17.06; 4, Otto Grigalka URS 16.78; 5, Roland Nilsson SWE 16.55; 6, John Savidge GBR 16.19.

DT: 1, Sim Iness USA 55.03; 2, Adolfo Consolini ITA 53.78; 3, Jim Dillion USA 53.28; 4, Fortune Gordien USA 52.66; 5, Ferenc Klics HUN 51.13; 6, Otto Grigalka URS 50.71.

HT: 1, József Csermák HUN 60.34 (world rec); 2, Karl Storch GER 58.86; 3, Imre Németh HUN 57.74; 4, Jiri Dadak TCH 56.81; 5, Nikolay Ryedkin URS 56.55; 6, Karl Wolf GER 56.49.

JT: 1, Cy Young USA 73.78; 2, Bill Miller USA 72.46; 3, Toivo Hyytiainen FIN 71.89; 4, Viktor Tsibulenko URS 71.72; 5, Branko Dangubic YUG 70.55; 6, Vladimir Kuznyetsov URS 70.37.

Dec: 1, Bob Mathias USA 7887 (world rec; 7592 on present tables) (10.9/11.08, 6.98, 15.30, 1.90, 50.2/50.38, 14.7/14.91, 46.89, 4.00, 59.21, 4:50.8/4:51.11); 2, Milt Campbell USA 6975 (6948); 3, Floyd Simmons USA 6788 (6903); 4, Vladimir Volkov URS 6674 (6868); 5, Sepp Hipp GER 6449 (6705); 6, Goran Widenfeldt SWE 6388 (6661).

10,000m Walk: 1, John Mikaelsson SWE 45:02.8; 2, Fritz Schwab SUI 45:41.0; 3, Bruno Junk URS 45:41.0; 4, Louis Chevalier FRA 45:50.4; 5, George Coleman GBR 46:06.8; 6, Ivan Yarmysch URS 46:07.0.

50k Walk: 1, Giuseppe Dordoni ITA 4:28:08; 2, Josef Dolezal TCH 4:30:18; 3, Antal Róka HUN 4:31:28; 4, Rex Whitlock GBR 4:32:21; 5, Sergey Lobastov URS 4:32:35; 6, Vladimir Ukhov URS 4:32:52.

Women's Events

100m: 1, Marjorie Jackson AUS 11.5/11.67 (eq world rec; 11.5/11.72 semi, eq world rec); 2, Daphne Hasenjager (née Robb) SAF 12.05; 3, Shirley Strickland AUS 12.12; 4, Winsome Cripps AUS 12.16; 5, Maria Sander GER 12.27; 6, Mae Faggs USA 12.27.

200m: 1, Marjorie Jackson AUS 23.7/23.89 (23.6/23.73 heat, eq world rec; 23.4/23.59 semi-final, world rec); 2, Bertha Brouwer NED 24.25; 3, Nadezhda Khnykina URS 24.37 (24.16sf); 4, Winsome Cripps AUS 24.40; 5, Helga Klein GER 24.72; 6, Daphne Hasenjager (née Robb) SAF 24.72.

80mH: 1, Shirley Strickland AUS 10.9/11.01 (world rec; 11.0/11.24 heat, eq world rec); 2, Maria Golubnichaya URS 11.24; 3, Maria Sander GER 11.38 (11.19w sf); 4, Anneliese Seonbuchner GER 11.46; 5, Jean Desforges GBR 11.75 (11.37w sf); Fanny Blankers-Koen NED dnf (11.34 ht).

4x100m Relay: 1, USA (Mae Faggs, Barbara Jones, Janet Moreau, Cathy Hardy) 45.9/46.14 (world rec); 2, Germany (Ursula Knab, Maria Sander, Helga Klein, Marga Petersen) 46.18; 3, Great Britain (Sylvia Cheeseman, June Foulds, Jean Desforges, Heather Armitage) 46.41; 4, USSR 46.42; 5, Australia 46.86 (46.1/46.22 heat, world rec); 6, Netherlands 47.16.

HJ: 1, Esther Brand SAF 1.67; 2, Sheila Lerwill GBR 1.65; 3, Aleksandra Chudina URS 1.63; 4, Thelma Hopkins GBR 1.58; 5, Olga Modrachova TCH 1.58; 6, Feodora Schenk AUT 1.58.

LJ: 1, Yvette Williams NZL 6.24; 2, Aleksandra Chudina URS 6.14; 3, Shirley Cawley GBR 5.92; 4, Irmgard Schmelzer GER 5.90; 5, Wilhelmina Lust NED 5.81; 6, Nina Tyurkina URS 5.81.

SP: 1, Galina Zybina URS 15.28 (world rec); 2, Marianne Werner GER 14.57; 3, Klavdia Tochenova URS 14.50; 4, Tamara Tyshkevich URS 14.42; 5, Gertrud Kille GER 13.84; 6, Yvette Williams NZL 13.35.

DT: 1, Nina Romashkova URS 51.42; 2, Yelisaveta Bagryantseva URS 47.08; 3, Nina Dumbadze URS 46.29; 4, Toyoko Yoshino JPN 43.81; 5, Lotte Haidegger AUT 43.49; 6, Lia Manoliu ROM 42.65.

JT: 1, Dana Zátopková TCH 50.47; 2, Aleksandra Chudina URS 50.01; 3, Yelena Gorchakova URS 49.76; 4, Galina Zybina URS 48.35; 5, Lily Kelsby-Carlstedt DEN 46.23; 6, Marlies Müller GER 44.37.

THE WORLD was in crisis as the Melbourne Olympics, the first to be staged in the Southern Hemisphere, opened on November 22 1956. The brutal suppression by Soviet troops of a popular uprising in Hungary, followed by Prime Minister Anthony Eden's controversial decision to send in British troops to wrest back control of the Suez Canal, created deep political divisions.

The Olympics themselves, although creating a welcome diversion from more important matters, were not immune from these events. Although, miraculously, a Hungarian team did compete, there was much ill feeling between their delegation and the Soviet Union's. The Netherlands and Spain decided to stay away altogether (as did Egypt and Lebanon), while the communist People's Republic of China withdrew in protest against the Republic of China (i.e. Taiwan) being allowed to compete. However, Avery Brundage – who took over as the International Olympic Committee President following the 1952 Games – did bring off a political coup by having a combined East/West German team participate.

Despite all the problems, plus the difficulty facing most of the world's leading athletes in having to reach peak form again in late November after having qualified for their teams during the summer, the Games proved a great success. Crowds of over 100,000 frequently packed the Melbourne Cricket Ground, although most Australian spectators exhibited more enthusiasm than knowledge. Norris McWhirter tells of the middle-aged Australian woman who, observing distressing scenes at the finish of the marathon, was heard to exclaim, "Cripes, how many qualify for the final?"

The Aussies had plenty to cheer, particularly in the women's events where all four (yes, still only four) track events were won by home athletes. Betty Cuthbert (18) was involved in three of those victories as she succeeded compatriot Marjorie Jackson as 100m and 200m champion and, unlike her predecessor, also went on to strike gold in the relay. Her team-mates in the 4x100m were Norma Croker, Fleur Mellor and 31 year-old Shirley de la Hunty (née Strickland), the latter also retaining her 80m hurdles title and bringing her total Olympic medal haul to a record seven (three golds, one silver and three bronzes), and that doesn't include the 200m bronze that should rightfully have been hers in 1948.

Cuthbert was everyone's image of the blonde, blue eyed, sporty Australian girl but, as she revealed in her autobiography Golden Girl, she was actually a shy person who had she not become a world renowned sprinter would have been perfectly happy to remain in the shadows. She never courted publicity or stardom, but her prowess was such that she could not escape from the pressures of fame.

At the age of 13 she began to be coached by June Ferguson (née Maston), herself a silver medallist in the 1948 Olympic relay. Overshadowed throughout most of her teens by Marlene Mathews, Cuthbert ran 11.0 for 100 yards and 24.8 for 220 yards in 1955 and, not expecting to win Olympic selection, went out and bought a set of stadium tickets for herself. But in 1956 she suddenly blossomed forth as an Olympic contender, running a wind assisted 11.2 for 100m and a world record 23.2 for 200m, and she was able to give away the tickets to her brother.

"When I trotted into the Olympic Village still a shy little thing at eighteen I could never have dreamt what was to follow," she wrote. "I was awestruck at the whole business. It was the first time I had been away from home for any length of time, away from my family, my friends

STAR OF THE GAMES

VLADIMIR KUTS
(born 7 Feb 1927; died 16 Aug 1975)

The stocky Ukrainian sailor Vladimir Kuts, the ultimate front runner, destroyed Britain's hope Gordon Pirie in a merciless 10,000m duel and then returned to win the 5000m by an even greater margin to prove a worthy successor to Emil Zátopek as the world's finest long distance runner.

SUCCESS DOWN UNDER CONTINUED

and June, my coach."

An Olympic record of 11.4 in her 100m heat helped settle her self-doubts and she went on to take the final against the wind in 11.5 (11.82 electrical) by a metre from the East German, Christa Stubnick, and Mathews. The finishing order in the 200m was the same, but this time Cuthbert had a good three metres to spare as she broke the tape in 23.4 (23.55).

The "Golden Girl", as she was now dubbed, completed a memorable week by anchoring the Australian relay team – from which Mathews was controversially omitted – to victory in a world record 44.5 (44.65), although she was run surprisingly close by Britain's Ceylon-born Heather Armitage. The British team of Anne Pashley (who became a noted opera singer), Jean Scrivens, June Paul and Armitage were also inside the previous world record of 44.9, achieved in the heats by Australia and Germany, with a time of 44.7 (44.70).

The Australian lead-off runner, de la Hunty, had earlier won the 80m hurdles in 10.7 (10.96), her task made easier by the shock elimination in the semis after a poor start of Germany's Zenta Gastl, credited with a world record 10.6 in July. De la Hunty became the first woman ever to retain an individual title.

The gold medal scoreline in the women's events was Australia 4, rest of world 5. The Soviet Union had only two winners: Tamara Tyshkevich (who weighed in at 116kg) deposed Galina Zybina in the shot with a put of 16.59 and the Latvian, Inese Yaunzeme – who had ranked only 25th in the world in 1955 with 46.84 – threw the javelin 53.86 for victory. Olga Fikotová, the Czechoslovak medical student who made bigger headlines from her romance with the American Hal Connolly, the hammer champion, won the discus with 53.69 and Elzbieta Krzesinska of Poland equalled her own world long jump record of 6.35.

The long jump silver medallist was Willye White (17), who would compete in four more Olympics, while another American youngster who came away with a medal was Wilma Rudolph, aged 16, who took a bronze in the relay after being eliminated in her 200m heat (24.83). Four years later she would be to Rome

what Betty Cuthbert was to Melbourne.

The American star of the women's events though, was high jumper Mildred McDaniel, who cleared the world record height of 1.76. Britain's Thelma Hopkins, who had briefly held the world record with 1.74 earlier in the year, tied for second at 1.67 ... a height cleared also by Romania's stork-like Iolanda Balas, who had held the record for four months until 1.75. Astonishingly, Balas would not be beaten again until 151 competitions later, in 1967!

The men's high jump also generated great interest with the appearance of 19 year-old Charley Dumas, who at the US Trials in Los Angeles in June had straddled over 2.15 to become the world's first seven-foot jumper. This time he cleared 2.12, second place going to Charles "Chilla" Porter, whose 2.10 was an Australian record. Americans won no fewer than 15 of the 24 men's events including six of the eight field events.

The Rev Bob Richards became the first pole vaulter to win for a second time, but not without some anxious moments when he failed twice at 4.15 in the qualifying contest. He won at 4.56, with team-mate Bob Gutowski clearing 4.53 for second place. Gutowski went on to break Cornelius Warmerdam's long standing world record the following year but was killed in a car accident in 1960 when still only 25. US-trained Georgios Roubanis placed third to become the first Greek for 44 years to win an Olympic athletics medal; he was also the first vault medallist to use a fibre glass pole.

Another repeat winner was Parry O'Brien, who halfway between his two shot put titles became the world's first 60-foot performer. Also the pioneering 18m (1953) and 19m (1956) exponent, he improved upon his 1952 Olympic record by over a metre with 18.57. Ridiculed at first when in 1951 he began to develop a new style in which he faced the back of the circle and rotated his right foot 180 degrees before despatching the shot, O'Brien – a 10.8 100m runner – revolutionised shot putting performances. Between July 1952 and June 1956 he won no fewer than 116 consecutive competitions!

Another legendary thrower, in his case at the outset of his international career, was Al

HISTORY OF THE OLYMPIC GAM

Oerter, who only two years after setting an American high school discus record found himself – as much to his amazement as anyone else's – Olympic champion. He wasn't expected to make the team after placing only sixth in the US Championships but he improved to second in the Trials while still 19. Aged 20 by the time of the Games, he exhibited the great competitive flair that was to net him four consecutive Olympic victories by unleashing a personal best and Olympic record of 56.36 with his opening throw.

The Americans swept the medals in the discus, but only just, for Mark Pharaoh achieved the finest ever British performance in the event to take fourth place with 54.27. That fifth round throw took him into third place but was edged out of the medals when the US third string Des Koch replied with 54.40.

Greg Bell, who had leapt 8.09 to threaten Jesse Owens' 1935 world record a few weeks earlier, won the long jump as anticipated, while Massachusetts-born Hal Connolly revived the great hammer traditions of his Irish forebears by winning a tense duel with world record holder Mikhail Krivonosov of the USSR, 63.19 to 63.03. Connolly, destined to become the world's first 70m thrower, succeeded despite a withered left arm, legacy of an accident at birth.

His romance with discus champion Olga Fikotova – he American and Catholic, she Czechoslovakian and Protestant – captured the hearts of the world and after many difficulties (initially the Czechoslovak government withheld permission) they were married in Prague in 1957 with Emil Zátopek as best man. It was not a case of "they lived happily ever after", though, for they divorced in 1973.

Brazil's Adhemar Ferreira da Silva registered 16.35 to retain his triple jump title but was pressed hard by Iceland's only Olympic medallist Vilhjalmur Einarsson, described by Norris McWhirter as the "blondest dark horse you ever saw" (he improved his best from 15.83 to 16.26). The only other field event to elude the Americans was the javelin.

That produced a phenomenal performance by Egil Danielsen, a 23 year-old Norwegian, who broke the world record by the biggest margin thus far. After three rounds he had thrown only 72.60 and just qualified in sixth place for another three attempts, but with his fourth throw – borrowing a steel javelin which Viktor Tsibulenko (USSR) had just thrown 79.50 – Danielsen smashed the world record of 83.66 by Poland's Janusz Sidlo with a mighty cast of 85.71.

Back to the Americans; on the track they won the 100m, 200m, 400m, 800m, both hurdle races and both relays, while Milt Campbell, a distant second to Bob Mathias in Helsinki, was dominant this time in the decathlon. He ran up the best ever first day score of 4654 on the tables of that era and only a poor pole vault cost him a world record. Needing to run 1500m in 4:44.2 to break Rafer Johnson's record of 7985 he clocked 4:50.6 for a score of 7937, which equates to 7565 on the tables used now. His individual performances included 14.0 for the hurdles, which would have gained third place in that Olympic final behind Lee Calhoun (13.5) and Jack Davis, who for the second Olympics shared the winning time but had to settle for silver. Campbell would, the following year, set a world 120 yards hurdles record of 13.4. Rafer Johnson, hampered by a knee injury, was second in the decathlon.

For the first time since Jesse Owens 20 years earlier, one man won both sprint events. He was the 20 year-old Texan, Bobby Joe Morrow, who attributed his success to "being so perfectly relaxed that I can feel my jaw muscles wiggle". Although far from outstanding as a youngster, with best times at 16 of 10.5 for 100 yards and 22.8 for 220 yards, he developed quickly in his late teens and in 1955 he won his first American title at 100 yards as well as clocking a sensational, if windy, time of 9.1. In 1956 he established himself as clear favourite for both sprint titles after three times equalling the world 100m record of 10.2 and also tying the 200m (turn) mark of 20.6.

Morrow opened in Melbourne with a 100m victory which was much more convincing than the official hand times (10.5 for both him and runner-up Thane Baker) would suggest. The electrical times were 10.62 for Morrow, 10.77 for Baker, with Australian Hec Hogan – who died of leukaemia in 1960 aged 29 – a close third. In the 200m, Morrow comfortably disposed of defending champion Andy Stanfield, equalling the world record of 20.6 in the process. Electric times were not considered for ratification in those days, but Morrow's 20.75 bettered Stanfield's Helsinki winning time of 20.81 as the best on record.

A third gold medal came Morrow's way in the 4x100m relay where he on the anchor leg linked up with Ira Murchison, Leamon King and Baker to break the 1936 world record of 39.8 by three-tenths. Although much slower per man, particularly slick baton enabled the Soviet team to match the former figures.

Hot favourite for the 400m was Lou Jones, winner of the US trial in a world record breaking 45.2, but he faded to fifth after leading for 300m and it was the American third string Charlie Jenkins who came through to win in 46.7. That was the slowest winning time since 1928 but the final was only 90 minutes after the semi-finals. Jenkins collected a second gold in the relay. The British foursome of John Salisbury, Mike Wheeler, Peter Higgins and Derek Johnson took the bronze medals.

Five days earlier Johnson had come so tantalisingly close to winning one of the most thrilling of all Olympic 800m races. The American, Arnie Sowell led at 400m in 52.9 ahead of team-mate Tom Courtney, Norway's Audun Boysen and Johnson. Courtney and Sowell entered the finishing straight level with Johnson boxed in behind in fourth place. Suddenly, with 70m to go, a gap appeared between the two Americans ... and, quick as a flash, Johnson darted through into the lead. Sowell could not hold the pace, so it was left to the powerfully built 6'2" Courtney to fight it out with the slight 5'9" Briton. There was absolutely nothing between them until the last ten metres, when Courtney's superior strength made itself felt. He snapped the tape first in 1:47.7, a tenth ahead of Johnson, with Britain's Mike Farrell – who went on to serve for several years as General Secretary of the AAA and BAAB – running the race of his life in fifth place.

As Johnson was to state: "Tom Courtney was an Olympic champion in the finest sense of the word. He had gathered his deepest resources at a time when many a man would have ceded the race."

Courtney revealed: "I had never run myself into such a state. My head was exploding, my stomach ripping and even the tips of my fingers ached. The only thing I could think was if I live I will never run again." Actually he turned out for the relay and won another gold medal!

Britain did win a title in Melbourne, thanks to Chris Brasher in the steeplechase (see page 74), while Sussex-born Norman Read scored an equally unexpected victory in the 50k walk ... but in the all-black of New Zealand. A former English junior champion, Read emigrated in 1954 and his request to represent Britain in the Games was rejected. Britain's loss was New Zealand's gain and Read won in 4:30:43. The 5000m yielded medals for both Gordon Pirie and Derek Ibbotson, but neither got anywhere near Vladimir Kuts, who had earlier destroyed Pirie in an epic 10,000m encounter (see page 73).

Britain had high hopes also in the 1500m, particularly after István Rózsavölgyi, who had established a world record of 3:40.6 in August, was eliminated in his heat. The Hungarian's demise was not surprising, for his mind and body were not equipped for the task at hand. In order to get out of Hungary he had to walk 200 miles to the Austrian border, leaving behind in Budapest his wife and young son.

Brian Hewson of Britain led into the finishing straight, but he tied up to finish fifth and the title went to Ireland's Ron Delany, who at the bell had been a boxed-in tenth but had extricated himself in time to produce a spectacular 25.6 last 200m. The 21 year-old from County Wicklow, who at the time was the youngest of the 11 men who had run a sub-four minute mile, set a personal best of 3:41.2 ahead of East Germany's Klaus Richtzenhain and Australia's world mile record holder John Landy.

As in the 200m, 110m hurdles and discus, American athletes scored a clean sweep in the 400m hurdles, although that might not have been the case had the South African contender, Gert Potgieter, not fallen at the last barrier when in third place. Glenn Davis, who had only run his first 440 yards hurdles race in April 1956 (54.4) and yet two months later at the US Trials reduced the world 400m hurdles record from 50.4 to 49.5, took the gold in 50.1 ahead of 18 year-old Eddie Southern.

At the other end of the age scale, 35 year-old Alain Mimoun, the Algerian-born Frenchman who had won three Olympic track silvers behind Emil Zátopek, finally came into his own ... as a marathoner. He became the third man running to make a winning debut in the Olympic marathon, and also maintained a cycle of French victories in this event. Michel Theato had won in 1900 and Boughera El Ouafi 28 years later, and now a further 28 years on it was Mimoun's turn. He won in 2:25:00, with Zátopek – not fully fit following a hernia operation – finishing sixth in his second and last marathon appearance.

Kuts v Pirie Epic

MOST OF the great duels in athletics history have been reflected in the results: Roger Bannister 3:58.8 v John Landy 3:59.6 in the Empire Games mile in Vancouver; Chris Chataway 13:51.6 v Vladimir Kuts 13:51.7 in the London v Moscow 5000m; Jamaica 3:03.9 v USA 3:04.0 in the 1952 Olympic 4x400m, and so on. On the face of it, Kuts 28:45.6 (1st) v Gordon Pirie 29:49.6 (8th) in the Melbourne Olympic 10,000m doesn't appear to qualify as one of the great head-to-head races of all time, but it most certainly was. Despite the eventual outcome the race turned on a knife's edge.

The stocky Ukrainian sailor and the tall, gaunt Briton came into the race at the top of their form. Kuts (29), the 1954 European 5000m champion, had smashed the world 10,000m record in Moscow in September with a time of 28:30.4. Pirie (25), whose UK record for that event was much slower at 29:17.2, had enjoyed a fabulous season over the shorter distances.

Back in 1953, when the world 5000m record stood at 13:58.2, Pirie claimed that one day he would run 13:40, a time that then appeared to be in the realm of science-fiction. But Pirie, whose inspiration was Emil Zátopek, knew better than most that man had only just begun to scratch the surface in distance running. By 1956 he was ready. Stronger and faster than ever following the introduction of weight training into his preparations he brought off his first coup on a rain-sodden track at Bergen in June. Not only did

he break the world record (and take 25.8 sec from his own previous best) with 13:36.8 but he also defeated Kuts (13:39.6) by 20m into the bargain. Kuts cut out a torrid pace yet was quite unable to drop Pirie, who sped through the final 300m in 41.2. Although Kuts had led, it was Pirie who had dictated the race. As he explained in his autobiography Running Wild, "Every straight I ran to Kuts's shoulder to hustle him along to a greater speed. At no time did I allow him to slacken to gather energy for a burst."

Three days later, at Trondheim, Pirie picked up another world record (7:55.5 for 3000m) and a second trip to Scandinavia in September found Pirie again in superlative form. Taking on the great

Hungarian trio of Sándor Iharos, László Tábori and István Rózsavölgyi over 3000m at Malmö he beat the lot in another world record of 7:52.8.

It's easy to be wise after the event but Pirie might have succeeded in the Melbourne 5000m had he concentrated on that event alone. Instead, he went first for the 10,000m and fell between two stools. On paper Kuts was over three quarters of a minute faster and a less uncompromising athlete than Pirie might, in the circumstances, have aimed for a fairly 'safe' silver medal. But Pirie, and all credit to him, wanted the gold or nothing.

Kuts, the ultimate front runner, unsettled everyone except Pirie with a blistering opening lap of 61.5 and it didn't take long before the pair had pulled well away from the rest of the field. They reached 5000m in 14:06.8, just a fifth of a second slower than Zátopek's Olympic record for that distance! Kuts tortured his rival with a series of bursts. Pirie takes over the story: "He was deliberately doing this fast-slow to put me off my rhythm. I was so tired that I couldn't lead to stop him doing it. He tried desperately to shake me off, sometimes running in the third lane ... I thought that with four laps to go I had passed the danger point and that it was only to be a matter of covering this last short distance before the gold medal was mine. This was not taking Kuts's strength into account. He put in another phenomenal burst after forcing me to take the lead momentarily. I broke with only three and a half laps left and Kuts's flagging spirit was renewed ... I staggered the last three laps at about walking pace. I was utterly exhausted, like a punch-drunk boxer, but I was still determined to cross the finishing line."

Kuts later admitted he was at breaking point himself when he inflicted the burst that finally caused his rival to crack. Had Pirie responded once more Kuts would have been the one to give up – that's how close it was despite the final result. Five days later, Kuts led all the way in the 5000m final to win by 70m in 13:39.6, followed home by Pirie (13:50.6) and Derek Ibbotson (13:54.4).

Kuts went on to recapture the world 5000m record in 1957 with 13:35.0 but only three years later suffered his first heart attack. The fourth attack, in 1975, killed him at the age of 48. Pirie was 60 when he died of cancer in December 1991.

"Well Done The Old Scrubber!"

IT IS one of the rich ironies of the sport that whereas the first four minute miler Roger Bannister and world 5000m record breaker Chris Chataway never won so much as an Olympic bronze medal between them it was their less exalted training companion, Chris Brasher, who was to become Britain's first Olympic champion since 1936.

Brasher, born in Georgetown, British Guiana (now Guyana) on August 21 1928, was for years merely a capable but unexceptional flat runner, and it was not until he switched to the steeplechase – an undulating event appropriate to his mountaineering skill (he was on the short list for an Everest expedition) - that he reached international standard. He made the 1952 Olympic team and in Helsinki improved by over 10 seconds with 9:03.2 in his heat. In the final he pluckily limped home 11th out of 12 after crashing into a barrier on the second lap.

He put his own ambitions on hold for the next two seasons, becoming better known to the public as Bannister's pacemaker and training colleague, and returned to serious steeplechasing in 1955, improving to 8:49.2. That ranked him tenth in the world that year, but he was still only third best in Britain behind John Disley (8:44.2) and Eric Shirley (8:47.6).

Brasher still appeared to be very much the third string at the 1956 AAA Championships where Shirley outsprinted Disley, 8:51.6 to 8:53.4. Brasher finished far behind in 9:02.6 and for a while he was in danger of being omitted from the Olympic team. He later ran Disley (8:46.6) close with a personal best of 8:47.2 to win his ticket.

The first indication that Brasher might fare best of the three came with the exciting news from Australia 15 days before the steeplechase final that he had run easily his fastest 2 miles time with 8:45.6. Reunited with his coach, Franz Stampfl, Brasher was obviously in the best form of his career.

At the bell in the Olympic final five men were still in contention. The order was Semyon Rzhishchin (USSR), Hungarian world record holder Sándor Rozsnyoi, Brasher, Ernst Larsen of Norway and Disley. As the Soviet runner flagged so Rozsnyoi, Brasher and Larsen challenged for the leadership. The Hungarian showed ahead briefly but, four barriers from home, Brasher attacked. Taking his rivals completely by surprise he quickly opened up a gap which stretched to 15m by the finish. Brasher, the British no 3, was Olympic champion!

Or was he? The result of the steeplechase, boomed the public address system: "First, Rozsnyoi". Brasher, it transpired, had been disqualified "for interference in the last lap"; more explicitly for obstructing Larsen over the fourth hurdle from home. The Norwegian immediately rallied to Brasher's cause. "Whatever happened," he said, "there was no need for disqualification. Brasher and I both tried to pass Rozsnyoi on the outside together when our elbows touched. It would be shocking to take the gold medal off Brasher." Rozsnyoi also supported Brasher. An appeal was lodged and, three nerve-racking hours after Brasher snapped the tape, the jury's verdict was announced. Brasher was reinstated, his time of 8:41.2 being a British and Olympic record.

For Brasher it was a triumphant finale to an otherwise unremarkable career, having never previously won either a national title or an international match event. "Well done the old scrubber" read the telegram he received from his training companions back in London. Chris Chataway, in Melbourne, said of Brasher: "He is five per cent ability and 95 per cent guts."

Brasher never raced again on the track but continued to be heavily involved in the sport. Nearly 25 years after his Olympic triumph he was responsible for another momentous happening when he conceived and masterminded (with Disley as his right-hand man) the London Marathon. He died in February 2003, aged 74.

1956 – MELBOURNE

100m: 1, Bobby Morrow USA 10.5/10.62 (10.47 ht & 10.52 sf); 2, Thane Baker USA 10.77 (10.61 sf); 3, Hec Hogan AUS 10.77 (10.62 sf); 4, Ira Murchison USA 10.79 (10.55 ht); 5, Manfred Germar GER 10.86; 6, Mike Agostini TRI 10.88.

200m: 1, Bobby Morrow USA 20.6/20.75 (eq world rec); 2, Andy Stanfield USA 20.97; 3, Thane Baker USA 21.05; 4, Mike Agostini TRI 21.35; 5, Boris Tokaryev URS 21.42; 6, Jose Telles da Conceicao BRA 21.56.

400m: 1, Charlie Jenkins USA 46.7/46.85 (46.19 sf); 2, Karl-Friedrich Haas GER 47.12 (46.29 sf); eq3, Voitto Hellsten FIN 47.15 (46.20 sf) & Ardalion Ignatyev URS 47.15 (46.88 ht); 5, Lou Jones USA 48.35; 6, Malcolm Spence SAF 48.40.

800m: 1, Tom Courtney USA 1:47.7/1:47.75; 2, Derek Johnson GBR 1:47.88; 3, Audun Boysen NOR 1:48.25; 4, Arnie Sowell USA 1:48.41; 5, Mike Farrell GBR 1:49.29; 6, Lon Spurrier USA 1:49.38.

1500m: 1, Ron Delany IRL 3:41.2/3:41.49; 2, Klaus Richtzenhain GER (GDR) 3:42.02; 3, John Landy AUS 3:42.03; 4, László Tábori HUN 3:42.55; 5, Brian Hewson GBR 3:42.69; 6, Stanislav Jungwirth TCH 3:42.80.

5000m: 1, Vladimir Kuts URS 13:39.6/13:39.86; 2, Gordon Pirie GBR 13:50.78; 3, Derek Ibbotson GBR 13:54.60; 4, Miklós Szabó HUN 14:03.38; 5, Albert Thomas AUS 14:05.03; 6, László Tábori HUN 14:09.99.

10,000m: 1, Vladimir Kuts URS 28:45.6/ 28:45.59; 2, József Kovács HUN 28:52.36; 3, Allan Lawrence AUS 28:53.59; 4, Zdzislaw Kryszkowiak POL 29:05.41; 5, Ken Norris GBR 29:21.6; 6, Ivan Chernyavskiy URS 29:31.6.

Marathon: 1, Alain Mimoun FRA 2:25:00; 2, Franjo Mihalic YUG 2:26.32; 3, Veikko Karvonen FIN 2:27:47; 4, Lee Chang-hoon KOR 2:28:45; 5, Yoshiaki Kawashima JPN 2:29:19; 6, Emil Zátopek TCH 2:29:34.

3000mSC: 1, Chris Brasher GBR 8:41.2/ 8:41.35; 2, Sándor Rozsnyoi HUN 8:43.68; 3, Ernst Larsen NOR 8:44.05; 4, Heinz Laufer GER 8:44.53; 5, Semyon Rzhishchin URS 8:44.58; 6, John Disley GBR 8:44.79.

110mH: 1, Lee Calhoun USA 13.5/13.70; 2, Jack Davis USA 13.73; 3, Joel Shankle USA 14.25 (14.20 ht); 4, Martin Lauer GER 14.67; 5, Stanko Lorger YUG 14.68; 6, Boris Stolyarov URS 14.71.

400mH: 1, Glenn Davis USA 50.1/50.29; 2, Eddie Southern USA 50.94 (50.26 sf); 3, Josh Culbreath USA 51.74 (50.97 sf); 4, Yuriy Lituyev URS 51.91; 5, Dave Lean AUS 51.93; 6, Gert Potgieter SAF 56.0 (fell).

4x100m Relay: 1, USA (Ira Murchison, Leamon King, Thane Baker, Bobby Morrow) 39.5/39.60 (world rec); 2, USSR (Leonid Bartenyev, Boris Tokaryev, Yuriy Konovalov, Vladimir Sukharyev) 39.93; 3, Germany (Lothar Knorzer, Leonhard Pohl, Heinz Fütterer, Manfred Germar) 40.34; 4, Italy 40.43; 5, Great Britain 40.74; 6, Poland 40.75.

4x400m Relay: 1, USA (Lou Jones 47.1, Jesse Mashburn 46.4, Charlie Jenkins 45.5, Tom Courtney 45.8) 3:04.8/3:04.81; 2, Australia (Leon Gregory 47.2, Dave Lean 46.3, Graham Gipson 46.6, Kevan Gosper 46.1) 3:06.19; 3, Great Britain (John

Salisbury 47.6, Mike Wheeler 46.8, Peter Higgins 46.3, Derek Johnson 46.4) 3:07.19; 4, Germany 3:08.27; 5, Canada 3:10.33; Jamaica disqualified.

HJ: 1, Charley Dumas USA 2.12; 2, Charles Porter AUS 2.10; 3, Igor Kashkarov URS 2.08; 4 Stig Pettersson SWE 2.06; 5, Ken Money CAN 2.03, 6, Vladimir Sitkin URS 2.00.

PV: 1, Bob Richards USA 4.56; 2, Bob Gutowski USA 4.53; 3, Georgios Roubanis GRE 4.50; 4, George Mattos USA 4.35; 5, Ragnar Lundberg SWE 4.25; 6, Zenon Wazny POL 4.25.

LJ: 1, Greg Bell USA 7.83; 2, John Bennett USA 7.68; 3, Jorma Valkama FIN 7.48; 4, Dmitriy Bondarenko URS 7.44; 5, Karim Olowu NGR 7.36; 6, Kazimierz Kropidlowski POL 7.30.

TJ: 1, Adhemar Ferreira da Silva BRA 16.35; 2, Vilhjalmur Einarsson ISL 16.26; 3, Vitold Kreyer URS 16.02; 4, William Sharpe USA 15.88; 5, Martin Rehák TCH 15.85; 6, Leonid Shcherbakov URS 15.80.

SP: 1, Parry O'Brien USA 18.57; 2, Bill Nieder USA 18.18; 3, Jiri Skobla TCH 17.65; 4, Ken Bantum USA 17.48; 5, Boris Balyayev URS 16.96; 6, Erik Uddebom SWE 16.65.

DT: 1, Al Oerter USA 56.36; 2, Fortune Gordien USA 54.81; 3, Des Koch USA 54.40; 4, Mark Pharaoh GBR 54.27; 5, Otto Grigalka URS 52.37; 6, Adolfo Consolini ITA 52.21.

HT: 1, Hal Connolly USA 63.19; 2, Mikhail Krivonosov URS 63.03; 3, Anatoliy Samotsvetov URS 62.56; 4, Albert Hall URS 61.96; 5, József Csermák HUN 60.70; 6, Kresimir Racic YUG 60.36.

JT: 1, Egil Danielsen NOR 85.71 (world rec); 2, Janusz Sidlo POL 79.98; 3, Viktor Tsibulenko URS 79.50; 4, Herbert Koschel GER 74.68; 5, Jan Kopyto POL 74.28; 6, Giovanni Lievore ITA 72.88.

Dec: 1, Milt Campbell USA 7937 (7565 on present tables) (10.8/10.91, 7.33, 14.76, 1.89, 48.8/48.83, 14.0/14.12, 44.98, 3.40, 57.08, 4:50.6/4:50.68); 2, Rafer Johnson USA 7587 (7422); 3, Vasiliy Kuznyetsov URS 7465 (7330); 4, Uno Palu URS 6930 (7028); 5, Martin Lauer GER 6853 (6910); 6, Walter Meier GER (GDR) 6773 (6910)

20k Walk: 1, Leonid Spirin URS 1:31:28; 2, Antanas Mikenas URS 1:32:03; 3, Bruno Junk URS 1:32:12; 4, John Ljunggren SWE 1:32:24; 5, Stan Vickers GBR 1:32:35; 6, Don Keane AUS 1:33:52.

50k Walk: 1, Norman Read NZL 4:30:43; 2, Yevgeniy Maskinskov URS 4:32:57; 3, John Ljunggren SWE 4:35:02; 4, Abdon Parnich ITA 4:39:00; 5, Antal Roka HUN 4:50:09; 6, Ray Smith AUS 4:56:08.

Women's Events

100m: 1, Betty Cuthbert AUS 11.5/11.82 (11.72 ht); 2, Christa Stubnick GER (GDR) 11.92 (11.89 ht) ; 3, Marlene Mathews AUS 11.94 (11.80 sf); 4, Isabelle Daniels USA 11.98 (11.91 ht); 5, Giuseppina Leone ITA 12.07; 6, Heather Armitage GBR 12.10.

200m: 1, Betty Cuthbert AUS 23.4/23.55; 2, Christa Stubnick GER (GDR) 23.89; 3, Marlene Mathews AUS 24.10; 4, Norma Croker AUS 24.22; 5, June Paul (née Foulds) GBR 24.30 (24.00 ht); 6, Gisela Köhler GER (GDR) 24.68.

80mH: 1, Shirley de la Hunty (née Strickland) AUS 10.7/10.96 (10.89 sf); 2, Gisela Köhler GER (GDR) 11.12 (10.93 sf); 3, Norma Thrower AUS 11.25 (10.94 ht); 4, Galina Bystrova URS 11.25 (11.09 ht); 5, Maria Golubnichaya URS 11.50; 6, Gloria Cooke AUS 11.60.

4x100m Relay: 1, Australia (Shirley de la Hunty, Norma Croker, Fleur Mellor, Betty Cuthbert) 44.5/44.65 (world rec; 44.9/45.00 heat, world rec); 2, Great Britain (Anne Pashley, Jean Scrivens, June Paul, Heather Armitage) 44.70; 3, USA (Isabelle Daniels, Mae Faggs, Wilma Rudolph, Margaret Matthews) 45.04; 4, USSR 45.81; 5, Italy 45.90; 6, Germany (Maria Sander, Christa Stubnick, Gisela Köhler, Barbara Mayer) 47.29 (44.9/45.07 heat, eq world rec)

HJ: 1, Mildred McDaniel USA 1.76 (world rec); eq 2, Thelma Hopkins GBR & Maria Pisaryeva URS 1.67; 4, Gunhild Larking SWE 1.67; 5, Iolanda Balas ROM 1.67; 6, Michele Mason AUS 1.67.

LJ: 1, Elzbieta Krzesinska POL 6.35 (eq world rec); 2, Willye White USA 6.09; 3, Nadezhda Dvalishvili URS 6.07; 4, Erika Fisch GER 5.89; 5, Marthe Lambert FRA 5.88; 6, Valentina Shaprunova URS 5.85.

SP: 1, Tamara Tyshkevich URS 16.59; 2, Galina Zybina URS 16.53; 3, Marianne Werner GER 15.61; 4, Zinaida Doynikova URS 15.54; 5, Valerie Sloper NZL 15.34; 6, Earlene Brown USA 15.12.

DT: 1, Olga Fikotová TCH 53.69; 2, Irina Beglyakova URS 52.54; 3, Nina Ponomaryeva (née Romashkova) URS 52.02; 4, Earlene Brown USA 51.35; 5, Albina Yelkina URS 48.20; 6, Isabel Avellan ARG 46.73.

JT: 1, Inese Yaunzeme URS 53.86; 2, Marlene Ahrens CHI 50.38; 3, Nadezhda Konyayeva URS 50.28; 4, Dana Zátopková TCH 49.83; 5, Ingrid Almqvist SWE 49.74; 6, Urszula Figwer POL 48.16.

I T WAS Rome which was responsible, over 15 centuries earlier, for the abolition of the Olympic Games, but handsome amends were made in the magnificent Stadio Olimpico. For the first time there was worldwide television coverage of an Olympics, there was a record entry of 83 nations (70 in athletics), and in many ways they were the greatest Games yet. World records were beaten or equalled in eight events, not counting a world best in the marathon, and there were Olympic records in 30 of the 34 events.

The only Olympic records to survive the onslaught were those for the 5000m (13:39.6 by Vladimir Kuts), 110m hurdles (13.5 by Lee Calhoun and Jack Davis), javelin (85.71 by Egil Danielsen) and 20k walk (1:31:28 by Leonid Spirin), all set in 1956. Emil Zátopek's Olympic marathon record was broken by the first 15 runners and Hal Connolly's hammer mark was exceeded on 29 occasions. A special case was the women's 800m, revived at last after 32 years. Of the 27 competitors, 25 were faster than the old Olympic record.

Among the plethora of brilliant performances it is perhaps invidious to select the very best but for this writer, attending his first Olympics, the memories of Herb Elliott utterly destroying the 1500m field in world record time (see page 82) and the gazelle-like speed and grace of Wilma Rudolph (see page 81) remain the most vivid and treasured.

For the British team, the Games got off to an appalling start on what was known as "Black Wednesday" as three of Britain's brightest hopes flopped. Mary Bignal (later Rand, later still Toomey and then Reese) had raised expectations by leading the long jump qualifiers with a UK record of 6.33, only 7cm short of the world record, but in the final she encountered acute approach problems, running through on her first attempt, misjudging her run on the second for another foul and reaching only 6.01 at her third and final try for ninth place. Victory went to the USSR's Vyera Krepkina, a co-holder of the world 100m record of 11.3, at 6.37. Gallingly, Bignal's qualifying distance would have sufficed for the silver in the final.

Another bitter disappointment for British fans on the opening day was the sight of

European shot champion and record holder Arthur Rowe, who had registered 19.19 in training three days earlier, reaching a mere 16.68 and failing to qualify for the final (in which the silver medal went at 19.11). He claimed that a combination of tummy troubles and lack of appetite brought on by the soaring heat and humidity had weakened him, and another apparent victim of inadequate acclimatisation was Gordon Pirie, who finished nearly 40 sec behind the winner of his 5000m heat in a pathetic 14:43.6. In his last major outing prior to Rome he had looked magnificent, clocking a 54.6 last lap in a race he won in 13:51.6.

Not that it was all doom and gloom for the British team. There were silver medals for Dorothy Hyman in the 100m, Carole Quinton in the 80m hurdles and Dorothy Shirley in the high jump; bronze medals for Peter Radford in the 100m (and another in the sprint relay along with David Jones, Dave Segal and Nick Whitehead), Stan Vickers in the 20k walk and Dorothy Hyman in the 200m, plus many other honourable placings, such as Mike Lindsay's fifth in the shot – the highest by a Briton in that event since 1908.

But it was il topolino ("the little mouse"), as Don Thompson was affectionately dubbed, who was the British hero. Recalling his ordeal in the sun at the Melbourne Olympics, when he collapsed from dehydration after 42k of the 50k walk and determined to be prepared for any cli-

STAR OF THE GAMES

HERB ELLIOTT
(born 25 Feb 1938)

He claims he was far less self-confident than he appeared, but Australia's Herb Elliott simply tore the opposition apart in the 1500m. A 56.0 third lap tested his opponents to the limit, and then he proceeded to accelerate still further to win by almost 20 metres, the biggest margin yet in an Olympic 1500m, in a world record breaking 3:35.6.

matic extremes next time, Thompson spent hours literally sweating it out by performing calisthenics in a small bathroom heated to a temperature of 38° celsius. It paid dividends, for although the weather was 30° at the start of the race the 27 year-old fire insurance clerk from Middlesex was able to cope with the conditions as well as the opposition.

Decked out in sunglasses and a head covering which made him look like a fugitive from the Foreign Legion, Thompson led by a minute at halfway, reached in 2:10:30, but was overtaken approaching 35k by 40 year-old John Ljunggren, the Swede who had won the title in 1948. At 45k, with the two men virtually abreast, Ljunggren halted for what Thompson described as "almost a wash and brush up", and the diminutive Briton seized his chance of building up a winning lead. At the finish he was 17 sec clear in 4:25:30. Thompson, a protégé of the 1936 champion Harold Whitlock, switched to marathon running in the eighties, with a best of 2:51, but in 1991 he returned to walking and became Britain's oldest ever international when, at 58, he competed in a 24 hour race in France.

Every Olympics produces upsets, and Rome was no exception. No one could have predicted that an unknown Ethiopian would win the marathon ... and, until he made an increasingly favourable impression in the preliminary rounds, few would have given much for Peter Snell's chances in the 800m. Another shock came in the high jump where world record holder John Thomas managed to salvage only the bronze medal.

North African runners, like defending marathon champion Alain Mimoun (an Algerian-born French citizen), had long been a force in distance running, and one or two Kenyan runners had been giving a good account of themselves in major competition, but there was no advance warning that Ethiopia had found a world-beating marathoner. If it had been known that Abebe Bikila had run 2:21:23 the previous month at high altitude Addis Ababa he might have been marked down as one worth looking out for in Rome, but he was completely overlooked in previews of the race which, for the only time in Olympic history, would not finish in the stadium. Instead, the marathon began on Capitol Hill and

ended by the Arch of Constantine.

The barefoot Ethiopian and the Moroccan, Rhadi ben Abdesselem (the international cross country champion) pulled clear of the field at 18k and by 20k were some 150m ahead. Their lead had grown to over 700m by 30k and they continued to fight it out until, in the final mile, Abebe Bikila succeeded in drawing away along the torch-lit Appian Way.

Not only did he become the first black African to win any Olympic title, but the 28 year-old member of Haile Selassie's Imperial Bodyguard also set a world's best time. That stood at 2:15:17.0 by Sergey Popov of the USSR when winning the 1958 European title, whereas the time in Rome was 2:15:16.2 – although, when rounding up to the nearest second above, Abebe Bikila's time of 2:15:17 equalled the record. Rhadi was second in 2:15:42 and New Zealander Barry Magee – coached, like the winners of the 800m and 5000m, by Arthur Lydiard – took third place. Popov finished fifth and Mimoun wound up 34th.

Nyandika Maiyoro, a trail blazer among Kenyan runners (he was fourth in the 1954 Empire Games 3 miles and seventh in the Melbourne 5000m), smashed his previous best with 13:52.8 for sixth in the 5000m, a race which saw New Zealander Murray Halberg bring off a courageous and dramatic victory. Not just a promising track career, but life itself, was threatened when at 17 he was grievously injured playing rugby in 1950. Doctors doubted at first whether he would survive; they predicted at best he would be permanently disabled. They reckoned without Halberg's fantastic will power. Although his left arm was withered as a result of the accident he fought his way to the top as an athlete. After scoring a brilliant 3 miles win at the 1958 Empire Games he was ready for Olympic glory.

Duplicating the tactics which had paid off in Cardiff two years earlier, he burst away with three laps remaining, covering the lap in 61.1 and opening up a 30m lead. It was a gamble, and the tension was almost unbearable as the pack began to reduce Halberg's hard won advantage on the last lap but he called on his final reserves to reach the tape eight metres ahead of East German Hans Grodotzki in a personal best of

13:43.4 to become the first non-European to win this title.

It completed a fabulous double for the Kiwis, as less than half an hour earlier the rugged 21 year-old Peter Snell had brought off an unexpected 800m victory over Roger Moens of Belgium. Snell, whose best time prior to Rome was a national half mile record of 1:49.2 (worth 1:48.5 metrically), as against Moens' 1955 world 800m record of 1:45.7, had attracted some attention by clocking a personal best of 1:48.1 for the fastest first-round heat time, and created a stir by finishing ahead of Moens in the semis in 1:47.2.

The final was fast, thanks to Christian Wägli of Switzerland, who sped through 400m in 51.8 and stayed ahead until the 700m mark. At that point Moens went in front, but in the closing stages Snell's great strength — developed from 22-mile training runs over a hilly course — won the day. Moens looked round despairingly as Snell charged past on the inside to snatch victory by half a metre in the Commonwealth record time of 1:46.3 ... but didn't realise he had won the race until he asked the crestfallen Moens! The Belgian said: "Don't tell me a silver medal is good to win. To me, it's as if I had finished last."

John Thomas probably felt likewise about his bronze medal in the high jump. The 19 year-old American had appeared untouchable after setting five world records in the space of nine weeks, culminating in 2.22 at the US Trials. In Rome, with the bar at 2.14, four straddle jumpers were left in: Thomas and the Soviet trio of Valeriy Brumel, the 18 year-old European record holder with 2.17, Viktor Bolshov and Robert Shavlakadze. The latter, a Georgian, cleared first time for a personal best, while the other three all made it on the second try.

A crowd of 70,000 sat transfixed as the four-hour contest neared its climax. Up went the bar to 2.16 ... and over at the first attempt, although the bar rattled, went Shavlakadze. Siberian-born Brumel went cleanly over at his second attempt; Bolshov failed three times and the atmosphere was electric as Thomas prepared for his final try at what was normally a routine height for him. The pressure was too much and it was left to Shavlakadze and Brumel to fight for the gold. Neither went higher, and so victory went to Shavlakadze.

That wasn't the only reverse for the Americans, whose men's team fell far short of their 1956 haul of 15 gold medals. This time they won nine and what hurt most was the complete absence of any victories in the sprint events (100m, 200m, 4x100m relay) for the first time in over half a century.

It was Europe which ruled supreme in that department as Armin Hary took the 100m, Livio Berruti the 200m and Germany the relay when the US squad was disqualified for a faulty first change between Frank Budd and Ray Norton. That completed a disastrous week for Norton, who had won both sprints at the US Trials. He was right out of form in Rome, finishing last in both finals, and it was the man who in June had run the world's first 10.0 century, Germany's Armin Hary, who turned up trumps in the short sprint.

Celebrated (or notorious?) for his blitz start, the Saarlander was penalised for a false start in the final. He got away fairly at the next attempt, yet such was the power of his pick-up that he quickly built up a significant lead. Both Dave Sime (USA) and Britain's Peter Radford were away poorly but finished strongly to take the silver and bronze medals respectively in 10.2 (10.35 electrical timing) and 10.3 (10.42), but Hary held on in 10.2 (10.32) to become the first German male athlete to win an Olympic track event.

Radford, who contracted a serious kidney disease when he was five which confined him to a wheelchair for two years, tied the UK record in the 100m and was hoping for better in the 200m, at which he was co-world record holder with 20.5. However, in his semi he was up against two other 20.5 men in Norton and his US colleague Stone Johnson, plus an inspired Livio Berruti of Italy (who won in a record equalling 20.5), and with only three to qualify, he was shut out in 20.9 — a time which would have gained second place in the other semi. In the final, Berruti produced another 20.5 (20.62 as compared to 20.65 in the semi) to become the first European winner of this title. There were world records also in the relay: Germany tied the USA's mark of 39.5 in the heats and duplicated that in the final although slower electrically, 39.66 to

39.61.

Of course, the Americans still had plenty to celebrate. Both Lee Calhoun (13.8 into the wind) and Glenn Davis (49.3) held on to their hurdling crowns and led American clean sweeps of the medals; and there were full points too in the shot, where reserve Bill Nieder (19.68) dethroned Parry O'Brien, and the discus, in which Al Oerter threw a personal best of 59.18 to capture the second of his four titles.

Otis Davis, with two golds and two world records, was one of the supreme performers at these Games. His was an extraordinary career, for he played basketball at college and did not start sprinting until he was 25. He moved up to the quarter the following year (1959), clocking a promising 46.2 for 440 yards, and improved slightly to 45.8 for 400m in Olympic year although he only just made the US team with third place in the Trials. In Rome he equalled the Olympic record of 45.9 in the second round, while in his semi he set new figures of 45.5 – with Indian-born Robbie Brightwell, in his first season at the event, narrowly failing to make the final with his British record of 46.1. The other semi was won by the Brooklyn-born German, Carl Kaufmann, in 45.7.

Their clash in the final next day was a thriller. After South African Malcolm Spence had led at 200m in 21.2, the seemingly backward leaning Davis (21.8) unleashed an incredible 10.8 third 100m to reach the start of the finishing straight in 32.6, four metres up on Kaufmann. Slowly but surely, the European record holder narrowed the gap but Davis managed to hold on by just one-hundredth as both men were credited with a barrier-breaking 44.9 ... actually 45.07 to 45.08 on electric timing. The pair met again on the anchor leg of the 4x400, with the US winning in a world record 3:02.2 (3:02.37).

Other American gold medallists were vaulter Don "Tarzan" Bragg, who used an aluminium pole to lever his 89kg (196lb) body over 4.70, long jumper Ralph Boston and decathlete Rafer Johnson. Boston, who had broken Jesse Owens' 1935 world record three weeks earlier with 8.21, surpassed the great man's 1936 Olympic record with a leap of 8.12 ... although team-mate "Bo" Roberson fell only a centimetre short with his final jump. Igor Ter-Ovanesyan,

these days the leading Russian athletics official, jumped a European record of 8.04 in third place.

The decathlon was another enthralling contest with world record holder Johnson defeating his UCLA fellow student, Yang Chuankwang of Taiwan (known as C K Yang in the US), by just 58 points with a score of 8392 (7901 on the present tables). Johnson had led by 55 points after a first day session which had ended after midnight, but he – a 13.8 performer – started the second day with a disastrous 15.3 hurdles, enabling Yang to set up a 128-point lead. Johnson struck back in the discus, opening up an advantage of 144 points but Yang whittled that down to 24 after the pole vault. Johnson's javelin throwing stretched that to 67 digits going into the 1500m. Yang would have to run about nine seconds quicker than his friend and rival to snatch the title, a difficult yet feasible task, but Johnson stayed close to finish barely a second behind. Johnson, who did not contest another decathlon, could point to a series of personal bests which stand comparison with later stars: 10.3 100m, 47.9 400m, 13.8 hurdles, 7.76 long jump, 16.75 shot, 52.50 discus, 76.74 javelin. He was weak at 1500m (4:49.7) but his high jump (1.89) and pole vault (4.10) would have been much better had the Fosbury Flop been invented earlier and had he mastered the fibre glass pole.

The Soviet Union picked up a total of 11 gold medals in the men's and women's events, as against the USA's 12. Pyotr Bolotnikov, a pupil of Vladimir Kuts, produced a 57.4 last lap to take the 10,000m in 28:32.2, narrowly missing Kuts' world record, with Welshman John Merriman setting a UK record of 28:52.6 in eighth place. Their other successes included a world record equalling 800m by Lyudmila Shevtsova. The Australian, Dixie Willis, led at 400m in a fast 60.3 and stayed ahead until, 150m from the finish, she suddenly threw up her arms and dramatically staggered off the track. Another Aussie, Brenda Jones, took up the running but was pipped for the gold by Shevtsova in 2:04.3. The Press sisters, Irina (80m hurdles) and Tamara (shot), took a title apiece, with Carole Quinton – only fifth fastest of the hurdles finalists on paper – excelling herself to finish second only half a metre down in British record time. Nina Ponomaryeva regained the discus title she had won in 1952, defending champion Olga Connolly (now representing the USA) placing seventh. Another former Czechoslovak Olympic champion, Dana Zátopková, became at 37 the oldest women's medallist up to that time as she finished second in the javelin to Elvira Ozolina of the USSR. There was heartache in that event for Britain's Sue Platt whose third round throw landed at around 54m and would have merited the silver medal. She was so excited and eager to see how far she had thrown that she unwittingly stepped over the line ... and up went the red flag.

Another Soviet javelin thrower, Viktor Tsibulenko, had a five metre winning margin at 84.64 – but spare a thought for Poland's Janusz Sidlo, who threw 85.14 in the qualifying competition but could manage only eighth place in the final. Nevertheless, Poland enjoyed a successful Games with eight medals, two of them gold through world record holders Zdzislaw Krzyszkowiak (steeplechase) and Józef Schmidt (triple jump). One of the silvers came from high jumper Jaroslawa Jozwiakowska, who tied at 1.71 with Dorothy Shirley, who thus notched up Britain's fifth successive second place in this event. The winner, inevitably, was Romania's Iolanda Balas, the world record holder at 1.86 when no one else had ever jumped higher than 1.78. She cleared 1.85 in Rome with her modified scissors style for the widest winning margin in this event, by a man or woman, since the 1896 Games.

The Human Gazelle

THAT WILMA Rudolph ever became an athlete, never mind the fastest sprinter up to that time, was little short of a miracle. Born prematurely and with polio in Tennessee on June 23 1940 the 20th of 22 children, her childhood was one long list of medical problems. She suffered scarlet fever and double pneumonia when she was four, causing one of her legs to be crooked with the foot turned inward, and much else besides. There seemed little hope that she would ever walk normally. For two years members of the family took turns to massage the stricken leg, four times a day. From the age of five to ten, she wore a steel leg brace all the time, and for another two years when the leg ached.

Yet, astonishingly, as a 13 year-old she won

all her races at school and just three years later made the 1956 Olympic team, setting an American 200m record of 24.6 despite being eliminated in her heat, and collecting a relay bronze.

After watching Betty Cuthbert win the sprint double she resolved that four years hence, "no matter where the Olympics were held, I was going to be there and I was going to win a gold medal or two for the United States". Little more was heard of her until in 1959, a year after the birth of her first child, she clocked 11.8 and won the US 100m title. In 1960, though, she was to rock the athletics world. At the US Championships she equalled the national 100m record of 11.5 and smashed Cuthbert's world 200m mark with a barrier-breaking 22.9 but her Olympic dreams came close to being shattered when, the day before the 100m heats in Rome, she twisted an ankle while training. Immediate treatment did the trick, though, and she equalled the world record of 11.3 (11.41 on electric timing) in her semi.

In the final she was timed in what was then considered an almost unbelievable 11.0 (11.18) with a 2.8m following wind and beat Britain's Dorothy Hyman by over two metres. In the 200m, after clocking 23.2 easing up in a heat, Rudolph ran 24.0 in the final against the wind, but she still had a good four metres to spare over the German, Jutta Heine, with Hyman third. The 20 year-old

American won her third gold medal in anchoring the relay squad, the team having established a new world record of 44.4 (44.50) in the heats.

The Wizard Of Oz

IN THE eyes of many, Herb Elliott was not only the greatest 1500m/mile runner of his time but of all-time. His career at the very top was all too brief – effectively just three seasons – but what an impact he made before retiring from international athletics at the age of 22. And the jewel in his crown was his Olympic 1500m victory in Rome in world record time, a race that will forever be remembered for the Australian's awesome superiority over the opposition.

Elliott, born at Subiaco, near Perth in Western Australia on February 25 1938, never lost a 1500m or mile race from the time he began serious training in 1954 until his final competition (for Cambridge against Oxford) in May 1961. He was a boy wonder and Percy Cerutty, the controversial "back to nature" coach and guru, said – after watching him run a 4:22 mile in his school sports in 1955 – "this boy can be coached to break John Landy's world mile record of 3:57.9 by the end of 1958". He did too.

Not that everything went smoothly. After breaking two bones in his foot Elliott missed the whole of the 1955/56 Australian season and might have drifted away from athletics, but fortunately the Melbourne Olympics reawoke his ambitions (Vladimir Kuts' front running victory in the 10,000m especially impressed him) and under Cerutty's direction he captured his first world junior record in January 1957 with a 4:06.0 mile. One year later, aged 19, he broke four minutes for the first time (he cut it fine with 3:59.9!) and improved to 3:57.8 on an American tour in May 1958.

Two months after that he triumphed in the Empire Games mile at Cardiff, followed 11 days later by his first world record. Racing at Dublin's celebrated Santry Stadium he pulverised Derek Ibbotson's mark of 3:57.2 with a startling 3:54.5 for the biggest single improvement since the IAAF began ratifying world records. Olympic 1500m champion Ron Delany, who finished third, quipped: "There's only one way to beat Elliott, and that's to tie his legs together". Later that summer, in Gothenburg, Elliott did a similar dem-olition job on the 1500m record (3:38.1 by Stanislav Jungwirth), running 3:36.0 to finish 20m clear of the Czechoslovak star.

Elliott had a low-key year in 1959, concentrating on cramming Latin for a scholarship to Cambridge as well as getting married. His best time was 3:58.9 for the mile and Cerutty was perturbed by his star pupil's lack of enthusiasm for running. "He has become lazy. Even if he starts training now he will be lucky to get to Rome". Elliott agreed he had lost much of his previous commitment, having achieved his primary goal of becoming the world's fastest miler and finding that running was not the be-all and end-all of his life.

With the Olympics looming, though, he did start to train very hard again, on one occasion covering 33 miles in four hours. The fearsome 80-foot sandhill at Cerutty's training camp at Portsea featured prominently in his preparations, with up to fifty ascents in a single session, and there was plenty of weight training too.

A 3:59.2 mile was his fastest time in the run-up to Rome and he admits he travelled to the Games "full of doubts", but that certainly wasn't apparent to anyone else in his 1500m heat. As he explained, "In the heats I had to try to frighten the others, so when I made my break in the final they would lose heart". His 3:41.4 heat, just 0.2 sec outside Ron Delany's Olympic record, had the desired effect and it's doubtful that any of his rivals in the final harboured any ambition higher than second place.

That the world record fell in that final was due to the Frenchman, Michel Bernard, who thought his own best chance of a medal was to burn off as many of the runners as possible. Bernard hared through the first 400m in 58.2 with Elliott showing 58.6, and reached 800m in 1:57.8, at which point the 22 year-old Australian was a close third in 1:58.0. It was soon afterwards that he challenged Bernard for the lead and, although the Frenchman resisted for a short while, Elliott hit the front with some 600m to run.

He savagely stepped up the pace, reaching 1000m in 2:25.4 (27.4 for that 200m!) and 1200m in 2:54.0 (56.0 for the third lap), with three men – ex-world record holder István Rózsavölgyi of Hungary, Michel Jazy of France and Zoltan Vamos of Romania – hanging on for grim death.

All three lost contact, though, when Elliott moved into another gear. The crowd gasped as, oozing strength, he powered his way into a ten metre lead in the space of the next 100m (covered in 13.6) and kept up the pressure with final segments of 13.6 and 14.4. The last lap had taken him 55.6 but it was the final 800m of 1:52.8 which had done the damage, and Elliott crossed the line in a world record breaking 3:35.6 some 20 metres clear of Jazy, a future world mile record holder.

It was the biggest winning margin thus far in an Olympic 1500m final and Elliott's devastating run will always burn brightly in the minds of those privileged to have witnessed it.

1960 - ROME

100m: 1, Armin Hary GER 10.2/10.32; 2, Dave Sime USA 10.35; 3, Peter Radford GBR 10.42; 4, Enrique Figuerola CUB 10.44; 5, Frank Budd USA 10.46; 6, Ray Norton USA 10.50.

200m: 1, Livio Berruti ITA 20.5/20.62 (eq world rec; 20.5/20.65 semi-final, eq world rec); 2, Les Carney USA 20.69; 3, Abdoulaye Seye FRA 20.83; 4, Marian Foik POL 20.90; 5, Stone Johnson USA 20.93; 6, Ray Norton USA 21.09 (20.81 sf).

400m: 1, Otis Davis USA 44.9/45.07 (world rec); 2, Carl Kaufmann GER 44.9/45.08 (world rec); 3, Malcolm Spence SAF 45.60; 4, Milkha Singh IND 45.73; 5, Manfred Kinder GER 46.04; 6, Earl Young USA 46.07.

800m: 1, Peter Snell NZL 1:46.3/1:46.48; 2, Roger Moens BEL 1:46.55; 3, George Kerr BWI (JAM) 1:47.25; 4, Paul Schmidt GER 1:47.82; 5, Christian Wägli SUI 1:48.19; 6, Manfred Matuschewski GER (GDR) 1:52.21.

1500m: 1, Herb Elliott AUS 3:35.6 (world rec); 2, Michel Jazy FRA 3:38.4; 3, István Rózsavölgyi HUN 3:39.2; 4, Dan Waern SWE 3:40.0; 5, Zoltan Vamos ROM 3:40.8; 6, Dyrol Burleson USA 3:40.9.

5000m: 1, Murray Halberg NZL 13:43.4/13:43.76; 2, Hans Grodotzki GER (GDR) 13:45.01; 3, Kazimierz Zimny POL 13:45.09; 4, Friedrich Janke GER (GDR) 13:47.14; 5, Dave Power AUS 13:52.38; 6, Nyandika Maiyoro KEN 13:53.25.

10,000m: 1, Pyotr Bolotnikov URS 28:32.2/ 28:32.18; 2, Hans Grodotzki GER (GDR) 28:37.22; 3, Dave Power AUS 28:37.65; 4, Aleksey Desyatchikov URS 28:39.72; 5, Murray Halberg NZL 28:49.11; 6, Max Truex USA 28:50.34.

Marathon: 1, Abebe Bikila ETH 2:15:17 (eq world best); 2, Rhadi ben Abdesselem MAR 2:15:42; 3, Barry Magee NZL 2:17:19; 4, Konstantin Vorobyev URS 2:19:10; 5, Sergey Popov URS 2:19:19; 6, Thyge Thøgersen DEN 2:21:04.

3000mSC: 1, Zdzislaw Krzyszkowiak POL 8:34.2/8:34.30; 2, Nikolay Sokolov URS 8:36.55; 3, Semyon Rzhishchin URS 8:42.34; 4, Gaston Roelants BEL 8:47.85; 5, Gunnar Tjörnebo SWE 8:58.87; 6, Ludwig Müller GER 9:01.57.

110mH: 1, Lee Calhoun USA 13.8/13.98 (13.88 sf); 2, Willie May USA 13.99 (13.87 sf); 3, Hayes Jones USA 14.17; 4, Martin Lauer GER 14.20 (14.06 ht); 5, Keith Gardner BWI (JAM) 14.55; 6, Valentin Chistyakov URS 14.71.

400mH: 1, Glenn Davis USA 49.3/49.51; 2, Cliff Cushman USA 49.77; 3, Dick Howard USA 49.90; 4, Helmut Janz GER 50.05; 5, Jussi Rintamäki FIN 50.98; 6, Bruno Galliker SUI 51.11.

4x100m Relay: 1, Germany (Bernd Cullmann, Armin Hary, Walter Mahlendorf, Martin Lauer) 39.5/39.66 (eq world rec; 39.5/39.61 heat, world rec); 2, USSR (Gusman Kosanov, Leonid Bartenyev, Yuriy Konovalov, Edvin Ozolin) 40.24; 3, Great Britain (Peter Radford, David Jones, Dave Segal, Nick Whitehead) 40.32 (40.27 ht); 4, Italy 40.33 (40.16 ht); 5, Venezuela 40.83; USA disqualified (39.60; 39.67 sf).

4x400m Relay: 1, USA (Jack Yerman 46.29, Earl Young 45.52, Glenn Davis 45.31, Otis Davis 45.25) 3:02.2/3:02.37 (world rec); 2, Germany (Hans-Joachim Reske 47.11, Manfred Kinder 45.04, Johannes Kaiser 45.83, Carl Kaufmann 44.86) 3:02.84; 3, British West Indies (Malcolm Spence JAM 46.58, James Wedderburn BAR 46.41, Keith Gardner JAM 45.70, George Kerr JAM 45.44) 3:04.13; 4, South Africa 3:05.18; 5, Great Britain 3:08.47; 6, Switzerland 3:09.55.

HJ: 1, Robert Shavlakadze URS 2.16; 2, Valeriy Brumel URS 2.16; 3, John Thomas USA 2.14; 4, Viktor Bolshov URS 2.14; 5, Stig Pettersson SWE 2.09; 6, Charles Dumas USA 2.03.

PV: 1, Don Bragg USA 4.70; 2, Ron Morris USA 4.60; 3, Eeles Landström FIN 4.55; 4, Rolando Cruz PUR 4.55; 5, Gunter Malcher GER (GDR) 4.50; eq6, Igor Petrenko URS & Matti Sutinen FIN 4.50.

LJ: 1, Ralph Boston USA 8.12; 2, Irvin "Bo" Roberson USA 8.11; 3, Igor Ter-Ovanesyan URS 8.04; 4, Manfred Steinbach GER 8.00; 5, Jorma Valkama FIN 7.69; 6, Christian Collardot FRA 7.68.

TJ: 1, Józef Schmidt POL 16.81; 2, Vladimir Goryayev URS 16.63; 3, Vitold Kreyer URS 16.43; 4, Ira Davis USA 16.41; 5, Vilhjalmur Einarsson ISL 16.37; 6, Ryszard Malcherczyk POL 16.01.

SP: 1, Bill Nieder USA 19.68; 2, Parry O'Brien USA 19.11; 3, Dallas Long USA 19.01; 4, Viktor Lipsnis URS 17.90; 5, Mike Lindsay GBR 17.80; 6, Alfred Sosgornik POL 17.57.

DT: 1, Al Oerter USA 59.18; 2, Rink Babka USA 58.02; 3, Dick Cochran USA 57.16; 4, József Szécsényi HUN 55.79; 5, Edmund Piatkowski POL 55.12; 6, Viktor Kompaneyets URS 55.06.

HT: 1, Vasiliy Rudenkov URS 67.10; 2, Gyula Zsivótzky HUN 65.79; 3, Tadeusz Rut POL 65.64; 4, John Lawlor IRL 64.95; 5, Olgierd Cieply POL 64.57; 6, Zvonko Bezjak YUG 64.21.

JT: 1, Viktor Tsibulenko URS 84.64; 2, Walter Krüger GER (GDR) 79.36; 3, Gergely Kulcsár HUN 78.57; 4, Valno Kuisma FIN 78.40; 5, Willy Rasmussen NOR 78.36; 6, Knut Fredriksson SWE 78.33 ... 8, Janusz Sidlo POL 76.46 (85.14q).

Dec: 1, Rafer Johnson USA 8392 (7901 on present tables) (10.9/11.07, 7.35, 15.82, 1.85, 48.3, 15.3/15.46, 48.49, 4.10, 69.76, 4:49.7); 2, Yang Chuan-kwang TAI 8334 (7820) (10.7/10.88, 7.46, 13.33, 1.90, 48.1, 14.6/14.80, 39.83, 4.30, 68.22, 4:48.5); 3, Vasiliy Kuznyetsov URS 7809 (7527); 4, Yuriy Kutyenko URS 7567 (7401); 5, Evert Kamerbeek NED 7236 (7212); 6, Franco Sar ITA 7195 (7140).

20k Walk: 1, Vladimir Golubnichiy URS 1:34:08; 2, Noel Freeman AUS 1:34:17; 3, Stan Vickers GBR 1:34:57; 4, Dieter Lindner GER 1:35:34, 5, Norman Read NZL 1:37:00; 6, Lennart Back SWE 1:37:17.

50k Walk: 1, Don Thompson GBR 4:25:30; 2, John Ljunggren SWE 4:25:47; 3, Abdon Pamich ITA 4:27:56; 4, Aleksandr Stcherbina URS 4:31:44; 5, Tom Misson GBR 4:33.03; 6, Alex Oakley CAN 4:33:09.

Women's Events

100m: (2.8) 1, Wilma Rudolph USA 11.0/11.18w (11.3/11.41 semi-final, eq world rec); 2, Dorothy Hyman GBR 11.43; 3, Giuseppina Leone ITA 11.48; 4, Maria Itkina URS 11.54; 5, Catherine Capdevielle FRA 11.64; 6, Jenny Smart GBR 11.72.

200m: 1, Wilma Rudolph USA 24.0/24.13 (23.30 ht); 2, Jutta Heine GER 24.58 (24.04 ht); 3, Dorothy Hyman GBR 24.82 (23.82 ht); 4, Maria Itkina URS 24.85; 5, Barbara Janiszewska POL 24.96; 6, Giuseppina Leone ITA 25.01 (23.90 ht).

800m: 1, Lyudmila Shevtsova URS 2:04.3/2:04.50 (eq world rec); 2, Brenda Jones AUS 2:04.58; 3, Ursula Donath GER (GDR) 2:05.73; 4, Vera Kummerfeldt GER 2:06.07; 5, Antje Gleichfeld GER 2:06.63; 6, Joy Jordan GBR 2:07.95.

80mH: 1, Irina Press URS 10.8/10.93 (10.77 sf); 2, Carole Quinton GBR 10.99; 3, Gisela Birkemeyer (née Köhler) GER (GDR) 11.13 (11.01 sf); 4, Mary Bignal GBR 11.22; 5, Galina Bystrova URS 11.26; 6, Rimma Kosheleva URS 11.28.

4x100m Relay: 1, USA (Martha Hudson, Lucinda Williams, Barbara Jones, Wilma Rudolph) 44.5/44.72 (44.4/44.50 heat, world rec); 2, Germany (Martha Langbein, Anni Biechl, Brunhilde Hendrix, Jutta Heine) 45.00; 3, Poland (Teresa Wieczorek, Barbara Janiszewska, Celina Jesionowska, Halina Richter) 45.19; 4, USSR 45.39; 5, Italy 45.80; Great Britain (Carole Quinton, Dorothy Hyman, Jenny Smart, Mary Bignal) disq.

HJ: 1, Iolanda Balas ROM 1.85; eq2, Jaroslawa Jozwiakowska POL & Dorothy Shirley GBR 1.71; 4, Galina Dolya URS 1.71; 5, Taisiya Chenchik URS 1.68; eq6, Helen Frith AUS, Inga-Britt Lorentzon SWE & Frances Slaap GBR 1.65.

LJ: 1, Vyera Krepkina URS 6.37; 2, Elzbieta Krzesinska POL 6.27; 3, Hildrun Claus GER (GDR) 6.21; 4, Renate Junker GER 6.19; 5, Lyudmila Radchenko URS 6.16; 6, Helga Hoffmann GER 6.11 ... 9, Mary Bignal GBR 6.01 (6.33q).

SP: 1, Tamara Press URS 17.32; 2, Johanna Lüttge GER (GDR) 16.61; 3, Earlene Brown USA 16.42; 4, Valerie Sloper NZL 16.39; 5, Zinaida Doynikova URS 16.13; 6, Renate Garisch GER (GDR) 15.94.

DT: 1, Nina Ponomaryeva URS 55.10; 2, Tamara Press URS 52.59; 3, Lia Manoliu ROM 52.36; 4, Kriemhild Hausmann GER 51.47; 5, Yevgenya Kuznyetsova URS 51.43; 6, Earlene Brown USA 51.29.

JT: 1, Elvira Ozolina URS 55.98; 2, Dana Zátopková TCH 53.78; 3, Birute Kalediene URS 53.45; 4, Vlasta Peskova TCH 52.56; 5, Urszula Figwer POL 52.33; 6, Anna Pazera AUS 51.15.

THE TOKYO Olympics occupy an honoured place in British athletics history. Subsequent to the "Chariots of Fire" Olympics of 1924 British athletes had never won more than two titles at any single Games (1928 – 2, 1932 – 2, 1936 – 2, 1948 – 0, 1952 – 0, 1956 – 1, 1960 – 1), yet in the Japanese capital no fewer than four gold medals were captured by Britons (see page 90).

Mary Rand set the ball rolling with her long jump success, to become the first British woman to win any Olympic athletics title, and she was followed by Ken Matthews in the 20 kilometres walk, long jumper Lynn Davies and Ann Packer in the women's 800m. Only two countries stacked up more victories: the United States with 14 and the Soviet Union with five.

This brilliant British team also came back with silver medals by Basil Heatley (marathon), Maurice Herriott (steeplechase), John Cooper (400m hurdles), Paul Nihill (50 kilometres walk), the men's 4x400m relay team, Ann Packer (400m) and Mary Rand (pentathlon), while the women's 4x100m relay squad captured the bronze. What with fourth places by Robbie Brightwell (400m), Alan Simpson (1500m), Brian Kilby (marathon), Fred Alsop (triple jump) and Mary Peters (pentathlon), it all added up to the finest ever British Olympic showing.

The Games, organised at vast expense by a nation which was just beginning to emerge as an economic super-power and which craved the world's respect and admiration, were the first to be staged on the Asian continent and attracted a record entry of 93 countries (79 in athletics).

Excluded, though, was South Africa. The previous year the International Olympic Committee had called upon the South African Olympic Committee to oppose all racial discrimination in sport, in keeping with the Olympic charter. When the South African Olympic Committee failed to comply, the IOC decided in January 1964 to rescind its invitation to compete in Tokyo and South Africans were subsequently excluded until dramatic political and social changes led to their return in Barcelona in 1992.

There were other political problems for the International Olympic Committee prior to the Tokyo Games. Communist China, which had left the Olympic movement in 1958, remained out and they were joined on the sidelines by North Korea and Indonesia as a result of the Games of the New Emergent Forces (GANEFO) staged in Jakarta in 1963. The IOC and IAAF warned that athletes who took part in those officially unsanctioned Games would not be eligible to compete in the Olympics, and as a consequence the Tokyo Games were deprived of the mysterious North Korean runner Sin Kim Dan, who was credited with 400m and 800m times of 51.4 and 1:58.0 when no other woman had ever clocked faster than 53.0 and 2:01.2!

The Tokyo Olympics were nevertheless an immense success and in retrospect were probably the last relatively innocent celebration. Future Games would be clouded by repression, terrorism, boycotts, drug abuse and over-commercialisation.

Japan may have been a major athletics power before the war, but few of the home athletes were anywhere near world class in 1964 and there was only one medallist to cheer. In his case the cheers turned to groans, for although marathoner Kokichi Tsuburaya entered the stadium in second place he was decisively outsprinted by Britain's Basil Heatley.

Tsuburaya committed suicide in January

STAR OF THE GAMES

BOB HAYES
(born 20 Dec 1942; died 18 Sep 2002)

Who is the world's fastest human? Carl Lewis maybe, Maurice Greene or Tim Montgomery perhaps. But for those who were privileged to witness Bob Hayes in Tokyo there is no argument. On a soft cinder track he won the 100m title by a full two metres in 10.06 after an incredible wind-aided 9.91 semi-final ... while on the last leg of the relay he went from fifth to first, from three metres down to three metres up!

TOKYO 1964 ASIA'S

1968 and the myth has developed that he took his life as a result of the humiliation experienced by being overtaken on the stadium lap. In fact he and the public were happy enough with any medal, the first by any Japanese athlete since 1936, but while in obsessive training for the 1968 Olympics he suffered a couple of serious injuries which led to a three-month spell in hospital and when he realised his Olympic dream was over he took his life, leaving a note which read "cannot run any more".

There was a tragic end in store also for the winner, Abebe Bikila. The Ethiopian (wearing running shoes this time) became the first athlete to win a second Olympic marathon crown and, as in Rome, he set a world record. That stood at 2:13:55 by Heatley on the Windsor to Chiswick course four months earlier in June, when Ron Hill was second in 2:14:12, and again hopes were high that a Briton would win the marathon title for the first time. The chances looked better still with the news that Abebe Bikila, who had run 2:16:19 at high altitude Addis Ababa in August, had – just six weeks before the Games – undergone an appendectomy.

However, the 32 year-old Ethiopian could not be adjudged by normal standards. Not only was he at the starting line, but he proceeded to run perhaps the greatest marathon race in history, for quite apart from smashing Heatley's world best with a time of 2:12:12 his winning margin was a staggering four minutes ... or over three quarters of a mile!

Three men quickly pulled away but the early pace proved suicidal for two of them as Bikila, Australian Ron Clarke (in his fourth race in a week) and Irishman Jim Hogan reached the 10k checkpoint in 30:14. By the halfway mark (1:04:28) only Hogan was still in contact, with Clarke an isolated third. The world 10,000m record holder had slipped out of medal contention by 30k, at which point Bikila (1:32:50) had built up a 40 sec lead over Hogan, who eventually dropped out at 37k in this his first marathon. Representing Britain, he would go on to win the European title two years later. Tsuburaya moved into second place when Hogan fell away and at 40k, although nearly three minutes behind the serene, unflagging Ethiopian, held a 75 sec margin over Heatley,

who had been bothered by stitch for much of the race.

At the finish Bikila was in such good condition that he straight away went into a routine of exercises, and he later said he could have kept the pace going for another 10k. Alas, this greatest of all marathon racers suffered spinal injuries in a car crash in 1969 which left him paralysed from the waist down, and he died of a brain haemorrhage in 1973 when he was 41.

Ron Clarke finished ninth in that marathon (2:20:27), while 14th place went to Billy Mills in 2:22:56. Exactly one week earlier both had been involved in a 10,000m race which matched anything before or since for excitement. Clarke, who at 19 carried the Olympic torch at the opening of the 1956 Games in Melbourne, was world record holder at 28:15.6 and went into the race as favourite but no one seriously considered Mills, the Marine Lieutenant whose best time was only 29:10.4 when finishing second in the US Trials.

Defending champion Pyotr Bolotnikov led through a fast first lap in 63.8 but then was swallowed up by the pack and eventually trailed home 25th, double lapped by the leaders. Clarke and Mamo Wolde of Ethiopia were in front most of the time and the halfway mark was reached in 14:04.6, inside world record pace. It was by then a four-man race involving Clarke, Wolde, Mills and the Tunisian, Mohamed Gammoudi. Wolde lost contact with two laps remaining, and at the bell it was Clarke and Mills together, with Gammoudi close behind.

Here is how I described that pulsating last lap at the time for the British magazine Athletics Weekly:

"Clarke, as he eases out to pass a lapped runner, elbows Mills in the ribs unintentionally. As both men momentarily falter Gammoudi rushes between them (committing a simultaneous foul, I would have thought) and opens up a ten yard lead in a flash. Everyone in the stadium is on his feet screaming, stamping, crying as the tiny red vested figure of Gammoudi twinkles along the back-straight and into the final bend. Can he pull off the sensation of the century by beating the great Ron Clarke? No, one senses, as Clarke's long stride bites into that all too insecure lead. Gammoudi is still ahead as he turns into the long finishing straight but within a few yards Clarke is past him. The race must be over – but no it isn't. Emerging at full tilt from amongst a bunch of lapped runners comes Mills. Can one believe one's eyes? Mills! And Mills it is who storms past to win by a couple of yards from the ever game Gammoudi, who repasses Clarke in the last few strides".

Mills, whose last lap took 59.8 seconds and whose final time of 28:24.4 was way inside his previous best, was as astonished as anybody at this unforeseen turn of events. "I'm flabbergasted. I can't believe it". Nor could Clarke, arguably the greatest athlete never to win an Olympic gold medal. "Crikey. I burn off all the regular distance runners and what am I left with? An Ethiopian, a Tunisian and a half-Sioux Indian!" Mills, seven-sixteenths Sioux to be precise, thus became the first American to win a 10,000m medal since Louis Tewanima, a Hopi Indian, finished second back in 1912. A film based on Mills' life, Running Brave, was released in 1983.

Another American, Bob Schul, won the 5000m but that was no great surprise as he topped the year's rankings with 13:38.0 and had set a world 2 miles record of 8:26.4 a few weeks before the Games. Again, Clarke led for much of the race but slipped out of contention after Frenchman Michel Jazy moved ahead with a kilometre to go. Jazy opened up a 10m advantage early on the last lap but he started his kick too early and began to tie up before the finishing straight was reached.

Despite the pouring rain and the cut-up clay track, Schul uncorked a fiery 54.8 last lap (38.7 for the final 300m) to win in 13:48.8 ahead of Germany's Harald Norpoth and another American in Bill Dellinger (who would later coach such stars as Steve Prefontaine and Alberto Salazar), who pipped the dispirited Jazy on the line. The race was notable also for the Olympic debut of 24 year-old Kip Keino. The Kenyan knocked a huge amount from his previous best with a 13:49.6 heat and was just outside that when finishing a commendable fifth in the final, a couple of strides away from a medal.

Keino, destined to win the 1500m title four years hence, set another personal best in that event, clocking 3:41.9 although not reaching the final. That was won in crushing fashion by New Zealander Peter Snell. His winning margin

of just over ten metres might not have been as wide as Herb Elliott's in Rome, and his time of 3:38.1 was not as quick ... but he had already retained the 800m title in 1:45.1 and had thus become the first runner since Albert Hill in 1920 to complete that fabulous double.

Snell had come a long way since he had brought off his shock victory over Roger Moens in Rome. Early in 1962 he clipped a tenth of a second from Herb Elliott's world mile record of 3:54.5 and followed up one week later with prodigious records at 800m (1:44.3) and 880 yards (1:45.1) in the same race, the previous marks standing at 1:45.7 and 1:46.8.

There had been a question mark over whether he intended to defend his 800m laurels in Tokyo, but a 1:47.1 time trial a week before the Games persuaded him to go for the double. He proved to be in irresistible form. Despite being badly boxed in at the bell, reached in 52.0, and having to veer out to lane four, he charged ahead at 600m and won by half a second from the Canadian, Bill Crothers, in 1:45.1 for the second fastest ever time. In third place, Wilson Kiprugut – whose pre-Tokyo best was 1:48.0 – ran 1:45.9 to win Kenya's first ever Olympic medal.

Snell was even more dominant in the 1500m final, his sixth race in a week. Remarkably, Snell had never before raced at 1500m. After loafing through his heat in 3:46.8, he took his semi in 3:38.8 and improved to 3:38.1 well clear of the Czechoslovak, Josef Odlozil, in the final. His finish was the fastest yet seen: 52.6 for the last 400m. Fellow New Zealander John Davies, born in London of Welsh descent, took third place, just pipping Yorkshireman Alan Simpson.

Snell apart, the only other athlete to capture two individual titles was Tamara Press (USSR) in the shot and discus, with her "little" sister Irina Press running up a world record score of 5246 points in the inaugural Olympic pentathlon.

Repeat winners from Rome, in addition to Snell in the 800m, Press in the shot and Abebe Bikila in the marathon, were Romanian high jumper Iolanda Balas (who cleared 1.90, a centimetre below her world record), Poland's Józef Schmidt in the triple jump (Fred Alsop placed fourth with a UK record 16.46), and Al Oerter (see page 89), who claimed his third discus victory.

Notwithstanding Oerter's gutsy triumph and Billy Mills' shock victory, the American who made the biggest impression on the Games was Bob Hayes, who set new standards of sprinting. Here was no stylist in the Jesse Owens and Bobby Morrow tradition; Hayes on the track was brute force personified. As a former French international sprinter, Guy Lagorce, wrote in the French sports daily L'Equipe: "It was a bison in the middle of a horse race".

Hayes had no weakness; he was a fast starter (he held the world indoor 60 yards record of 5.9) and as a former unofficial co-holder of the world 220 yards record of 20.5 had no problems going the full 100m distance. The first man to run 100 yards in 9.1, the powerfully built 21 year-old from Florida hit devastating form in Tokyo. He was electrically timed at an amazing 9.91 with a 5.3m wind in his semi, while in the final – despite running in a particularly soft lane (these were the last Games to be staged on a cinder or clay track) and with the wind a legal 1.1m – he posted a 10.06. The official winning time was given as 10.0, which equalled the world record, although it should be noted that when Armin Hary ran the first hand timed 10.0 the electrical time was actually 10.25. His winning margin was equally awesome, for he had fully two metres to spare over Enrique Figuerola, who became Cuba's first ever Olympic medallist.

Hayes was even more dazzling on the anchor leg of the sprint relay. Team-mates Paul Drayton, Gerry Ashworth and Dick Stebbins had not excelled themselves on the first three legs and when Hayes grabbed the baton he was in fifth place, some three metres down on the Frenchman in the lead. No other man on earth could have won from that position, but Hayes made light of his task. "It was like a crack express overtaking the local stopping train", was how I described it at the time as Hayes powered past everybody within the first 30 metres and went on to score by three metres in a world record 39.0 (39.06). It was – and probably remains – the greatest piece of sprinting in history. A disgruntled European rival said to Drayton, "you haven't anything except Hayes," to which the American, proudly displaying his gold medal, replied, "that's all we need, pal".

Who knows what Hayes might have gone on to achieve on the track but that proved to be his last race. On returning to the USA he signed a professional football contract as a wide receiver with the Dallas Cowboys and became one of the game's outstanding players.

Another who quit athletics all too soon for the financial inducements of American football was Henry Carr, who as a native son of Motown was known as "the fastest Carr to come out of Detroit". He took the 200m, into a slight breeze, in 20.3 – just a tenth outside his world record – and anchored the 4x400m team to victory in a world record 3:00.7 with the fastest split of the race, 44.5.

The first leg was run by Ollan Cassell, who later became the executive director of the US track and field athletics governing body. He handed over just behind the British revelation Tim Graham (45.9), who had never run faster than 46.7 before the Games and had excelled himself by placing sixth in the 400m final. On the second leg, Mike Larrabee (at 30, the oldest man to win the 400m title) ran 44.8 to take the lead as Britain's Adrian Metcalfe handed over third. Ulis Williams maintained the Americans' advantage over Trinidad with a 45.4 stint, while although 400m hurdler John Cooper (45.4) out of his socks he slipped back to fourth as Mel Spence of Jamaica edged past him. Carr flew round his lap unopposed but there was an almighty scrap for second place with British team captain Robbie Brightwell the hero. Disappointed by his fourth place finish in the 400m final (in the UK record time of 45.75), Brightwell made amends by catching Jamaica's George Kerr 60m from the finish and taking Trinidad's Wendell Mottley (the 400m silver medallist) in the last few strides for a 44.8 leg which lifted the British team into second place in the European record time of 3:01.6.

John Cooper had won an earlier silver medal in the 400m hurdles, won by Rex Cawley (USA) in 49.6 despite leading with the "wrong" leg for the first seven hurdles. Cooper, who lowered his UK record to 50.1, was to perish in a plane crash over Paris ten years later, aged 33. Britain's other silver medallists included Maurice Herriott, who set a national steeplechase record of 8:32.4 ten metres behind Gaston Roelants (8:30.8) who was some 50m clear at the bell, and Paul Nihill whose 50k walk time of 4:11:32, only 19 sec behind Italy's Abdon Pamich's new world best, was a UK record.

Even though Wilma Rudolph had retired, the USA held on to the women's sprint titles. Wyomia Tyus (19) tied Rudolph's 100m world record of 11.2 (actually she ran a new electrical best of 11.23) in a heat and comfortably won the final, while Edith McGuire was successful in the 200m, ahead of an 18 year-old Russian-born Pole by the name of Irena Kirszenstein, who had earlier finished second to Mary Rand in the long jump. Kirszenstein went on to strike gold in the sprint relay.

Perhaps the most frustrated athlete of the Games was the Soviet javelin thrower Yelena Gorchakova. With a previous best of 55.62, she shocked everyone with a world record shattering 62.40. Unfortunately for her, that was in the qualifying round, and in the final she couldn't do better than 57.06 and had to settle for the bronze medal, the title going to the statuesque (1.86m/94kg) Romanian schoolgirl Mihaela Penes (17), whose timing was somewhat better. She chose the first round of the final to improve from 55.58 to 60.54!

Penes demonstrated that the dividing line between success and failure at the Olympics can be so narrow, for in the qualifying round she very nearly stepped into obscurity. Her first throw went only 43.00 and she fouled the second before a final-gasp 51.19 took her through to her date with destiny. Even more distraught than Gorchakova, though, was her compatriot, defending champion Elvira Ozolina. Deprived of her title and the world record she previously held, she was so disgusted with her performance (fifth with 54.81) that on her return to the Olympic Village she had all her hair cut off.

There was heartbreak, too, in the men's javelin, won by Pauli Nevala with a throw of 82.66. Terje Pedersen, the Norwegian who had established a phenomenal world record of 91.72 six weeks earlier, lived up to his unpredictable reputation by being eliminated in the qualifying contest with a mere 72.10. Actually, the only thrower to qualify automatically by reaching the 77 metre standard was Switzerland's Urs von Wartburg but that distinction counted for nothing as eleven others were advanced to the final in which he placed only

fifth. However, his final throw of over 83m was ruled to have landed flat – a tough decision for the official to make and for the athlete to accept.

One To Go

THE GRITTIEST of all the Olympic champions crowned in Tokyo was Al Oerter, winner of the discus for the third time.

The odds were heavily stacked against the American legend, who was suffering from acute physical problems. A cervical disc injury had necessitated wearing a neck harness in competition for most of the year and in Tokyo, six days before the competition, he tore cartilages in his lower rib cage. With his ribs heavily taped and his right side packed in ice as a safeguard against internal haemorrhaging he was advised by doctors not to throw and he did think of withdrawing, but that intense competitive spirit of his won the argument going on his mind.

Oerter was hoping that he could unleash a winning effort with his first throw, realising it could also be his last, but it went only 57.65. "It felt like somebody was trying to tear out my ribs", he noted. The early leader was Czechoslovakia's Ludvik Danek, the world record holder at 64.54. He opened with 59.73 and improved to 60.52 in the fourth round, whereas Oerter's best was 58.34 with his second throw and after four rounds he was in third place. But, despite the pain, Oerter wasn't ready to give in. "These are the Olympics," he said. "You die for them". In the fifth round he decided to use a slower spin and a higher trajectory ... and the throw landed at an Olympic record of 61.00, Danek could make no effective response and Oerter had pulled it off again!

His first triumph in Melbourne had come as a complete surprise. Aged only 20 he threw a personal best and Olympic record of 56.36 in the first round. Four years later in Rome he again summoned up a timely lifetime best and Olympic record (59.18), this time in the fifth round, to lead another American clean sweep of the medals. By winning a third consecutive Olympic title in Tokyo, Oerter equalled the achievement of fellow discus thrower Martin Sheridan (1904/1906/1908), hammer thrower John Flanagan (1900/1904/1908) and javelin thrower Eric Lemming (1906/1908/1912) ... and there was more to come, as we shall discover in the next chapter covering the 1968 Games in Mexico City.

Great Britons

THE LAST time prior to Tokyo that British athletes won as many as four titles at a single Olympics was way back in 1920 when Albert Hill completed the 800m/1500m double, Percy Hodge took the steeplechase and the 4x400m team came home first. Those Games in Antwerp were supported by just 29 countries; in 1964 there were 93 countries competing. For Britain to gain more golds than anyone other than the USA (14) and the USSR (5) was a momentous achievement. Here, in chronological order, is how the four titles were won:

October 14: Mary Rand (long jump)

Four years previously, in Rome, Mary Bignal had finished only ninth in a long jump competition she had been capable of winning. This time, Mary Rand (now the wife of international sculler Sidney Rand and mother of a two year-old daughter) fulfilled the highest of expectations by achieving the ultimate in athletic endeavour ... winning an Olympic title with a world record.

After leading the qualifiers with an Olympic record of 6.52, the 24 year-old (born at Wells, Somerset, on February 10 1940) got down to serious business in the final. She opened with a UK record of 6.59 (+ 1.4m wind), consolidated with leaps of 6.56 and 6.57 into the swirling wind, improved to 6.63 (+1.2) and then, in the fifth round, produced an extraordinary jump of 6.76. It was a performance ahead of its time, for there was a headwind of 1.6m blowing at the time and the clay runway was rainsoaked. Off a synthetic surface and with that amount of wind in her favour it's possible she would have jumped very close to seven metres – the sort of distance that would not be attained for another dozen years. Rand completed her series with a 6.61, again into the wind, to become the first British woman athlete ever to win an Olympic title.

Tatyana Shchelkanova (USSR), expected to be Rand's main rival, was well below her best with 6.42 in third place; the silver went instead to the lanky 18 year-old Polish sprinter, Irena Kirszenstein, who had only taken up long jumping the previous season and improved in Tokyo from 6.39 to a world junior record of 6.60. Later, as Irena Szewinska she would make Olympic history herself.

In the pentathlon, which started two days later, Rand again competed brilliantly to become only the second woman ever to exceed 5000 points. She totalled 5035 and finished ahead of Irina Press in three of the five events. However, she lost so many points to Press in the shot – no fewer than 384 – that the Russian ran out the winner 211 points clear with a record breaking score of 5246. Mary

Peters, whose own golden moments were still eight years in the future, placed fourth. Rand, who was coached by John Le Masurier, completed a set of medals by winning a bronze in the 4x100m relay.

October 15: Ken Matthews (20k walk)

Like Mary Rand, Chris Brasher and Don Thompson, Ken Matthews succeeded in striking Olympic gold at the second attempt. He had been among the favourites in Rome but fell victim to a combination of the after effects of flu, his own ruthless pace and the searing heat. He led for 8k and was second at 10k before collapsing and being taken to hospital. Victory went to the USSR's Vladimir Golubnichiy in 1:34:08.

During the next few years Matthews won all the major titles open to him: he scored individual victories in the 1961 and 1963 editions of the Lugano Cup (the world walking team championship) and became European champion in 1962. Apart from a judge's warning early in the race, he encountered no problems in Tokyo. Matthews forged ahead to reach the 5k checkpoint in 22:19 and inflicted great damage on the rest of the field by covering the second 5k in 22:04. At 10k (44:23) he held a 24 sec advantage over Germany's Dieter Lindner with defending champion Golubnichiy another four seconds in arrears. Although Matthews was slower over the second half of the journey he increased his lead and at the finish (Olympic record of 1:29:34) his margin over Lindner was 1 min 40 sec. Matthews, born in Birmingham on June 21 1934, promptly retired from competition.

October 18: Lynn Davies (long jump)

Welshman Lynn Davies (born at Nantymoel, near Bridgend, on May 20 1942) was asked towards the end of 1963 about his long jumping ambitions, his personal best at the time being 25' 4" or 7.72. His aim for 1964, he replied, was a jump of 26' 4" (8.03), "which should place me in the final six in Tokyo". His all-time goal was "to win an Olympic medal in Mexico City" in 1968. However, so quickly did he develop in 1964 under coach Ron Pickering that he wildly exceeded those aims.

Stronger and faster (9.5 for 100 yards) than ever before, and technically much more proficient now that he was using a two-and-a-half hitchkick, Davies reached the eight metre mark for the first time in May 1964 and improved the UK record to 8.02 in July. Defending champion Ralph Boston, who had raised the world record to 8.34 (plus a wind assisted 8.49) at the US Trials, started as favourite, with the USSR's Igor Ter-Ovanesyan, a previous world record holder at 8.31 and credited in 1964 with 8.18, considered the man most likely to upset Boston.

Davies' Olympic challenge came perilously close to ending in the qualifying round. Needing 7.60 to automatically reach the final, he opened with 7.39 and followed with a foul. All depended on his last attempt ... happily, he jumped 7.78 and the crisis was over.

Conditions for the final later in the day were deplorable: the runway was covered with puddles, the wind blew against the jumpers and the temperature was a chilly 13 deg. Not surprisingly the length of the jumps was adversely affected and after four rounds Boston led with 7.88 from Ter-Ovanesyan (7.80) and Davies (7.78). The bronze medal was as good as his but Davies sensed he could win the coveted gold medal. All too accustomed to such weather, he knew he was being unsettled by the damp and dismal conditions to a lesser degree than his opponents. He put his whole body and soul into the fifth jump and, generating a combination of speed, spring, strength and technique that would have spelt 27 feet (8.23) in more reasonable circumstances, he cut the sand at 8.07. Incredibly, in spite of the adverse breeze, the state of the runway and the pressure of an Olympic final, he had managed to jump further than ever before. "The suspense was agony", he admitted, as his rivals took their remaining attempts. Ter-Ovanesyan replied with a fifth-round 7.99 to move into second place, but in the final round Boston — landing heart-stoppingly close to Davies' mark — recaptured second position with 8.03. For the first time in Olympic athletics history, Wales could hail an individual event winner. The remarkably youthful-looking Davies is currently President of the governing body, UK Athletics.

October 20: Ann Packer (800m)

Just in time, Ann Packer discovered her best event. Whereas Fanny Blankers-Koen began her career at 800m and found fame as a sprinter, hurdler and jumper, Packer started as a sprinter, hurdler and jumper and found fame at 800m. And whereas the Dutchwoman was 30 when she achieved Olympic immortality and continued in serious competition for a further eight years, the British athlete (born at Moulsford, Berkshire, on March 8 1942) decided to retire immediately after her Olympic success aged only 22.

She could look back upon an extraordinarily varied career. She won the 100 yards title at the 1959 English Schools Championships, took the WAAA long jump in 1960, unexpectedly reached the 200m final at the 1962 European Championships and later that year placed sixth in the Commonwealth Games 80m hurdles and won a silver medal in the relay. In 1963 she moved up to 400m and swiftly burst into world class with 53.4. Finally, in 1964, she took up the 800m – with astonishing results.

She travelled to Tokyo with only five two-lap races behind her, her best time being 2:05.3. Her main objective was to win the 400m and she came so very close, clocking a European record of 52.2 (52.20) but having to settle for the silver as Betty Cuthbert, who won the sprint double at the 1956 Games, held off her opponent in 52.0 (52.01). Packer might have reduced her chances by running faster than necessary in the preliminaries: she recorded 53.1 winning her heat, while Cuthbert finished third in 56.0 in hers; in the semis Packer won in 52.7 (52.77) as Cuthbert conserved further energy with 53.8 behind her.

Packer took a leaf out of Cuthbert's book in the 800m. She was content to place fifth (2:12.6) in a heat won by Frenchwoman Maryvonne Dupureur in 2:04.5. Dupureur ran another fast race (2:04.1) in her semi, while Packer virtually jogged home third in hers in 2:06.0.

Although on paper Packer was the slowest of the eight finalists, and most accounts claim she was given no chance of winning, a glance at the forecast in Athletics Weekly for October 10 1964 reveals that Dixie Willis, the Australian who held the official world record of 2:01.2, was picked for first, Ann Packer for second,

Maryvonne Dupureur for third and Marise Chamberlain (New Zealand) for fourth. Modesty forbids revealing the identity of the prognosticator in question, but as Willis was ill and never competed in Tokyo his tip to win therefore became Packer.

Racing the distance for the eighth and last time in her life, Packer – advised by Denis Watts and inspired by her fiancé Robbie Brightwell – was sixth at the bell in 59.1, just a couple of strides behind the leader, Dupureur (58.6); she was in third place at 600m and second around the final turn. The French runner was still five metres ahead entering the final straight but as she began to flag so Packer's stride lengthened and her spirits soared. She passed her opponent without encountering any resistance and, with a beatific smile on her face, Packer broke the tape five metres clear of Dupureur, with Chamberlain third. Her time: a world record 2:01.1. "It was so easy, I couldn't believe I had won," said Ann Packer, who became Mrs Brightwell a couple of months later and, explaining her immediate retirement, said "running a home is more important than running races".

1964 - TOKYO

100m: (1.1) 1, Bob Hayes USA 10.0/10.06 (eq world rec; 9.91w sf); 2, Enrique Figuerola CUB 10.25; 3, Harry Jerome CAN 10.27; 4, Wieslaw Maniak POL 10.42 (10.15w sf); 5, Heinz Schumann GER 10.46; eq6, Gaoussou Kone CIV & Mel Pender USA 10.47; 8, Tom Robinson BAH 10.57.

200m: (-0.7) 1, Henry Carr USA 20.3/20.36; 2, Paul Drayton USA 20.58; 3, Ed Roberts TRI 20.63; 4, Harry Jerome CAN 20.79; 5, Livio Berruti ITA 20.83; 6, Marian Foik POL 20.83; 7, Dick Stebbins USA 20.89; 8, Sergio Ottolina ITA 20.94.

400m: 1, Mike Larrabee USA 45.1/45.15; 2, Wendell Mottley TRI 45.24; 3, Andrzej Badenski POL 45.64; 4, Robbie Brightwell GBR 45.75; 5, Ulis Williams USA 46.01; 6, Tim Graham GBR 46.08; 7, Peter Vassella AUS 46.32; 8, Edwin Skinner TRI 46.8 (hand).

800m: 1, Peter Snell NZL 1:45.1; 2, Bill Crothers CAN 1:45.6; 3, Wilson Kiprugut KEN 1:45.9; 4, George Kerr JAM 1:45.9; 5, Tom Farrell USA 1:46.6; 6, Jerry Siebert USA 1:47.0; 7, Dieter Bogatzki GER 1:47.2; 8, Jacques Pennewaert BEL 1:50.5.

1500m: 1, Peter Snell NZL 3:38.1; 2, Josef Odlozil TCH 3:39.6 (3:39.3 sf); 3, John Davies

NZL 3:39.6; 4, Alan Simpson GBR 3:39.7; 5, Dyrol Burleson USA 3:40.0; 6, Witold Baran POL 3:40.3 (3:38.9 sf); 7, Michel Bernard FRA 3:41.2; 8, John Whetton GBR 3:42.4.

5000m: I, Bob Schul USA 13:48.8; 2, Harald Norpoth GER 13:49.6; 3, Bill Dellinger USA 13:49.8; 4, Michel Jazy FRA 13:49.8; 5, Kip Keino KEN 13:50.4 (13:49.6 ht); 6, Bill Baillie NZL 13:51.0; 7, Nikolay Dutov URS 13:53.8; 8, Thor Helland NOR 13:57.0; 9, Ron Clarke AUS 13:58.0 (13:48.4 ht).

10,000m: I, Billy Mills USA 28:24.4; 2, Mohamed Gammoudi TUN 28:24.8; 3, Ron Clarke AUS 28:25.8; 4, Mamo Wolde ETH 28:31.8; 5, Leonid Ivanov URS 28:53.2; 6, Kokichi Tsuburaya JPN 28:59.4; 7, Murray Halberg NZL 29:10.8; 8, Tony Cook AUS 29:15.8.

Marathon: I, Abebe Bikila ETH 2:12:12 (world best); 2, Basil Heatley GBR 2:16:20; 3, Kokichi Tsuburaya JPN 2:16:23; 4, Brian Kilby GBR 2:17:03; 5, József Sütö HUN 2:17:56; 6, Leonard "Buddy" Edelen USA 2:18:13; 7, Aurele Vandendriessche BEL 2:18:43; 8, Kenji Kimihara JPN 2:19:49.

3000mSC: I, Gaston Roelants BEL 8:30.8; 2, Maurice Herriott GBR 8:32.4; 3, Ivan Belyayev URS 8:33.8; 4, Manuel de Oliveira POR 8:36.2; 5, George Young USA 8:38.2; 6, Guy Texereau FRA 8:38.6; 7, Adolfas Aleksiejunas URS 8:39.0 (8:31.8 ht); 8, Lars-Erik Gustafsson SWE 8:41.8.

110mH: (2.0) I, Hayes Jones USA 13.6/13.67; 2, Blaine Lindgren USA 13.74; 3, Anatoliy Mikhailov URS 13.78; 4, Eddy Ottoz ITA 13.84; 5, Gurbachan Singh IND 14.09; 6, Marcel Duriez FRA 14.09; 7, Giovanni Cornacchia ITA 14.12; 8, Giorgio Mazza ITA 14.17.

400mH: I, Warren "Rex" Cawley USA 49.6; 2, John Cooper GBR 50.1; 3, Salvatore Morale ITA 50.1; 4, Gary Knoke AUS 50.4; 5, James Luck USA 50.5; 6, Roberto Frinolli ITA 50.7; 7, Vasiliy Anisimov URS 51.1; 8, Wilfried Geeroms BEL 51.4.

4x100m Relay: I, USA (Paul Drayton, Gerry Ashworth, Dick Stebbins, Bob Hayes) 39.0/39.06 (world rec); 2, Poland (Andrzej Zielinski, Wieslaw Maniak, Marian Foik, Marian Dudziak) 39.36; 3, France (Paul Genevay, Bernard Laidebeur, Claude Piquemal, Jocelyn Delecour) 39.36; 4, Jamaica 39.49; 5, USSR 39.50; 6, Venezuela 39.53; 7, Italy 39.54; 8, Great Britain 39.69.

4x400m Relay: I, USA (Ollan Cassell 46.0,

Mike Larrabee 44.8, Ulis Williams 45.4, Henry Carr 44.5) 3:00.7 (world rec); 2, Great Britain (Tim Graham 45.9, Adrian Metcalfe 45.5, John Cooper 45.4, Robbie Brightwell 44.8) 3:01.6; 3, Trinidad (Edwin Skinner 46.0, Kent Bernard 45.3, Ed Roberts 45.4, Wendell Mottley 45.0) 3:01.7; 4, Jamaica 3:02.3; 5, Germany 3:04.3; 6, Poland 3:05.3; 7, USSR 3:05.9; 8, France 3:07.4.

HJ: I, Valeriy Brumel URS 2.18; 2, John Thomas USA 2.18; 3, John Rambo USA 2.16; 4, Stig Pettersson SWE 2.14; 5, Robert Shavlakadze URS 2.14; eq6, Ralf Drecoll GER & Kjell-Ake Nilsson SWE 2.09; 8, Ed Caruthers USA 2.09.

PV: I, Fred Hansen USA 5.10; 2, Wolfgang Reinhardt GER 5.05; 3, Klaus Lehnertz GER 5.00; 4, Manfred Preussger GER (GDR) 5.00; 5, Gennady Bliznyetsov URS 4.95; 6, Rudolf Tomasek TCH 4.90; 7, Pentti Nikula FIN 4.90; 8, Billy Pemelton USA 4.80.

LJ: I, Lynn Davies GBR 8.07; 2, Ralph Boston USA 8.03; 3, Igor Ter-Ovanesyan URS 7.99; 4, Wariboko West NGR 7.60; 5, Jean Cochard FRA 7.44; 6, Luis Felipe Areta ESP 7.34; 7, Mike Ahey GHA 7.30; 8, Andrzej Stalmach POL 7.26.

TJ: I, Józef Schmidt POL 16.85; 2, Oleg Fyedoseyev URS 16.58; 3, Viktor Kravchenko URS 16.57; 4, Fred Alsop GBR 16.46; 5, Serban Ciochina ROM 16.23; 6, Manfred Hinze GER (GDR) 16.15; 7, Georgi Stoikovski BUL 16.10; 8, Hans-Jürgen Rückborn GER (GDR) 16.09.

SP: I, Dallas Long USA 20.33; 2, Randy Matson USA 20.20; 3, Vilmos Varju HUN 19.39; 4, Parry O'Brien USA 19.20; 5, Zsigmond Nagy HUN 18.88; 6, Nikolay Karasyov URS 18.86; 7, Les Mills NZL 18.52; 8, Adolfas Varanauskas URS 18.41.

DT: I, Al Oerter USA 61.00; 2, Ludvik Danek TCH 60.52; 3, Dave Weill USA 59.49; 4, Jay Silvester USA 59.09; 5, József Szécsényi HUN 57.23; 6, Zenon Begier POL 57.06; 7, Edmund Platkowski POL 55.81; 8, Vladimir Trusenyov URS 54.78.

HT: I, Romuald Klim URS 69.74; 2, Gyula Zsivótzky HUN 69.09; 3, Uwe Beyer GER 68.09; 4, Yuriy Nikulin URS 67.69; 5, Yuriy Bakarinov URS 66.72; 6, Hal Connolly USA 66.65; 7, Ed Burke USA 65.66; 8, Olgierd Cieply POL 64.83.

JT: I, Pauli Nevala FIN 82.66; 2, Gergely Kulcsar HUN 82.32; 3, Janis Lusis URS 80.57; 4, Janusz Sidlo POL 80.17; 5, Urs von Wartburg SUI 78.72; 6, Jorma Kinnunen FIN 76.94; 7, Rolf Herings GER 74.72; 8, Vladimir Kuznyetsov URS 74.26.

Dec: I, Willi Holdorf GER 7887 (7726 on present tables) (10.7, 7.00, 14.95, 1.84, 48.2, 15.0, 46.05, 4.20, 57.37, 4:34.3); 2, Rein Aun URS 7842 (7677); 3, Hans-Joachim Walde GER 7809 (7666); 4, Paul Herman USA 7787 (7651); 5, Yang Chuan-kwang TAI 7650 (7539); 6, Horst Beyer GER 7647 (7488); 7, Vasiliy Kuznyetsov URS 7569 (7454); 8, Mikhail Storozhenko URS 7464 (7307).

20k Walk: I, Ken Matthews GBR 1:29:34; 2, Dieter Lindner GER (GDR) 1:31:14; 3, Vladimir Golubnichiy URS 1:32:00; 4, Noel Freeman AUS 1:32:07; 5, Gennadiy Solodov URS 1:32:33; 6, Ron Zinn USA 1:32:43; 7, Boris Khrolovich URS 1:32:46; 8, John Edgington GBR 1:32:46.

50k Walk: I, Abdon Pamich ITA 4:11:13 (world best); 2, Paul Nihill GBR 4:11:32; 3, Ingvar Pettersson SWE 4:14:18; 4, Burkhard Leuschke GER (GDR) 4:15:27; 5, Bob Gardiner AUS 4:17:07; 6, Christoph Hohne GER (GDR) 4:17:42; 7, Anatoliy Vedyakov URS 4:19:56; 8, Kurt Sakowski GER (GDR) 4:20:31.

Women's Events

100m: (-1.2) I, Wyomia Tyus USA 11.4/11.49 (11.2/11.23 heat, eq world rec); 2, Edith McGuire USA 11.62 (11.47 ht); 3, Ewa Klobukowska POL 11.64 (11.42 sf); 4, Marilyn White USA 11.67; 5, Miguelina Cobian CUB 11.72; 6, Marilyn Black AUS 11.73; 7, Halina Gorecka POL 11.83; 8, Dorothy Hyman GBR 11.90.

200m: (0.8) I, Edith McGuire USA 23.0/23.05; 2, Irena Kirszenstein POL 23.13; 3, Marilyn Black AUS 23.18; 4, Una Morris JAM 23.58; 5, Lyudmila Samotyosova URS 23.59; 6, Barbara Sobotta (née Janiszewska) POL 23.97; 7, Janet Simpson GBR 23.98; 8, Daphne Arden GBR 24.01.

400m: I, Betty Cuthbert AUS 52.0/52.01; 2, Ann Packer GBR 52.20; 3, Judy Amoore AUS 53.4 (53.39 sf); 4, Antonia Munkácsi HUN 54.4; 5, Maria Itkina URS 54.6; 6, Tilly van der Zwaard NED 55.2; 7, Gertrud Schmidt GER (GDR) 55.4; 8, Evelyne Lebret FRA 55.5.

800m: I, Ann Packer GBR 2:01.1 (world rec); 2, Maryvonne Dupureur FRA 2:01.9; 3, Marise Chamberlain NZL 2:02.8; 4, Zsuzsa Szabó HUN 2:03.5; 5, Antje Gleichfeld GER 2:03.9; 6, Laine Erik URS 2:05.1; 7, Gerda Kraan NED 2:05.8; 8, Anne Smith GBR 2:05.8.

80mH: (2.3) I, Karin Balzer GER (GDR) 10.5/10.54w; 2, Teresa Ciepla POL 10.55; 3, Pam Kilborn AUS 10.56; 4, Irina Press URS 10.62; 5, Ikuko Yoda JPN 10.72; 6, Maria Piatkowska POL 10.76; 7, Draga Stamejcic YUG 10.86; 8, Rosie Bonds USA 10.88.

4x100m Relay: I, Poland (Teresa Ciepla, Irena Kirszenstein, Halina Gorecka (née Richter), Ewa Klobukowska) 43.6/43.69 (world rec but later deleted by IAAF as Klobukowska failed chromosome test in 1967); 2, USA (Willye White, Wyomia Tyus, Marilyn White, Edith McGuire) 43.9/43.92 (world rec); 3, Great Britain (Janet Simpson, Mary Rand (née Bignal), Daphne Arden, Dorothy Hyman) 44.0/44.09; 4, USSR 44.4/44.44; 5, Germany 44.7; 6, Australia 45.0; 7, Hungary 45.2; 8, France 46.1.

HJ: I, Iolanda Balas ROM 1.90; 2, Michele Brown (née Mason) AUS 1.80; 3, Taisiya Chenchik URS 1.78; 4, Aida dos Santos BRA 1.74; 5, Dianne Gerace CAN 1.71; 6, Frances Slaap GBR 1.71; 7, Olga Pulic YUG 1.71; 8, Eleanor Montgomery USA 1.71.

LJ: I, Mary Rand (née Bignal) GBR 6.76 (world rec); 2, Irena Kirszenstein POL 6.60; 3, Tatyana Shchelkanova URS 6.42; 4, Ingrid Becker GER 6.40; 5, Viorica Viscopoleanu ROM 6.35; 6, Diana Yorgova BUL 6.24; 7, Hildrun Laufer (née Claus) GER (GDR) 6.24; 8, Helga Hoffmann GER 6.23 (6.44q).

SP: I, Tamara Press URS 18.14; 2, Renate Garisch GER (GDR) 17.61; 3, Galina Zybina URS 17.45; 4, Val Young (née Sloper) NZL 17.26; 5, Margitta Helmboldt GER (GDR) 16.91; 6, Irina Press URS 16.71; 7, Nancy McCredie CAN 15.89; 8, Ana Salagean ROM 15.83.

DT: I, Tamara Press URS 57.27; 2, Ingrid Lotz GER (GDR) 57.21; 3, Lia Manoliu ROM 56.97; 4, Virzhinia Mikhailova BUL 56.70; 5, Yevgenya Kuznyetsova URS 55.17; 6, Jolán Kleiber HUN 54.87; 7, Kriemhild Limberg (née Hausmann) GER 53.81; 8, Olimpia Catarama ROM 53.08.

JT: I, Mihaela Penes ROM 60.54; 2, Márta Rudas HUN 58.27; 3, Yelena Gorchakova URS 57.06 (62.40 qualifying, world rec); 4, Birute Kalediene URS 56.31; 5, Elvira Ozolina URS 54.81; 6, Maria Diaconescu ROM 53.71; 7, Hiroko Sato JPN 52.48; 8, Anneliese Gerhards GER 52.37.

Pen: I, Irina Press URS 5246 (world rec) (80mH-10.7, SP-17.16, HJ-1.63, LJ-6.24, 200m-24.7); 2, Mary Rand GBR 5035 (10.9, 11.05, 1.72, 6.55, 24.2); 3, Galina Bystrova URS 4956; 4, Mary Peters GBR 4797; 5, Draga Stamejcic YUG 4790; 6, Helga Hoffman GER 4737; 7, Pat Winslow USA 4724; 8, Ingrid Becker GER 4717.

MEXICO CITY 1968

EVEN AFTER all these many years the International Olympic Committee's irresponsibility in awarding the Games to Mexico City still rankles. There were world records galore in those events in which performances benefit from the thin air of the Mexican capital, which stands at 2248 metres (7347 feet), demoralising later generations of sprinters and long jumpers who competed without hope of matching such performances at or near sea level. Far more damaging, though, was the effect of the high altitude on the running events from 1500m upwards. Athletes from lowland countries, unless they had trained at altitude for a long period, had no chance of competing on anything approaching level terms against opponents who lived permanently at an elevation of several thousand feet.

Take the case of the Australian, Ron Clarke. He was far and away the greatest distance runner of that era, his numerous world records including 13:16.6 for 5000m and 27:39.4 for 10,000m whereas the next fastest ever runners at those distances as at 1968 were Kip Keino of Kenya with 13:24.2 and Jürgen Haase of the GDR with 28:04.4. Clarke, who ran 27:49.4 in very windy conditions in London on August 29, ran himself into oblivion in Mexico City on October 13 ... for a time of 29:44.8. The first lowlander to finish, in sixth place behind a Kenyan, an Ethiopian, a Tunisian (who trained almost exclusively in the mountains for the preceding two years), a Mexican and a Soviet runner based at altitude, Clarke was in a very bad way as he crossed the line.

As I reported at the time for Athletics Weekly: "The arena afterwards resembled a battlefield, with bodies sprawled all over the place. One in particular attracted the profound sympathy of all who care anything about athletics. The man on the stretcher, gasping for air until oxygen was administered, was Ron Clarke – his hopes shattered not so much by the opposition as by the folly of the men who, five years ago, glibly agreed to award these Games to an oxygen-starved city. He deserved a better fate". Clarke himself has said that his greatest frustration was not his failure to win an Olympic title "but the fact it was in Mexico City and I didn't have a chance to show if I could have won or not".

The Games were also controversial for other reasons. They opened uneasily in the wake of student riots at the University of Mexico City which were mercilessly put down by the authorities at the cost of numerous lives, while during the Games passions would be inflamed by "Black Power" demonstrations.

Even without the altitude factor, African runners would have made their best showing yet but with their inbuilt advantage the men from Kenya and Ethiopia, plus the aforementioned Tunisian (Mohamed Gammoudi), dominated the longer races. They won the 1500m, 5000m, 10,000m, marathon and steeplechase, with medal sweeps in the 5000m and 10,000m.

The distinction of becoming the first Kenyan gold medallist (and first black African to win an Olympic track title) fell to Naftali Temu in the 10,000m – a far cry from his Olympic baptism in Tokyo when, as a 19 year-old, he failed to finish in the 10,000m and placed 49th in the marathon in 2:40:47. He had gone on to score a brilliant 6 miles victory at the 1966 Commonwealth Games in Jamaica, knocking over a minute off his best time to finish well ahead of Clarke in 27:14.6 (equivalent to around 28:15 for 10,000m). In Mexico he clocked 29:27.40 to win narrowly from Mamo Wolde of Ethiopia with Gammoudi third. Britain's Ron Hill, running barefoot, excelled himself in the circumstances by placing seventh in 29:53.2 but there was little satisfaction, only frustration. As he

STAR OF THE GAMES

BOB BEAMON
(born 29 Aug 1946)

If there is one single performance in Olympic athletics history which will be remembered for ever it must surely be Bob Beamon's 8.90 leap in Mexico City. Admittedly the high altitude and maximum legal wind helped, but it remains as one of the greatest advances in measurable human achievement. It broke the previous world record by 55cm, while in the 35 years since the record has progressed by just 5cm.

THE HEIGHT OF FOLLY CONTINUED

wrote in his autobiography, The Long Hard Road: "There was a tremendous feeling of anti-climax, a sort of emptiness. I knew I had had a good run and yet seventh place meant nothing. People congratulated me, but I said seventh was no good; I felt it was a tragedy to have such a good performance, but there at altitude, where it could do nothing for me".

Temu wound up third in the 5000m behind Gammoudi (14:05.01) and fellow Kenyan Kip Keino, with Clarke fifth in 14:12.45. European record holder Harald Norpoth of the Federal Republic of Germany (for the first time at the Olympics there were separate teams from East and West Germany) dropped out after 3000m. Gammoudi, who produced a 54.8 last lap, had prepared thoroughly for the conditions and had run an outstanding 13:52.6 time trial at Font Romeu, high up in the French Pyrenees, a few weeks earlier.

Keino simply got better as the Games progressed. Third fastest of all-time with 28:06.4 that summer, Keino ran in the 10,000m and was with the leaders with just over a kilometre to go when he dropped out of the race suffering from stomach cramps. Two days later he won his 5000m heat, followed another two days after that by his silver medal in the final. Then, on successive days, he won his 1500m heat by a 30m margin, cruised home behind arch-rival Jim Ryun (USA) in the semis and took the title with one of the most astonishing runs in middle distance history.

Keino, whose best stood at 3:36.7, had never beaten Ryun, who at the time held world records for 880 yards (1:44.9), 1500m (3:33.1) and mile (3:51.1) and had not lost a race at either 1500m or mile for three years. The Kenyan knew the altitude factor would be in his favour but, on the other hand, Ryun would be fresh for this clash. In view of Ryun's legendary finishing speed (52.5 final quarter in his world record mile; 50.6 last 400m in a 3:38.2 1500m), Keino had resolved to neutralise the American's kick by setting a very fast pace. He was aided and abetted by team-mate Ben Jipcho, who hared around the first lap in 56.0. By 800m (1:55.3), with Keino ahead, Ryun was some 20m back. The margin widened to over 30m as Keino reached 1200m in 2:53.4. Keino finished in an astonishing 3:34.91, a time that intrinsically was superior to the world record and is still regarded in awe. Ryun narrowed the deficit on the last lap but the gap at the end was still wider than when

Herb Elliott won in Rome although Ryun surpassed his own expectations by clocking 3:37.89.

Keino would become Olympic steeplechase champion four years hence and the man he would succeed was another Kenyan, the unforgettable Amos Biwott. His best time of 8:44.8 (just 0.2 inside the qualifying standard) two months earlier did not rank him among the top 70 in the world that year but that did not inhibit him. He was over 60m ahead after the first lap of his heat, astonishing experienced observers by hurdling the entire water jump, and he went on to finish 70m clear in 8:49.4. In the final, Biwott – a schoolboy aged anything between 19 and 21, running maybe the sixth steeplechase of his life – ran much more cautiously. With two laps to go he was ninth and seemingly out of contact; at the bell he was sixth but still some 20m down. At the last hurdle it was fellow Kenyan Ben Kogo leading from American George Young (from high altitude Arizona) and Australian lowlander Kerry O'Brien, with Biwott now fourth, but on the run-in it was the novice who overtook everybody to snatch the title in 8:51.02. Asked why Biwott cleared the entire water jump, coach John Velzian suggested "if you've got only one pair of shoes in the world you don't want to get them wet".

Africa's remaining gold medal came in the marathon which, for the third time running, went to an Ethiopian. This time Abebe Bikila was forced to drop out injured after 17k but was succeeded by 36 year-old Mamo Wolde, who pulled away from his 10,000m conqueror Temu after 30k for victory in 2:20:27, the Kenyan blowing up and finishing 19th. Kenji Kimihara of Japan was second, with Scottish-born New Zealander Mike Ryan third. For Wolde it was a glorious finale (or was it?) to a long and amazingly varied Olympic career. He had competed in Melbourne in 1956, finishing last in his 800m and 1500m heats and even competing on the 4x400m relay team; he missed the 1960 Games but in 1964 was fourth in the 10,000m and a non-finisher in the marathon. This time he came away with gold and silver medals.

The rarefied air, the first synthetic track to be used for an Olympics and some suspicious wind readings all contributed to a flood of world records, several of which stood for many years. First and foremost, Bob Beamon (see page 100) long jumped 8.90 – which survived

HISTORY OF THE OLYMPIC GAM

as the world record until 1991. The USA's 4x400m relay time of 2:56.16 stood for 24 years; the 43.86 400m by Lee Evans was not surpassed until 1988. The other world records set by Americans (who won 15 of the 36 events with Kenya and the USSR next best with three each) were Jim Hines's 9.95 100m, Tommie Smith's 19.83 200m, the 4x100m team's 38.24, Wyomia Tyus's 11.08 100m and the women's sprint relay squad's 42.88.

David Hemery of Britain (see page 101) set new 400m hurdles figures of 48.12, three men broke the triple jump record with Viktor Saneyev of the USSR having the final word with a leap of 17.39, Irena Szewinska of Poland ran 22.58 for 200m and Romania's Viorica Viscopoleanu long jumped 6.82, while Australian Maureen Caird clocked 10.39 for 80m hurdles which was the best ever electrical time for that event (which was soon after replaced by 100m hurdles) but was never ratified. There was, in addition, a world record set in the 800m, where the advantages and disadvantages of altitude just about cancel each other out, by Australia's Ralph Doubell, whose time of 1:44.3 tied the listed mark, and shot put marks of 19.07 and 19.61 by Margitta Gummel of the GDR for a massive improvement on her previous record of 18.87.

Although electronic 1/100th second timing was used in every event, the times officially released were to a tenth of a second. Hines was credited with a world record equalling 9.9 in the 100m although the electronic timing registered 9.95, which in 1977 was ratified by the IAAF as the first such world record. Off to what he called the best start of his life, Hines emerged as the clear leader after 70m and had a metre to spare at the finish over Jamaican Lennox Miller. For the first time at an Olympics there were eight finalists in the shorter track events, and in the 100m none was white. Hines collected another gold medal and world record (38.24) in the sprint relay, taking over for the anchor leg in third place but storming through for victory over Cuba by nearly two metres with Jamaica, who had set the previous world record of 38.39 in a heat, third. That was the end of Hines' international track career although he was only 22; he became a footballer with the Miami Dolphins.

Tommie Smith, the 200m winner, also retired prematurely to play for the Cincinnati Bengals. He was the most gifted all-round male sprinter the world has seen, only Michael Johnson rivalling his exploits. In 1966 he set world records for 200m and 220 yards of 20.0 (turn) and 19.5 (straight track), ran a 43.8 400m relay leg and missed the world 100m record by just a tenth with 10.1. He accumulated further world records in 1967 with 44.5 for 400m and 44.8 for 440 yards. At the Olympics he captured the 200m title in a world record 19.83 (19.8) and would have been quicker still had he not flung up his arms in triumph a few metres before the finish. Barely two hours earlier he had suffered leg cramp while winning his semi in 20.14 and feared he might have to miss the final.

His biggest rival, John Carlos (who had beaten Smith, 19.92 to 20.18, in the US Olympic Trials at high altitude Echo Summit), led by more than a metre entering the finishing straight but Smith drew level with 50m to go. At that moment, Carlos glanced to his left to see how Smith was faring and that lapse in concentration cost him the silver. Peter Norman of Australia, who had set a fleeting Olympic record of 20.23 (20.2) in his heat and was only sixth at halfway, stormed along the straight to overhaul the American a few strides from the line to clock an inspired 20.06.

Norman, a Salvation Army officer, later shared the medal dais with Smith and Carlos when they staged a protest to highlight black Americans' struggle for civil rights. Smith and Carlos, each wearing one black glove, bowed their heads and thrust out a clenched fist in a black power gesture as the American anthem was played at the medal ceremony. The International Olympic Committee accused the pair of contravening one of the basic principles of the Olympic Games by using the ceremony "to advertise domestic political views" and the US Olympic Committee swiftly suspended them and expelled them from the Olympic Village.

Lee Evans, favourite for the 400m, learned on the day of his final that Smith and Carlos had been thrown off the team and was so shocked that he considered withdrawing in a show of solidarity. Wearing long black socks (as had Smith and Carlos) as a gesture of his support for the cause, Evans went ahead in pursuit of his athletic dream, and here is how he described his race: "I ran the first bend hard and then thought about

THE HEIGHT OF FOLLY CONTINUED

form and relaxation on the back stretch. After that I ran the second turn hard and mustered up some kind of kick or finish to hold on and win, which I did, though just barely". The time was a barrier-busting 43.86 (43.8) with Larry James just a metre back in 43.97, and Ron Freeman completing a US clean sweep. There had never been such a display of one-lap running: even in the first round of heats 15 men broke 46 sec, and Amadou Gakou of Senegal improved from a pre-Games best of 46.7 to an African record of 45.01 in the final, while Tanzania's Claver Kamanya progressed from 48.5 to 45.7.

IOC officials watched carefully as the three Americans participated in the victory ceremony. All wore black berets and raised their fists when introduced but during the anthem the usual proprieties were observed. They could not afford to behave otherwise if the USA were to field a 4x400m relay team. And what a team it was. Vince Matthews covered the first stage in 45.0 although unexpectedly he found himself three metres down on Kenya's Charles Asati (44.6). On the second leg Freeman produced the then fastest split in history – 43.2 – to open up a lead of over 15m. James added another ten metres or so with a 43.8 leg and Evans (44.1) brought the team home in a staggering 2:56.16 (2:56.1) to chop three and a half seconds off the previous world record. Kenya finished second in a time (2:59.6) which tied the old mark, while Britain's national record of 3:01.2, with David Hemery contributing the fastest leg of 44.6, sufficed only for fifth place.

There were world records also for American women sprinters. Barbara Ferrell tied the 100m record of 11.1 (actually 11.12) in her second-round heat, as did Poland's Irena Szewinska (née Kirszenstein) although her electronic time was 11.20, while in a rainsoaked final Wyomia Tyus was timed at 11.0/11.08 in becoming the first athlete to retain an Olympic 100m title. Silver medallist Ferrell, 17 year-old Margaret Bailes (who promptly retired after the Games), Mildrette Netter and Tyus combined to win the relay in a record 42.8/42.88, while Szewinska – aided by the maximum permissible wind of 2.0 metres per second in the straight – set new figures of 22.5/22.58 to win the 200m ahead of the Australians, Raelene Boyle (17) and Jennifer Lamy.

Australians did well in these Games,

despite the inevitable demise of Ron Clarke, for over and above the 200m medals by Boyle, Lamy and Peter Norman there were victories for Ralph Doubell and Maureen Caird.

Doubell, who won his 800m semi-final in a national record of 1:45.7, was up against a great front runner in Kenya's Wilson Kiprugut in the final and a classic race ensued. Kiprugut blazed through splits of 24.0 and 51.0, and was five metres clear at 600m (77.6). However, Doubell gradually pegged back his rival, passed him some 40m from the finish and held on grimly as the Kenyan remained tenaciously close. The time of 1:44.3 (1:44.40 electronic) tied Peter Snell's world record. Doubell, who had never broken 1:46 prior to the Games, thus became the first Aussie to lift the Olympic 800m crown since Edwin Flack (time of 2:11.0) back in 1896.

Favourite for the last edition of the Olympic 80m hurdles was 29 year-old Pam Kilborn, but it was her 17 year-old team-mate Maureen Caird, who had never previously beaten her, who took the title. Caird won by a clear half metre in 10.3, a tenth outside the world record although the electronic timing of 10.39 was the fastest ever. Chi Cheng of Taiwan, in third place, became the first Asian woman since 1928 to win a medal in any event. During 1969 and 1970 she was to set world records at 100 yards (10.0), 100m (11.0), 200m (22.4), 220 yards (22.6), 100m hurdles (12.8) and 200m hurdles (26.2) and win a staggering 153 competitions out of 154, the only loss being a disputed 100 yards verdict against Ferrell.

Apart from the 400m hurdles, won by David Hemery with John Sherwood third, Britain's most successful event in Mexico City was the women's 400m. Lillian Board (19), born in South Africa of British parents, ran splendidly to break Ann Packer's UK record with 52.1/52.12 but in the final few strides the French outsider, Colette Besson (who had run no faster than 53.8 before the Games), edged past for victory in a European record of 52.0/52.03, with Janet Simpson excelling herself with 52.5 in fourth place. At the European Championships the following year Board won the 800m title and turned the tables on Besson on the anchor leg of a nail-biting 4x400m relay. The most popular figure in British athletics at the time, she was shaping up as the woman most likely to win the 1972 Olympic 800m crown in Munich. But tragedy struck; she developed cancer and died, aged 22, on Boxing Day of 1970 in a clinic ... in Munich.

Britain's only other medallist was Sheila Sherwood, who long jumped a personal best of 6.68 to finish second to Viorica Viscopoleanu, a Romanian who leapt 6.82 to succeed Mary Rand as world record holder as well as Olympic champion. The latter was present at the Games as a television commentator, having been thwarted by injury in her bid to win selection for the pentathlon, but although her last remaining athletics ambition went unfulfilled she did witness a gold medal performance by her future husband, Bill Toomey. The American led the decathlon by 115 points after the first day, including a remarkable 45.6 400m, but an ordeal awaited him in the pole vault where he had two failures at his opening height of 3.60 before eventually equalling his best of 4.20 and proceeding to victory.

Talking of pole vault, that was the most closely contested event of the Games as three men cleared the winning height of 5.40, one centimetre under Bob Seagren's world record. To be accurate, four men did – but John Pennel (USA) had his clearance disallowed as his pole passed under the uprights, a rule which the IAAF had just decided to scrap but only with effect from May 1969. The Americans had won the pole vault at every Olympics (excluding the interim Games of 1906) since their revival in 1896, and Seagren kept that amazing streak alive ... if only just. "This kind of competition is like poker or Russian roulette: you have to gamble", said Seagren, and the first chance he took was entering the contest later than most of his main rivals with the bar at 5.05. The second was opting, alone among the seven still left in, to sit out the potentially vital height of 5.35 – although he later admitted he would not have done so had he realised what that was in feet and inches! At 5.40 he and the inspired Claus Schiprowski (whose pre-Olympic best was 5.18) went over at the second attempt, the FIFTH personal best clearance of the contest for the West German. Wolfgang Nordwig of East Germany cleared third time and with all three failing at 5.45 the title went to Seagren on countback.

American field eventers, with five wins out of eight in the men's events, would never again

be as successful. As well as Seagren and Beamon, world record holder Randy Matson won the shot title (20.54), Dick Fosbury created a sensation with his seemingly bizarre but undoubtedly effective new method of clearing a high jump bar (he flopped over 2.24 on this occasion), and Al Oerter proved himself the supreme Olympic competitor as he won his fourth discus gold medal. Competing in a different continent each time, he simply got better every four years with Olympic records of 56.36 in Melbourne, 59.18 in Rome, 61.00 in Tokyo and now 64.78 in Mexico City.

As in his three previous Olympic appearances, Oerter did not start as favourite based on that year's form. Yet again he would raise his game as others cracked under the pressure. This time the man in form was team-mate Jay

DID YOU KNOW?
WILLIE DAVENPORT, the 110m hurdles champion, competed as a bobsledder in the 1980 Winter Olympics ... Inger Miller (USA), world 200m champion in 1999, is the daughter of Jamaica's Lennox Miller, the 100m silver medallist in Mexico City ... Father of Jutta Stöck, 8th in the 200m, is Gerhard Stöck, Germany's 1936 Olympic javelin champion ... Klaus Beer, second to Bob Beamon in the long jump, has two children who became internationals: son Ron long jumped 8.23 in 1988 and daughter Peggy was heptathlon bronze medallist in the 1990 European Championships ... Other father/son combinations: Gyula Zsivótzky (1st hammer) and Attila Zsivóczky (8554 decathlon in 2000), Janis Lusis (1st javelin) and Voldemars (84.19 in 2003), Jorma Kinnunen (2nd javelin) and Kimmo (1991 world javelin champion), Eddy Ottoz (3rd 110m hurdles) and Laurent (world best 22.55 for 200m hurdles in 1995) ... Natalya Pechenkina (3rd in 400m) is the mother of Australia's 5.90 pole vaulter Viktor Chistiakov ... Giuseppe Gentile, who broke the world triple jump record but finished third, starred with Maria Callas in a film of Medea ... Lia Manoliu became at 36 the oldest women's champion to that time when winning the discus title at the fifth attempt after placing 6th in 1952, 9th in 1956, 3rd in 1960 and 3rd in 1964; she made a record sixth appearance in 1972, finishing 9th.

THE HEIGHT OF FOLLY

Silvester, who had raised the world record to 68.40 that year. By comparison, Oerter's lifetime best was 63.22. Even Oerter later confessed: "I didn't think I had a chance this time". An Olympic record of 63.34 in the qualifying round boosted Silvester's confidence but, not for the first time , he "choked" with the chips down in the final. Oerter started quietly but in the third round he produced a timely personal best of 64.78 which destroyed Silvester, who fouled three throws in a row and wound up fifth with 61.78. As Silvester once remarked: "When you throw against Oerter you don't expect to win; you just hope".

Oerter weighed 100kg (nearly 16 stones) at the time of his 1956 triumph, 114kg in 1960, 118kg in 1964 and 129kg (over 20 stones) in 1968, but he laid to rest any suspicions that anabolic steroids – which had infiltrated the sport in the previous few years – had anything to do with his increasing bodyweight and longer distances. "I just can't imagine going in for that kind of thing in order to win a sports competition. It surely shows the wrong kind of values. And it's counter-productive because it defeats the sense of accomplishment the athlete is looking for". Oerter announced his retirement after the 1969 season in order to spend more time with his two daughters. But it was not the end; he returned to competition in 1976, set a world veterans (40 and over) record of 62.52 the following year and in 1979 he improved upon his personal best with throws of 67.00 and 67.46. Another Olympics ("the ultimate physiological and psychological challenge") were on the horizon and in 1980 – aged 43 – he progressed still further to 69.46, ranking him second in the world that year. But the US boycott of the Moscow Games put paid to his dream ... although he was still in the running for an Olympic comeback in 1984 after throwing 67.90 in 1983. However, an achilles tendon strain kept him out of the Olympic trials. Even in his 50th year, and by then a grandfather, he threw beyond 62 metres!

The only contemporary who would seriously challenge Oerter's four successive victories in any event was triple jumper Viktor Saneyev, of the USSR. Oerter's last gold medal was won two days before Saneyev's first. The triple jump contest in Mexico City produced distances that bordered on the unimaginable for that era thanks to the altitude and benign wind readings, but it will always be remembered for its sheer excitement. The sensations started in the qualifying round when Józef Schmidt's venerated world record of 17.03, set in 1960, was obliterated by Giuseppe Gentile, who progressed all the way from 16.74 to 17.10 (nil wind). The Italian also struck the first blow in the final with a leap of 17.22 (nil wind), but he was replaced as leader in the third round when Saneyev, whose previous best was 16.87, soared out to 17.23 with the wind reading dead on the limit at 2.0m per second. But Saneyev himself was ousted in the fifth round when Nelson Prudencio of Brazil – who came to the Olympics with a best of 16.46 – landed at an amazing 17.27 with the gauge registering precisely 2.0m/sec. Going into the final round it was Prudencio from Saneyev, Gentile and Nikolay Dudkin (USSR), who also topped Schmidt's listed record with 17.09. The tension was tremendous; clearly anything could yet happen ... and did. Saneyev, from Georgia, rose to the occasion with a colossal leap of 17.39. The wind reading? Yes, you guessed. It was all over. Or was it? The American, Art Walker, back in 7th place with 16.77, got inspired too and landed at 17.12, didn't even come away with a medal. Even more galling was that from lift off to landing his estimated distance was 17.45. What a narrow dividing line it is between fame and obscurity at an Olympic Games.

Leap Of A Lifetime

THE LONG jump was one of the most keenly awaited events in Mexico City. For the first time, the "big four" would be clashing and lips were licked in anticipation at the prospect of Britain's defending champion Lynn Davies (best of 8.23) up against the joint holders of the world record at 8.35, Ralph Boston (USA) and Igor Ter-Ovanesyan (USSR), and the 1968 world leader Bob Beamon (USA), whose best was 8.33.

Of the four, Beamon was the most unpredictable, having a tendency to mess up his approach run, but also had the most potential. Both Boston, the 1960 champion, and Davies proved prophetic in assessing Beamon's possibilities. "Don't get him angry or he'll jump right out of the pit", remarked Boston, while the pride of Wales commented "it only needs Beamon to hit the board once, and we can all go home".

Just a few minutes into the competition and Davies's tongue in cheek observation was translated into reality, transforming his own dream of successfully defending the title into a nightmare. Beamon, utilising his great speed, had everything going for him as he flew down the runway. The thin air, a superb synthetic Tartan surface, a tailwind of precisely the maximum allowable for records (2m/sec), the advantage of being the first of the big guns to fire – all those factors, plus a once in a lifetime occasion when all the technical components fell into place to perfection, resulted in an astonishing performance.

It was such a mighty jump that Beamon's heels cut the sand beyond the new-fangled optical measuring device and a good old fashioned steel tape had to be brought into service. There were gasps of disbelief as the figures eventually went up on the board ... 8.90! For Beamon and other Americans (and Britons) the full impact of that achievement did not register until metric conversion tables had been consulted. Not only had he broken through the 28-foot barrier (8.35 equalled 27ft 5in), but he had leapt beyond 29 feet too with a measurement of 29ft 2.5in.

Like Jesse Owens in 1936 and Lynn Davies in 1964, Beamon had earlier experienced an uncomfortable time qualifying for the final. The standard was a derisory 7.65 but an over excited Beamon fouled his first two attempts before Boston calmed him down. Slowing his run and taking off with plenty to spare on the board he qualified safely with an 8.19 which ranked him second to Boston's own new Olympic record of 8.27.

Boston fancied his own chances of another Olympic victory but Beamon's awe-inspiring 8.90 put paid to those hopes before he even had a chance of opening his account in the final. He had been physically and psychologically prepared to jump over 28 feet (8.53), but knew he couldn't reach 29 feet. With the contest for the gold medal already over, even such normally competitive animals as Boston, Davies and Ter-Ovanesyan had the stuffing knocked out of them. They were not men content to be fighting for the lesser medals, which is why the silver

went to an athlete who had harboured no pretensions of winning: the East German, Klaus Beer, who produced a personal best of 8.19.

Boston salvaged the bronze with 8.16 and Ter-Ovanesyan, competing in his fourth Olympic final, jumped 8.12 for fourth, but Davies had a totally wretched time. The best of his three jumps of 7.94 placed him equal eighth and he should have been offered another three attempts, but the officials erred and by the time the mistake was acknowledged Davies had no wish to continue in the competition.

It took a while for Beamon to realise just what he had achieved when those figures of 8.90 flashed up. Dick Schaap, author of Beamon's biography The Perfect Jump, described the scene in graphic terms:"Suddenly, the enormity of what he had done sank in, and Beamon fell to his knees, leaned his head against the Tartan running track, almost as if he were kissing the ground, then clasped his head in his hands. Waves of nausea rolled over him, and his heart pounded as it had never pounded before, and he could see stars in front of his eyes. 'Tell me I am not dreaming,' he mumbled. 'It's not possible. I can't believe it. Tell me I am not dreaming.'"

That was no fantasy for the 22 year-old New Yorker, but for the rest of his athletics career he was chasing after moonbeams. After achieving the jump of a lifetime there was no more incentive. Although he continued to compete for a few more years he never again succeeded in jumping beyond 8.20. The magic had gone.

Record Smasher Hemery

THERE HAS been no more convincing British Olympic champion in history than David Hemery. What he achieved in the 400m hurdles final in Mexico City was the ultimate in athletic achievement. Not only did he win the race and smash the world record, but his domination over the opposition at such a level was quite extraordinary.

Born in Cirencester, Gloucestershire on July 18 1944, he moved with his family to the United States when he was 12, but returned to Britain for two years from 1962 after graduating from his high school in Massachusetts. In 1964 he entered Boston University and early in 1966 set European indoor records of 1:09.8 for

600 yards and 7.1 for 60 yards hurdles; outdoors he ran only a few quarter hurdles (52.8 in 1965, 51.8 in 1966) and concentrated on the "highs". He won the 1966 Commonwealth title and equalled the UK record of 13.9. Hamstring trouble caused him to miss the 1967 outdoor season but, discouraging as it was at the time, that enforced rest enabled him to undertake a gruelling non-stop 60-week build up for the Mexico City Olympics.

Coached in Boston by Billy Smith and in Britain by Fred Housden, he improved practically week by week so that in his final US race he won the National Collegiate title in 49.8 and he trimmed that to 49.6 in Britain. Although his three American opponents had faster times, with Geoff Vanderstock having achieved a world record 48.8 (48.94) in the US Trials at high altitude, Hemery sensed he was in with as good a chance as anyone.

Fastest in the heats was Ron Whitney (USA), who set a needless Olympic record of 49.0 (49.06), while the semi-finals saw seven men clocking between 49.1 and 49.3, both John Sherwood and Hemery running 49.3 (49.37) to break Hemery's UK record.

The line-up for the final was the greatest yet assembled in this event, but Hemery made his opponents look almost ordinary. Drawn in lane six, he blasted from the blocks and in practically no time had made up the stagger on Whitney, in seven. He whizzed along the back straight at breakneck speed, the hurdles hardly disturbing the graceful flow of his stride. He flashed past the 200m mark in an unheard of 23.0 and it became clear that he was either going to win the race by a street or he was going to die a dreadful death in the closing stages.

But it was when the going got toughest that Hemery's prodigious stamina training paid rich dividends. As coach Smith had reminded him: "There are a thousand hills and sand-dunes behind you and there isn't time for the others to catch up." He never flagged and the outcome was that he crossed the finish line at least seven metres clear of European record holder Gerhard Hennige. Or rather, ex-European record holder, for Hemery's staggering time of 48.12 (48.1) smashed the world record. Almost unnoticed, as all eyes were on Hemery's triumphal progression, John Sherwood (whose long jumping wife Sheila had finished second

the previous day) also ran the race of his life as he snatched the bronze medal in 49.03 (49.0). The last time Britain collected two medals in the same event was the 400m in 1924, and it was appropriate that the medals should be presented by the Marquess of Exeter, who as Lord Burghley won this very title in 1928.

"I had to start out fairly fast because Whitney has a very strong finish and I thought he would be the man to watch at the finish," Hemery explained. "John went out fast in the eighth lane, which helped me. At the sixth hurdle I changed from 13 to 15 strides and from there I had to push, though I tried to relax so I wouldn't tie up in the straight." Such was his tunnel vision during the race that at the finish he wasn't even sure he had won!

1968 - MEXICO CITY

100m: (0.3) 1, Jim Hines USA 9.95 (inaugural auto timing world rec); 2, Lennox Miller JAM 10.04; 3, Charlie Greene USA 10.07 (10.02 ht); 4, Pablo Montes CUB 10.14; 5, Roger Bambuck FRA 10.16; 6, Mel Pender USA 10.17; 7, Harry Jerome CAN 10.20; 8, Jean-Louis Ravelomanantsoa MAD 10.28.

200m: (0.9) 1, Tommie Smith USA 19.83 (inaugural auto timing world rec); 2, Peter Norman AUS 20.06; 3, John Carlos USA 20.10; 4, Ed Roberts TRI 20.34; 5, Roger Bambuck FRA 20.51; 6, Larry Questad USA 20.62; 7, Michael Fray JAM 20.63; 8, Joachim Eigenherr FRG 20.66.

400m: 1, Lee Evans USA 43.86 (inaugural auto timing world rec); 2, Larry James USA 43.97; 3, Ron Freeman USA 44.41; 4, Amadou Gakou SEN 45.01; 5, Martin Jellinghaus FRG 45.33; eq6, Tegegne Bezabeh ETH & Andrzej Badenski POL 45.42; 8, Amos Omolo UGA 47.61.

800m: 1, Ralph Doubell AUS 1:44.40 (ratified as 1:44.3, eq world rec); 2, Wilson Kiprugut KEN 1:44.57; 3, Tom Farrell USA 1:45.46; 4, Walter Adams FRG 1:45.83; 5, Josef Plachy TCH 1:45.99; 6, Dieter Fromm GDR 1:46.30; 7, Thomas Saisi KEN 1:47.59; 8, Benedict Cayenne TRI 1:54.40.

1500m: 1, Kip Keino KEN 3:34.91; 2, Jim Ryun USA 3:37.89; 3, Bodo Tümmler FRG 3:39.08; 4, Harald Norpoth FRG 3:42.57; 5, John Whetton GBR 3:43.90; 6, Jacques Boxberger FRA 3:46.65; 7, Henryk Szordykowski POL 3:46.69; 8, Josef Odlozil TCH 3:48.69.

5000m: 1, Mohamed Gammoudi TUN 14:05.01; 2, Kip Keino KEN 14:05.16; 3, Naftali Temu KEN 14:06.41; 4, Juan Martinez MEX 14:10.76; 5, Ron Clarke AUS 14:12.45; 6, Wohib Masresha ETH 14:17.70; 7, Nikolay Sviridov URS 14:18.40; 8, Fikru Deguefu ETH 14:18.98.

10,000m: 1, Naftali Temu KEN 29:27.40; 2, Mamo Wolde ETH 29:27.75; 3, Mohamed Gammoudi TUN 29:34.2; 4, Juan Martinez MEX 29:35.0; 5, Nikolay Sviridov URS 29:43.2; 6, Ron Clarke AUS 29:44.8; 7, Ron Hill GBR 29:53.2; 8, Wohib Masresha ETH 29:57.0.

Marathon: 1, Mamo Wolde ETH 2:20:27; 2, Kenji Kimihara JPN 2:23:31; 3, Mike Ryan NZL 2:23:45; 4, Ismail Akcay TUR 2:25:19; 5, Bill Adcocks GBR 2:25:33; 6, Gebru Merawi ETH 2:27:17; 7, Derek Clayton AUS 2:27:24; 8, Tim Johnston GBR 2:28:05.

3000mSC: 1, Amos Biwott KEN 8:51.02 (8:49.39 ht) ; 2, Ben Kogo KEN 8:51.56; 3, George Young USA 8:51.86; 4, Kerry O'Brien AUS 8:52.08; 5, Aleksandr Morozov URS 8:55.61; 6, Mikhail Zhelev BUL 8:58.41, 7, Gaston Roelants BEL 8:59.50; 8, Arne Risa NOR 9:08.98.

110mH: (nil wind) 1, Willie Davenport USA 13.33; 2, Ervin Hall USA 13.42; 3, Eddy Ottoz ITA 13.46; 4, Leon Coleman USA 13.67; 5, Werner Trzmiel FRG 13.68; 6, Bo Forssander SWE 13.73; 7, Marcel Duriez FRA 13.77; 8, Pierre Schoebel FRA 14.02.

400mH: 1, David Hemery GBR 48.12 (ratified as world rec of 48.1); 2, Gerhard Hennige FRG 49.02; 3, John Sherwood GBR 49.03; 4, Geoff Vanderstock USA 49.07; 5, Vyacheslav Skomorokhov URS 49.12; 6, Ron Whitney USA 49.27; 7, Rainer Schubert FRG 49.30; 8, Roberto Frinolli ITA 50.13.

4x100m Relay: 1, USA (Charlie Greene, Mel Pender, Ronnie Ray Smith, Jim Hines) 38.24 (ratified as world rec of 38.2); 2, Cuba (Hermes Ramirez, Juan Morales, Pablo Montes, Enrique Figuerola) 38.40; 3, France (Gerard Fenouil, Jocelyn Delecour, Claude Piquemal, Roger Bambuck) 38.43; 4, Jamaica 38.47 (38.39 semifinal, ratified as world rec of 38.3); 5, GDR 38.66; 6, FRG 38.76; 7, Italy 39.22; 8, Poland 39.22.

4x400m Relay: 1, USA (Vince Matthews 45.0, Ron Freeman 43.2, Larry James 43.8, Lee Evans 44.1) 2:56.16 (inaugural auto timing world rec); 2, Kenya (Charles Asati 44.6, Munyoro Nyamau 45.5, Naftali Bon 45.1, Daniel Rudisha 44.4) 2:59.64; 3, FRG (Helmar Müller 46.4, Gerhard Hennige 44.7, Manfred Kinder 44.7, Martin Jellinghaus 44.7) 3:00.57; 4, Poland 3:00.58; 5, Great Britain 3:01.21; 6, Trinidad 3:04.52; 7, Italy 3:04.64; 8, France 3:07.51.

HJ: 1, Dick Fosbury USA 2.24; 2, Ed Caruthers USA 2.22; 3, Valentin Gavrilov URS 2.20; 4, Valeriy Skvortsov URS 2.16; 5, Reynaldo Brown USA 2.14; 6, Giacomo Crosa ITA 2.14; 7, Gunther Spielvogel FRG 2.14; 8, Lawrie Peckham AUS 2.12.

PV: 1, Bob Seagren USA 5.40; 2, Claus Schiprowski FRG 5.40; 3, Wolfgang Nordwig GDR 5.40; 4, Christos Papanicolaou GRE 5.35; 5, John Pennel USA 5.35; 6, Gennadiy Bliznyetsov URS 5.30; 7, Herve D'Encausse FRA 5.25; 8, Heinfried Engel FRG 5.20.

LJ: 1, Bob Beamon USA 8.90 (world rec); 2, Klaus Beer GDR 8.19; 3, Ralph Boston USA 8.16 (8.27q); 4, Igor Ter-Ovanesyan URS 8.12; 5, Tonu Lepik URS 8.09; 6, Allen Crawley AUS 8.02; 7, Jack Pani FRA 7.97; 8, Andrzej Stalmach POL 7.94.

TJ: 1, Viktor Saneyev URS 17.39 (world rec); 2, Nelson Prudencio BRA 17.27; 3, Giuseppe Gentile ITA 17.22; 4, Art Walker USA 17.12w; 5, Nikolay Dudkin URS 17.09w; 6, Phil May AUS 17.02; 7, Józef Schmidt POL 16.89; 8, Mansour Dia SEN 16.73w

SP: 1, Randy Matson USA 20.54 (20.68q); 2, George Woods USA 20.12; 3, Eduard Gushchin URS 20.09; 4, Dieter Hoffmann GDR 20.00; 5, Dave Maggard USA 19.43; 6, Wladyslaw Komar POL 19.28; 7, Uwe Grabe GDR 19.03; 8, Heinfried Birlenbach FRG 18.80.

DT: 1, Al Oerter USA 64.78; 2, Lothar Milde GDR 63.08; 3, Ludvik Danek TCH 62.92; 4, Hartmut Losch GDR 62.12; 5, Jay Silvester USA 61.78; 6, Gary Carlsen USA 59.46; 7, Edmund Piatkowski POL 59.40; 8, Ricky Bruch SWE 59.28.

HT: 1, Gyula Zsivótzky HUN 73.36; 2, Romuald Klim URS 73.28; 3, Lázár Lovász HUN 69.78; 4, Takeo Sugawara JPN 69.78; 5, Sándor Eckschmidt HUN 69.46; 6, Gennadiy Kondrashov URS 69.08; 7, Reinhard Theimer GDR 68.84; 8, Helmut Baumann GDR 68.26.

JT: 1, Janis Lusis URS 90.10; 2, Jorma Kinnunen FIN 88.58; 3, Gergely Kulcsár HUN 87.06; 4, Wladyslaw Nikiciuk POL 85.70; 5, Manfred Stolle GDR 84.42; 6, Karl-Ake Nilsson SWE 83.48; 7, Janusz Sidlo POL 80.58; 8, Urs von

Wartburg SUI 80.56.

Dec: 1, Bill Toomey USA 8193 (8158 on present tables) (10.41, 7.87, 13.75, 1.95, 45.68, 14.95, 43.68, 4.20, 62.80, 4:57.18); 2, Hans-Joachim Walde FRG 8111 (8120); 3, Kurt Bendlin FRG 8064 (8096); 4, Nikolay Avilov URS 7909 (7884); 5, Joachim Kirst GDR 7861 (7791); 6, Tom Waddell USA 7720 (7694); 7, Rick Sloan USA 7692 (7553); 8, Steen Smidt-Jensen DEN 7648 (7507).

20k Walk: 1, Vladimir Golubnichiy URS 1:33:59; 2, Jose Pedraza MEX 1:34:00; 3, Nikolay Smaga URS 1:34:04; 4, Rudy Haluza USA 1:35.01; 5, Gerhard Sperling GDR 1:35:28; 6, Otto Bartsch URS 1:36.17; 7, Hans-Georg Reimann GDR 1:36:32; 8, Stefan Ingvarsson SWE 1:36:44.

50k Walk: 1, Christoph Höhne GDR 4:20:14; 2, Antal Kiss HUN 4:30:17; 3, Larry Young USA 4:31:56; 4, Peter Selzer GDR 4:33:10; 5, Stig-Erik Lindberg SWE 4:34:05; 6, Vittorio Visini ITA 4:36:34; 7, Brian Eley GBR 4:37:33; 8, José Pedraza MEX 4:37:52.

Women's Events

100m: (1.2) 1, Wyomia Tyus USA 11.08 (inaugural auto timing world rec); 2, Barbara Ferrell USA 11.15 (11.12 heat; eq ratified world rec of 11.1); 3, Irena Szewinska (née Kirszenstein) POL 11.19 (11.20 heat, eq ratified world rec of 11.1); 4, Raelene Boyle AUS 11.20; 5, Margaret Bailes USA 11.37; 6, Dianne Burge AUS 11.44; 7, Chi Cheng TAI 11.53; 8, Miguelina Cobian CUB 11.61.

200m: (2.0) 1, Irena Szewinska (née Kirszenstein) POL 22.58 (ratified as world rec of 22.5); 2, Raelene Boyle AUS 22.74; 3, Jennifer Lamy AUS 22.88; 4, Barbara Ferrell USA 22.93; 5, Nicole Montandon FRA 23.08; 6, Wyomia Tyus USA 23.08; 7, Margaret Bailes USA 23.18; 8, Jutta Stöck FRG 23.25.

400m: 1, Colette Besson FRA 52.03; 2, Lillian Board GBR 52.12; 3, Natalya Pechenkina URS 52.25; 4, Janet Simpson GBR 52.57; 5, Aurelia Pentón CUB 52.75; 6, Jarvis Scott USA 52.79; 7, Helga Henning FRG 52.89; 8, Myrna van der Hoeven NED 53.02.

800m: 1, Madeline Manning USA 2:00.92; 2, Ileana Silai ROM 2:02.58; 3, Maria Gommers NED 2:02.63; 4, Sheila Taylor GBR 2:03.81; 5, Doris Brown USA 2:03.98; 6, Pat Lowe GBR 2:04.25; 7, Abby Hoffman CAN 2:06.99; 8, Maryvonne Dupureur FRA 2:08.28.

80mH: (nil wind) 1, Maureen Caird AUS 10.39; 2, Pam Kilborn AUS 10.46 (10.41 ht); 3, Chi Cheng TAI 10.51; 4, Pat Van Wolvelaere USA 10.60; 5, Karin Balzer GDR 10.61; 6, Danuta Straszynska POL 10.66; 7, Elzbieta Zebrowska POL 10.66; 8, Tatyana Talysheva URS 10.72.

4 x100m Relay: 1, USA (Barbara Ferrell, Margaret Bailes, Mildrette Netter, Wyomia Tyus) 42.88 (ratified as world rec of 42.8; 43.4 heat, world rec; 43.50); 2, Cuba (Marlene Elejarde, Fulgencia Romay, Violetta Quesada, Miguelina Cobian) 43.36; 3, USSR (Lyudmila Zharkova, Galina Bukharina, Vyera Popkova, Lyudmila Samotysova) 43.41; 4, Netherlands 43.44 (43.4 heat, eq world rec; 43.49); 5, Australia 43.50; 6, FRG 43.70; 7, Great Britain 43.78; 8, France 44.30.

HJ: 1, Milena Rezková TCH 1.82; 2, Antonina Okorokova URS 1.80; 3, Valentina Kozyr URS 1.80; 4, Jaroslava Valentová TCH 1.78; 5, Rita Schmidt GDR 1.78; 6, Maria Faithová TCH 1.78; 7, Karin Schulze GDR 1.76; 8, Ilona Gusenbauer AUT 1.76.

LJ: 1, Viorica Viscopoleanu ROM 6.82 (world rec); 2, Sheila Sherwood GBR 6.68; 3, Tatyana Talysheva URS 6.66; 4, Burghild Wieczorek GDR 6.48; 5, Miroslawa Sarna POL 6.47; 6, Ingrid Becker FRG 6.43; 7, Berit Berthelsen NOR 6.40; 8, Heide Rosendahl FRG 6.40.

SP: 1, Margitta Gummel (née Helmboldt) GDR 19.61 (world rec); 2, Marita Lange GDR 18.78; 3, Nadezhda Chizhova URS 18.19; 4, Judit Bognár HUN 17.78; 5, Renate Boy (née Garisch) GDR 17.72; 6, Ivanka Khristova BUL 17.25; 7, Marlene Fuchs FRG 17.11; 8, Els van Noorduyn NED 16.23.

DT: 1, Lia Manoliu ROM 58.28; 2, Liesel Westermann FRG 57.76; 3, Jolán Kleiber HUN 54.90; 4, Anita Otto GDR 54.40; 5, Antonina Popova URS 53.42; 6, Olga Connolly (née Fikotová) USA 52.96; 7, Christine Spielberg GDR 52.86; 8, Brigitte Berendonk FRG 52.80.

JT: 1, Angéla Németh HUN 60.36; 2, Mihaela Penes ROM 59.92; 3, Eva Janko AUT 58.04; 4, Márta Rudas HUN 56.38; 5, Daniela Jaworska POL 56.06; 6, Natasa Urbancic YUG 55.42; 7, Ameli Koloska FRG 55.20; 8, Kaisa Launela FIN 53.96.

Pen: 1, Ingrid Becker FRG 5098 (10.95w, 11.48, 1.71, 6.43, 23.55); 2, Liese Prokop AUT 4966; 3, Annamaria Toth HUN 4959; 4, Valentina Tikhomirova URS 4927; 5, Marion Bornholdt FRG 4890; 6, Pat Winslow USA 4877; 7, Inge Bauer GDR 4849; 8, Meta Antenen SUI 4848.

THE ORGANISERS of the first Olympics to be staged in Germany since the Nazi-influenced festival of 1936 were hoping for a Games free of political influences. Their hopes were dashed. Pressurised by threats of a boycott by African nations, the IOC expelled the Rhodesian team, but that was of little consequence (except, it would seem, to the IOC president Avery Brundage) by comparison to the tragedy which befell the Israeli team on the eleventh day (September 5) of the Munich Games.

A squad of eight Palestinian terrorists, from the "Black September" movement, burst into the Israeli quarters in the supposedly security-tight Olympic Village and killed two members of the team and held nine others as hostages. That night helicopters lifted the terrorists and their captives to Fuerstenfeldbruck airport as the first step to being flown to an Arab country, but after police opened fire on the gang all of the Israeli hostages were murdered. It was the grimmest day in Olympic history – the day that the worst excesses of power politics invaded the cosy world of the Games.

While the terrifying drama was played out, the Games were put on hold. Officials agonised over whether they should be cancelled as a mark of respect to the slain; eventually – with the approval of what was left of the Israeli delegation – it was decided that the Games would resume following a memorial service in the main stadium. Alas, Avery Brundage, in almost his last appearance as IOC president (he was succeeded after the Games by Lord Killanin), managed to demean what was otherwise a sombre and moving occasion by using his address as an excuse for condemning what he termed the "naked political blackmail" of those countries which had been strongly opposed to Rhodesian participation. This observer got the impression that to Brundage that issue mattered more than the reason for the service. It was a disgraceful speech, and all too characteristic of a man of so little sensitivity.

Until the massacre, the Games had been setting new standards of excellence. Enthusiastic crowds packed the stadium each day (there were even 70,000-plus fans in place to watch the morning sessions of heats and qualifying rounds) and they were treated to world records by John Akii-Bua of Uganda in the 400m hurdles, Britain's Mary Peters (see page 110) in the pen-

tathlon, Lasse Viren of Finland (see page 111) in the 10,000m and Ulrike Meyfarth – who at 16 years and 123 days became the youngest ever individual champion – in the women's high jump.

There was a magical atmosphere in the stadium on that evening of September 4 as the West German schoolgirl flopped over 1.92 to equal the record and bring the first half of the athletics programme to a close. The terrible events of the next day would also bring to an end any last vestiges of the hope and belief that the Olympic Games were a refuge from the problems of the outside world. Other great performances did follow, with further world records in the 110m hurdles, decathlon, 4x100m relay, women's 200m, 1500m, shot and both relays, but the Olympic spell – the feeling that what was happening in the stadium was absolutely the most important thing going on in the world that moment – had forever been broken.

German athletes, from both the Democratic Republic (GDR) and the Federal Republic (FRG), performed magnificently to accumulate almost as many gold medals as the USA and USSR combined. The East Germans, subsequently discredited by evidence of systematic drug taking programmes, took eight titles and the West Germans six, as against nine by the Soviet athletes and just six by the Americans,

STAR OF THE GAMES

LASSE VIREN
(born 22 Jul 1949)

The great Finnish Olympic distance running tradition was revived after 36 years thanks to a 23 year-old policeman by the name of Lasse Viren. He produced an astounding run in the 10,000m when, despite falling over approaching halfway, he sprinted to victory in world record time. One week later, in the 5000m final, he covered the final four laps in four minutes to become the first Finn to complete that Olympic double since Hannes Kolehmainen in 1912.

who experienced their worst ever Games.

Vince Matthews won the 400m, Dave Wottle the 800m, Frank Shorter the marathon, Rod Milburn the 110m hurdles, Randy Williams the long jump and the 4×100m relay team struck gold, but otherwise it was a catalogue of disasters for the Americans.

It has long been a topic for heated debate as to whether Valeriy Borzov of the USSR would have won the 100m title had the two top Americans been up against him in the final. The majority of unbiased followers feel Borzov would have won anyway. After running 10.07 in a heat, the fastest electronic time of the year, the Ukrainian was such a clearcut winner of the final that he was able to fling up his arms in triumph before crossing the finish line with no need to dip and his time of 10.14 into a slight headwind was a full tenth of a second faster than runner-up Robert Taylor (USA). He reckoned he was operating at only 90% of capacity and declared to reporters: "I'm Olympic 100m champion. The circumstances surrounding the Americans were unfortunate, but all I can say is that I have beaten American sprinters six times out of six in the past".

What happened was that on the opening day Taylor, along with the two men who had tied the world hand-timed record of 9.9 ahead of him in the US Trials two months earlier, Eddie Hart and Rey Robinson, were watching TV at around 4.15 pm at the ABC building by the Olympic Village when pictures of a 100m heat came up. At first they assumed it was a recording from the first round that morning; but no, it was live coverage of the second round – in which they were due to be competing! They had been told by team coach Stan Wright that the races would not be until around 7 pm, but it transpired that he had been consulting a long out-of-date timetable. A car from ABC rushed them over to the stadium, but Hart and Robinson were too late. Taylor just made it in time and, without a proper warm up and with the loss of much nervous energy, he managed a remarkable 10.16 behind Borzov's 10.07 to proceed on his way.

Borzov proved his point that he was the world's top sprinter that year by completing the double, the only European man ever to do so. Second to the American, Larry Black, with 70m to run in the 200m final, he won by two metres

in the European record time of 20.00. Even he couldn't make up all the deficit he inherited on the anchor leg of the sprint relay and collected a silver medal as Black, Taylor, Gerald Tinker (Black's first cousin) and Hart scorched to victory in a world record 38.19.

The longer relay looked a good thing for the Americans too, but they never even managed to field a team. John Smith, now a successful coach and then holder of the world 440 yards record of 44.5, dropped out during the 400m final with a hamstring injury, but the USA still scored a one-two as Vince Matthews, nominally the American third string, triumphed in 44.66 ahead of Wayne Collett. However, for what was deemed "insulting behaviour" during the medal ceremony, Matthews and Collett were immediately banned by the IOC and thus ineligible for the relay. Their offence was that they talked and fidgeted while the Star Spangled Banner was being played, something Avery Brundage referred to a a "disgusting display" in a letter to the US Olympic Committee.

The athletes, both black, explained the incident from their point of view. "It's hard for Wayne or I to come to a thing like the Olympic Games and forget about the conditions we left at home," said Matthews. "It would be almost hypocritical on my part to stand erect and listen to something like this knowing my family had to go through so much." Collett added: "I think it's been six or seven years since I've stood at attention because the national anthem was playing. I just can't do it with a clear conscience, seeing the way things are in the country."

With only three of their six nominated relay runners available, the Americans had to scratch from an exciting race which was won by Kenya in 2:59.83. At the final exchange it was West Germany a couple of metres ahead of Poland with Kenya, France and Britain all close behind, but Germany's anchorman Karl Honz (the European record holder) went out too fast – 20.1 for his first 200m from a flying start – and crumpled in the finishing straight. Julius Sang, the individual bronze medallist in a Commonwealth record of 44.92, judged his effort to perfection to bring Kenya home first, his split being a spectacular 43.6, while European champion David Jenkins made up for his disappointment in failing to reach the 400m final by anchoring Britain to the silver medals in European record time with a 44.2 leg.

Another American disaster occurred in the 1500m, where Jim Ryun, the world record holder at 3:33.1, was hoping it would be a case of third time lucky at the Olympics. In Tokyo, as a 17 year-old prodigy, he had been drained by flu and failed to reach the final, while the effects of high altitude in Mexico City put paid to his gold medal chances although he did finish a brave if distant second to Kip Keino.

It was not to be. An official's error, failing to make clear that the 1972 best submitted on behalf of Ryun of 3:52.8 was a mile, not 1500m, time resulted in the American being unseeded and drawn against Keino in the heats. With four to proceed to the semis that was not in itself a problem but it was his misfortune to encounter a couple of inexperienced runners as he began to thread his way through from the back of the field and he was brought down with some 500m to go. He did scramble back into the race with the leaders some 80m ahead but he had no chance of qualifying, finishing ninth in 3:51.5 while fourth place went in 3:40.4.

In the final, Finland's Pekka Vasala produced a storming finish to outkick Keino in 3:36.33, covering the last 400m in 53.6 ... but one had to recall that Ryun, in his record 3:33.1, had covered the final 400m in 53.3, and had clocked 52.5 for the last quarter (equals 52.2 for 400m) in his record 3:51.1 mile. New Zealander Rod Dixon surpassed his own expectations by taking third place while another who would make more of a mark at longer distances, Brendan Foster, finished fifth after setting new British figures of 3:38.20 in his semi-final.

Six days earlier Keino, virtually a novice in the event and in his own words "jumping like a horse", had become Olympic steeplechase champion. Fastest in the heats was another Kenyan, defending champion Amos Biwott, in an Olympic record of 8:23.73, but it was a third Kenyan, Ben Jipcho, who proved to be Keino's main rival in the final. The early pace was slow (4:22.0 at halfway) but when Keino hit the front with over a lap to go the tempo quickened considerably and a 59.0 last lap carried him over the line six metres ahead of Jipcho (who became world record holder the following year) in a personal best of 8:23.64. He had covered the second half of the race in close to 4:01!

Another East African to strike gold was John Akii-Bua, who performed sensationally in the 400m hurdles. He had first attracted attention by finishing fourth in the 1970 Commonwealth Games and in 1971 had established himself as a possible medallist by winning in an Africa v USA match in 49.0, the world's second fastest time that year. The lanky 22 year-old Ugandan, a fine all-rounder who scored 6933 in his decathlon debut, trained hard under his British coach Malcolm Arnold (who, many years later, would guide Colin Jackson to stardom) and although prior to Munich in 1972 he didn't run faster than 49.4 in competition he knew from a 48.8 time trial that he was peaking at just the right time.

Akii-Bua, one of 43 children (his father took eight wives), clocked the fastest time of 49.25 in the semis but nevertheless was drawn in the tight inside lane for the final, a particular disadvantage for a man who hurdled with a right-leg lead. He certainly did not permit that to psyche him out, nor was he awestruck by the astonishing speed generated by defending champion, David Hemery. The Briton was even quicker at 200m (22.8) than he was in Mexico City, but Akii-Bua paced himself sensibly and early in the finishing straight he overtook Hemery and the USA's Ralph Mann. Moving further away with each powerful stride, Akii-Bua went on to win by some six metres in the startling time of 47.82, a full three-tenths faster than Hemery's celebrated world record ... and without the benefit of altitude. Mann pipped Hemery for second, 48.51 to 48.52.

Africans were overshadowed this time in the longer distance events, although Mohamed Gammoudi of Tunisia (the defending champion) and the new Ethiopian star Miruts Yifter picked up medals in the 5000m and 10,000m respectively behind Finland's all-conquering Lasse Viren. As for 40 year-old Mamo Wolde, the 1968 marathon champion, he recorded his fastest ever time of 2:15:09 to finish third.

The marathon winner was, for the first time since 1908, an American – although, by an extraordinary coincidence, Frank Shorter was actually born (of American parents) in Munich. His victory would have immense ramifications for road racing, for he helped inspire the phenomenal running and jogging boom which swept the USA later in the seventies, leading to the mass city marathons which have become such a welcome and distinctive feature of the athletics scene.

It was one of the minor irritations of a tragic Games that Shorter did not receive the public acclaim he so richly deserved as he covered the lap of the stadium to win the race. A practical joker, who had earlier entered the stadium posing as the winner, so thoroughly confused the crowd that Shorter himself was accorded at best a mixed reception, for the derisive jeers aimed at the imposter were still emanating from the spectators as Shorter entered the arena. He had utterly dominated the race, moving away after about 7 miles and extending his lead to over two minutes by the finish, which he reached in a personal best time of 2:12:20.

Another American success story was Dave Wottle, who although he had fancied his chances more in the 1500m (where he failed to reach the final) triumphed in the 800m with a display of even pace running which would have delighted the late Tom Hampson. Wottle, who had improved a full three seconds when sensationally equalling the world record of 1:44.3 in the US Olympic Trials with lap times of 52.9 and 51.4, had subsequently sustained an achilles tendon injury which had caused him to lose form in European races prior to Munich, and the favourite was the ultra-consistent European champion Yevgeniy Arzhanov of the USSR.

For most of the race it looked as though Arzhanov would indeed be the winner; he led at 600m and as he reached the finishing straight his main dangers appeared to be the Kenyan pairing of Mike Boit and Robert Ouko. The latter faded, but Boit (1:46.01) continued to press Arzhanov (1:45.89) hard all the way to the finish ... only for Wottle to come from nowhere and pip both of them in 1:45.86. In fact the American, wearing an old golf cap as was his custom, ran a remarkably even paced race even though he had looked completely out of it for much of the time. His 200m splits were 26.4 (the leader went through in 24.5), 26.9, 26.4 and 26.2, and Wottle overtook Arzhanov – who was in the process of falling to the track – in just the last metre or two.

Wottle's US team-mate Rod Milburn won his event, the 110m hurdles, by a wider margin. The man who had in 1971 run the first 13-flat 120 yards hurdles equalled the world record for the fractionally longer metric distance of 13.2, his electronic time of 13.24 being the first to be ratified by the IAAF when they began officially accepting such times in 1977. Guy Drut (later France's Minister for Sport), took second place. The other American success was 19 year-old Randy Williams, although he jumped farther in the qualifying round (8.34) than in the final (8.24). It was the end of an era as Igor Ter-Ovanesyan (contesting his fifth Olympics) and Lynn Davies failed to reach the final.

For the first time in Olympic history, excluding the interim Games of 1906, the pole vault was not won by an American. Defending champion Bob Seagren was in the form of his life, having set a world record of 5.63 in the US Trials, but the newly developed Cata-Pole he had used since April was not allowed in Munich by the IAAF on the grounds that the model was not widely available. Not until two days before the qualifying round did the IAAF make it clear the Cata-Pole would not be allowed, and so Seagren had little time to adjust to another model. He went on to clear 5.40 in the final but the East German Wolfgang Nordwig, three times European champion, made first 5.45 and then a personal best of 5.50 to take the title.

Controversy surrounded the shot final too, with another American feeling embittered about finishing second. Wladyslaw Komar, who had been banned "for life" some years earlier for misbehaviour but reinstated by the Polish Federation, opened with a personal best of 21.18. That remained the winning distance although Woods was unlucky. His fourth round put fell just a centimetre short at 21.17, while with his final attempt the shot thudded into a flag, marking Komar's Olympic record distance, before it had landed. It might have cost Woods several inches and yet still was measured at 21.05.

Another mighty close throwing result occurred in the javelin. Defending champion Janis Lusis, who had recently regained the world record with 93.80, began with 88.88 and improved to 89.54 in the third round. But, with his fifth throw, West Germany's Klaus Wolfermann thrilled the home fans with an Olympic record of 90.48. Now the pressure was on the Latvian; he too cast the spear beyond the 90m mark and the crowd held its breath as officials measured the throw. It was recorded as 90.46, and Wolfermann had won by just one inch.

Another defending Soviet champion, Viktor Saneyev from Georgia, retained his laurels in the triple jump, but it was close as his first jump of 17.35 (+2.2m wind) held up ahead of the fifth round 17.31 (+1.5m) of East Germany's Jorg Drehmel. Jüri Tarmak, an Estonian, became the last straddle exponent to win the Olympic high jump, and other Soviet successes came in the hammer through Anatoliy Bondarchuk (who would later coach Yuriy Sedykh to two Olympic titles) and in the decathlon where Nikolay Avilov, like Bondarchuk a Ukrainian, scored 8454 (8466 on today's tables) for a world record and 419-point victory. Avilov was second to East Germany's Joachim Kirst overnight (4345 to 4364) but Kirst fell in the first event of the second day, the hurdles. Another casualty was British record holder Peter Gabbett, whose outstanding 46.1 400m had helped him place fourth after seven events, but a knee injury ruined his chances in the pole vault and he withdrew. Avilov set seven new personal bests; needing to run 1500m in 4:28.0 for the world record, he ran his fastest ever of 4:22.8. A spectacular 4:05.9 1500m carried team-mate Leonid Litvinenko (16th overnight) from eighth to second place!

Another who left it late was the Czechoslovak discus thrower Ludvik Danek, second to Al Oerter in 1964 and third in 1968. He was lying fifth until, with his final attempt, he threw 64.40.

German athletes, from West and East, dominated the women's events. The only non-German winners were Mary Peters in the pentathlon (where Germans filled the next three places), Lyudmila Bragina in the 1500m (a German was second), Nadezhda Chizhova in the shot (German second) and Faina Melnik in the discus.

East Germans claimed six titles, with Renate Stecher taking two of them. After winning the 100m by a wide margin in 11.07, a hundredth inside Wyomia Tyus's altitude-assisted world record at the 1968 Games, the powerfully built Stecher took the 200m in 22.40, which was ratified at 22.4 to equal Chi Cheng's record but on

electrical timing easily bettered Irena Szewinska's 1968 Olympic mark of 22.58. In both races she was followed home by Australian Raelene Boyle, whose 200m time of 22.45 was also inside the old world figures. Stecher, who won 90 consecutive sprint races between August 1970 and June 1974, went on to anchor the GDR team in the 4x100m relay but, surprisingly, Heide Rosendahl preserved a one metre margin for the FRG squad which clocked a world record 42.81 and Stecher had to settle for silver.

Rosendahl enjoyed a great Games, for she also won the long jump (by a single centimetre) with 6.78 and broke the world pentathlon record with a score of 4791 ... although Mary Peters pipped her for the gold medal with a score of ten points more.

West Germany's other triumphs were provided by Hildegard Falck in the 800m and young Ulrike Meyfarth in the high jump. The 1.84m (6ft) tall schoolgirl, whose best before the Games was 1.85 and who had placed only third in her national championships, produced a staggering display by improving to 1.88, 1.90 and ultimately a world record equalling 1.92, while Britain's Barbara Inkpen also excelled by finishing fourth with a UK record-tying 1.85. There was another British record in the 800m, by New Zealand-born Rosemary Stirling whose 2:00.15 in seventh place bettered Ann Packer's 1964 gold medal winning time. After a thrilling race, Falck held on to win by half a stride from the Lithuanian, Niole Sabaite, in 1:58.55 – missing her own world record by just a tenth of a second.

A world record also narrowly eluded Monika Zehrt, a 19 year-old schoolgirl, in the 400m which she won in 51.08 but she gained a plaque in the inaugural 4x400m relay championship where she anchored the GDR team to a time of 3:22.95, over five seconds faster than the world record they set in a heat. That represented an average of 50.74 per leg at a time when the individual 400m record stood at 51.02.

Other East German winners were Ruth Fuchs in the javelin and Annelie Ehrhardt in the 100m hurdles. In the latter event, Israel's star athlete, Esther Shakhamorov, was likely to have become her nation's first Olympic finalist, but poignantly her lane in the semi-finals was empty. Her coach, Amizur Shapira, was among the

Israelis killed by the terrorists.

There was a Jewish winner, however, in the women's events in Munich, for Faina Melnik lifted the discus title. Her Soviet team-mate, Nadezhda Chizhova, added 40cm to her own world shot record with a barrier-breaking put of 21.03, while Lyudmila Bragina broke the world record in all three of her 1500m races. She went to the Games as record holder with 4:06.9 and proceeded to run 4:06.47 in her heat, 4:05.07 in her semi and a resounding 4:01.38 in the first Olympic women's 1500m final, covering the final 800m in 2:06.1. Such was the upsurge in standards that Sheila Carey (who improved by over 11 seconds in Munich!) set a UK record of 4:04.81 – inside the world record – but could finish no higher than fifth. Joyce Smith, later to find greater fame as a marathon runner, had ear- lier posted British records of 4:11.27 and 4:09.37 but failed to reach the final.

Mary Peters: An Overnight Star ... After 17 Years

IT WAS not until she was 33, after 17 years of pentathlon competition, that Mary Peters "overnight" became one of the world's great sports stars and a household name throughout the British Isles when in Munich she joined the immortals by winning an Olympic title with a world record performance – in the tradition established by Britain's only previous female Olympic champions, Mary Rand and Ann Packer.

Her story is one of perseverance. Overshadowed as a pentathlete by Rand and never quite making world class as a shot putter, her career might well have ended after a disappointing showing at the 1968 Olympics where, hampered by an injured ankle, she placed ninth. She was already 29 and had she quit then she would have been remembered as a very good and big hearted athlete (she placed fourth in the 1964 Games) but not truly a great one.

Instead she took off 1969 in order to regain her zest and, competing at her fourth Commonwealth Games, in 1970, she won gold medals in both the shot and pentathlon, representing Northern Ireland. Although born at Halewood in Lancashire on July 6 1939, she had lived in Ulster from the age of 11. Her pentathlon score of 5148 (4515 on the later tables) re-established her among the world's elite after a gap of six years.

Again she passed up competition in 1971 as, with her coach Buster McShane, she prepared for the following year's Olympics, and the indoor season of 1972 saw her transformed as a high jumper. Previously just a competent straddle jumper with a best of 1.67, she emerged as a Fosbury-flopper of close to world class. This dramatic improvement was worth over 100 points in that one event and was the key to her Olympic aspirations.

During the Olympic build-up period she raised the UK record to 4630, which ranked her fifth among the pentathlon contenders, and from the very first event in Munich it was apparent she was in superb form and afraid of

DID YOU KNOW?

AMONG THE competitors in the 100m was a man who, 16 years later, would be closely involved in the biggest ever Olympic scandal as Ben Johnson's coach: Charlie Francis of Canada placed eighth in his second round heat in 10.51w ... Fernando Mamede, the Portuguese who would become world 10,000m record holder 12 years later, finished fourth in his 800m heat in 1:48.6, sixth in his 1500m heat in 3:45.1 and ran a 48.0 anchor leg for the 4x400m team, while his compatriot Carlos Lopes, who would win the Olympic marathon in 1984, was eliminated in the heats of the 5000m and 10,000m, finishing ninth both times in 14:29.6 and 28:53.6 ... A first glimpse of African women's middle distance running talent came from 5ft tall Kenyan, Cherono Maiyo (18), who clocked 2:04.9 in her 800m heat ... Danny Ecker, who vaulted 6.00 indoors in 2001, is the son of Heide Rosendahl, the Munich Olympic long jump champion ... Japanese hammer thrower Shigenobu Murofushi placed eighth with 70.88; his son Koji finished ninth in the 2000 Olympics, improving to second in the World Championships next year ... American long jump contestant Kim Attlesey (dnq with 5.80) is the daughter of 110m hurdles ex-world record holder Dick Attlesey.

nobody. She clocked 13.29 for the 100m hurdles, a UK record on electrical timing; put the shot 16.20, which was only 11cm below her UK record; and ended the first day with an inspired high jump of 1.82 with the predominantly German crowd taking the bouncy blonde with the flashing smile and cheery wave to its collective heart despite the fact that with each successful clearance she was widening her points advantage over West Germany's big hope, the European champion Heide Rosendahl. Mary's overnight score of 2969, the highest ever recorded, gave her a handsome lead over the GDR's world record holder Burglinde Pollak (2872) with Rosendahl only fifth on 2668 ... but with her two strongest events to come.

On the second day Peters went close to her personal best with a long jump of 5.98, but Rosendahl — world record holder for the event — cleared a massive 6.83 to narrow the gap considerably. The scores going into the final event, the 200m, were: 1, Peters 3871; 2, Pollak 3824; 3, Rosendahl 3750.

Bearing in mind that Peters' personal best for 200m stood at 24.2, compared to 23.1 by Rosendahl and 23.8 by Pollak, it was clear that it was still anybody's title. A duplication of those times would result in Peters finishing with a score of 4790 ahead of Pollak 4781 and Rosendahl 4776. What it amounted to was that Peters would have to finish no more than 1.2 sec behind Rosendahl and 0.4 behind Pollak. It would be the ultimate test of nerve as well as speed.

"My legs went like jelly about 40 yards from home and I had to get those arms going and just drive like hell", recalled Peters. It was immediately obvious that she had finished close enough to Pollak, as there was not much more than a metre between them at the line. But Rosendahl had finished about ten metres ahead, her time flashing up as 22.96 — a wonderful run into a slight headwind. Hasty consultation of the scoring tables indicated Peters would need 24.18 to win. The suspense was unbearable during the minutes that passed before the other times became available. It was 24.08! Technically, Rosendahl had held the world record for 1.12 sec but Peters had won by 10 points, her final score of 4801 points being a world record for good measure. She is now Dame Mary Peters.

Lasse Comes Home
A National Hero

BETWEEN 1912 and 1936 there were 12 Olympic 5000m or 10,000m races, ten of them won by Finnish runners! Hannes Kolehmainen ... Paavo Nurmi ... Ville Ritola ... Lauri Lehtinen ... Gunnar Hockert ... Ilmari Salminen. These were the men who struck gold; great runners, still held in high esteem by a population steeped in athletics tradition. But where was the heir to this glorious tradition?. Decades passed in disappointment but at last, in 1971, the Finns hailed a potential Olympic winner in Juha Väätäinen, who sprinted away with both the 5000m and 10,000m titles at the European Champs, staged appropriately in Helsinki — only it was not he but the man who had finished seventh in the 5000m and 17th in the 10,000m who was to revive that tradition in Munich. His name: Lasse Viren.

Born at Myrskyla on July 22 1949, Viren had begun to make a name for himself in his own country in 1967 when setting Finnish age-18 bests at 3000m and 5000m, and in 1969 he won his first senior national 5000m title. He reached top class levels in 1971 with times of 13:29.8 for 5000m (a Finnish record) and 28:17.4 for 10,000m, ranking him fifth and 12th respectively in the world that year, but it wasn't until the end of July 1972, just a few weeks before the Games, that he leapt into contention as a serious medal contender. Until then his best marks for the season were 13:33.8 and 28:39.0, but in rapid succession he ran Finnish records of 13:19.0, 7:43.2 (3000m) and 27:52.4, followed by a world two miles record of 8:14.0 when destroying an all-star field including Emiel Puttemans, Anders Garderud, Ian Stewart, Dick Quax and Dave Bedford in Stockholm. Viren, who covered the second mile in 4:04.6, was ready for anything in Munich ... even, as it turned out, falling over in the 10,000m, picking himself up, chasing after the leaders, and winning the race in world record time!

His Olympic programme began on August 31, and while Puttemans and Bedford smashed the Olympic record with times of 27:53.4 and 27:53.6 in their heat Viren was content to ease home in fifth place in his in 28:04.4. In the final, on September 3, British record holder Bedford predictably set a furious pace (60.0 opening lap!), reaching 3000m in 8:06.4 and 5000m in 13:44.0. In the leading pack a few metres behind Bedford was Viren, which was remarkable considering that just over a lap previously he had fallen over, with Mohamed Gammoudi tripping over him. The Tunisian played no further effective role in the race and soon dropped out, but Viren – who lay sprawled on the track for about three seconds – almost effortlessly closed the gap. Indeed, he went on to take the lead at 6000m and, with Bedford slipping out of contact during the eighth kilometre, there were five men left in contention with two kilometres to run: Viren, Mariano Haro, Miruts Yifter, Puttemans and Frank Shorter (a week before his marathon triumph). The five were still close with two laps remaining, but from 600m out Viren began a murderously fast drive for the finish. The penultimate lap was covered in 60.0, with Puttemans and Yifter gamely clinging on, but they had no answer to Viren's final lap of 56.6 which carried the 23 year-old policeman to a brilliant victory in 27:38.4 (27:38.35 electrical), a second inside Ron Clarke's world record.

Four days later Viren returned to the track for the 5000m heats and was one of 13 men to break Vladimir Kuts' Olympic record of 13:39.6. He won his heat in 13:38.4, the fastest time of the round being 13:31.8 by Puttemans. For the final, on September 10, Viren's intention was to take the lead after 3000m and gradually wind up the pace, but he had to defer his plan as he was hemmed in by other runners at that stage. It wasn't surprising the field was tightly bunched as the pace was exceedingly slow. The first lap was covered in a funereal 69.6 and the 3000m time of 8:20.2 represented only 13:53.6 pace for the full distance.

It was the charismatic American, Steve Prefontaine, who pre-empted Viren's move. He surged ahead with four laps to go and the race sparked into life as he ran laps of 62.6 and 61.0, burning off everyone but Viren, Puttemans, defending champion Gammoudi and Ian Stewart. That was fine by Viren, who moved ahead on the penultimate lap (60.4), but Gammoudi wasn't going to concede his title without a fight and went in front along the final back straight. However, Viren was ahead entering the final straight and completed the final lap in 56.0 to score in 13:26.42, a remarkable time in view of the sluggish start. The last four laps took just four minutes!

Gammoudi rounded off a superb Olympic career with a silver medal to add to his 10,000m silver from 1964 and 5000m gold and 10,000m bronze from 1968. He was very nearly pipped, though, by Scotland's Commonwealth champion Stewart, who stormed past Prefontaine and came close to catching the Tunisian on the line. The American, who said "The Israeli tragedy affected me very much emotionally; I almost didn't want to compete", died in a car crash three years later, aged 24. For Viren, though, there was more glory ahead.

1972 - MUNICH

100m: (-0.3) 1, Valeriy Borzov URS 10.14 (10.07 ht); 2, Robert Taylor USA 10.24 (10.16 ht); 3, Lennox Miller JAM 10.33; 4, Aleksandr Kornelyuk URS 10.36; 5, Mike Fray JAM 10.40; 6, Jobst Hirscht FRG 10.40; 7, Zenon Nowosz POL 10.46; Hasely Crawford TRI dnf (10.18 ht).

200m: (nil wind) 1, Valeriy Borzov URS 20.00; 2, Larry Black USA 20.19; 3, Pietro Mennea ITA 20.30; 4, Larry Burton USA 20.37; 5, Chuck Smith USA 20.55; 6, Siegfried Schenke GDR 20.56; 7, Martin Jellinghaus FRG 20.65; 8, Hans-Joachim Zenk GDR 21.05.

400m: 1, Vince Matthews USA 44.66; 2, Wayne Collett USA 44.80; 3, Julius Sang KEN 44.92; 4, Charles Asati KEN 45.13; 5, Horst-Rüdiger Schlöske FRG 45.31; 6, Markku Kukkoaho FIN 45.49; 7, Karl Honz FRG 45.68; John Smith USA dnf.

800m: 1, Dave Wottle USA 1:45.86; 2, Yevgeniy Arzhanov URS 1:45.89; 3, Mike Boit KEN 1:46.01 (1:45.87 sf); 4, Franz-Josef Kemper FRG 1:46.50; 5, Robert Ouko KEN 1:46.53; 6, Andy Carter GBR 1:46.55; 7, Andrzej Kupczyk POL 1:47.10; 8, Dieter Fromm GDR 1:47.96.

1500m: 1, Pekka Vasala FIN 3:36.33; 2, Kip Keino KEN 3:36.81; 3, Rod Dixon NZL 3:37.46; 4, Mike Boit KEN 3:38.41; 5, Brendan Foster GBR 3:39.02 (3:38.20 sf); 6, Herman Mignon BEL 3:39.05; 7, Paul-Heinz Wellmann FRG 3:40.08; 8, Vladimir Panteley URS 3:40.24.

5000m: 1, Lasse Viren FIN 13:26.42; 2, Mohamed Gammoudi TUN 13:27.33; 3, Ian Stewart GBR 13:27.61; 4, Steve Prefontaine USA 13:28.25; 5, Emiel Puttemans BEL 13:30.82; 6, Harald Norpoth FRG 13:32.58; 7, Per Halle NOR 13:34.38; 8, Nikolay Sviridov URS 13:39.31.

10,000m: 1, Lasse Viren FIN 27:38.35 (world rec); 2, Emiel Puttemans BEL 27:39.58; 3, Miruts Yifter ETH 27:40.96; 4, Mariano Haro ESP

27:48.14; 5, Frank Shorter USA 27:51.32; 6, Dave Bedford GBR 28:05.44 (27:53.64 ht); 7, Daniel Korica YUG 28:15.18; 8, Abdelkader Zaddem TUN 28:18.17.

Marathon: 1, Frank Shorter USA 2:12:20; 2, Karel Lismont BEL 2:14:32; 3, Mamo Wolde ETH 2:15:09; 4, Kenny Moore USA 2:15:40; 5, Kenji Kimihara JPN 2:16:27; 6, Ron Hill GBR 2:16:31; 7, Don Macgregor GBR 2:16:35; 8, Jack Foster NZL 2:16:57.

3000mSC: 1, Kip Keino KEN 8:23.64; 2, Ben Jipcho KEN 8:24.62; 3, Tapio Kantanen FIN 8:24.66; 4, Bronislaw Malinowski POL 8:27.92; 5, Dusan Moravcik TCH 8:29.06; 6, Amos Biwott KEN 8:33.48 (8:23.73 ht); 7, Romualdas Bitte URS 8:34.64; 8, Pekka Päivärinta FIN 8:37.17.

110mH: (0.3) 1, Rod Milburn USA 13.24 (inaugural IAAF electronic world rec); 2, Guy Drut FRA 13.34; 3, Tom Hill USA 13.48 (13.47 sf); 4, Willie Davenport USA 13.50; 5, Frank Siebeck GDR 13.71; 6, Leszek Wodzynski POL 13.72; 7, Lubomir Nadenicek TCH 13.76; 8, Petr Cech TCH 13.86.

400mH: 1, John Akii-Bua UGA 47.82 (world rec); 2, Ralph Mann USA 48.51; 3, David Hemery GBR 48.52; 4, Jim Seymour USA 48.64; 5, Rainer Schubert FRG 49.65; eq6, Yevgeny Gavrilenko URS & Stavros Tziortzis GRE 49.66; 8, Yuriy Zorin URS 50.25.

4x100m Relay: 1, USA (Larry Black, Robert Taylor, Gerald Tinker, Eddie Hart) 38.19 (inaugural IAAF electronic world rec); 2, USSR (Aleksandr Kornelyuk, Vladimir Lovetskiy, Juris Silovs, Valeriy Borzov) 38.50; 3, FRG (Jobst Hirscht, Karl-Heinz Klotz, Gerhard Wucherer, Klaus Ehl) 38.79; 4, Czechoslovakia 38.82; 5, GDR 38.90; 6, Poland 39.03; 7, France 39.14; 8, Italy 39.14.

4x400m Relay: 1, Kenya (Charles Asati 45.3, Hezekiah Nyamau 45.3, Robert Ouko 45.6, Julius Sang 43.6) 2:59.83; 2, Great Britain (Martin Reynolds 46.3, Alan Pascoe 45.1, David Hemery 44.9, David Jenkins 44.2) 3:00.46; 3, France (Gilles Bertould 46.2, Daniel Velasquez 44.1, Francis Kerbiriou 45.6, Jacques Carette 44.8) 3:00.65; 4, FRG 3:00.88; 5, Poland 3:01.05; 6, Finland 3:01.12; 7, Sweden 3:02.57; 8, Trinidad 3:03.58.

HJ: 1, Jüri Tarmak URS 2.23; 2, Stefan Junge GDR 2.21; 3, Dwight Stones USA 2.21; 4, Hermann Magerl FRG 2.18; 5, Adám Szepesi HUN 2.18; eq6, John Beers CAN & István Major HUN 2.15; 8, Rustam Akhmetov URS 2.15.

PV: 1, Wolfgang Nordwig GDR 5.50; 2, Bob Seagren USA 5.40; 3, Jan Johnson USA 5.35; 4, Reinhard Kuretzky FRG 5.30; 5, Bruce Simpson CAN 5.20; 6, Volker Ohl FRG 5.20; 7, Hans Lagerqvist SWE 5.20; 8, Francois Tracanelli FRA 5.10.

LJ: 1, Randy Williams USA 8.24 (8.34q); 2, Hans Baumgartner FRG 8.18; 3, Arnie Robinson USA 8.03; 4, Josh Owusu GHA 8.01; 5, Preston Carrington USA 7.99 (8.22q); 6, Max Klauss GDR 7.96; 7, Alan Lerwill GBR 7.91; 8, Leonid Borkovskiy URS 7.75.

TJ: 1, Viktor Saneyev URS 17.35w; 2, Jörg Drehmel GDR 17.31; 3, Nelson Prudencio BRA 17.05; 4, Carol Corbu ROM 16.85w; 5, John Craft USA 16.83; 6, Mansour Dia SEN 16.83w; 7, Michal Joachimowski POL 16.69; 8, Kristen Flogstad NOR 16.44.

SP: 1, Wladyslaw Komar POL 21.18; 2, George Woods USA 21.17; 3, Hartmut Briesenick GDR 21.14; 4, Hans-Peter Gies GDR 21.14; 5, Al Feuerbach USA 21.01; 6, Brian Oldfield USA 20.91; 7, Heinfried Birlenbach FRG 20.37; 8, Vilmos Varju HUN 20.10.

DT: 1, Ludvik Danek TCH 64.40; 2, Jay Silvester USA 63.50; 3, Ricky Bruch SWE 63.40; 4, John Powell USA 62.82; 5, Géza Fejér HUN 62.62; 6, Detlef Thorith GDR 62.42; 7, Ferenc Tégla HUN 60.60; 8, Tim Vollmer USA 60.24.

HT: 1, Anatoliy Bondarchuk URS 75.50; 2, Jochen Sachse GDR 74.96; 3, Vasiliy Khmelevskiy URS 74.04; 4, Uwe Beyer FRG 71.52; 5, Gyula Zsivótzky HUN 71.38; 6, Sándor Eckschmidt HUN 71.20; 7, Edwin Klein FRG 71.14; 8, Shigenobu Murofushi JPN 70.88.

JT: 1, Klaus Wolfermann FRG 90.48; 2, Janis Lusis URS 90.46; 3, Bill Schmidt USA 84.42; 4, Hannu Siitonen FIN 84.32; 5, Bjorn Grimnes NOR 83.08; 6, Jorma Kinnunen FIN 82.08; 7, Miklós Németh HUN 81.98; 8, Fred Luke USA 80.06.

Dec: 1, Nikolay Avilov URS 8454 (world rec; 8466 on present tables) (11.00, 7.68, 14.36, 2.12, 48.45, 14.31, 46.98, 4.55, 61.66, 4:22.8); 2, Leonid Litvinenko URS 8035 (7970); 3, Ryszard Katus POL 7984 (7936); 4, Jeff Bennett USA 7974 (7920); 5, Stefan Schreyer GDR 7950 (7907); 6, Freddy Herbrand BEL 7947 (7897); 7, Steen Smidt-Jensen DEN 7947 (7908); 8, Tadeusz Janczenko POL 7861 (7791).

20k Walk: 1, Peter Frenkel GDR 1:26:43; 2, Vladimir Golubnichiy URS 1:26:56; 3, Hans-Georg Reimann GDR 1:27:17; 4, Gerhard Sperling GDR 1:27:55; 5, Nikolay Smaga URS 1:28:17; 6, Paul Nihill GBR 1:28:45; 7, Jan Ornoch

POL 1:32:02; 8, Vittorio Visini ITA 1:32:30.

50k Walk: 1, Bernd Kannenberg FRG 3:56:12; 2, Veniamin Soldatenko URS 3:58:24; 3, Larry Young USA 4:00:46; 4, Otto Barch URS 4:01:36; 5, Peter Selzer GDR 4:04:06; 6, Gerhard Weidner FRG 4:06:26; 7, Vittorio Visini ITA 4:08:32; 8, Gabriel Hernandez MEX 4:12:09.

Women's Events

100m: (-0.2) 1, Renate Stecher GDR 11.07 (world rec); 2, Raelene Boyle AUS 11.23; 3, Silvia Chivas CUB 11.24 (11.18 ht); 4, Iris Davis USA 11.32; 5, Annegret Richter FRG 11.38; 6, Alice Annum GHA 11.41; 7, Barbara Ferrell USA 11.45; 8, Eva Glesková TCH 12.48 (injured).

200m: (1.1) 1, Renate Stecher GDR 22.40 (world rec); 2, Raelene Boyle AUS 22.45; 3, Irena Szewinska POL 22.74; 4, Ellen Stropahl GDR 22.75; eq5, Christina Heinich GDR & Annegret Kroniger FRG 22.89; 7, Alice Annum GHA 22.99; 8, Rosie Allwood JAM 23.11.

400m: 1, Monika Zehrt GDR 51.08; 2, Rita Wilden FRG 51.21; 3, Kathy Hammond USA 51.64; 4, Helga Seidler GDR 51.86; 5, Mable Fergerson USA 51.96; 6, Charlene Rendina AUS 51.99; 7, Dagmar Käsling GDR 52.19; 8, Györgyi Balogh HUN 52.39.

800m: 1, Hildegard Falck FRG 1:58.55; 2, Niole Sabaite URS 1:58.65; 3, Gunhild Hoffmeister GDR 1:59.19; 4, Svetla Zlateva BUL 1:59.72 (1:58.93 ht); 5, Vera Nikolic YUG 1:59.98; 6, Ileana Silai ROM 2:00.04; 7, Rosemary Stirling GBR 2:00.15; 8, Abby Hoffman CAN 2:00.17.

1500m: 1, Lyudmila Bragina URS 4:01.38 (world rec; world recs of 4:06.47 in heat & 4:05.07 in semi-final); 2, Gunhild Hoffmeister GDR 4:02.83; 3, Paola Cacchi ITA 4:02.85; 4, Karin Burneleit GDR 4:04.11; 5, Sheila Carey (née Taylor) GBR 4:04.81; 6, Ilja Keizer NED 4:05.13; 7, Tamara Pangelova URS 4:06.45; 8, Jenny Orr AUS 4:12.15.

100mH: (-0.6) 1, Annelie Ehrhardt GDR 12.59; 2, Valeria Bufanu ROM 12.84; 3, Karin Balzer GDR 12.90; 4, Pam Ryan (née Kilborn) AUS 12.98; 5, Teresa Nowak POL 13.17; 6, Danuta Straszynska POL 13.18; 7 Annerose Krumpholz GDR 13.27; 8, Grazyna Rabsztyn POL 13.44.

4x100m Relay: 1, FRG (Christiane Krause, Ingrid Mickler (née Becker), Annegret Richter, Heide Rosendahl) 42.81 (world rec); 2, GDR (Evelyn Kaufer, Christina Heinich, Bärbel Struppert, Renate Stecher) 42.95 (42.88 ht); 3, Cuba (Marlene Elejarde, Carmen Valdes,

Fulgencia Romay, Silvia Chivas) 43.36; 4, USA 43.39 (43.07 ht); 5, USSR 43.59; 6, Australia 43.61; 7, Great Britain 43.71; 8, Poland 44.20.

4x400m Relay: 1, GDR (Dagmar Käsling 52.2, Rita Kühne 50.0, Helga Seidler 51.0, Monika Zehrt 49.8) 3:22.95 (world rec; world rec of 3:28.48 in heat); 2, USA (Mable Fergerson 51.8, Madeline Manning 51.9, Cheryl Toussaint 51.2, Kathy Hammond 50.2) 3:25.15; 3, FRG (Anette Rückes 53.1, Inge Bödding 51.6, Hildegard Falck 51.2, Rita Wilden 50.6) 3:26.51; 4, France 3:27.52; 5, Great Britain 3:28.74; 6, Australia 3:28.84; 7, Finland 3:29.44; 8, USSR 3:31.89.

HJ: 1, Ulrike Meyfarth FRG 1.92 (eq world rec); 2, Yordanka Blagoyeva BUL 1.88; 3, Ilona Gusenbauer AUT 1.88; 4, Barbara Inkpen GBR 1.85; 5, Rita Schmidt GDR 1.85; 6, Sara Simeoni ITA 1.85; 7, Rosemarie Witschas GDR 1.85; 8, Debbie Brill CAN 1.82.

LJ: 1, Heide Rosendahl FRG 6.78; 2, Diana Yorgova BUL 6.77; 3, Eva Suranová TCH 6.67; 4, Marcia Garbey CUB 6.52w; 5, Heidi Schüller FRG 6.51; 6, Meta Antenen SUI 6.49; 7, Viorica Viscopoleanu ROM 6.48w; 8, Margrit Olfert GDR 6.46.

SP: 1, Nadezhda Chizhova URS 21.03 (world rec); 2, Margitta Gummel GDR 20.22; 3, Ivanka Khristova BUL 19.35; 4, Esfir Dolzhenko URS 19.24; 5, Marianne Adam GDR 18.94; 6, Maritta Lange GDR 18.85; 7, Helena Fibingerová TCH 18.81; 8, Yelena Stoyanova BUL 18.34.

DT: 1, Faina Melnik URS 66.62; 2, Argentina Menis ROM 65.06; 3, Vasilka Stoyeva BUL 64.34; 4, Tamara Danilova URS 62.86; 5, Liesel Westermann FRG 62.18; 6, Gabriele Hinzmann GDR 61.72; 7, Carmen Ionescu ROM 60.42; 8, Lyudmila Muravyova URS 59.00.

JT: 1, Ruth Fuchs GDR 63.88; 2, Jacqueline Todten GDR 62.54; 3, Kate Schmidt USA 59.94; 4, Lutvian Mollova BUL 59.36; 5, Natasa Urbancic YUG 59.06; 6, Eva Janko AUT 58.56; 7, Ewa Gryziecka POL 57.00; 8, Svetlana Korolyova URS 56.36.

Pen: 1, Mary Peters GBR 4801 (world rec) (13.29, 16.20, 1.82, 5.98, 24.08); 2, Heide Rosendahl FRG 4791 (13.34, 13.86, 1.65, 6.83, 22.96); 3, Burglinde Pollak GDR 4768 (13.53, 16.04, 1.76, 6.21, 23.93); 4, Christine Bodner GDR 4671; 5, Valentina Tikhomirova URS 4597; 6, Nedyalka Angelova BUL 4496; 7, Karen Mack FRG 4449; 8, Ilona Bruzsenyak HUN 4419.

ALREADY SERIOUSLY damaged by the security lapses which led to the terrorist outrage in Munich, the Olympic movement experienced further problems at the Montreal Games. There were fears that the facilities would not be ready in time (they were, although the roof of the ambitiously designed main stadium was not completed), and the costs escalated to such a degree that the Games, which were supposed to be self-financing, cost the city and its taxpayers an astronomical sum. The Games were also adversely affected by a boycott by 22 African countries plus Guyana on the grounds that New Zealand, whose rugby team had toured South Africa, should have been expelled from the Montreal Olympics. The International Olympic Committee justifiably refused, insisting that the actions of rugby teams were outside its jurisdiction.

Apart from Tanzania, who led the protest, the African teams travelled to Montreal hoping for a last-minute change of heart by the IOC and there were emotional scenes when the athletes had to return home shortly before the opening ceremony. Among those who missed their big chance of Olympic glory were world 1500m record holder Filbert Bayi of Tanzania and Kenyan 800m star Mike Boit, while Uganda's John Akii-Bua was unable to defend his 400m hurdles title.

Despite that, the Games were a tremendous success, with world records achieved by Alberto Juantorena of Cuba (see page 120), 1:43.50 for 800m; Anders Gärderud of Sweden, 8:08.02 steeplechase; Edwin Moses (USA), 47.64 400m hurdles; Miklos Nemeth of Hungary, 94.58 javelin; Bruce Jenner (USA), 8618 decathlon; Annegret Richter of West Germany, 11.01 100m; Irena Szewinska of Poland (see page 120), 49.29 400m; Tatyana Kazankina (USSR), 1:54.94 800m; and the East German women's 4x400m relay team (3:19.23). Lasse Viren of Finland made history by winning a second 5000m/10,000m double and Viktor Saneyev (USSR) chalked up his third Olympic triple jump title.

On the men's side, the USA (six golds) and the East European bloc (seven golds) accounted for more than half the titles, while the women's events saw an awesome if dubious display of strength by the East Europeans who took no fewer than 33 of the 42 available medals, including 13 out of 14 golds. The East Germans won nine titles and in only one event did they fail to gain a medal.

The British team, which travelled to Montreal with high hopes, returned deflated with just one medal – a bronze by Brendan Foster in the 10,000m – to show for their efforts. There were numerous placings between fourth and eighth for the aficionado to appreciate, but that was not what the general public had been led to expect.

The British women had a particularly miserable time, for never before in 44 years of Olympic competition had they failed to win a medal. This time only Andrea Lynch reached the first eight of an individual event, placing seventh in the 100m, although it was unfortunate that Britain's main sprinting hope, Sonia Lannaman, had to withdraw after injuring a hamstring during relay practice. Another big disappointment was the failure of the British team to reach the final of the men's 4x400m, in which they were considered medal contenders; Alan Pascoe had the baton knocked out of his hand in his heat.

Britain's finest showing came in the 10,000m where Foster not only finished third but Welsh-born Tony Simmons was close behind in fourth place and Bernie Ford was

STAR OF THE GAMES

ALBERTO JUANTORENA
(born 3 Dec 1950)

Prior to 1976 the tall muscular Cuban, known as "El Caballo" (the horse), was a 400m specialist with an 800m best of 1:49.8. But in Montreal, having meanwhile improved to 1:44.9 although still a novice at the distance, he became Olympic champion in the world record time of 1:43.50. Later he completed a stupendous double by taking the 400m in 44.26, at that time the fastest ever electrical mark at low altitude.

eighth. With seven laps to go, Portugal's Carlos Lopes (whose greatest Olympic moment would come eight years later), Lasse Viren and Foster had broken clear, with Lopes trying hard to drop the other two. He succeeded with Foster, who wasn't at his best because of an upset stomach, but Viren clung to the international cross country champion and raced away approaching the bell. The elegant Finn, who covered the second half of the race in a then unheard of 13:31.4, won by 30m in 27:40.38 to join Paavo Nurmi and Emil Zátopek as the only runners to win a second Olympic 10,000m crown. "Viren is simply the greatest runner there has ever been", said Foster.

Viren, who had achieved little of note since Munich due to a lack of training in 1973 and leg injuries during the following two years, was – in the manner of Al Oerter – a man who needed the stimulus of Olympic competition to bring the best out of him. He hadn't run a really quick 5000m for four years but, when it counted, he was ready.

Content to qualify in fourth place in his heat in 13:33.39 while Foster won his in the Olympic record time of 13:20.34, Viren outwitted and outran his opponents in the final. Knowing he was up against men who, in a last lap sprint, might be faster than himself, he began his drive for the finish from a full kilometre out. Commandeering the inside lane throughout, while his rivals ran wide in increasingly desperate attempts to wrest the lead, Viren was never headed as he cranked out a final 800m of 1:57.5, the last lap taking 55.0. The winning time was 13:24.76, with the Dutch-born New Zealander, Dick Quax, three metres behind in second place, while Quax's teammate Rod Dixon was pipped for the bronze by West Germany's Klaus-Peter Hildenbrand, who literally fell over the line in a dip finish. Foster, who would continue to hold the Olympic record until 1984, placed fifth although finishing barely ten metres behind the winner, who became the first to successfully defend a 5000m title and thus completed a fabulous "double double".

The very next day Viren was back in action, to make his marathon debut in an attempt to emulate Zátopek's historic triple of 1952. Zátopek had won the 10,000m (a straight final) in 29:17.0, taken the 5000m four

days later in 14:06.6 (14:26.0 heat) and triumphed in the marathon three days after the 5000m in 2:23:04. Viren's sequence was vastly superior in terms of the stopwatch. He ran a 28:14.95 10,000m heat on July 23, 27:40.38 in the final on July 26, 13:33.39 for his 5000m heat on July 28 and 13:24.76 in the final on July 30. His marathon time on July 31 was 2:13:11 which, although it netted him "only" fifth place, was a monumental achievement in the circumstances. Frank Shorter (USA) ran somewhat faster than when he won in Munich but had to be content with second as the former East German steeplechase international, Waldemar Cierpinski, chopped over two minutes from his previous best to win in 2:09:55.

The other East German men's winner was also unexpected. Shot putter Udo Beyer, aged 20, was only added to the team at the last moment but whereas more favoured candidates like world record holder Aleksandr Baryshnikov of the USSR, the Americans Al Feuerbach and George Woods, and British record holder Geoff Capes grew increasingly edgy as they found themselves unable to recapture their best form Beyer was able to relax in the knowledge that no one was counting upon him to win. "I started feeling extraordinarily calm, while my competitors were all going crazy, almost hysterical. I was cool, and focused all my concentration on my technique". He pushed out the winning put of 21.05, far behind the Olympic record set by Baryshnikov when qualifying, in the fifth round and the others were left to rue the golden chance that slipped away.

The East German women collected 19 medals (as against 13 in Munich), of which nine were gold (compared to six last time), but the title of Olympic 100m champion passed from Renate Stecher to the West German, Annegret Richter, who set a world 100m record of 11.01 in her semi-final and, despite suffering cramp in her right calf after that run, went on to win the final two hours later in 11.08, half a metre ahead of the once unbeatable East German.

Two youngsters who would go on to amass the highest honours during lengthy careers made that final: 19 year-old Evelyn Ashford (USA), still a world class sprinter 16 years later, and 18 year-old Marlies Oelsner (later Göhr) of the GDR. Stecher lost her

200m title also, placing third to her less well known team-mate Barbel Eckert, who edged Richter by 2/100ths in 22.37. Eckert captured another gold in the sprint relay, while the East Germans also won the 4x400m in which the world record was lowered by a massive 3.72 sec with 3:19.23 – the first sub-50 sec average.

The outstanding women's 400m runner, though, was Poland's Irena Szewinska who added further lustre to an already brilliant Olympic career by smashing her own world record with a time of 49.29. Standing in the wings, though, was another East German, who would develop into the fastest ever female 400m runner. Marita Koch (19) reached the semis but had to withdraw injured ... costing her also a place in the relay team.

Another unlucky East German was Christine Laser in the pentathlon. She didn't go away empty handed, for she took the silver medal with 4745 points – but with exactly the same score it was her colleague Sigrun Siegl who achieved athletic immortality by being crowned Olympic champion. At the end of the first day Laser was in fifth place and Siegl, world record holder for the long jump at 6.99, only ninth. Siegl was best in her speciality, but managed only 6.49 to move up to seventh (3718 points) with just the 200m to go, while Laser remained fifth on 3757. The leader with 3788 was Nadezhda Tkachenko of the USSR. However, Siegl's sparkling 23.09 did the trick and Laser also ran faster than ever before. Siegl was declared the overall winner as she outscored Laser in three of the five events.

A year before the Games no one would have correctly predicted the winners of the 800m in Montreal. Alberto Juantorena was known to be a great 400m runner but his best 800m was only 1:49.8; likewise Tatyana Kazankina had begun to make a mark at 1500m and 3000m but with a best of 2:01.70 was not rated in the two-lap event. Yet both went on not only to win their 800m races in Montreal but break the world record!

The small, skinny and pale Russian (who, six years earlier, had suffered a heart problem) had not established herself as a prospective Olympic medallist in any event until June 1976 when she set a personal best of 4:02.8 for 1500m, covering the final 800m in 2:03.6. A few days later she shook the athletics world by rip-ping through 400m in 59.5, 800m in 2:05.5 and 1200m in 3:09.5 on the way to a 3:56.0 timing – an incredible 5.4 sec improvement on Lydumila Bragina's world record. Just prior to the Games she hacked her fastest 800m time down to 1:56.6 and, contrary to her own wishes, was picked for that event too by the Olympic selectors.

Their faith in her ability and recuperative powers was justified. After running 1:57.49 in her semi-final, Kazankina bided her time as team-mate Svetlana Styrkina blazed through the first lap in 55.05 and reached 600m in 85.0. Her deceptive strength came into play in the final straight as, while the others paid for that searing early pace, she moved from fifth to first. Her time of 1:54.94 took over a second off the world record of 1:56.0, which was broken also by the next three finishers.

Kazankina virtually played with the opposition in the 1500m final, her sixth race of the Games. The 1.62m (5'4"), 47kg (7st 5lb) graduate student of economics at Leningrad University was content to sit in through leisurely laps of 68.2 and 70.7. The third lap was appreciably quicker at 64.5 but in the closing stages no one could match the formidable speed of Kazankina (4:05.48), whose last 400m took just 56.9!

The men's 1500m final was similarly slow overall but notable for the rapidity of the last lap. New Zealander John Walker who had, the previous year, set a barrier-breaking world mile record of 3:49.4, was the red-hot favourite in the regrettable absence (because of the political boycott) of Tanzanian Filbert Bayi, the world 1500m record holder at 3:32.16. The winning time at 3:39.17 may have been the slowest for 20 years but Walker's kick, from 250m out, was brutal. He covered the 200m stretch between 1200 and 1400m in 24.7, the final lap taking 52.7.

He was pressed hard all the way, though, by Belgium's Ivo Van Damme, who had earlier finished a brilliant runner-up to Juantorena in the 800m. Alas, this great talent died in a car crash just a few months later at the age of 22. So close was the finish of that 1500m that Scotsman Frank Clement, the UK record holder, wound up fifth although less than half a second behind Walker. Fellow Briton Steve Ovett, who would emerge as the world's number one at the distance the following year, posted a personal best of 3:37.89 in his heat but – having earlier finished fifth in the 800m – ran out of steam in his semi.

Future Olympic glory lay in store for Ovett and for another 20 year-old in Tessa Sanderson, who on this occasion placed tenth in the javelin after setting a UK record of 57.18 in the qualifying round.

Another, more youthful, Olympic debutant was Daley Thompson, who celebrated his 18th birthday on the second day of the decathlon. The competition proved to be a priceless education for Thompson ("Bruce Jenner has been fantastic, pointing things out and being very helpful to me"), who gave an excellent account of himself on the first day by scoring 4055 points in 11th place. He dropped back to 18th (7434) eventually, but learned much that contributed to his future success.

Competing in his final decathlon, Jenner enjoyed a dream competition, reeling off one personal best after another and ending up with a world record score of 8618 (8634 on the tables used today). The American was a true all-rounder, not particularly brilliant in any one event but with no real weaknesses either. The highlight for him was the final stages of the 1500m. As he reflected: "I've always imagined myself coming off the final turn knowing I'm Olympic champion and just running that last straight. I thought here it is, I've finally done it. I came off the turn and I tried to take a mental picture of it so I'd have it for the rest of my life. I felt great. How can you feel bad when you've won the Olympic Games and broken the world record wide open?" Like his predecessors Glenn Morris, Bob Mathias and Rafer Johnson, Jenner was signed up to make films in Hollywood.

The Americans' other world record wrecker was a 20 year-old newcomer by the name of Edwin Moses. Rarely has an athlete catapulted from total obscurity to the ultimate in athletic achievement so quickly. At high school, Moses had broken neither 50 sec for the flat quarter nor 15 sec for the sprint hurdles, yet by 1975 he was running 45.5 for 440 yards in a relay and 14.0 for 120 yards hurdles. His coach realised that this combination of talents pointed towards the longer hurdles event and a start was made with a 52.0 timing over

440 yards hurdles (worth 51.7 for 400m) which didn't rank him among the world's top 100 that year.

Moses began the 1976 season with 50.1 in March and his rise towards greatness was relentless: 49.8 in April, 48.8 in May, an American record of 48.30 in June. At the Games he clocked 48.29 in his semi and a world record shattering 47.64 in the final, which he won by the widest margin in Olympic history – some eight metres – and that despite making mistakes worth in his estimation at least half a second as he strode thirteens all the way. Britain's European champion Alan Pascoe, top ranked in the world in 1975, pulled out all the stops in the first half of the race in a do or die attempt to hold Moses but, well short of peak fitness following injury, he faded to last place.

Unlike Moses, two other world record breakers in Montreal were seasoned campaigners who previously had been labelled as flops in major championships.

A dazzling future was predicted for Anders Gärderud, when he front-ran to victory in the European junior 1500m steeplechase in 1964. The lanky Swede did indeed make good as a senior in terms of producing fast times – on the flat (3:36.7 1500m, 13:17.6 5000m) as well as the steeplechase – but for much of his career he was regarded as a poor competitor on the big occasion. He was eliminated in the heats at the 1966 European Championships and at the Olympics of 1968 and 1972, while he "choked" again in the 1971 European final to place tenth after clocking the fastest heat time. He put up a better showing at the 1974 European Championships, finishing second to his arch-rival Bronislaw Malinowski of Poland, and the following season he became the first to break 8:10 for the event.

However, it was not until Montreal that Gärderud finally, and decisively, convinced doubters that he was temperamentally as well as physically equipped to land the supreme prize. This time Malinowski could not drop the Swede and 300m from home Gärderud burst ahead to win in a world record 8:08.02. It was a dramatic finish, though, for Frank Baumgartl, a young East German, drew level with Gärderud as they rose for the final barrier. Gärderud took it cleanly but Baumgartl struck the solid hurdle with his knee and crashed to the track. He was up quickly but the golden opportunity had passed and he finished third. Gärderud covered the second half of the race in 4:01.5, the final kilometre in a sizzling 2:38.95.

Hungarian javelin thrower Miklós Németh also redeemed himself in some style. As the son of 1948 Olympic hammer champion Imre Németh, he spent most of his career in his father's shadow and was usually a big disappointment in major competitions. Nursing an elbow injury he failed to qualify for the 1968 Olympic final and placed seventh in 1972, while in the European Championships he finished ninth in 1971 and seventh in 1974. It wasn't until 1975, aged 28, that he began to tap his obvious potential; that year he topped the world list with a throw of 91.38, though even then he was only world ranked fifth on merit due to his wildly fluctuating results.

The moment of truth came in Montreal: would he confirm the widely held opinion that he was a rotten competitor when the chips were down, or would he seize the opportunity to show the world his true form? His very first throw said it all – as the spear sailed on and on to touch down at the remarkable world record distance of 94.58. That knocked the stuffing out of his rivals and his winning margin of more than six metres was the widest in Olympic field event history. He was so excited by his historic throw that he was unable to calm down sufficiently to take his next two attempts.

One who had nothing further to prove in the matter of competitive ability was Viktor Saneyev, and the Soviet triple jumper came up trumps for the third time running to become only the third man in Olympic history to gain a hat-trick of gold medals at four-yearly intervals in the same individual event, his predecessors being hammer thrower John Flanagan and four-time discus champion Al Oerter. James Butts (USA) created a stir by jumping 17.18 in the fourth round only for Saneyev to respond in the next round with 17.29. Team-mate Yuriy Sedykh, a legendary Olympian in the making, won his first hammer throwing title at the age of 21, leading a Soviet clean sweep of the medals with defending champion Anatoliy Bondarchuk, Sedykh's coach, placing third.

As stated earlier, the Games were a disaster for the British team, and in view of what was to happen at the next Olympics and the current rich state of British men's sprinting it's interesting to note that no 100m runner was considered worth selecting. However, the Commonwealth did well in that event, as Trinidad's Hasely Crawford won from Jamaica's Don Quarrie, who went on to take the 200m, but that was not much consolation for British fans ... nor was the success of France's Guy Drut in the 110m hurdles even if his mother was English!

A Pole Apart

AS AN 18 year-old in 1964 she had struck gold in the sprint relay in world record time to go with silvers in the 200m (in a European record 23.1) and long jump (Polish record of 6.60); in 1968 she won the 200m in a world record 22.5 and was third in the 100m after matching the world record of 11.1 in a heat; in 1972, by then a mother, she placed third in the 200m.

This time Irena Szewinska (née Kirszenstein) concentrated on the 400m, an event in which she was the first to break 50 sec in 1974, and smashed her own world record of 49.75 with a time of 49.29. Reaching 200m in 23.5 and 300m in 35.4, she drew away from a former world record breaker, 18 year-old Christina Brehmer (GDR), to win by a resounding ten metres. That time was faster than when Bevil Rudd won the 1920 Olympic crown in Antwerp and it was hailed as one of the greatest performances in the history of women's athletics.

Born in Leningrad on May 24 1946, Szewinska was 30 and with a dozen years of top-class competition behind her at the time of her Montreal triumph, but her career was by no means at an end. In 1977 she maintained her position as world's number one at both 200m and 400m. At that year's World Cup she first disposed of Olympic champion Bärbel Wöckel (née Eckert) in the 200m and then prevailed over up and coming Marita Koch in the 400m, and added yet another string to her bow by running 400m hurdles in 56.62, less than a second outside the world record at that time.

However, even Szewinska could not reign supreme for ever. Koch won the 1978 European title in a world record 48.94 with Szewinska third in 50.40, but that and another bronze in the 4x400m relay brought her tally of European Championship medals to ten. Her final fling, aged 34, came at the Moscow Games of 1980 - her fifth Olympics - but an Achilles tendon injury caused her to be eliminated at the semi-final stage. She has ever since been a prominent official both nationally and internationally. Her personal bests included 11.13 for 100m, 22.21 for 200m, 49.29 for 400m, 56.62 for 400m hurdles, 1.68 for high jump, 6.67 for long jump and 4705 points (old tables) for pentathlon.

Caribbean Carnival

PRIOR TO 1976 the only Caribbean island to have won an Olympic gold medal in athletics was Jamaica, thanks to Arthur Wint in 1948 and George Rhoden and the 4x400m team in 1952. Jamaica added to that tally in Montreal when Don Quarrie won the 200m, while both Trinidad (Hasely Crawford in the 100m) and Cuba (Alberto Juantorena in the 400m and 800m) supplied their first ever Olympic champions. Another Central American nation, Mexico, also struck gold for the first time with Daniel Bautista taking the 20k walk.

Juantorena was the most exciting star of the Games. The tall, muscular Cuban – known as El Caballo (the horse) – completed a double unique in Olympic annals if one excludes the Interim Games of 1906. Even such earlier competitive giants as Ted Meredith, Arthur Wint and Mal Whitfield never quite achieved what he did in Montreal.

It was only at the last moment that Juantorena decided to go for both titles. Certainly he was among the favourites for the 400m title, topping the 1976 world rankings with a time of 44.70, but no one quite knew of his intentions at 800m. His pre-1976 best of 1:49.8 gave no indication of his possibilities but a Cuban record of 1:45.2 in Italy in May catapulted him into world class. However, he denied any Olympic ambitions at that distance. "The 800 will have to wait until next year. I want to be Olympic 400 champion first". He had second thoughts, though, after running 1:44.9 back in Havana just a couple of weeks before the Games.

The favourite for the 800m, which came before the 400m, was probably Rick Wohlhuter, who headed the season's world rankings at 1:44.8 and whose 1974 world 880 yards record of 1:44.1 translated to about 1:43.5 for 800m. The American would live to regret his statement that "Juantorena will not be a factor because he is basically a 400m runner who will have trouble running three 800m races in as many days".

Talk about famous last words! It was Wohlhuter, not Juantorena, who ran out of steam in the final, which was run at a cracking pace throughout. The 1.88m, 84kg Cuban was ahead at the bell in 50.85 and never looked like faltering. He held a three metre lead over Wohlhuter at 600m in 77.0, and was still that far ahead at the finish as Belgium's tragically destined Ivo Van Damme overtook the American for second place. Steve Ovett, who was considered to have an outside chance of winning, never recovered from too slow a start out in the blind eighth lane and finished fifth although he ran a personal best of 1:45.44.

Juantorena's time of 1:43.50 broke the world record of 1:43.7 held by the South African-born Italian Marcello Fiasconaro. As Mal Whitfield, himself a two-time Olympic 800m champion, enthused: "He's phenomenal. He's got about a nine-foot stride and reminds me of myself out there. He's what the future's going to be like in running".

Juantorena, who thus became the first man from a non-English speaking country to win that title (since 1896 it had always been won by an Australian, Briton, American or New Zealander), dedicated his medal "to Fidel Castro and the revolution" and returned to the stadium next day for the first two rounds of the 400m which he negotiated with the minimum of effort. Two days later he won his semi in 45.10, virtually jogging in after being left at the start, and the day after that he let rip in the final — his seventh race of the Games. He trailed the Americans, Fred Newhouse and Herman Frazier, at 200m and was still two metres down on Newhouse (32.1) at 300m, but it was in the finishing straight that his immense strength and stride length came into play and at the finish he was a metre clear. His time of 44.26, the fastest ever electrical time other than at high altitude, made it one of the greatest doubles in Olympic history.

Another powerfully built athlete came out top in the 100m. He was Hasely Crawford, the Trinidadian who had the misfortune in 1972 to drop out during the Olympic final with a leg injury. A hand-timed run of 10.0 into the wind at a warm-up meeting in Montreal indicated he had reached top form at the right time and so it proved as he powered to victory in 10.06. It was close, though, as the pride of Jamaica, the diminutive Don Quarrie, ran him to just 2/100ths of a second. Defending champion Valeriy Borzov of the USSR placed third for his first defeat in a lengthy championship career but had the distinction of becoming the

first 100m winner to gain a medal in the same event four years later. For the first time since 1928 no American broke into the medals.

Quarrie, another casualty of the Munich Games (he was stretchered off after pulling a hamstring in his 200m semi), enjoyed his golden moment this time over the distance at which he was co-holder of the world record with 19.8 at altitude. "I figured I was strong enough. I was just hoping my legs held up and I didn't get too tired. I didn't because I decided to run just to win rather than trying for a world record". He succeeded with a time of 20.23 ahead of Americans Millard Hampton and Dwayne Evans (17), with the man who was to succeed him as champion and world record holder, Pietro Mennea of Italy, fourth. Crawford pulled a muscle in the final and walked home, but wasn't too distressed. He had won what he came for.

1976 - MONTREAL

100m: (nil wind) 1, Hasely Crawford TRI 10.06; 2, Don Quarrie JAM 10.08; 3, Valeriy Borzov URS 10.14; 4, Harvey Glance USA 10.19; 5, Guy Abrahams PAN 10.25; 6, Johnny Jones USA 10.27; 7, Klaus-Dieter Kurrat GDR 10.31; 8, Petar Petrov BUL 10.35.

200m: (0.8) 1, Don Quarrie JAM 20.23; 2, Millard Hampton USA 20.29; 3, Dwayne Evans USA 20.43; 4, Pietro Mennea ITA 20.54; 5, Ruy da Silva BRA 20.84; 6, Bogdan Grzejszczak POL 20.91; 7, Colin Bradford JAM 21.17; 8, Hasely Crawford TRI 79.60 (injured).

400m: 1, Alberto Juantorena CUB 44.26; 2, Fred Newhouse USA 44.40; 3, Herman Frazier USA 44.95; 4, Alfons Brijdenbach BEL 45.04; 5, Maxie Parks USA 45.24; 6, Richard Mitchell AUS 45.40; 7, David Jenkins GBR 45.57; 8, Jan Werner POL 45.63.

800m: 1, Alberto Juantorena CUB 1:43.50 (world rec); 2, Ivo van Damme BEL 1:43.86; 3, Rick Wohlhuter USA 1:44.12; 4, Willi Wülbeck FRG 1:45.26; 5, Steve Ovett GBR 1:45.44; 6, Luciano Susanj YUG 1:45.75; 7, Sriram Singh IND 1:45.77; 8, Carlo Grippo ITA 1:48.39.

1500m: 1, John Walker NZL 3:39.17 (3:36.87 ht); 2, Ivo van Damme BEL 3:39.27; 3, Paul-Heinz Wellmann FRG 3:39.33; 4, Eamonn Coghlan IRL 3:39.51; 5, Frank Clement GBR 3:39.65; 6, Rick Wohlhuter USA 3:40.64; 7, Dave Moorcroft GBR 3:40.94; 8, Graham Crouch AUS 3:41.80.

5000m: 1, Lasse Viren FIN 13:24.76; 2, Dick Quax NZL 13:25.16; 3, Klaus-Peter

Hildenbrand FRG 13:25.38; 4, Rod Dixon NZL 13:25.50 (13:20.48 ht); 5, Brendan Foster GBR 13:26.19 (13:20.34 ht); 6, Willy Polleunis BEL 13:26.99; 7, Ian Stewart GBR 13:27.65; 8, Aniceto Simoes POR 13:29.38.

10,000m: 1, Lasse Viren FIN 27:40.38; 2, Carlos Lopes POR 27:45.17; 3, Brendan Foster GBR 27:54.92; 4, Tony Simmons GBR 27:56.26; 5, Ilie Floroiu ROM 27:59.93; 6, Mariano Haro ESP 28:00.28; 7, Marc Smet BEL 28:02.80; 8, Bernie Ford GBR 28:17.78.

Marathon: 1, Waldemar Cierpinski GDR 2:09:55; 2, Frank Shorter USA 2:10:46; 3, Karel Lismont BEL 2:11:13; 4, Don Kardong USA 2:11:16; 5, Lasse Viren FIN 2:13:11; 6, Jerome Drayton CAN 2:13:30; 7, Leonid Moseyev URS 2:13:34; 8, Franco Fava ITA 2:14:25.

3000mSC: 1, Anders Gärderud SWE 8:08.02 (world rec); 2, Bronislaw Malinowski POL 8:09.11; 3, Frank Baumgartl GDR 8:10.36; 4, Tapio Kantanen FIN 8:12.60; 5, Michael Karst FRG 8:20.14; 6, Euan Robertson NZL 8:21.08; 7, Dan Glans SWE 8:21.53; 8, Antonio Campos ESP 8:22.65.

110mH: (nil wind) 1, Guy Drut FRA 13.30; 2, Alejandro Casanas CUB 13.33; 3, Willie Davenport USA 13.38; 4, Charles Foster USA 13.41; 5, Thomas Munkelt GDR 13.44; 6, James Owens USA 13.73; 7, Vyacheslav Kulebyakin URS 13.93; 8, Viktor Myasnikov URS 13.94.

400mH: 1, Edwin Moses USA 47.64 (world rec); 2, Mike Shine USA 48.69; 3, Yevgeniy Gavrilenko URS 49.45; 4, Quentin Wheeler USA 49.86; 5, José Carvalho POR 49.94; 6, Yanko Bratanov BUL 50.03; 7, Damaso Alfonso CUB 50.19; 8, Alan Pascoe GBR 51.29.

4x100m Relay: 1, USA (Harvey Glance, Johnny Jones, Millard Hampton, Steve Riddick) 38.33; 2, GDR (Manfred Kokot, Jörg Pfeifer; Klaus-Dieter Kurrat, Alexander Thieme) 38.66; 3, USSR (Aleksandr Aksinin, Nikolay Kolesnikov, Juris Silovs, Valeriy Borzov) 38.78; 4, Poland 38.83; 5, Cuba 39.01; 6, Italy 39.08; 7, France 39.16; 8, Canada 39.47.

4x400m Relay: 1, USA (Herman Frazier 45.3, Benny Brown 44.6, Fred Newhouse 43.8, Maxie Parks 45.0) 2:58.65; 2, Poland (Ryszard Podlas 46.7, Jan Werner 44.0, Zbigniew Jaremski 45.5, Jerzy Pietrzyk 45.2) 3:01.43; 3, FRG (Franz-Peter Hofmeister 46.0, Lothar Krieg 45.3, Harald Schmid 45.8, Bernd Herrmann 44.9) 3:01.98; 4, Canada 3:02.64; 5, Jamaica 3:02.84 (Seymour Newman 43.8); 6, Trinidad 3:03.46; 7, Cuba 3:03.81; 8, Finland 3:06.51.

HJ: 1, Jacek Wszola POL 2.25; 2, Greg Joy CAN 2.23; 3, Dwight Stones USA 2.21; 4, Sergey Budalov URS 2.21; 5, Sergey Senyukov URS 2.18; 6, Rodolfo Bergamo ITA 2.18; 7, Rolf Beilschmidt GDR 2.18; 8, Jesper Tørring DEN 2.18.

PV: 1, Tadeusz Slusarski POL 5.50; 2, Antti Kalliomaki FIN 5.50; 3, Dave Roberts USA 5.50; 4, Patrick Abada FRA 5.45; 5, Wojciech Buciarski POL 5.45; 6, Earl Bell USA 5.45; 7, Jean-Michel Bellot FRA 5.40; 8, Itsuo Takanezawa JPN 5.40.

LJ: 1, Arnie Robinson USA 8.35; 2, Randy Williams USA 8.11; 3, Frank Wartenberg GDR 8.02; 4, Jacques Rousseau FRA 8.00; 5, Joao Carlos de Oliveira BRA 8.00; 6, Nenad Stekic YUG 7.89; 7, Valeriy Podluzhniy URS 7.88; 8, Hans Baumgartner FRG 7.84.

TJ: 1, Viktor Saneyev URS 17.29; 2, James Butts USA 17.18; 3, Joao Carlos de Oliveira BRA 16.90; 4, Pedro Pérez CUB 16.81; 5, Tommy Haynes USA 16.78; 6, Wolfgang Kolmsee FRG 16.68; 7, Eugeniusz Biskupski POL 16.49; 8, Carol Corbu ROM 16.43.

SP: 1, Udo Beyer GDR 21.05; 2, Yevgeniy Mironov URS 21.03; 3, Aleksandr Baryshnikov URS 21.00 (21.32q); 4, Al Feuerbach USA 20.55; 5, Hans-Peter Gies GDR 20.47; 6, Geoff Capes GBR 20.36; 7, George Woods USA 20.26; 8, Hans Höglund SWE 20.17.

DT: 1, Mac Wilkins USA 67.50 (68.28q); 2, Wolfgang Schmidt GDR 66.22; 3, John Powell USA 65.70; 4, Norbert Thiede GDR 64.30; 5, Siegfried Pachale GDR 64.24; 6, Pentti Kahma FIN 63.12; 7, Knut Hjeltnes NOR 63.06; 8, Jay Silvester USA 61.98.

HT: 1, Yuriy Sedykh URS 77.52; 2, Aleksey Spiridonov URS 76.08; 3, Anatoliy Bondarchuk URS 75.48; 4, Karl-Hans Riehm FRG 75.46; 5, Walter Schmidt FRG 74.72; 6, Jochen Sachse GDR 74.30; 7, Chris Black GBR 73.18; 8, Edwin Klein FRG 71.34.

JT: 1, Miklós Németh HUN 94.58 (world rec); 2, Hannu Siitonen FIN 87.92; 3, Gheorghe Megelea ROM 87.16; 4, Piotr Bielczyk POL 86.50; 5, Sam Colson USA 86.16; 6, Vasiliy Yershov URS 85.26; 7, Seppo Hovinen FIN 84.26 (89.76q); 8, Janis Lusis URS 80.26.

Dec: 1, Bruce Jenner USA 8618 (world rec; 8634 on present tables) (10.94, 7.22, 15.35, 2.03, 47.51, 14.84, 50.04, 4.80, 68.52, 4:12.61); 2, Guido Kratschmer FRG 8411 (8416); 3, Nikolay Avilov URS 8369 (8403); 4, Raimo Pihl SWE 8218 (8216); 5, Ryszard Skowronek POL

8113 (8099); 6, Siegfried Stark GDR 8048 (8051); 7, Leonid Litvinenko URS 8025 (7963); 8, Lennart Hedmark SWE 7974 (8002).

20k Walk: 1, Daniel Bautista MEX 1:24:41; 2, Hans-Georg Reimann GDR 1:25:14; 3, Peter Frenkel GDR 1:25:30; 4, Karl-Heinz Stadtmuller GDR 1:26:51; 5, Raul González MEX 1:28:19; 6, Armando Zambaldo ITA 1:28:26; 7, Vladimir Golubnichiy URS 1:29:25; 8, Vittorio Visini ITA 1:29:32.

50k Walk: not held.

Women's Events

100m: (nil wind) 1, Annegret Richter FRG 11.08 (11.01 semi-final, world rec); 2, Renate Stecher GDR 11.13 (11.10 sf); 3, Inge Helten FRG 11.17; 4, Raelene Boyle AUS 11.23; 5, Evelyn Ashford USA 11.24; 6, Chandra Cheeseborough USA 11.31; 7, Andrea Lynch GBR 11.32; 8, Marlies Oelsner GDR 11.34.

200m: (nil wind) 1, Bärbel Eckert GDR 22.37; 2, Annegret Richter FRG 22.39; 3, Renate Stecher GDR 22.47; 4, Carla Bodendorf GDR 22.64; 5, Inge Helten FRG 22.68; 6, Tatyana Prorochenko URS 23.03; 7, Denise Robertson AUS 23.05; 8, Chantal Rega FRA 23.09.

400m: 1, Irena Szewinska POL 49.29 (world rec); 2, Christina Brehmer GDR 50.51; 3, Ellen Streidt GDR 50.55 (50.51 sf); 4, Pirjo Häggman FIN 50.56; 5, Rosalyn Bryant USA 50.65; 6, Sheila Ingram USA 50.90; 7, Riitta Salin FIN 50.98; 8, Debra Sapenter USA 51.66.

800m: 1, Tatyana Kazankina URS 1:54.94 (world rec); 2, Nikolina Shtereva BUL 1:55.42; 3, Elfi Zinn GDR 1:55.60; 4, Anita Weiss GDR 1:55.74; 5, Svetlana Styrkina URS 1:56.44; 6, Svetla Zlateva BUL 1:57.21; 7, Doris Gluth GDR 1:58.99; 8, Mariana Suman ROM 2:02.21.

1500m: 1, Tatyana Kazankina URS 4:05.48; 2, Gunhild Hoffmeister GDR 4:06.02 (4:02.45 sf); 3, Ulrike Klapezynski GDR 4:06.09 (4:02.13 sf); 4, Nikolina Shtereva BUL 4:06.57 (4:02.33 sf); 5, Lyudmila Bragina URS 4:07.20 (4:02.41 sf); 6, Gabriella Dorio ITA 4:07.27; 7, Ellen Wellmann FRG 4:07.91; 8, Jan Merrill USA 4:08.54.

100mH: (nil wind) 1, Johanna Schaller GDR 12.77; 2, Tatyana Anisimova URS 12.78; 3, Natalya Lebedyeva URS 12.80; 4, Gudrun Berend GDR 12.82; 5, Grazyna Rabsztyn POL 12.96; 6, Esther Rot ISR 13.04; 7, Valeria Stefanescu ROM 13.35; 8, Ileana Ongar ITA 13.51.

4x100m Relay: 1, GDR (Marlies Oelsner, Renate Stecher, Carla Bodendorf, Bärbel Eckert) 42.55; 2, FRG (Elvira Possekel, Inge Helten, Annegret Richter, Annegret Kroniger) 42.59; 3, USSR (Tatyana Prorochenko, Lyudmila Maslakova, Nadezhda Besfamilnaya, Vera Anisimova) 43.09; 4, Canada 43.17; 5, Australia 43.18; 6, Jamaica 43.24; 7, USA 43.35; 8, Great Britain 43.79.

4x400m Relay: 1, GDR (Doris Maletzki 50.5, Brigitte Rohde 49.5, Ellen Streidt 49.5, Christina Brehmer 49.7) 3:19.23 (world rec); 2, USA (Debra Sapenter 51.8, Sheila Ingram 50.0, Pam Jiles 51.3, Rosalyn Bryant 49.7) 3:22.81; 3, USSR (Inta Klimovicha, Lyudmila Aksyonova, Natalya Sokolova, Nadezhda Ilyina) 3:24.24; 4, Australia 3:25.56; 5, FRG 3:25.71; 6, Finland 3:25.87; 7, Great Britain 3:28.01; 8, Canada 3:28.91.

HJ: 1, Rosi Ackermann (née Witschas) GDR 1.93; 2, Sara Simeoni ITA 1.91; 3, Yordanka Blagoyeva BUL 1.91; 4, Maria Mracnová TCH 1.89; 5, Joni Huntley USA 1.89; 6, Tatyana Shlyakhto URS 1.87; 7, Annette Tannander SWE 1.87; 8, Cornelia Popa ROM 1.87.

LJ: 1, Angela Voigt GDR 6.72; 2, Kathy McMillan USA 6.66; 3, Lidia Alfeyeva URS 6.60; 4, Sigrun Siegl 6.59; 5, Ildikó Szabó HUN 6.59; 6, Jarmila Nygrynová TCH 6.54; 7, Heidemarie Wycisk GDR 6.39; 8, Elena Vintila ROM 6.38.

SP: 1, Ivanka Khristova BUL 21.16; 2, Nadezhda Chizhova URS 20.96; 3, Helena Fibingerová TCH 20.67; 4, Marianne Adam GDR 20.55; 5, Ilona Schoknecht GDR 20.54; 6, Margitta Droese GDR 19.79; 7, Eva Wilms FRG 19.29; 8, Yelena Stoyanova BUL 18.89.

DT: 1, Evelin Schlaak GDR 69.00; 2, Maria Vergova BUL 67.30; 3, Gabriele Hinzmann GDR 66.84; 4, Faina Melnik URS 66.40; 5, Sabine Engel GDR 65.88; 6, Argentina Menis ROM 65.38; 7, Maria Betancourt CUB 63.86; 8, Natalya Gorbachova URS 63.46.

JT: 1, Ruth Fuchs GDR 65.94; 2, Marion Becker FRG 64.70 (65.14q); 3, Kate Schmidt USA 63.96; 4, Jacqueline Hein (née Todten) GDR 63.84; 5, Sabine Sebrowski GDR 63.08; 6, Svetlana Babich (née Korolyova) URS 59.42; 7, Nadezhda Yakubovich URS 59.16; 8, Karin Smith USA 57.50.

Pen: 1, Sigrun Siegl GDR 4745 (13.31, 12.92, 1.74, 6.49, 23.09); 2, Christine Laser (née Bodner) GDR 4745 (13.55, 14.29, 1.78, 6.27, 23.48); 3, Burglinde Pollak GDR 4740 (13.30, 16.25, 1.64, 6.30, 23.64); 4, Lyudmila Popovskaya URS 4700; 5, Nadezhda Tkachenko URS 4669; 6, Diane Jones CAN 4582; 7, Jane Frederick USA 4566; 8, Margit Papp HUN 4535.

CHEATS NEVER PROSPER?

IT WAS ironic that sports-loving Jimmy Carter, a former cross country competitor and the first Presidential jogger, should – by a cheap political gesture – have sabotaged the 1980 Games and gone close to destroying the Olympic movement. As a protest against the Soviet invasion of Afghanistan he decreed that if Soviet troops were not withdrawn by February 20 1980 the United States would boycott the Games, to be held in Moscow in July. The troops remained and the boycott went ahead. The Americans could have exerted real pressure had they threatened to stop trading with the USSR, which might have caused the Kremlin to reconsider, but no such action was forthcoming.

The boycott appears to have been just a weak ploy to bolster his re-election prospects that year. As Bert Nelson, editor of Track & Field News, wrote in the February 1980 issue of his magazine: "He is taking full advantage of the situation. He knows the American people are mad and are looking for some way to strike back at foreign enemies. He offers the Olympics as a sacrificial weapon and the public grabs it. After all, few of them have anything to lose."

The people who were sacrificed were the athletes of the USA and other countries who (in deference to American aid and influence) were ordered by their governments to join in the boycott – including West Germany, Kenya, Japan, Canada and New Zealand. Instead of the 125-130 countries expected, only 81 were represented (69 in athletics). Had Prime Minister Margaret Thatcher got her way, Britain would have stayed away too, but the British Olympic Association refused to bow to political pressure and a large team was sent to Moscow.

As a consequence of the boycott, many events were severely devalued – as would be the case four years later when, predictably, the Soviet Union and its allies retaliated by refusing to compete in Los Angeles. Potential gold medallists who were denied their chance of glory in Moscow included the Americans Stanley Floyd (100m), Renaldo Nehemiah (110m hurdles), Edwin Moses (400m hurdles), Mac Wilkins (discus) and the men's relay teams, together with the Germans Thomas Wessinghage (5000m) and Guido Kratschmer (decathlon), marathoner Toshihiko Seko of Japan and Kenya's Henry Rono (10,000m). In their world merit rankings for 1980, Track & Field News included among the top three in each event a total of 24 men who were prevented from competing in Moscow.

Obviously, athletes from Communist countries dominated the proceedings (making it a propaganda coup for the hosts), with no fewer than 31 of the 38 titles going to competitors from the Soviet Union, its satellites in Eastern Europe and its client states of Cuba and Ethiopia. The only western athletes to triumph were four from Britain (Allan Wells, 100m; Steve Ovett, 800m; Sebastian Coe, 1500m; Daley Thompson, decathlon) and three from Italy (Pietro Mennea, 200m; Maurizio Damilano, 20k walk; Sara Simeoni, women's high jump).

Few athletes of medal potential were missing from the women's events where the standard was the highest yet seen. There were world records for Nadezhda Olizarenko (USSR) with 1:53.43 in the 800m, Nadezhda Tkachenko (USSR) with a pentathlon score of 5083, and the GDR sprint relay team with a time of 41.60, while Olympic records tumbled in every other event with the exception of the 100m and 4x400m. There were a few "cheap" medals in the men's events but mostly performances were of a high calibre and world records fell to Gerd Wessig (GDR) in the high jump with 2.36, Wladyslaw Kozakiewicz of Poland in the pole

STAR OF THE GAMES

SEBASTIAN COE
(born 29 Sep 1956)

You don't often get a second chance in the cauldron of Olympic competition. Make a serious mistake and you face a four-year wait for the opportunity of redemption. Seb Coe was fortunate. After a tactically naive showing in the event he was expected to win, the 800m (the silver medal was scant consolation for a man of his ambition), he came back to run a perfectly planned and executed race against his 800m conqueror Steve Ovett in the 1500m.

vault at 5.78 and Yuriy Sedykh (USSR) with a hammer throw of 81.80. Olympic records were achieved in the shot and both walks.

The British team performed brilliantly to notch up four gold, two silver and four bronze medals ... a far cry from the solitary bronze in Montreal four years earlier. Gary Oakes, who ran out of his socks to clock 49.11 and take third place in the 400m hurdles, clearly benefitted from the absence of world record holder Moses and European record holder Harald Schmid of West Germany, and the American women might well have finished ahead of Britain in the 4x400m relay, but otherwise the medals were absolutely merited. Coe and Ovett (see page 129), the two most exciting and talented middle distance runners in the world, dominated the 800m and 1500m as expected – even if each won the other's speciality – and it's difficult to imagine anyone else snatching victory in those races. Thompson, the supreme competitor on the big occasion, would surely have responded to the West German challenge. As for Wells, the Americans might claim that their champion, Stanley Floyd, would have beaten the Scotsman ... but it should be noted that in their first clash of the summer, in Cologne a fortnight after the Olympic final, it was Wells who came out on top.

Wells (born in Edinburgh on May 3 1952) had an unlikely background for a man who would win the Blue Riband of sprinting, the first Briton to do so since Harold Abrahams 56 years earlier. Who could have predicted in 1970 that the lad raking the long jump pit at the Commonwealth Games in his native city, enabling him to watch at close quarters his idol Lynn Davies, would – ten years later – become an Olympic champion himself? At the time Wells was the Scottish junior triple jump champion, and it was as a long jumper (7.32 in 1972) that he primarily developed. Ironically, though, he was handicapped by a lack of speed on the runway and it was not until 1976 that he first managed to break 11 sec for 100m without wind assistance. That season he improved to 10.55 but neither he nor any other British 100m runner was deemed worthy of Olympic selection. Indeed, at the time of Abrahams' death, early in 1978, British sprinting was at its lowest ebb and had anyone predicted that two years hence a Briton would win the Olympic 100m crown that person would have been adjudged insane!

However, in the summer of 1978 it became apparent that the muscular Scot was quickly developing into world class; in the space of a week he first equalled Peter Radford's UK record of 10.29 and then smashed it with 10.15 ... without using starting blocks. However in Moscow it was compulsory to use blocks as they were fitted with an electronic device to register false starts and Wells adapted hastily and successfully to them in 1980.

He peaked perfectly for the Games, trimming his UK record to 10.11 in the heats. The final, run into the wind, was one of the closest in Olympic history as Wells and Cuba's Silvio Leonard – drawn the width of the track apart – crossed the line simultaneously. Neither was sure who had won, until the TV action replay suggested what the photo finish was to confirm: that Wells' lunge had won him the race by the narrowest of margins. It was so close that the two men could not be separated even by 1/100th of a second at 10.25. The 28 year-old Wells thus became not only the oldest man (until Linford Christie in 1992) to win the 100m title but the first Scottish Olympic champion since Eric Liddell in 1924.

While Wells was sprinting his way to immortality, Daley Thompson (born in London on July 30 1958) was busy piling up the points on the first day of the decathlon. Four years earlier, in Montreal, he had served his Olympic apprenticeship encouraged by Bruce Jenner; now he was ready to succeed the American as champion.

Daley (real name: Francis Morgan Thompson) had first topped 8000 points in 1977, the year he won the European junior title, and the following season – at the Commonwealth Games – he piled up the third highest score (using electrical timing) in decathlon history although his total of 8467 couldn't be ratified as a Commonwealth record because of excessive wind assistance in the long jump, where he achieved the spectacular distance of 8.11. Three weeks later he scored a valid 8289 at the European Championships but was inconsolable as that placed him only second. He resolved never to lose another decathlon ... and that was the case until injury ruined his chances in the 1987 World Championships!

Training for up to eight hours a day to perfect the diverse skills required of the decathlete,

Thompson was one of the new breed of full-time athlete, unable due to training demands (and the recuperation needed) to contemplate a job and therefore existing on officially channelled sponsorship money. He prepared for the Olympics brimming with self-confidence and in May 1980 he not only comfortably beat Guido Kratschmer, who would have been his main rival in Moscow but for West Germany joining the boycott, but broke Jenner's world record with a score of 8622 (8648 on the tables used today).

In Moscow Thompson proved unstoppable. A 10.62 100m, half a second quicker than his main rivals, laid the foundations and after enjoying an overnight lead of 264 with 4542 points, which included an eight metre long jump into the wind, he looked set for a massive score. But, hampered by the weather on the second day, he was content practically to jog home in the final event for a score of 8495 (8522). He had fulfilled his destiny of becoming the world's greatest all-round athlete ... and this was only the start.

Wells went agonisingly close to completing the double. Drawn in lane seven, with world record holder Mennea on the outside, he went off at such a lick that he had cancelled out the Italian's stagger in the first 50 metres. Wells must have had at least three metres to spare over Mennea entering the straight but he had expended too much energy too soon and, as he began to tie up, so his smooth-striding rival closed the gap. He drew level ten metres from the finish and won by just 2/100ths of a second. Wells set a British record of 20.21 in second place, with defending champion Don Quarrie of Jamaica third.

Five champions from Montreal did manage to hang on to their crowns, the most resounding defence being put up by Yuriy Sedykh, whose opening hammer throw of 81.80 was a world record and enabled him to surpass the achievement of his coach, Anatoliy Bondarchuk, Olympic champion in 1972 and bronze medallist four years later. A later throw of 81.46 by Sedykh was shown in a TV replay to be clearly a foul, and although the Soviet athletes did not need any help in this event it was a major talking point at the Games that judging decisions tended to favour the home team.

The result of the triple jump shows that Estonian Jaak Uudmae won with 17.35 ahead of

Soviet colleague Viktor Saneyev (17.24) – who so nearly emulated Al Oerter's record of four wins in the same event – with Brazil's Joao Carlos de Oliveira, Britain's Keith Connor and Australia's Ian Campbell next. However, both Campbell and de Oliveira were, in the view of expert observers, robbed of possible victory. In the third round Campbell landed beyond the Olympic record marker set at 17.39 only to find the red flag being raised. The jump was ruled a foul on the grounds that his left foot had dragged along the runway during the step phase, which was against the rule then in force, but Campbell denied that was the case – as borne out by scrutiny of videotape. But his demand for the referee to be summoned was ignored and the sandpit raked over before any further protest could be made. Similarly, two huge jumps by de Oliveira of beyond 17.50 were inexplicably ruled out.

There was controversy also in the discus and javelin, won respectively by Viktor Rashchupkin (66.64) and Dainis Kula (91.20), both of the USSR. With his final effort in the discus, Cuba's Luis Delis threw what might have been a winning distance but an official was seen to place the marker some way short of where the discus landed. The official measurement was 66.32 and Delis had to settle for the bronze. Kula was another to benefit from questionable judging. After two fouls he had to land a decent throw in the third round to stay in the competition, but although he did get off a long throw the spear landed tail first and should have been ruled out. Not so; up went the white flag, the throw was measured at 88.88 and the Latvian lived to fight another day. Curiously, that particular throw was never replayed on TV. In the next round Kula threw the winning distance of 91.20.

The rules were bent also in the men's and women's 4x400m relay. At that time, substitutions were permitted only on production of a medical certificate and yet individual 400m champion Viktor Markin plus two of their best women runners in Nina Zyuskova and Irina Nazarova were all somehow too ill to run in the heats but, miraculously recovered (not to mention rested), were able to play their part in the final. As the victory margin over the GDR was just 0.2 sec in each race the Soviets' manipulation of the rules was probably crucial.

Sedykh apart, the repeat winners were

Tatyana Kazankina (USSR) in a swift 1500m and the East German trio of marathoner Waldemar Cierpinski, discus thrower Evelin Jahl (née Schlaak) and 200m runner Bärbel Wöckel (née Eckert).

Kazankina, who broke the Olympic record with 3:59.12 in her heat, went into the lead with 600m to go in the final and a 57.7 last lap (and around two minutes flat for the final 800m) brought her to the finish in 3:56.56, as compared to her recent world record of 3:55.0 – which she was to lower to a sensational 3:52.47 in Zürich 12 days after the Games. Kazankina thus became only the fourth woman ever to win a third individual Olympic title, following in the footsteps of Fanny Blankers-Koen, Betty Cuthbert and Tamara Press. She did not defend her 800m title, but the USSR captured all the medals anyway with Nadezhda Olizarenko front-running through laps of 56.41 and 57.02 for a phenomenal time of 1:53.43. Runner-up Olga Mineyeva also finished inside Olizarenko's previous world mark of 1:54.85. Olizarenko, whose husband Sergey reached the steeple-chase semi-finals, was possessed of outstanding speed (50.96 400m) and stamina (3:56.8 1500m and a bronze medal in that event at the Games) and her career has been one of prodigious longevity. She won the European 800m title in 1986 and was still running inside 1:59 as recently as 1990 when she was 36.

Cierpinski emulated the feat of Abebe Bikila in winning the Olympic marathon for a second time. Running two days before his 30th birthday, the East German – who had achieved little of note since his Montreal success – ran with cool judgment in the sweltering conditions to surge clear of his rivals over the final 6k to win in 2:11:03. Lasse Viren, who had earlier placed fifth in the 10,000m, was a non-finisher ... as were all three Britons: Ian Thompson (high temperature), Bernie Ford (heat exhaustion) and Dave Black (toe injury). Indeed, it was a poor Games for British distance runners; nobody reached the 5000m final and Brendan Foster was highest placed at 11th in the 10,000m.

The man who dominated both those events may have been physically unimposing ... but how he could move at the end of a race! He was Ethiopia's mysterious and enigmatic Miruts Yifter; all 1.62m (5'4") and 53kg (8st 5lb) of him.

No one, not even Yifter himself, knew exactly how old he was – the best guess being that he was born between 1943 and 1945, although in Moscow he looked even older than 35-37. Little was known about his lifestyle (the father of six children, he was an officer in the Ethiopian Air Force) or his training methods. What was known was that he benefitted from living and training at high altitude and he possessed the deadliest finishing kick in distance running. Any sympathy the fans might have had at the start of a race when they saw this tiny, balding figure lining up with much more athletic looking opponents would almost certainly have been transferred to his luckless rivals by the finish!

He had become an international celebrity back in 1971 when, in a match between the USA and Africa in North Carolina, he miscounted the laps in the 5000m, sprinted to what he thought was victory over the redoubtable Steve Prefontaine and then discovered, to his horror, there was another lap to go. The race went to the American but next day he defeated Frank Shorter in the 10,000m and a new star was born. He encountered mixed fortunes at the 1972 Olympics. He ran bravely to come within two seconds of Ron Clarke's previous world record in finishing third in the 10,000m behind Viren and Emiel Puttemans, but his 5000m hopes were shattered when he spent too long in the toilet and missed the start of the final. With the African boycott preventing him from challenging Viren at the 1976 Games he had to wait eight years for his next Olympic opportunity. In the meantime he bolstered his reputation with 5000/10,000m doubles at both the 1977 and 1979 World Cup meetings.

"Yifter the Shifter", as he was affectionately and admiringly dubbed, seized his belated chance of Olympic glory in Moscow, sprinting away to victory in both the 10,000m (27:42.69 with a 54.4 last lap) and 5000m (13:20.91 with a 54.9 finish). Had the timetable allowed, he would have gone also for the marathon, but that race was held on the same day as the 5000m.

Another who had to wait eight years for a second Olympic chance as a consequence of the 1976 boycott was the Tanzanian, Filbert Bayi. He was only a 19 year-old novice in Munich, where he showed promise with times of 3:45.4 for 1500m and 8:41.4 for the steeplechase but failed to survive the heats. By the following year, though, he was among the world's elite at

CHEATS NEVER PROSPER?

1500m and in 1974 he led from gun to tape to beat John Walker for the Commonwealth title in a world record 3:32.16. A world mile record of 3:51.0 followed in 1975. Injuries and illness took their toll in the next three seasons but in 1980 he once again struck superb form ... as a steeple-chaser.

In Moscow he set a fiendish pace, passing 1000m in 2:38.8 and 2000m in a world's best of 5:20.3, which represents 8:00.5 pace for the full distance. At that point he was over 25m ahead of Ethiopia's Eshetu Tura with Bronislaw Malinowski, fourth in 1972 and second in 1976, holding back some 35m in arrears in the belief that Bayi would wilt in the closing stages. The Pole's confidence in his own pace judgment proved to be justified. With 600m to go he over-took Tura and at the bell he had reduced Bayi's lead to 20m. Malinowski steamed past his opponent approaching the final water jump and romped to victory in 8:09.70 with Bayi second in a personal best of 8:12.48 and proud to be his nation's first ever Olympic medallist. Sadly, Malinowski – who had dreams of emigrating to Scotland (his mother's birthplace) and wearing the blue vest at the 1982 Commonwealth Games – perished in a car crash barely a year after his Olympic triumph, aged 30.

Poland's other hero in Moscow was Wladyslaw Kozakiewicz, who became the first vaulter to win an Olympic title with a world record since Frank Foss (USA) in 1920. On that occasion the record leap measured 4.09; this time it was 5.78. The Lithuanian-born Kozakiewicz, whose vaulting career had begun as a 10 year-old but who was 15 before he first cleared three metres, deserved his success. Injury had cost him his chance at the 1976 Games, where he had the galling experience of watching the title go to a compatriot, Tadeusz Slusarski, who had long played second fiddle to himself, but in Moscow he couldn't put a foot wrong despite unsporting attempts by some Soviet fans to distract him during the competition. Just five vaults clinched the gold medal for him: first time clearances at 5.35, 5.50, 5.60, 5.65 and 5.70. He then went on to make 5.75 at the first attempt and 5.78 at the second.

A far less expected world record breaker was the East German high jumper, Gerd Wessig, who hadn't even ranked among the world's top 50 the previous year with an outdoor mark of

2.21. He went to the Games with bests of 2.27 outdoors and 2.29 indoors but his competitive temperament in Moscow was remarkable as he repeatedly jumped higher than ever before and one rival after another dropped by the wayside. Not until he cleared 2.31 was he assured of a medal, but at the next height of 2.33 the gold medal became his as he cleared on the second attempt and his two remaining opponents (Poland's defending champion Jacek Wszola and GDR team-mate Jörg Freimuth) were eliminated. It would have been understandable if all incentive had drained away in the excitement of winning as the bar was raised to the world record height of 2.36, but at his second try Wessig succeeded with something to spare.

The East Germans picked up another world record when the women's sprint relay squad of Romy Müller, Bärbel Wöckel, Ingrid Auerswald and Marlies Göhr swept round the track in 41.60 for a five-metre margin over the USSR with Heather Hunte (later to marry 400m hurdles medallist Gary Oakes), Kathy Smallwood, Bev Goddard and Sonia Lannaman setting a UK and Commonwealth record of 42.43 in third place. For Wöckel, the former Bärbel Eckert, it was her fourth gold medal – equalling the most by any female athlete. She had earlier retained her 200m title in 22.03 ahead of Natalya Bochina (USSR), whose 22.19 is still the world junior record, and a 20 year-old Jamaican by the name of Merlene Ottey. Göhr, who had in 1977 become the first woman to break 11 sec for 100m with an astonishing 10.88, was surprisingly beaten in that event. A poor start saw her only fourth at halfway and although she finished well she failed by a hundredth to catch Lyudmila Kondratyeva (USSR), 11.06 to 11.07.

Göhr's colleague, Marita Koch, also came away with a gold and a silver, but in her case the victory was in an individual event. If ever an athlete was destined to become Olympic 400m champion it was Koch who, as a 19 year-old, had to withdraw, injured, from the semi-finals at the 1976 Games. Some consolation came in taking the 1977 European indoor title with a world indoor best of 51.14, while that summer she improved to 49.53 when winning at the European Cup Final. Three weeks later, in a classic duel at the World Cup, the experience and determination of world record holder Irena

Szewinska proved just too much for the youthful exuberance of Koch, 11 years her junior, but the writing was on the wall. At the 1978 European Championships Koch demolished her Polish rival in a world record 48.94, while in 1979 she improved to 48.60 as well as setting an astonishing 200m record of 21.71.

A sad sight in Moscow was that of Szewinska (34), in her fifth Olympics, limping in last in her semi-final with an Achilles tendon injury, but no one would have stopped Koch in that final. She ran the second fastest time in history of 48.88, although significantly she was run closer than expected by the much improved Jarmila Kratochvilová of Czechoslovakia, who would in 1983 beat Koch to the distinction of being the first woman to break 48 sec. Even Koch could not wipe out the Soviet team's lead in the 4x400m relay, although she tried hard with a 48.27 anchor leg. The bronze medals went to Britain's squad of Linsey Macdonald (who had placed eighth in the 400m to become, at 16, the youngest Briton ever to reach an Olympic track final), Michelle Probert, Joslyn Hoyte-Smith and Donna Hartley.

Although no one failed a drugs test at the Games, the Moscow Olympics were notorious in that, for the first time, two proven cheats were crowned as champions. Ilona Slupianek, the East German winner of the shot in Moscow with 22.41, was banned after the 1977 European Cup Final when a doping test proved she had been taking anabolic steroids ... but penalties imposed by the IAAF were so lenient in those days that she came back to win the European title barely a year later. It was at those 1978 championships that Nadezhda Tkachenko (USSR) was stripped of the European pentathlon title, again as a result of steroid use. Her suspension was for 18 months (although she continued to compete domestically) and she reached new heights in 1980. In her third attempt at the title, having placed ninth in Munich and a tearful fifth in Montreal after leading prior to the final event, Tkachenko added no fewer than 227 points to the previous world record with a score of 5083 points.

Other cheats came to light years afterwards. Kaarlo Maaninka of Finland, whose pre-1980 bests were 13:34.0 for 5000m and 28:13.6 for 10,000m, ran 13:22.00 and 27:44.28 in Moscow to win the bronze and silver medals

respectively ... but later admitted he resorted to the practice of blood boosting. As for Vladimir Kiselyov (USSR), who won the shot title with 21.35, he revealed in 1991 that the long-term use of hormone-based drugs came close to killing him.

Coe v Ovett: 1-1

NEVER HAVE two athletes been subjected to so much media hype and speculation as were Sebastian Coe and Steve Ovett prior to their 800m and 1500m clashes at the Moscow Games. It was as if no one else was involved in those two races ... that the Olympic gold medals would, by divine right, be awarded to one or other of the Britons.

The consensus was that Coe, who had established a phenomenal world record of 1:42.33 the previous year, would be untroubled

DID YOU KNOW?

ABDERRAHMANE MORCELI, brother and coach of world record breaking Noureddine, finished 7th in his 1500m heat in Moscow in 3:45.96. He set Algerian records of 3:36.26 for 1500m in 1977 (placing fourth, aged 19, in the World Cup) and 3:54.63 for the mile in 1983 ... Olga Rukavishnikova technically held the world pentathlon record for 0.4 sec when finishing first in the 800m (2:04.8) but her score of 4937 was surpassed by Nadezhda Tkachenko (2:05.2) ... Lutz Dombrowski, the East German who won the long jump with a European record (and world sea level best) of 8.54, admitted in 1992 that he was an informer on fellow athletes for the dreaded Stasi secret police ... Pascal and Patrick Barré became the first twins to win Olympic athletics medals, forming half of the French team which finished third in the 4x100m relay ... Irina Nazarova, who anchored the winning Soviet 4x400m team, is the daughter of Yelisaveta Bagryantseva, who was second in the discus at the 1952 Games ... Gisela Beyer (GDR), at 1.85m and 88kg the 1976 shot champion Udo Beyer's "little sister", placed fourth in the discus ... Sergey Makarov, son of Moscow javelin silver medallist Aleksandr Makarov, gained the bronze medal in that event at the Sydney Olympics of 2000 and became world champion in 2003.

in winning the 800m, and that Ovett – unbeaten at the distance for three years – would start favourite in the 1500m, an event at which the two protagonists were co-holders of the world record at 3:32.1.

Adding to the mystique was that the pair had raced each other on the track only once before. That was at the 1978 European Championships, in which Ovett set a UK 800m record of 1:44.09 and Coe (after shooting round the first lap in 49.32) finished in 1:44.76, and yet both were beaten by the unconsidered East German, Olaf Beyer, in 1:43.84.

Ovett (born in Brighton on October 9 1955) had been hailed as a major star in the making since 1973 when, as a 17 year-old, he had won the European junior 800m title and run exactly four minutes for his miling debut. In 1974 he did well to finish second in the European senior championship in his best time of 1:45.8 but his attitude – one of dismay that by being boxed in at the crucial moment he lost his chance of victory – earmarked this tall, strongly built youngster, coached by Harry Wilson, as a very special breed of athlete.

Another aspect of Ovett's talent was his versatility. He had in 1974 improved his 400m time to 47.5 and yet he opened his 1975 campaign by winning the English junior cross country title with 200m to spare. At the 1976 Olympics he produced a personal best of 1:45.44 in the 800m final but, too slow into his running, he was never in the hunt and placed fifth some 15m behind Alberto Juantorena's world record 1:43.50. He later picked up another personal best as he won his 1500m heat in 3:37.9 but ran out of energy in the semis.

It was from 1977 onwards that Ovett's trademarks, the burst of acceleration 200m from the finish and his cheeky waves to the crowd well before the race was over, made him a charismatic and controversial figure known the world over.

Previously content to win in slowish times, he ran a devastating race in the 1977 World Cup 1500m to clock a UK record of 3:34.45 ... having, a fortnight earlier, won a half marathon in 65:38! In 1978 he followed up his silver medal in the European 800m with gold in the 1500m (covering the final 200m in 24.8), and set a world 2 miles best of 8:13.51.

Coe (born in London on September 29 1956) started off as a sprinter but, realising his light build wasn't ideally suited to that activity, he switched to cross country and 1500/3000m races. Whereas Ovett's first significant title was the English Schools under-15 400m, Coe's was the English Schools under-17 3000m three years later. In 1975 Coe took the bronze medal in the European junior 1500m and appeared to be well along the conventional path leading to the longer track events.

But Seb and his father/coach Peter Coe came to a momentous decision: if Seb was first to approach his limits as a 1500m runner his basic speed had to be improved drastically. The result of this policy became apparent in 1976 when, at 19, he improved his 800m time from 1:53.8 to 1:47.7 and clocked 3:58.4 for the mile. The following winter he captured the European indoor 800m title and in the summer of 1977 posted his first UK record of 1:44.95.

In 1979 Coe created a sensation by setting three world records in the space of 41 days with 1:42.33 for 800m, 3:48.95 for the mile and 3:32.03 (rounded up for record purposes to 3:32.1) for 1500m. Ovett, who had previously expressed disdain for record chasing, quickly realised he had to reply in kind if his reputation was not to suffer by comparison. He fell just short of Coe's records with 3:49.57 and 3:32.2 (3:32.11), but in July 1980 he succeeded with a 3:48.8 mile and a record equalling 3:32.1 (actually 3:32.09). Coe set a 1000m record of 2:13.40 also within weeks of the Olympics and clearly both men were in stupendous form at the right time.

Not that this was apparent watching Coe in the 800m final. Running an appalling tactical race and seemingly not concentrating on the job at hand, he struggled to salvage second place in 1:45.85 while Ovett seized his golden opportunity with both elbows, so to speak, as he barged his way through to a good position and raced away from the opposition early in the finishing straight to score convincingly in 1:45.40. Round one to Steve.

The rematch over 1500m was even more intriguing now that the "wrong man" had triumphed in the 800m. Surely Ovett, having won his supposedly weaker event, would be unbeatable in his speciality. Yet, with a gold medal already in the bank, would he be as hungry for success as Coe, whose whole reputation as a championship racer as distinct from a great time triallist was now on the line? As Coe said at the time, "I've got to come back and climb the mountain again. I MUST win it".

In terms of fitness and physical ability there was probably little to choose between the two men but, in that 1500m final, it was Coe's stronger will which made the difference. It was no longer – in athletic terms – a matter of life and death for Ovett whether he won; for Coe it was.

Coe this time was always in touch with the leaders, well placed to take advantage of the sharp acceleration in pace injected by East Germany's Jürgen Straub 700m from the finish. Coe was in his element as Straub covered the third lap of the race in a sizzling 54.2, safely tucked away in second place with Ovett third and no jostling as in the 800m. Straub held a four metre lead with 200m to go but Coe and Ovett were gathering themselves for the final strike.

Decisively, it was Coe who got his blow in first, producing a double kick along the finishing straight which carried him over the line three metres clear in 3:38.40, an unremarkable time until you consider he covered the last lap in 52.2 and the final 700m was run at sub-1:47 800m pace! Ovett, defeated at last over 1500m or mile after a winning streak of 45 races stretching back to May 1977, just could not get past the inspired Straub and had to settle for third in 3:39.0. Back in eighth place, soaking up the experience, was a gangling 19 year-old by the name of Steve Cram.

"I'm proud of my bronze as I am of my gold because I did my best," said Ovett. Coe commented: "I was able to do what I'm best at ... running freely and uncluttered, thanks to Straub." The last word comes from Peter Coe: "You've seen an athlete come back from the grave. In the last analysis it's all about character".

1980 - MOSCOW

100m: (-1.1) 1, Allan Wells GBR 10.25 (10.11 ht); 2, Silvio Leonard CUB 10.25 (10.16 ht); 3, Petar Petrov BUL 10.39 (10.13 ht); 4, Aleksandr Aksinin URS 10.42; 5, Osvaldo Lara CUB 10.43; 6, Vladimir Muravyov URS 10.44; 7, Marian Woronin POL 10.46; 8, Hermann Panzo FRA 10.49.

200m: (0.9) 1, Pietro Mennea ITA 20.19; 2, Allan Wells GBR 20.21; 3, Don Quarrie JAM 20.29; 4, Silvio Leonard CUB 20.30; 5, Bernard Hoff GDR 20.50; 6, Leszek Dunecki POL 20.68; 7, Marian Woronin POL 20.81; 8, Osvaldo Lara CUB 21.19.

400m: 1, Viktor Markin URS 44.60; 2, Richard Mitchell AUS 44.84; 3, Frank Schaffer GDR 44.87; 4, Alberto Juantorena CUB 45.09; 5, Alfons Brijdenbach BEL 45.10; 6, Michael Solomon TRI 45.55; 7, David Jenkins GBR 45.56; 8, Joseph Coombs TRI 46.33.

800m: 1, Steve Ovett GBR 1:45.40; 2, Seb Coe GBR 1:45.85; 3, Nikolay Kirov URS 1:45.94; 4, Agberto Guimaraes BRA 1:46.20; 5, Andreas Busse GDR 1:46.81; 6, Detlef Wagenknecht GDR 1:46.91; 7, José Marajo FRA 1:47.26; 8, David Warren GBR 1:49.25.

1500m: 1, Seb Coe GBR 3:38.40; 2, Jürgen Straub GDR 3:38.80 (3:36.95 ht); 3, Steve Ovett GBR 3:38.99 (3:36.80 ht); 4, Andreas Busse GDR 3:40.17; 5, Vittorio Fontanella ITA 3:40.37; 6, Josef Plachy TCH 3:40.66; 7, José Marajo FRA 3:41.48; 8, Steve Cram GBR 3:41.98.

5000m: 1, Miruts Yifter ETH 13:20.91; 2, Suleiman Nyambui TAN 13:21.60; 3, Kaarlo Maaninka FIN 13:22.00; 4, Eamonn Coghlan IRL 13:22.74; 5, Markus Ryffel SUI 13:23.03; 6, Dietmar Millonig AUT 13:23.25; 7, John Treacy IRL 13:23.62; 8, Aleksandr Fedotkin URS 13:24.10.

10,000m: 1, Miruts Yifter ETH 27:42.69; 2, Kaarlo Maaninka FIN 27:44.28; 3, Mohammed Kedir ETH 27:44.64; 4, Tolossa Kotu ETH 27:46.47; 5, Lasse Viren FIN 27:50.46; 6, Jörg Peter GDR 28:05.53; 7, Werner Schildhauer GDR 28:10.91; 8, Enn Sellik URS 28:13.72.

Marathon: 1, Waldemar Cierpinski GDR 2:11:03; 2, Gerard Nijboer NED 2:11:20; 3, Setymkul Dzhumanazarov URS 2:11:35; 4, Vladimir Kotov URS 2:12:05; 5, Leonid Moseyev URS 2:12:14; 6, Rodolfo Gomez MEX 2:12:39; 7, Dereje Nedi ETH 2:12:44; 8, Massimo Magnani ITA 2:13:12.

3000mSC: 1, Bronislaw Malinowski POL 8:09.70; 2, Filbert Bayi TAN 8:12.48; 3, Eshetu Tura ETH 8:13.57; 4, Domingo Ramón ESP 8:15.74; 5, Francisco Sánchez ESP 8:17.93; 6, Giuseppe Gerbi ITA 8:18.47; 7, Boguslaw Maminski POL 8:19.43; 8, Anatoliy Dimov URS

8:19.75.

110mH: (0.9) 1, Thomas Munkelt GDR 13.39; 2, Alejandro Casanas CUB 13.40; 3, Aleksandr Puchkov URS 13.44; 4, Andrey Prokofiev URS 13.49; 5, Jan Pusty POL 13.68; 6, Arto Bryggare FIN 13.76; 7, Javier Moracho ESP 13.78; 8, Yuriy Chervanyev URS 15.80.

400mH: 1, Volker Beck GDR 48.70; 2, Vasiliy Arkhipenko URS 48.86; 3, Gary Oakes GBR 49.11; 4, Nikolay Vasilyev URS 49.34; 5, Rok Kopitar YUG 49.67; 6, Horia Toboc ROM 49.84; 7, Franz Meier SUI 50.00; 8, Yanko Bratanov BUL 56.35.

4x100m Relay: 1, USSR (Vladimir Muravyov, Nikolay Sidorov, Aleksandr Aksinin, Andrey Prokofiev) 38.26; 2, Poland (Krzysztof Zwolinski, Zenon Licznerski, Leszek Dunecki, Marian Woronin) 38.33; 3, France (Antoine Richard, Pascal Barre, Patrick Barre, Hermann Panzo) 38.53; 4, Great Britain 38.62; 5, GDR 38.73; 6, Bulgaria 38.99; 7, Nigeria 39.12; 8, Brazil 39.54.

4x400m Relay: 1, USSR (Remigius Valiulis 45.90, Mikhail Linge 45.13, Nikolay Chernetsky 44.89, Viktor Markin 45.16) 3:01.08; 2, GDR (Klaus Thiele 45.88, Andreas Knebel 45.32, Frank Schaffer 44.91, Volker Beck 45.15) 3:01.26; 3, Italy (Stefano Malinverni, Mauro Zuliani, Roberto Tozzi, Pietro Mennea) 3:04.3 (3:03.5 ht); 4, France 3:04.8; 5, Brazil 3:05.9; 6, Trinidad 3:06.6 ; 7, Czechoslovakia 3:07.0 (3:03.5 ht); Great Britain dnf.

HJ: 1, Gerd Wessig GDR 2.36 (world rec); 2, Jacek Wszola POL 2.31; 3, Jörg Freimuth GDR 2.31; 4, Henry Lauterbach GDR 2.29; 5, Roland Dalhauser SUI 2.24; 6, Vaso Komnenic YUG 2.24; 7, Adrian Proteasa ROM 2.21; 8, Aleksandr Grigoriev URS 2.21.

PV: 1, Wladyslaw Kozakiewicz POL 5.78 (world rec); eq2, Tadeusz Slusarski POL & Konstantin Volkov URS 5.65; 4, Philippe Houvion FRA 5.65; 5, Jean-Michel Bellot FRA 5.60; 6, Mariusz Klimczyk POL 5.55; 7, Thierry Vigneron FRA 5.45; 8, Sergey Kulibaba URS 5.45.

LJ: 1, Lutz Dombrowski GDR 8.54; 2, Frank Paschek GDR 8.21; 3, Valeriy Podluzhniy URS 8.18; 4, László Szalma HUN 8.13; 5, Stanislaw Jaskulka POL 8.13; 6, Viktor Belskiy URS 8.10; 7, Antonio Corgos ESP 8.09; 8, Yordan Yanev BUL 8.02.

TJ: 1, Jaak Uudmae URS 17.35; 2, Viktor Saneyev URS 17.24; 3, Joao Carlos de Oliveira BRA 17.22; 4, Keith Connor GBR 16.87; 5, Ian Campbell AUS 16.72; 6, Atanas Chochev BUL 16.56; 7, Béla Bakosi HUN 16.47; 8, Ken Lorraway AUS 16.44.

SP: 1, Vladimir Kiselyov URS 21.35; 2, Aleksandr Baryshnikov URS 21.08; 3, Udo Beyer GDR 21.06; 4, Reijo Stahlberg FIN 20.82; 5, Geoff Capes GBR 20.50; 6, Hans-Jürgen Jacobi GDR 20.32; 7, Jaromir Vlk TCH 20.24; 8, Vladimir Mili YUG 20.07.

DT: 1, Viktor Rashchupkin URS 66.64; 2, Imrich Bugár TCH 66.38; 3, Luis Delis CUB 66.32; 4, Wolfgang Schmidt GDR 65.64; 5, Yuriy Dumchev URS 65.58; 6, Igor Duginets URS 64.04; 7, Emil Vladimirov BUL 63.18; 8, Velko Velev BUL 63.04.

HT: 1, Yuriy Sedykh URS 81.80 (world rec); 2, Sergey Litvinov URS 80.64; 3, Jüri Tamm URS 78.96; 4, Roland Steuk GDR 77.54; 5, Detlef Gerstenberg GDR 74.60; 6, Emanouil Dulgherov BUL 74.04; 7, Gianpaolo Urlando ITA 73.90; 8, Ireneusz Golda POL 73.74.

JT: 1, Dainis Kula URS 91.20; 2, Aleksandr Makarov URS 89.64; 3, Wolfgang Hanisch GDR 86.72; 4, Heino Puuste URS 86.10; 5, Antero Puranen FIN 85.12; 6, Pentti Sinersaari FIN 84.34; 7, Detlef Fuhrmann GDR 83.50; 8, Miklós Németh HUN 82.40 ... 10, Ferenc Paragi HUN 79.52 (88.76q).

Dec: 1, Daley Thompson GBR 8495 (8522 on present tables) (10.62, 8.00, 15.18, 2.08, 48.01, 14.47, 42.24, 4.70, 64.16, 4:39.9); 2, Yuriy Kutsenko URS 8331 (8369); 3, Sergey Zhelanov URS 8135 (8135); 4, Georg Werthner AUT 8050 (8084); 5, Josef Zeilbauer AUT 8007 (7989); 6, Dariusz Ludwig POL 7978 (7972); 7, Atanas Andonov BUL 7927 (7887); 8, Steffen Grummt GDR 7892 (7840).

20k Walk: 1, Maurizio Damilano ITA 1:23:36; 2, Pyotr Pochenchuk URS 1:24:46; 3, Roland Wieser GDR 1:25:59; 4, Yevgeniy Yevsyukov URS 1:26:29; 5, José Marin ESP 1:26:46; 6, Raul González MEX 1:27:49; 7, Bohdan Bulakowski POL 1:28:37; 8, Karl-Heinz Stadtmuller GDR 1:29:22.

50k Walk: 1, Hartwig Gauder GDR 3:49:24; 2, Jorge Llopart ESP 3:51:25; 3, Yevgeniy Ivchenko URS 3:56:32; 4, Bengt Simonsen SWE 3:57:08; 5, Vyacheslav Fursov URS 3:58:32; 6, José Marin ESP 4:03:08; 7, Stanislaw Rola POL 4:07:07; 8, Willi Sawall AUS 4:08:25.

Women's Events

100m: (1.0) 1, Lyudmila Kondratyeva URS 11.06; 2, Marlies Göhr (née Oelsner) GDR 11.07; 3, Ingrid Auerswald GDR 11.14 (11.12 ht); 4, Linda Haglund SWE 11.16; 5. Romy Müller GDR 11.16 (11.09 ht); 6, Kathy Smallwood GBR 11.28; 7, Chantal Rega FRA 11.32; 8, Heather Hunte GBR 11.34.

200m: (1.5) 1, Bärbel Wöckel (née Eckert) GDR 22.03; 2, Natalya Bochina URS 22.19; 3, Merlene Ottey JAM 22.20; 4, Romy Müller GDR 22.47; 5, Kathy Smallwood GBR 22.61; 6, Bev Goddard GBR 22.72; 7, Denise Boyd (née Robertson) AUS 22.76; 8, Sonia Lannaman GBR 22.80.

400m: 1, Marita Koch GDR 48.88; 2, Jarmila Kratochvilová TCH 49.46; 3, Christina Lathan (née Brehmer) GDR 49.66; 4, Irina Nazarova URS 50.07; 5, Nina Zyuskova URS 50.17; 6, Gabriele Löwe GDR 51.33; 7, Pirjo Häggman FIN 51.35; 8, Linsey Macdonald GBR 52.40.

800m: 1, Nadezhda Olizarenko URS 1:53.43 (world rec); 2, Olga Mineyeva URS 1:54.81; 3, Tatyana Providokhina URS 1:55.46; 4, Martina Kämpfert GDR 1:56.21; 5, Hildegard Ullrich GDR 1:57.20; 6, Jolanta Januchta POL 1:58.25; 7, Nikolina Shtereva BUL 1:58.71; 8, Gabriella Dorio ITA 1:59.12.

1500m: 1, Tatyana Kazankina URS 3:56.56; 2, Christiane Wartenberg GDR 3:57.71; 3, Nadezhda Olizarenko URS 3:59.52 (3:59.48 ht); 4, Gabriella Dorio ITA 4:00.30; 5, Ulrike Bruns GDR 4:00.62; 6, Lyubov Smolka URS 4:01.25; 7, Maricica Puica ROM 4:01.26; 8, Ileana Silai ROM 4:02.98.

100mH: (1.0) 1, Vera Komisova URS 12.56; 2, Johanna Klier (née Schaller) GDR 12.63; 3, Lucyna Langer POL 12.65; 4, Kerstin Claus GDR 12.66; 5, Grazyna Rabsztyn POL 12.74 (12.64 sf); 6, Irina Litovchenko URS 12.84; 7, Bettina Gärtz GDR 12.93; 8, Zofia Bielczyk POL 13.08.

4x100m Relay: 1, GDR (Romy Müller, Bärbel Wöckel, Ingrid Auerswald, Marlies Göhr) 41.60 (world rec); 2, USSR (Vera Komisova, Lyudmila Maslakova, Vera Anisimova, Natalya Bochina) 42.10; 3, Great Britain (Heather Hunte, Kathy Smallwood, Bev Goddard, Sonia Lannaman) 42.43; 4, Bulgaria 42.67; 5, France 42.84; 6, Jamaica 43.19; 7, Poland 43.59; Sweden dnf.

4x400m Relay: 1, USSR (Tatyana Prorochenko 50.2, Tatyana Goistchik 51.5, Nina Zyuskova 49.7, Irina Nazarova 48.8) 3:20.12; 2, GDR (Gabriele Löwe 50.6, Barbara Krug 50.5, Christina Lathan 51.0, Marita Koch 48.3) 3:20.35; 3, Great Britain (Linsey Macdonald, Michelle Probert, Joslyn Hoyte-Smith, Donna Hartley) 3:27.5; 4, Romania 3:27.7; 5, Hungary 3:27.9; 6, Poland 3:27.9; 7, Belgium 3:31.6; Bulgaria dnf.

HJ: 1, Sara Simeoni ITA 1.97; 2, Urszula Kielan POL 1.94; 3, Jutta Kirst GDR 1.94; 4, Rosi Ackermann (née Witschas) GDR 1.91; 5, Marina Sysoyeva URS 1.91; eq6, Christine Stanton AUS & Andrea Reichstein GDR 1.91; 8, Cornelia Popa ROM 1.88.

LJ: 1, Tatyana Kolpakova URS 7.06; 2, Brigitte Wujak GDR 7.04; 3, Tatyana Skachko URS 7.01; 4, Anna Wlodarczyk POL 6.95; 5, Sigrun Siegl GDR 6.87; 6, Jarmila Nygrynová TCH 6.83; 7, Sigrid Heimann GDR 6.71; 8, Lidiya Alfeyeva URS 6.71.

SP: 1, Ilona Slupianek (née Schoknecht) GDR 22.41; 2, Svetlana Krachevskaya URS 21.42; 3, Margitta Pufe (née Droese) GDR 21.20; 4, Nunu Abashidze URS 21.15; 5, Verzinia Vesselinova BUL 20.72; 6, Elena Stoyanova BUL 20.22; 7, Natalya Akhrimenko URS 19.74; 8, Ines Reichenbach GDR 19.66.

DT: 1, Evelin Jahl (née Schlaak) GDR 69.96; 2, Maria Petkova (née Vergova) BUL 67.90; 3, Tatyana Lesovaya URS 67.40; 4, Gisela Beyer GDR 67.08; 5, Margitta Pufe (née Droese) GDR 66.12; 6, Florenta Tacu ROM 64.38; 7, Galina Murashova URS 63.84; 8, Svetla Bozhkova BUL 63.14.

JT: 1, Maria Colon CUB 68.40; 2, Saida Gunba URS 67.76; 3, Ute Hommola GDR 66.56; 4, Ute Richter GDR 66.54 (66.66q); 5, Ivanka Vancheva BUL 65.38; 6, Tatyana Biryulina URS 65.08; 7, Eva Raduly-Zorgo ROM 64.08; 8, Ruth Fuchs GDR 63.94.

Pen: 1, Nadezhda Tkachenko URS 5083 (world rec; 13.29, 16.84, 1.84, 6.73, 800m-2:05.2); 2, Olga Rukavishnikova URS 4937; 3, Olga Kuragina URS 4875; 4, Ramona Neubert GDR 4698; 5, Margit Pápp HUN 4562; 6, Burglinde Pollak GDR 4553; 7, Valentina Dimitrova BUL 4458; 8, Emilia Kounova BUL 4431.

FAILED DRUGS TESTS

THE FIRST athlete in Olympic history to be disqualified and banned for failing a drugs test was a female Polish discus thrower Danuta Rosani in 1976. During the past quarter century or so, no fewer than 49 athletes who had either gained or would win Olympic medals have served drug suspensions of a year or longer ... 21 of them gold medallists. Clearly, some of them set out to cheat and were caught; others might have been unlucky in that their samples contained banned performance enhancing substances of which they had no prior knowledge. However, the rules are clear. The athlete is ultimately responsible for what he or she ingests.

Bear in mind that this deeply depressing list contains the names only of those who failed tests. How many others managed to avoid detection? Dozens of East German athletes for a start. Only one star, shot putter Ilona Slupianek, was ever caught out while representing the GDR but as there is incontrovertible evidence that during the 1970s and 1980s there was a state supported drugs programme for athletes from that nation it is obvious that a vast number of their Olympic medals were effectively gained under false pretences.

In the list which follows, the year is that in which the athlete was banned (in some cases there were subsequent suspensions and life bans). The details refer to Olympic placings. * = athlete refused to take test

1977 Ilona Slupianek GDR 1st 1980 Shot
1978 Yevgeniy Mironov URS 2nd 1980 Shot
1978 Nadezhda Tkachenko URS 1st 1980 Pentathlon
1979 Ileana Silai ROM 2nd 1968 800m
1981 Gael Martin AUS 3rd 1984 Shot
1984 Martti Vainio FIN 2nd 1984 10,000m
1984 Tatyana Kazankina URS* 1st 1976 800m & 1500m, 1st 1980 1500m
1986 Daniela Costian ROM 3rd 1992 Discus (representing AUS)
1988 Ben Johnson CAN 3rd 1984 100m & 4x100m, 1st 1988 100m
1989 Aleksandr Bagach URS 3rd 1996 Shot (representing UKR)
1990 Butch Reynolds USA 2nd 1988 400m, 1st 4x400m
1990 Larry Myricks USA 3rd 1988 Long Jump
1990 Randy Barnes USA 2nd 1988 Shot, 1st 1996 Shot

1990 Mike Stulce USA 1st 1992 Shot
1990 Jim Doehring USA 2nd 1992 Shot
1990 Luis Delis CUB 3rd 1980 Discus
1990 LaVonna Martin USA 2nd 1992 100mH
1990 Patricia Girard FRA 3rd 1996 100mH
1991 Sui Xinmei CHN 2nd 1996 Shot
1992 Danny Harris USA 2nd 1984 400mH
1992 Chioma Ajunwa NGR 1st 1996 Long Jump
1992 Ellina Zvereva BLR 3rd 1996 Discus, 1st 2000 Discus
1992 Charity Opara NGR 2nd 1996 4x400m
1992 Grit Breuer GER 3rd 1996 4x400m
1993 John Ngugi KEN* 1st 1988 5000m
1993 Romas Ubartas LTU 2nd 1988 Discus, 1st 1992 Discus
1993 Liliya Nurutdinova RUS 2nd 1992 800m
1993 Tatyana Dorovskikh-Samolenko UKR 3rd 1988 1500m, 1st 3000m; 2nd 1992 3000m
1993 Ludmila Engquist SWE (Lyudmila Narozhilenko RUS at time of ban) 1st 1996 100mH
1993 Tsvetanka Khristova BUL 3rd 1988 Discus, 2nd 1992 Discus
1993 Irina Belova RUS 2nd 1992 Heptathlon
1993 Lyudmila Dzhigalova UKR 1st 1992 4x400m
1994 Chidi Imoh NGR 2nd 1992 4x100m
1994 Olga Bogoslovskaya RUS 2nd 1992 4x100m
1995 Violeta Szekely ROM 2nd 2000 1500m
1996 Daniel Plaza ESP 1st 1992 20k Walk
1996 Olga Nazarova RUS 3rd 1988 400m, 1st 4x400m; 1st 1992 4x400m
1996 Olga Shishigina KAZ 1st 2000 100mH
1996 Yelena Ruzina RUS 1st 1992 4x400m
1997 Irina Khudorozhkina RUS 2nd 1996 Shot
1998 Dennis Mitchell USA 3rd 1992 100m, 1st 4x100m; 2nd 1996 4x100m
1999 Linford Christie GBR 2nd 1988 100m & 4x100m, 1st 1992 100m
1999 Dieter Baumann GER 2nd 1988 5000m, 1st 1992 5000m
1999 Davidson Ezinwa NGR 2nd 1992 4x100m
1999 Mark Richardson GBR 2nd 1996 4x400m
2000 Inessa Kravets UKR 3rd 1992 Long Jump, 1st 1996 Triple Jump
2001 Ali Saïdi-Sief ALG 2nd 2000 5000m
2001 Tony Dees USA 2nd 1992 110mH
2003 Yanina Korolchik BLR 1st 2000 Shot

WORLD RECORDS

(best performances at January 1 1980)
(A = high altitude mark;
mx = mixed race against men)

100: 9.95A Jim Hines USA 1968
200: 19.72A Pietro Mennea ITA 1979
400: 43.86A Lee Evans USA 1968
800: 1:42.33 Sebastian Coe GBR 1979
1500: 3:32.1 Sebastian Coe GBR 1979
5000: 13:08.4 Henry Rono KEN 1978
10,000: 27:22.4 Henry Rono KEN 1978
Marathon: 2:08:34 Derek Clayton AUS 1969
3000SC: 8:05.4 Henry Rono KEN 1978
110H: 13.00 Renaldo Nehemiah USA 1979
400H: 47.45 Edwin Moses USA 1977
4x100: 38.03 USA 1977
4x400: 2:56.16A USA 1968
HJ: 2.34 Volodymyr Yashchenko URS 1978
PV: 5.70 Dave Roberts USA 1976
LJ: 8.90A Bob Beamon USA 1968
TJ: 17.89A Joao Carlos de Oliveira BRA 1975
SP: 22.15 Udo Beyer GDR 1978
DT: 71.16 Wolfgang Schmidt GDR 1978
HT: 80.32 Karl-Hans Riehm FRG 1978
JT: 94.58 Miklos Németh HUN 1976
Decathlon: 8618 (8634 on present tables)
Bruce Jenner USA 1976
20kW: 1:18:49 Daniel Bautista MEX 1979
50kW: 3:41:20 Raul González MEX 1978

Women

100: 10.88 Marlies Oelsner GDR 1977
200: 21.71 Marita Koch GDR 1979
400: 48.60 Marita Koch GDR 1979
800: 1:54.9 Tatyana Kazankina URS 1976
1500: 3:56.0 Tatyana Kazankina URS 1976
3000: 8:27.1 Lyudmila Bragina URS 1976
5000: 15:08.8mx Loa Olafsson DEN 1978
10,000: 31:45.4mx Loa Olafsson DEN 1978
Marathon: 2:27:33 Grete Waitz NOR 1979
100H: 12.48 Grazyna Rabsztyn POL 1978/79
400H: 54.78 Marina Makeyeva URS 1979
4x100: 42.09 GDR 1979
4x400: 3:19.23 GDR 1976
HJ: 2.01 Sara Simeoni ITA 1978 (twice)
LJ: 7.09 Vilma Bardauskiene URS 1978
SP: 22.32 Helena Fibingerová TCH 1977
DT: 70.72 Evelin Jahl GDR 1978
JT: 69.52 Ruth Fuchs GDR 1979
Pentathlon: (with 800m) 4839 Nadezhda
Tkachenko URS 1977

METRIC CONVERSIONS

For the benefit of American readers not fully
conversant with the metric system, here are
some key conversions from metres to feet and
inches. The figures have been extracted from
tables compiled by the late Bob Sparks.

HIGH JUMP

1.60	5ft 3in	2.10	6ft 10.75in
1.70	5ft 7in	2.15	7ft 0.5in
1.80	5ft 10.75in	2.20	7ft 2.5in
1.85	6ft 0.75in	2.25	7ft 4.5in
1.90	6ft 2.75in	2.30	7ft 6.5in
1.95	6ft 4.75in	2.35	7ft 8.5in
2.00	6ft 6.75in	2.40	7ft 10.5in
2.05	6ft 8.75in	2.45	8ft 0.5in

POLE VAULT

3.80	12ft 5.5in	5.20	17ft 0.75in
4.00	13ft 1.5in	5.40	17ft 8.5in
4.20	13ft 9.25in	5.50	18ft 0.5in
4.40	14ft 5.25in	5.60	18ft 4.5in
4.50	14ft 9in	5.80	19ft 0.25in
4.60	15ft 1in	6.00	19ft 8.25in
4.80	15ft 9in	6.10	20ft 0.25in
5.00	16ft 4.75in	6.20	20ft 4.25in

LONG JUMP

6.30	20ft 8in	7.80	25ft 7.25in
6.50	21ft 4in	8.00	26ft 3in
6.70	21ft 11.75in	8.20	26ft 11in
6.90	22ft 7.75in	8.40	27ft 6.75in
7.00	22ft 11.75in	8.50	27ft 10.75in
7.20	23ft 7.5in	8.60	28ft 2.75in
7.40	24ft 3.5in	8.80	28ft 10.5in
7.60	24ft 11.25in	9.00	29ft 6.5in

TRIPLE JUMP & SHOT

14.00	45ft 11.25in	18.20	59ft 8.5in
15.00	49ft 2.5in	18.40	60ft 4.5in
16.00	52ft 6in	19.00	62ft 4in
17.00	55ft 9.25in	20.00	65ft 7.5in
17.40	57ft 1in	21.00	68ft 10.75in
17.80	58ft 4.75in	22.00	72ft 2.25in
18.00	59ft 0.75in	23.00	75ft 5.5in

LONG THROWS

40m	131ft 3in	75m	246ft 1in
45m	147ft 8in	78m	255ft 11in
50m	164ft 0in	80m	262ft 5in
55m	180ft 5in	83m	272ft 4in
60m	196ft 10in	85m	278ft 10in
63m	206ft 8in	88m	288ft 8in
65m	213ft 3in	90m	295ft 3in
68m	223ft 1in	93m	305ft 1in
70m	229ft 8in	95m	311ft 8in
73m	239ft 6in	98m	321ft 6in

ANOTHER DEVALUED GAMES

ON THE positive side, the Games of the 23rd Olympiad attracted the greatest number of countries (121) ever to be represented in the Olympic athletics events, the crowds in the memorial Coliseum were huge (well over a million in aggregate), the organisation was generally commendable and a handsome profit was made. Many scintillating performances were recorded and there was much stimulating competition. Nevertheless, there was no getting away from the fact that the Communist bloc boycott did cast a giant shadow over the proceedings.

Stars like Carl Lewis, Joaquim Cruz, Seb Coe, Said Aouita, Carlos Lopes, Ed Moses and Daley Thompson would have won their titles regardless, but the absence of Soviet and East German athletes in particular did devalue the worth of several events, including practically the whole of the women's programme. Previous boycotts in 1976 (by the African nations) and 1980 (led by the USA) were damaging enough but never had the Olympic athletics events been marred to such an extent by the non-appearance of so many prime medal contenders.

Hypothetical, of course, but roughly a third of the men and over half of the women who won medals in Los Angeles might not have done so had the events been at full strength. Of course, the athletes can only beat those who actually turn up, and it's not their fault if political considerations remove much of the top opposition, but on this occasion the Games suffered by comparison to the IAAF's inaugural World Athletics Championships staged in Helsinki the previous year when all the world's best athletes – other than those who were ill or injured – did battle.

The individual star of the Los Angeles Olympics was Carl Lewis (see page 139), who emulated the legendary feat of Jesse Owens in 1936 by winning gold medals in the 100m, 200m, long jump and 4 x 100m, contributing to the USA's world record time of 37.83 in the relay. On the women's side, Valerie Brisco-Hooks – known only to close followers of the sport beforehand – collected three gold medals (200m, 400m, 4x400m relay), and these two athletes helped the United States win 16 of the 41 titles on offer. Next most successful was West Germany (FRG) with four, followed by Britain, Italy and Romania (the only Soviet bloc nation to compete) with three apiece.

Helped, admittedly, by the absence of certain East Europeans, the Games proved to be Britain's most successful Olympics. Even the haul of 12 medals in Tokyo in 1964 was easily topped as British athletes collected three gold (Coe, Thompson and Tessa Sanderson), seven silver and six bronze medals. Only the USA (40) won more medals, while on the basis of athletes placed in the first eight Britain (40) ranked second to the USA (74) with West Germany third on 27.

Coe made Olympic history by becoming the first man to retain the 1500m title, silencing British critics who thought that Peter Elliott, and not he, should have been awarded the vacant spot in that event after Steve Cram and Steve Ovett had been pre-selected. As in Moscow four years earlier his 1500m triumph followed a silver medal in the 800m, the difference this time being that Coe was perfectly happy with his showing in the shorter event. While Brazil's Joaquim Cruz won in 1:43.00, then the third fastest ever time, Coe ran a fine race too to clock 1:43.64 against the strongest two-lap field yet assembled.

Coe might have looked frail, but he possessed the endurance to cap four tough 800m

STAR OF THE GAMES

CARL LEWIS
(born 1 Jul 1961)

He didn't win over the fans in Los Angeles like his predecessor did in Berlin in 1936, but Carl Lewis carved out a niche for himself in Olympic history by matching Jesse Owens' colossal haul of four gold medals – in the 100m, 200m, long jump and 4x100m relay. All his performances were remarkable: he won the 100m by two metres in 9.99, long jumped 8.54 before retiring after the second round, ran 19.80 for 200m into the wind and anchored the relay team to a world record races and two rounds of the 1500m with a devastating display in the final. Always in good position, he pre-empted world champion Cram's move by striking first with 200m to go. He never wavered as he completed the last lap in 53.3 (1:50.0 for the final 800m) to score in 3:32.53, breaking Kip Keino's Olympic record. With two gold and two silver medals to his name, he became Britain's most successful Olympic athlete ever.

Cram, not at his fittest following injury, was a clear second but hopes of a British clean sweep were dashed when world record holder Steve Ovett dropped out shortly after the bell when in fourth place, suffering once again from the chest pains (later diagnosed as a viral heart condition) which had reduced him to last place in the 800m final.

Daley Thompson also joined the select ranks of British athletes who have retained their Olympic laurels, and for good measure somehow managed - belatedly - to be credited with a world record too (see page 140).

Britain's other gold medallist, Tessa Sanderson, may have benefitted from the absence - due to the boycott - of the GDR's Petra Felke (who beat her, 74.24 to 67.92, in Potsdam two weeks before the Olympic final) but hers was one of the most heart-warming stories of the Games. The 1980 Olympics in Moscow had been the nadir of her career when, rated an almost certain medallist and possible winner, she had seized up with nerves in the qualifying round and failed to reach the final. That was a tearful occasion for the Jamaican-born all-rounder; and so too was Los Angeles – for happier reasons.

Having in the meantime overcome injuries which would have spelt premature retirement for many an athlete, Sanderson rose magnificently to the occasion. Her opening throw was an Olympic record of 69.56, and it stood up as the winner although world record holder Tiina Lillak, nursing an ankle injury, came uncomfortably close with her second throw of 69.00. That was literally the Finn's final fling; the ankle gave and she did not throw again. The only other realistic challenger was British team colleague Fatima Whitbread, but her best was 67.14 for the bronze medal. Sanderson thus became Britain's first Olympic women's champion since Mary Peters in 1972 and the only

Briton ever to win an Olympic throwing title.

Another Jamaican-born medallist at these Games was Merlene Ottey, who picked up a couple of sprinting bronze medals, the honours going to the American duo of Evelyn Ashford and Valerie Brisco-Hooks. World record holder Ashford thus at last won the big title that had eluded her for so long. Fifth as a youngster in the 1976 Olympic final, she was deprived by the boycott of her chance of Olympic glory in 1980, and she broke down at the 1983 World Championships. In the absence of her toughest rival – world champion Marlies Göhr – Ashford was the clear favourite ... as long as her injury-prone legs could stand up to the strain. They did, and she sped to a comfortable victory in 10.97, superb running into a 1.2m wind.

With a 400m gold medal already to her name, Brisco-Hooks had less to prove than her rivals and was able to approach the 200m final in a relaxed, though still determined, mood. Even a poor start did not throw her; she relied on strength to pull her through and on this occasion she took the lead from Florence Griffith (who would metamorphose into Flo Jo four years later) early in the finishing straight and strode to a two metre victory margin in 21.81. She became the first athlete, male or female, to complete an Olympic 200/400m double.

In the 400m Brisco-Hooks had been considered the USA's second string prior to the Games. Chandra Cheeseborough, after all, had won the USA Olympic Trial in 49.28 (ahead of Brisco-Hooks' 49.79). However, in the final it was Brisco-Hooks who came out on top, becoming the first woman from outside Eastern Europe to break 49 sec. She had not bettered 52 sec before 1984! Shadowing Kathy Cook through 200m (23.5 to the Briton's 23.4), she moved ahead around the final turns and held on to win by two metres from Cheeseborough. Cook, already Britain's most bemedalled athlete, took the bronze with a Commonwealth record time of 49.43, and went on to finish fourth a whisker behind Ottey in the 200m with a UK record 22.10. Brisco-Hooks capped a great display by helping the US team win the 4x400m relay by a big margin.

Another American woman to triumph was Joan Benoit. Her bold tactics paid handsome dividends in the first ever Olympic women's marathon. While her main rivals, including world champion Grete Waitz and European record holder Ingrid Kristiansen, were daunted by the prospect of very hot weather and adjusted their pace accordingly, the diminutive American threw caution to the winds. Between 10 and 20k, a section she covered in the extraordinary time of 33:08, she built up a lead of some 400m. At 30k her advantage was close to two minutes and although Waitz did eat into that in the closing stages Benoit still had over 400m in hand at the finish, which she reached in 2:24:52, then the third quickest on record.

"I don't know how to say this without sounding cocky, but it was a very easy run for me," she explained diffidently. At 1.60m (5'3") and 47.5kg (105lb) she became the smallest of Olympic athletics champions up until that time. Waitz, beset by back pains, ran gallantly to finish second, and European champion Rosa Mota took the bronze in her best time.

Not everything went the Americans' way in the women's events, though. There was an upset in the first Olympic heptathlon (it replaced the pentathlon) when Jackie Joyner - in the days before she was married to Bobby Kersee - was beaten by Australia's Glynis Nunn. It could hardly have been much closer. Going into the final event, Nunn trailed by 31 points but by running the 800m nearly two and a half seconds faster than her rival Nunn finished just 5 points ahead with a total of 6390 points.

Actually it was the long jump that proved to be Joyner's demise. Already a world class performer with a best of 6.81 (she would later become Olympic and world champion), she fouled two massive jumps and had to settle for a very nervous (and consequently mediocre) safety jump of 6.11 in order to guarantee staying in the competiton. That cost her a good 100 points. In the individual long jump a few days later Joyner (whose brother, Al, won the triple jump) leapt 6.77. JJK, as she became, did not lose another completed heptathlon until 12 years later!

Much more traumatic for the public, though, was Mary Decker's demise in the 3000m. The sight of America's sporting sweetheart sprawled on the infield, crying tears of pain and anguish as her Olympic dream turned into a nightmare, has remained one of the most vivid images of these Games.

Whether Decker's downfall was her own fault, or whether Zola Budd - a South African

who, with indecent haste, was made eligible to represent Britain - was responsible, has been debated heatedly ever since that fateful incident on the fifth lap which spelt disaster for both athletes. Decker, the world champion, was out of the race; while Budd was booed by sections of the 85,000 crowd and, deeply upset as well as bleeding from spike wounds, trailed home a despondent seventh.

Television replays indicated that Budd was in front at the time and that Decker's fall was prompted by her insistence on challenging on the inside when there just wasn't sufficient room. Budd was at first disqualified, but that decision was overturned. Even if Decker had got through the race unscathed there is no guarantee she would have beaten Maricica Puica, the tough 34-year-old Romanian who had won the world cross-country title earlier in the year. Puica ran out a worthy inaugural champion, overtaking Britain's Wendy Sly along the final back straight to win by 20 metres in 8:35.96.

The reigning men's world cross country champion also came away with a gold medal. It was unfortunate that Waldemar Cierpinski (GDR) was deprived by the boycott of the chance of scoring an unprecedented third Olympic marathon victory, but there was no indication from his form that year that he could have lived with Portugal's 37 year-old Carlos Lopes during the closing stages.

Lopes, completing only the second marathon of his career, showed tremendous pace over the final miles, including a fantastic 5k stretch timed in 14:33, to clock 2:09:21. Some 200m behind him there was a titanic struggle for the silver medal, with former world cross country champion John Treacy of Ireland (making an exceptional marathon debut) just getting the better of Britain's Charlie Spedding.

Lopes' Portuguese colleague, world record holder Fernando Mamede, was a notable casualty in the 10,000m. Victim once more of the nerves which plagued him on the big occasions, he swung off the track halfway through a final which would live in Olympic notoriety.

For the first time, an athlete was stripped of an Olympic medal after failing a drug test. That dubious distinction befell Finland's Martti Vainio, who finished second to Alberto Cova after a dramatic race ... and then, five days later, was turned away from the 5000m final after laboratory analysis had shown he had taken anabolic steroids.

Following a slow first half (14:19.84) the race hotted up when Vainio, aware he would not outsprint Cova, threw in one fast lap after another in an attempt to shake off his Italian rival. He didn't succeed and Cova, covering the second 5000m in a remarkable 13:26.98, kicked to victory by 25m in 27:47.54. However, with Vainio being removed from the official results, the winning margin grew by another 100m over the new silver medallist, Mike McLeod, whose second place was the highest ever by a Briton in this event.

The timetable precluded the possibility of a 1500/5000m double and as the year's fastest performer at both events Morocco's Said Aouita had a tricky decision to make. He chose well. Although Aouita was quoted as saying "if I'd run in the 1500 I'd have won that ... Seb is a champion by default", a more objective assessment would question whether he, or anyone else, could have beaten such an inspired Coe on the day.

At 5000m, though, he was untroubled as a 55.08 last lap carried him to victory in 13:05.59, at the time the third fastest run ever at the distance behind Dave Moorcroft's world record of 13:00.41 and his own African record of 13:04.78 – and that in hot, humid conditions. Moorcroft could only go through the motions, painfully, as a result of a pelvic injury and the British medal challenge was provided by Tim Hutchings, now well known as a TV commentator for Eurosport. His fourth placing in a time (13:11.50) that was 8.74 sec inside his previous best was one of the most under-rated British performances of the Games.

Three days earlier Aouita had been pipped for the honour of becoming Morocco's first ever gold medallist by Nawal El Moutawakil (54.61 in women's 400m hurdles). Africa's only other winner was Julius Korir of Kenya, who took the steeplechase in 8:11.80, followed home by the Moroccan-born Frenchman Joseph Mahmoud.

Mostly, it was Americans who cleaned up, as in the 400m hurdles in which Ed Moses' victory may have been one of the most predictable of the Games but was also probably the most popular. Moses had not lost a race since August 1977 and he wasn't about to

break the habit before 85,000 adoring fans. Exuding power, grace and dignity, he was almost five metres clear of Germany's Harald Schmid (the last man to beat him) at halfway and although he conceded a metre or two in the finishing straight as Schmid and 18 year-old Danny Harris fought out the other medals, he was never in danger as he notched up his 105th consecutive victory (90th counting finals only) in the event. In fact, his win streak would stretch to 122 (107 finals) before he finally lost to Harris in June 1987.

Carl Lewis Emulates Jesse Owens' Feat

"As far as I'm concerned, 60 per cent of it is over. This is by far the toughest event for me because so much can happen." So spoke a relieved Carl Lewis after safely taking the first step in his 1984 bid to duplicate Jesse Owens' quadruple Olympic success in Berlin in 1936. He need not have worried, for he outclassed the opposition to win the

LOS ANGELES 1984

race by over two metres.

During the long jump final Lewis found that even superstars are not immune to criticism. It made good sense to him that, after running a pair of 200m heats in the morning and not wishing to take chances with a slightly sore leg, he would not take the full complement of jumps. He settled for two: an opener of 8.54 and a second round foul. When it became evident that Lewis was sitting out the rest of the contest many fans gave vent to their feelings by booing Lewis as he walked up to receive the second of his four gold medals.

In winning his third gold, Lewis produced what may have been the finest ever 200m until that time. When Pietro Mennea set his world record of 19.72 he enjoyed the twin advantages of high altitude and a following wind close to the allowable limit. In Los Angeles, clocking 19.80, Lewis encountered a *headwind* in the straight of 0.9m. He entered the straight two metres up, and held almost all of that advantage at the finish over his training colleague Kirk Baptiste

Lewis completed his momentous Games by anchoring the relay team to victory in a world record 37.83. Competing in his 13th event in eight days, he was timed at 8.94 from a flying start as he more than doubled the team's lead to eight metres.

Carl Lewis went on to achieve many more triumphs and in practically every poll was voted the outstanding athlete of the century. Let's look first at what he did at 100 m:

• He is the only man ever to have won two Olympic titles in the event. On the first occasion he won by 0.20 for the widest margin in Olympic 100m history; second time around, in Seoul, he set a world record of 9.92.

• Had separate world records set at low altitude (less than 1000 metres up) been recognised by the IAAF, he would have set his first world mark in 1981 and been credited with the first sub-10.00 clocking (9.97) in 1983.

• He won three world titles, his 9.93 behind the subsequently disqualified Ben Johnson in 1987 equalling the listed world record and the 9.86 he registered in 1991 taking 4/100ths off the old record.

• In 1988 he ran what was then the absolute fastest ever time of 9.78 with a 5.2m wind.

• He finished first in the US Olympic Trials or American Championships seven times between 1981 and 1990.

• He ran under 10.00 legally what was then a record total of 15 times.

Those achievements alone, in the most highly developed of all events, would suffice to rank him among the all-time greats, but to that we can add his accomplishments over 200m.

• At or near sea level he would have held the world record from 1983 (19.75 easing up) until Michael Marsh ran 19.73 in 1992.

• Falling just 4/100ths short with 19.79 in Seoul after winning in Los Angeles in 19.80, he has come closer than any other man to winning a second Olympic 200m title.

Yet even that stunning catalogue of success as a sprinter is surpassed by his long jumping career. Just consider this ...

• He retired in 1997 but the last time he was beaten indoors was by Larry Myricks at the US Championships in February 1981; outdoors he went undefeated from July 1980 until he was beaten for the world title by Mike Powell in August 1991. Indoors and outdoors combined, he won 65 consecutive competitions.

• He is the only athlete to have won four Olympic long jump titles (1984-1996), equalling Al Oerter's record sequence for any event; he was world champion in 1983 and 1987, and it took a world record to beat him in 1991.

• He set world low-altitude bests of 8.62 in 1981, 8.76 in 1982 and 8.79 in 1983, duplicating that last distance in 1984 for a world indoor record.

• He jumped beyond 28 feet (8.53) 71 times and produced the greatest ever series when placing second to Powell in the 1991 World Championships: 8.68, foul, 8.83w, 8.91w, 8.87, 8.84.

World's greatest ever athlete? Who else could it be?

Supreme All-Rounder

IT WAS a case of hope over experience for West Germany's world decathlon record holder Jürgen Hingsen when he faced Britain's Daley Thompson, the reigning champion, in Los Angeles. They had clashed six times between 1977 and 1983 ... but Thompson, who could never even contemplate defeat, always managed to pysche out his rival and the outcome was six wins out of six. The nearest Hingsen got was 105 points at the inaugural World Championships in 1983.

Any belief that Hingsen, still without an international title, could turn the tables this time must have disappeared very quickly when Thompson - unbeaten in a decathlon for six years - blazed to his fastest legal 100m time of 10.44, followed by a wind-free personal best long jump of 8.01 to open up a devastating lead of 164 points. The shot brought little comfort to Hingsen although he did make inroads in the high jump, but a superb 46.97 400m by Thompson enabled him to end the day 114 points clear of the towering German with a world's best halfway score of 4633.

Significantly faster than his rival at 110m hurdles, Hingsen failed to gain more than a few points in th e opening event of day two. But in the discus he must have felt that his luck was about to change. He threw a lifetime best of 50.82 whereas Thompson managed only a feeble 37.90 and 41.42. If he couldn't improve upon that with his final attempt then Hingsen would sail into a 68 point lead and strike an immense psychological blow. It was just the sort of challenge that Thompson relished. He threw 46.56, close to his best, and the crisis was over, even if his lead had been narrowed to 32 points.

There was no stopping Thompson now. He easily outvaulted Hingsen and threw the javelin nearly five metres farther, so that after nine events his score was a colossal 8241 points to his opponent's 8032. Barring disaster in the 1500m, not only was victory certain but Hingsen's world record of 8798 set two months earlier looked doomed.

In fact, Thompson was happy to use the 1500m as a protracted lap of honour instead of hurting himself in pursuit of the record and finished on 8797 to Hingsen's still meritorious 8673. However, in a bizarre twist, Thompson's hurdles time was later corrected from 14.34 to 14.33, thus equalling the world record 8798, and even that wasn't the end of the story. The new IAAF scoring tables which came into effect the following April converted Thompson's score to 8847 as against Hingsen's 8832 and so he became sole record holder! Poor Hingsen never could beat him.

1984 - LOS ANGELES

100m: (0.2) 1, Carl Lewis USA 9.99; 2, Sam Graddy USA 10.19 (10.15 ht); 3, Ben Johnson CAN 10.22; 4, Ron Brown USA 10.26; 5, Mike McFarlane GBR 10.27; 6, Ray Stewart JAM 10.29; 7, Donovan Reid GBR 10.33; 8, Tony Sharpe CAN 10.35.

200m: (-0.9) 1, Carl Lewis USA 19.80; 2, Kirk Baptiste USA 19.96; 3, Thomas Jefferson USA 20.26; 4, Joao Batista da Silva BRA 20.30; 5, Ralf Lübke FRG 20.51; 6, Jean-Jacques Boussemart FRA 20.55; 7, Pietro Mennea ITA 20.55; 8, Ade Mafe GBR 20.85.

400m: 1, Alonzo Babers USA 44.27; 2, Gabriel Tiacoh CIV 44.54; 3, Antonio McKay USA 44.71; 4, Darren Clark AUS 44.75; 5, Sunder Nix USA 44.75; 6, Sunday Uti NGR 44.93; 7, Innocent Egbunike NGR 45.35; Bert Cameron JAM dns.

800m: 1, Joaquim Cruz BRA 1:43.00; 2, Sebastian Coe GBR 1:43.64; 3, Earl Jones USA 1:43.83; 4, Billy Konchellah KEN 1:44.03; 5, Donato Sabia ITA 1:44.53; 6, Edwin Koech KEN 1:44.86 (1:44.12 sf); 7, Johnny Gray USA 1:47.89; 8, Steve Ovett GBR 1:52.28 (1:44.81 sf).

1500m: 1, Sebastian Coe GBR 3:32.53; 2, Steve Cram GBR 3:33.40; 3, José Abascal ESP 3:34.30; 4, Joseph Chesire KEN 3:34.52; 5, Jim Spivey USA 3:36.07; 6, Peter Wirz SUI 3:36.97; 7, Andrés Vera ESP 3:37.02; 8, Omer Khalifa SUD 3:37.11.

5000m: 1, Said Aouita MAR 13:05.59; 2, Markus Ryffel SUI 13:07.54; 3, Antonio Leitao POR 13:09.20; 4, Tim Hutchings GBR 13:11.50; 5, Paul Kipkoech KEN 13:14.40; 6, Charles Cheruiyot KEN 13:18.41; 7, Doug Padilla USA 13:23.56; 8, John Walker NZL 13:24.46.

10,000m: 1, Alberto Cova ITA 27:47.54; 2, Mike McLeod GBR 28:06.22; 3, Mike Musyoki KEN 28:06.46; 4, Salvatore Antibo ITA 28:06.50; 5, Christoph Herle FRG 28:08.21; 6, Sosthenes Bitok KEN 28:09.01; 7, Yutaka Kanai JPN 28:27.06; 8, Steve Jones GBR 28:28.08; Martti Vainio FIN (27:51.10) disq.

Marathon: 1, Carlos Lopes POR 2:09:21; 2, John Treacy IRL 2:09:56; 3, Charlie Spedding GBR 2:09:58; 4, Takeshi Soh JPN 2:10:55; 5, Rob de Castella AUS 2:11:09; 6, Juma Ikangaa TAN 2:11:10; 7, Joe Nzau KEN 2:11:28; 8, Djama Robleh DJI 2:11:39.

3000mSC: 1, Julius Korir KEN 8:11.80; 2, Joseph Mahmoud FRA 8:13.31; 3, Brian Diemer USA 8:14.06; 4, Henry Marsh USA 8:14.25; 5, Colin Reitz GBR 8:15.48; 6, Domingo Ramon ESP 8:17.27; 7, Julius Kariuki KEN 8:17.47; 8, Pascal Debacker FRA 8:21.51.

110mH: (-0.4) 1, Roger Kingdom USA 13.20; 2, Greg Foster USA 13.23; 3, Arto Bryggare FIN 13.40 (13.35 ht); 4, Mark McKoy CAN 13.45

(13.30 sf); 5, Tonie Campbell USA 13.55; 6, Stéphane Caristan FRA 13.71; 7, Carlos Sala ESP 13.80; 8, Jeff Glass CAN 14.15.

400mH: 1, Ed Moses USA 47.75; 2, Danny Harris USA 48.13; 3, Harald Schmid FRG 48.19; 4, Sven Nylander SWE 48.97; 5, Amadou Dia Ba SEN 49.28; 6, Tranel Hawkins USA 49.42; 7, Michel Zimmerman BEL 50.69; 8, Henry Amike NGR 53.78.

4 x 100m Relay: 1, USA (Sam Graddy, Ron Brown, Calvin Smith, Carl Lewis) 37.83 (world rec); 2, Jamaica (Albert Lawrence, Gregory Meghoo, Don Quarrie, Ray Stewart) 38.62; 3, Canada (Ben Johnson, Tony Sharpe, Desai Williams, Sterling Hinds) 38.70; 4, Italy 38.87; 5, Germany/FRG 38.99; 6, France 39.10; 7, Great Britain 39.13 (38.68 sf); 8, Brazil 39.40.

4 x 400m Relay: 1, USA (Sunder Nix 45.59, Ray Armstead 43.97, Alonzo Babers 43.75, Antonio McKay 44.60) 2:57.91; 2, Great Britain (Kriss Akabusi 45.87, Garry Cook 44.74, Todd Bennett 44.17, Phil Brown 44.35) 2:59.13; 3, Nigeria (Sunday Uti 45.34, Moses Ugbisie 44.48, Rotimi Peters 44.94, Innocent Egbunike 44.56) 2:59.32; 4, Australia 2:59.70 (Darren Clark 43.86); 5, Italy 3:01.44; 6, Barbados 3:01.60; 7, Uganda 3:02.09; 8, Canada 3:02.82.

HJ: 1, Dietmar Mögenburg FRG 2.35; 2, Patrik Sjöberg SWE 2.33; 3, Zhu Jianhua CHN 2.31; 4, Dwight Stones USA 2.31; 5, Doug Nordquist USA 2.29; 6, Milt Ottey CAN 2.29; 7, Liu Yunpeng CHN 2.29; 8, Cai Shu CHN 2.27.

PV: 1, Pierre Quinon FRA 5.75; 2, Mike Tully USA 5.65; eq3, Earl Bell USA & Thierry Vigneron FRA 5.60; 5, Kimmo Pallonen FIN 5.45; 6, Doug Lytle USA 5.40; 7, Felix Böhni SUI 5.30; 8, Mauro Barella ITA 5.30.

LJ: 1, Carl Lewis USA 8.54; 2, Gary Honey AUS 8.24; 3, Giovanni Evangelisti ITA 8.24; 4, Larry Myricks USA 8.16; 5, Liu Yuhuang CHN 7.99; 6, Joey Wells BAH 7.97; 7, Junichi Usui JPN 7.87; 8, Kim Jong-Il KOR 7.81.

TJ: 1, Al Joyner USA 17.26w; 2, Mike Conley USA 17.18 (17.36q); 3, Keith Connor GBR 16.87; 4, Zhou Zhenxian CHN 16.83; 5, Peter Bouschen FRG 16.77; 6, Willie Banks USA 16.75; 7, Ajayi Agbebaku NGR 16.67 (16.93q); 8, Eric McCalla GBR 16.66 (17.01q).

SP: 1, Alessandro Andrei ITA 21.26; 2, Mike Carter USA 21.09; 3, Dave Laut USA 20.97; 4, Augie Wolf USA 20.93; 5, Werner Günthör SUI 20.28; 6, Marco Montelatici ITA 19.98; 7, Sören

Tallhem SWE 19.81; 8, Erik De Bruin NED 19.65.

DT: 1, Rolf Danneberg FRG 66.60; 2, Mac Wilkins USA 66.30; 3, John Powell USA 65.46; 4, Knut Hjeltnes NOR 65.28; 5, Art Burns USA 64.98; 6, Alwin Wagner FRG 64.72; 7, Luciano Zerbini ITA 63.50; 8, Stefan Fernholm SWE 63.22.

HT: 1, Juha Tiainen FIN 78.08; 2, Karl-Hans Riehm FRG 77.98; 3, Klaus Ploghaus FRG 76.68; 4, Orlando Bianchini ITA 75.94; 5, Bill Green USA 75.60; 6, Harri Huhtala FIN 75.28; 7, Walter Ciofani FRA 73.46; 8, Robert Weir GBR 72.62; Giampaolo Urlando ITA (75.96) disq.

JT: 1, Arto Härkönen FIN 86.76; 2, Dave Ottley GBR 85.74; 3, Kenth Eldebrink SWE 83.72; 4, Wolfram Gambke FRG 82.46; 5, Masami Yoshida JPN 81.98; 6, Einar Vilhjálmsson ISL 81.58; 7, Roald Bradstock GBR 81.22; 8, Laslo Babits CAN 80.68 ... 10, Tom Petranoff USA 78.40 (85.96q).

Dec: 1, Daley Thompson GBR 8798 (8847 on present tables, world rec) (10.44, 8.01, 15.72, 2.03, 46.97, 14.33, 46.56, 5.00, 65.24, 4:35.00); 2, Jürgen Hingsen FRG 8673 (8695) (10.91, 7.80, 15.87, 2.12, 47.69, 14.29, 50.82, 4.50, 60.44, 4:22.60); 3, Siggy Wentz FRG 8412 (8416); 4, Guido Kratschmer FRG 8326 (8357); 5, William Motti FRA 8266 (8278); 6, John Crist USA 8130 (8115); 7, Jim Wooding USA 8091 (8054); 8, Dave Steen CAN 8047 (8034).

20k Walk: 1, Ernesto Canto MEX 1:23:13; 2, Raul Gonzáles MEX 1:23:20; 3, Maurizio Damilano ITA 1:23:26; 4, Guillaume LeBlanc CAN 1:24:29; 5, Carlo Mattioli ITA 1:25:07; 6, José Marin ESP 1:25:32; 7, Marco Evoniuk USA 1:25:42; 8, Erling Andersen NOR 1:25:54.

50k Walk: 1, Raul Gonzáles MEX 3:47:26; 2, Bo Gustafsson SWE 3:53:19; 3, Sandro Bellucci ITA 3:53:45; 4, Reima Salonen FIN 3:58:30; 5, Raffaello Ducceschi ITA 3:59:26; 6, Carl Schueler USA 3:59:46; 7, Jorge Llopart ESP 4:03:09; 8, José Pinto POR 4:04:42.

Women's Events

100m: (-1.2) 1, Evelyn Ashford USA 10.97; 2, Alice Brown USA 11.13; 3, Merlene Ottey JAM 11.16; 4, Jeanette Bolden USA 11.25; 5, Grace Jackson JAM 11.39; 6, Angela Bailey CAN 11.40; 7, Heather Oakes (née Hunte) GBR 11.43; 8, Angella Taylor CAN 11.62.

200m: (-0.1) 1, Valerie Brisco-Hooks USA 21.81; 2, Florence Griffith USA 22.04; 3, Merlene Ottey JAM 22.09; 4, Kathy Cook (née Smallwood) GBR

22.10; 5, Grace Jackson JAM 22.20; 6, Randy Givens USA 22.36; 7, Rose-Aimée Bacoul FRA 22.78; 8, Liliane Gaschet FRA 22.86.

400m: 1, Valerie Brisco-Hooks USA 48.83; 2, Chandra Cheeseborough USA 49.05; 3, Kathy Cook (née Smallwood) GBR 49.43; 4, Marita Payne CAN 49.91; 5, Lillie Leatherwood USA 50.25; 6, Ute Thimm FRG 50.37; 7, Charmaine Crooks CAN 50.45; 8, Ruth Waithera KEN 51.56.

800m: 1, Doina Melinte ROM 1:57.60; 2, Kim Gallagher USA 1:58.63; 3, Fita Lovin ROM 1:58.83; 4, Gabriella Dorio ITA 1:59.05; 5, Lorraine Baker GBR 2:00.03; 6, Ruth Wysocki USA 2:00.34; 7, Margrit Klinger FRG 2:00.65; 8, Caroline O'Shea IRL 2:00.77.

1500m: 1, Gabriella Dorio ITA 4:03.25; 2, Doina Melinte ROM 4:03.76; 3, Maricica Puica ROM 4:04.15; 4, Roswitha Gerdes FRG 4:04.41; 5, Chris Benning GBR 4:04.70; 6, Chris Boxer GBR 4:05.53; 7, Brit McRoberts CAN 4:05.98; 8, Ruth Wysocki USA 4:08.92.

3000m: 1, Maricica Puica ROM 8:35.96; 2, Wendy Sly GBR 8:39.47; 3, Lynn Williams CAN 8:42.14; 4, Cindy Bremser USA 8:42.78; 5, Cornelia Bürki SUI 8:45.20; 6, Aurora Cunha POR 8:46.37; 7, Zola Budd GBR 8:48.80; 8, Joan Hansen USA 8:51.53 ... Mary Decker USA dnf (8:44.38 ht).

Marathon: 1, Joan Benoit USA 2:24:52; 2, Grete Waitz NOR 2:26:18; 3, Rosa Mota POR 2:26:57; 4, Ingrid Kristiansen NOR 2:27:34; 5, Lorraine Moller NZL 2:28:34; 6, Priscilla Welch GBR 2:28:54; 7, Lisa Martin AUS 2:29:03; 8, Sylvie Ruegger CAN 2:29:09.

100mH: (-0.7) 1, Benita Fitzgerald-Brown USA 12.84; 2, Shirley Strong GBR 12.88; eq3, Kim Turner USA & Michele Chardonnet FRA 13.06; 5, Glynis Nunn AUS 13.20; 6, Marie-Noelle Savigny FRA 13.28; 7, Ulrike Denk FRG 13.32; 8, Pamela Page USA 13.40.

400mH: 1, Nawal El Moutawakil MAR 54.61; 2, Judi Brown USA 55.20; 3, Cristina Cojocaru ROM 55.41 (55.24 sf); 4, P T Usha IND 55.42; 5, Ann-Louise Skoglund SWE 55.43 (55.17 sf); 6, Debbie Flintoff AUS 56.21; 7, Tuija Helander FIN 56.55; 8, Sandra Farmer JAM 57.15.

4 x 100m Relay: 1, USA (Alice Brown, Jeanette Bolden, Chandra Cheeseborough, Evelyn Ashford) 41.65; 2, Canada (Angela Bailey, Marita Payne, Angella Taylor, France Gareau) 42.77; 3, Great Britain (Simmone Jacobs, Kathy Cook, Bev Callender (née Goddard), Heather

Oakes) 43.11; 4, France 43.15; 5, Germany/FRG 43.57; 6, Bahamas 44.18; 7, Trinidad 44.23; 8, Jamaica 53.54 (43.05 ht).

4 x 400m Relay: 1, USA (Lillie Leatherwood 50.50, Sherri Howard 48.83, Valerie Brisco-Hooks 49.23, Chandra Cheeseborough 49.73) 3:18.29; 2, Canada (Charmaine Crooks 50.30, Jillian Richardson 50.22, Molly Killingbeck 50.62, Marita Payne 50.07) 3:21.21; 3, Germany/FRG (Heike Schulte-Mattler 51.73, Ute Thimm 50.25, Heike-Elke Gaugel 50.65, Gaby Bussmann 50.35) 3:22.98; 4, Great Britain 3:25.51; 5, Jamaica 3:27.51; 6, Italy 3:30.82; 7, India 3:32.49; Puerto Rico dns.

HJ: 1, Ulrike Meyfarth FRG 2.02; 2, Sara Simeoni ITA 2.00; 3, Joni Huntley USA 1.97; 4, Maryse Ewanje-Epée FRA 1.94; 5, Debbie Brill CAN 1.94; 6, Vanessa Browne AUS 1.94; 7, Zheng Dazhen CHN 1.91; 8, Louise Ritter USA 1.91.

LJ: 1, Anisoara Stanciu ROM 6.96; 2, Vali Ionescu ROM 6.81; 3, Sue Hearnshaw GBR 6.80w; 4, Angela Thacker USA 6.78w; 5, Jackie Joyner USA 6.77; 6, Robyn Lorraway AUS 6.67; 7, Glynis Nunn AUS 6.53w; 8, Shonel Ferguson BAH 6.44.

SP: 1, Claudia Losch FRG 20.48; 2, Mihaela Loghin ROM 20.47; 3, Gael Martin AUS 19.19; 4, Judy Oakes GBR 18.14; 5, Li Meisu CHN 17.96; 6, Venissa Head GBR 17.90; 7, Carol Cady USA 17.23; 8, Florenta Craciunescu ROM 17.23.

DT: 1, Ria Stalman NED 65.36; 2, Leslie Deniz USA 64.86; 3, Florenta Craciunescu (née Tacu) ROM 63.64; 4, Ulla Lundholm FIN 62.84; 5, Meg Ritchie GBR 62.58; 6, Ingra Manecke FRG 58.56; 7, Venissa Head GBR 58.18; 8, Gael Martin AUS 55.88.

JT: 1, Tessa Sanderson GBR 69.56; 2, Tiina Lillak FIN 69.00; 3, Fatima Whitbread GBR 67.14; 4, Tuula Laaksalo FIN 66.40; 5, Trine Solberg NOR 64.52; 6, Ingrid Thyssen FRG 63.26; 7, Beate Peters FRG 62.34; 8, Karin Smith USA 62.06.

Hep: 1, Glynis Nunn AUS 6390 (6387 on 1985 tables) (100mH-13.02, HJ-1.80, SP-12.82, 200m-24.06, LJ-6.66, JT-35.58, 800m-2:10.57); 2, Jackie Joyner USA 6385 (6363) (13.63, 1.80, 14.39, 24.05, 6.11, 44.52, 2:13.03); 3, Sabine Everts FRG 6363 (6388) (13.54, 1.89, 12.49, 24.05, 6.71, 32.62, 2:09.05); 4, Cindy Greiner USA 6281 (6236); 5, Judy Simpson GBR 6280 (6264); 6, Sabine Braun FRG 6236 (6195); 7, Tineke Hidding NED 6147 (6085); 8, Kim Hagger GBR 6127 (6103).

THE ULTIMATE SCANDAL

SPRINTERS HAVE often attracted the biggest headlines at the Olympics. The men's 100 metres is the most basic test of athletic endeavour, a contest of sheer speed, and the winner enjoys a special status at the Games. The title of "world's fastest human" or "fastest man on earth" captures the imagination and such great performers as Jesse Owens in 1936, Bob Hayes in 1964 and Carl Lewis in 1984 occupy a revered place in the pantheon of Olympic heroes. Thus when Ben Johnson won the 100m in Seoul in the incredible time of 9.79, leaving even an in-form Lewis a metre and a half behind, he was hailed as a mega-star. The adulation lasted only until the news broke that Johnson had failed a drugs test; the fastest man in history was revealed as a cheat and he flew home in disgrace.

Johnson was the only track and field athlete to provide a positive doping sample in Seoul but it would be naive to deduce that he alone was guilty of using performance enhancing substances. In his case it was carelessness that led to his downfall after years of steroid use during which he sailed through numerous doping controls. The Dubin Inquiry in Canada, set up in the wake of the Johnson scandal, revealed the extent of the problem in just one nation and several Olympic medallists have at one time or another been suspended for drug use (see page 134). The Americans have a particularly bad record, and there is now solid evidence from the former German Democratic Republic confirming what was long suspected: that the carefully controlled administration of drugs was an integral part of that state's hugely successful sports programme.

What no one in Seoul could have suspected was that the GDR would be participating as a separate entity for the last time in Olympic competition, nor that the Soviet Union would shortly disintegrate. After two Olympics which were ruined by large scale boycotts, the Seoul Games – supported by a record 159 countries (139 taking part in athletics) – brought together the world's best athletes with the notable exceptions of Cuba and Ethiopia, who stayed away in support of North Korea's ludicrous objections to not being awarded half of the Games.

The Ethiopian marathoners were missed, but African runners did very nicely all the same, winning all the men's track events from 800m to 10,000m, including the steeplechase, with other medals coming in the marathon and 400m hurdles.

Star of the Games, although not free of controversy herself, was Florence Griffith Joyner, more popularly known as Flo-Jo (see page 150). Her 10.49 100m in the US Trials, with a reported nil wind reading, was widely disbelieved but in Seoul she proved she was in a class of her own by winning the title in a windy 10.54 after a legal heat time of 10.62. Better still was her 200m winning performance of 21.34 following a 21.56 semi. For nine years the world record had been stuck at 21.71 but in one day it was improved by 37/100ths of a second or nearly four metres of track! Flo-Jo also also ran a 48.08 400m relay leg but had to settle for silver as the Soviet team held on for victory in a world record 3:15.18.

The removal of Ben Johnson led to Carl Lewis being credited with a world 100m record of 9.92, while Jackie Joyner-Kersee (see page

STAR OF THE GAMES

FLORENCE GRIFFITH JOYNER
(born 21 Dec 1959; died 21 Sep 1998)

There has been no more controversial figure in track and field history than "Flo Jo". She was for several years a world class sprinter, but in 1988 – her last season – she metamorphosed into a woman who ran times that could not previously have even been fantasized about ... 10.49 100m and 21.34 200m. In Seoul she won both events, smiling broadly, by huge margins, won a third gold in the 4x100m and finished up with a 48.08 anchor leg and silver in the 4x400m. She never failed a drugs test, but suspicions remained for the rest of her all too brief life.

151) broke her own world heptathlon record with 7291 points and the Americans equalled the long standing 4x400m relay mark of 2:56.16.

No golds this time, but the British team came back laden with medals – silver for Linford Christie in the 100m (and sprint relay along with Elliot Bunney, John Regis and Mike McFarlane), Peter Elliott in the 1500m, Colin Jackson in the 110m hurdles, Liz McColgan in the 10,000m and Fatima Whitbread in the javelin; bronze for Mark Rowland in the steeplechase and Yvonne Murray in the 3000m.

But back to that 100 metres. Ben Johnson has gone down in athletics history as the athlete who cheated his way to an Olympic title and was found out. His reign as champion lasted less than three days, and that 9.79 never did make the record lists. The news of Johnson's disqualification, following a test which revealed the presence of an anabolic steroid, cast a shadow over the race, but it would be unfair to devalue the splendid achievements of Lewis and Christie because of Johnson's cheating. Both ran faster than ever before, and Christie's time of 9.97 made him the first European to crack 10 seconds.

Lewis was timed at 9.92 – which subsequently was recognised as a world record when Johnson's 9.83 from 1987 was removed from the books after he confessed he was using steroids at the time. Thus, Lewis became the first man to win the Olympic 100m crown for a second time. Having registered the quickest ever time of 9.78w in the US Trials, Lewis started favourite in Seoul but by halfway through the final it was all over. Johnson leapt out of the blocks for an immediate advantage but it was his dynamic pick-up which clinched the race for him. By 50m (5.52) Johnson was 13/100ths clear ... his eventual 'winning' margin. The Canadian, who reached 60m in an unprecedented 6.37 as against 6.53 for Lewis and 6.55 for Christie, thus covered the first half of the race in 5.52 and the second in 4.27. Lewis was also timed in 4.27, with Christie on 4.28.

Notching up his 56th consecutive victory, Lewis not only became the first man ever to retain an Olympic long jump title but Mike Powell and Larry Myricks completed the first clean sweep in this event since 1904. Although Lewis was drawn to jump first he was given dis-

pensation to jump 12th to allow him maximum recovery following his 200m quarter-final an hour earlier, and he leapt into an immediate lead with 8.41 as against 8.23 by Powell and 8.14 by Myricks. In the second round he went further ahead with 8.56, while Myricks slipped into second with 8.27. In the third round, though, Powell produced a lifetime best of 8.49 to regain second place and pressurise Lewis, whose third jump measured 8.52, but a great fourth round leap of 8.72 by Lewis totally demoralised the opposition.

However, his dream of retaining all four Olympic titles was ended by one of his closest friends in Joe DeLoach. The 200m final was almost a carbon copy of the US Olympic trial. On that occasion Lewis led until ten metres from the finish, with DeLoach nipping past to win, 19.96 to 20.01. The times in Seoul were faster but the pattern of the race and the winning margin were similar. Both men bettered Lewis's Olympic record of 19.80, as DeLoach scored by 4/100ths in 19.75 – equalling his opponent's world sea level record. DeLoach, who trained with Lewis, remarked: "I couldn't have done it without Carl. He has been instrumental in making me the athlete I am, and there's no doubt he is the greatest athlete of them all." Christie followed up his fastest ever 100m with his swiftest 200m, clocking a UK record of 20.09 in fourth place, and later picked up another silver medal in the relay. The surprise winners were the USSR as the US team were disqualified in their heat.

The Americans made no mistakes in the 4x400m. A fabulous first leg off blocks by Danny Everett, timed at 43.79, laid the foundations of a runaway win in a world record equalling 2:56.16. As the time they tied was set at high altitude in Mexico City 20 years before this performance was clearly the best yet. Subsequent legs by Steve Lewis (43.69), Kevin Robinzine (44.74) and Butch Reynolds (43.94) enabled the Americans to score by more than 35m for the biggest winning margin in 40 years. Jamaica, reviving memories of past glories, took second.

In the individual 400m, the hot favourite – Butch Reynolds – misjudged his pace and came away 'only' with silver. His victories in the US Trials (43.93 over Danny Everett 43.98 and Steve Lewis 44.37) and Zürich (world record

43.29 ahead of Everett 44.20 and Lewis 44.26) pointed to Olympic victory. However, Reynolds left himself with too much to do in the final straight. While Lewis (32.08) and Everett (32.13) blasted away to lead at 300m, Reynolds (32.53) was lagging back in fifth place. He came through in breathtaking fashion but the inspired 19 year-old Lewis dug in and held on to win by half a metre in a world junior record of 43.87.

The Kenyan runners enjoyed fabulous success in Seoul, providing the winners of the 800m, 1500m, 5000m and steeplechase, and picking up lesser medals in the 10,000m and marathon.

You would have looked in vain for the name of Paul Ereng among any list of 800m contenders prior to 1988, for the simple reason that the 20-year-old Kenyan – a 45.6 400m runner in 1987 – had never raced at two laps! He broke 1:47 for the first time in April 1988, and in June improved to 1:44.82 although he only just scraped into the Kenyan team.

The final was a cracker. Under pressure from Nixon Kiprotich, José Luis Barbosa of Brazil reached the bell in 49.53, with the Kenyan, defending champion Joaquim Cruz and Britain's Peter Elliott in close attendance. At that stage the versatile 1984 Olympic 5000m champion Said Aouita was sixth and Ereng seventh in 51.07. Cruz struck round the turn to lead into the finishing straight ahead of Elliott, Ereng and Aouita but he started to run out of steam in the last 30m, enabling Ereng to stride past for a remarkable victory in a lifetime best of 1:43.45. Cruz clung on for second while Aouita outlegged Elliott for the bronze to become the first athlete to gain an Olympic medal in both 800m and 5000m.

Peter Rono was another virtually unknown Kenyan to strike gold. His best 1500m time before 1988 was 3:39.2 in 1985; in 1986 he placed second in the World Junior Championships. A run of 3:35.96 sufficed for victory in Seoul. What with the controversial non-selection of Seb Coe, the withdrawal of injured world champion Abdi Bile and the hamstring trouble which caused world record holder Aouita to pull out of the semis, the line-up for the final was less distinguished than anticipated. It was a race which Steve Cram would normally have expected to win but the world mile record holder was not in the best of health and the supreme prize again slipped from his grasp. Gritty is an adjective often used to describe Peter Elliott, and never was it more deserved than in Seoul. Suffering from a groin injury necessitating daily pain-killing injections, he did well enough in the 800m but his second place in the 1500m was quite remarkable in the circumstances. The early pace was slow until Rono began to stretch the field on the third lap, covered in 56.38. With 200m to go, he held a two metre lead over Elliott, and that margin remained substantially unaltered until the line, the last 300m taking 39.27 and the final 400m 52.8. Rono thus became the most unexpected Olympic 1500m champion since Luxembourg's Josy Barthel in 1952.

John Ngugi produced a daring front running triumph in the 5000m. A cautious first kilometre was not to his liking, so he launched out on his own. He quickly opened up a 30m gap – not surprising considering that breakaway lap was covered in 58.22! That was followed by a 62.03 and by 2000m he was 40m clear of the pack. The gap remained constant until 3000m, at which stage Domingos Castro realised that drastic action was required if the race was not to be conceded. He set about reducing the deficit and by 4000m Ngugi's lead over Castro was down to 25m, and the Portuguese runner was a similar margin ahead of the rest of the field. Ngugi produced a 60.28 last lap to run out a safe and deserving winner in a personal best of 13:11.70, but there was a terrific burn-up behind him for the other medals. Poor Castro was ill-rewarded for his initiative as Dieter Baumann (FRG) and Hansjörg Kunze (GDR) turned in a 55 last lap to edge him out of the medals.

It seemed a good bet that a Kenyan would win the steeplechase ... but which one? Peter Koech had the fastest time with 8:11.61 as against Patrick Sang's 8:12.00 and Julius Kariuki's 8:15.71, but Kariuki had the best competitive record. In the event it was Kariuki who not only came out on top but improved by 10 sec and practically broke the world record in the process. That stood to the credit of yet another Kenyan, Henry Rono (no relation to the 1500m winner), with a hand timed 8:05.4, whereas Kariuki's electrically registered time was 8:05.51.

Tantalisingly, had he not eased up before the finish Kariuki would surely have broken 8:05.

Only one man dared track Kariuki and Koech during the final kilometre, and that was Mark Rowland. It was a crucial move for the Briton, for he found the strength and resolve to hold a tremendous pace which carried him well clear of everyone else. At the bell Kariuki was 10m ahead of Koech, with Rowland only a stride or two behind, and the postion remained much the same throughout the last lap. Rowland finished with a UK record of 8:07.96, a massive improvement on his previous personal best of 8:16.34 and an astounding achievement by someone who had only run his first steeplechase in 1987.

Africa's other victory was provided by a Moroccan. When Brahim Boutayeb clocked the startling 5000m time for a 19-year-old of 13:17.47 in 1987 it was apparent that a major new talent had emerged, but one could hardly have envisaged that only a year later he would run away with the Olympic 10,000m title! When Moses Tanui made a break at 2000m with a 62.70 lap Boutayeb was one of only three men able or willing to cover the Kenyan's move. The halfway time of 13:35.32 conjured up visions of a world record. Kipkemboi Kimeli of Kenya led at that point, with Boutayeb breathing down his neck. Boutayeb moved ahead at 5400m and a 64 sec lap enabled him to open up a 10m advantage. He reached the bell 40m clear and could easily have cracked 27:20 had he not celebrated victory along the final straight. He finished in the African record time of 27:21.46, with Salvatore Antibo closing on the last lap to clock an Italian record of 27:23.55 for the silver.

An Italian saw off the African challenge in the marathon, though, as European champion Gelindo Bordin fought it out with the men who had finished ahead of him in the previous year's World Championships: Douglas Wakiihuri of Kenya and Ahmed Salah from Djibouti.

In cool weather on such a flat course the winning time might have been inside 2:08. Instead it was outside 2:10, for in order to provide a dramatic lead-up to the closing ceremony the organising committee made sacrificial lambs of the marathoners, their event being run during the hottest part of the day. At 38k an African victory looked assured. Salah burst away into a 15m lead over Wakiihuri, while Bordin appeared to have settled for third. Not so. As the leading duo weakened approaching the stadium, so the Italian found renewed hope and strength. Bordin passed Wakiihuri at 40k and some 500m later he strode past Salah to bring off Italy's first ever Olympic marathon victory – 80 years after Dorando Pietri came so agonisingly close in London.

Apart from Carl Lewis, the only athlete to retain a title was sprint hurdler Roger Kingdom. In the second round he broke his own Olympic record with 13.17, and dominated the final to become the second man (after Lee Calhoun in 1960) to make a successful defence of this title. In clocking 12.98 he registered the second best time thus far at sea level and his winning margin of three metres had only once been surpassed in the Olympics ... and that was in 1908. Colin Jackson, the first Welshman to win an individual Olympic medal on the track since steeplechaser John Disley in 1952, took the silver. Previously, no Briton had reached the Olympic final since Don Finlay in 1936; this time all three representatives did so.

An era drew to a close with the first defeat in a 400m hurdles championship of Ed Moses, aged 33 and the supremo in his event for the past dozen years. In losing only his second race in 11 years Moses still proved a tough customer as he strove to become the first athlete to win a third Olympic 400m hurdles title. He and Andre Phillips were level at halfway and Moses was second at the final barrier. At his very best, Moses might yet have retrieved the situation but Phillips was not to be denied. He pulled clear on the run-in, although he had a scare when, with an amazing finishing burst, Amadou Dia Ba of Senegal came to within 4/100ths of him. Phillips' 47.19 broke Moses' Olympic record and moved him to second on the all-time list. Of Moses, he said: "I watched him in Montreal 12 years ago and I've been chasing him ever since. He's been my motivation, my incentive, my idol. I don't know if I would have kept it up this long if it weren't for the way Edwin has been running for the last 12 years". Dia Ba, a former 2.18 high jumper who had not previously broken 48 sec, ran 47.23 to relegate Moses to third.

A chapter of athletics history closed also in the decathlon when Daley Thompson failed in his bid to become the first man in Olympic history to win a third decathlon title but won plaudits for his courage and tenacity in the face of mounting adversity. The Thompson of old would have destroyed this field, weakened as it was by the withdrawal of the injured Siggi Wentz and the disqualification of Jürgen Hingsen for three false starts in the 100m, but he was handicapped by a thigh injury.

The leader after four events was Christian Schenk, the 2.01m tall East German who – using the dated but effective straddle style – jumped a spectacular 2.27, equalling the highest ever recorded in a decathlon. At halfway, it was Schenk in the lead with 4470, followed by Christian Plaziat (4375) and Thompson (4332). The pole vault was critical to Thompson's fast receding medal chances, but the gods were not with him. His pole snapped at his first attempt at 4.70; yet, despite the shock and pain (he aggra-

DID YOU KNOW?

World 200m record holder Pietro Mennea (36) made his fifth Italian Olympic team but failed to appear in his 200m quarter-final ... Troy Douglas of Bermuda made his Olympic debut, reaching the 200m semis and 400m quarter-finals. Now a Dutch citizen, he set a world masters record of 20.64 for 200m in 2003, aged 40, and could be a competitor in Athens ... Abel Antón, later to win two world marathon titles, reached the semis of the 5000m; future world indoor 60m champion Bruny Surin competed in the long jump, narrowly failing to reach the final... Among the non-qualifiers for the triple jump final was future world and Olympic champion and world record smasher Jonathan Edwards, who jumped just 15.88 in 23rd place... The Olympic javelin record of 94.58 by Miklós Németh in 1976 became irrelevant as a new specification javelin was used at the Games for the first time; Jan Zelezny threw 85.90, but that was in the qualifying round and he had to settle for the silver behind Finland's Tapio Korjus (84.28) in the final ... The first 20 finishers were inside the old Olympic 20k walk record ... Olga Bryzgina (400m) and her husband Viktor Bryzgin (4x100m) both won gold medals ... A 15 year-old novice from Mozambique by the name of Maria Mutola placed seventh in her heat of the 800m in 2:04.36.

vated his leg injury and hurt his shoulder), he refused to quit. He went on to clear 4.90 in a gutsy display but effectively lost further ground. Off a limp-up rather than a run-up, Thompson threw 64.04 for a personal best with the new-specification javelin, and with Plaziat experiencing a disaster Thompson was back in third place. His left thigh bandaged, Thompson gave his all to run the 1500m in 4:45.11, but fell back to fourth overall as the title went to Schenk with 8488 points.

Another of the sport's legends, pole vaulter Sergey Bubka, made his Olympic debut a winning one and the other medals went to his Soviet compatriots Rodion Gataullin and Grigoriy Yegorov for the first clean sweep in this event for 60 years. No man was more deserving of the title than Bubka, who had dominated the vaulting scene since his upset win in the 1983 World Championships but who was deprived of his Olympic chance in 1984 because of the Soviet boycott. Not that he was handed victory on a plate; there were anxious moments when he went under the bar at his first attempt at his opening height of 5.70, and after only just scraping clear at the second (the bar bounced) he gambled by sitting out 5.80 and 5.85. The pressure was on Bubka after two bad misses at 5.90. If he failed again not only would the title pass on to one of his colleagues, but he himself would be out of the medals. He made it.

There was a Soviet sweep also in the hammer. The three Olympic medallists from Moscow in 1980 shared the spoils again. Jüri Tamm picked up another bronze medal, but Yuriy Sedykh was foiled in his bid to win a third title. Although he threw much further than when he won in Montreal (77.52) and Moscow (a then world record of 81.80), 33-year-old Sedykh found that even four throws beyond 83m were insufficient to beat world champion Sergey Litvinov, the silver medallist eight years previously. Litvinov always held the edge over Sedykh, and all six of his throws were in excess of the old Olympic record. Throwing ahead of Sedykh, Litvinov produced this brilliant series: — 84.76, 83.82, 83.86, 83.98, 84.80 and 83.80.

Flo-Jo may have been the supreme star of the Seoul Games, but her sister-in-law Jackie Joyner-Kersee ran her close and more than made up for her galling experience at the previous Games. Right from the start of the heptathlon a world record was a possibility. The target was her score of 7215 in the US Trials and she began brilliantly with 12.69 for the hurdles. Although subsequent marks of 1.86 high jump, 15.80 shot and 22.56 200m brought her a first day total of 4262 as compared to 4367 in Indianapolis there was scope for catching up with herself on the second day. She leapt a glorious 7.27 – breaking the Olympic long jump record – but the javelin (45.66) was down on expectations, so she needed to run 800m in 2:13.67 to break the record – her best ever being 2:09.32 back in 1982. She went for it, covering the first lap in close to 63 sec and finishing in a magnificent 2:08.51 for a final score of 7291. The icing on the cake for JJK was her subsequent long jump victory. She overhauled her great East German rival Heike Drechsler (7.22) with a fifth round 7.40 for another Olympic record.

A far less expected American victory came in the high jump. Stefka Kostadinova of Bulgaria had cleared 2.03 or higher no fewer than 29 times, as against ten such clearances by the rest of the world's jumpers lumped together. But, when she most needed it, she found that height beyond her. She and Lou Ritter traded blow for blow throughout a gripping contest: 1.80, 1.85, 1.90, 1.93, 1.96, 1.99, 2.01 – each cleared without a failure. When both missed three times at 2.03 a jump-off was ordered. It was a sudden death situation, starting with a fourth try at 2.03 before the bar would begin to be lowered. Kostadinova, jumping first, failed. But moments later Ritter succeeded to bring about one of the biggest upsets of the Games.

Having earlier finished a brilliant second in the 3000m, Paula Ivan produced one of the most impressive front runs in the history of women's 1500m running ... an equivalent of Herb Elliott's immortal display at the 1960 Games. The Romanian poured on the pace right from the start. She dashed through the first 400m in a scorching 62.52 and slowed only slightly to reach 800m in 2:05.76. By 1200m, reached in 3:08.25 (62.49 third lap!), her margin was more than 20m. At the finish Ivan's lead was an incredible 40m and her time of 3:53.96 was the second fastest in history, surpassed only by Tatyana Kazankina's 3:52.47 in 1980.

Earlier, in the 3000m, Ivan had fought for the gold medal with world champion Tatyana Samolenko, originally selected by the USSR only for the 1500m. Concerned she might be at the mercy of faster finishers, Yvonne Murray spurted ahead 50m before the bell (7:26.58) – a bold move which assured her of a medal, for only Ivan and Samolenko were able to respond. Ivan took over with 300m to go, while Samolenko moved into second along the back straight. The Romanian led into the final straight but Samolenko had the stronger finish. Completing her last lap in under a minute she won in 8:26.53 - a time only Tatyana Kazankina (8:22.62) and Mary Slaney (8:25.83) had bettered. Ivan was timed at 8:27.15, and an elated Murray took bronze in 8:29.02, the fastest ever by a British-born athlete. She became the first Scotswoman to win an individual Olympic medal, beating Liz McColgan to the honour by five days.

The 10,000m had been seen by many as a straight duel between world champion and record holder Ingrid Kristiansen and the only woman to have beaten her in a 10,000m track race, McColgan. But the fates decreed otherwise. Kristiansen impressed with an inaugural Olympic record of 31:44.69 in her heat, but in the final she veered off the track at 2800m, victim of a foot injury. From 13 laps out McColgan (15:37.89 at 5000m) did all the leading and her remorseless pace dropped everyone except former world record holder Olga Bondarenko. The Soviet runner simply would not give up and was perfectly content to follow the Scot's every move, biding her time. It was with precisely 200m to go that Bondarenko made her move. In a flash it was all over and she drew 20m clear to win in 31:05.21.

It was the tiny Portuguese runner, Rosa Mota, who carried off the first gold medal of the Games – pulling away over the last 4k to add the Olympic crown (2:25:40) to her world and European marathon titles. She thus became her country's first female Olympic champion and she dedicated her victory to women's rights in Portugal. In her earlier days, before she became a national heroine, she was subjected to abuse on the streets of Oporto because it was not considered fitting for a woman to run in shorts! At 1.57m (5ft 2 ins) and 45kg (99lb) she dethroned her predecessor, Joan Benoit, as the smallest Olympic athletics champion in history.

FLO-JO & JJK

FLORENCE GRIFFITH-JOYNER

NEXT TO the Ben Johnson affair, the big talking point from Seoul was the phenomenal sequence of sprints by Florence Griffith Joyner, or Flo-Jo as she was more familiarly known.

One of the enduring images of the Seoul Games was that of the American sprinting to glory with a huge smile on her face. We are used to sprinters with agonised, distorted features ... but grins well before the finish line is reached? Truly, Flo-Jo was a one-off. There has never been a female sprinter like her, before or since. Not only did she run like the wind, but her grace, relaxation and muscular power set her apart from all others. Her speed, appearance and demeanour also gave rise to accusations and rumours that, years later, have not totally abated.

For many seasons she was a world class sprinter, an Olympic relay silver medallist in 1984 and second in the 200m at the 1987 World Championships, but her transformation – physically and statistically – in 1988 was quite astonishing.

It was at the USA Trials that she created the first big stir. She reduced her best 100m time of 10.89 to a staggering 10.49 in a quarter-final, making a nonsense of the highly respected world record of 10.76 by Evelyn Ashford. Although it was a windy afternoon and the triple jump being held at the same time on a parallel runway threw up several high readings, the wind gauge for the 100m registered zero and the mark was ratified by the IAAF. She won the final next day in 10.61 (+1.2m wind), which sounded more reasonable although still an amazing time. In the 200m she improved her best from 21.96 to an American record of 21.77.

In Seoul she started off with an Olympic 100m record of 10.88, and then improved to 10.62 (+1.0m wind) in her quarter final. In the semi-finals she coasted to a windy 10.70, while in the final she sped to another Olympic record of 10.54. The wind was over the limit at 3.0m per second, but it was the astonishingly relaxed nature of that run, plus the margin of victory, which rendered it as an almost unbelievable achievement. Ashford, although running as well as ever, was fully three metres behind in second

place in 10.83.

It was over 200m that we saw the full flowering of Flo-Jo's talent. She kicked off with a sedate 22.51 heat before stretching those muscular legs in the quarter-finals with an American and Olympic record of 21.76, six metres ahead of a discomfited Heike Drechsler of East Germany. In the semi final the next day, Merlene Ottey ran 22.07 and Silke Möller 22.15, good times by any standards, but some five metres in front of them was Flo-Jo in 21.56. The wind was below the limit at 1.7m per second and the world record of 21.71, first established by Marita Koch and then equalled by Drechsler, had been shattered.

One hundred minutes later the finalists settled into their blocks. Griffith Joyner, running her eighth race in five days, held a narrow lead at the half distance in 11.11 ahead of Ottey (11.13), but powered away in spectacular style along the straight to stop the timing device in an amazing 21.34! The wind reading was 1.3m per second. Grace Jackson used her raking stride to good effect to finish second in the Commonwealth record time of 21.72 with Drechsler pipping Ottey for the bronze.

There was another gold medal to come. A bungled exchange between Flo-Jo and Ashford came close to costing the USA the 4x100m relay title. By the time Ashford was away and running she was in third place some four metres behind the GDR and the USSR, but Flo-Jo's predecessor as the fastest woman on earth seized her chance of renewed glory with a super run which took her past both of her rivals, one of whom – Marlies Göhr – she had been duelling with since they both reached the 1976 Olympic 100m final as teenagers.

Still she hadn't finished! Despite formidable Soviet and East German opposition, the inclusion of Flo-Jo in the US 4x400m squad made possible the prospect of her equalling Fanny Blankers-Koen's record haul of four gold medals from one Games.

The race turned out to be a titanic battle between the USSR and the USA, with both teams finishing inside the GDR's world record of 3:15.92 and relegating the East Germans to a distant third.

Denean Howard ran well on the opening leg (49.82), two metres ahead of the Soviet

400m hurdles revelation Tatyana Ledovskaya (50.12), but on the second leg a tremendous contribution by Olga Nazarova (47.82) enabled her to open a lead of nearly ten metres over Diane Dixon (49.17). Valerie Brisco ran heroically on the third stage (48.44) to close right up on Maria Pinigina (49.43), and so we had the intriguing situation of a last lap duel between the world's number one, Olga Bryzgina, and an athlete who had never before raced 400m at international level and whose personal best of 50.94 dated back to 1983. With 200m to go Bryzgina had lengthened her lead to four metres but Flo-Jo came back a little in the finishing straight to end up barely a stride behind. The times were tremendous – Bryzgina 47.80, Griffith Joyner 48.08 – with the Soviet squad clocking 3:15.17 and the Americans 3:15.51.

Despite rumours of taking up the marathon seriously and of attacking the world 400m record, this most enigmatic of athletes did not race again on the track.

Unhappily, she was to hit the world's headlines again ten years after Seoul when she died in her sleep at home in California on September 21 1998, aged just 38. Born in Los Angeles on December 21 1959, she married 1984 Olympic triple jump champion Al Joyner in 1987 and produced a daughter, Mary Ruth, in 1990.

JACKIE JOYNER-KERSEE

HER SISTER-IN-LAW, Jackie Joyner-Kersee (Al Joyner is her brother, Bobby Kersee her husband and coach), would probably have been hailed as the star of the Games but for Flo-Jo's exploits. First she won the heptathlon with a score (7291) which remains unapproached as the world record to this day, and then she won the long jump with 7.40, breaking the Olympic record of 7.27 she had herself set during the heptathlon! She thus became the first woman to win both an individual and multi-event gold medal at the Olympics, a feat achieved only once by a man: Harold Osborn, winner of the high jump and decathlon at the 1924 Games.

In 2003 young Carolina Klüft of Sweden produced one of the outstanding performances of the World Championships in Paris when winning the heptathlon with a score of 7001, the world's highest total for 11 years. Along the way she set personal bests in five of the seven

events, but she still has a long way to go before she can eclipse JJK. Here is how their individual personal bests compare (JJK's first): 100m hurdles – 12.61 to 13.18, high jump – 1.93 to 1.94, shot – 16.84 to 14.48, 200m – 22.30 to 22.98, long jump – 7.49 to 6.92, javelin – 50.12 to 50.24, 800m – 2:08.51 to 2:12.12.

Born in East St Louis, Illinois, on March 3 1962 and named by her grandmother after Jacqueline Kennedy, she began long jumping at the age of 12 and won the Pan-American junior title in 1980. She took up the heptathlon in 1981 and the following year topped 6000 points and claimed her first American title.

She failed to finish in the 1983 World Championships but came away from the 1984 Olympics in Los Angeles with a medal. However, it was not the medal she had hoped for. Holding a 31 point lead going into the final event, the 800m, she was devastated to find herself five points behind Australia's Glynis Nunn at the end. Although hampered throughout the two days by a strained hamstring, she attributed her defeat to a "poor mental approach" and resolved she would never again allow herself to be defeatist before or during a competition. She was as good as her word ... and never lost a completed heptathlon until narrowly beaten for the US title 12 years later!

She set her first world heptathlon records in 1986, scoring 7148 at the Goodwill Games in Moscow (an enormous improvement on the previous mark of 6946 as rescored on the present tables) and 7158 in Houston. In 1987 she equalled Heike Drechsler's world long jump record of 7.45 at the Pan-American Games in Indianapolis prior to becoming world heptathlon and long jump champion in Rome. In a final tune-up prior to Seoul in 1988 she boosted her world record score to 7215, again in Indianapolis, this time at the US Olympic Trials.

JJK reached what can now be seen as the peak of her career at those Games. She opened brilliantly with a hurdles time which would have gained the bronze medal in the individual event, and by the end of day one she was a whopping 181 points ahead. She began the second day with that Olympic long jump record and finished with her fastest ever 800m time to break the world record and stretch her winning margin to an almost indecent 394 points.

Five days later she took on the world's best long jump specialists and triumphed again. Heike Drechsler took the lead in the third round with 7.18 and increased it with her next jump of 7.22 but JJK rose to the challenge. With her fifth leap she landed at 7.40. "I always said the impossible was possible," she remarked. "I never gave in. This was only my third actual long jump competition of the season because I've been concentrating on the heptathlon, so to win the gold is fantastic."

JJK continued at the highest level for many years. She won 14 consecutive heptathlons from 1985 until retiring injured at the 1991 World Championships (where she retained her long jump title), pulling up in the 200m after leading by 165 points after three events. At the 1992 Olympics she won two more medals: heptathlon gold and long jump bronze. She regained the world heptathlon title in 1993, while in 1994 she improved her US long jump record to 7.49, the second longest ever legal distance. Injuries were always a problem and at the 1996 Olympics, by then aged 34, she had to withdraw with a hamstring problem after winning her heat of the 100m hurdles. That was not how she planned to end her fabulous Olympic career, and – despite the pain – she returned to take a bronze medal in the long jump.

1988 - SEOUL

100m: (1.1) 1, Carl Lewis USA 9.92 (world rec); 2, Linford Christie GBR 9.97; 3, Calvin Smith USA 9.99; 4, Dennis Mitchell USA 10.04; 5, Robson da Silva BRA 10.11; 6, Desai Williams CAN 10.11; 7, Ray Stewart JAM 12.26; Ben Johnson CAN (9.79) disq

200m: (1.7) 1, Joe DeLoach USA 19.75; 2, Carl Lewis USA 19.79; 3, Robson da Silva BRA 20.04; 4, Linford Christie GBR 20.09; 5, Atlee Mahorn CAN 20.39; 6, Gilles Quenéhervé FRA 20.40; 7, Mike Rosswess GBR 20.51; 8, Bruno Marie-Rose FRA 20.58.

400m: 1, Steve Lewis USA 43.87; 2, Butch Reynolds USA 43.93; 3, Danny Everett USA 44.09; 4, Darren Clark AUS 44.55 (44.38 sf); 5, Innocent Egbunike NGR 44.72; 6, Bert Cameron JAM 44.94 (44.50 sf); 7, Ian Morris TRI 44.95 (44.60 sf); 8, Mohamed Al Malky OMN 45.03 (44.69 sf).

800m: 1, Paul Ereng KEN 1:43.45; 2, Joaquim Cruz BRA 1:43.90; 3, Said Aouita MAR 1:44.06; 4, Peter Elliott GBR 1:44.12; 5, Johnny Gray USA 1:44.80; 6, José Luis Barbosa BRA 1:46.39 (1:44.99 sf); 7, Donato Sabia ITA 1:48.03 (1:44.90 sf); 8, Nixon Kiprotich KEN 1:49.55 (1:44.71 sf).

1500m: 1, Peter Rono KEN 3:35.96; 2, Peter Elliott GBR 3:36.15; 3, Jens-Peter Herold GDR 3:36.21; 4, Steve Cram GBR 3:36.24; 5, Steve Scott USA 3:36.99; 6, Han Kulker NED 3:37.08; 7, Kip Cheruiyot KEN 3:37.94; 8, Marcus O'Sullivan IRL 3:38.39.

5000m: 1, John Ngugi KEN 13:11.70; 2, Dieter Baumann FRG 13:15.52; 3, Hansjörg Kunze GDR 13:15.73; 4, Domingos Castro POR 13:16.09; 5, Sydney Maree USA 13:23.69; 6, Jack Buckner GBR 13:23.85; 7, Stefano Mei ITA 13:26.17; 8, Evgeni Ignatov BUL 13:26.41.

10,000m: 1, Brahim Boutayeb MAR 27:21.46; 2, Salvatore Antibo ITA 27:23.55; 3, Kipkemboi Kimeli KEN 27:25.16; 4, Jean-Louis Prianon FRA 27:36.43; 5, Arturo Barrios MEX 27:39.32; 6, Hansjörg Kunze GDR 27:39.35; 7, Paul Arpin FRA 27:39.36; 8, Moses Tanui KEN 27:47.23.

Marathon: 1, Gelindo Bordin ITA 2:10:32; 2, Douglas Wakiihuri KEN 2:10:47; 3, Ahmed Salah DJI 2:10:59; 4, Takeyuki Nakayama JPN 2:11:05; 5, Steve Moneghetti AUS 2:11:49; 6, Charlie Spedding GBR 2:12:19; 7, Juma Ikangaa TAN 2:13:00; 8, Rob de Castella AUS 2:13:07.

3000mSC: 1, Julius Kariuki KEN 8:05.51; 2, Peter Koech KEN 8:06.79; 3, Mark Rowland GBR 8:07.96; 4, Alessandro Lambruschini ITA 8:12.17; 5, William Van Dijck BEL 8:13.99; 6, Henry Marsh USA 8:14.39; 7, Patrick Sang KEN 8:15.22; 8, Boguslaw Maminski POL 8:15.97.

110mH: (1.5) 1, Roger Kingdom USA 12.98; 2, Colin Jackson GBR 13.28; 3, Tonie Campbell USA 13.38; 4, Vladimir Shishkin URS 13.51; 5, Jon Ridgeon GBR 13.52; 6, Tony Jarrett GBR 13.54; 7, Mark McKoy CAN 13.61; 8, Arthur Blake USA 13.96.

400mH: 1, Andre Phillips USA 47.19; 2, Amadou Dia Ba SEN 47.23; 3, Ed Moses USA 47.56; 4, Kevin Young USA 47.94; 5, Winthrop Graham JAM 48.04; 6, Kriss Akabusi GBR 48.69; 7, Harald Schmid FRG 48.76; 8, Edgar Itt FRG 48.78.

4 x 100m Relay: 1, USSR (Viktor Bryzgin, Vladimir Krylov, Vladimir Muravyov, Vitaliy Savin) 38.19; 2, Great Britain (Elliot Bunney, John Regis, Mike McFarlane, Linford Christie) 38.28; 3,

France (Bruno Marie-Rose, Daniel Sangouma, Gilles Quenéhervé, Max Moriniere) 38.40; 4, Jamaica 38.47; 5, Italy 38.54; 6, FRG 38.55; 7, Canada 38.93; 8, Hungary 39.19.

4 x 400m Relay: 1, USA (Danny Everett 43.79, Steve Lewis 43.69, Kevin Robinzine 44.74, Butch Reynolds 43.94) 2:56.16 (eq world rec); 2, Jamaica (Howard Davis 45.05, Devon Morris 44.90, Winthrop Graham 45.80, Bert Cameron 44.55) 3:00.30; 3, FRG (Norbert Dobeleit 45.30, Edgar Itt 45.10, Jörg Vaihinger 45.52, Ralf Lübke 44.64) 3:00.56; 4, GDR 3:01.13; 5, Great Britain 3:02.00; 6, Australia 3:02.49; 7, Nigeria 3:02.50; 8, Kenya 3:04.69.

HJ: 1, Gennadiy Avdeyenko URS 2.38; 2, Hollis Conway USA 2.36; eq3, Rudolf Povarnitsyn URS & Patrik Sjöberg SWE 2.36; 5, Nick Saunders BER 2.34; 6, Dietmar Mögenburg FRG 2.34; eq7, Carlo Thränhardt FRG, Igor Paklin URS & Dalton Grant GBR 2.31.

PV: 1, Sergey Bubka URS 5.90; 2, Rodion Gataullin URS 5.85; 3, Grigoriy Yegorov URS 5.80; 4, Earl Bell USA 5.70; eq5, Thierry Vigneron FRA & Philippe Collet FRA 5.70; 7, István Bagyula HUN 5.60; 8, Philippe D'Encausse FRA 5.60.

LJ: 1, Carl Lewis USA 8.72; 2, Mike Powell USA 8.49; 3, Larry Myricks USA 8.27; 4, Giovanni Evangelisti ITA 8.08w; 5, Antonio Corgos ESP 8.03; 6, László Szalma HUN 8.00; 7, Norbert Brige FRA 7.97; 8, Leonid Voloshin URS 7.89.

TJ: 1, Khristo Markov BUL 17.61; 2, Igor Lapshin URS 17.52; 3, Aleksandr Kovalenko URS 17.42; 4, Oleg Protsenko URS 17.38; 5, Charlie Simpkins USA 17.29; 6, Willie Banks USA 17.03; 7, Ivan Slanar TCH 16.75; 8, Jacek Pastusinski POL 16.72.

SP: 1, Ulf Timmermann GDR 22.47; 2, Randy Barnes USA 22.39; 3, Werner Günthör SUI 21.99; 4, Udo Beyer GDR 21.40; 5, Remigius Machura TCH 20.57; 6, Gert Weil CHI 20.38; 7, Alessandro Andrei ITA 20.36; 8, Sergey Smirnov URS 20.36.

DT: 1, Jürgen Schult GDR 68.82; 2, Romas Ubartas URS 67.48; 3, Rolf Danneberg FRG 67.38; 4, Yuriy Dumchev URS 66.42; 5, Mac Wilkins USA 65.90; 6, Gejza Valent TCH 65.80; 7, Knut Hjeltnes NOR 64.94; 8, Alois Hannecker FRG 63.28.

HT: 1, Sergey Litvinov URS 84.80; 2, Yuriy Sedykh URS 83.76; 3, Jüri Tamm URS 81.16; 4, Ralf Haber GDR 80.44; 5, Heinz Weis FRG

79.16; 6, Tibor Gécsek HUN 78.36; 7, Imre Szitas HUN 77.04; 8, Ivan Tanev BUL 76.08.

JT: 1, Tapio Korjus FIN 84.28; 2, Jan Zelezny TCH 84.12 (85.90q); 3, Seppo Räty FIN 83.26; 4, Klaus Tafelmeier FRG 82.72; 5, Viktor Yevsyukov URS 82.32; 6, Gerald Weiss GDR 81.30; 7, Vladimir Ovchinnikov URS 79.12; 8, Dag Wennlund SWE 78.30.

Decathlon: 1, Christian Schenk GDR 8488 (11.25, 7.43, 15.48, 2.27, 48.90, 15.13, 49.28, 4.70, 61.32, 4:28.95); 2, Torsten Voss GDR 8399 (10.87, 7.45, 14.97, 1.97, 47.71, 14.46, 44.36, 5.10, 61.76, 4:33.02); 3, Dave Steen CAN 8328 (11.18, 7.44, 14.20, 1.97, 48.29, 14.81, 43.66, 5.20, 64.16, 4:23.20); 4, Daley Thompson GBR 8306; 5, Christian Plaziat FRA 8272; 6, Alain Blondel FRA 8268; 7, Tim Bright USA 8216; 8, Robert de Wit NED 8189.

20k Walk: 1, Jozef Pribilinec TCH 1:19:57; 2, Ronald Weigel GDR 1:20:00; 3, Maurizio Damilano ITA 1:20:14; 4, José Marin ESP 1:20:34; 5, Roman Mrazek TCH 1:20:43; 6, Mikhail Shchennikov URS 1:20:47; 7, Carlos Mercenario MEX 1:20:53; 8, Axel Noack GDR 1:21:14.

50k Walk: 1, Vyacheslav Ivanenko URS 3:38:29; 2, Ronald Weigel GDR 3:38:56; 3, Hartwig Gauder GDR 3:39:45; 4, Aleksandr Potashov URS 3:41:00; 5, José Marin ESP 3:43:03; 6, Simon Baker AUS 3:44:07; 7, Bo Gustafsson SWE 3:44:49; 8, Raffaello Ducceschi ITA 3:45:43.

Women's Events

100m: (3.0) 1, Florence Griffith Joyner USA 10.54w (10.62 qf. +1.0m); 2, Evelyn Ashford USA 10.83 (legal 10.88 qf); 3, Heike Drechsler GDR 10.85 (10.96 qf); 4, Grace Jackson JAM 10.97 (11.13 qf); 5, Gwen Torrence USA 10.97 (10.99 qf); 6, Natalya Pomoshnikova URS 11.00 (10.98 qf); 7, Juliet Cuthbert JAM 11.26 (11.03 qf); 8, Anelia Nuneva BUL 11.49 (11.00 sf) ... Merlene Ottey JAM did not start in semi (11.03 qf).

200m: (1.3) 1, Florence Griffith Joyner USA 21.34 (world rec; 21.56 semi-final, world rec); 2, Grace Jackson JAM 21.72; 3, Heike Drechsler GDR 21.95; 4, Merlene Ottey JAM 21.99; 5, Silke Möller GDR 22.09; 6, Gwen Torrence USA 22.17; 7, Maia Azarashvili URS 22.33; 8, Galina Malchugina URS 22.42.

400m: 1, Olga Bryzgina URS 48.65; 2, Petra Müller GDR 49.45; 3, Olga Nazarova URS 49.90 (49.11 sf); 4, Valerie Brisco USA 50.16 (49.90 sf);

5, Diane Dixon USA 50.72 (49.84 sf); 6, Denean Howard USA 51.12 (49.87 sf); 7, Helga Arendt FRG 51.17; 8, Maree Holland AUS 51.25.

800m: 1, Sigrun Wodars GDR 1:56.10; 2, Christine Wachtel GDR 1:56.64; 3, Kim Gallagher USA 1:56.91; 4, Slobodanka Colovic YUG 1:57.50; 5, Delisa Floyd USA 1:57.80; 6, Inna Yevseyeva URS 1:59.37; 7, Teresa Zuniga ESP 1:59.82; 8, Diane Edwards GBR 2:00.77.

1500m: 1, Paula Ivan ROM 3:53.96; 2, Laima Baikauskaite URS 4:00.24; 3, Tatyana Samolenko URS 4:00.30; 4, Chris Cahill (née Boxer) GBR 4:00.64; 5, Lynn Williams CAN 4:00.86; 6, Andrea Hahmann GDR 4:00.96; 7, Shireen Bailey GBR 4:02.32; 8, Mary Slaney USA 4:02.49.

3000m: 1, Tatyana Samolenko URS 8:26.53; 2, Paula Ivan ROM 8:27.15; 3, Yvonne Murray GBR 8:29.02; 4, Yelena Romanova URS 8:30.45; 5, Natalya Artyomova URS 8:31.67; 6, Vicki Huber USA 8:37.25; 7, Wendy Sly GBR 8:37.70; 8, Lynn Williams CAN 8:38.43.

10,000m: 1, Olga Bondarenko URS 31:05.21; 2, Liz McColgan GBR 31:08.44; 3, Yelena Zhupiyova URS 31:19.82; 4, Kathrin Ullrich GDR 31:29.27; 5, Francie Larrieu Smith USA 31:35.52; 6, Lynn Jennings USA 31:39.93; 7, Wang Xiuting CHN 31:40.23; 8, Susan Lee CAN 31:50.51.

Marathon: 1, Rosa Mota POR 2:25:40; 2, Lisa Martin AUS 2:25:53; 3, Katrin Dörre GDR 2:26:21; 4, Tatyana Polovinskaya URS 2:27:05; 5, Zhao Youfeng CHN 2:27:06; 6, Laura Fogli ITA 2:27:49; 7, Daniele Kaber LUX 2:29:23; 8, Maria Curatolo ITA 2:30:14.

100mH: (0.2) 1, Yordanka Donkova BUL 12.38; 2, Gloria Siebert GDR 12.61 (12.60 sf); 3, Claudia Zaczkiewicz FRG 12.75; 4, Natalya Grigoryeva URS 12.79; 5, Florence Colle FRA 12.98; 6, Julie Rocheleau CAN 12.99; 7, Monique Ewanje-Epée FRA 13.14; 8, Cornelia Oschkenat GDR 13.73 (12.63 sf) ... Lyudmila Narozhilenko URS dnf semi (12.62 qf).

400mH: 1, Debbie Flintoff-King AUS 53.17; 2, Tatyana Ledovskaya URS 53.18; 3, Ellen Fiedler GDR 53.63; 4, Sabine Busch GDR 53.69; 5, Sally Gunnell GBR 54.03; 6, Gudrun Abt FRG 54.04; 7, Tatyana Kurochkina URS 54.39; 8, Latanya Sheffield USA 55.32.

4 x 100m Relay: 1, USA (Alice Brown, Sheila Echols, Florence Griffith Joyner, Evelyn Ashford) 41.98; 2, GDR (Silke Möller, Kerstin Behrendt, Ingrid Lange, Marlies Göhr) 42.09; 3, USSR (Lyudmila Kondratyova, Galina Malchugina, Marina Zhirova, Natalya Pomoshnikova) 42.75 (42.01 sf); 4, FRG 42.76 (42.69 sf); 5, Bulgaria 43.02; 6, Poland 43.93; 7, France 44.02; Jamaica dns.

4 x 400m Relay: 1, USSR (Tatyana Ledovskaya 50.12, Olga Nazarova 47.82, Maria Pinigina 49.43, Olga Bryzgina 47.80) 3:15.17 (world rec); 2, USA (Denean Howard 49.82, Diane Dixon 49.17, Valerie Brisco 48.44, Florence Griffith Joyner 48.08) 3:15.51; 3, GDR (Dagmar Neubauer 50.58, Kirsten Emmelmann 49.91, Sabine Busch 48.81, Petra Müller 48.99) 3:18.29; 4, FRG 3:22.49; 5, Jamaica 3:23.13; 6, Great Britain 3:26.89; 7, France 3:29.37; Canada dnf.

HJ: 1, Lou Ritter USA 2.03 (in jump off); 2, Stefka Kostadinova BUL 2.01; 3, Tamara Bykova URS 1.99; 4, Olga Turchak URS 1.96; eq5, Galina Astafei ROM & Lyudmila Andonova BUL 1.93; 7, Chris Stanton AUS 1.93; eq8, Diana Davies GBR & Kim Hee-Sun KOR 1.90.

LJ: 1, Jackie Joyner-Kersee USA 7.40; 2, Heike Drechsler GDR 7.22; 3, Galina Chistyakova URS 7.11; 4, Yelena Byelevskaya URS 7.04 (7.06q); 5, Nicole Boegman AUS 6.73w; 6, Fiona May GBR 6.62; 7, Agata Karczmarek POL 6.60; 8, Sabine John GDR 6.55.

SP: 1, Natalya Lisovskaya URS 22.24; 2, Kathrin Neimke GDR 21.07; 3, Li Meisu CHN 21.06; 4, Ines Müller GDR 20.37; 5, Claudia Losch FRG 20.27 (20.39q); 6, Heike Hartwig GDR 20.20; 7, Natalya Akhrimenko URS 20.13; 8, Huang Zhihong CHN 19.82.

DT: 1, Martina Hellmann GDR 72.30; 2, Diana Gansky GDR 71.88; 3, Tzvetanka Khristova BUL 69.74; 4, Svetla Mitkova BUL 69.14; 5, Ellina Zveryova URS 68.94; 6, Zdenka Silhavá TCH 67.84; 7, Gabriele Reinsch GDR 67.26; 8, Hou Xuemei CHN 65.94.

JT: 1, Petra Felke GDR 74.68; 2, Fatima Whitbread GBR 70.32; 3, Beate Koch GDR 67.30; 4, Irina Kostyuchenkova URS 67.00; 5, Silke Renk GDR 66.38; 6, Natalya Yermolovich URS 64.84; 7, Donna Mayhew USA 61.78; 8, Ingrid Thyssen FRG 60.76.

Heptathlon: 1, Jackie Joyner-Kersee USA 7291 (world rec; 12.69, 1.86, 15.80, 22.56, 7.27, 45.66, 2:08.51); 2, Sabine John GDR 6897 (12.85, 1.80, 16.23, 23.65, 6.71, 42.56, 2:06.14); 3, Anke Behmer GDR 6858 (13.20, 1.83, 14.20, 23.10, 6.68, 44.54, 2:04.20); 4, Natalya Shubenkova URS 6540; 5, Remigija Sablovskaite URS 6456; 6, Ines Schulz GDR 6411; 7, Jane Flemming AUS 6351; 8, Cindy Greiner USA 6297.

WITH CUBA and Ethiopia back in the fold for the first time since Moscow in 1980, every nation of consequence in athletics was present in Barcelona. The era of boycotts was over. Politically, many momentous events had occurred since the previous Games. The misleadingly named German Democratic Republic (Communist East Germany) had ceased to exist and Germany was represented by one team; the dismembered Soviet Union competed under the title "Unified Team" while the Baltic States previously under its control proudly participated as Estonia, Latvia and Lithuania; and back from the sporting wilderness came a reconstituted South Africa, welcome at an Olympics for the first time since 1960.

Perhaps the most indelible image of the Games was the sight of Derartu Tulu, a black Ethiopian, and Elana Meyer, a white South African, running a joint lap of honour following the 10,000m in which they finished first and second respectively. It was an emotional scene which proved that for all their shortcomings – as with every other human endeavour – the Olympic Games remain an important force for harmony and friendship transcending political and racial differences.

That women's 10,000m was highly significant also in underlining the progress of Africa's women athletes. Thirty two years after Ethiopian marathon legend Abebe Bikila became the first black African to strike Olympic gold, Tulu opened a new era for the women. She had first attracted attention by winning the 1990 World Junior 10,000m title, while the following year she was the last runner to be dropped by Liz McColgan in the 1991 World Championships 10,000m, even if she did fade to eighth place. Her talent and ambition would not long be denied and in Barcelona the 20 year-old prison administrator superseded Rosa Mota as the smallest of all Olympic champions at 1.55m (5ft 1in) and 44kg (97lb). McColgan, who finished fifth, led for the first 6k and then Meyer took over, with only Tulu able to respond. Tulu raced away at the bell to win in the African record time of 31:06.02.

The next day Algeria's Hassiba Boulmerka took the Olympic 1500m crown to add to her world title. Thanks to the fierce pace set by Lyudmila Rogachova, of the Unified Team (60.66,

2:05.02, 3:09.88) it was a very fast race with the first four all inside 3:58. With 200m to go, Boulmerka launched her attack and sped home ten metres up in an African record of 3:55.30, nearly 5 sec inside her previous fastest. An equally significant result was the Asian record of 3:57.08 in third place by China's 19 year-old Qu Yunxia, whose pre-1992 best stood at 4:07.71. A year later Qu would become world 3000m champion and world 1500m record holder with 3:50.46.

In all, Africa's athletes garnered 19 medals from a dozen events as against 11 medals from seven disciplines in Seoul. Their parade events were the men's 10,000m and steeplechase, in which clean sweeps were achieved.

Controversy reared its head in the 10,000m. Did Khalid Skah cheat his way to the gold medal, or was the intervention by the lapped runner, fellow Moroccan Hammou Boutayeb, unplanned? The referee's immediate reaction was that Skah had indeed transgressed the rule which forbids assistance during an event, and he was accordingly disqualified. But next morning, following a protest by the Moroccan team management, the Jury of Appeal reinstated Skah as winner, declaring there had been no contravention of the rules by him.

In view of Skah's devastating finishing kick –

STAR OF THE GAMES

KEVIN YOUNG
(born 16 Sep 1966)

A time of 46.78 would have sufficed for victory in the flat 400m at the 1956 Olympics, but that was Kevin Young's amazing barrier-breaking performance when winning the 400m hurdles in Barcelona. The lanky American would have gone even faster had he not hit the final hurdle and savoured his victory before crossing the finish line. After over a decade it remains unapproached as the world record.

he covered the last 200m in 26.0 – it's probable that he would have beaten the young Kenyan, Richard Chelimo, anyway, but Boutayeb's actions did have an effect on the pattern of the race which must have been to Chelimo's detriment. He slowed the race down during the two laps he was in front, which was to the advantage of a big kicker like Skah, who vehemently denied any collusion. He declared: "Boutayeb and I are friends, but on the track we are enemies. We never run as a team. I was the best in the race and I didn't need any help to win."

Duplicating their achievement at the 1991 World Championships but for the first time in the Olympics, Kenyans took all three medals in their speciality, the steeplechase. The winner in a swift 8:08.44, despite falling soon after a kilometre and rejoining the race in ninth place, was the 1990 world junior champion Matthew Birir.

Kenyans were dominant also in the 800m, even though defending champion Paul Ereng trailed home last in his semi. For only the second time in 80 years, one country gained a one-two in this race (Steve Ovett and Seb Coe for Great Britain in 1980 was the other incidence) as William Tanui (1:43.66) and Nixon Kiprotich caught and passed Johnny Gray in a fast and thrilling race. The lanky 32 year-old American, author of so many fast times but never before a major force in a big championship, sped around the first lap in 49.99 and led into the finishing straight, when first Kiprotich (who only qualified for the final as a fastest loser) and then Tanui took command.

Africans also held justifiably high hopes of winning the 1500m and 5000m but both titles surprisingly went to Europeans.

While the overwhelming favourite, Algeria's world champion Noureddine Morceli, ran the worst race of his glittering career to finish seventh, Fermin Cacho was transformed into a national hero by winning the coveted title in front of his own fans. The Spaniard, noted for his finishing speed, was delighted by the slow early pace; indeed the first two laps were slower than in the women's final. The race sprang to life in the third lap, covered in 55.72, and Cacho took the lead on the final turn to win in 3:40.12 from Morocco's Rachid El Basir, who moved from eighth to second in the final straight. The last lap was covered

in 50.5 and Spain could celebrate her first Olympic running champion, 20 kilometre walker Daniel Plaza having earlier become that nation's first ever athletics gold medallist.

Barely half an hour after Cacho's triumph another European lifted the gold medal in the 5000m, the next five men home all being Africans. In a thrilling last lap, for much of which he was boxed in, Dieter Baumann of Germany extricated himself in time to produce a scintillating sprint along the finishing straight to win by a metre or so in 13:12.52, his last 200m taking just 24.9.

Of the record number of 157 countries to participate in the athletics events, 35 provided medallists – way beyond the previous record of 25 in 1968 and indicative of the way in which athletics talent is becoming more widespread throughout the world. The USA. however, remained the dominant power as Uncle Sam's representatives grabbed 12 titles (next best was seven by the Unified Team and four by Germany) and a total of 30 medals as against 21 by the former Soviet Union and 10 by Germany. The British team picked up six medals, two of which were gold thanks to Linford Christie and Sally Gunnell (see page 160).

There wasn't much argument over the best performance of the Games ... Kevin Young's 46.78 400m hurdles. Such a time would have sufficed to win the 400m flat title at the Melbourne Games

Number of Competing Nations in Olympic Athletics

1896	10	1952	55
1900	16	1956	59
1904	10	1960	70
1906	21	1964	79
1908	21	1968	91
1912	27	1972	102
1920	25	1976	71
1924	40	1980	69
1928	40	1984	121
1932	33	1988	139
1936	42	1992	157
1948	52	1996	197
		2000	194

of 1956! The long-legged American, unique in his mixture of 12 and 13-stride intervals between the hurdles, thus broke Ed Moses' world record of 47.02 set nine years earlier. The 50 sec barrier was broken in 1956, 49 sec in 1968, 48 sec in 1972 ... now 47 sec had been breached, and Young's time would have been even swifter had he not rammed the final hurdle and celebrated his victory well short of the line. He explained: "As I was coming to the finish I was listening for other hurdlers. When I didn't hear anyone coming near I just threw up my hands, something I have always wanted to do."

Kriss Akabusi, who placed third with a British record of 47.82, commented: "Edwin Moses was, for me, the man of 400m hurdling, and I didn't think his record would be broken in my generation. I can't believe he [Young] did it. It's great".

The flat 400m threw up another brilliant performance by an American as Quincy Watts, in only his second serious season at the event, removed Lee Evans' 1968 Olympic (and former world) record of 43.86 with 43.71 in his semi-final, followed by 43.50 in the final – second fastest on record to Butch Reynolds' 43.29. He overhauled defending champion Steve Lewis around the final turn to win by some six metres, the biggest Olympic winning margin since Eric Liddell back in 1924. His coach, former 400m star John Smith, remarked: "He really doesn't know how to run the race yet".

Even closer to setting a world record was Michael Marsh in the 200m, an event that was marred by the illness which led to the favourite, Michael Johnson, being eliminated in the semi-finals. Despite appearing to relax before crossing the line, Marsh won his semi in 19.73, fastest ever at sea level and just one tantalising hundredth of a second shy of Pietro Mennea's record. In the final next day there was a headwind to contend with in the straight and everybody ran slower than in the preliminaries as Marsh raced to a clear win over Namibia's Frank Fredericks (earlier second to Christie in the 100m) in 20.01.

Michael Johnson and Noureddine Morceli were not the only major casualties of these Games. Britain's Colin Jackson posted the fastest 110m hurdles time in Barcelona with 13.10 but that was in a heat and he wound up only seventh in the final (won by his training companion, Mark McKoy of Canada in 13.12) as a hip muscle injury hampered him severely; and another surprise was the failure of Swiss shot putting ace Werner Günthör to win a medal.

The biggest upset, though, came in the pole vault. Many thought defending champion Sergey Bubka had only to turn up at the stadium to collect another gold medal, particularly as he had been showing his best ever form in 1992 with world records indoors of 6.13 and outdoors of 6.11. But, in the final, the Ukrainian failed to clear a height. Due to a combination of a swirling wind, problems preparing to vault within the allotted time and a misjudgment over the choice of his poles, he contrived to miss twice at 5.70 and did no better when he elected to save up his remaining try for 5.75. His demise was a bonus to everyone else and Russian Maksim Tarasov cleared 5.80 for victory. "Of course I wasn't expecting to win a gold medal," he admitted, "but I just took my chance. Sergey's elimination was a big surprise to us".

The pole vault was keenly contested, with Igor Trandenkov taking the silver also at 5.80, but the high jump was even more closely fought as no fewer than five men cleared the winning height of 2.34. For the first time in Olympic history there was a three-way tie for one of the medals. Bronze awards were presented to Artur Partyka (POL), Tim Forsyth (AUS) and Hollis Conway (USA), all of whom made 2.34 on the second attempt after one failure apiece at a lower height. The silver went to Sweden's Patrik Sjöberg, also over at the second try but with no other failures, while the gold went to world record holder Javier Sotomayor, who had missed his chance of Olympic glory in 1988 because of the Cuban boycott. Sotomayor, the first man to leap 8 feet (2.44), chalked up a potentially costly failure at his opening height of 2.24 but that error was wiped out when he succeeded first time at 2.34.

Perhaps the most eagerly awaited confrontation of the Games was the long jump re-match between Mike Powell, who had the previous year lifted the world title with a world record 8.95, and Carl Lewis, runner-up in that memorable contest with a windy 8.91 and now seeking an unprecedented third Olympic long jump crown.

A WHOLE NEW WORLDCONTINUED

While the stadium was still buzzing from the excitement of Kevin Young's 400m hurdles exploit, Lewis opened his account with 8.67 - a mark that was to prove to be his best of the day. Would it be enough? Powell started with a modest 7.95 but gradually got into his stride with jumps of 8.22, 8.33, a foul of around 8.50, and 8.53. At his final attempt, Powell knew he had to jump at least 8.67 for victory. Hearts fluttered as the measurement was awaited ... but at 8.64 it was an inch short of what he needed and so the result was a repeat of the Seoul Games and Lewis had won his sixth individual Olympic gold medal.

By contrast, the triple jump - yet another American success story - was a one-man show. Mike Conley won from his team-mate Charlie Simpkins by the enormous distance of 57cm, or nearly two feet, for the biggest Olympic winning margin since the inaugural Games in 1896. Conley, a superbly talented athlete who has wind assisted marks of 8.63 for the long jump and 20.12 for 200m, was unlucky though in that his final effort of 18.17 was aided by a wind of 2.1m per second. Had the reading been 2.0m he would have been credited with smashing Willie Banks' world record of 17.97. Philosophically and prophetically, Conley commented: "I will always have this [the gold medal] and Willie won't always have the world record". Three years later, Britain's Jonathan Edwards (who failed to reach the Barcelona final, 35th with 15.76) would succeed Banks as record holder.

World records were smashed by the Americans in both the men's relays. The "dream team" of Michael Marsh, Leroy Burrell, Dennis Mitchell and Carl Lewis (for his eighth Olympic gold medal) stormed around in 37.40, while Andrew Valmon, Quincy Watts, Michael Johnson (still not in the best of health) and Steve Lewis averaged under 44 sec per leg for a 4x400m time of 2:55.74. The fastest splits of the race came from Watts (a best on record 43.00) and Lewis (43.41), both running solo far ahead of the opposition.

American women dominated the sprints as Gail Devers (see page 159) snatched a very closely contested 100m in 10.82, Gwen Torrence emerged a clear winner of the 200m in 21.81 and with Evelyn Ashford (16 years after her first Olympic appearance) on the first leg and Torrence on the anchor the USA took the 4x100m relay in 42.11. Torrence, who was also a close fourth in the 100m, picked up a silver medal in the 4x400m won by the Unified Team.

Devers, who had not been expected to win the 100m (she improved her best time by 13/100ths), looked all set to complete a golden double in her "better" event, the 100m hurdles, even more so when her main rival, Lyudmila Narozhilenko, had to scratch injured from the semi-finals. In the final Devers held a big lead as she rose to the final hurdle but, unable to control her blazing speed, she clipped that final barrier with the heel of her lead leg. Almost falling, she staggered over the finish line in fifth place while the title went to a complete outsider, Paraskevi Patoulidou of Greece in 12.64. She had never run faster than 12.96 prior to the Games and her previous best showing in a major championship was reaching the European semis in 1990. The former basketball player became the first Greek woman ever to win an Olympic gold medal, 80 years after the last Greek man to succeed.

A more significant 'first' occurred in the inaugural women's 10k road walk when Chen Yueling won China's first ever Olympic athletics title. It was a controversial result, for Alina Ivanova of the Unified Team crossed the finish line seven seconds ahead but was subsequently disqualified for lifting. Ivanova, the 1991 world champion, was so disgusted that she proceeded to retire from race walking and turned to marathon running instead.

Former Soviet athletes did have their successes, though, in the women's events and with 14 medals outscored the USA (10). They won the 4x400m relay, 3000m (Yelena Romanova unleashing a savage final 200m of 28.1), marathon (Valentina Yegorova toughing it out up the merciless hill to the finish) and the shot (Svetlana Krivelyova). Next best were the German women with six medals, three of them gold thanks to Heike Henkel and Heike Drechsler in the jumps and Silke Renk in the javelin. Notable among other winners were elegant Marie-José Perec, who took the 400m in a French record of 48.83; Ellen van Langen, 800m victor in a Dutch record of 1:55.54; and Jackie Joyner-Kersee, who retained her heptathlon title with a score of 7044.

From Death's Door To Olympic Gold

THERE ARE numerous examples of athletes who have recovered from severe injury or illness and gone on to great triumphs, but only one who went from death's door to a World Championship medal in the space of a few months, followed a year later by Olympic victory. This athlete's story was so extraordinary that when a made-for-television drama based on the events was shown in the USA many viewers must have assumed it was dreamt up by Hollywood scriptwriters.

Gail Devers (born in Seattle on November 19 1966) reached world class as a sprinter in 1985, aged 18, and won the Pan American 100m title two years later. Her future looked bright indeed when in 1988 she set an American 100m hurdles record of 12.61. On form, she should have made the final at that year's Seoul Olympics but she finished a lack-lustre last in her semi-final – plagued by a severe headache.

On returning home it became evident she was really ill. The migraine headaches continued, along with fainting spells, blurred vision, shaky hands and loss of sleep and memory. Some of her hair fell out and her bodyweight – normally 52 kilograms (114lb) – fluctuated alarmingly between 45 and 60kg (99-132lb). Believing she had over-taxed herself, doctors advised her to rest. That didn't help and it was not until September 1990 that she was diagnosed as suffering from Graves' disease, a potentially fatal hyperthyroid condition. "The doctors told me that my disease was two weeks away from being cancerous. If it had been cancerous I would have died within a matter of months," she said.

She was given chemotherapy and radiation treatment, but with dreadful side effects. Her feet became so badly burned by the radiation that in March 1991 she came close to having them amputated.

After such an ordeal most people would have been happy just to walk again and live a normal life, but Gail Devers wanted more; she still had unfulfilled athletic ambitions. In April 1991 she stepped onto a track for the first time in over two years, her "training" consisting of gingerly walking around in her socks. Incredibly, the following month she made a successful return to competition!

In her first season back she proved better than ever, finishing a close second in the 100m hurdles at the World Championships and improving the US record to 12.48. At 1.60 (5ft 3in) tall Devers may be the shortest of top hurdlers but her blazing speed between the barriers more than compensates.

That speed was seen to devastating effect in Barcelona in 1992 when, unexpectedly, she snatched the Olympic 100m gold medal in 10.82, a startling improvement of 13/100ths of a second. With her "better" event to follow she was tipped to become the first since "The Flying Dutchwoman" Fanny Blankers-Koen in 1948 to complete the sprint/hurdles double. Sure enough, she held a substantial lead rising to the final hurdle but, unable to control her speed, she clipped the barrier with the heel of her lead leg. Almost falling, she staggered over the line in fifth place.

Devers remained philosophical. "My illness taught me so much," she says. "I wouldn't wish it on anyone, but I'm happy I went through it. There is nothing that can come up in my life that I can't get over. I learned never to give up."

Nor has she as further honours piled up. A dynamic starter, she captured the world indoor 60m title in 1993 and later that year achieved that elusive 100m flat and hurdles double at the outdoor World Championships. She retained her world hurdles crown two years later, and won a second Olympic 100m gold medal (plus victory in the 4x100m relay) in Atlanta in 1996.

Still more gold medals came her way: at 60m in the 1997 World Indoors, in the 4x100m relay at that year's World Championships, a third world title at 100m hurdles in 1999 and her first world indoor 60m hurdles triumph in 2003 ... a total of ten global gold medals. She was 33 when she set the current US hurdles record of 12.33 in 2000. Just one ambition remains: to become Olympic 100m hurdles champion. World ranked no 1 by *Athletics International* in that event in 2003, she could at the age of 37 yet achieve that ultimate goal!

THE PRIDE OF BRITAIN

AUGUST 1 1992 was the day that Linford Christie won the blue riband event of the Olympics and became one of the sport's immortals. Although he had considered he stood as good a chance as anybody else, even he could not have dreamed of winning the biggest race of his life by such a convincing margin.

At the finish he had 6/100ths of a second – more than half a metre – to spare over Frank Fredericks, with Dennis Mitchell third. Former world record holder Leroy Burrell, who had earlier shaded Christie in their semi-final, 9.97 to 10.00 into a 1.3m wind, wound up a metre and a half behind Christie in the final, fifth behind Bruny Surin. Reinstated Ben Johnson came nowhere near to making the final, while Carl Lewis failed to make the US squad for the 100m.

Prior to the semi-finals Christie had reckoned he stood a 90% chance of winning; afterwards he was convinced he would win. His coach Ron Roddan and Colin Jackson's coach Malcolm Arnold pointed out how he could improve his pick-up, Christie adjusted his block setting to that used by Jackson and Europe's

DID YOU KNOW?

Who would have predicted that the last two finishers in the heptathlon would eventually blossom into global champions? Ghada Shouaa of Syria, 25th with 5278 points, became world champion in 1995 and Olympic champion in 1996, while Eunice Barber from Sierra Leone, who placed 26th with 4530 (scoring no points in the javelin), was destined to win the 1999 world title in French colours. Barber fared little better in two individual events. She finished 30th in the long jump qualifying competition with 5.55 (this the woman who would win the world long jump title in 2003!) and last in her 100m hurdles heat in 15.01 ... Two other bright stars of the future also dwelt in obscurity in Barcelona: Ato Boldon of Trinidad failed to survive his first round sprint heats with times of 10.77 and 21.65 and Tegla Loroupe of Kenya came home 17th of the 18 finishers in the 10,000m final in 32:53.09 ... Competing in the Olympics for the first time, Namibia gained two silver medals through sprinter Frank Fredericks ... John Regis equalled Linford Christie's UK 200m record of 20.09 in his semi-final ... Britain's Roger Black gained the unwanted distinction of becoming the fastest ever non-qualifier at 400m when he ran 44.72 for fifth place in his semi; one position ahead of him was David Grindley (19) in a UK record of 44.47 ... Prior to Fermín Cacho's triumph, the last man to win the Olympic 1500m title on home soil was James Lightbody (USA) in St Louis in 1904, in a world record 4:05.4 ... Mohamed Suleiman, third in the 1500m to become Qatar's first ever Olympic medallist, was actually born in Somalia ... Marathon runner Hwang Young-Jo became the first athlete representing Korea to win an Olympic title, although Kitei Son – the 1936 marathon champion representing Japan – was in fact a Korean whose real name was Sohn Kee-chung. Korea was under Japanese occupation at the time and he was obliged to change his name to a Japanese equivalent ... Laurent Ottoz of Italy, a semi-finalist in the 110m hurdles, is the son of the 1968 Olympic bronze medallist Eddy Ottoz; Kimmo Kinnunen of Finland, fourth in the javelin, is the son of 1968 silver medallist and former world record holder Jorma Kinnunen; Peggy Beer of Germany, sixth in the heptathlon, is the daughter of Klaus Beer, the man who finished a totally unnoticed second to Bob Beamon in the long jump at the 1968 Games... Mark McKoy, winner of the 110m hurdles in Canada's colours, was born in Guyana and spent much of his childhood in Britain; his wife is German and he went on to represent Austria ... High jump runner-up Patrik Sjöberg of Sweden became the first man to win three Olympic medals in that event ... All three medallists in the men's shot were reinstated drugs offenders, while discus winner Romas Ubartas (the first athlete representing Lithuania to strike Olympic gold) failed a doping control in 1993 ... Sandra Farmer-Patrick (USA), second in the 400m hurdles, had placed 8th in 1984, running for Jamaica ... Destined to create walking history in later Games, Poland's Robert Korzeniowski made an inauspicious Olympic debut; he failed to finish in the 20k and was disqualified in the 50k event.

fastest ever sprinter went to the start confident and totally focussed. Ten seconds or less of supreme physical and mental effort that could change his life lay ahead.

The capacity crowd of 64,800 was hushed as the eight men settled in their blocks. The tension was heightened when Burrell caused a false start and a second attempt to get the runners away was aborted when Mitchell signalled he was not ready. At the third try they were away ... and Christie got a beauty of a start. For once, and on absolutely the right occasion, Christie found himself on level terms with his main rivals almost from the outset. By 60 metres, which he reached in 6.48, he was clear and sprinting towards gold and glory.

He crossed the line upright in 9.96 as his well beaten rivals lunged desperately for the other spoils. It was at the time the second fastest mark of his career, behind the 9.92 he recorded when placing fourth to Lewis, Burrell and Mitchell in Tokyo but by any other criterion it was the race of his life.

After so narrowly failing to win a medal in those 1991 World Championships, Christie considered taking his leave of the sport but, as he said after his Olympic victory, "I'm just glad I didn't retire then. That's the best decision I've ever made. This is something that Ron and I have been working for over the last 10 to 12 years".

Although he doesn't like to be reminded, Christie made Olympic history by becoming the oldest man to win the 100m crown, at 32, the previous 'record holder' being Allan Wells – the last Briton to beat Christie in a 100m final, back in 1986 – when he won in Moscow at the age of 28. The only other British winner of the title was Harold Abrahams in the "Chariots of Fire" Games of 1924.

Christie also earned the distinction of becoming the first Jamaican-born athlete to strike gold at 100m. Herb McKenley had previously come closest. losing by 1/100th in 1952; Lennox Miller and Don Quarrie also finished second in 1968 and 1976 respectively, while Christie himself took silver in Seoul in 9.97 when Ben Johnson (also a native of Jamaica) was disqualified.

Until Sally Gunnell's success in Barcelona, the only British woman to have won an Olympic track event was Ann Packer back in 1964. Packer was a sprinter, long jumper and 80m hurdler before finding her forte was really the 800m; similarly, Gunnell graduated from the long jump (at 13 she was the national under-15 champion), pentathlon (13th in the 1983 European Junior Championships) and 100m hurdles, winning the 1986 Commonwealth title and setting a British record of 12.82 in 1988, before discovering what many had long been predicting ... that the 400m hurdles event was made for her.

After making a tentative 59.9 debut in 1987, she progressed rapidly to 54.03 and fifth place in the 1988 Olympics; she became Commonwealth champion in 1990, while the following year she finished second in the World Championships in her best time of 53.16. She went to Barcelona as co-favourite along with the flamboyant American, Sandra Farmer-Patrick. Here is how Sally described her Olympic experience in an interview the author conducted for *Athletics Today* a few weeks later:

"Quite a few training sessions I had about two weeks before the Games indicated I was getting into shape. Once I had finished my last race [winning at Crystal Palace in 54.40] and was completing my build-up for Barcelona the sessions were going really well. I had a certain amount of confidence beforehand, and was talking about medals, but as I went through the heats and semis that's when I realised I could win.

"I had been visualising the final ever since about last November, I did a lot of mental preparation for it. It really helps. I would think about every possible situation I could be in, working through the heats and semis as well. I would visualise running in lane one right through to lane eight, just making sure every time I got the stride pattern right and won.

"I was lucky; I had the easier semi for sure, had a good run [53.78] and was given the best lane [three with Farmer-Patrick in four] for the final. I was really quite calm for the final. I was quite surprised; I thought I would be a nervous wreck.

"The race that I ran was one of the races that I had been running in my mind, so it just went to plan. I ran fifteens to hurdle six, changed down at seven and then sixteens home. It was the first time I had ever managed that.

"I remember going down the back straight thinking 'okay, I haven't lost too much on Sandra, I'm in a good position.' Then my next thought was coming off the eighth hurdle, being level almost and realising that a lot of people had said to me that if I could be up there at the eighth hurdle it was mine on the way home. That gave me a lot of positive thought and I just concentrated so hard down the home straight. I ran very conservatively at the beginning just to keep my energy for the last part of the race. So many people went off so fast and that's why, apart from Sandra [53.69] and I [53.23], the times were very slow. They all hammered it out.

"I really stretched for the last hurdle. Last year I had a negative thought at that stage, but this time I was so determined and had run it so often in my mind that I was going to get there. I was still running scared, waiting for Sandra to come up, but I was just as determined that she wasn't going to be able to. All the way around that lap of honour I just couldn't believe I had done it. It was like being in a dream world."

1992 - BARCELONA

100m: (0.5) 1, Linford Christie GBR 9.96; 2, Frank Fredericks NAM 10.02; 3, Dennis Mitchell USA 10.04; 4, Bruny Surin CAN 10.09; 5, Leroy Burrell USA 10.10 (9.97 sf); 6, Olapade Adeniken NGR 10.12; 7, Ray Stewart JAM 10.22; 8, Davidson Ezinwa NGR 10.26.
200m: (-1.0) 1, Michael Marsh USA 20.01 (19.73 sf); 2, Frank Fredericks NAM 20.13 (20.02 qf); 3, Michael Bates USA 20.38; 4, Robson da Silva BRA 20.45 (20.15 sf); 5, Olapade Adeniken NGR 20.50; 6, John Regis GBR 20.55 (20.09 sf); 7, Oluyemi Kayode NGR 20.67; 8, Marcus Adam GBR 20.80.
400m: 1, Quincy Watts USA 43.50 (43.71 sf); 2, Steve Lewis USA 44.21; 3, Samson Kitur KEN 44.24 (44.18 sf); 4, Ian Morris TRI 44.25 (44.21 sf); 5, Roberto Hernández CUB 44.52; 6, David Grindley GBR 44.75 (44.47 sf); 7, Ibrahim Ismail QAT 45.10; 8, Susumu Takano JPN 45.18.
800m: 1, William Tanui KEN 1:43.66; 2, Nixon Kiprotich KEN 1:43.70; 3, Johnny Gray USA 1:43.97; 4, José Luis Barbosa BRA 1:45.06; 5, Andrea Benvenuti ITA 1:45.23; 6, Curtis Robb GBR 1:45.57; 7, Réda Abdenouz ALG 1:48.34; Mark Everett USA dnf.
1500m: 1, Fermín Cacho ESP 3:40.12 (3:34.93 sf);

2, Rachid El Basir MAR 3:40.62; 3, Mohamed Suleiman QAT 3:40.69 (3:34.77 sf); 4, Joseph Chesire KEN 3:41.12; 5, Jonah Birir KEN 3:41.27 (3:35.41 sf); 6, Jens-Peter Herold GER 3:41.53; 7, Noureddine Morceli ALG 3:41.70; 8, Jim Spivey USA 3:41.74.
5000m: 1, Dieter Baumann GER 13:12.52; 2, Paul Bitok KEN 13:12.71; 3, Fita Bayissa ETH 13:13.03; 4, Brahim Boutayeb MAR 13:13.27; 5, Yobes Ondieki KEN 13:17.50; 6, Worku Bikila ETH 13:23.52; 7, Rob Denmark GBR 13:27.76; 8, Abel Antón ESP 13:27.80.
10,000m: 1, Khalid Skah MAR 27:46.70; 2, Richard Chelimo KEN 27:47.72; 3, Addis Abebe ETH 28:00.07; 4, Salvatore Antibo ITA 28:11.39; 5, Arturo Barrios MEX 28:17.79; 6, German Silva MEX 28:20.19; 7, William Koech KEN 28:25.18; 8, Moses Tanui KEN 28:27.11.
Marathon: 1, Hwang Young-Jo KOR 2:13:23; 2, Koichi Morishita JPN 2:13:45; 3, Stephan Freigang GER 2:14:00; 4, Takeyuki Nakayama JPN 2:14:02; 5, Salvatore Bettiol ITA 2:14:15; 6, Salah Kokaich MAR 2:14:25; 7, Jan Huruk POL 2:14:32; 8, Hiromi Taniguchi JPN 2:14:42.
3000mSC: 1, Matthew Birir KEN 8:08.44; 2, Patrick Sang KEN 8:09.55; 3, William Mutwol KEN 8:10.74; 4, Alessandro Lambruschini ITA 8:15.52; 5, Steffen Brand GER 8:16.60; 6, Tom Hanlon GBR 8:18.14; 7, Brian Diemer USA 8:18.77; 8, Azzedine Brahmi ALG 8:20.71.
110mH: (0.8) 1, Mark McKoy CAN 13.12; 2, Tony Dees USA 13.24; 3, Jack Pierce USA 13.26 (13.17 qf); 4, Tony Jarrett GBR 13.26; 5, Florian Schwarthoff GER 13.29 (13.23 sf); 6, Emilio Valle CUB 13.41; 7, Colin Jackson GBR 13.46 (13.10 ht); 8, Hugh Teape GBR 14.00.
400mH: 1, Kevin Young USA 46.78 (world rec); 2, Winthrop Graham JAM 47.66 (47.62 sf); 3, Kriss Akabusi GBR 47.82; 4, Stéphane Diagana FRA 48.13; 5, Niklas Wallenlind SWE 48.63; 6, Oleg Tverdokhleb EUN/UKR 48.63; 7, Stéphane Caristan FRA 48.86; 8, Dave Patrick USA 49.26.
4x100m Relay: 1, USA (Michael Marsh, Leroy Burrell, Dennis Mitchell, Carl Lewis) 37.40 (world rec); 2, Nigeria (Oluyemi Kayode, Chidi Imoh, Olapade Adeniken, Davidson Ezinwa) 37.98; 3, Cuba (Andrés Simón, Joel Lamela, Joel Isasi, Jorge Aguilera) 38.00; 4, Great Britain 38.08; 5, Unified Team 38.17; 6, Japan 38.77; 7, Austria 39.30; 8, Ivory Coast 39.31.
4x400m Relay: 1, USA (Andrew Valmon 44.6, Quincy Watts 43.00, Michael Johnson 44.73, Steve Lewis 43.41) 2:55.74 (world rec); 2, Cuba (Lazaro

Martinez 45.5, Hector Herrera 44.45, Norberto Tellez 45.04, Roberto Hernandez 44.52) 2:59.51 (2:59.13 ht); 3, Great Britain (Roger Black 45.2, David Grindley 44.65, Kriss Akabusi 45.14, John Regis 44.74) 2:59.73; 4, Brazil 3:01.61; 5, Nigeria 3:01.71; 6, Italy 3:02.18; 7, Trinidad & Tobago 3:03.31; Kenya dnf (2:59.63 ht).

HJ: 1, Javier Sotomayor CUB 2.34; 2, Patrik Sjöberg SWE 2.34; eq3, Artur Partyka POL, Hollis Conway USA & Tim Forsyth AUS 2.34; 6, Ralf Sonn GER 2.31; 7, Troy Kemp BAH 2.31; eq8, Charles Austin USA, Dragutin Topic IOP/YUG & Marino Drake CUB 2.28.

PV: 1, Maksim Tarasov EUN/RUS 5.80; 2, Igor Trandenkov EUN/RUS 5.80; 3, Javier Garcia ESP 5.75; 4, Kory Tarpenning USA 5.75; 5, Dave Volz USA 5.65; 6, Asko Peltoniemi FIN 5.60; 7, Philippe Collet FRA 5.55; 8, Yevgeniy Krasnov ISR 5.40.

LJ: 1, Carl Lewis USA 8.67 (8.68q); 2, Mike Powell USA 8.64; 3, Joe Greene USA 8.34; 4, Iván Pedroso CUB 8.11; 5, Jaime Jefferson CUB 8.08; 6, Konstantinos Koukodimos GRE 8.04 (8.22q); 7, Dmitriy Bagryanov EUN/RUS 7.98; 8, Huang Geng CHN 7.87 (8.22q).

TJ: 1, Mike Conley USA 18.17w (17.63); 2, Charlie Simpkins USA 17.60; 3, Frank Rutherford BAH 17.36; 4, Leonid Voloshin EUN/RUS 17.32; 5, Brian Wellman BER 17.24; 6, Yoelvis Quesada CUB 17.18; 7, Aleksandr Kovalenko EUN/BLR 17.06; 8, Zou Sixin CHN 17.00 ... 11, Pierre Camara FRA 16.52 (17.34q).

SP: 1, Mike Stulce USA 21.70; 2, Jim Doehring USA 20.96; 3, Vyacheslav Lykho EUN/RUS 20.94; 4, Werner Günthör SUI 20.91; 5, Ulf Timmermann GER 20.49; 6, Klaus Bödenmüller AUT 20.48; 7, Dragan Peric IOP/YUG 20.32; 8, Aleksandr Klimenko EUN/RUS 20.23.

DT: 1, Romas Ubartas LTU 65.12 (66.08q); 2, Jürgen Schult GER 64.94; 3, Roberto Moya CUB 64.12; 4, Costel Grasu ROM 62.86; 5, Attila Horváth HUN 62.82; 6, Juan Martinez CUB 62.64; 7, Dmitriy Kovtsun EUN/UKR 62.04; 8, Dmitriy Shevchenko EUN/RUS 61.78.

HT: 1, Andrey Abduvaliyev EUN/TJK 82.54; 2, Igor Astapkovich EUN/BLR 81.96; 3, Igor Nikulin EUN/RUS 81.38; 4, Tibor Gécsek HUN 77.78; 5, Jüri Tamm EST 77.52; 6, Heinz Weis GER 76.90; 7, Lance Deal USA 76.84; 8, Sean Carlin AUS 76.16; Jud Logan USA (79.00) disq.

JT: 1, Jan Zelezny TCH 89.66; 2, Seppo Räty FIN 86.60; 3, Steve Backley GBR 83.38; 4, Kimmo Kinnunen FIN 82.62; 5, Sigurdur Einarsson ISL 80.34; 6, Juha Laukkanen FIN 79.20; 7, Mike Barnett

USA 78.64; 8, Andrey Shevchuk EUN/RUS 77.74.

Decathlon: 1, Robert Zmelik TCH 8611 (10.78, 7.87, 14.53, 2.06, 48.65, 13.95, 45.00, 5.10, 59.06, 4:27.21); 2, Antonio Penalver ESP 8412 (11.09, 7.54, 16.50, 2.06, 49.66, 14.58, 49.68, 4.90, 58.64, 4:38.02); 3, Dave Johnson USA 8309 (11.16, 7.33, 15.28, 2.00, 49.76, 14.76, 49.12, 5.10, 62.86, 4:36.63); 4, Deszö Szabó HUN 8199; 5, Robert Muzzio USA 8195; 6, Paul Meier GER 8192; 7, William Motti FRA 8164; 8, Ramil Ganiyev EUN/UZB 8160.

20k Walk: 1, Daniel Plaza ESP 1:21:45; 2, Guillaume LeBlanc CAN 1:22:25; 3, Giovanni De Benedictis ITA 1:23:11; 4, Maurizio Damilano ITA 1:23:39; 5, Chen Shaoguo CHN 1:24:06; 6, Jimmy McDonald IRL 1:25:16; 7, Daniel Garcia MEX 1:25:35; 8, Sándor Urbanik HUN 1:26:08.

50k Walk: 1, Andrey Perlov EUN/RUS 3:50:13; 2, Carlos Mercenario MEX 3:52:09; 3, Ronald Weigel GER 3:53:45; 4, Valeriy Spitsyn EUN/RUS 3:54:39; 5, Roman Mrázek TCH 3:55:21; 6, Hartwig Gauder GER 3:56:47; 7, Valentin Kononen FIN 3:57:21; 8, Miguel Rodriguez MEX 3:58:26.

Women's Events

100m: (-1.0) 1, Gail Devers USA 10.82; 2, Juliet Cuthbert JAM 10.83; 3, Irina Privalova EUN/RUS 10.84; 4, Gwen Torrence USA 10.86; 5, Merlene Ottey JAM 10.88; 6, Anelia Nuneva BUL 11.10; 7, Mary Onyali NGR 11.15; 8, Liliana Allen CUB 11.19.

200m: (-0.6) 1, Gwen Torrence USA 21.81 (21.72 sf); 2, Juliet Cuthbert JAM 22.02 (21.75 sf); 3, Merlene Ottey JAM 22.09 (21.94 qf); 4, Irina Privalova EUN/RUS 22.19 (22.08 sf); 5, Carlette Guidry USA 22.30; 6, Grace Jackson JAM 22.58; 7, Michelle Finn USA 22.61; 8, Galina Malchugina EUN/RUS 22.63.

400m: 1, Marie-José Perec FRA 48.83; 2, Olga Bryzgina EUN/UKR 49.05; 3, Ximena Restrepo COL 49.64; 4, Olga Nazarova EUN/RUS 49.69; 5, Jill Richardson CAN 49.93; 6, Rochelle Stevens USA 50.11; 7, Sandie Richards JAM 50.19; 8, Phylis Smith GBR 50.87.

800m: 1, Ellen van Langen NED 1:55.54; 2, Lilia Nurutdinova EUN/RUS 1:55.99; 3, Ana Quirot CUB 1:56.80; 4, Inna Yevseyeva EUN/UKR 1:57.20; 5, Maria Mutola MOZ 1:57.49; 6, Ella Kovacs ROM 1:57.95; 7, Joetta Clark USA 1:58.06; 8, Lyubov Gurina EUN/RUS 1:58.13.

1500m: 1, Hassiba Boulmerka ALG 3:55.30; 2, Lyudmila Rogachova EUN/RUS 3:56.91; 3, Qu Yunxia CHN 3:57.08; 4, Tatyana Dorovskikh (formerly Samolenko) EUN/UKR 3:57.92; 5, Li Liu CHN

4:00.20; 6, Teresa Zuniga ESP 4:00.59; 7, Malgorzata Rydz POL 4:01.91; 8, Yekaterina Podkopayeva EUN/RUS 4:02.03.

3000m: 1, Yelena Romanova EUN/RUS 8:46.04; 2, Tatyana Dorovskikh (formerly Samolenko) EUN/UKR 8:46.85 (8:42.45 ht); 3, Angela Chalmers CAN 8:47.22 (8:42.85 ht); 4, Sonia O'Sullivan IRL 8:47.41; 5, PattiSue Plumer USA 8:48.29; 6, Yelena Kopytova EUN/RUS 8:49.55; 7, Shelly Steely USA 8:52.67; 8, Yvonne Murray GBR 8:55.85 ... Marie-Pierre Duros FRA dnf (8:42.32 ht).

10,000m: 1, Derartu Tulu ETH 31:06.02; 2, Elana Meyer RSA 31:11.75; 3, Lynn Jennings USA 31:19.89; 4, Zhong Huandi CHN 31:21.08; 5, Liz McColgan GBR 31:26.11; 6, Wang Xiuting CHN 31:28.06; 7, Uta Pippig GER 31:36.45; 8, Judi St Hilaire USA 31:38.04.

Marathon: 1, Valentina Yegorova EUN/RUS 2:32:41; 2, Yuko Arimori JPN 2:32:49; 3, Lorraine Moller NZL 2:33:59; 4, Sachiko Yamashita JPN 2:36:26; 5, Katrin Dörre GER 2:36:48; 6, Mun Gyong-ae PRK 2:37:03; 7, Manuela Machado POR 2:38:22; 8, Ramilya Burangulova EUN/RUS 2:38:46; Madina Biktagirova EUN/BLR (2:35:39) disq.

100mH: (0.4) 1, Paraskevi Patoulidou GRE 12.64; 2, LaVonna Martin USA 12.69; 3, Yordanka Donkova BUL 12.70; 4, Lynda Tolbert USA 12.75; 5, Gail Devers USA 12.75; 6, Aliuska López CUB 12.87; 7, Natalya Kolovanova EUN/UKR 13.01; 8, Odalys Adams CUB 13.57.

400mH: 1, Sally Gunnell GBR 53.23; 2, Sandra Farmer-Patrick USA 53.69; 3, Janeene Vickers USA 54.31; 4, Tatyana Ledovskaya EUN/BLR 54.31; 5, Vera Ordina EUN/RUS 54.83; 6, Margarita Ponomaryova EUN/RUS 54.83 (53.98 sf); 7, Deon Hemmings JAM 55.58; Myrtle Bothma RSA dnf.

4x100m Relay: 1, USA (Evelyn Ashford, Esther Jones, Carlette Guidry, Gwen Torrence) 42.11; 2, Unified Team/Russia (Olga Bogoslovskaya, Galina Malchugina, Marina Trandenkova, Irina Privalova) 42.16; 3, Nigeria (Beatrice Utondu, Faith Idehen, Christy Opara-Thompson, Mary Onyali) 42.81 (42.39 ht); 4, France 42.85 (42.58 ht); 5, Germany 43.12; 6, Australia 43.77; Jamaica (42.28 ht) & Cuba dnf.

4x400m Relay: 1, Unified Team (Yelena Ruzina 51.5, Lyudmila Dzhigalova 50.1, Olga Nazarova 49.1, Olga Bryzgina 49.5) 3:20.20; 2, USA (Natasha Kaiser 51.4, Gwen Torrence 49.8, Jearl Miles 49.5, Rochelle Stevens 50.2) 3:20.92; 3,

Great Britain (Phylis Smith 51.3, Sandra Douglas 52.0, Jennifer Stoute 50.5, Sally Gunnell 50.4) 3:24.23; 4, Canada 3:25.20; 5, Jamaica 3:25.68; 6, Germany 3:26.37; 7, Australia 3:26.42; 8, Portugal 3:36.85.

HJ: 1, Heike Henkel GER 2.02; 2, Alina Astafei ROM 2.00; 3, Ioamnet Quintero CUB 1.97; 4, Stefka Kostadinova BUL 1.94; 5, Sigrid Kirchmann AUT 1.94; 6, Silvia Costa CUB 1.94; 7, Megumi Sato JPN 1.91; 8, Alison Inverarity AUS 1.91.

LJ: 1, Heike Drechsler GER 7.14; 2, Inessa Kravets EUN/UKR 7.12; 3, Jackie Joyner-Kersee USA 7.07; 4, Mirela Dulgheru ROM 6.71; 5, Irina Mushayilova EUN/RUS 6.68; 6, Sharon Couch USA 6.66; 7, Sheila Echols USA 6.62; 8, Susen Tiedtke GER 6.60; Niole Medvedeva LTU (6.76) disq.

SP: 1, Svetlana Krivelyova EUN/RUS 21.06; 2, Huang Zhihong CHN 20.47; 3, Kathrin Neimke GER 19.78; 4, Belsis Laza CUB 19.70; 5, Zhou Tianhua CHN 19.26; 6, Svetla Mitkova BUL 19.23; 7, Stephanie Storp GER 19.10; 8, Vita Pavlysh EUN/UKR 18.69.

DT: 1, Maritza Marten CUB 70.06; 2, Tzvetanka Khristova BUL 67.78; 3, Daniela Costian AUS 66.24; 4, Larisa Korotkevich EUN/RUS 65.52 (67.92q); 5, Olga Burova EUN/RUS 64.02; 6, Hilda Ramos CUB 63.80; 7, Irina Yatchenko EUN/BLR 63.74; 8, Stefania Simova BUL 63.42.

JT: 1, Silke Renk GER 68.34; 2, Natalya Shikolenko EUN/BLR 68.26; 3, Karen Forkel GER 66.86; 4, Tessa Sanderson GBR 63.58; 5, Trine Hattestad NOR 63.54 (67.20q); 6, Heli Rantanen FIN 62.34; 7, Petra Meier (née Felke) GER 59.02; 8, Dulce Garcia CUB 58.26.

Heptathlon: 1, Jackie Joyner-Kersee USA 7044 (12.85, 1.91, 14.13, 23.12, 7.10, 44.98, 2:11.78); 2, Irina Belova EUN/RUS 6845 (13.25, 1.88, 13.77, 23.34, 6.82, 41.90, 2:05.08); 3, Sabine Braun GER 6649 (13.25, 1.94, 14.23, 24.27, 6.02, 51.12, 2:14.35); 4, Liliana Nastase ROM 6619; 5, Svetla Dimitrova BUL 6464; 6, Peggy Beer GER 6434; 7, Birgit Clarius GER 6388; 8, Urszula Wlodarczyk POL 6333; Jackie Joyner-Kersee USA dnf.

10k Walk: 1, Chen Yueling CHN 44:32; 2, Yelena Nikolayeva EUN/RUS 44:33; 3, Li Chunxiu CHN 44:41; 4, Sari Essayah FIN 45:08; 5, Cui Yingxi CHN 45:15; 6, Madelein Svensson SWE 45:17; 7, AnnaRita Sidoti ITA 45:23; 8, Yelena Saiko EUN/RUS 45:23; Alina Ivanova EUN/RUS (44:25) & Ileana Salvador ITA (44:40) disq.

The Ultimate Olympians

Here is a list of those immortals who have won Olympic titles with a world record since 1912, the year world records were subject to official ratification. Also included where relevant are world bests (* unratified world record).

100m: Eddie Tolan USA 10.3 (= rec) 1932
Bob Hayes USA 10.0 (= rec) 1964
Jim Hines USA 9.95A 1968
Carl Lewis USA 9.92 1988
Donovan Bailey CAN 9.84 1996

200m: Jesse Owens USA 20.7* 1936
Bobby Morrow USA 20.6 (= rec) 1956
Livio Berruti ITA 20.5 (= rec) 1960
Tommie Smith USA 19.83A 1968
Michael Johnson USA 19.32 1996

400m: Bill Carr USA 46.2 1932
Otis Davis USA 44.9 1960
Lee Evans USA 43.86A 1968

800m: Ted Meredith USA 1:51.9 1912
Tom Hampson GBR 1:49.8 1932
Ralph Doubell AUS 1:44.3A (= rec) 1968
Alberto Juantorena CUB 1:43.50 1976

1500m: Jack Lovelock NZL 3:47.8 1936
Herb Elliott AUS 3:35.6 1960

5000m: Hannes Kolehmainen FIN 14:36.6 1912

10,000m: Ville Ritola FIN 30:23.2 1924
Lasse Viren FIN 27:38.35 1972

Mar: Hannes Kolehmainen FIN 2:32:36 1920
Abebe Bikila ETH 2:15:17 (= rec) 1960
Abebe Bikila ETH 2:12:12 1964

3000SC: Toivo Loukola FIN 9:21.8* 1928
Volmari Iso-Hollo FIN 9:03.8 1936
Horace Ashenfelter USA 8:45.4 1952
Anders Gärderud SWE 8:08.02 1976

110mH: Earl Thomson CAN 14.8 1920
Rod Milburn USA 13.24 1972

400mH: Frank Loomis USA 54.0 1920
Morgan Taylor USA 52.6* 1924
Bob Tisdall IRL 51.7* 1932
David Hemery GBR 48.12A 1968
John Akii-Bua UGA 47.82A 1972
Ed Moses USA 47.64 1976
Kevin Young USA 46.78 1992

HJ: Gerd Wessig GDR 2.36 1980

PV: Frank Foss USA 4.09 1920
Wladyslaw Kozakiewicz POL 5.78 1980

LJ: Bob Beamon USA 8.90A 1968

TJ: Nick Winter AUS 15.52 1924
Chuhei Nambu JPN 15.72 1932
Naoto Tajima JPN 16.00 1936
Adhemar F da Silva BRA 16.22 1952
Viktor Saneyev URS 17.39A 1968

SP: John Kuck USA 15.87 1928

HT: József Csermák HUN 60.34 1952
Yuriy Sedykh URS 81.80 1980

JT: Egil Danielsen NOR 85.71 1956
Miklos Németh HUN 94.58 1976

Dec: Jim Thorpe USA 8412 (tables then in use)/6564 (today's tables) 1912
Harold Osborn USA 7711/6476 1924
Paavo Yrjölä FIN 8053/6587 1928
Jim Bausch USA 8462/6735 1932
Glenn Morris USA 7900/7254 1936
Bob Mathias USA 7887/7592 1952
Nikolay Avilov URS 8454/8466 1972
Bruce Jenner USA 8618/8634 1976
Daley Thompson GBR 8798/8847 1984

50k Walk: Abdon Pamich ITA 4:11:13 1964

Women's Events

100m: Stanislawa Walasiewicz POL 11.9 (= rec) 1932
Marjorie Jackson AUS 11.5 (= rec) 1952
Wyomia Tyus USA 11.08A 1968
Renate Stecher GDR 11.07 1972

200m: Irena Szewinska POL 22.58A 1968
Renate Stecher GDR 22.40 1972
Florence Griffith Joyner USA 21.34 1988

400m: Irena Szewinska POL 49.29 1976

800m: Lina Radke GER 2:16.8 1928
Lyudmila Shevtsova URS 2:04.3 (= rec) 1960
Ann Packer GBR 2:01.1 1964
Tatyana Kazankina URS 1:54.94 1976
Nadezhda Olizarenko URS 1:53.43 1980

1500m: Lyudmila Bragina URS 4:01.38 1972

80mH: Babe Didrikson USA 11.7 1932
Shirley Strickland AUS 10.9 1952

HJ: Ethel Catherwood CAN 1.59 1928
Jean Shiley USA 1.65 1932
Mildred McDaniel USA 1.76 1956
Ulrike Meyfarth FRG 1.92 (= rec) 1972

LJ: Elzbieta Krzesinska POL 6.35 (= rec) 1956
Mary Rand GBR 6.76 1964
Viorica Viscopoleanu ROM 6.82A 1968

SP: Galina Zybina URS 15.28 1952
Margitta Gummel GDR 19.61A 1968
Nadezhda Chizhova URS 21.03 1972

DT: Halina Konopacka POL 39.62 1928

Pen: Irina Press URS 5246 (with 80mH & hand times) 1964
Mary Peters GBR 4801 (with 100mH & electrical times) 1972
Nadezhda Tkachenko URS 5083 (with 800m instead of 200m) 1980
Jackie Joyner-Kersee USA 7291 1988

THE STARS AND STRIPES FOREVER

ALTHOUGH THE sheer scale and over-commercialisation of the Games attracted press criticism, the track and field athletics programme of the Centennial Olympics in Atlanta was nothing short of superb. The competition was great, performances outstanding with many events being the best ever for depth. The weather was kinder than expected and the number of spectators - over a million - was unprecedented.

That wasn't the only Olympic record. All 197 countries within the Olympic movement were represented, and far more nations than ever came away with medals: 45 as against the previous highest of 35 in Barcelona. The number of countries claiming Olympic champions rose to 24. The USA was the most successful team with 23 medals, 13 of them gold. No other country won more than three golds (France, Germany and Russia), and next best in medal terms were Russia (10), Kenya (8), Germany (7), Great Britain and Jamaica (6 each).

There was no problem nominating THE athlete of the Games. The timetable was altered for the benefit of Michael Johnson (see page 183) and his bid to become the first man to win both the 200m and 400m, and he grasped the opportunity to become an Olympic legend. After win-

ning the 400m in an Olympic record of 43.49 he returned to take the 200m in the "sci-fi" time of 19.32.

Johnson's exploit eclipsed the other world record: Donovan Bailey's 9.84 100m. The winner of the 1995 world title went on to share in another gold medal and add to the US sprinters' discomfiture by anchoring Canada to victory in the 4x100m relay. This was the only occasion in the event's Olympic history that the American team has lost other than through disqualification.

Many defending champions lost their laurels. Not so Carl Lewis. Only his most faithful supporters believed that at 35 he could win the long jump again but he twice delivered a big leap when it mattered most to join discus thrower Al Oerter as the only athlete to win the same event four times. If Michael Johnson was the king of Atlanta then Carl Lewis was the brightest star of the Olympic pantheon.

Lewis brought his total of golds to nine, equal to Paavo Nurmi's record if one does not take into account Ray Ewry's victories in the Interim Games of 1906, while Merlene Ottey expanded her collection of medals to seven (spread over a 16-year period), matching the women's record.

MEN'S EVENTS
100 Metres

An Olympic 100m final is rarely lacking in drama, but the 1996 version proved to be an even more theatrical event than usual. As the eight men settled in their blocks the atmosphere was electric. The predominantly American crowd of over 80,000 were willing on Dennis Mitchell and Michael Marsh while the Canadian fans had eyes only for their world champion Donovan Bailey. Less biased observers felt, on the basis of the preliminaries, that the race might be between Frank Fredericks (9.93 quarter final, 9.94 semi) and Ato Boldon (9.95 and 9.93), those 9.93 clockings being the fastest ever recorded outside of a final.

Linford Christie, the defending champion, was the unknown factor. He had established a season's best of 10.03 in his quarter final and with a big-time record like his he could never be discounted. Frustratingly, we shall never know if the 36 year-old Briton would have stunned his younger rivals one more time. He of all people, the steadiest of starters during a long career at

---

STAR OF THE GAMES

MICHAEL JOHNSON
(born 13 Sep 1967)

Illness ruined his chances of individual Olympic glory in 1992, but in Atlanta the Texan sprinter with the unique running action made his mark on athletics history. Not only did he become the first man to complete a 200/400m double but in the 200m final, his eighth race of the Games, he clocked the almost unbelievable time of 19.32 – nearly four metres quicker than any other man before or since.

the top, was thrown out for two false starts. He couldn't, wouldn't, believe it and refused an initial request to leave the track.

Some eight minutes elapsed before they were back in their blocks - an eternity for seven keyed-up sprinters. The one man who appeared to be totally unfazed by it all ("it gave me more time to relax and think about my race") was Bailey who, despite a typically sluggish start, generated the prodigious speed of 12.1m/sec (over 27 mph) at 60m and won by over half a metre. The time was a glittering world record breaking 9.84 and the Jamaican-born Canadian thus completed the triple crown of sprinting: world title, Olympic title, world record. Fredericks (9.89) finished second as he had in 1992 and Boldon ran a national record of 9.90 to become the fastest third placer in history.

(0.7) 1, Donovan Bailey CAN 9.84 (world rec); 2, Frank Fredericks NAM 9.89; 3, Ato Boldon TRI 9.90; 4, Dennis Mitchell USA 9.99; 5, Michael Marsh USA 10.00; 6, Davidson Ezinwa NGR 10.14; 7, Michael Green JAM 10.16; Linford Christie GBR disq (10.03qf). Note: Kim Collins SKN 5q4 10.34.

200 Metres

Not since the figures 8.90 flashed up for Bob Beamon in Mexico City in 1968 has there been such an incredulous reaction. Michael Johnson's demolition job against a great 200m field was awesome enough but his time sent a shock wave through those with an appreciation of the sport's statistics. Even Johnson could hardly believe it when he saw the digits 19.32 displayed.

That time represents probably the greatest performance in all athletics history. According to the IAAF's decathlon scoring tables that time equates to 9.72 for 100m as against Donovan Bailey's new world record of 9.84! No wonder Johnson was shocked. He had been confident of breaking 19.60, perhaps even 19.50, but a time such as 19.32 never came into his reckoning.

That 0.34 sec improvement on his month-old mark represents close to four metres of track, an immense margin. Adding to the amazing quality of Johnson's run is that it came in his eighth race of the Games, following 400's in 45.80 (July 26), 44.63 (27), 44.59 (28) and 43.49 (29) plus 200's in 20.55 and 20.37 (31) and a 20.27 semi just under two hours before the final on August 1.

What were the ingredients which combined to produce such a phenomenal time? A hard, super-fast track certainly helped, as did the support of nearly 83,000 fans. It was warm but the following wind of 0.4m/sec was negligible. Mostly it was down to Johnson himself. Once he had the 400m title safely tucked away he was able to direct all his energy to fulfilling his ambition of becoming the first man to complete the 400/200 double. He knew the 400m was the 'easier' part, for in the 200m he was not necessarily the outright favourite. Frank Fredericks had beaten him in their most recent clash, 19.82-19.85, the previous month. Johnson sensed it would take something really special to beat the Namibian, who also had plenty of motivation to win after three successive Olympic sprint silvers.

Despite a slight stumble at the start, Johnson ran a screamingly fast bend. He was timed at 10.12 for that first curved 100m, only 3/100ths outside his personal best on the straight, but Fredericks was only slightly slower at 10.14 with Ato Boldon still in contention at 10.18. It was Johnson's speed along the straight that practically defied belief. Fredericks was running faster than anyone else in history other than Johnson and yet he lost close to four metres. Johnson covered the second 100m in 9.20 as against 9.54 by Fredericks (19.68) and 9.62 by Boldon (19.80). The winning margin was the widest in an Olympic 200m since the 1936 race, dominated by the man Johnson with his upright stance and pitter-patter stride is most often compared to ... Jesse Owens.

(0.4) 1, Michael Johnson USA 19.32 (world rec); 2, Frank Fredericks NAM 19.68; 3, Ato Boldon TRI 19.80; 4, Obadele Thompson BAR 20.14; 5, Jeff Williams USA 20.17; 6, Iván Garcia CUB 20.21; 7, Patrick Stevens BEL 20.27; 8, Michael Marsh USA 20.48.

400 Metres

Michael Johnson hadn't lost a 400m race since 1989 and ever since he missed his chance of Olympic glory at 200m in Barcelona when, weakened by food poisoning, he didn't even reach the final, he had been planning to achieve what no man had done before on the Olympic stage: the 200/400m double. The nearest anyone had got was when Britain's Eric Liddell won the 400m after placing third in the 200m at the 1924 Games.

Only one man had ever run 400m faster than Johnson's best of 43.39 and that was Butch Reynolds (43.29 in 1988), and having run 43.91 in the US Trials he was rated the only rival with even the remotest chance of defeating Johnson. When he pulled up with a hamstring injury on the first bend of his semi-final that left Roger Black as Johnson's main opponent ... and the British record holder was the first to admit he was essentially running for second place.

In posting his 55th consecutive victory in a 400m final, Johnson ran 43.49 (21.22 at 200m), an Olympic record, the fourth fastest ever and his own twelfth mark inside 44 sec. His winning margin over Black of 0.92 sec was effectively the widest in Olympic history. Black was not dismayed by the distance he finished behind. He knew he had run his best possible race, and his silver medal equalled the highest placing by a European in this event since Liddell. Clocking 44.41 he became the first male Briton since Godfrey Brown in 1936 to win a 400m medal.

1, Michael Johnson USA 43.49; 2, Roger Black GBR 44.41; 3, Davis Kamoga UGA 44.53; 4, Alvin Harrison USA 44.62; 5, Iwan Thomas GBR 44.70; 6, Roxbert Martin JAM 44.83; 7, Davian Clarke JAM 44.99; Ibrahim Ismail QAT dnf (44.96qf).

800 Metres

It was like Hamlet without the Prince of Denmark. This Olympic 800m was a fast and fascinating race, and Vebjørn Rodal ran out a worthy winner ... but the absence of world champion Wilson Kipketer cast a shadow over the proceedings. He had, after all, beaten Rodal (1:42.76 to 1:42.95) in Oslo on July 5 and five days later in Nice ran 1:42.51 for the world's quickest time since 1985. But although granted dispensation by the IAAF to represent Denmark, his home since 1990, at the 1995 World Championships the Olympic rules are more stringent and Kenyan-born Kipketer was unable to compete in Atlanta for his new country.

Still, even without him the first four finishers broke Joaquim Cruz's 1984 Olympic record of 1:43.00, the highest ever standard for an 800m race. Johnny Gray (36) zipped through the first 400m in 49.55. He was still ahead at 600 (75.85) as Rodal moved into second around the final turn but then the US veteran faded out of contention.

Rodal it was who led into the straight and he held on grimly to become Norway's first Olympic winner since Egil Danielsen smashed the world javelin record at the 1956 Games. Rodal clocked his fastest time of 1:42.58 and barely a metre behind, moving up four places in the final straight, was Hezekiel Sepeng, becoming the first black South African to win an Olympic medal.

1, Vebjørn Rodal NOR 1:42.58; 2, Hezekiel Sepeng RSA 1:42.74; 3, Fred Onyancha KEN 1:42.79; 4, Norberto Tellez CUB 1:42.85; 5, Nico Motchebon GER 1:43.91; 6, David Kiptoo KEN 1:44.19; 7, Johnny Gray USA 1:44.21; 8, Benyounes Lahlou MAR 1:45.52. Note: André Bucher SUI 4s1 1:46.41.

1500 Metres

The clash between world record holder and three-time world champion Noureddine Morceli and the man who would prove to be his successor, Hicham El Guerrouj, was among the most keenly awaited of the Games. Although Morceli's last defeat at 1500m or mile was back in 1992 and he had brought the world record down to 3:27.37, he had not appeared to be at his brilliant best in 1996, his fastest being 3:29.50 while El Guerrouj had run 3:29.59.

The preliminary rounds were rich in promise, Morceli's 3:32.88 semi being not only the swiftest ever outside of a final but only 0.35 sec away from Seb Coe's 1984 Olympic record, but the final proved a major disappointment. It was slow with 61.03 at 400m and 2:01.63 at 800m until Morceli took the lead early on the third lap and hotted up the proceedings with a 53.4 circuit. Approaching the bell, reached in 2:42.27, El Guerrouj tucked in behind Morceli but the Moroccan got too close to his opponent and tripped. Morceli was spiked in the process, although it did not appear to hinder him, and several other runners were adversely affected. Defending champion Fermin Cacho, losing an estimated five metres while so doing, had to leap over the sprawled figure of El Guerrouj ... just about the margin he lost by. Morceli raced round the last lap in 53.51 for his 54th successive 1500m/mile victory, winning the only honour to have eluded him.

1, Noureddine Morceli ALG 3:35.78 (3:32.88sf); 2, Fermin Cacho ESP 3:36.40 (3:33.12sf); 3, Stephen Kipkorir KEN 3:36.72

(3:35.35sf); 4, Laban Rotich KEN 3:37.39 (3:33.73sf); 5, William Tanui KEN 3:37.42 (3:33.57sf); 6, Abdi Bile SOM 3:38.03 (3:33.30sf); 7, Marko Koers NED 3:38.18; 8, Ali Hakimi TUN 3:38.19 ... 12, Hicham El Guerrouj MAR 3:40.75 (3:35.29sf).

5000 Metres

Venuste Niyongabo took a calculated gamble ... and it paid off. At 1500m, the distance at which he had placed third in the 1995 World Championships behind Morceli and El Guerrouj, he knew that although he would win an Olympic medal it was realistically most likely to be the bronze. At 5000m, though, the sky was the limit, although equally there was a risk that his total lack of experience of stringing together three 5000m races in the space of four days could prove to be his downfall. He opted to take a chance at the longer distance, an event he had contested only twice in his life before the Games, winning in Italy in April in 13:24.20 and in France in June in 13:03.29.

The thin man from Burundi might have won regardless, but luck was certainly with him. Daniel Komen failed to make the Kenyan team, Salah Hissou restricted himself to the 10,000m and Haile Gebrselassie scratched from the 5000m after badly damaging his feet when winning the 10,000m. The final was run at a slow pace until Bob Kennedy made a move 800m out but his bid for glory was brief and Niyongabo overtook him before the bell. Niyongabo sped round the last lap in 54.93 for victory - Burundi's first ever Olympic medal.

1, Vénuste Niyongabo BDI 13:07.96; 2, Paul Bitok KEN 13:08.16; 3, Khalid Boulami MAR 13:08.37; 4, Dieter Baumann GER 13:08.81; 5, Thomas Nyariki KEN 13:12.29; 6, Bob Kennedy USA 13:12.35; 7, Enrique Molina ESP 13:12.91; 8, Brahim Lahlafi MAR 13:13.26.

10,000 Metres

The weather proved less stifling than normal and the 27°C registered during the 10,000m final enabled the top runners to turn in some nifty performances. Khalid Skah (27:46.98) produced practically the identical time which won him the title four years earlier and yet wound up seventh. The first eight placings went to Africans, unprecedented in any event in Olympic athletics history.

The race developed into a classic duel between an Ethiopian and a Kenyan: Haile Gebrselassie v Paul Tergat. The early pace was fairly cautious (halfway was reached in 13:55.22) but the second half was sensationally quick ... faster than the 13:12.52 it took Dieter Baumann to win the 5000m title in Barcelona! It was with five laps remaining that Tergat took off, throwing in a 29 sec 200m which only Gebrselassie could handle. The ninth kilometre was covered in 2:33.90, the final one was swifter still at 2:31.46. Gebrselassie waited until just before the bell to pounce, covering the last lap in 57.5 to smash the Olympic record with 27:07.34. He had covered the second half in an extraordinary 13:11.5 with Tergat only six metres back.

1, Haile Gebrselassie ETH 27:07.34; 2, Paul Tergat KEN 27:08.17; 3, Salah Hissou MAR 27:24.67; 4, Aloÿs Nizigama BDI 27:33.79; 5, Josephat Machuka KEN 27:35.08; 6, Paul Koech KEN 27:35.19; 7, Khalid Skah MAR 27:46.98; 8, Mathias Ntawalikura RWA 27:50.73.

Marathon

Josia Thugwane made history by becoming the first black South African ever to lift an Olympic title. It was a victory of symbolic importance ... and totally unanticipated. Thugwane (25) had excelled himself by placing fifth in the 1995 World Half Marathon Championship and had won the hot, sticky Honolulu Marathon in December 1995 in 2:16:08 and the Cape Town Marathon in February 1996 in 2:11:46, but he would not have figured on many people's lists to finish even in the top ten.

An Olympic record number of 124 runners lined up for the 7.05 am start in a temperature of 23°C (rising to 27°C) and with a humidity rating of 73-92%. In deference to the weather and an undulating course the runners set off cautiously. At 30k (1:35:24) there was still a leading group of 22 runners. When Thugwane moved ahead soon afterwards that pack began to fragment and only Lee Bong-ju was able to stay with the leader. Eric Wainaina, a Japan-based Kenyan, succeeded in closing the gap and from the 35th kilometre the first three constantly exchanged the lead. The pace by now was savage with the fourth 10k stretch covered in 30:44.

As the three leaders remained locked in combat it became evident that this would be the closest ever Olympic marathon. Up to then the narrowest winning margin was 13 sec in 1920 but as they entered the stadium for a final lap of the track Thugwane was less than 30m ahead of Lee with Wainaina another 10m back. At the finish just 8 sec covered the three of them with Thugwane speeding through the second half in 65:00.

1, Josia Thugwane RSA 2:12:36; 2, Lee Bong-ju KOR 2:12:39; 3, Eric Wainaina KEN 2:12:44; 4, Martin Fíz ESP 2:13:20; 5, Richard Nerurkar GBR 2:13:39; 6, Germán Silva MEX 2:14:29; 7, Steve Moneghetti AUS 2:14:35; 8, Benjamin Paredes MEX 2:14:55. Note: 44, Abdelkader El Mouaziz MAR 2:20:39.

3000 Metres Steeplechase

That a Kenyan runner should win this particular title came as no surprise. Kenya and steeplechasing are synonymous, the African nation having supplied the gold medallist at every Olympics it has contested since Amos Biwott won in 1968. That the new champion would be Joseph Keter and not the strong favourite, Moses Kiptanui, was a shock. The pair fought it out during a final kilometre (2:37.97) which was fast and furious. They took the last water jump abreast before Keter edged ahead early in the finishing straight to complete the last lap in 59.27 and win in his best ever time.

1, Joseph Keter KEN 8:07.12; 2, Moses Kiptanui KEN 8:08.33; 3, Alessandro Lambruschini ITA 8:11.28; 4, Matthew Birir KEN 8:17.18; 5, Mark Croghan USA 8:17.84; 6, Steffen Brand GER 8:18.52; 7, Brahim Boulami MAR 8:23.13; 8, Jim Svenøy NOR 8:23.39.

110 Metres Hurdles

If life were fair, Colin Jackson would have been Olympic champion. Second to Roger Kingdom at the 1988 Games, he was strong favourite to succeed him in 1992 before injury held him back to seventh in a race won by his training partner Mark McKoy. The following year he won the world title with a world record of 12.91 and subsequently he amassed an astounding number of top class marks.

Nonetheless, the gold medal goes to the best athlete on the day regardless of what may have occurred before and, in Atlanta, Jackson - who underwent a double knee cartilage operation after the 1995 season - was far below his best form in placing fourth in 13.19. Not that the title went by default for Allen Johnson was indeed a worthy champion.

Johnson, whose credentials included an 8.14 long jump, 20.77 200m and 2.11 high jump, broke into world class at 110m hurdles in 1994, and the following year he ended Jackson's 44-win streak prior to winning the world indoor and outdoor titles. In 1996 he equalled Kingdom's American record of 12.92, second only to Jackson, and in the Olympic final he clipped Kingdom's Olympic record with a convincing one and a half metre victory over Mark Crear (running with a broken left arm!) in 12.95. Florian Schwarthoff, at 2.01m the tallest of top class hurdlers, shaded Jackson for the bronze.

(0.6) 1, Allen Johnson USA 12.95; 2, Mark Crear USA 13.09; 3, Florian Schwarthoff GER 13.17 (13.13sf); 4, Colin Jackson GBR 13.19 (13.17sf); 5, Emilio Valle CUB 13.20; 6, Eugene Swift USA 13.23; 7, Kyle Vander-Kuyp AUS 13.40; 8, Erik Batte CUB 13.43. Note: Anier García CUB 6q2 13.58.

400 Metres Hurdles

Prior to this final Derrick Adkins and Samuel Matete had clashed no fewer than 37 times since 1991, with Matete holding a 22-15 advantage, including 4-1 thus far in 1996. However, while Adkins sailed to victory in his semi in 47.76, Matete ran into some technical problems in the other race and only a hectic scramble at the end got him into the final. Calvin Davis won comfortably in his fastest time of 47.91 - not bad for someone who did not contest his first ever 400m hurdles race until April 1996.

That below-par showing had an unfortunate consequence for Matete, for whereas Adkins was drawn in lane six for the final Matete found himself in the tight inside lane. Adkins, an Atlanta resident, went on to equal his personal best of 47.54 while Matete overcame his handicap by finishing just two metres down for second ahead of Davis. The standard was the highest ever as 15 men broke 49 sec.

1, Derrick Adkins USA 47.54; 2, Samuel Matete ZAM 47.78; 3, Calvin Davis USA 47.96 (47.91sf); 4, Sven Nylander SWE 47.98; 5, Rohan Robinson AUS 48.30; 6, Fabrizio Mori ITA 48.41; 7, Everson Teixeira BRA 48.57; 8, Eronilde Araujo BRA 48.78. Note: Llewellyn Herbert RSA 8h3 51.13.

4x100 Metres Relay

From the time that Carl Lewis won his fourth long jump title and brought his total of Olympic golds to a record equalling nine a big issue for the American media was whether he should be included in the 4x100m relay team to enable him to boost his gold tally to ten. The underlying assumption was that, whether Lewis was in the squad or not, the USA were going to win that race. It hardly occurred to them that their northern neighbours were the reigning world champions and just might prove tough to beat!

Jon Drummond, timed at 10.37 for 100m around the turn, led on the first leg but a strong showing by Glenroy Gilbert (9.02 along the back straight) took Canada into a lead of close to three metres by the halfway mark. There was little to choose between Bruny Surin (9.25 around the turn) and Michael Marsh (9.27), and Donovan Bailey (8.95 easing up!) gained another metre over Dennis Mitchell to win untroubled. The Canadians' time of 37.69 was a new Commonwealth record and the sixth quickest in history. "We got barbecued out there", admitted Marsh. It was the first time, other than by disqualification, that the USA had ever lost the Olympic 4x100m relay ... and the inclusion of Lewis would not have made a difference.

1, Canada (Robert Esmie, Glenroy Gilbert, Bruny Surin, Donovan Bailey) 37.69; 2, USA (Jon Drummond, Tim Harden, Michael Marsh, Dennis Mitchell) 38.05 (37.96sf); 3, Brazil (Arnaldo Silva, Robson da Silva, Edson Ribeiro, Andre Silva) 38.41; 4, Ukraine 38.55; 5, Sweden 38.67; 6, Cuba 39.39; France dnf; Ghana dns.

4x400 Metres Relay

The 400m result at the US Olympic Trials suggested the Americans would field a squad capable of breaking the world record of 2:54.29. Michael Johnson had won in 43.44, followed by Butch Reynolds in 43.91, Alvin Harrison in 44.09 and LaMont Smith in 44.30. However, with Reynolds and Johnson injuring themselves at the Games (Johnson sustained a hamstring problem in the closing strides of his record shattering 200m) the US squad was reduced to human proportions and both Britain and Jamaica could at least hope for an upset. It was still going to be tough: the US team of Smith, Jason Rouser, Derek Mills and Anthuan Maybank ran 2:57.87 for the fastest ever

semi-final time.

The first leg in the final saw Smith (44.62) hand over nearly three metres ahead of Britain's Iwan Thomas (44.92) with Michael McDonald of Jamaica (45.05) a close third. Jamie Baulch of Britain dashed ahead with a spectacular first 200m but Harrison bided his time to finish well clear, running 43.84 to the Welshman's 44.19, while faster still was Roxbert Martin (43.81) who took Jamaica into second place. Unfortunately all his good work was wasted when the outgoing Greg Haughton fell as he struggled to take the baton and it was left to Britain's Mark Richardson to chase after Mills. Richardson clocked the fastest split of the race with 43.62 but still gained very little on the American, timed at 43.66. Maybank, the only sub-45 sec 400m runner ever to long jump over 27 feet (8.23), took over for the anchor stage five metres up on Roger Black, the individual silver medallist, and the margin at the end was precisely the same as both men ran 43.87. The Americans' time of 2:55.99 was the third fastest ever; Britain broke the European record with 2:56.60 and despite Haughton's mishap Jamaica clung to third.

1, USA (LaMont Smith 44.62, Alvin Harrison 43.84, Derek Mills 43.66, Anthuan Maybank 43.87) 2:55.99; 2, Great Britain (Iwan Thomas 44.92, Jamie Baulch 44.19, Mark Richardson 43.62, Roger Black 43.87) 2:56.60; 3, Jamaica (Michael McDonald 45.05, Roxbert Martin 43.81, Greg Haughton 45.87, Davian Clarke 44.69) 2:59.42; 4, Senegal 3:00.64; 5, Japan 3:00.76; 6, Poland 3:00.96; 7, Bahamas 3:02.71; Kenya dns.

High Jump

World record holder Javier Sotomayor, reduced by ankle and knee injuries to failing at heights which previously would have been derisory by his standards, went out at 2.32, placing equal 11th at 2.25. Gone was his dream of becoming the first man to retain an Olympic high jump title.

Seven athletes were still in contention when the bar was raised to 2.37. Four (Dragutin Topic, Steinar Hoen, Lambros Papakostas and Tim Forsyth) were swiftly eliminated as they had only one remaining attempt after carrying forward two failures from 2.35, which left Charles Austin, Artur Partyka and Steve Smith to fight for the medals.

The only one successful at 2.37 was Partyka,

born of an Algerian father and Polish mother, and he must have believed the gold was his as he flopped clear at his second attempt, equalling the Polish record. After two failures apiece Austin and Smith reserved their final attempt for the next height, an Olympic record of 2.39.

Partyka, jumping first, failed ... but Austin made it. Smith's turn was next and he came agonisingly close. Still, the bronze was his - the first ever in this event by an Englishman. Partyka elected to take his remaining attempts at 2.41, failed and had to settle for silver. As for Austin, the first American winner since Dick Fosbury revolutionised the whole business in 1968, he ended his competition by shooting for a world record 2.46m.

1, Charles Austin USA 2.39; 2, Artur Partyka POL 2.37; 3, Steve Smith GBR 2.35; 4, Dragutin Topic YUG 2.32; 5, Steinar Hoen NOR 2.32; 6, Lambros Papakostas GRE 2.32; 7, Tim Forsyth AUS 2.32; 8, Lee Jin-taek KOR 2.29.

Pole Vault

From the time when he catapulted to fame as a 19 year-old by winning the title at the inaugural meeting in Helsinki in 1983, Sergey Bubka had not put a foot wrong at the World Championships. He retained the title in 1987, 1991, 1993 and 1995 ... and would succeed again in 1997. His Olympic career has been altogether less momentous. He would have been heavily favoured to win at the 1984 Games but the Soviet Union boycotted. In 1988 he won with an Olympic record of 5.90 but 1992 proved disastrous and he failed to register a height in the final. In Atlanta the Ukrainian didn't even get that far. He was in too much pain from an Achilles tendon injury while warming up for the qualifying round to compete.

The final nonetheless was the classiest ever in-depth contest as the first three all cleared 5.92 and three others made 5.86. Dmitriy Markov and Tim Lobinger bade farewell at 5.92, while two others - Igor Potapovich and Pyotr Bochkaryov - registered one and two failures respectively and saved up their remaining attempts for 5.97. Igor Trandenkov was the first over 5.92. It was a last-ditch attempt, for he had chalked up two misses at 5.86 and carried over his remaining trial to 5.92. His hold on the gold medal was short lived as Jean Galfione, the pin up boy of French athletics, went clear at his first try, having earlier made 5.86

also first time. Andrei Tivontchik, formerly of Belarus but a German citizen since 1994, raised the German record by clearing at the second try to clinch the bronze medal.

1, Jean Galfione FRA 5.92; 2, Igor Trandenkov RUS 5.92; 3, Andrei Tivontchik GER 5.92; 4, Igor Potapovich KAZ 5.86; 5, Pyotr Bochkaryov RUS 5.86; 6, Dmitriy Markov BLR 5.86; 7, Tim Lobinger GER 5.80; 8, Lawrence Johnson USA 5.70. Note: Okkert Brits RSA no height in qualifying contest.

Long Jump

Already widely acknowledged as the greatest athlete in history, Carl Lewis still had one more ambition ... to win a fourth Olympic long jump crown. His detractors may have scoffed; they felt he was yesterday's man and pointed to the US Trials at which Lewis only just scraped into the team with 3cm to spare. His final pre-Olympic competition, in North Carolina on July 13, had been profoundly disappointing as he jumped a mere 8.00. At 35, his critics argued, the magic had gone.

But Lewis continued to dream about matching discus thrower Al Oerter's unique feat of four successive golds in the same event, convinced he could rise to the challenge one more time. First he had to reach the final by jumping 8.05 or placing in the top twelve. It should have been merely a formality but Lewis was in deep trouble after two rounds. His first leap had been only 7.93 and on the second try he had run through. He was looking into a chasm as, languishing in 15th place, he prepared for his last attempt. Surely his glittering Olympic career was not simply going to fizzle out with an ignominious "dnq".

What a fine dividing line there is between triumph and disaster. One moment Lewis is sinking into an abyss, the next he is scaling a mountain as a clearance of 8.29 propels him not just to safety but to top place among the qualifiers! This is a man NEVER to be under-estimated on the big occasion.

After passing that test of nerve the final was practically a breeze for him. In the third round Lewis harnessed all his skill, determination and experience into a jump which, despite a 1.3m/sec headwind, dented the sand at 8.50. The master conjuror had pulled out one last rabbit from his hat and even those who had doubted him saluted the ultimate competitor. No one came close. Joe Greene moved into second with 8.24 and remained there until James Beckford's final attempt of 8.29. World record holder Mike Powell, in pain and despair, finished fifth while the previous year's number one Ivan Pedroso, not yet fully fit following leg surgery, was never in contention (12th at 7.75). Lewis thus gained a ninth gold medal to equal the record of Paavo Nurmi, many of whose victories came in events no longer on the Olympic programme.

1, Carl Lewis USA 8.50; 2, James Beckford JAM 8.29; 3, Joe Greene USA 8.24 (8.28q); 4, Emmanuel Bangué FRA 8.19; 5, Mike Powell USA 8.17; 6, Gregor Cankar SLO 8.11; 7, Aleksandr Glovatskiy BLR 8.07; 8, Mattias Sunneborn SWE 8.06.

Triple Jump

Kenny Harrison had been "the invisible man" of triple jumping. After just missing the world record in 1990 with 17.93 and winning the world title the next year, injuries played havoc with what had promised to be such a brilliant career. Not having competed since the 1995 indoor season no one knew what to expect of him at the US Trials in June 1996. There he jumped a windy 18.01 ... he was back in a big way!

After qualifying for the Olympic final with 17.58, his best legitimate mark for five years, he opened up with a legal Olympic record of 17.99 for second place on the world all-time list behind Jonathan Edwards. The Briton was himself encountering a crisis. He fouled his first two trials, only to produce 17.13 and a reprieve at the third attempt. The real action came in round four. Defending champion Mike Conley moved into second place with 17.40 but that was overtaken by Edwards' 17.88 while a 17.44 by Yoelbi Quesada pushed Conley out of the medals. Harrison completed the round with a breathtaking 18.09, the third longest legal jump in history after Edwards' 18.29 and 18.16 in Gothenburg. Edwards' last two efforts, although way beyond 18m, were fouls and his 22-win streak came to an end. His 17.88 ranked as the longest ever non-winning mark.

1, Kenny Harrison USA 18.09; 2, Jonathan Edwards GBR 17.88; 3, Yoelvis Quesada CUB 17.44; 4, Mike Conley USA 17.40; 5, Armen Martirosyan ARM 16.97; 6, Brian Wellman BER 16.95; 7, Galin Georgiev BUL 16.92; 8, Robert Howard USA 16.90.

Shot

Eight years after his Olympic silver medal in Seoul, following a chequered career which included setting a world record of 23.12 in 1990 and serving a two-year drugs ban, Randy Barnes returned to the Olympic arena. Although physically in top form, as indicated by a 22.40 shortly before the Games, his best after five rounds was a mere 20.44 and he was sixth with John Godina the leader at 20.79. It was a tense moment as he entered the circle for the last time, only at last the elements of his spin technique knitted together and the shot thudded down at 21.62. Godina fouled in response and the gold medal was Barnes'.

1, Randy Barnes USA 21.62; 2, John Godina USA 20.79; 3, Aleksandr Bagach UKR 20.75; 4, Paolo Dal Soglio ITA 20.74; 5, Oliver-Sven Buder GER 20.51; 6, Roman Virastyuk UKR 20.45; 7, C J Hunter USA 20.39; 8, Dragan Peric YUG 20.07.

Discus

Widely acknowledged as the finest big-time discus competitor since Al Oerter, Lars Riedel had won the last three world titles without yet making his mark in the Olympics, for he failed to make the final at the 1992 Games. In Atlanta it was expected that he would put that right, but as the German giant entered the circle for the third time in the final he was just one spin away from a humiliatingly early exit as he had fouled his first two throws.

To make the top eight and qualify for a further three trials he had to throw in excess of 62.70. Strong nerves as well as muscles saved the day. He threw 65.40 to slot into third place and in round five Riedel harnessed all his technical prowess and competitive fire to produce a mighty throw of 69.40, breaking Jürgen Schult's Olympic record and establishing the longest ever distance in a global championship. He won by 2.80 metres, easily the widest Olympic margin since 1912.

1, Lars Riedel GER 69.40; 2, Vladimir Dubrovshchik BLR 66.60; 3, Vasiliy Kaptyukh BLR 65.80; 4, Anthony Washington USA 65.42; 5, Virgilijus Alekna LTU 65.30; 6, Jürgen Schult GER 64.62; 7, Vitaliy Sidorov UKR 63.78; 8, Vaclavas Kidykas LTU 62.78.

Hammer

Lance Deal plumbed the depths of despair and experienced the joy of fulfilment ... and all in the same competition. The 34 year-old American fouled his first two throws and his third was measured at 76.94, same as the eighth best thrower but - thought Deal - good only for ninth place. He believed his Olympic bid was over. But no it wasn't. Under the relevant rule Deal was considered to be equal eighth; he was still in the contest ... and with his final attempt he came close to winning the gold medal! Balázs Kiss had led for most of the competition, reaching 81.24 in the third round, and his position was not seriously challenged until Deal's throw landed at 81.12, making him the USA's first medallist in this event since Hal Connolly's victory in 1956. "I had to restart my heart," said Kiss. "It was amazing how his hammer kept going and going".

1, Balázs Kiss HUN 81.24; 2, Lance Deal USA 81.12; 3, Oleksiy Krykun UKR 80.02; 4, Andrey Skvaruk UKR 79.92; 5, Heinz Weis GER 79.78; 6, Ilya Konovalov RUS 78.72; 7, Igor Astapkovich BLR 78.20; 8, Sergey Alay BLR 77.38. Note: dnq (28) Adrián Annus HUN 72.58.

Javelin

Steve Backley, who had undergone an Achilles tendon operation in April and only returned to competition a month before the Games, put everything into the first throw of the final and it soared to 87.44, his best of the year. Would it be good enough? Jan Zelezny came up with the answer by throwing 88.16 in the second round. It was a distance he had exceeded in eight other competitions that year, led by his stupendous world record of 98.48 in May, but it proved to be sufficient to enable the Czech to become the first man to claim a second Olympic javelin title since Jonni Myyrä of Finland in 1924.

1, Jan Zelezny CZE 88.16; 2, Steve Backley GBR 87.44; 3, Seppo Räty FIN 86.98; 4, Raymond Hecht GER 86.88; 5, Boris Henry GER 85.68; 6, Sergey Makarov RUS 85.30; 7, Kimmo Kinnunen FIN 84.02; 8, Tom Pukstys USA 83.58 ... 10, Kostas Gatsioudis GRE 81.46 (87.12q).

Decathlon

Judged by most criteria, Dan O'Brien - world record breaker and three times world champion - was already one of the all-time greats of his event, but there was one glaring omission from his credentials. There was no Olympic title, no Olympic medal, no Olympic anything. He had famously failed to make the team for Barcelona when no-heighting in the pole vault at the US Trials.

O'Brien took the overall lead after three events but his overnight advantage over Frank Busemann (4592-4468) was not as commanding as anticipated. The 21 year-old German, the 1994 world junior 110m hurdles champion, was on a roll. In all, he would establish personal bests in five events and go close in all the others. He opened the second day with a world decathlon hurdles best of 13.47, leaving O'Brien four metres behind. After six events O'Brien led by 71 points but the discus and pole vault went the American's way and after eight events it was O'Brien 7338, Eduard Hämäläinen 7196, Busemann and Steve Fritz 7129.

Busemann threw the javelin a personal best of 66.86, but O'Brien responded with his longest ever throw of 66.90 to lead by 209 points prior to the 1500m. It meant O'Brien had to stay within 32 sec of Busemann to clinch the title. Busemann ran 4:31.41 but O'Brien never got too far behind and his 4:45.89 brought his score to 8824 for his eleventh consecutive decathlon win. Busemann scored 8706, amazing for someone with less than two years of decathlon experience, and Tomás Dvorák (destined to succeed O'Brien as world record holder in 1999) broke the Czech record with 8664 in third place. No fewer than 16 men topped 8200 as against the previous record of eight.

1, Dan O'Brien USA 8824 (10.50, 7.57, 15.66, 2.07, 46.82, 13.87, 48.78, 5.00, 66.90, 4:45.89); 2, Frank Busemann GER 8706 (10.60, 8.07, 13.60, 2.04, 48.34, 13.47, 45.04, 4.80, 66.86, 4:31.41); 3, Tomás Dvorák CZE 8664 (10.64, 7.60, 15.82, 1.98, 48.29, 13.79, 46.28, 4.70, 70.16, 4:31.25); 4, Steve Fritz USA 8644; 5, Eduard Hämäläinen BLR 8613; 6, Erki Nool EST 8543; 7, Robert Zmelik CZE 8422; 8, Ramil Ganiyev UZB 8318.

20 Kilometres Walk

Jefferson Pérez became, at 22, the youngest ever Olympic walking champion, winning Ecuador's first Olympic medal in any sport. He walked a canny race, ignoring the early jousting at the front.

He was only 21st after 6k but by halfway, in 40:59, he was joint fourth. With just 2k remaining the situation was tense. Ilya Markov had the lead, pursued by Pérez, Miguel Rodriguez, Bernardo Segura and Nick A'Hern. Markov was caught by Pérez and Rodriguez at 19k but, agonisingly late in the race, Rodriguez was disqualified and Pérez entered the stadium ahead, followed by Markov and Segura. The winner covered the second half in a very fast 39:08.

1, Jefferson Pérez ECU 1:20:07; 2, Ilya Markov RUS 1:20:16; 3, Bernardo Segura MEX 1:20:23; 4, Nick A'Hern AUS 1:20:31; 5, Rishat Shafikov RUS 1:20:41; 6, Aigars Fadejevs LAT 1:20:47; 7, Mikhail Shchennikov RUS 1:21:09; 8, Robert Korzeniowski POL 1:21:13.

50 Kilometres Walk
Robert Korzeniowski walked a shrewd and fair race, receiving no red cards. He clocked a cautious 46:20 at 10k; by 20k (1:31:37) he was third, and shortly after 30k he took the lead. Moving increasingly faster with 10k splits of 46:20, 45:17, 44:35 and 43:54 he scorched through the final segment in 43:24. His time of 3:43:30, with the last 20k covered in 1:27:18, gave him a 16 sec advantage over Mikhail Shchennikov, who was contesting this distance for only the second time and after a conservative start clocked a final 20k of just 1:26:58.

1, Robert Korzeniowski POL 3:43:30; 2, Mikhail Shchennikov RUS 3:43:46; 3, Valentin Massana ESP 3:44:19; 4, Arturo Di Mezza ITA 3:44:52; 5, Viktor Ginko BLR 3:45:27; 6, Ignacio Zamudio MEX 3:46:07; 7, Valentin Kononen FIN 3:47:40; 8, Sergey Korepanov KAZ 3:48:42.

Women's Events
100 Metres
Nobody has had better luck in photo finishes than Gail Devers. Remember the 1992 Olympic 100m in Barcelona? Devers won by 1/100th of a second over Juliet Cuthbert in 10.82. Recall the World Championships a year later in Stuttgart? She and Merlene Ottey could not be separated on the clock at 10.82 but again it was Devers who snatched the verdict - by 1/1000th of a second!. Again in Atlanta, Devers and Ottey shared the winning time - 10.94 on this occasion - and yes, it was Devers who prevailed, by 5/1000ths of a second. Ottey did at least win her first Olympic silver,

after four bronzes dating back to 1980, but that wasn't much of a consolation after coming so close to winning the biggest prize of all.

Earlier in the year Gwen Torrence had a realistic chance of amassing four gold medals (100m, 200m and both relays) but she came down to earth at the US Trials when, after beating Devers by a metre in 10.82, a sore hip muscle reduced her to fourth in the 200m - removing the opportunity to defend her Olympic crown. She still wasn't back to her best form at the Games and it says much for her renowned competitive qualities that she was able to go so near to winning. She was only 2/100ths behind Devers and Ottey as she swept into third place.

(-0.7) 1, Gail Devers USA 10.94 (10.92ht); 2, Merlene Ottey JAM 10.94 (10.93sf); 3, Gwen Torrence USA 10.96; 4, Chandra Sturrup BAH 11.00; 5, Marina Trandenkova RUS 11.06; 6, Natalya Voronova RUS 11.10; 7, Mary Onyali NGR 11.13; 8, Zhanna Pintusevich UKR 11.14. Note: Ekaterini Thánou GRE 6q3 11.48; Irina Privalova RUS 7s2 11.31.

200 Metres
This was Merlene Ottey's final chance of Olympic glory. Clearly she was in excellent shape, making light of her 36 years, and with 1992 champion Gwen Torrence unable to make the US team and an out of form Irina Privalova failing to appear in her semi, Ottey's chances of success were never better. There was just one problem ... and her name was Marie-José Pérec (see page 182).

Pérec was attempting the same double as Michael Johnson and seeking to emulate the feat of Valerie Brisco-Hooks (USA) in 1984. Pérec clocked her fastest ever 400m time of 48.25 and looked ominously relaxed as she sauntered through her quarter-final in 22.24 and semi-final in 22.07, the year's quickest time. Ottey took the other semi in 22.08 after speeding through the opening 100m in 11.09.

A repetition of that devastating speed around the turn in the final might have ensured victory for Ottey, but although she did enter the straight in the lead her time was markedly slower at 11.28 with Pérec fifth in 11.38. Gradually that long elegant stride of Perec's cancelled out Ottey's lead and carried her past for a clearcut victory in 22.12. Strength had won out: Pérec covered her flying 100m in 10.74, Ottey in 10.96.

Pérec thus completed her double 15 minutes before Johnson, while Ottey made some Olympic history of her own by becoming the first runner to reach the final of the same event in five celebrations. She was third in Moscow (22.20), third in Los Angeles (22.09), fourth in Seoul (21.99), third in Barcelona (22.09) and now second in Atlanta (22.24).

(0.3) 1, Marie-José Pérec FRA 22.12 (22.07sf); 2, Merlene Ottey JAM 22.24 (22.08sf); 3, Mary Onyali NGR 22.38 (22.16sf); 4, Inger Miller USA 22.41; 5, Galina Malchugina RUS 22.45; 6, Chandra Sturrup BAH 22.54; 7, Juliet Cuthbert JAM 22.60 (22.24sf); 8, Carlette Guidry USA 22.61. Note: Zhanna Pintusevich UKR 8q4 23.68; Cathy Freeman AUS 6s1 22.78; Irina Privalova RUS dns s1.

400 Metres

Marie-José Pérec's long-term domination at 400m rivalled that of Michael Johnson. He had not been beaten since 1989; while she, since placing third in the 1990 European Championships, had lost only twice and one of those defeats was for stepping out of her lane. Along the way she has garnered two world and two Olympic titles at 400m, a better collection than the other MJ.

That the Guadeloupe-born French woman was at the peak of her powers became obvious in the semi-final when she clocked an easy looking 49.19, the fastest time in the world since 1992. Cathy Freeman, the Australian acknowledged as Pérec's most dangerous rival, won the other semi in 50.32 and the stage was set for the finest 400m duel for years. Furthermore, for the first time ever in one race, six women broke 50 sec. The first four finishers set national records and 1993 world champion Jearl Miles ran 49.55, the fastest by an American since 1984, to wind up fifth!

Pérec, the first athlete - male or female - to retain an Olympic 400m title, was pushed by Freeman to the quickest time the world had seen for ten years: an Olympic record of 48.25. She passed 200m in 23.25, just behind Pauline Davis (23.23) and ahead of Freeman (23.27), and she and Freeman fought it out in the final straight. Although she tied up a little at the end, the Australian hacked almost a full second from her best to clock 48.63, a Commonwealth record. Falilat Ogunkoya and Davis also finished inside the old Commonwealth mark of 49.43, the Nigerian's

49.10 being an African record and the Bahamian's 49.28 a Central American & Caribbean record.

1, Marie-José Pérec FRA 48.25; 2, Cathy Freeman AUS 48.63; 3, Falilat Ogunkoya NGR 49.10; 4, Pauline Davis BAH 49.28; 5, Jearl Miles USA 49.55; 6, Fatima Yusuf NGR 49.77; 7, Sandie Richards JAM 50.45; 8, Grit Breuer GER 50.71.

800 Metres

The pundits were in agreement. This would be the true "world title" race which failed to materialise the year before at the World Championships in Gothenburg. On that occasion, Maria Mutola had been disqualified in her semi-final, leaving the door open for a moving victory by Ana Quirot, returning almost literally from the dead.

The fastest time in Atlanta at 1:57.62 was indeed recorded by Mutola - but that was at the semi-final stage and she was beaten in the final by Quirot. But the Cuban didn't win, either. She was outpaced by front running Svetlana Masterkova in 1:57.73.

Masterkova led practically from the start of the final. With Quirot and Britain's Kelly Holmes in close attendance, she reached 400m in 58.43 and, with a look of disbelief, proceeded to hold off every subsequent challenge. The result ended a win-streak (counting finals only) of 50 races by Mutola, who was suffering from a cold and was coughing at the finish.

1, Svetlana Masterkova RUS 1:57.73; 2, Ana Quirot CUB 1:58.11 (1:57.99sf); 3, Maria Mutola MOZ 1:58.71 (1:57.62sf); 4, Kelly Holmes GBR 1:58.81 (1:58.49sf); 5, Yelena Afanasyeva RUS 1:59.57 (1:57.77sf); 6, Patricia Djaté FRA 1:59.61 (1:57.93sf); 7, Natalya Dukhnova BLR 2:00.32 (1:58.67sf); 8, Toni Hodgkinson NZL 2:00.54 (1:58.25sf).

1500 Metres

Anyone attempting to predict the outcome based on the previous year's results would surely have considered world champion Hassiba Boulmerka and her runner-up Kelly Holmes, together with 3:58.85 performer Sonia O'Sullivan. No one could have thought of Svetlana Masterkova. Not only was her 800m career on hold during maternity leave but, as far as anyone was aware, she had never run 1500m in her life. In fact she did actually run the distance once, clocking 4:24 in 1984 when she was 16. On more recent form the prospects changed drastically. Masterkova won the Russian title in 3:59.30 to head the 1996 world rankings and the strength she demonstrated in her 800m victory marked her out as a definite contender for a second gold medal. O'Sullivan, however, was completely out of sorts; she dropped out of the 5000m final and trailed in tenth in her 1500m heat (4:19.77).

Another to make an early departure was Boulmerka. She stumbled during her semi and jogged in 12th and last (4:23.86) with a sprained ankle. Holmes was also out of luck. Suffering from a hairline fracture of the lower left leg, a condition for which she had to take painkillers, she was in no condition to contest the 1500m final, her sixth race of the Games, but, typically, refused to quit. She bravely led the field through to 1200m in 3:16.63 before she fell apart to finish eleventh (4:07.46). She returned from Atlanta on crutches.

The race was made for Masterkova as a 60.0 last lap (28.7 for the final 200m) propelled her to victory in 4:00.83, emulating the 1976 double of Tatyana Kazankina. An equally joyful second in a personal best of 4:01.54 was Gabriela Szabo, bouncing back after acclimatisation problems saw her fail to qualify for the final of the 5000m for which she was one of the favourites.

1, Svetlana Masterkova RUS 4:00.83; 2, Gabriela Szabo ROM 4:01.54; 3, Theresia Kiesl AUT 4:03.02; 4, Leah Pells CAN 4:03.56; 5, Margaret Crowley AUS 4:03.79; 6, Carla Sacramento POR 4:03.91; 7, Lyudmila Borisova RUS 4:05.90; 8, Malgorzata Rydz POL 4:05.92.

5000 Metres

Although officially Wang Junxia's best 5000m time was 14:51.87 she did cover the second half during her phenomenal 29:31.78 10,000m from 1993 in 14:26.09 - way inside the world record. She didn't need to operate at anything like that speed to run away with the inaugural Olympic title. The race started slowly with a 3:06.15 first kilometre and got faster throughout with splits of 3:02.61, 2:59.26 (by 3000m Pauline Konga and Wang were out on their own), 2:57.23 and 2:54.63. Wang launched her drive for home with two laps remaining and became China's first ever Olympic gold medallist in a track event.

1, Wang Junxia CHN 14:59.88; 2, Pauline Konga KEN 15:03.49; 3, Roberta Brunet ITA 15:07.52; 4, Michiko Shimizu JPN 15:09.05; 5,

Paula Radcliffe GBR 15:13.11; 6, Yelena Romanova RUS 15:14.09; 7, Elena Fidatov ROM 15:16.71; 8, Rose Cheruiyot KEN 15:17.33 ... Sonia O'Sullivan IRL dnf. Note: Gabriela Szabo ROM 7h3 15:42.35.

10,000 Metres

With the 5000m title safely in the bag, and four days clear rest before the 10,000m final, Wang Junxia must have fancied her chances of becoming the first woman to complete such a double in a global championship. Her confidence would have soared higher still when, with just over 600m to go, she opened up a small but potentially decisive margin over world champion Fernanda Ribeiro. Ultimately, however, she was foiled by a combination of her own heavy legs and the unquenchable fighting spirit of her fresher Portuguese opponent. To which Wang would add the worrisome presence of Kenya's Sally Barsosio. The Chinese star was seen to remonstrate with Barsosio (who set a world junior record of 31:36.00 in her heat) and afterwards was very critical of the Kenyans. "Their tactics prevented me from controlling the race and, without this, I could have won," she claimed.

Ribeiro led at halfway in 15:35.83 and covered the second 5000m in 15:25.80 with a final kilometre of 2:50.0. Wang held a five metre lead entering the finishing straight but it was insufficient as Ribeiro dug deep into her final reserves to overtake Wang on the inside 50m from the line and win in an Olympic record. It was Wang's first ever defeat in a four-year career at 10,000m.

1, Fernanda Ribeiro POR 31:01.63; 2, Wang Junxia CHN 31:02.58; 3, Gete Wami ETH 31:06.65; 4, Derartu Tulu ETH 31:10.46; 5, Masako Chiba JPN 31:20.62; 6, Tegla Loroupe KEN 31:23.22; 7, Yuko Kawakami JPN 31:23.23; 8, Iulia Negura ROM 31:26.46 ... 18, Birhane Adere ETH 32:57.35.

Marathon

Four years after another Ethiopian, Derartu Tulu, blazed the trail in women's athletics by winning the 10,000m to become black Africa's first female Olympic champion it was Fatuma Roba's turn to bring the women's marathon into Africa's catalogue of Olympic triumphs. Earlier in 1996 she had chalked up wins in Marrakesh (2:30:50) and Rome (2:29:05), yet even so ranked only 29th on

STARS AND STRIPES FOREVERCONTINUED

time in the Atlanta field.

For reasons best known to herself, Uta Pippig went off like a bat out of hell (she was 28 sec ahead at 10k) and succeeded only in self-destructing, eventually dropping out. At halfway Roba held a nine second lead in 1:12:31 and she covered the second half nearly as quickly to win by a staggering two-minute margin over defending champion Valentina Yegorova in 2:26:05. She had built up a minute's advantage by 30k and continued to stretch her lead to the finish.

1, Fatuma Roba ETH 2:26:05; 2, Valentina Yegorova RUS 2:28:05; 3, Yuko Arimori JPN 2:28:39; 4, Katrin Dörre-Heinig GER 2:28:45; 5, Rocio Rios ESP 2:30:50; 6, Lidia Simon ROM 2:31:04; 7, Manuela Machado POR 2:31:11; 8, Sonja Krolik GER 2:31:16.

100 Metres Hurdles
Until a few months before the Games the prospect of someone winning Sweden's first ever gold medal in women's athletics was about as likely as Dan O'Brien beating Noureddine Morceli over 1500m. Yet it happened, thanks to the sudden ending of a drugs ban and a quick naturalisation process.

As Lyudmila Narozhilenko from Russia, Ludmila Engquist had been world indoor and outdoor champion in 1991, still held the world indoor 60m hurdles record of 7.69 and her 1992 100m hurdles time of 12.26 ranked her third fastest of all time. When, in February 1993, she was banned for four years for a drugs offence it looked as though her Olympic career was over. However, in December 1995 the IAAF reinstated her under its "exceptional circumstances" rule and by now divorced from her Russian husband and married to her Swedish agent, Johan Engquist, she was on her way to becoming a Swedish citizen. Her new nationality was granted just in time for her to be selected.

Despite losing three seasons of competition the 32 year-old quickly regained world class form and travelled to Atlanta as the fastest in the world that year with 12.52 and was expected to be the main rival of world champion Gail Devers. In fact it was Brigita Bukovec - improving on her Slovenian record for the third time at the Games - who ran Engquist closest in the final. It was close all right as Engquist, recovering well after a poor start, dipped just 1/100th ahead.

(0.2) 1, Ludmila Engquist SWE (former Lyudmila Narozhilenko, USSR) 12.58 (12.47qf); 2, Brigita Bukovec SLO 12.59; 3, Patricia Girard FRA 12.65 (12.59sf); 4, Gail Devers USA 12.66 (12.62sf); 5, Dionne Rose JAM 12.74 (12.64sf); 6, Michelle Freeman JAM 12.76 (12.57qf); 7, Lynda Goode USA 13.11; disqualified after positive drugs test: Natalya Shekhodanova RUS (12.80).

400 Metres Hurdles
The honour of becoming the first Jamaican woman to win an Olympic title (not counting Tessa Sanderson as she was representing Britain) fell to Deon Hemmings. She gave a warning of what lay ahead when finishing three metres clear of Tonja Buford-Bailey in her semi in 52.99, a new Olympic and national record. In the final Hemmings, not a great technician but blessed with 50.63 flat speed at 400m, went faster still. She ran 52.82, drawing away on the run-in from Kim Batten and Buford-Bailey, who a year earlier had beaten her in Gothenburg in world record time. For the first time, all eight finalists broke 55 sec. Defending champion Sally Gunnell broke down injured in her semi.

1, Deon Hemmings JAM 52.82; 2, Kim Batten USA 53.08; 3, Tonja Buford-Bailey USA 53.22; 4, Debbie Ann Parris JAM 53.97; 5, Heike Meissner GER 54.03; 6, Rosey Edeh CAN 54.39; 7, Ionela Tirlea ROM 54.40; 8, Silvia Rieger GER 54.57.

4x100 Metres Relay
With a typically dazzling run on the anchor leg to overtake Russia's Irina Privalova and hoist Jamaica into third place behind the USA and Bahamas, Merlene Ottey was timed at 9.83 for her flying 100m, the next quickest being 9.90 by Nigeria's Mary Onyali. That brought her tally of Olympic medals to seven, equalling the women's all-time record held by Shirley Strickland-Delahunty of Australia (1948-56) and Irena Szewinska of Poland (1964-76). More Olympic history was made by the USA's third leg runner Inger Miller, who was born in Los Angeles a few weeks before the Munich Olympics of 1972. Her gold completed a set of Olympic medals for the family as her father, Lennox Miller, gained a silver (1968) and bronze (1972) at 100m in the colours of Jamaica.

The first two stages of the race featured a neck and neck struggle between the USA and

178

HISTORY OF THE OLYMPIC GAMES

Bahamas. Miller opened up nearly a metre on the third leg and Gwen Torrence completed the job for the fourth consecutive American victory in this event. Not that the Bahamian team were crestfallen; they had smashed their national record, won their nation's first ever medal in a women's event and were whooping with as much glee as the Americans.

1, USA 41.95 (Chryste Gaines, Gail Devers, Inger Miller, Gwen Torrence); 2, Bahamas 42.14 (Eldece Clarke, Chandra Sturrup, Savatheda Fynes, Pauline Davis); 3, Jamaica 42.24 (Michelle Freeman, Juliet Cuthbert, Nikole Mitchell, Merlene Ottey); 4, Russia 42.27; 5, Nigeria 42.56; 6, France 42.76; 7, Australia 43.70; 8, Gt Britain & NI 43.93.

4x400 Metres Relay

The Nigerians seized the initiative thanks to Bisi Afolabi, whose 51.13 lead-off gave her a lead of nearly two metres over Russia. Fatima Yusuf kept up the good work with a 49.72 split, widening the lead over Russia to some eight metres while Maicel Malone moving the Americans up to third. On the third leg Charity Opara over-reached herself and 'died', enabling Kim Graham (49.49) to open up a five metre lead for the USA. With the capacity crowd at fever pitch, the 1993 world 400m champion Jearl Miles kept the USA in front with a 49.47 leg ... but only just as Falilat Ogunkoya ran a storming 48.90 to finish barely a metre down in a Commonwealth and African record time. But finishing more strongly than anyone was Grit Breuer, whose 48.63 split swept Germany into third place and fell only a couple of metres short of victory in a tingling finale. The 400m hurdles champion Deon Hemmings ran a valiant 49.34 but was powerless to keep Jamaica among the medals.

1, USA 3:20.91 (Rochelle Stevens 51.68, Maicel Malone 50.27, Kim Graham 49.49, Jearl Miles 49.47); 2, Nigeria 3:21.04 (Bisi Afolabi 51.13, Fatima Yusuf 49.72, Charity Opara 51.29, Falilat Ogunkoya 48.90); 3, Germany 3:21.14 (Uta Rohländer 51.72, Linda Kisabaka 50.43, Anja Rücker 50.36, Grit Breuer 48.63); 4, Jamaica 3:21.69; 5, Russia 3:22.22; 6, Cuba 3:25.85; 7, Czech Republic 3:26.99; 8, France 3:28.46.

High Jump

Back in 1988, the Olympic contest went to a jump-off after both Lou Ritter and Stefka Kostadinova cleared 2.01 without incurring any failures. The American created a major upset by clearing 2.03 at the fourth try. At that time Kostadinova was already a high jump legend, the world champion and record holder. Since then the Bulgarian had gone on to achieve further honours, such as winning the 1995 world title just seven months after producing a son and boosting her tally of competitions in which she had cleared at least 2 metres to well in excess of 100. At 31 time was starting to run out if she were ever to crown a glorious career with Olympic gold (she was only fourth in 1992) but in Atlanta she emerged triumphant at last, becoming the oldest ever champion in this event.

As in Seoul she was faultless to 2.01 and this time she prolonged her no-failure sequence to include 2.03. That height proved beyond Inga Babakova, expected to be her main rival, but Kostadinova still had company as Niki Bakogianni chose this occasion to display form she had never before hinted at. Not content with adding 2cm to her Greek record with 1.99 she proceeded to clear 2.01 and 2.03! The magic came to an end at 2.05 but by then the silver medal was safely hers. Kostadinova meanwhile made 2.05 at the second try for a new Olympic record. She was unsuccessful with three attempts at a world record 2.10. The contest produced the highest ever standards. No one before Babakova had ever cleared 2.01 in third place, and 13 over 1.93 were the best figures ever recorded. It would have been 14 but Antonella Bevilacqua, originally placed fourth at 1.99, was ruled ineligible to compete as she had failed an earlier drugs test.

1, Stefka Kostadinova BUL 2.05; 2, Niki Bakogianni GRE 2.03; 3, Inga Babakova UKR 2.01; 4, Yelena Gulyayeva RUS 1.99; 5=, Alina Astafei GER, Tatyana Motkova RUS & Nelé Zilinskiené LTU 1.96; 8, Hanne Haugland NOR 1.96; dq: Antonella Bevilacqua ITA (1.99). Note: Kajsa Bergqvist SWE dnq (16) 1.90, Amy Acuff USA dnq (25=) 1.85.

Long Jump

In the absence of the 1992 champion Heike Drechsler of Germany, who was not yet sufficiently recovered from injury to compete, the logical co-favourites were world champion Fiona May and Jackie Joyner-Kersee if fit enough following the hamstring injury which caused her early withdrawal from the heptathlon. Few would have considered Chioma Ajunwa. Indeed, only the closest observers of the sport would have realised that, after serving a four-year drugs suspension, she was competing again.

Ajunwa kicked off the final with 7.12, an African record which was to bring Nigeria its first ever Olympic title in any sport. Not that the opposition stopped trying, for in the second round May raised her Italian record from 6.96 to 7.02, thus becoming also the first British-born athlete to join the 7m club. In the final round the indestructible JJK (34) – ignoring the ever increasing pain from her damaged right hamstring – snatched the bronze medal with a jump of precisely 7 metres. That made it four Olympics in a row where she gained a medal: heptathlon silver in 1984, long jump and heptathlon gold in 1988, heptathlon gold again in 1992, long jump bronze in 1992 and 1996. Ajunwa, incidentally, was banned for life in 2002 after a second doping positive.

1, Chioma Ajunwa NGR 7.12; 2, Fiona May ITA 7.02; 3, Jackie Joyner-Kersee USA 7.00; 4, Niki Xanthou GRE 6.97; 5, Iryna Chekhovtsova UKR 6.97; 6, Agata Karczmarek POL 6.90; 7, Nicole Boegman AUS 6.73; 8, Tünde Vaszi HUN 6.60; dq: (drugs suspension) Iva Prandzheva BUL (6.82). Note: Eunice Barber SLE dnq (20) 6.45.

Triple Jump

That this event fully justified its elevation to Olympic status was apparent from the quality of performance in the qualifying round. New records for depth were achieved when six women, led by Inna Lasovskaya with 14.75, exceeded 14.50 and another six went over the 14.20 qualifying mark.

Lasovskaya set the standard in the final with 14.98, a distance matched by Sárka Kaspárková, a 1.85m tall former Olympic high jumper. A 14.84 leap by world record holder Inessa Kravets carried her into third place at the halfway point. Kaspárková jumped 14.69 in round four, followed moments later by 14.66 from Lasovskaya, but their grim battle for the lead took another twist in round five when Lasovskaya landed at 14.70 to go in front by 1cm on the basis of their second best jumps. However, all that became academic in terms of the gold medal when, with her penultimate effort, Kravets uncorked a monster of a leap to kill the competition stone dead, just as she had at the 1995 World Championships with her stunning world record of 15.50. This time she cut the sand at 15.33, the second longest in history.

1, Inessa Kravets UKR 15.33; 2, Inna Lasovskaya RUS 14.98; 3, Sárka Kaspárková CZE 14.98; 4, Ashia Hansen GBR 14.49; 5, Olga Vasdeki GRE 14.44; 6, Ren Ruipeng CHN 14.30; 7, Rodica Mateescu ROM 14.21; 8, Jelena Blazevica LAT 14.12; dq: (drugs suspension) Iva Prandzheva BUL (14.92).

Shot

Unbeaten outdoors since placing third in the 1994 World Cup and making her Olympic debut, Astrid Kumbernuss chalked up her 40th consecutive victory. Again, her margin of supremacy was colossal. At the 1995 World Championships her 1.18m advantage was the widest ever at global title level, and in Atlanta she had 68cm to spare over the runner-up. She wrapped up the title in the first round with 20.56. Apart from her own final round effort of 20.47 the nearest approach to that was 19.88 in round three by Sui Xinmei, China's former world indoor champion who was banned for two years in 1991 for a drugs offence.

1, Astrid Kumbernuss GER 20.56; 2, Sui Xinmei CHN 19.88; 3, Irina Khudorozhkina RUS 19.35; 4, Vita Pavlysh UKR 19.30; 5, Connie Price-Smith USA 19.22; 6, Stephanie Storp GER 19.06; 7, Kathrin Neimke GER 18.92; 8, Irina Korzhanenko RUS 18.65. Note: Svetlana Krivelyova RUS dnq (15) 18.23.

Discus

Ilke Wyludda's winning distance in Atlanta of 69.66 was her best since she threw 70.96 four years earlier. In 1993 she underwent surgery on both knees and subsequently competed with them strapped up for protection. That throw came in the second round, following an opener of 68.02, and the German dominated the proceedings to such an extent that all five of her valid throws were superior to the best that anyone else achieved. Her winning margin of more than three metres was the widest at the Olympics since 1952.

1, Ilke Wyludda GER 69.66; 2, Natalya Sadova RUS 66.48; 3, Ellina Zvereva BLR 65.64;

4, Franka Dietzsch GER 65.48; 5, Xiao Yanling CHN 64.72; 6, Olga Chernyavskaya (formerly Burova) RUS 64.70; 7, Nicoleta Grasu ROM 63.28; 8, Lisa-Marie Vizaniari AUS 62.48 ... 12, Irina Yatchenko BLR 60.46. Note: Anastasia Kelesídou GRE dnq (18) 59.60, Ekaterini Voggoli GRE dnq (22) 58.70.

Javelin
With Tiina Lillak beaten into second place at the 1984 Games by Tessa Sanderson (who in Atlanta made a record-equalling sixth Olympic appearance) the Finns had yet to celebrate an Olympic women's javelin title - or indeed any Olympic women's gold medal - until Heli Rantanen brought it off. Sixth in the 1992 Olympics and fourth in the 1995 World Championships, she was regarded as a potential medallist but her best ever throw of 66.18 ranked her only eighth on 1996 performances by those entered. Rantanen, who improved to 66.54 in the qualifying contest, was first to throw in the final and never did an athlete capitalise more from that opportunity to dishearten the opposition with a mighty opener. She launched the spear out to 67.94 ... and nobody, herself included, came within two metres of that.

1, Heli Rantanen FIN 67.94; 2, Louise McPaul AUS 65.54; 3, Trine Hattestad NOR 64.98; 4, Isel López CUB 64.68; 5, Xiomara Rivero CUB 64.48; 6, Karen Forkel GER 64.18; 7, Mikaela Ingberg FIN 61.52; 8, Li Lei CHN 60.74; 9, Steffi Nerius GER 60.20; 10, Felicia Tilea ROM 59.94 (66.94q). Note: Mirela Manjani ALB dnq (24) 55.64.

Heptathlon
From the time she finished second just five points behind Australia's Glynis Nunn at the 1984 Olympics to her three-point defeat by Kelly Blair in the 1996 US Olympic Trials, Jackie Joyner-Kersee never lost a heptathlon she completed. It's a record of long-term supremacy unsurpassed by any athlete. Having won the Olympic crown in 1988 and 1992, JJK was bidding to become the first woman ever to win the same individual event three times in a row at the Olympics. It was not to be. Troubled by the hamstring injury which had hampered her in the Trials, she limped off after winning her heat of the opening event, the 100m hurdles, in 13.24.

Her successor was the statuesque Ghada Shouaa, who built up a first day score of 3992 and a 112-point lead over Urszula Wlodarczyk. Hopes of a huge score evaporated at the start of day two when in the long jump she managed only 6.26, a loss of 165 points as compared to her personal best of 6.77. It cost her the lead, too, as Natasha Sazanovich went ahead by 6 points. Shouaa immediately bounced back by improving her javelin best to 55.70, which took her into a 182pt lead over Sazanovich and a 2:15.43 800m extended that still further. With a score of 6780, her second highest, she became Syria's first Olympic champion in any sport. A personal best javelin throw of 54.82 and a tenacious 800m enabled Denise Lewis, only 8th after a disappointing long jump, to hold on for the bronze.

1, Ghada Shouaa SYR 6780 13.72, 1.86, 15.95, 23.85, 6.26, 55.70, 2:15.43); 2, Natasha Sazanovich BLR 6563 (13.56, 1.80, 14.52, 23.72, 6.70, 46.00, 2:17.92); 3, Denise Lewis GBR 6489 (13.45, 1.77, 13.92, 24.44, 6.32, 54.82, 2:17.41); 4, Urszula Wlodarczyk POL 6484; 5, Eunice Barber SLE 6342; 6, Rita Ináncsi HUN 6336; 7, Sabine Braun GER 6317; 8, Kelly Blair USA 6307; JJK USA dnf.

10 Kilometres Walk
Here's one for the trivia buffs. In which event is the women's Olympic record superior to the men's? It's the 10k walk. There is a catch, as the men's event (actually 10,000m on the track) was last staged in 1952 but the record was 45:02.8 by John Mikaelsson of Sweden ... which would have placed 17th in the Atlanta women's road walk! The first 14 broke the inaugural Olympic record of 44:32 established in Barcelona by Chen Yueling of China.

On that occasion Yelena Nikolayeva finished just one second behind, but in 1996 the Russian achieved new standards of excellence. She produced the extraordinary time of 41:04 in April, knocking 25 seconds off the previous world best, and she led the way in Atlanta to win by 23 sec in 41:49.

1, Yelena Nikolayeva RUS 41:49; 2, Elisabetta Perrone ITA 42:12; 3, Wang Yan CHN 42:19; 4, Gu Yan CHN 42:34; 5, Rossella Giordano ITA 42:43; 6, Olga Kardapoltseva BLR 43:02; 7, Katarzyna Radtke POL 43:05; 8, Valya Tsybulskaya BLR 43:21.

A MODEL ATHLETE

AMID ALL the hype surrounding Michael Johnson's successful bid to become the first man to win both the Olympic 200m and 400m, Marie-José Perec almost unobtrusively landed the same double. She did not break any world records and it had been accomplished once before by a woman (Valerie Brisco-Hooks of the USA in the boycott-diminished Games of 1984), but it was nevertheless a stunning achievement by the tall, elegant Frenchwoman.

Pérec had come a long way since she ran her first 400m race in 61 sec, aged 16, in her native Caribbean island of Guadeloupe. She moved to Paris to further her career but it was not until she was 20 that she made the transition to international level. She didn't get beyond the 200m quarter-finals at the 1988 Olympics but only months later won the European indoor 200m title.

With her long, loping stride (measured at 2.50m or over 8 feet) Pérec looked more at home over 400m and signalled her exciting possibilities by finishing first in the 1989 World Cup race in 50.30, although disqualified for running out of her lane. Third in the 1990 European Championships, she did not lose another 400m race until July 1995.

In the year (1991) she claimed her first world 400m title in 49.13, the fastest time in the world for three years, she reduced her 100m best to a spectacular 10.96. At the 1992 Olympics she improved to 48.83 for a great victory but, although running 21.99 for 200m in 1993 and winning the world 400m title again in 1995, she stagnated at her main event until Atlanta in 1996. There, in becoming the first athlete to retain an Olympic 400m title, she advanced to 48.25 – a time bettered to this day only by Marita Koch (GDR) and Jarmila Kratochvilová of Czechoslovakia.

For the first time Pérec started to believe that Koch's world record of 47.60 might just be within her reach. Previously she had implied that such a time was possible only with "biological aid." Pérec's American coach at this time, John Smith, who himself set a world 440 yards record of 44.5 in 1971, felt she could run 47.2-47.3!

Pérec's decision to tackle the 200m also in Atlanta came only a few weeks beforehand after a 22.29 victory in Nice persuaded her that she

had nothing to lose as her main event would be completed two days before the heats of the 200m. A relaxed looking 22.07 semi-final, fastest in the world that year, indicated all was well and in the final that giant, remorseless stride of hers ate steadily into Merlene Ottey's lead along the finishing straight for a 22.12 victory.

"It was like icing on the cake for me," said Pérec, whose joy was tinged with compassion for her 36 year-old Jamaican rival. "When I passed the finish line I was quite happy, but also inside I was a little bit sad. I was not overjoyed because I admire Merlene a lot. I was bothered. It disturbed me."

Now there were other worlds to conquer. Based in California from 1994 to escape the hassles of being France's most recognised sportswoman, Pérec stated that her ambitions included furthering her burgeoning modelling career, for which she certainly possessed the requisite hauteur and carriage, and breaking the world record for 400m hurdles. That stood at 52.61 by Kim Batten (USA) and both Pérec and coach John Smith felt a time of around 51.5 was possible.

In her first serious season at the event (1995) she ran 53.21 and defeated world champion Batten in all three of their races, but she never hurdled again. Indeed, she barely raced at anything following that triumphant 1996 campaign.

The 1997 season was practically a write-off after losing training due to a virus and a stress fracture of the shin (best of 22.67 for 200m, no 400m races), while she did not compete at all in 1998 due to a form of mononucleosis, Epstein-Barr Syndrome, and ensuing cardiac problems. She did make a tentative return in 1999 but ran only 11.67 and 23.25 and abandoned plans to contest the World Championships.

Things looked more promising in 2000. Under the seventh coach of her career, none other than Wolfgang Meier, the man who guided (and married) Marita Koch, she clocked 22.71 and – in her first 400m for four years – 50.32, but this notoriously temperamental athlete cracked under the pressure and fled Sydney shortly before her clash with Cathy Freeman in the Olympic 400m. Various claims of a comeback have failed to materialise, but – who knows – she might have one more surprise in store for us.

MICHAEL JOHNSON

NOBODY RUNS like Michael Johnson. The Texan's distinctive style of sprinting, ridiculed at first, was the key to his fabulous success and although that upright stance, low knee lift and piston-like stride didn't win prizes for grace or beauty the technique worked perfectly for him. It's the way he ran naturally, and all credit to the coaches who resisted the temptation to alter it.

Biomechanically, for a man of Michael Johnson's build, it made sense. Although he is 1.85m (just over 6ft) tall his legs are short in proportion and suited to an exceptionally rapid cadence.

As Clyde Hart, Johnson's coach for the past ten years, explained in an interview with *Track & Field News*: "Foot placement is a real key to speed. Many athletes place a foot slightly in front of their centre of gravity and that actually causes a blocking effect. It's like they're putting on the brakes all the time."

Johnson, though, made contact with the track beneath his centre of gravity. "While Michael may give up a little in stride length, he never stops moving," said Hart. "While one foot is hitting the track, the other is coming all the time and it forms nearly a complete circle. Also Michael doesn't strain, which is often overlooked in running. Stride rate and stride length, **with** relaxation, is the ideal."

It wasn't only Johnson's running style which was unique; so were his accomplishments. Just look at his 400m career. From the time he was beaten when placing second to Antonio McKay in the US Indoor Championships in February 1989 he went undefeated until finishing fifth in Paris in June 1997, a race won by Antonio Pettigrew. That was a win streak, counting finals only, of 58 races. He won the world title in 1993, 1995, 1997 and 1999 (finally breaking Butch Reynolds' world record with 43.18) and he took the gold medal in Atlanta by the widest winning margin in Olympic history.

Britain's Roger Black, a delighted runner-up in Atlanta, was honest: "I've always said there are two races with that guy in the race. People who say they are going to beat Michael Johnson are idiots."

Johnson retained the 400m title in Sydney in 2000 to become the first man to win the event a second time and no one has come close to his tally of marks inside 44 sec. He had 23 such times, the rest of the world's 400m runners 13. Oh, and he also ran the swiftest ever 400m relay leg of 42.94.

That's an awesome catalogue of triumphs ... and yet he made an equally profound impact at 200m. True, he lost the occasional race, but at the 1996 Olympics he put the world record out of sight with a time that even he, in his wildest dreams, had never envisaged.

Prior to 1996 Italy's Pietro Mennea held the oldest of all standard event world records with his altitude-assisted 19.72 in 1979. Johnson finally broke that in the US Olympic Trials in Atlanta with 19.66, which was regarded as fairly phenomenal until he ran 19.32 in the Olympic final on the same track a few weeks later. It represented the biggest ever single improvement of the 200m record, and this at a time when it would be logical to assume that records in such highly developed activities as sprinting would be chipped away, not demolished. Frank Fredericks ran the race of his life to clock 19.68 and still finished nearly four metres back as Johnson produced the widest margin of victory in this event at the Olympics since Jesse Owens in 1936.

Another remarkable feature was that it came in his eighth race of the Games; in the process Johnson became the first man ever to win the Olympic 200/400m double, emulating his feat at the previous year's World Championships.

Was 19.32 his limit? Not necessarily, believed Johnson, who described the 1996 Olympic final as "definitely the closest I've ever come to a perfect race." Never complacent, even immediately after achieving arguably THE greatest of all performances in athletics history, he admitted: "There were a few mistakes - like I stumbled about my fourth step out of the blocks - which tells me I'm capable of going faster."

In fact, as he concentrated more on 400m, he never again ran faster than 19.71 and that at altitude, but again his tally of 22 sub-20 marks is unmatched. In 2000, his final year of individual competition, he also let rip over 300m at altitude in South Africa, clocking a world's best of 30.85. Johnson, born in Dallas on September 13 1967, is now a highly regarded TV athletics analyst.

HUGE CROWDS FOR "BEST" GAMES

FOR THE first time since 1948 there were no world records set at the Olympic athletics, but despite that and the fact that winning marks were inferior to those set in the unfairly maligned Atlanta Games in 26 of the 43 events common to both occasions (plus two the same), the Sydney Olympics proved wildly successful. Many observers described them as the best Olympic Games ever. Unprecedented crowds, with attendances of between 85,806 and 97,432 for each of the morning sessions and from 99,428 to 112,524 for the evening sessions, totalling 1,597,104 in all (over 300,000 more than in Atlanta), provided a fantastic atmosphere and the athletes responded accordingly.

The Americans, led by Marion Jones' three gold and two bronze medals, were easily the strongest nation on view although their tally must have sounded alarm bells at home: "only" 10 golds, including the inaugural women's pole vault, as against 13 in 1988, 12 in 1992 and 13 in 1996. They also had many disappointing results from their athletes below the super-star level so that on the points table for top eight placings the US scored 185 ahead of Russia (132), whereas the figures for 1996 were 246 and 130 respectively. Next came Germany with 100 (114 in Atlanta) and Britain with 95, compared to 69 for equal fifth place four years earlier. In all 44 nations won medals as against 42 in Atlanta.

STAR OF THE GAMES

MARION JONES
(born 12 Oct 1975)

The aim was to win five gold medals. She didn't succeed, but Marion Jones still made Olympic history by becoming the first woman to pick up five medals in a single Games. On September 23rd she won the 100m by almost four metres in 10.75; on the 28th she took the 200m in 21.84; on the 29th she long jumped 6.92 for the bronze medal; while on the 30th she collected bronze (4x100m) and gold (4x400m) in the relays!

The competition was superb and the fourth day was one of the greatest in the history of our sport. The highlight for the crowd was undoubtedly Cathy Freeman's victory at 400m run in a massive roar of popular support and illuminated by the flashing of thousands of cameras as she strode around the track. But there was much else besides, with victories for all-time greats such as Michael Johnson, Jonathan Edwards, Maria Mutola and Gabriela Szabo, the closest approach to a world record at the Games from pole vault attempts by Stacy Dragila and Tatiana Grigorieva, and above all one of the greatest races we have ever seen, the men's 10,000m, which culminated in an epic sprint to the finish in which the sheer mental strength of Haile Gebrselassie, below par all year, overcame the challenge from Paul Tergat.

MEN'S EVENTS
100 Metres

Having lost four 100m races in 2000, Maurice Greene might have appeared more vulnerable than he was the previous year. Not so. As his last race, winning in Berlin in 9.86, had indicated, he was back to top form when it mattered and coach John Smith had suggested he was in 9.75 shape for the Games. In fact 9.87 into a slight wind, the second fastest ever Olympic time, sufficed to make Greene (26) the first American 100m champion since Carl Lewis in 1988 and his winning margin of 0.12 over training companion Ato Boldon was the widest since Lewis in 1984. Dwain Chambers looked set for bronze until he dipped too early and was edged by Obadele Thompson, winning a first ever Olympic medal for Barbados. On reaction times Boldon was fastest away at 0.136 sec with Greene at a slow 0.197 and Thompson worst at 0.216.

A frustrated and tearful spectator in Atlanta four years earlier, Greene now uniquely held every short sprint honour available: Olympic and world champion and world record holder at 100m, world champion and record holder at the indoor 60m. He was also the reigning world 200m champion. Defending champion Donovan Bailey suffered one injury too many and trailed home last in his quarter-final in 11.36.

(-0.3) 1, Maurice Greene USA 9.87; 2, Ato Boldon TRI 9.99; 3, Obadele Thompson BAR 10.04; 4, Dwain Chambers GBR 10.08; 5, Jon

Drummond USA 10.09; 6, Darren Campbell GBR 10.13; 7, Kim Collins SKN 10.17; Abdul Aziz Zakari GHA dnf (10.16sf). Note: Deji Aliu NGR 6s2 10.32, Patrick Johnson AUS 5q5 10.44.

200 Metres

The absence of Michael Johnson and Maurice Greene made the event wide open … but who could have predicted, at least before the quarter finals, that Konstadinos Kedéris and Darren Campbell would take gold and silver? Prior to 2000 the Greek had a best of 20.50 and was better known as a 45.60 400m runner, while European 100m champion Campbell was a 20.48 performer.

The first quarter-final brought Kedéris and Campbell together with startling results: Campbell ran 20.13 to rank third fastest ever Briton behind John Regis and his own coach Linford Christie, and Kedéris clocked 20.14. In their semi Kedéris ran 20.20 and Campbell 20.23 but US champion John Capel clocked 20.10 in the other race, looking round. Capel finished last in the final, however; he was left at the start as he moved early and then rocked back onto his blocks as the gun went. Campbell led into the straight from Ato Boldon and Obadele Thompson but Kedéris (27) inched past to become the first Greek man to win an Olympic running title since 1896. It was the first time the USA has been out of the medals (excluding 1980 of course) since 1928!

(-0.6) 1, Konstadinos Kedéris GRE 20.09; 2, Darren Campbell GBR 20.14 (20.13qf); 3, Ato Boldon TRI 20.20; 4, Obadele Thompson BAR 20.20 (20.16qf); 5, Christian Malcolm GBR 20.23 (20.19qf & sf); 6, Claudinei da Silva BRA 20.28; 7, Coby Miller USA 20.35; 8, John Capel USA 20.49 (20.10sf). Note: Shingo Suetsugu JPN 8s2 20.69.

400 Metres

It's not often that Michael Johnson plays second fiddle to anyone but, with 112,000 fans still emotionally drained after Cathy Freeman's triumph, his lap of the track proved something of an anti-climax even though he became the first man to win a second Olympic 400m title. There had been talk of his breaking 43 sec but that target was put on hold as he concentrated on ensuring victory. "I train with Greg Haughton every day, so I know what sort of shape he is in, and I know

Alvin Harrison's form, so I couldn't take any chances," he explained. Harrison had completed an impressive 44.25 quarter-final with a smile on his face and Johnson let him win their semi in 44.53. Haughton, in lane 8, went off fast in the final and was second to Johnson (lane 6) at 300m. The great man drew away while Harrison (lane 4) overtook the Jamaican for a US 1-2. Johnson's 43.84 has been bettered by only three other men yet it ranked merely 13th on his own all-time list! At 33 he became the oldest man to win any Olympic title under 5000m.

1, Michael Johnson USA 43.84; 2, Alvin Harrison USA 44.40 (44.25qf); 3, Greg Haughton JAM 44.70; 4, Sanderlei Parrela BRA 45.01; 5, Robert Mackowiak POL 45.14; 6, Hendrik Mokganyetsi RSA 45.26; 7, Antonio Pettigrew USA 45.42; 8, Danny McFarlane JAM 45.55. Note: Marc Raquil FRA 5q4 45.56

800 Metres

After eight men broke 1:45 in the semis, the final proved a disappointingly slow race. A brilliant line-up included world record holder Wilson Kipketer, entitled now to bid for the Olympic crown denied him four years earlier; Hezekiel Sepeng (who ran Kipketer to 2/100ths in the 1999 World Championships); European champion Nils Schumann; the world's two quickest in 2000 in André Bucher and Djabir Saïd-Guerni; and the exciting if often exasperating Yuriy Borzakovskiy, who reduced his European junior record to 1:44.33 in his semi.

The first lap took 53.43, with Borzakovskiy way behind even at that pedestrian pace. At 600m Andrea Longo pushed Bucher momentarily off the track, an action which led to his disqualification after finishing sixth. Entering the final straight it was Longo from Bucher and Schumann and it was the 22 year-old German, who had set a personal best of 1:44.22 winning his semi, who timed his effort best and was indeed the only finalist who ran a sensible race. With less than a stride separating the first four he held on for Germany's first ever Olympic win in the men's 800m. Kipketer and (especially) Saïd-Guerni left themselves too much to do, finishing out in lanes 4 and 5 respectively! Kipketer revealed he was spiked at the moment he intended making a break but was pleased with the silver. Defending champion Vebjørn Rodal went out in the semis.

1, Nils Schumann GER 1:45.08 (1:44.22sf); 2, Wilson Kipketer DEN 1:45.14 (1:44.22sf); 3, Djabir Saïd-Guerni ALG 1:45.16 (1:44.19sf); 4, Hezekiel Sepeng RSA 1:45.29 (1:44.85sf); 5, André Bucher SUI 1:45.40 (1:44.38sf); 6, Yuriy Borzakovskiy RUS 1:45.83 (1:44.33sf); 7, Glody Dube BOT 1:46.24 (1:44.70sf); Andrea Longo ITA dq (1:45.66; 1:44.49sf).

1500 Metres

Unbeaten at 1500m since falling in Atlanta four years earlier, Hicham El Guerrouj had hinted he might challenge his world record of 3:26.00 to win the gold medal, and when team-mate Youssef Baba hared round the first lap in 54.14 with El Guerrouj in close attendance it looked as though he might indeed be going for it. However, Baba took 60.63 for lap two (1:54.77) and, with no prospect of a record, El Guerrouj took charge. He stepped up the pace with a 56.90 (2:51.67) yet, ominously, Noah Ngeny, Bernard Lagat and Mehdi Baala remained in contact. Although Baala (who was to prove the most successful French athlete of the Games with 4th place!) dropped back during the 54.27 last lap, the Kenyan pair stayed close and for the first time serious doubts were raised over whether the Moroccan could find another gear to dispose of his pursuers. With some 30m remaining Ngeny (21) moved ahead to claim a famous victory in 3:32.07, breaking Seb Coe's 1984 Olympic record, while El Guerrouj only just salvaged second ahead of Lagat.

Despite his world 1000m record of 2:11.96 the previous year, Ngeny's triumph still came as a shock. El Guerrouj hasn't lost a single race at 1500m or mile since then, while Ngeny's career has since proved to be a chequered one. Defending champion Noureddine Morceli, who had not raced all year, jogged in last in his semi following a collision in the finishing straight.

1, Noah Ngeny KEN 3:32.07; 2, Hicham El Guerrouj MAR 3:32.32; 3, Bernard Lagat KEN 3:32.44; 4, Mehdi Baala FRA 3:34.14; 5, Kevin Sullivan CAN 3:35.50; 6, Daniel Zegeye ETH 3:36.78; 7, Andrés Diaz ESP 3:37.27; 8, Juan Carlos Higueuro ESP 3:38.91.

5000 Metres

Having decided to tackle the 5000m rather than the 1500m, Ali Saïdi-Sief was most people's favourite to win despite having seriously run the distance only twice before. However, like El Guerrouj, he was found wanting in the finishing straight, enabling Million Wolde to sprint past and become at 21 the youngest winner of this event for 80 years. In the slowest Olympic final since 1968, Jirka Arndt led at 1k in 2:45.36, Dagne Alemu at 2k in 5:39.54, Brahim Lahlafi at 3k in 8:21.79 and 4k in 11:09.84, at which point the entire field was still bunched. Saïdi-Sief threw in a 60.36 lap to the bell, where he was 3m up on Wolde with Lahlafi third, but had no answer to the Ethiopian's 53.83 last lap. The final kilometre took just 2:25.64. For the first time in this event all of the top six placings were occupied by Africans. The 1996 champion Vénuste Niyongabo, still struggling to recapture form after injury, finished 15th in his heat.

1, Million Wolde ETH 13:35.49 (13:22.75ht); 2, Ali Saïdi-Sief ALG 13:36.20 (13:29.24ht); 3, Brahim Lahlafi MAR 13:36.47 (13:22.70ht); 4, Fita Bayissa ETH 13:37.03 (13:22.92ht); 5, David Chelule KEN 13:37.13 (13:29.98ht); 6, Dagne Alemu ETH 13:37.17 (13:29.93ht); 7, Sergey Lebed UKR 13:37.80 (13:29.69ht); 8, Jirka Arndt GER 13:38.57 (13:26.18ht).

10,000 Metres

Winning by a smaller margin than Maurice Greene in the 100m, and seemingly travelling as fast at the finish, Haile Gebrselassie (27) joined the Olympic greats by becoming the fourth man – after Nurmi, Zátopek and Viren – to capture a second Olympic 10,000m title. Poor Paul Tergat, so often his runner-up on the track, could have been excused for believing he had pulled it off at last when he spurted ahead 200m from home and unleashed a prodigious kick. It didn't seem possible that Gebrselassie, at one time a doubtful starter due to an Achilles tendon injury, could close the gap ... but he did and, in the last ten metres, summoned up one final superhuman effort to edge past and maintain a seven-year unbeaten record at the distance. It was the closest ever finish to an Olympic distance race at 9/100ths. The last lap took 56.56 with the last 200m in 26.0 by Gebrselassie as he stopped the clock in 27:18.20, the second 5000m covered in 13:32.32. East Africans occupied the top five places, Assefa Mezgebu taking bronze ahead of Patrick Ivuti and John Korir (18). The first European home was Britain's Karl Keska (8th) who set personal bests in heat and final.

1, Haile Gebrselassie ETH 27:18.20; 2, Paul Tergat KEN 27:18.29; 3, Assefa Mezgebu ETH 27:19.75; 4, Patrick Ivuti KEN 27:20.44; 5, John Korir KEN 27:24.75; 6, Saïd Bérioui MAR 27:37.83; 7, Toshinari Takaoka JPN 27:40.44; 8, Karl Keska GBR 27:44.09.

Marathon

For the first time in Olympic marathon history all three medals went to Africans, with fourth place – only 7 seconds away from the bronze – unexpectedly going to Britain's Jon Brown, whose comment "that is the first marathon I've run where there has been a level playing field" was clearly about the influence of the introduction of EPO testing prior to the Games.

The race began in warm, windy conditions at 4pm. At 35k the leaders were Gezahegne Abera, fellow Ethiopian Tesfaye Tola and Kenya's Eric Wainaina, the 1996 bronze medallist, with Brown one second behind. The Briton had to let them go soon afterwards when he suffered stitch and Tola dropped back during the 39th kilometre, after beckoning to Abera to go on to challenge the Japanese-based Wainaina who had been pressing on hardest. The 22 year-old Ethiopian pulled clear of Wainaina at 39k and had 20 sec to spare at the end in 2:10:11, a formidable time in the conditions on a hilly course and all the more remarkable as he fell after 17k, hurting his knee and losing about 20m in the process.

1, Gezahegne Abera ETH 2:10:11; 2, Eric Wainaina KEN 2:10:31; 3, Tesfaye Tola ETH 2:11:10; 4, Jon Brown GBR 2:11:17; 5, Giacomo Leone ITA 2:12:14; 6, Martín Fiz ESP 2:13:06; 7, Abdelkader El Mouaziz MAR 2:13:49; 8, Mohamed Ouaadi FRA 2:14:04; ... 20, Josia Thugwane RSA 2:16:59; 24, Lee Bong-ju KOR 2:17:57; Stefano Baldini ITA dnf.

3000 Metres Steeplechase

This always shaped up as a Kenyan/Moroccan affair and so it proved, although Brahim Boulami – then the fastest non-Kenyan ever with 8:02.90 in 2000 – placed no higher than seventh due to some fine running by the two Martíns from Spain. Luis Martín led at 1k in 2:55.85 with Reuben Kosgei just ahead of the leading pack of 11 men at 2k in 5:43.91. Kosgei (21), the 1998 world junior champion with a best of 8:03.92, held off all challenges during a 61.38 last lap, the most serious coming from 1997 world champion Wilson Boit Kipketer who drew level on the run in before a clash of arms caused him to falter, while Ali Ezzine edged world record holder Bernard Barmasai for bronze. The final kilometer in this the slowest final since 1972 was covered in 2:37.52. Kenya has now won this title at every Games they have contested since 1968 and this was their fourth successive 1-2.

1, Reuben Kosgei KEN 8:21.43; 2, Wilson Boit Kipketer KEN 8:21.77; 3, Ali Ezzine MAR 8:22.15; 4, Bernard Barmasai KEN 8:22.23; 5, Luis M Martín ESP 8:22.75; 6, Eliseo Martín ESP 8:23.00; 7, Brahim Boulami MAR 8:24.32; 8, Günther Weidlinger AUT 8:26.70. Note: Bob Tahri FRA 6h1 8:34.69.

110 Metres Hurdles

At 33 Colin Jackson, clearly one of the all-time greats of sprint hurdling, reconciled himself to the fact that he will never be Olympic champion. Second in 1988, seventh in 1992 when as strong favourite he was hampered by an injury and fourth in 1996, Sydney was his final chance. With his greatest rival, defending champion Allen Johnson, in questionable form following injury the opportunity for victory at the fourth attempt was there but in the final Jackson placed fifth, admitting "I made mistakes during the race and paid the penalty." Johnson also finished outside the medals as Anier García (24) ran out a splendid, clearcut winner in a Cuban and Central American record of 13.00, followed by the American pair of 10.04 100m man Terrence Trammell (in a pb 13.16) and Mark Crear, who was responsible for one false start.

(0.6) 1, Anier García CUB 13.00; 2, Terrence Trammell USA 13.16; 3, Mark Crear USA 13.22; 4, Allen Johnson USA 13.23; 5, Colin Jackson GBR 13.28; 6, Florian Schwarthoff GER 13.42; 7, Dudley Dorival HAI 13.49; 8, Robert Kronberg SWE 13.61. Note: Stanislav Olijar LAT 6s2 13.50.

400 Metres Hurdles

He may not be the prettiest of hurdlers but there is no denying Angelo Taylor's speed (43.6

"BEST" GAMES CONTINUED

SYDNEY 2000, HUGE CROWDS

relay split) and effectiveness. The 21 year-old US champion had plenty of motivation after failing dismally in the previous year's World Championships and seized the opportunity to prove he was the world's no 1. He lowered his personal best to 47.50 – and, like Morgan Taylor in 1924 and John Akii-Bua in 1972 – he did it from the inside lane, the penalty for finishing second to Llewellyn Herbert in his semi with only the seventh quickest time of the round. Fastest was Hadi Al-Somaily, whose 48.14 was an Asian record and he became the first Saudi Arabian ever to make an Olympic athletics final. There he went much faster still, leading in to the final straight and clocking 47.53 for a very close second ahead of fast finishing Herbert whose 47.81 was a South African record.

1, Angelo Taylor USA 47.50; 2, Hadi Al-Somaily KSA 47.53; 3, Llewellyn Herbert RSA 47.81; 4, James Carter USA 48.04; 5, Eronilde de Araujo BRA 48.34; 6, Pawel Januszewski POL 48.44; 7, Fabrizio Mori ITA 48.78; 8, Gennadiy Gorbenko UKR 49.01. Note: Felix Sánchez DOM 7s2 49.69.

4x100 Metres Relay

Britain had high hopes of taking the silver medals as in the 1999 World Championships, perhaps even defeating the Americans, but the team didn't even survive the first round. Appalling baton passing led to last place (40.36) and subsequent disqualification whereas the US was fastest in the heats (38.15) and semis (37.82) before taking the final by three metres in 37.61, sixth fastest ever behind five other US combinations. Chasing Maurice Greene on the anchor, Brazil's Claudinei da Silva overtook Cuba's Freddy Mayola for silver in the South American record time of 37.90. Japan tied the Asian record of 38.31 in their semi. In addition to Jon Drummond, Bernard Williams, Brian Lewis and Greene, Kenny Brokenburr and Tim Montgomery received gold medals as they ran in the heats.

1, USA (Jon Drummond, Bernard Williams, Brian Lewis, Maurice Greene) 37.61; 2, Brazil (Vicente Lima, Edson Ribeiro, André da Silva, Claudinei da Silva) 37.90; 3, Cuba (José César, Luis Pérez-Rionda, Iván García, Freddy Mayola) 38.04; 4, Jamaica 38.20; 5, France 38.49; 6, Japan 38.66; 7, Italy 38.67; 8, Poland 38.96.

4x400 Metres Relay

With four runners whose best times added up to 2:56.12 from standing starts there was a chance that the US team might threaten the world record of 2:54.20. Had Michael Johnson on the anchor run full out they would have been quite close. Alvin Harrison established a substantial lead on the first leg with a time of 44.5, Antonio Pettigrew followed with a 44.1 and Calvin Harrison (who had clocked a 43.56 split in the semis) covered his lap in 43.55. Needing a somewhat unlikely 42.07 for the record, Johnson contented himself with an unstraining 44.22 for a time of 2:56.35, the no 7 mark of all-time. In his final Olympic appearance Johnson thus brought his total of gold medals to five. Jerome Young and Angelo Taylor also won golds for their contribution in the heats and semis, the 400m hurdles champion being timed at 44.2 in his semi. Alvin and Calvin Harrison became the first twins to win an Olympic gold medal apiece. The Bahamas were second for much of the final but were squeezed out of the medals on the last leg with Nigeria setting an African record of 2:58.68 just ahead of Jamaica.

1, USA (Alvin Harrison 44.5, Antonio Pettigrew 44.1, Calvin Harrison 43.55, Michael Johnson 44.22) 2:56.35; 2, Nigeria (Clement Chukwu 45.2, Jude Monye 44.5, Sunday Bada 44.7, Enefiok Udo-Obong 44.3) 2:58.68; 3, Jamaica (Michael Blackwood 44.7, Greg Haughton 44.8, Chris Williams 44.8, Danny McFarlane 44.5) 2:58.78; 4, Bahamas 2:59.23 (2:59.02sf); 5, France 3:01.02; 6, Gt Britain 3:01.22; 7, Poland 3:03.22; 8, Australia 3:03.91.

High Jump

A clear favourite was the world champion Vyacheslav Voronin, but he was completely out of sorts, clearing 2.29 only on his final attempt before going out at 2.32. It was his less celebrated training companion Sergey Klyugin (26) who triumphed. It was Klyugin's good fortune that his initial clearance at 2.35 (at a time when he had been in fourth place behind Javier Sotomayor, Abderahmane Hammad and Stefan Holm) came before the heavens opened. The heavy rain ruined the rest of the contest and none of the other six men left in came close to succeeding, but as they would have had to jump 2.38 to beat Klyugin it is unlikely that the gold medal was affected. The controversially reinstated Sotomayor took silver to add to his 1992 gold and Hammad became the first African male athlete to win an Olympic field event medal.

1, Sergey Klyugin RUS 2.35; 2, Javier Sotomayor CUB 2.32; 3, Abderahmane Hammad ALG 2.32; 4, Stefan Holm SWE 2.32; 5, Konstantin Matusevich ISR 2.32; 6=, Staffan Strand SWE & Mark Boswell CAN 2.32; 8, Wolfgang Kreissig GER 2.29.

Pole Vault

An era came to an end when the greatest ever pole vaulter, Sergey Bubka (36), bade farewell. He departed not in a blaze of glory but with a typically audacious gesture; although injury had restricted him to a best of only 5.55 that summer he did not enter the qualifying competition until 5.70 … and failed to clear. Out too went defending champion Jean Galfione. The final was full of surprises, one of which was the fact that only two Europeans made the top seven. Eight men were still in as the bar was raised to 5.90 and four cleared: Nick Hysong (28) at the first attempt (even if the bar did bounce), Lawrence Johnson at the second, Maksim Tarasov and Michael Stolle at the third, and as all four (along with Dmitriy Markov who carried forward one final try) failed at 5.96 the result was the USA's first victory for 32 years. The Americans had won all of the first 15 quadrennial Olympic titles but since Bob Seagren's 1968 success had played second fiddle to the Europeans. Now they had their first 1-2 since 1960, and remember that the year 2000 world leader at 6.03, Jeff Hartwig, no-heighted in the US Trials.

1, Nick Hysong USA 5.90; 2, Lawrence Johnson USA 5.90; 3, Maksim Tarasov RUS 5.90; 4, Michael Stolle GER 5.90; 5=, Dmitriy Markov AUS & Viktor Chistyakov AUS 5.80; 7, Okkert Brits RSA 5.80; 8, Danny Ecker GER 5.80 … 10=, Aleksandr Averbukh ISR & Giuseppe Gibilisco ITA 5.50; 13, Tim Lobinger GER 5.50.

Long Jump

For the first time since 1980 the Olympic long jump champion was assured to be someone other than Carl Lewis. The universal favourite was Iván Pedroso but he had to dig deep before the gold medal became a reality. In the qualifying contest he faced possible elimination after jump- ing merely 7.70 and 7.99, only to pull out an 8.32 to head the field. From round 2 onwards the final became a riveting duel between Pedroso and the flamboyant Australian, Jai Taurima. The latter took the lead with his second jump of 8.18, only to be overtaken in that round by Pedroso's 8.34. In round 3 Taurima himself leapt 8.34 to take the lead on countback, but Pedroso struck back with a fourth round 8.41. Jumping next, Taurima fell 1cm short with a new Oceania record of 8.40, but in the fifth round, in which Pedroso fouled, Taurima drew a huge roar from the 106,000 crowd as he landed at 8.49. Even Pedroso can't jump that far to order but, amid unbearable tension, he produced an 8.55. Taurima finished with 8.28 and the 27 year-old Cuban had won an Olympic crown to add to his seven world outdoor and indoor titles. The only American finalist was Dwight Phillips, who placed eighth for an all-time worst US showing.

1, Iván Pedroso CUB 8.55; 2, Jai Taurima AUS 8.49; 3, Roman Shchurenko UKR 8.31; 4, Aleksey Lukashevich UKR 8.26; 5, Kofi Amoah Prah GER 8.19; 6, Peter Burge AUS 8.15; 7, Luis Felipe Meliz CUB 8.08; 8, Dwight Phillips USA 8.06. Note: James Beckford JAM dnq (14) 7.98, Yago Lamela ESP dnq (19) 7.89, Savanté Stringfellow USA dnq (22) 7.84.

Triple Jump

Four years after he was expected to become Olympic champion, the world record holder finally fulfilled his destiny. Now 34 (thus becoming easily the oldest ever winner of this event), Jonathan Edwards had remained the world's no 1 for most of the time since Atlanta and, with the virtual retirement of Kenny Harrison, no truly outstanding challenger had emerged. Edwards' compatriot Larry Achike, the Commonwealth champion, started the final on a high note. The leading qualifier with a personal best of 17.30, he opened with 17.29 – a distance which would keep him in a medal position until close to the end. Edwards went ahead with his second jump of 17.37, minutes later Denis Kapustin responded with 17.46, but in round 3 Edwards leapt to a winning 17.71. That's how it stayed until in the final round Yoelbi Quesada knocked Achike out of the medals with 17.37, only to be deposed himself by team-mate Yoel García's last gasp silver medal winning 17.47. With three in the top

"BEST" GAMES CONTINUED

six this was Britain's best ever performance in an Olympic field event.

1, Jonathan Edwards GBR 17.71; 2, Yoel García CUB 17.47; 3, Denis Kapustin RUS 17.46; 4, Yoelbi Quesada CUB 17.37; 5, Larry Achike GBR 17.29; 6, Phillips Idowu GBR 17.08; 7, Robert Howard USA 17.05; 8, Paolo Camossi ITA 16.96 ... 11, Walter Davis USA 16.61. Note: Christian Olsson SWE dnq (17) 16.64.

Shot

The surprise leader in the qualifying round was Arsi Harju, who improved his best from 21.04 to 21.39, and he consolidated that form in the final. He opened with 21.20, a distance matched in the second round by Adam Nelson, but with his second put the Finn, looking like a gigantic pirate, reached what proved to be the winning distance of 21.29. Nelson improved slightly to 21.21 in round 3, while 1995 & 1997 world champion John Godina (a late substitute for C J Hunter, who had failed a drugs test) went close with a fifth round 21.20, moving from fifth to third. With just 9cm covering the medallists it was one of the closest ever Olympic contests. Harju (26) became the first Finnish winner of the event since Ville Pörhölä 80 years earlier. All three medallists used the rotational technique.

1, Arsi Harju FIN 21.29 (21.39q); 2, Adam Nelson USA 21.21; 3, John Godina USA 21.20; 4, Andy Bloom USA 20.87; 5, Yuriy Bilonog UKR 20.84; 6, Manuel Martínez ESP 20.55; 7, Janus Robberts RSA 20.32; 8, Oliver-Sven Buder GER 20.18; 9, Andrey Mikhnevich BLR 19.48.

Discus

Virgilijus Alekna (28), the Lithuanian who had clearly been the world's no 1 in 2000, 5-1 v Lars Riedel and with 11 competitions beyond 68m, opened with a dreadful 58.55 before getting down to business. In the second round he threw 67.54 to take second place behind Frantz Kruger's 67.89 opener and a momentous third round saw, in sequence, defending champion Riedel take the lead with 68.50, Kruger improve to 68.19 and Alekna move ahead with 68.73. Although the other two were over 68m again in the next round their challenge ultimately petered out, particularly when Alekna progressed to 69.30 in round 5. The three medallists were respectively 2.00, 1.99 and 2.03 tall! World

record holder Jürgen Schult placed eighth at the age of 40.

1, Virgilijus Alekna LTU 69.30; 2, Lars Riedel GER 68.50; 3, Frantz Kruger RSA 68.19; 4, Vasiliy Kaptyukh BLR 67.59; 5, Adam Setliff USA 66.02; 6, Jason Tunks CAN 65.80; 7, Vladimir Dubrovshchik BLR 65.13; 8, Jürgen Schult GER 64.41. Note: Róbert Fazekas HUN dnq (16) 61.76.

Hammer

The leading qualifier was Igor Astapkovich at 79.81 and he started as the sentimental favourite; four times a silver medallist in Olympics and World Championships and that year's world leader at 82.58 this was his big chance. But although he did make the podium again it was only as bronze medallist. The 1994 world junior champion Szymon Ziółkowski (24) took the lead with a second round 79.87 and improved to 80.02 with his fourth effort. That was commendable throwing considering the event started in rain, the circle remained wet and slippery, and the Pole had brought only one pair of shoes, designed for dry conditions. Meanwhile, the left handed Nicola Vizzoni produced a personal best silver medal winning 79.64, and Astapkovich nudged his compatriot Ivan Tikhon out of the bronze when he threw the same distance but finished ahead on the basis of a superior second best.

1, Szymon Ziółkowski POL 80.02; 2, Nicola Vizzoni ITA 79.64; 3, Igor Astapkovich BLR 79.17 (79.81q); 4, Ivan Tikhon BLR 79.17; 5, Ilya Konovalov RUS 78.56; 6, Loris Paoluzzi ITA 78.18; 7, Tibor Gécsek HUN 77.70; 8, Vladimir Maska CZE 77.32; 9, Koji Murofushi JPN 76.60; 10, Andrey Skvaruk UKR 75.50 (79.55q). Note: Adrián Annus HUN dnq (17) 75.41.

Javelin

Bidding for a record breaking third Olympic javelin title, despite a rib injury sustained in training the previous month, Jan Zelezny opened with a daunting 89.41, followed in quick succession by 88.67 from Sergey Makarov and 87.76 by Raymond Hecht. It was shaping up as a titanic contest (there were a record seven men over 85m), and early in round 2 Backley threw an Olympic record (with current model) of 89.85, a distance which he might reasonably have expected to win gold. But Zelezny, irritated at having to hold fire while the women's 100m victory ceremony was being staged, ploughed all his frustration as well as strength and skill into his third round effort. It landed at 90.17 and Backley knew he was destined once again to finish second best to the man who must now surely be acknowledged as the greatest ever javelin thrower. At 34 he had become the oldest ever Olympic javelin winner. Backley could only console himself with the thought that once again he had raised his game on the big occasion (his season's best had been 86.70) and had become the first Briton in any event to win an Olympic medal in three Games. Makarov's opener held up for bronze, his father having won silver in 1980.

1, Jan Zelezny CZE 90.17; 2, Steve Backley GBR 89.85; 3, Sergey Makarov RUS 88.67; 4, Raymond Hecht GER 87.76; 5, Aki Parviainen FIN 86.62; 6, Konstadínos Gatsioúdis GRE 86.53; 7, Boris Henry GER 85.78; 8, Emeterio González CUB 83.33.

Decathlon
In a perfect world Tomás Dvorák would have succeeded Dan O'Brien as Olympic champion, just as he had as world record holder. But the Czech started with abdominal and knee injuries and was unable to do himself justice. That opened the door for another medallist and what a scrap there was for a place on the podium. Chris Huffins set the pace right through to the last event and although this remained his weakest discipline the American hung on for the bronze behind Erki Nool and Roman Sébrle, leaving Britain's Dean Macey – despite a personal best score of 8567 – to end up fourth.

Unfortunately, a controversial decision involving Nool in the discus cast a shadow over the proceedings. Following two fouls the 30 year-old European champion faced oblivion when his third attempt was measured but was declared a foul. A protest by the Estonians succeeded as the referee overruled the judges, but experts who viewed the video were in no doubt that Nool foot faulted and should have been awarded "nool points" and it was amazing that the Jury of Appeal upheld the referee's decision when they examined the video evidence.

Huffins led after day 1 with 4554 but only by 8pts from Macey who posted personal bests in the long jump and 400m (a magnificent 46.41). Next came Nool 4505, Tom Pappas 4476 and Sébrle 4460. Huffins widened his advantage after the hurdles to 87 over Macey, who was handicapped in all the throws following a right elbow operation and had a poor discus. After 7 events it was: Huffins 6401, Sébrle 6205, Macey 6186, Nool 6157.

Although Huffins vaulted only 4.70 he was still well clear after 8 events with 7220. Nool, who had a best of 5.60, went no higher than 5.00 but even so moved to second with 7067 just ahead of Sébrle 7054 and Macey 7035, who raised his best of 4.60 to 4.70 and 4.80. Nool's vastly superior javelin throwing whittled the American's lead down to just 14pts (7907-7893) after nine events with Sébrle on 7853 and Macey (in agony from his elbow but heroically throwing over 60m) on 7779. Nool ran a solid 1500m to become Estonia's first Olympic athletics champion, 35pts ahead of Sébrle (who would the following year break through the 9000 barrier), but although Macey set another personal best he was foiled by Huffins' determined run.

1, Erki Nool EST 8641 (10.68, 7.76, 15.11, 2.00, 46.71, 14.48, 43.66, 5.00, 65.82, 4:29.48); 2, Roman Sébrle CZE 8606 (10.92, 7.62, 15.22, 2.12, 48.20, 13.87, 44.39, 4.80, 64.04, 4:28.79); 3, Chris Huffins USA 8595 (10.48, 7.71, 15.27, 2.09, 48.31, 13.91, 49.55, 4.70, 56.62, 4:38.71); 4, Dean Macey GBR 8567; 5, Tom Pappas USA 8425; 6, Tomás Dvorák CZE 8385; 7, Frank Busemann GER 8351; 8, Attila Zsivóczky HUN 8277.

20 Kilometres Walk
Robert Korzeniowski would make further history in the 50 kilometres seven days later but by winning the 20 kilometres he became the first to win Olympic road walking titles at both distances, the previous closest being Raul González, winner of the 50 kilometres and 2nd at 20 kilometres in 1984. Not that Korzeniowski (32), the 50 kilometres champion in Atlanta, knew that he had won when he crossed the line for he assumed he had finished a close second to Bernardo Segura. Only 15 minutes later, after a lap of honour and while he was speaking on the phone to his nation's President, was it revealed that the Mexican had been disqualified, leaving the Pole the winner in an Olympic record

"BEST" GAMES CONTINUED

1:18:59 with halves of 39:55 and 39:04. Noe Hernández finished just 4 sec behind in a personal best of 1:19:03 while Vladimir Andreyev took bronze well clear of defending champion Jefferson Pérez

1, Robert Korzeniowski POL 1:18:59; 2, Noe Hernández MEX 1:19:03; 3, Vladimir Andreyev RUS 1:19:27; 4, Jefferson Pérez ECU 1:20:18; 5, Andreas Erm GER 1:20:25; 6, Roman Rasskazov RUS 1:20:57; 7, Francisco Fernández ESP 1:21:01; 8, Nathan Deakes AUS 1:21:03.

50 Kilometres Walk

Having won the 20 kilometres, which he had regarded in the nature of a warm up for his best distance, Robert Korzeniowski was fired up for the defence of his 50 kilometres title and history was made as he became the first road walker to win a third Olympic gold. Competing in hot, humid conditions he covered the first 20 kilometres in 1:30:00, the next in a murderous 1:26:28, eventually winning by over a minute in 3:42:22. His 10 kilometre splits were 45:53, 44:07, 43:30, 42:58 and 45:54.

Joel Sánchez was his closest rival but a warning prompted the Mexican to throttle back after being just a second down at 40 kilometres, and Korzeniowski, who received one caution during the race, pulled away at 43k. Aigars Fadejevs, the European 20k silver medallist, finished strongly to overtake Sánchez for second after being 55 sec behind the Mexican at 40 kilometres and 19 sec down at 45 kilometres. A great reception was accorded the last finisher, an injured Chris Maddocks (43), the first British male athlete to compete in five Olympics.

1, Robert Korzeniowski POL 3:42:22; 2, Aigars Fadejevs LAT 3:43:40; 3, Joel Sánchez MEX 3:44:36; 4, Valentí Massana ESP 3:46:01; 5, Nikolay Matyukhin RUS 3:46:37; 6, Nathan Deakes AUS 3:47:29; 7, Miguel Rodríguez MEX 3:48:12; 8, Roman Magdziarczyk POL 3:48:17.

WOMEN'S EVENTS
100 Metres

Marion Jones (24) began her much publicised quest for five golds with a breathtaking display. To win her first Olympic title by nearly four metres was a staggering achievement. Even Flo-Jo in Seoul won by "only" 3m. It was the widest ever margin of victory at 100m for men or women;

Marjorie Jackson, one of the Australian legends who played such a moving part in the Sydney opening ceremony, won by 0.38 in 1952 (11.67) but at today's higher speeds Jones' margin of 0.37 represents more track space. Her 10.75, into a slight wind, was the year's fastest. She ran her lap of honour holding the flag of Belize (her mother's home country) as well as the Stars and Stripes. Tayna Lawrence, who edged out her much more celebrated fellow Jamaican, Merlene Ottey (40), for the bronze by 1/100th, was fastest away at 0.163 followed by Ottey 0.179 and Jones 0.189. Ekaterini Thánou, penalised for a false start, showed 0.206 but came through for silver. Three Bahamians reached the final, underlining their golden chance in the relay.

(-0.4) 1, Marion Jones USA 10.75; 2, Ekaterini Thánou GRE 11.12 (10.99qf); 3, Tayna Lawrence JAM 11.18 (11.11qf); 4, Merlene Ottey JAM 11.19 (11.08qf); 5, Zhanna Pintusevich (now Block) UKR 11.20 (11.08qf); 6, Chandra Sturrup BAH 11.21; 7, Savatheda Fynes BAH 11.22 (11.10qf); 8, Debbie Ferguson BAH 11.29 (11.10ht). Note: Chryste Gaines USA 5s2 11.23 (11.06ht), Christine Arron FRA 7s1 11.42, Torri Edwards USA 5q1 11.32.

200 Metres

Remaining remarkably focused and upbeat, at least in public, while the furore over her then husband C J Hunter's drugs positives raged all week, Marion Jones posted another world leading mark for the year of 21.84 for gold no 2, her winning margin this time being a good four metres and she gave the impression that there was something in reserve as she became the seventh woman, but first since Flo-Jo in 1988, to complete the Olympic 100/200m double. Not counting her breakdown in the 1999 World Championships in Seville, Jones had not lost a 200m race since May 1995. Finishing an ecstatic second was Pauline Davis-Thompson (34), competing in her fifth Olympics and winning her first medal after being a 100/200m semi-finalist in 1984, 1988 and 1992 and placing fourth over 400m in Atlanta. She ran a personal best of 22.27 to edge Susanthika Jayasinghe, who set a Sri Lankan record. The medals were presented, aptly enough, by the Marion Jones of her day – the legendary Irena Szewinska.

(0.7) 1, Marion Jones USA 21.84; 2, Pauline

Davis-Thompson BAH 22.27; 3, Susanthika Jayasinghe SRI 22.28; 4, Bev McDonald JAM 22.35; 5, Debbie Ferguson BAH 22.37; 6, Melinda Gainsford-Taylor AUS 22.42; 7, Cathy Freeman AUS 22.53; 8, Zhanna Pintusevich (now Block) UKR 22.66. Note: Torri Edwards USA 6s2 23.06, Muriel Hurtis FRA 7s2 23.13.

400 Metres

The dramatic departure from Sydney of reigning champion Marie-José Pérec, initially claiming she had feared for her safety but later admitting she had run away from the prospect of taking on Cathy Freeman, robbed the Games of what might have been one of the great Olympic duels ... but the vast majority of the 112,524 fans who packed the stadium for the final could not have cared less. It was unthinkable that Freeman (27), an icon of modern Australia who has become a symbol of reconciliation between the white community and the indigenous population, could lose this race and – despite the unbearable pressure of all the public expectation – she rose to the occasion despite having to work hard to overcome her rivals.

Lorraine Graham (lane 4) ran hard to enter the finishing straight narrowly ahead of Freeman (6) and Katharine Merry (3), and although the local heroine powered past for victory in 49.11, the world's fastest for four years, the Jamaican finished second four metres back in a personal best of 49.58. Merry and fast finishing Donna Fraser (lane 2) became (after Kathy Cook in 1984) the second and third Britons ever to crack 50 sec, Fraser improving at the Games from 50.85 to 50.77 in round 2, 50.21 in her semi and 49.79 in the final. For the first time since 1964 (with the obvious exception of 1980) no American made the final; they didn't even have a semi-finalist ... and yet the US would go on to win the 4x400 relay!

1, Cathy Freeman AUS 49.11; 2, Lorraine Graham (now Fenton) JAM 49.58; 3, Katharine Merry GBR 49.72; 4, Donna Fraser GBR 49.79; 5, Ana Guevara MEX 49.96; 6, Heide Seyerling RSA 50.05; 7, Falilat Ogunkoya NGR 50.12; 8, Olga Kotlyarova RUS 51.04. Note: Amy Mbacké Thiam SEN 7s2 51.60.

800 Metres

It was an astonishing sight: Kelly Holmes, so short of training after her latest round of injuries that making the British Olympic team had for most of the year seemed a forlorn hope and with a season's best pre-Sydney of 2:00.35, was well clear of the field entering the finishing straight in the Olympic final. It was the stuff of dreams. Okay, Maria Mutola and Stephanie Graf did steam past to take gold and silver but Holmes could not have been more delighted with her bronze. Helena Fuchsová set a tremendous pace, reaching 400m in 55.04 with the main contenders well back. Holmes took the field by surprise with an early strike and led until 50m out, finishing in a remarkable 1:56.80. Mutola, still only 27 yet contesting her fourth Olympics, became the first athlete from Mozambique to win an Olympic title, the time of 1:56.15 being the world's best for the year, while Graf set an Austrian record.

1, Maria Mutola MOZ 1:56.15; 2, Stephanie Graf AUT 1:56.64; 3, Kelly Holmes GBR 1:56.80; 4, Brigita Langerholc SLO 1:58.51; 5, Helena Fuchsová CZE 1:58.56; 6, Zulia Calatayud CUB 1:58.66; 7, Hazel Clark USA 1:58.75; 8, Hasna Benhassi MAR 1:59.27.

1500 Metres

For all but the winner this event proved to be full of anguish. Regina Jacobs never even got to the Games due to a viral infection, defending champion Svetlana Masterkova hobbled off the track in her heat, while the final – described by Kelly Holmes as "the dirtiest 1500 I've ever been in" – was marred when Hayley Tullett fell at 800m, Gabriela Szabo (then in last place) having to hurdle her, losing valuable ground.

The race started slowly with Marla Runyan, the first near-blind athlete to reach an Olympic final, passing 400m in 70.56, but then Suzy Favor-Hamilton, the world's fastest in 2000 at 3:57.40, pushed on and was ahead at 800m in 2:15.93. Carla Sacramento took over at the bell and led at 1200m (3:17.85). Favor-Hamilton then went ahead with just over 200m to go, only for Bouria Mérah-Benida (29), running in her first major final, to dash in front early in the finishing straight and open up a significant lead. The American, trying to respond but suffering from severe dehydration (the effects of anti-inflammatory pills), hit the kerb and later her legs buckled while she was in sixth place, causing her to fall. The most dangerous challenge to Mérah-Benida came from

Szabo (who was some 30m down at one point and sixth with 40m to go, finishing out in lane 4), but the Algerian scraped home ahead of Szekely with the last lap taking 63.0.

1, Nouria Mérah-Benida ALG 4:05.10; 2, Violeta Szekely ROM 4:05.15; 3, Gabriela Szabo ROM 4:05.27; 4, Kutre Dulecha ETH 4:05.33; 5, Lidia Chojecka POL 4:06.42; 6, Anna Jakubczak POL 4:06.49; 7, Kelly Holmes GBR 4:08.02; 8, Marla Runyan USA 4:08.30; ... 11, Hayley Tullett GBR 4:22.29; 12, Suzy Favor-Hamilton USA 4:23.05. Note: Süreyya Ayhan TUR 8s2 4:09.42.

5000 Metres

Gabriela Szabo's renowned kick had reaped a golden reward in the 5000m five days before the 1500m final. Leah Malot, who had sensationally beaten her in Berlin, never did make the Kenyan team but unexpectedly Gete Wami decided to double and with Sonia O'Sullivan also in the field this looked as though it would develop into a mighty burn-up on the last lap. Szabo cheekily held the early lead for no other reason than to slow the pace and succeeded as the first kilometre took 3:03.84. Wami made it more respectable with a second kilometre of 2:53.49 (5:57.33), during which O'Sullivan fell 20m behind, but a 3:01.00 (8:58.33) enabled her to catch up. At around 3700m Wami signalled for her colleague, the junior Werknesh Kidane, to move ahead and at 4k (11:53.60; 2:55.27 kilometre) it was an Ethiopian 1-2-3 (Kidane, Worku, Wami) ahead of Szabo and O'Sullivan. Szabo showed ahead a lap later and, after resisting a challenge from Kazakhstan-born Irina Mikitenko (whose father Leonid ran for the USSR in the 1968 Olympics) along the final back straight, she held off O'Sullivan in a fantastic sprint for the line. With a lap of 60.01 (28.6 last 200m) and final kilometre of 2:47.19, Szabo (24) smashed the Olympic record with 14:40.79 with O'Sullivan setting a national record while becoming Ireland's first ever female Olympic medallist. Wami and Worku battled for bronze, Ethiopia's first medal by a woman at a distance below 10,000m.

1, Gabriela Szabo ROM 14:40.79; 2, Sonia O'Sullivan IRL 14:41.02; 3, Gete Wami ETH 14:42.23; 4, Ayelech Worku ETH 14:42.67; 5, Irina Mikitenko GER 14:43.59; 6, Lydia Cheromei KEN 14:47.35; 7, Werknesh Kidane ETH 14:47.40; 8,

Olga Yegorova RUS 14:50.31; ... 12, Jo Pavey GBR 14:58.27; 13, Tatyana Tomashova RUS 15:01.28. Note: Marta Domínguez ESP 10h2 15:45.07.

10,000 Metres

Long after many a medallist from Sydney is forgotten, the vision of Paula Radcliffe's brave front running will remain. Lacking the finishing powers of her main rivals her tactic was to make the pace so fast that the opposition fell back exhausted before the last lap was reached. In the previous year's World Championships she burned off everyone except Gete Wami, clocking a Commonwealth record of 30:27.13. This time she ran even faster with 30:26.97, a time only four women had ever bettered prior to Sydney ... and yet came fourth.

By 3000m (9:01.99) even Sonia O'Sullivan – destined to smash the Irish record – had been dropped, but four formidable runners in Gete Wami, 1992 champion Derartu Tulu, defending champion Fernanda Ribeiro and Tegla Loroupe (seemingly unscathed after a distressing marathon experience) clung to the tall tortured-looking Briton through halfway in a searing 15:05.70 and on to 7k in 21:17.05. Just before 7800m the Ethiopians went ahead in order to slow it down (8k Wami 24:21.27), But before long Radcliffe was in charge again to 9k in 27:29.34. Loroupe was dropped on the penultimate lap and the heroic Radcliffe went from first to fourth as her three remaining opponents accelerated approaching the bell. Tulu (28) produced a stunning 60.26 finale, while Wami narrowly prevailed over Ribeiro. Tulu's Olympic and African record of 30:17.49 shattered her previous best of 30:56.4 and there were best ever times for places 3-7 and 10-20.

1, Derartu Tulu ETH 30:17.49; 2, Gete Wami ETH 30:22.48; 3, Fernanda Ribeiro POR 30:22.88; 4, Paula Radcliffe GBR 30:26.97; 5, Tegla Loroupe KEN 30:37.26; 6, Sonia O'Sullivan IRL 30:53.37; 7, Li Ji CHN 31:06.94; 8, Elana Meyer RSA 31:14.70; ... 12, Berhane Adere ETH 31:40.52. Note: Galina Bogomolova RUS 16h2 34:06.21, Deena Drossin USA 18h2 34:40.86.

Marathon

When Naoko Takahashi won the 1998 Asian Games title in Bangkok in hot and humid weather in 2:21:47, a world best for a women-only race, the sceptics raised doubts as to the authen-ticity of that performance. Injury ruled her out of the 1999 World Championships but she con-firmed her outstanding talent by winning in Nagoya earlier in 2000 in 2:22:19 with a 69:39 second half. In Sydney she showed the world just how good she is by becoming the first Japanese-born winner of an Olympic marathon title – a feat that will practically deify her in a marathon-crazy country. You have to go back to the triple jump of 1936 to find the last Japanese gold medallist. The temperature for the race was rea-sonable but the high humidity and the severity of the course did not make for fast times, and yet the first three broke Joan Benoit's Olympic record of 2:24:52.

Takahashi (28), with her minimal arm action, led at halfway in 71:45 with only Ari Ichihashi (who would finish 15th) and Lidia Simon for company. At 30k Ichihashi was 47 sec behind Simon and Takahashi (1:41:39). By 35k Joyce Chepchumba was a clear third and at 40k Takahashi (2:15:19) held a 28 sec lead over Simon, although the Romanian narrowed that to eight seconds by the finish. Defending champion Fatuma Roba placed 9th (2:27:38) while world record holder Tegla Loroupe, who had been ill before the race, finished 13th (2:29:45) and was put on a drip after the race. Fourteen women under 2:30 was a record for any marathon as was 26 under 2:35.

1, Naoko Takahashi JPN 2:23:14; 2, Lidia Simon ROM 2:23:22; 3, Joyce Chepchumba KEN 2:24:45; 4, Esther Wanjiru KEN 2:26:17; 5, Madina Biktagirova RUS 2:26:33; 6, Elfenesh Alemu ETH 2:26:54; 7, Eri Yamaguchi JPN 2:27:03; 8, Ham Bong-sil PRK 2:27:07.

100 Metres Hurdles

Next to Marion Jones, 33 year-old Gail Devers was just about the hottest favourite in the women's events. She had run 12.33, 12.39 and 12.47 that summer while no one else had clocked faster than 12.52 and she was really hun-gry for the title which had so tantalisingly eluded her in 1992. Despite two 100m titles and a relay gold she had never collected any Olympic medal as a hurdler. That looked about to change after running a 12.62 heat – the fastest time of the entire competition – but in her semi she pulled up beyond the fourth hurdle, citing a hamstring

problem.

Suddenly a group of athletes previously resigned to fighting for silver could dream of being crowned Olympic champion, and it was Asian record holder Olga Shishigina, making her Olympic debut at 31 (she was serving a drugs ban at the time of the 1996 Games), who grabbed the opportunity. Off to a sluggish start (reaction time 0.237) she ran a brilliant second half to pip Glory Alozie in 12.65 and give Kazakhstan its first ever Olympic athletics victo-ry, and indeed the first medal of any colour.

(0.0) 1, Olga Shishigina KAZ 12.65; 2, Glory Alozie NGR 12.68; 3, Melissa Morrison USA 12.76; 4, Delloreen Ennis-London JAM 12.80; 5, Aliuska López CUB 12.83; 6, Nicole Ramalalanirina FRA 12.91; 7, Linda Ferga FRA 13.11; 8, Brigitte Foster JAM 13.49 (12.70sf). Note: Gail Devers USA dnf s1 (12.62ht), Perdita Felicien CAN 6h4 13.21.

400 Metres Hurdles

Although it's not unprecedented for an athlete to strike Olympic gold in their first year. Irina Privalova, a world record holder for the indoor 60m, made history by winning at 400m hurdles! She made a sensational debut two months before the Games with 54.49 and since then had taken the Russian title in 54.21 and won in Monaco (54.06) and Moscow (54.52). In Sydney she ran with the assurance of a veteran, lower-ing her best to 54.02 when winning her semi and, in the fifth 400m hurdles final of her life, a full second faster in the final. Hurdling confidently off either leg (although jumping higher than neces-sary), and with the luxury of the flat speed which enabled her to run a 48.47 relay leg in 1993, she finished four metres ahead of defending champi-on Deon Hemmings, with former world cham-pion Nezha Bidouane and current world cham-pion Daimi Pernía a further one and two metres behind. No less an authority than Ed Moses stat-ed she could go under 52 sec. At 31 she became the oldest, male or female, to win an Olympic 400m hurdles title.

1, Irina Privalova RUS 53.02; 2, Deon Hemmings JAM 53.45; 3, Nezha Bidouane MAR 53.57; 4, Daimi Pernia CUB 53.68; 5, Tatyana Tereshchuk UKR 53.98; 6, Ionela Tirlea ROM 54.35; 7, Gudrun Arnardóttir ISL 54.63; 8, Natasha Danvers GBR 55.00. Note: Sandra

Glover USA 6s2 54.98, Jana Pittman AUS 3h3 56.76.

4x100 Metres Relay

It was just as well that Marion Jones' five golds dream had already been shattered, for the US team – without Inger Miller or Gail Devers – was no match for the Caribbean islands. Jones pulled well clear of Christine Arron (France) on the anchor, but that was for the bronze. Up front the Bahamas, fielding the same personnel and running order as when they won the 1999 world title in 41.92 (and three of the Atlanta silver medal team), this time whizzed the stick around in 41.95 – a gold medal for a nation of 275,000 and for Pauline Davis-Thompson in her fifth Olympics. Jamaica took second place, anchored by Merlene Ottey who at 40 became the oldest women's medallist in Olympic history. She also became the most prolific female medal-list ever with a total of eight spread over an astonishing 20-year period … three silvers and five bronzes. Eldece Clarke-Lewis also won a gold as she ran for the Bahamas in the heats and semis.

1, Bahamas (Savatheda Fynes, Chandra Sturrup, Pauline Davis-Thompson, Debbie Ferguson) 41.95; 2, Jamaica (Tayna Lawrence, Veronica Campbell, Bev McDonald, Merlene Ottey) 42.12; 3, USA (Chryste Gaines, Torri Edwards, Nanceen Perry, Marion Jones) 42.20; 4, France 42.42; 5, Russia 43.02; 6, Germany 43.11; 7, Nigeria 44.05; 8, China 44.87.

4x400 Metres Relay

Marion Jones completed her marathon stint in style, bringing her tally to three golds and two bronzes. That total of five medals is the most ever amassed by a woman at one Games but she continued to believe that the target of five golds had been a feasible one. "I still feel in my heart that I could have won the long jump and we had a chance in the 4x100. Still I guess at the end of the day it has been a productive Olympics." She certainly made all the difference to the US 4x400m squad. After legs of 51.1 by Jearl Miles-Clark and 51.4 by Monique Hennagan she took over for the third leg about level with Jamaica's Deon Hemmings but hand-ed over some 15m clear after completing her lap in 49.40. That gave LaTasha Colander-Richardson

a good safety margin as Lorraine Graham (49.6), Irina Privalova (49.6), Falilat Ogunkoya (49.7) and Cathy Freeman (49.4) set off in pursuit, and she won by five metres with a 50.68 leg. There were swift legs also for the British team by Donna Fraser (50.3) and Katharine Merry (49.6). Andrea Anderson ran in the heats for the USA and was also awarded a gold medal.

1, USA 3:22.62 (Jearl Miles-Clark 51.1, Monique Hennagan 51.4, Marion Jones 49.40, LaTasha Colander-Richardson 50.68); 2, Jamaica 3:23.25 (Sandie Richards 51.0, Catherine Scott 51.5, Deon Hemmings 51.2, Lorraine Graham 49.6); 3, Russia 3:23.46 (Yuliya Sotnikova 52.3, Svetlana Goncharenko 51.7, Olga Kotlyarova 49.8, Irina Privalova 49.6); 4, Nigeria 3:23.80 (3:22.99ht); 5, Australia 3:23.81; 6, Gt Britain 3:25.67; 7, Czech Republic 3:29.17; 8, Cuba 3:29.47.

High Jump

A major shock at the previous year's World Championships was the elimination in the quali-fying round of Hestrie Cloete, who had not long before cleared a world leading 2.04. This time she did herself justice, fighting all the way before losing on countback to 30 year-old Olympic debutante Yelena Yelesina, twice a world silver medallist whose lifetime best of 2.02 dated back to 1990, topping the world list that year. The medals were determined from 1.99. First Cloete (who had incurred one costly failure at 1.96) and then Yelesina made it first time, followed at the second attempt by Kajsa Bergqvist and the astonishing Oana Pantelimon who had equalled her personal best of 1.94 to qualify for the final and had raised it first to 1.96 and now 1.99 for a share of the bronze medal. After seeing Cloete and Yelesina clear 2.01 second time round, Bergqvist saved up her final two attempts at the next bar setting of 2.03 … and came closer than anyone else to succeeding.

1, Yelena Yelesina RUS 2.01; 2, Hestrie Cloete RSA 2.01; 3=, Kajsa Bergqvist SWE & Oana Pantelimon ROM 1.99; 5, Inga Babakova UKR 1.96; 6, Svetlana Zalevskaya KAZ 1.96; 7, Viktoriya Palamar UKR 1.96; 8, Amewu Mensah GER 1.93. Note: Blanka Vlasic CRO dnq (17) 1.92, Marina Kuptsova RUS dnq (26=) 1.85, Amy Acuff USA dnq (31) 1.80.

Pole Vault

Stacy Dragila was at this stage of her career turning out to be the Sergey Bubka of women's pole vaulting. Not only did she hold the world record but she had now won all three inaugural global titles: World Indoors in 1997, World in 1999 and Olympics in 2000. Most of her main opponents fell by the wayside long before the climax; all three Russians no-heighted in the qualifying competition and European champion Anzhela Balakhonova did the same in the final. It was left to a former Russian turned Australian, Tatiana Grigorieva, to test Dragila and thrill the home fans. However, the leader for a long time was Vala Flosadóttir, who had a clean sheet up to and including 4.50. Former world record holder Daniela Bártová, with last ditch clearances at 4.35 and 4.45, also made 4.50 first time, whereas Grigorieva needed two tries and Dragila her full quota. Flosadóttir (who became the first Icelandic woman to win an Olympic medal) and Bártová didn't get any higher but Grigorieva literally leapt into the lead by clearing a personal best 4.55 first time and Dragila followed at the second. At 4.60, Dragila (29) finally got her act together, flying clear at the first attempt while still chewing gum. Grigorieva failed and carried her two remaining attempts to a world record 4.65 but neither she nor Dragila succeeded.

1, Stacy Dragila USA 4.60; 2, Tatiana Grigorieva AUS 4.55; 3, Vala Flosadóttir ISL 4.50; 4, Daniela Bártová CZE 4.50; 5, Nicole Humbert GER 4.45; 6, Yvonne Buschbaum GER 4.40; 7, Monika Pyrek POL 4.40; 8, Marie Rasmussen DEN 4.35. Note: Yelena Isinbayeva RUS, Svetlana Feofanova RUS & Yelena Belyakova RUS dnq (no height).

Long Jump

Marion Jones' bid for five golds came to an end in her third event. She had her chances, with at least three of her four fouls being a potential winning jump, but her best valid mark of 6.92 gave her third place. "I don't regret it at all," she said. "I had a shot at it and it didn't pan out." Fiona May jumped the same distance but took her second Olympic silver by virtue of a superior second best: 6.82 to 6.68. The gold went to an athlete who has enjoyed an even more remarkable and diverse career than Jones. Even before Sydney, Heike Drechsler had done it all ... former holder of world records at 200m and long jump, still holder of the world indoor long jump record, Olympic champion (1992), twice world champion (the first time in 1983, aged 18), reigning European champion, one of the world's great heptathletes as well as sprinters and with a 50.0 400m relay leg to her credit. When she had to miss the 1999 World Championships through injury one might have assumed her chance of one last global title had passed, but in Sydney she was in exuberant form. Heading the qualifiers at 6.84, she jumped 6.99 at the start of round 3 – adding 4cm to her world masters record and making her at 35 by far the oldest winner of this Olympic gold. The 17-year span separating her first and latest global title is the widest in the history of athletics, surpassing Sergey Bubka's 14 years and Carl Lewis's 13 years.

1, Heike Drechsler GER 6.99; 2, Fiona May ITA 6.92; 3, Marion Jones USA 6.92; 4, Tatyana Kotova RUS 6.83; 5, Olga Rublyova RUS 6.79; 6, Susen Tiedtke GER 6.74; 7, Jackie Edwards BAH 6.59; 8, Tünde Vaszi HUN 6.59.

Triple Jump

For several athletes it wasn't the first time they had competed in Sydney for a global title as the World Junior Championships were staged there in 1996. The only athlete to win on both occasions was Tereza Marinova, who set a world junior record of 14.62 the first time and a Bulgarian record of 15.20 on her return visit. That jump, the equal fourth longest of all time, came in the first round and had a devastating effect on most of the opposition but also came before the heavy rain which influenced the rest of the competition. Only two of her rivals managed anything in excess of 14.30. However, Yelena Govorova responded later in round 1 with a personal best of 14.96, which held up for second place until the pre-event favourite Tatyana Lebedeva leapt 15.00 in round 5. An injured Inessa Kravets did not defend her title. Marinova (23) is the daughter of former Bulgarian 800m record holder Monche Marinov (1:47.7 in 1974) and her brother Tsvetomir was third in the 1995 European Junior 400m in 46.66. Competing outdoors for the first time in 2000, Ashia Hansen jumped 14.29 after two fouls to qualify but two more no-jumps in the final led to her taking off much too far behind the board with her third 'safety' jump.

1, Tereza Marinova BUL 15.20; 2, Tatyana Lebedeva RUS 15.00; 3, Yelena Govorova UKR 14.96; 4, Yamilé Aldama CUB 14.30; 5, Baya Rahouli ALG 14.17; 6, Cristina Nicolau ROM 14.17; 7, Olga Vasdéki GRE 14.15; 8, Oxana Rogova RUS 13.97; ... 10, Francoise Mbango CMR 13.53; 11, Ashia Hansen GBR 13.44.

Shot

The first round determined the medal winners. Yanina Korolchik led with 19.43 to 19.38 by 1996 champion Astrid Kumbernuss and 19.16 by Larisa Peleshenko, who led the world year list with her startling 21.46. Peleshenko moved ahead with a second round 19.92 and kept up the pressure with 19.79 in the third. The 1992 champion Svetlana Krivelyova pressed Kumbernuss for the bronze with 19.37 in the fifth round but Peleshenko's hold on the event looked secure as Korolchik had nothing better than 19.11 to show between rounds 2 and 5. In the final round Krivelyova reached 19.36 followed by 19.62 from Kumbernuss to lift her into second place ... for a minute or two. Then came Korolchik, the 23 year-old Belarussian who had placed third in the 1998 European and fourth in the 1999 World Championships. Inspiration came from somewhere as she despatched the shot a lifetime best of 20.56. A thunderstruck Peleshenko had her chance to counterpunch but her effort went only 19.60.

1, Yanina Korolchik BLR 20.56; 2, Larisa Peleshenko RUS 19.92; 3, Astrid Kumbernuss GER 19.62; 4, Svetlana Krivelyova RUS 19.37; 5, Krystyna Zabawska POL 19.18; 6, Yumileidi Cumbá CUB 18.70; 7, Kalliópi Ouzoúni GRE 18.63; 8, Nadine Kleinert-Schmitt GER 18.49.

Discus

With 2000 world leader Nicoleta Grasu failing to qualify after two fouls and world champion Franka Dietzsch scraping through as the 12th and last qualifier there were shocks even before the final. In the event Ellina Zvereva was in unbeatable form, all four of her valid throws exceeding anything thrown by the opposition. She opened with 67.00, followed by 65.71 from Anastasia Kelesídou which remained the silver medal throw throughout and 65.00 by Natalya Sadova. Zvereva improved to 68.40 in the third

round, while her Belarus team-mate Irina Yatchenko crept past Sadova to snatch bronze with 65.20 in round 5; her husband, Igor Astapkovich, had won a bronze in the hammer three days earlier. Zvereva, only weeks short of her 40th birthday, thus became the oldest ever woman to lift an Olympic title, the previous record being held by fellow discus thrower Lia Manoliu, who was 36 when she won in 1968. World champion in 1995, Zvereva was fifth in the 1988 Olympics, third in 1996 – she missed 1992 due to a drugs suspension.

1, Ellina Zvereva BUL 68.40; 2, Anastasia Kelesídou GRE 65.71; 3, Irina Yatchenko BLR 65.20; 4, Natalya Sadova RUS 65.00; 5, Stiliani Tsikoúna GRE 64.08; 6, Franka Dietzsch GER 63.18; 7, Ilke Wyludda GER 62.97; 8, Lisa-Marie Vizaniari AUS 62.57; 9, Ekaterini Vóggoli GRE 61.57.

Hammer

It was drama all the way. Mihaela Melinte, the world record holder and co-favourite with Olga Kuzenkova for this inaugural title, was led away from the arena just prior to her pool of the hammer qualifying starting, having just been informed that she had failed a drugs test. The qualifying contest also saw the end of Manuela Montebrun, no. 3 on the world list for 2000 with 71.18 but able to throw only a mere 57.77. That left Kuzenkova, world leader at 75.68, seemingly in a class of her own. Next best on form was 17 year-old Skolimowska (70.62), who cut loose in the third round with a stunning world junior record of 71.16. That was still a routine distance for Kuzenkova, who had qualified with 70.60, but after throwing 69.77 in round 4 she fouled her remaining two efforts. Skolimowska, who has inherited her strength from her father, a world junior weightlifting champion in 1976, became the youngest Olympic athletics champion since Ulrike Meyfarth won the 1972 high jump title at 16.

1, Kamila Skolimowska POL 71.16; 2, Olga Kuzenkova RUS 69.77 (70.60q); 3, Kirsten Münchow GER 69.28; 4, Yipsi Moreno CUB 68.33; 5, Debbie Sosimenko AUS 67.95; 6, Lyudmila Gubkina BLR 67.08; 7, Dawn Ellerbe USA 66.80; 8, Amy Palmer USA 66.15. Note: Manuela Montebrun FRA dnq (24) 57.77.

Javelin

World junior champion Osleidys Menéndez, who led the qualifying round with 67.34, opened with 66.03 but her lead lasted only a minute or two as Trine Hattestad's response was a mighty 68.91, an Olympic record with the new implement and a distance which only the 34 year-old Norwegian herself had surpassed with that model. Although the Cuban improved a little to 66.18 with her final throw the main challenge came from the Albanian-born world champion Miréla Tzelili, who threw a Greek record of 67.51 in round 3 and matched that with her last throw. Hattestad (née Solberg), competing in her fifth Olympics (5th 1984, non-qualifier 1988, 5th 1992, 3rd 1996), became the first Norwegian woman ever to win an Olympic athletics title.

1, Trine Hattestad NOR 68.91; 2, Miréla Tzelili (now Manjani) GRE 67.51; 3, Osleidys Menéndez CUB 66.18 (67.34q); 4, Steffi Nerius GER 64.84; 5, Sonia Bisset CUB 63.26; 6, Xiomara Rivero CUB 62.92; 7, Tatyana Shikolenko RUS 62.91; 8, Nikola Tomecková CZE 62.10; 9, Mikaela Ingberg FIN 58.56.

Heptathlon

With all three having been beset by injuries this year, no one quite knew what to expect from world champion Eunice Barber, defending champion Ghada Shouaa and World Championships silver medallist Denise Lewis. Shouaa pulled up almost immediately in the hurdles, but Barber looked to be in fine shape as she flew to a 12.97 win and Lewis performed well for 13.23. Barber kept up the pressure with the equal highest jump of 1.84 but Lewis made an error by passing 1.78 before failing at 1.81 and dropped to eighth place after two events, 152pts behind Barber. Lewis made up with fine shot putting (over 4m better than Barber!) and the positions were transformed: Atlanta silver medallist Natalya Sazanovich led by 30 points from Lewis. For Barber, down to eighth, it was the beginning of the end; she was nearly a second behind her best at 200m and the overnight placings were: 1, Sazanovich 3903; 2, Natalya Roshchupkina 3872; 3, Lewis 3852.

Barber took only one long jump, a mediocre 5.93, before retiring injured. Lewis, too, was having problems with her left Achilles tendon but stayed in the hunt with a 6.48 leap.

Disaster for Roshchupkina; after two fouls she mustered only 5.47 and dropped from second to eighth. After five events: Sazanovich 4910, Lewis 4853, Yelena Prokhorova 4807.

As so often, the javelin came to Lewis's rescue. She threw 50.19 to take the lead with 5717 ahead of Sazanovich 5654 and Prokhorova 5571. All would depend on Lewis staying close enough to Sazanovich in the 800m to preserve her lead and hope that Prokhorova would not repeat the fabulous 2:04.27 she ran when winning the Russian title (6765) earlier in the year. Prokhorova went for it with a first lap of 62.38 but could not sustain the pace this time and finished in 2:10.32, good for the silver, but Lewis (28) did enough to win by 53 points with a total of 6584. "It's not a great score," she admitted. "It was simply about winning."

1, Denise Lewis GBR 6584 (13.23, 1.75, 15.55, 24.34, 6.48, 50.19, 2:16.83); 2, Yelena Prokhorova RUS 6531 (13.63, 1.81, 13.21, 23.72, 6.59, 45.05, 2:10.32); 3, Natalya Sazanovich BLR 6527 (13.45, 1.84, 14.79, 24.12, 6.50, 43.97, 2:16.41); 4, Urszula Wlodarczyk POL 6470; 5, Sabine Braun GER 6355; 6, Natalya Roshchupkina RUS 6237; 7, Karin Ertl GER 6209; 8, Tiia Hautala FIN 6173; Eunice Barber FRA & Ghada Shouaa SYR dnf.

20 Kilometres Walk

Three athletes were disqualified while in the lead: world champion Liu Hongyu (17th kilometre), Atlanta 10k silver medallist Elisabetta Perrone (18th kilometre), and – most galling of all – Australia's own Jane Saville just a few strides outside the Olympic stadium with over 100,000 inside bursting to greet her. Asked later if there was anything she needed, Saville replied only half jokingly "a gun to shoot myself." To almost complete silence, it was Wang Liping (24), ranked no. 10 on times that year among those competing (1:28:33), who entered the stadium for victory in 1:29:05. She had received one warning, for a bent knee.

1, Wang Liping CHN 1:29:05; 2, Kjersti Plätzer NOR 1:29:33; 3, María Vasco ESP 1:30:23; 4, Erica Alfridi ITA 1:31:25; 5, Guadalupe Sánchez MEX 1:31:33; 6, Norica Cimpean ROM 1:31:50; 7, Kerry Saxby-Junna AUS 1:32:02; 8, Tatyana Gudkova RUS 1:32:35 ... 10, Gillian O'Sullivan IRL 1:33:10.

FIVE MEDALS IN ONE GAMES!

SHE MIGHT never match Flo-Jo's controversial world record time of 10.49 for 100m but Marion Jones has no rival in female sprinting history when it comes to high level consistency.

Flo-Jo bettered 10.83 without wind assistance just four times during her career, whereas Jones has 21 such marks ... and there could well be many more to come if she can regain her old form after giving birth to a baby in June 2003. She has raced 200m far less often but has still amassed six times faster than 21.85 (equalling Merlene Ottey's "record"), while Flo-Jo's total was four.

And how's this for a competitive streak? Between 1997 and 2002 she lost just one of 60 finals at 100m, to Zhanna Pintusevich-Block in the 2001 World Championships (10.82-10.85), and up to that race had a winning sequence of 42 100m finals spread over four years. The figures for 200m are if anything even more impressive. She pulled up with back spasms in her semi-final at the 1999 World Championships but she has not actually lost a final at the distance since 1995! At both events she was voted no 1 in the Athletics International World Merit Rankings for six successive years, 1997 to 2002.

But that's not the end of her talents. She is also a brilliant if unpredictable and technically unsophisticated long jumper, and if she ever concentrated on the 400m for a year even Marita Koch's world record of 47.60 would be endangered.

Born in Los Angeles on October 12 1975, her mother a native of Belize (Marion holds dual citizenship), she was an infant prodigy when it came to athletics. She set world age bests of 11.17 for 100m and 22.76 for 200m at 15, and 11.14/22.58 at 16. She qualified for the US Olympic 4x100m relay squad in 1992, but declined as she felt she was too young. After that season she virtually disappeared from the track scene due to a combination of concentrating on college basketball and a series of injuries, and for a time it looked as though she had joined the ranks of precocious athletes who never went on to fulfil their potential.

That appeared to be confirmed in 1995 when, at age 19, she had best times of 11.68 and 23.96w ... slower than she was running at 14. In 1996, after breaking her foot, she didn't compete at all.

However, the desire to succeed had never deserted her and in 1997 she made a stunning comeback. She won the world 100m title, clocked the year's fastest times both in that event (10.76) and 200m (21.76), and even beat the legendary Jackie Joyner-Kersee for the US long jump title with a leap of 6.93.

Her versatility was even more apparent in 1998. In addition to becoming the second fastest of all-time at 100m and 200m with high altitude times of 10.65 and 21.62 (that thin air advantage being largely cancelled out by the cold weather in Johannesburg), she ran 6.95 for equal second place on the indoor 60m all-time list, ran 50.36 in her first 400m race for six years and long jumped 7.31, the best in the world for four years. In the process she became the highest paid female athlete up to that time, netting over three quarters of a million dollars of prize money from the IAAF's Golden League, Grand Prix and World Cup alone. Soon after the season ended she married C J Hunter, destined to become world shot put champion the following year.

Injury restricted Jones to just the 100m title and long jump bronze medal at those 1999 World Championships, but she was in fine fettle physically leading up to the Sydney Olympics, although her mental preparation must have been affected by her husband's drugs ban. Earlier in the season she had reduced her 400m personal best to 49.59, clinching selection for the 4x400m relay and sustaining her dream of winning an unprecedented five gold medals at a single Olympics. In reality she had to settle for three, plus two bronze ... itself a record haul.

Since then the lanky Miss Jones has remained the biggest name in sprinting, despite the 100m loss to Pintusevich-Block in the 2001 World Championships (she won the 200m). Although she has not run quicker than 10.84 or 22.11 since 2000, or long jumped at all, she is as ambitious as ever. Having divorced Hunter, she is now the partner of world 100m record holder Tim Montgomery and following maternity leave in 2003 she has her sights on achieving even more in Athens than she did in Sydney.

FOR DECADES it was accepted that the greatest distance runner of all time was Emil Zátopek, the only other plausible candidate being his predecessor Paavo Nurmi. However, during the past decade the glittering achievements, year after year, of Haile Gebrselassie have brought him to the point where even Zátopek's most fervent fans have to concede that the diminutive Ethiopian with the biggest smile in athletics might have done enough to warrant the accolade.

No one is ever likely to emulate Zátopek's feat of winning the 5000m, 10,000m and marathon at the same Games, or win an Olympic 10,000m title by some 300m, or run up a string of 38 consecutive victories at 10,000m. But Gebrselassie can point to a host of astonishing performances also.

In 1994 he became the first Ethiopian track runner to break a world record, and to date has set 17 global records or bests, indoors and out, including the existing marks of 5000m in 12:39.36 and 10,000m in 26:22.75 in 1998. He went undefeated at 10,000m throughout seven seasons (1994-2000 inclusive), during which time he won four world titles plus the Olympic crowns of 1996 and 2000. At 5000m outdoors he built up a four-year unbeaten sequence. As for versatility, his range is awesome. This is a man who has run 1:46 for 800m in training, and at the other end of the scale 2:06:35 in his first serious marathon. In between he won the world indoor 1500m title in his first and only international championship at the distance and set world indoor records at 2000m and 3000m.

Born at Arssi on April 18 1973, and inspired as a young boy by the 1980 Olympic double of Miruts Yifter, he was only 15 when in 1989 he completed a marathon in high altitude Addis Ababa in 2:48. Three years later he emerged fully formed to complete a 5000/10,000m double at the 1992 World Junior Championships. A year later he was the world senior 10,000m champion and would never look back. With his cheerful demeanour, smooth running action and spectacular finishing kick, he developed into the world's most popular athlete ... and he has not finished yet!

Jonathan Edwards – The Human Kangaroo

HOW FORTUNATE for Jonathan Edwards and athletics as a whole that, after being struck down by the debilitating Epstein Barr virus in 1994 he did not decide that, aged 28 and with a highly respectable triple jumping career behind him, it was time to move on to other things. This vicar's son who, prior to 1993, would not compete on a Sunday, had competed in the Olympics of 1988 and 1992, failing both times to get anywhere near qualifying for the final, but had displayed competitive flair to place third in the 1993 World Championships and he had two Commonwealth Games silver medals to his credit from 1990 and 1994. His best showing, however, had been in the World Cup. In the 1989 edition he improved from 16.74 to 17.28 for third place, while in 1992 he emerged as the winner. By the end of 1994 his personal best had advanced just 16cm in the five years since his breakthrough.

As far as he knew, he might have gone as far as he could, but he decided to persevere.

Echoing the sentiments of 1924 Olympic hero Eric Liddell, he felt that as a committed Christian it was his duty to develop to the full his God-given talent. His objective for 1995 was simply to re-establish himself in international competition. No one, least of all himself, ever imagined he was destined to take triple jumping into a new era. His metamorphosis from just another world-class jumper to a trail-blazer for the event bordered on the miraculous.

At the European Cup in June 1995 the news that he had registered a wind aided 18.43 was greeted with incredulity, but it was no fluke as the following month he succeeded Willie Banks as world record holder with 17.98. It was at that summer's World Championships in Gothenburg that Edwards achieved athletic immortality. First he advanced the world record to 18.16 and one round later he cut the sand at 18.29, a fraction over 60 feet ... and watching him in full flow was one of the sport's greatest aesthetic as well as athletic experiences. He would never approach such distances again but after finishing second in Atlanta in 1996 he fulfilled his ultimate dream by becoming Olympic champion in Sydney at the age of 34.

WORLD RECORDS

OLYMPIC RECORDS

Men

100m	9.84	Donovan Bailey CAN 96
200m	19.32	Michael Johnson USA 96
400m	43.49	Michael Johnson USA 96
800m	1:42.58	Vebjørn Rodal NOR 96
1500m	3:32.07	Noah Ngeny KEN 00
5000m	13:05.59	Said Aouita MAR 84
10,000m	27:07.34	Haile Gebrselassie ETH 96
Marathon	2:09:21	Carlos Lopes POR 84
3000mSC	8:05.51	Julius Kariuki KEN 88
110mH	12.95	Allen Johnson USA 96
400mH	46.78	Kevin Young USA 92
HJ	2.39	Charles Austin USA 96
PV	5.92	Jean Galfione FRA 96
	5.92	Igor Trandenkov RUS 96
	5.92	Andrei Tivontchik GER 96
LJ	8.90	Bob Beamon USA 68
TJ	18.09	Kenny Harrison USA 96
		note: 18.17w
		Mike Conley USA 92
SP	22.47	Ulf Timmermann GDR 88
DT	69.40	Lars Riedel GER 96
HT	84.80	Sergey Litvinov URS 88
JT	90.17	Jan Zelezny CZE 00
Dec	8847	Thompson GBR 84
20k Walk	1:18:59	Robert Korzeniowski POL 00
50k Walk	3:38:29	Vyacheslav Ivanenko URS 88
4x100m	37.40	United States 92
4x400m	2:55.74	United States 92

Women

100m	10.62	Florence Griffith Joyner USA 88 (qf)
	note:	10.54w Griffith Joyner 88
200m	21.34	F Griffith Joyner USA 88
400m	48.25	Marie-José Pérec FRA 96
800m	1:53.43	Nad. Olizarenko URS 80
1500m	3:53.96	Paula Ivan ROM 88
5000m	14:40.79	Gabriela Szabo ROM 00
10,000m	30:17.49	Derartu Tulu ETH 00
Marathon	2:23:14	Naoko Takahashi JPN 00
100mH	12.38	Yordanka Donkova BUL 88
400mH	52.82	Deon Hemmings JAM 96
HJ	2.05	Stefka Kostadinova BUL96
PV	4.60	Stacy Dragila USA 00
LJ	7.40	Jackie Joyner-Kersee USA 88
TJ	15.33	Inessa Kravets UKR 96
SP	22.41	Ilona Slupianek GDR 80
DT	72.30	Martina Hellmann GDR 88
HT	71.16	Kamila Skolimowska POL 00
JT	68.91	Trine Hattestad NOR 00
Hep	7291	Jackie Joyner-Kersee USA 88
20k Walk	1:29:05	Wang Liping CHN 00
4x100m	41.60	GDR (East Germany) 80
4x400m	3:15.17	Soviet Union 88

WORLD RECORDS

Men

9.78	Tim Montgomery USA 14.9.2002
19.32	Michael Johnson USA 1.8.1996
43.18	Michael Johnson USA 26.8.1999
1:41.11	Wilson Kipketer DEN 24.8.1997
3:26.00	Hicham El Guerrouj MAR 14.7.1998
12:39.36	Haile Gebrselassie ETH 13.6.1998
26:22.75	Haile Gebrselassie ETH 1.6.1998
2:04:55	Paul Tergat KEN 28.9.2003
7:55.28	Brahim Boulami MAR 24.8.2001
12.91	Colin Jackson GBR 20.8.1993
46.78	Kevin Young USA 6.8.1992
2.45	Javier Sotomayor CUB 27.7.1993
6.14	Sergey Bubka UKR 31.7.1994
	(+ 6.15 indoors on 21.2.1993)
8.95	Mike Powell USA 30.8.1991
18.29	Jonathan Edwards GBR 7.8.1995
23.12	Randy Barnes USA 20.5.1990
74.08	Jürgen Schult GDR 6.6.1986
86.74	Yuriy Sedykh URS 30.8.1986
98.48	Jan Zelezny CZE 25.5.1996
9026	Roman Sebrle CZE 27.5.2001
1:17:21	Jefferson Pérez ECU 23.8.2003
3:36:03	Robert Korzeniowski POL 27.8.2003
37.40	United States 8.8.1992 & 21.8.1993
2:54.20	United States 22.7.1998

Women

10.49	Florence Griffith Joyner USA 16.7.1988
21.34	Florence Griffith Joyner USA 29.9.1988
47.60	Marita Koch GDR 6.10.1985
1:53.28	Jarmila Kratochvilová TCH 26.7.1983
3:50.46	Qu Yunxia CHN 11.9.1993
14:28.09	Jiang Bo CHN 23.10.1997
29:31.78	Wang Junxia CHN 8.9.1993
2:15:25	Paula Radcliffe GBR 13.4.2003
12.21	Yordanka Donkova BUL 20.8.1988
52.34	Yuliya Pechonkina RUS 8.8.2003
2.09	Stefka Kostadinova BUL 30.8.1987
4.82	Yelena Isinbayeva RUS 13.7.2003
7.52	Galina Chistyakova URS 11.6.1988
15.50	Inessa Kravets UKR 10.8.1995
22.63	Natalya Lisovskaya URS 7.6.1987
76.80	Gabriele Reinsch GDR 9.7.1988
76.07	Mihaela Melinte ROM 29.8.1999
71.54	Osleidys Menéndez CUB 1.7.2001
7291	Jackie Joyner-Kersee USA 24.9.1988
1:26:22	Yan Wang CHN 19.11.2001
41.37	GDR (East Germany) 6.10.1985
3:15.17	Soviet Union 1.10.1988

US OLYMPIC LEGENDS

American athletes who have won two or more individual gold medals

Tom Burke: 1896 100m & 400m
Ellery Clark: 1896 High Jump & Long Jump
Bob Garrett: 1896 Shot & Discus
Alvin Kraenzlein: 1900 60m, 110mH, 200mH & Long Jump
Walter Tewksbury: 1900 200m & 400mH
Irving Baxter: 1900 High Jump & Pole Vault
Meyer Prinstein: 1900 Triple Jump; 1904 Long Jump & Triple Jump; 1906 Long Jump
Ray Ewry: 1900 & 1904 Standing High Jump, Long Jump & Triple Jump; 1906 & 1908 Standing High Jump & Long Jump
John Flanagan: 1900, 1904 & 1908 Hammer
Archie Hahn: 1904 60, 100m & 200m; 1906 100m
Harry Hillman: 1904 400m, 200mH & 400mH
James Lightbody: 1904 800m, 1500m & 2590mSC; 1906 1500m
Ralph Rose: 1904 & 1908 Shot; 1912 Shot (agg)
Paul Pilgrim: 1906 400m & 800m
Martin Sheridan: 1904 Discus; 1906 Shot & Discus; 1908 Discus & Discus (Greek)
Mel Sheppard: 1908 800m & 1500m
Ralph Craig: 1912 100m & 200m
Pat McDonald: 1912 Shot; 1920 56lb Weight
Jim Thorpe: 1912 Decathlon & Pentathlon
Harold Osborn: 1924 High Jump & Decathlon
Bud Houser: 1924 Shot & Discus; 1928 Discus
Eddie Tolan: 1932 100m & 200m
Jesse Owens: 1936 100, 200m & Long Jump
Harrison Dillard: 1948 100m; 1952 110mH
Mal Whitfield: 1948 & 1952 800m
Bob Mathias: 1948 & 1952 Decathlon
Bob Richards: 1952 & 1956 Pole Vault
Parry O'Brien: 1952 & 1956 Shot
Bobby Morrow: 1956 100m & 200m
Lee Calhoun: 1956 & 1960 110mH
Glenn Davis: 1956 & 1960 400mH
Al Oerter: 1956, 1960, 1964 & 1968 Discus
Ed Moses: 1976 & 1984 400mH
Carl Lewis: 1984 100m, 200m & Long Jump; 1988 100m & Long Jump; 1992 & 1996 Long Jump
Roger Kingdom: 1984 & 1988 110mH
Michael Johnson: 1996 200m & 400m; 2000 400m

Women

Babe Didrikson: 1932 80mH & Javelin
Wilma Rudolph: 1960 100m & 200m
Wyomia Tyus: 1964 & 1968 100m
Valerie Brisco-Hooks: 1984 200m & 400m
Florence Griffith Joyner: 1988 100m & 200m
Jackie Joyner-Kersee: 1988 Long Jump & Heptathlon; 1992 Heptathlon
Gail Devers: 1992 & 1996 100m
Marion Jones: 2000 100m & 200m

Most Olympic Gold Medals:

10	Ray Ewry USA (8 excluding 1906)
9	Paavo Nurmi FIN
9	Carl Lewis USA
5	Ville Ritola FIN
5	Martin Sheridan USA (3 excluding 1906)
5	Michael Johnson USA
4	Alvin Kraenzlein USA
4	Mel Sheppard USA
4	Hannes Kolehmainen FIN
4	Jesse Owens USA
4	Fanny Blankers-Koen NED
4	Harrison Dillard USA
4	Emil Zátopek TCH
4	Betty Cuthbert AUS
4	Al Oerter USA
4	Lasse Viren FIN
4	Barbel Eckert-Wöckel GDR
4	Evelyn Ashford USA

Most Olympic Medals:

12	Paavo Nurmi FIN
10	Ray Ewry USA (8 excluding 1906)
10	Carl Lewis USA
9	Martin Sheridan USA (4 excluding 1906)
8	Ville Ritola FIN
8	Merlene Ottey JAM (now SLO)

Most Gold Medals In A Single Games:

5	Paavo Nurmi FIN 1924
4	Alvin Kraenzlein USA 1900
4	Ville Ritola FIN 1924
4	Jesse Owens USA 1936
4	Fanny Blankers-Koen NED 1948
4	Carl Lewis USA 1984

Oldest Olympic Champions:

Men: (*current Olympic events)
42y 23d	Pat McDonald USA (56lb WT)
*37y 176d	Carlos Lopes POR (Mar)

Women:
39y 316d	Ellina Zvereva BLR (DT)

Oldest Olympic Medallists:

Men:
48y 115d	Tebbs Lloyd-Johnson GBR (50kW)

Women:
40y 143d	Merlene Ottey JAM (4x100m)

Youngest Olympic Champions:

Men:
17y 263d	Bob Mathias USA (Dec)

Women: (also youngest medallist)
15y 123d	Barbara Jones USA (4x100m)

Youngest Olympic Medallists:

Men: (* current Olympic events)
17y 168d	Frank Castleman USA (200mH)
* 17y 229d	Ture Persson SWE (4x100m)

Most Successful Nations:

(Gold medals) USA 310; USSR/Unified Team 71; Finland 49; Gt Britain & NI 45 (49 inc Gt Britain/Ireland). (All medals) USA 715; USSR/Unified Team 214; Gt Britain & NI 180 (192 inc Gt Britain/Ireland).

BY COUNTRY

Men

ALG	1996 Noureddine Morceli, 1500m
ARG	1932 Juan Carlos Zabala, Marathon
AUS	1896 Edwin Flack, 1500m
BDI	1996 Vénuste Niyongabo, 5000m
BEL	1948 Gaston Reiff, 5000m
BRA	1952 Adhemar F da Silva, Triple Jump
BUL	1988 Khristo Markov, Triple Jump
CAN	1900 George Orton, 2500mSC
CUB	1976 Alberto Juantorena, 800m
CZE	see under TCH
ECU	1996 Jefferson Pérez, 20k Walk
ESP	1992 Daniel Plaza, 20k Walk
EST	2000 Erki Nool, Decathlon
ETH	1960 Abebe Bikila, Marathon
FIN	1906 Verner Järvinen, Discus (Greek)
FRA	1900 Michel Théato, Marathon
GBR	1900 Charles Bennett, 1500m
GER	1936 Hans Woellke, Shot
GRE	1896 Spiridon Louis, Marathon
HUN	1900 Rudolf Bauer, Discus
IRL	1904 Tom Kiely, All-Round Contest
ITA	1920 Ugo Frigerio, 10,000m Walk
JAM	1948 Arthur Wint, 400m
JPN	1928 Mikio Oda, Triple Jump
KEN	1968 Naftali Temu, 10,000m
KOR	1992 Hwang Young-Jo, Marathon
LTU	1992 Romas Ubartas, Discus
LUX	1952 Josy Barthel, 1500m
MAR	1984 Saïd Aouita, 5000m
MEX	1976 Daniel Bautista, 20k Walk
NOR	1920 Helge Lövland, Decathlon
NZL	1936 Jack Lovelock, 1500m
POL	1932 Janusz Kusocinski, 10,000m
POR	1984 Carlos Lopes, Marathon
RSA	see under SAF
RUS	1992 Maksim Tarasov, Pole Vault & Andrey Perlov, 50k Walk
SAF	1908 Reggie Walker, 100m
SWE	1906 Eric Lemming, Javelin
TCH	1948 Emil Zátopek, 10,000m
TJK	1992 Andrey Abduvaliyev, Hammer
TRI	1976 Hasely Crawford, 100m
TUN	1968 Mohamed Gammoudi, 5000m
UGA	1972 John Akii-Bua, 400mH
URS	1956 Vladimir Kuts, 10,000m
USA	1896 James Connolly, Triple Jump

Women

ALG	1992 Hassiba Boulmerka, 1500m
AUS	1952 Marjorie Jackson, 100m
AUT	1948 Herma Bauma, Javelin
BAH	2000 4x100m Relay Team
BLR	2000 Ellina Zvereva, Discus
BUL	1976 Ivanka Khristova, Shot
CAN	1928 Ethel Catherwood, High Jump

	& 4x100m Relay Team
CHN	1992 Chen Yueling, 10k Walk
CUB	1980 María Colon, Javelin
CZE	see under TCH
ETH	1992 Derartu Tulu, 10,000m
FIN	1996 Heli Rantanen, Javelin
FRA	1948 Micheline Ostermeyer, Discus
GBR	1964 Mary Rand, Long Jump
GER	1928 Lina Radke, 800m
GRE	1992 Paraskevi Patoulidou, 100mH
HUN	1936 Ibolya Csak, High Jump
ITA	1936 Trebisonda Valla, 80mH
JAM	1996 Deon Hemmings, 400mH
JPN	2000 Naoko Takahashi, Marathon
KAZ	2000 Olga Shishigina, 100mH
MAR	1984 Nawal El Moutawakil, 400mH
MOZ	2000 Maria Mutola, 800m
NED	1948 Fanny Blankers-Koen, 100m
NGR	1996 Chioma Ajunwa, Long Jump
NOR	2000 Trine Hattestad, Javelin
NZL	1952 Yvette Williams, Long Jump
POL	1928 Halina Konopacka, Discus
POR	1988 Rosa Mota, Marathon
ROM	1960 Iolanda Balas, High Jump
RSA	see under SAF
RUS	1992 Valentina Yegorova, Marathon
SAF	1952 Esther Brand, High Jump
SWE	1996 Ludmila Engquist, 100mH
SYR	1996 Ghada Shouaa, Heptathlon
TCH	1952 Dana Zátopková, Javelin
UKR	1996 Inessa Kravets, Triple Jump
URS	1952 Nina Romashkova, Discus
USA	1928 Betty Robinson, 100m

(see next page for key to national abbreviations)

ATHENS TIMETABLE 2004 (Finals)

Aug 18 or 19: Shot (M & W), at Olympia.
Aug 20: 20k Walk, Heptathlon (W; day 1), 10,000m.
Aug 21: Heptathlon (W; day 2), Discus (W), 100m (W).
Aug 22: Marathon (W), Hammer, High Jump, Triple Jump, 100m.
Aug 23: 20k Walk (W), Decathlon (day 1), Triple Jump (W), Discus, 800m (W), 400m, 5000m (W).
Aug 24: Decathlon (day 2), Pole Vault (W), 3000mSC, 400m (W), 100mH (W), 1500m.
Aug 25: 400mH (W), Hammer (W), 200m (W).
Aug 26: Long Jump, 400mH, 200m.
Aug 27: 50k Walk, Pole Vault, Long Jump (W), Javelin (W), 110mH, 10,000m (W), 4x100m (W).
Aug 28: High Jump (W), Javelin, 1500m (W), 800m, 5000m, 4x100m, 4x400m (W), 4x400m.
Aug 29: Marathon.

KEY TO NATIONAL ABBREVIATIONS

Athletes from the following countries appear in the Olympic results in this book:

ALB	Albania
ALG	Algeria
ARG	Argentina
ARM	Armenia
AUS	Australia
AUT	Austria
BAH	Bahamas
BAR	Barbados
BDI	Burundi
BEL	Belgium
BER	Bermuda
BLR	Belarus
BOH	Bohemia
BOT	Botswana
BRA	Brazil
BUL	Bulgaria
BWI	British West Indies
CAN	Canada
CEY	Ceylon
CHI	Chile
CHN	China
CIV	Ivory Coast
CMR	Cameroon
COL	Colombia
CRO	Croatia
CUB	Cuba
CZE	Czech Republic
DEN	Denmark
DJI	Djibouti
DOM	Dominican Republic
ECU	Ecuador
ESP	Spain
EST	Estonia
ETH	Ethiopia
EUN	Unified Team (ex-USSR)
FIN	Finland
FRA	France
FRG	Federal Rep of Germany
GBR	Great Britain & N Ireland
GDR	German Dem Rep (E Ger)
GER	Germany
GHA	Ghana
GRE	Greece
HAI	Haiti
HUN	Hungary
IND	India
IRL	Ireland
ISL	Iceland
ISR	Israel
ITA	Italy
JAM	Jamaica
JPN	Japan
KAZ	Kazakhstan
KEN	Kenya
KOR	Korea (S Korea)
KSA	Saudi Arabia
LAT	Latvia
LTU	Lithuania
LUX	Luxembourg
MAD	Madagascar
MAR	Morocco
MEX	Mexico
MOZ	Mozambique
NAM	Namibia
NED	Netherlands
NGR	Nigeria
NOR	Norway
NZL	New Zealand
OMN	Oman
PAN	Panama
PHI	Philippines
POL	Poland
POR	Portugal
PRK	DPR Korea (N Korea)
PUR	Puerto Rico
QAT	Qatar
ROM	Romania
RSA	Republic of South Africa
RUS	Russia
RWA	Rwanda
SAF	South Africa
SEN	Senegal
SKN	St Kitts & Nevis
SLE	Sierra Leone
SLO	Slovenia
SOM	Somalia
SRI	Sri Lanka
SUD	Sudan
SUI	Switzerland
SVK	Slovak Republic
SWE	Sweden
SYR	Syria
TAI	Taiwan
TAN	Tanzania
TCH	Czechoslovakia (to 1991)
TJK	Tajikistan
TRI	Trinidad & Tobago
TUN	Tunisia
TUR	Turkey
UGA	Uganda
UKR	Ukraine
URS	Soviet Union
USA	United States of America
UZB	Uzbekistan
VEN	Venezuela
YUG	Yugoslavia
ZAM	Zambia

ACKNOWLEDGEMENTS

I WISH to acknowledge the main sources for my research. Having been fortunate enough to attend eight Olympic Games between 1960 and 1996 and watched those of 1980, 1988 and 2000 on television I have drawn heavily on my own reports and notes over that period.

For information on earlier celebrations I have referred to a multitude of books, the primary source being Ekkehard zur Megede's fantastic 700-page book The Modern Olympic Century 1896-1996 (published by Deutsche Gesellschaft für Leichtathletik-Dokumentation 1999), which lists every athletics result in Olympic history!

Other invaluable sources of information have included Whitaker's Olympic Almanack 2004 by Stan Greenberg (A & C Black Ltd 2004), The Complete Book of the Olympics by David Wallechinsky (Aurum Press 1996), The Olympic Games Complete Track & Field Results 1896-1988 by Barry J Hugman & Peter Arnold (The Arena Press 1988), Quest For Gold by Bill Mallon & Ian Buchanan (Leisure Press 1984), British Olympians by Ian Buchanan (Guinness Publishing 1991), Progression of World Best Performances & Official IAAF World Records by Richard Hymans (IAAF 2003), History of Ancient Olympic Games by Lynn & Gray Poole (Vision Press 1965), Greek Athletes & Athletics by H A Harris (Hutchinson 1964), The Olympic Games: The First Thousand Years by M I Finley & H W Pleket (Chatto & Windus 1976), five editions of Encyclopaedia of Athletics by Mel Watman (Robert Hale 1964-81), History of British Athletics by Mel Watman (Robert Hale 1968), The Modern Olympic Games by Dr Ferenc Mezo (Pannonia Press 1956), The Olympic Games edited by Lord Killanin & John Rodda (Macdonald & Jane's 1979), The Complete Book of Track & Field edited by Gene Brown (Arno 1980), The Games edited by Marshall Brant (Proteus 1980), Olympic Track & Field by the editors of Track & Field News (Tafnews Press 1979), The Evolution of the Olympic Games by F A M Webster (Heath, Cranton & Ouseley 1914), Olympic Cavalcade by F A M Webster (Hutchinson 1948), Athletics of Today for Women by F A M Webster (Warne 1930), The Fastest Men On Earth by Neil Duncanson (Willow Books 1988), Athletics: A History of Modern Track & Field Athletics by Roberto L Quercetani (Vallardi 1991), Ireland's Olympic Heroes by David Guiney (Philip Roderick 1965), Scottish Athletics by John W Keddie (Scottish AAA 1982), The Marathon Footrace by David E Martin & Roger W H Gynn (Charles C Thomas 1979), Olympic Odyssey by Stan Tomlin (Modern Athlete Publications 1956), The Decathlon by Frank Zarnowski (Leisure Press 1989), Flying Finns by Matti Hannus (Tietosanoma 1990), Track's Greatest Women by Jon Hendershott (Tafnews Press 1987), Track's Greatest Champions by Cordner Nelson (Tafnews Press 1986), Tales of Gold by Lewis H Carlson & John J Fogarty (Contemporary Books 1987), The Nazi Olympics by Richard D Mandell (Souvenir Press 1972), Athletics 1977 by Ron Pickering & Mel Watman (Macdonald & Jane's 1977), International Running Guide 1985 edited by Mel Watman (Tantivy Press 1985), and Magic of Athletics: A Century of Great Moments by Alain Billouin, Roberto L Quercetani & Mel Watman (IAAF 1999), plus various statistical publications of the ATFS and IAAF.

I also consulted numerous magazines, notably Athletics Today, Athletics Weekly, Athletics International, Track & Field News, Track Newsletter, Athletics World, World Sports, IAAF Magazine and Leichtathletik.

My thanks also to Peter Matthews, Sir Eddie Kulukundis, Stan Greenberg, Matti Hannus, Randall Northam, Nick Davies, Larry Eder, Mark Shearman, the IAAF and, last but by no means least, my wife Pat for her continuing encouragement and support for a project which she knows is so close to my heart.

—**Mel Watman**

There is only one way to keep up to date with track & field performances from around the globe in Olympic Year... by subscribing to

ATHLETICS INTERNATIONAL

Launched in 1993, this newsletter edited by Mel Watman and Peter Matthews has readers in over 60 countries. You can't consider yourself well informed without its deep and accurate worldwide results service. The aim is to include all marks which would qualify for the ATFS Annual (150-200 deep world performances at senior level), together with reports on major events, news items, statistical compilations etc. There are 30 issues per year of A5 size, usually of between 8 and 16 pages. It is published weekly during the busiest part of the season.

Annual print subscription rates (30 issues)
UK subscribers £70; rest of Europe (by airmail) £80 or 120 euros, USA & elsewhere in the world (by airmail): £95 or $165

E-mail edition
A quicker and cheaper alternative to the printed edition of "Athletics International" is the e-mail version. Everything that appears in the printed edition is included, but as a Microsoft Word attachment without columns or boxes – just straight text. Depending on where they live, subscribers can expect to receive the e-mail version at least two to four days earlier than the printed edition ... and the annual subscription rate (30 issues) is cheaper too at £60 or 90 euros or $105.

You can pay by credit card (Visa, Mastercard, Amex only). Please send details (type of card, name on card, card number & date of expiry, amount to be deducted in pounds sterling), or send cash or cheque, drawn on a British bank and payable to Athletics International Ltd, to: Mel Watman, 13 Garden Court, Marsh Lane, Stanmore, HA7 4TE, England (UK).

Free sample copy sent on request

OLYMPIC TRACK & FIELD HISTORY

By Mel Watman

No one is better qualified to write a history of Olympic track and field athletics than Mel Watman, who has been a professional observer of the sport for more than 45 years and who has attended eight Olympic celebrations between 1960 and 1996.

In this fully revised and updated edition of the History of Olympic Track & Field Athletics he published in 2000 the author recalls the highlights, stars and trends of every Games from Athens in 1896 to Sydney in 2000, provides detailed results, and profiles such Olympic legends as Jim Thorpe, Paavo Nurmi, Jesse Owens, Fanny Blankers-Koen, Emil Zátopek, Herb Elliott, Wilma Rudolph, Bob Beamon, Al Oerter, Lasse Viren, Seb Coe and Steve Ovett, Daley Thompson, Florence Griffith Joyner, Jackie Joyner-Kersee, Carl Lewis, Michael Johnson, Marion Jones, Haile Gebrselassie and Jonathan Edwards

A former editor of the British magazines Athletics Weekly and (with Randall Northam) Athletics Today, Mel Watman now co-edits and publishes (with Peter Matthews) the newsletter Athletics International. His previous books include The Encyclopaedia of Athletics (in five editions), History of British Athletics, The Coe & Ovett File, several editions of Who's Who in World Athletics and (with Roberto Quercetani and Alain Billouin) The Magic of Athletics: A Century of Great Moments. As well as being a member of the ATFS (Association of Track & Field Statisticians), he is a co-founder of the British offshoot, the NUTS (National Union of Track Statisticians), and the British Athletics Writers Association, and a member of the Track & Field Writers of America. He and his wife Pat live in the north London suburb of Stanmore.

Published by Athletics International Ltd in association
with Shooting Star Media, Inc

ISBN 0 9528011 6 7   £12

SEE YOU
IN ATHENS!

ATHENS 2004

OFFICIAL PROVIDER
TRACK & FIELD SURFACES • EQUIPMENT
VOLLEYBALL SURFACES

MONDO

 MONDO

ENGINEERED FOR HUMAN VITALITY

sales office: 800 441 6645   email: mondo@mondousa.com   website: www.mondousa.com

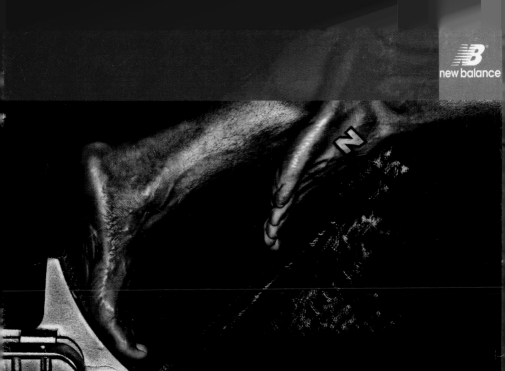

www.newbalance.com   N is for dash, not flash.   achieve **new balance**

AMERICAN
Track&Field

PRESENTS

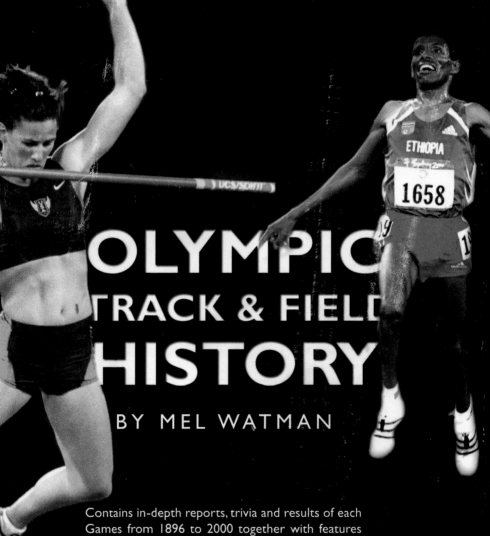

OLYMPIC
TRACK & FIELD
HISTORY

BY MEL WATMAN

Contains in-depth reports, trivia and results of each
Games from 1896 to 2000 together with features
on numerous Olympic greats from Jim Thorpe,
Paavo Nurmi, Jesse Owens and Emil Zatopek
through to Carl Lewis, Michael Johnson, Haile
Gebrselassie, Jonathan Edwards and Marion Jones.

Published by Athletics International Ltd.
in Association with Shooting Star Media, Inc.

LIFE'S A RUSH. LOVE YOUR FEET.

SPENCO

INSOLES & FOOTCARE SOLUTI